PHILOSOPHY
the Cutting Edge

PHILOSOPHY
the Cutting Edge

DAVID BERLINSKI
University of Puget Sound

ALFRED PUBLISHING CO., INC.
75 Channel Drive, Port Washington, New York 11050

Published by Alfred Publishing Co., Inc.
75 Channel Drive, Port Washington, N.Y. 11050

Copyright © 1976 by Alfred Publishing Co., Inc.
All rights reserved.

Printed in the United States of America

Library of Congress Cataloging in Publication Data
Main entry under title:

Philosophy: The Cutting edge.

Includes index.
1. Philosophy—Addresses, essays, lectures.
I. Berlinski, David J.
B29.C83   190   76-7548
ISBN 0-88284-029-0

"There is a difference between someone gnashing his teeth, and the gnashing of someone's teeth."
— Paul Ziff

CONTENTS*

*Articles arranged in opposing pairs.

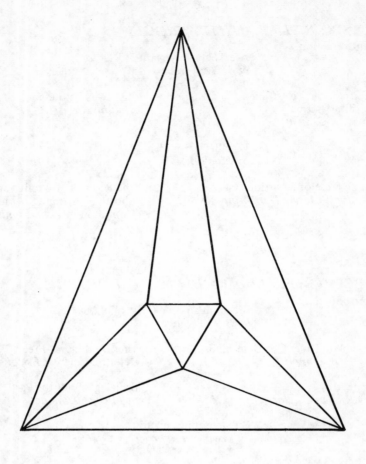

One of the most surprising theorems in elementary geometry was discovered in 1899 by F. Morely ... He mentioned it to his friends, who spread it over the world in the form of mathematical gossip. At last, after ten years, a trigonometrical proof by M. Satyanarayana and an elementary proof by M. T. Naraniengar were published.

Morley's Theorem. The three points of intersection of the adjacent trisectors of the angles of any triangle form an equilateral triangle.

— H. S. M. Coxeter
Introduction to Geometry

PREFACE

Philosophy is an old and a difficult discipline. Students are asked to study it because in its essentials philosophy involves nothing less than the activities of the intellect as it makes efforts to understand itself. So it is very often claimed, at least by philosophers.

My aim in putting this collection together is to assemble readings that exhibit the overwhelmingly argumentative nature of modern philosophy. Having read these selections, the student will have some knowledge of philosophy and some feel for its characteristic arguments. Modern philosophy does give to the uninitiated a sense of solemn and incomprehensible combat——the inconceivable with fearful snorts gradually swallowing the unimaginable. But there is also in the best of the philosophical tradition a sense of the playful and a spirit of elegant intellectual banter, and I have tried to arrange the selections to suggest some of this.

The Cutting Edge is divided into seven self-contained sections. Most of the pieces were composed between 1940 and 1970—dates that mark the last stage in the difficult revolution in philosophy that began with Frege and Russell. I have included nothing of contemporary Continental philosophy in the volume. Although great soupy volumes pour off the European presses with the inevitability of death, much of what results calls to mind only the perfect vacuum. Neither have I included readings from the history of western philosophy. I agree that a student who has not read Plato, Aristotle, Hume or Kant is somehow unpardonably deficient; I urge only that undergraduates spend a semester at the lamp with the classics *after* and not *before* they have learned something of modern philosophy. My own experience has convinced me that most students are simply not prepared to cope with the vagaries of translation and the strangeness of historical idioms while they are simultaneously struggling to make sense of arguments that are novel, difficult and very often quite abstract. Thus the very student who rejects Berkeley as being insufficiently attentive to the needs of the Third World and Minority Communities, quite often finds himself hopelessly captivated by A. J. Ayer and spends endless hours looking for loopholes in the argument from illusion.

I have arranged almost all of the selections in the book in argumentative pairs. The philosopher who brings a thesis to the attention of his colleagues is sure to find at least half of them prepared to deny it. So within each section, authors are matched to their natural antagonists. There is real opposition here, not some vague setting out of alternative points of view. The student coming on a group of papers contradicted regularly in most points of detail will come to the conclusion that only half of the readings can be correct. This reduces his proverbial awe of the printed page even if it encourages him in the conviction that the authors he is reading must be every bit as unqualified to speak to the issues as he is himself.

Although the sections of the book, together with my introductions, are pretty much self-contained, their order involves a sequence that I have found natural and useful for a course in introductory philosophy. The device of having readings matched in argumentative pairs makes it very easy to integrate the readings with other text material. In this respect, the simplest tactic is also the best.

I have appended a small glossary to the readings; the entries are really quite brief and students should use the glossary strictly to assure themselves that their sense of what a given word or phrase means comes tolerably close to what it in fact does mean. Also included within each introduction are biographical matters; these too make no pretense at completeness but together with my notes on the literature they should give the student some feeling that the authors of these essays actually displaced space in the real world.

D.B.
New York
1976

PHILOSOPHY
the Cutting Edge

1

MAN AND MACHINES

"The analogies between a living organism and a machine hold true to a remarkable extent at all levels at which it is investigated."

— Jean Pierre Changeux

"This is not to say that comparisons of the life dynamic with some manifestation of human technology (automata, electronic computers, etc.) are pointless, but rather that these comparisons have validity only for partial mechanisms, fully developed with their complete functional activity, and they can never be applied to the global living structure or to its epigenesis and physiological maturation."

— René Thom

INTRODUCTION

Philosophers since the time of Descartes have found the hypothesis that human beings are very much like extraordinarily complicated machines compelling. And for obvious reasons. The thought that human beings stand separate from the natural world studied so successfully by means of physics or chemistry is aesthetically dissatisfying. But if strong analogies do hold between machines and living creatures, a theory that explains the first might well explain the second.

Mathematicians, curiously enough, have had something of a proprietary interest in the idea that purely mechanical devices could produce recognizably human behavior. This is not quite the hypothesis that men are machines but rather its inverse, that machines are in certain respects very much like men. Leibnitz wrote of a universal calculating device in the 17th century; his successors have been looking for it ever since. Alan Turing brought to his important paper experiences as an immensely distinguished mathematician. His researches, carried out in the 1930s and 1940s, were very much in the spirit of Leibnitz. The great papers that he wrote involved the effort to understand abstractly the concept of *computability*. It is this notion that some measure provides the mathematical framework for the modern computer. But "Computing Machinery and Intelligence" is addressed to the philosophical issue of whether computing machines can carry out such distinctly human activities as thought and speech. The paper has become something of a fixed point in contemporary discussions largely, I think, because Turing recognizes so clearly that the bald question, "Can computer think?" invites by its unclarity arguments that are passionate but unfocused. What is required, before an intelligent answer to the question may be framed is some sense of the conditions under which we would be prepared to say, however reluctantly, that a purely mechanical object evinced human intellectual powers. This is a typical maneuver in philosophy. Call it *epistemological prefixing.* Epistemology has to do broadly with the means by which we acquire knowledge and epistemological prefixing (taken simply as a tactic) involves the reorganization of certain kinds of questions. Instead of asking simply whether something is such and such, the philosopher asks first how we would know whether such and such really is true of something. Having thus reformulated the fundamental question, Turing uses the rest of his paper to take on, with what he judges considerable success, a variety of hypothetical opponents arguing against the thesis that computers might at some stage in their development exhibit sophisticated intellectual powers.

Some ten years after his death, Norbert Wiener retains a secure if somewhat shady reputation as the author of *Cybernetics,* a book devoted to what Wiener himself thought of as the basics of a science of control and communication. Like Turing, Wiener was a research mathematician of distinction, and like Turing, Wiener found himself impressed with the degree to which some mechanical systems could come to seem remarkably like human beings. In both there is an aesthetic preference for a point of view in which men and machines seem similar. This gives rise to a philosophic program that works to perfection, one might think, only so long as one sticks to observations roughly on the order that the heart is like a pump or the lungs like a bellows. Going further, one encounters human attributes and capacities that seem to have no machine analogues whatsoever. Human beings, for example, conceive, carry out and execute their ordinary actions according to fixed goals and purposes and in the usual run of things most people would not look to a mechanical device for evidence of goal directed or teleological powers. But Wiener and his collaborator Rosenblueth argue bluntly that this is a mistake. A scientifically satisfying theory of human behavior can refer only to human behavior. Goal direction is an achievement that reflects merely the organization of certain acts, and many machines,

4

such as thermostats, regulators and automata are arranged so as to exhibit in their operation behavior that is plainly purposeful.

Professional philosophers often observe that scientists and mathematicians reach certainty on difficult philosophical issues with remarkable celerity. And once having formed an opinion they hang on to it like a bulldog. Professors Wiener and Rosenblueth, for example, looked on their work as reflecting the glacial but inevitable progress of Science itself. Those people who were not quite prepared to read pure teleological powers into the operation of a wall thermostat Wiener and Rosenblueth tended to dismiss as hopelessly humanistic. A certain happy ferocity is therefore required of their critics. This Richard Taylor provided. An American philosopher with no special expertise in mathematics or science, Taylor took the view that what made Wiener and Rosenblueth's position possible was nothing less than gross philosophical confusion. To their high-toned arguments Taylor responded with infuriatingly self-assured scepticism. Taylor's piece moved Wiener and Rosenblueth to response; that essay provoked yet another suave (if savage) reply from Taylor. There the issues remained with enthusiasts for both camps persuaded that only intellectual perversity prevented the other side from recognizing the hopelessness of their position. Since it seems to touch on all of the chief arguments, I have reprinted only the first exchange here.

In the third and last exchange of this section, Simon and Newell and Hubert Dreyfus argue the merits of research programs in the development of artificial intelligence. Simon and Newell both are American scientists and both have since the 1950s been involved in research concerning artificial intelligence. Their aim, in brief, has been to understand the structure of what they dub *information processing systems*. The human brain is such a system but so they claim is the digital computer, at least when properly programmed. A theory that explained them both as information processing systems would go some distance toward extinguishing our natural sense that information processing is the prerogative of creatures with just our kind of complicated nervous systems.

It is against this point of view (and the voluptuous optimism with which it is expressed) that Professor Dreyfus sets himself. Dreyfus is a young American philosopher. During the 1960s he found himself at the Rand Corporation and while there he seems to have stumbled indignantly over the voluminous literature on artificial intelligence. He declared the discipline bogus in a Rand monograph. The monograph led to papers, the papers to a book; and for his efforts Dreyfus has evoked denunciation of a sort habitually reserved for the philosopher, who without formal training, announces grandly that the methods and conclusions of a scientific discipline resemble nothing so much as Scientology or the theory of the Orgone Box.

The reader who wishes to pursue the themes discussed in this section might begin with a collection such as Alan Ross Anderson's *Mind and Machines* (Prentice-Hall). Michael A. Arbib has written an interesting account of research in machine computability and artificial intelligence, *Brains, Machines and Mathematics* (McGraw-Hill) and readers who wish to have Professor Dreyfus's critique at book length may consult his text *What Computers Cannot Do* (Harper & Row). Norbert Wiener's *Cybernetics* is, of course, a contemporary classic.

COMPUTING MACHINERY AND INTELLIGENCE*

Alan Turing

THE IMITATION GAME

I propose to consider the question "Can machines think?" This should begin with definitions of the meaning of the terms "machine" and "think." The definitions might be framed so as to reflect so far as possible the normal use of the words, but this attitude is dangerous. If the meanings of the words "machine" and "think" are to be found by examining how they are commonly used, it is difficult to escape the conclusion that the meaning and the answer to the question, "Can machines think?" is to be sought in a statistical survey such as a Gallup poll. But this is absurd. Instead of attempting such a definition I shall replace the question by another, which is closely related to it and is expressed in relatively unambiguous words.

The new form of the problem can be described in terms of a game which we call the "imitation game." It is played with three people, a man (A), a woman (B), and an interrogator (C) who may be of either sex. The interrogator stays in a room apart from the other two. The object of the game for the interrogator is to determine which of the other two is the man and which is the woman. He knows them by labels X and Y, and at the end of the game he says either "X is A and Y is B" or "X is B and Y is A." The interrogator is allowed to put questions to A and B thus:

C: Will X please tell me the length of his or her hair? Now suppose X is actually A, then A must answer. It is A's object in the game to try to cause C to make the wrong identification. His answer might therefore be "My hair is shingled, and the longest strands are about nine inches long."

*From Turing: "Computing Machinery and Intelligence." *Mind*, 59 (1950). Reprinted by permission of the Editor of *Mind*.

In order that tones of voice may not help the interrogator the answers should be written, or better still, typewritten. The ideal arrangement is to have a teleprinter communicating between the two rooms. Alternatively the question and answers can be repeated by an intermediary. The object of the game for the third player (B) is to help the interrogator. The best strategy for her is probably to give truthful answers. She can add such things as "I am the woman, don't listen to him!" to her answers, but it will avail nothing, as the man can make similar remarks.

We now ask the question, "What will happen when a machine takes the part of A in this game?" Will the interrogator decide wrongly as often when the game is played like this as he does when the game is played between a man and a woman? These questions replace our original, "Can machines think?"

CRITIQUE OF THE NEW PROBLEM

As well as asking, "What is the answer to this new form of the question," one may ask, "Is this new question a worthy one to investigate?" This latter question we investigate without further ado, thereby cutting short an infinite regress.

The new problem has the advantage of drawing a fairly sharp line between the physical and the intellectual capacities of a man. No engineer or chemist claims to be able to produce a material which is indistinguishable from the human skin. It is possible that at some time this might be done, but even supposing this invention available we should feel there was little point in trying to make a "thinking machine" more human by dressing it up in such artificial flesh. The form in which we have set the problem reflects this fact in the condition which prevents the interrogator from seeing or touching the other competitors, or hearing their voices. Some other advantages of the proposed criterion may be shown up by specimen questions and answers. Thus:

Q: Please write me a sonnet on the subject of the Forth Bridge.

A: Count me out on this one. I never could write poetry.

Q: Add 34,957 to 70,764.

A: (Pause about 30 seconds and then give as answer) 105,621.

Q: Do you play chess?

A: Yes.

Q: I have K at my K1 and no other pieces. You have only K at K6 and R at R1. It is your move. What do you play?

A: (After a pause of 15 seconds) R-R8 mate.

The question and answer method seems to be suitable for introducing almost any one of the fields of human endeavor that we wish to include. We do not wish to penalize the machine for its inability to shine in beauty competitions, nor to penalize a man for losing in a race against an airplane. The conditions of our game make these disabilities irrelevant. The "witnesses" can brag, if they consider it advisable, as much as they please about their charms, strength, or heroism, but the interrogator cannot demand practical demonstrations.

THE MACHINES CONCERNED IN THE GAME

It is natural that we should wish to permit every kind of engineering technique to be used in our machines. We also wish to allow the possiblity that an engineer or team of engineers may construct a machine which works, but whose manner of operation cannot be satisfactorily described by its constructors because they have applied a method which is largely experimental. Finally, we wish to exclude from the machines men born in the usual manner. It is difficult to frame the definitions so as to satisfy these three conditions. One might for instance insist that the team of engineers should be all of one sex, but this would not really be satisfactory, for it is probably possible to rear a complete individual from a single cell of the skin (say) of a man. To do so would be a feat of biological technique deserving of the very highest praise, but we would not be inclined to regard it as a case of "constructing a thinking machine." This prompts us to abandon the requirement that every kind of technique should be permitted. We are the more ready to do so in view of the fact that the present interest in "thinking machines" has been aroused by a particular kind of machine, usually called an "electronic computer" or "digital computer." Following this suggestion we only permit digital computers to take part in our game.

This restriction appears at first glance to be a very drastic one. I shall attempt to show that it is not so in reality. To do this necessitates a short account of the nature and properties of these computers.

DIGITAL COMPUTERS

The idea behind digital computers may be explained by saying that these machines are intended to carry out any operations which could be done by a human computer. The human computer is supposed to be following fixed rules; he has no authority to deviate from them in any detail. We may suppose that these rules are supplied in a book, which is altered whenever he is put on to a new job. He also has unlimited supply of paper on which he does his calculations. He may also do his multiplications and additions on a "desk machine," but this is not important.

If we use the above explanation as a definition we shall be in danger of circularity of argument. We avoid this by giving an outline of the means by which the desired effect is achieved. A digital computer can usually be regarded as consisting of three parts:

(1) store
(2) executive unit
(3) control

The store is a store of information and corresponds to the human computer's paper, whether this is the paper on which he does his calculations or that on which his book of rules is printed. Insofar as the human computer does calculations in his head a part of the store will correspond to his memory.

The executive unit is the part which carries out the various individual operations involved in a calculation. What these individual operations are will vary from machine to machine. Usually fairly lengthy operations can be done such as "Multiply 3,540,675,445 by 7,076,345,687," but in some machines only very simple ones such as "Write down o" are possible.

We have mentioned that the "book of rules" supplied to the computer is replaced in the machine by a part of the store. It is then called the "table of instructions." It is the duty of the control to see that these instructions are obeyed correctly and in the right order. The control is so constructed that this necessarily happens.

The information in the store is usually broken up into packets of moderately small size. In one machine, for instance, a packet might consist of 10 decimal digits. Numbers are assigned to the parts of the store in which the various packets of information are stored, in some systematic manner. A typical instruction might say—

Add the number stored in position 6809 to that in 4302 and put the result back into the latter storage position.

Needless to say, it would not occur in the machine expressed in English. It would more likely be coded in a form such as 6809430217. Here 17 says which of various possible operations is to be performed on the two numbers. In this case the operation is that described above, namely, "Add the number. . . ." It will be noticed that the instruction takes up 10 digits and so forms one packet of information very conveniently. The control will normally take the instructions to be obeyed in the order of the positions in which they are stored, but occasionally an instruction such as

Now obey the instruction stored in position 5606, and continue from there may be encountered, or again

If position 4505 contains o obey next the instruction stored in 6707, otherwise continue straight on.

Instructions of these latter types are very important because they make it possible for a sequence of operations to be repeated over and over again until some condition is fulfilled, but in doing so to obey, not fresh instructions on each repetition, but the same ones over and over again. To take a domestic analogy, suppose Mother wants Tommy to call at the cobbler's every morning on his way to school to see if her shoes are done; she can ask him afresh every morning. Alternatively she can stick up a notice once and for all in the hall which he will see when he leaves for school and which tells him to call for the shoes, and also to destroy the notice when he comes back if he has the shoes with him.

The reader must accept it as a fact that digital computers can be constructed, and indeed have been constructed, according to the principles we have described, and that they can in fact mimic the actions of a human computer very closely.

CONTRARY VIEWS ON THE MAIN QUESTION

We may consider the ground to have been cleared. We are ready to proceed to the debate on our question, "Can machines think?" and the variant of it quoted at the end of the last section. We cannot altogether abandon the original form of the problem, for opinions will differ as to the appropriateness of the substitution and we must at least listen to what has to be said in this connection.

It will simplify matters for the reader if I explain first my own beliefs in the matter. Consider first the more accurate form of the question. I believe that in about 50 years' time it will be possible to program computers, with a storage capacity of about 10^9, to make them play the imitation game so well that an average interrogator will not have more than a 70 percent chance of making the right identification after five minutes of questioning. The original question, "Can machines think?" I believe to be too meaningless to deserve discussion. Nevertheless I believe that at the end of the century the use of words and general educated opinion will have altered so much that one will be able to speak of machines thinking without expecting to be contradicted. I believe further that no useful purpose is served by concealing these beliefs. The popular view that scientists proceed inexorably from well-established fact to well-established fact, never being influenced by any unproved conjecture, is quite mistaken. Provided it is made clear which are proved facts and which are conjectures, no harm can result. Conjectures are of great importance since they suggest useful lines of research.

11

I now proceed to consider opinions opposed to my own.

THE THEOLOGICAL OBJECTION

Thinking is a function of man's immortal soul. God has given an immortal soul to every man and woman, but not to any other animal or to machines. Hence no animal or machine can think.

I am unable to accept any part of this, but will attempt to reply in theological terms. I should find the argument more convincing if animals were classed with men, for there is a greater difference, to my mind, between the typical animate and the inaminate than there is between man and the other animals. The arbitrary character of the orthodox view becomes clearer if we consider how it might appear to a member of some other religious community. How do Christians regard the Moslem view that women have no souls? But let us leave this point aside and return to the main argument. It appears to me that the argument quoted above implies a serious restriction of the omnipotence of the Almighty. It is admitted that there are certain things that He cannot do, such as making one equal to two, but should we not believe that He has freedom to confer a soul on an elephant if He sees fit? We might expect that He would only exercise this power in conjunction with a mutation which provided the elephant with an appropriately improved brain to minister to the needs of this soul. An argument of exactly similar form may be made for the case of machines. It may seem different because it is more difficult to "swallow." But this really only means that we think it would be less likely that He would consider the circumstances suitable for conferring a soul. The circumstances in question are discussed in the rest of this article. In attempting to construct such machines we should not be irreverently usurping His power of creating souls any more than we are in the procreation of children. Rather we are, in either case, instruments of His will providing mansions for the souls that He creates.

However, this is mere speculation. I am not very impressed with theological arguments whatever they may be used to support. Such arguments have often been found unsatisfactory in the past. In the time of Galileo it was argued that the texts, "And the sun stood still . . . and hasted not to go down about a whole day" (Joshua x. 13) and "He laid the foundations of the earth, that it should not move at any time" (Psalm cv. 5) were an adequate refutation of the Copernican theory. With our present knowledge such an argument appears futile. When that knowledge was not available it made a quite different impression.

THE "HEADS IN THE SAND" OBJECTION

"The consequences of machines thinking would be too dreadful. Let us hope and believe that they cannot do so."

This argument is seldom expressed quite so openly as in the form above. But it affects most of us who think about it at all. We like to believe that man is in some subtle way superior to the rest of creation. It is best if he can be shown to be *necessarily* superior, for then there is no danger of him losing his commanding position. The popularity of the theological argument is clearly connected with this feeling. It is likely to be quite strong in intellectual people, since they value the power of thinking more highly than others and are more inclined to base their belief in the superiority of man on this power.

I do not think that this argument is sufficiently substantial to require refutation. Consolation would be more appropriate; perhaps this should be sought in the transmigration of souls.

THE MATHEMATICAL OBJECTION

There are a number of results of mathematical logic which can be used to show there are limitations to the powers of discrete state machines. The best known of these results is known as Gödel's theorem; it shows that in any sufficiently powerful logical system statements can be formulated which can neither be proved nor disproved within the system, unless possibly the system itself is inconsistent. There are other, in some respects similar, results due to Church, Kleene, Rosser, and Turing. The latter result is the most convenient to consider since it refers directly to machines. The result in question refers to a type of machine which is essentially a digital computer with an infinite capacity. It states that there are certain things that such a machine cannot do. If it is rigged up to give answers to questions as in the imitation game, there will be some questions to which it will either give a wrong answer or fail to give an answer at all however much time is allowed for a reply. There may, of course, be many such questions, and questions which cannot be answered by one machine may be satisfactorily answered by another. We are, of course, supposing for the present that the questions are of the kind to which an answer "yes" or "no" is appropriate, rather than questions such as "What do you think of Picasso?" The questions that we know the machines must fail on are of this type, "Consider the machine specified as follows. . . . Will this machine ever answer 'yes' to any question?" The dots are to be replaced by a description of some machine in a standard form. When the machine described bears a certain comparatively simple relation to the machine which is under interrogation, it can be shown that the answer is either wrong or not forthcoming. This is the mathematical result; it is argued that it proves a disability of machines to which the human intellect is not subject.

The short answer to this argument is that although it is established that there are limitations to the powers of any particular machine, it has only been stated, without any sort of proof, that no such limitations apply to the human intellect. But I do not think this view can be dismissed quite so lightly. Whenever one of these machines is asked the appropriate critical question, and gives a definite answer, we know that this answer must be wrong, and this gives us a certain feeling of superiority. Is this feeling illusory? It is no doubt quite genuine, but I do not think very much importance should be attached to it. We too often give wrong answers to questions ourselves to be justified in being very pleased at such evidence of fallibility on the part of the machines. Further, our superiority can only be felt on such an occasion in relation to the one machine over which we have scored our petty triumph. There would be no question of triumphing simultaneously over *all* machines. In short, then, there might be men cleverer than any given machine, but then again there might be other machines cleverer again, and so on.

Those who hold to the mathematical argument would, I think, mostly be willing to accept the imitation game as a basis for discussion. Those who believe in the two previous objections would probably not be interested in any criteria.

THE ARGUMENT FROM CONSCIOUSNESS

This argument is very well expressed in Professor Jefferson's Lister Oration for 1949, from which I quote. "Not until a machine can write a sonnet or compose a concerto because of thoughts and emotions felt, and not by the chance fall of symbols, could we agree that machine equals brain—that is, not only write it but know that it had written it. No mechanism could feel (and not merely artificially signal, an easy contrivance) pleasure at its successes, grief when its valves fuse, be warmed by flattery, be made miserable by its mistakes, be charmed by sex, be angry or depressed when it cannot get what it wants."

This argument appears to be a denial of the validity of our test. According to the most extreme form of this view the only way by which one could be sure that a machine thinks is to *be* the machine and to feel oneself thinking. One could then describe these feelings to the world, but of course no one would be justified in taking any notice. Likewise according to this view the only way to know that a *man* thinks is to be that particular man. It is, in fact, the solipsist point of view. It may be the most logical view to hold, but it makes communication of ideas difficult. A is liable to believe "A thinks but B does not" while B believes "B thinks but A does not." Instead of arguing continually over this point it is usual to have the polite convention that everyone thinks.

I am sure that Professor Jefferson does not wish to adopt the extreme and solipsist point of view. Probably he would be quite willing to accept the imitation game as a test. The game (with the player B omitted) is frequently used in practice under the name of *viva voce* to discover whether someone really

14

understands something or has "learned it parrot fashion." Let us listen in to a part of such a *viva voce:*

Interrogator: In the first line of your sonnet which reads "Shall I compare thee to a summer's day," would not "a spring day" do as well or better?

Witness: It wouldn't scan.

Interrogator: How about "a winter's day"? That would scan all right.

Witness: Yes, but nobody wants to be compared to a winter's day.

Interrogator: Would you say Mr. Pickwick reminded you of Christmas?

Witness: In a way.

Interrogator: Yet Christmas is a winter's day, and I do not think Mr. Pickwick would mind the comparison.

Witness: I don't think you're serious. By a winter's day one means a typical winter's day, rather than a special one like Christmas.

And so on. What would Professor Jefferson say if the sonnet-writing machine was able to answer like this in the *viva voce*? I do not know whether he would regard the machine as "merely artificially signaling" these answers, but if the answers were as satisfactory and sustained as in the above passage I do not think he would describe it as "an easy contrivance." This phrase is, I think, intended to cover such devices as the inclusion in the machine of a record of someone reading a sonnet, with appropriate switching to turn it on from time to time.

In short, then, I think most of those who support the argument from consciousness could be persuaded to abandon it rather than be forced into the solipsist position. They will then probably be willing to accept our test.

I do not wish to give the impression that I think there is no mystery about consciousness. There is, for instance, something of a paradox connected with any attempt to localize it. But I do not think these mysteries necessarily need to be solved before we can answer the question with which we are concerned here.

ARGUMENTS FROM VARIOUS DISABILITIES

These arguments take the form, "I grant you that you can make machines do all the things you have mentioned, but you will never be able to make one to do X." Numerous features X are suggested in this connection. I offer a selection:

Be kind, resourceful, beautiful, friendly, have initiative, have a sense of humor, tell right from wrong, make mistakes, fall in love, enjoy strawberries and cream, make someone fall in love with it, learn from experience, use words properly, be the subject of its own thought, have as much diversity of behavior as a man, do something really new.

15

Support is seldom offered for these statements. I believe they are founded mostly on the principle of scientific induction. A man has seen thousands of machines in his lifetime. From what he sees of them he draws a number of general conclusions. They are ugly, each is designed for a very limited purpose, when required for a minutely different purpose they are useless, the variety of behavior of any one of them is very small, and so on. Naturally he concludes that these are necessary properties of machines in general. Many of these limitations are associated with the very small storage capacity of most machines. (I am assuming that the idea of storage capacity is extended in some way to cover machines other than discrete state machines. The exact definition does not matter, as no mathematical accuracy is claimed in this discussion.) A few years ago, when very little had been heard of digital computers, it was possible to elicit much incredulity concerning them if one mentioned their properties without describing their construction. That was presumably due to a similar application of the principle of scientific induction. These applications of the principle are, of course, largely unconscious. When a burned child fears the fire and shows that he fears it by avoiding it, I should say that he was applying scientific induction. (I could, of course, also describe his behavior in many other ways.) The works and customs of mankind do not seem to be very suitable material to which to apply scientific induction. A very large part of space-time must be investigated if reliable results are to be obtained. Otherwise we may (as most English children do) decide that everybody speaks English and that it is silly to learn French.

There are, however, special remarks to be made about many of the disabilities that have been mentioned. The inability to enjoy strawberries and cream may have struck the reader as frivolous. Possibly a machine might be made to enjoy this delicious dish, but any attempt to make one do so would be idiotic.

The claim that "machines cannot make mistakes" seems a curious one. One is tempted to retort, "Are they any the worse for that?" But let us adopt a more sympathetic attitude and try to see what is really meant. I think this criticism can be explained in terms of the imitation game. It is claimed that the interrogator could distinguish the machine from the man simply by setting them a number of problems in arithmetic. The machine would be unmasked because of its deadly accuracy. The reply to this is simple. The machine (programed for playing the game) would not attempt to give the *right* answers to the arithmetic problems. It would deliberately introduce mistakes in a manner calculated to confuse the interrogator. A mechanical fault would probably show itself through an unsuitable decision as to what sort of a mistake to make in the arithmetic. Even this interpretation of the criticism is not sufficiently sympathetic. But we cannot afford the space to go into it much further. It seems to me that this criticism depends on a confusion between two kinds of mistakes. We may call them "errors of functioning" and "errors of conclusion." Errors of functioning are due to some mechanical or electrical fault which causes the machine to behave otherwise than it was designed to do. In philosophical discussions one likes to ignore the possiblity of such errors; one is therefore discussing "abstract machines." These abstract machines are mathematical fictions rather than physical objects. By definition, they are incapable of errors of functioning. In this sense we can truly say that "machines can never make mistakes." Errors of conclusion can arise only when some meaning is attached to the output signals from the machine. The machine might, for instance, type out mathematical equations or sentences in English. When a false proposition is typed we say that the machine has committed an error of conclusion. There is clearly no reason for saying that a machine cannot make this kind of mistake. It might do nothing but type out repeatedly "0 = 1." To take a less perverse example, it might have some method for drawing conclusions by scientific induction. We must expect such a method to lead occasionally to erroneous results.

The claim that a machine cannot be the subject of its own thought can, of course, be answered only if it can be shown that the machine has *some* thought with *some* subject matter. Nevertheless, "the subject matter of a machine's operations" does seem to mean something, at least to the people who deal with it. If, for instance, the machine was trying to find a solution to the equation, $x^2 - 40x - 11 = 0$, one would be tempted to describe this equation as part of the machine's subject matter at that moment. In this sense a machine undoubtedly can be its own subject matter. It may be used to help in making up its own programs or to predict the effect of alterations in its own structure. By observing the results of its own behavior it can modify its own programs so as to achieve some purpose more effectively. These are possibilities of the near future rather than Utopian dreams.

The criticism that a machine cannot have much diversity of behavior is just a way of saying that it cannot have much storage capacity. Until fairly recently a storage capacity of even a thousand digits was very rare.

The criticisms that we are considering here are often disguised forms of the argument from consciousness. Usually if one maintains that a machine *can* do one of these things and describes the kind of method that the machine could use, one will not make much of an impression. It is thought that the method (whatever it may be, for it must be mechanical) is actually rather base. Compare the parenthesis in Jefferson's statement quoted above.

LADY LOVELACE'S OBJECTION

A variant of Lady Lovelace's objection states that a machine can "never do anything really new." This may be parried for a moment with the saw, "There is nothing new under the sun." Who can be certain that "original work" that he has done was not simply the growth of the seed planted in him by teaching or the effect of following well-known general principles? A better variant of the objection says that a machine can never "take us by surprise." This statement is a more direct challenge and can be met directly. Machines take me by surprise with great frequency. This is largely because I do not do sufficient calculation to decide what to expect them to do, or rather because, although I do a calculation, I do it in a hurried, slipshod fashion, taking risks. Perhaps I say to myself, "I suppose the voltage here ought to be the same as there; anyway let's assume it is." Naturally I am often wrong, and the result is a surprise for me, for by the time the experiment is done, these assumptions have been forgotten. These admissions leave me open to lectures on the subject of my vicious ways, but do not throw any doubt on my credibility when I testify to the surprises I experience.

I do not expect this reply to silence my critic. He will probably say that such surprises are due to some creative mental act on my part, and reflect no credit on the machine. This leads us back to the argument from consciousness, and far from the idea of surprise. It is a line of argument we must consider closed, but it is perhaps worth remarking that the appreciation of something as surprising requires as much of a "creative mental act" whether the surprising event originates from a man, book, machine, or anything else.

The view that machines cannot give rise to surprises is due, I believe, to a fallacy to which philosophers and mathematicians are particularly subject. This is the assumption that as soon as a fact is presented to a mind all consequences of that fact spring into the mind simultaneously with it. It is a very useful assumption under many circumstances, but one too easily forgets that it is false. A natural consequence of doing so is that one then assumes that there is no virtue in the mere working out of consequences from data and general principles.

ARGUMENT FROM CONTINUITY
IN THE NERVOUS SYSTEM

The nervous system is certainly not a discrete state machine. A small error in the information about the size of a nervous impulse impinging on a neuron may make a large difference to the size of the outgoing impulse. It may be argued that, this being so, one cannot expect to be able to mimic the behavior of the nervous system with a discrete state system.

It is true that a discrete state machine must be different from a continuous machine. But if we adhere to the conditions of the imitation game, the interrogator will not be able to take any advantage of this difference. The situation can be made clearer if we consider some other simpler continuous machine. A differential analyzer will do very well. (A differential analyzer is a certain kind of machine not of the discrete state type used for some kinds of calculations.)

Some of these provide their answers in a typed form and so are suitable for taking part in the game. It would not be possible for a digital computer to predict exactly what answers the differential analyzer would give to a problem, but it would be quite capable of giving the right sort of answer. For instance, if asked to give the value of π (actually about 3.1416), it would be reasonable to choose at random between the values 3.12, 3.13, 3.14, 3.15, 3.16 with the probabilities of, say, 0.05, 0.15, 0.55, 0.19, 0.06. Under these circumstances it would be very difficult for the interrogator to distinguish the differential analyzer from the digital computer.

THE ARGUMENT FROM INFORMALITY OF BEHAVIOR

It is not possible to produce a set of rules purporting to describe what a man should do in every conceivable set of circumstances. One might, for instance, have a rule that one is to stop when one sees a red traffic light and to go if one sees a green one, but what if by some fault both appear together? One may perhaps decide that it is safest to stop. But some further difficulty may well arise from this decision later. To attempt to provide rules of conduct to cover every eventuality, even those arising from traffic lights, appears to be impossible. With all this I agree.

From this it is argued that we cannot be machines. I shall try to reproduce the argument, but I fear I shall hardly do it justice. It seems to run something like this. "If each man had a definite set of rules of conduct by which he regulated his life he would be no better than a machine. But there are no such rules, so men cannot be machines." The undistributed middle is glaring. I do not think the argument is ever put quite like this, but I believe this is the argument used nevertheless. There may, however, be a certain confusion between "rules of conduct" and "laws of behavior" to cloud the issue. By "rules of conduct" I mean precepts such as "Stop if you see red lights," on which one can act and of which one can be conscious. By "laws of behavior" I mean laws of nature as applied to a man's body, such as "if you pinch him he will squeak." If we substitute "laws of behavior which regulate his life" for "laws of conduct by which he regulates his life" in the argument quoted the undistributed middle is no longer insuperable. For we believe that it is not only true that being regulated by laws of behavior implies being some sort of machine (though not necessarily a discrete state machine), but that conversely being such a machine implies being regulated by such laws. However, we cannot so easily convince ourselves of the absence of complete laws of behavior as of complete rules of conduct. The only way we know of for finding such laws is scientific observation, and we certainly know of no circumstances under which we could say, "We have searched enough. There are no such laws."

We can demonstrate more forcibly that any such statement would be unjustified. For suppose we could be sure of finding such laws if they existed. Then given a discrete state machine, it should certainly be possible to discover, by observation enough about it to predict its future behavior and this within a reasonable time, say a thousand years. But this does not seem to be the case. I have set up on the Manchester computer a small program using 100 units of storage, whereby the machine supplied with one 16-figure number replies with another within two seconds. I would defy anyone to learn from these replies enough about the program to be able to predict any replies to untried values.

The reader will have noticed that I have no very convincing arguments of a positive nature to support my views. If I had, I should not have taken such pains to point out the fallacies in contrary views. Such evidence as I have I will now give.

Let us return for a moment to Lady Lovelace's objection, which stated that the machine can only do what we tell it to do. One could say that a man can "inject" an idea into the machine and that it will respond to a certain extent and then drop into quiescence, like a piano string struck by a hammer. Another simile would be an atomic pile of less than critical size: an injected idea is to correspond to a neutron entering the pile from outside. Each such neutron will cause a certain disturbance which eventually dies away. If, however, the size of the pile is sufficiently increased, the disturbance caused by such an incoming neutron will very likely go on and on, increasing until the whole pile is destroyed. Is there a corresponding phenomenon for minds, and is there one for machines? There does seem to be one for the human mind. The majority of them seem to be "subcritical," that is, to correspond in this analogy to piles of subcritical size. An idea presented to such a mind will, on an average, give rise to less than one idea in reply. A smallish proportion are supercritical. An idea presented to such a mind may give rise to a whole "theory" consisting of secondary, tertiary, and more remote ideas. Animals' minds seem to be very definitely subcritical. Adhering to this analogy we ask, "Can a machine be made to be supercritical?"

The "skin of an onion" analogy is also helpful. In considering the functions of the mind or the brain we find certain operations which we can explain in purely mechanical terms. This we say does not correspond to the real mind; it is a sort of skin which we must strip off if we are to find the real mind. But then in what remains we find a further skin to be stripped off, and so on. Proceeding in this way do we ever come to the "real" mind or do we eventually come to the skin which has nothing in it? In the latter case the whole mind is mechanical. (It would not be a discrete state machine, however. We have discussed this.)

The two preceding paragraphs do not claim to be convincing arguments. They should rather be described as "recitations tending to produce belief."

As I have explained, the problem is mainly one of programing. Advances in engineering will have to be made too, but it seems unlikely that these will not be adequate for the requirements. Estimates of the storage capacity of the brain vary from 10^{10} to 10^{15} binary digits. I incline to the lower values and believe that only a very small fraction is used for the higher types of thinking. Most of it is probably used for the retention of visual impressions. I should be surprised if more than 10^9 was required for satisfactory playing of the imitation game, at any rate against a blind man. (Note: The capacity of the *Encyclopaedia Britannica,* 11th edition, is 2×10^9.) A storage capacity of 10^7 would be a very practicable possibility even by present techniques. It is probably not necessary to increase the speed of operations of the machines at all. Parts of modern machines which can be regarded as analogues of nerve cells work about a thousand times faster than the latter. This should provide a "margin of safety" which could cover losses of speed arising in many ways. Our problem, then, is to find out how to program these machines to play the game. At my present rate of working I produce about a thousand digits of program a day, so that about 60 workers working steadily through the 50 years might accomplish the job, if nothing went into the wastepaper basket. Some more expeditious method seems desirable.

We may hope that machines will eventually compete with men in all purely intellectual fields. But which are the best ones to start with? Even this is a difficult decision. Many people think that a very abstract activity, like playing chess, would be best. It can also be maintained that it is best to provide the machine with the best sense organs that money can buy and then teach it to understand and speak English. This process could follow the normal teaching of a child. Things would be pointed out and named, etc. Again, I do not know what the right answer is, but I think both approaches should be tried.

We can only see a short distance ahead, but we can see plenty there that needs to be done.

BEHAVIOR, PURPOSE, and TELEOLOGY *

Arturo Rosenblueth, Norbert Wiener,
and Julian Bigelow

This essay has two goals. The first is to define the behavioristic study of natural events and to classify behavior. The second is to stress the importance of the concept of purpose.

Given any object, relatively abstracted from its surroundings for study, the behavioristic approach consists in the examination of the output of the object and of the relations of this output to the input. By *output* is meant any change produced in the surroundings by the object. By *input,* conversely, is meant any event external to the object that modifies this object in any manner.

The above statement of what is meant by the behavioristic method of study omits the specific structure and the intrinsic organization of the object. This omission is fundamental because on it is based the distinction between the behavioristic and the alternative functional method of study. In a functional analysis, as opposed to a behavioristic approach, the main goal is the intrinsic organization of the entity studied, its structure and its properties; the relations between the object and the surroundings are relatively incidental.

From this definition of the behavioristic method a broad definition of behavior ensues. By behavior is meant any change of an entity with respect to its surroundings. This change may be largely an output from the object, the input being then minimal, remote, or irrelevant; or else the change may be immediately traceable to a certain input. Accordingly, any modification of an object, detectable externally, may be denoted as behavior. The term would be, therefore, too extensive for usefulness were it not that it may be restricted by apposite adjectives—that is, that behavior may be classified.

* From Arturo Rosenblueth, Norbert Wiener, and Julian Bigelow, "Behavior, Purpose, and Teleology," *Philosophy of Science,* 10 (1943), 18–24. Copyright ©1943, The Williams & Wilkins Co. Reproduced by permission.

The consideration of the changes of energy involved in behavior affords a basis for classification. Active behavior is that in which the object is the source of the output energy involved in a given specific reaction. The object may store energy supplied by a remote or relatively immediate input, but the input does not energize the output directly. In passive behavior, on the contrary, the object is not a source of energy; all the energy in the output can be traced to the immediate input (for example, the throwing of an object), or the object may control energy which remains external to it throughout the reaction (for example, the soaring flight of a bird).

Active behavior may be subdivided into two classes: purposeless (or random) and purposeful. The term *purposeful* is meant to denote that the act or behavior may be interpreted as directed to the attainment of a goal—that is, to a final condition in which the behaving object reaches a definite correlation in time or in space with respect to another object or event. Purposeless behavior, then, is that which is not interpreted as being directed to a goal.

The vagueness of the phrase "may be interpreted" as used above might be considered so great that the distinction would be useless. Yet the recognition that behavior may sometimes be purposeful is unavoidable and useful, as follows. The basis of the concept of purpose is the awareness of *voluntary activity*. Now the purpose of voluntary acts is not a matter of arbitrary interpretation but a physiological fact. When we perform a voluntary action what we select voluntarily is a specific purpose, not a specific movement. Thus if we decide to take a glass containing water and carry it to our mouth we do not command certain muscles to contract to a certain degree and in a certain sequence; we merely trip the purpose and the reaction follows automatically. Indeed, experimental physiology has so far been largely incapable of explaining the mechanism of voluntary activity. We submit that this failure is due to the fact that when an experimenter stimulates the motor regions of the cerebral cortex he does not duplicate a voluntary reaction; he trips efferent, "output" pathways, but does not trip a purpose, as is done voluntarily.

The view has often been expressed that all machines are purposeful. This view is untenable. First may be mentioned mechanical devices such as a roulette, designed precisely for purposelessness. Then may be considered devices such as a clock, designed, it is true, with a purpose, but having a performance which, although orderly, is not purposeful—that is, there is no specific final condition toward which the movement of the clock strives. Similarly, although a gun may be used for a definite purpose, the attainment of a goal is not intrinsic to the performance of the gun; random shooting can be made, deliberately purposeless.

Some machines, on the other hand, are intrinsically purposeful. A torpedo with a target-seeking mechanism is an example. The term *servomechanisms* has been coined precisely to designate machines with intrinsic purposeful behavior. It is apparent from these considerations that although the definition of purposeful behavior is relatively vague and hence operationally largely meaning-less, the concept of purpose is useful and should therefore be retained.

Purposeful active behavior may be subdivided into two classes: *feedback* (or teleological) and *nonfeedback* (or nonteleological). The expression feedback is used by engineers in two different senses. In a broad sense it may denote that some of the output energy of an apparatus or machine is returned as input; an example is an electrical amplifier with feedback. The feedback is in these cases positive—the fraction of the output which reenters the object has the same sign as the original input signal. Positive feedback adds to the input signals, it does not correct them. The term feedback is also used in a more restricted sense to signify that the behavior of an object is controlled by the margin of error at which the object stands at a given time with reference to a relatively specific goal. The feedback is then negative; that is, the signals from the goal are used to restrict outputs which would otherwise go beyond the goal. It is this second meaning of the term feedback that is used here.

All purposeful behavior may be considered to require negative feedback. If a goal is to be attained, some signals from the goal are necessary at some time to direct the behavior. By nonfeedback behavior is meant that in which there are no signals from the goal which modify the activity of the object *in the course of the behavior.* Thus a machine may be set to impinge on a luminous object al-though the machine may be insensitive to light. Similarly, a snake may strike at a frog or a frog at a fly, with no visual or other report from the prey after the movement has started. Indeed, the movement is in these cases so fast that it is not likely that nerve impulses would have time to arise at the retina, travel to the central nervous system and set up further impulses which would reach the muscles in time to modify the movement effectively.

As opposed to the examples considered, the behavior of some machines and some reactions of living organisms involve a continuous feedback from the goal that modifies and guides the behaving object. This type of behavior is more effective than that mentioned above, particularly when the goal is not stationary. But continuous feedback control may lead to very clumsy behavior if the feed-back is inadequately damped and becomes therefore positive instead of negative for certain frequencies of oscillation. Suppose, for example, that a machine is designed with the purpose of impinging on a moving luminous goal; the path followed by the machine is controlled by the direction and intensity of the light from the goal. Suppose further that the machine overshoots seriously when it follows a movement of the goal in a certain direction; an even stronger stimulus will then be delivered, which will turn the machine in the opposite direction. If that movement again overshoots, a series of increasingly larger oscillations will ensue, and the machine will miss the goal.

This picture of the consequences of undamped feedback is strikingly similar to that seen during the performance of a voluntary act by a cerebellar patient.

At rest the subject exhibits no obvious motor disturbance. If he is asked to carry a glass of water from a table to his mouth, however, the hand carrying the glass will execute a series of oscillatory motions of increasing amplitude as the glass approaches his mouth, so that the water will spill and the purpose will not be fulfilled. This test is typical of the disorderly motor performance of patients with cerebellar disease. The analogy with the behavior of a machine with un-damped feedback is so vivid that we venture to suggest that the main function of the cerebellum is the control of the feedback nervous mechanisms involved in purposeful motor activity.

Feedback purposeful behavior may again be subdivided. It may be extrapolative (predictive), or it may be nonextrapolative (nonpredictive). The reactions of unicellular organisms known as tropisms are examples of nonpredictive performances. The amoeba merely follows the source to which it reacts; there is no evidence that it extrapolates the path of a moving source. Predictive animal behavior, on the other hand, is a commonplace. A cat starting to pursue a running mouse does not run directly toward the region where the mouse is at any given time, but moves toward an extrapolated future position. Examples of both predictive and nonpredictive servomechanisms may also be found readily.

Predictive behavior may be subdivided into different orders. The cat chasing the mouse is an instance of first-order prediction; the cat merely predicts the path of the mouse. Throwing a stone at a moving target requires a second-order prediction; the paths of the target and of the stone should be foreseen. Examples of predictions of higher order are shooting with a sling or with a bow and arrow.

Predictive behavior requires the discrimination of at least two coordinates, a temporal and at least one spatial axis. Prediction will be more effective and flexible, however, if the behaving object can respond to changes in more than one spatial coordinate. The sensory receptors of an organism or the corresponding elements of a machine may therefore limit the predictive behavior. Thus a bloodhound *follows* a trail; that is, it does not show any predictive behavior in trailing, because a chemical, olfactory input reports only spatial information: distance as indicated by intensity. The external changes capable of affecting auditory, or even better, visual receptors, permit more accurate spatial localization, hence the possibility of more effective predictive reactions when the input affects those receptors.

In addition to the limitations imposed by the receptors on the ability to perform extrapolative actions, limitations may also occur that are due to the internal organization of the behaving object. Thus a machine which is to trail predictively a moving luminous object should not only be sensitive to light (for example, by the possession of a photoelectric cell), but should also have the structure adequate for interpreting the luminous input. It is probable that limitations of internal organization, particularly of the organization of the central nervous system, determine the complexity of predictive behavior which a

25

mammal may attain. Thus it is likely that the nervous system of a rat or dog is such that it does not permit the integration of input and output necessary for the performance of a predictive reaction of the third or fourth order. Indeed, it is possible that one of the features of the discontinuity of behavior observable when comparing humans with other high mammals may lie in that the other mammals are limited to predictive behavior of a low order, whereas man may be capable potentially of quite high orders of prediction.

The classification of behavior suggested so far is tabulated below.

It is apparent that each of the dichotomies established arbitrarily singles out one feature, deemed interesting, leaving an amorphous remainder: the nonclass. It is also apparent that the criteria for the several dichotomies are heterogeneous. It is obvious, therefore, that many other lines of classification are available which are independent of that developed above. Thus behavior in general, or any of the groups in the table, could be divided into linear (that is, output proportional to input) and nonlinear. A division into continuous and discontinuous might be useful for many purposes. The several degrees of freedom which behavior may exhibit could also be employed as a basis of systematization.

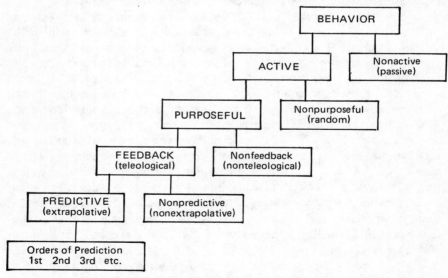

The classification tabulated above was adopted for several reasons. It leads to the singling out of the class of predictive behavior, a class particularly interesting since it suggests the possibility of systematizing increasingly more complex tests of the behavior of organisms. It emphasizes the concepts of purpose and of teleology, concepts which, although rather discredited at present, are shown to be important. Finally, it reveals that a uniform behavioristic analysis is applicable to both machines and living organisms, regardless of the complexity of the behavior.

It has sometimes been stated that the designers of machines merely attempt to duplicate the performances of living organisms. This statement is uncritical. That the gross behavior of some machines should be similar to the reactions of organisms is not surprising. Animal behavior includes many varieties of all the possible modes of behavior, and the machines devised so far have far from exhausted all those possible modes. There is, therefore, a considerable overlap of the two realms of behavior. Examples, however, are readily found of manmade machines with behavior that transcends human behavior. A machine with an electrical output is an instance, for men, unlike the electric fishes, are incapable of emitting electricity. Radio transmission is perhaps an even better instance, for no animal is known with the ability to generate short waves, even if so-called experiments on telepathy are considered seriously.

A further comparison of living organisms and machines leads to the following inferences. The methods of study for the two groups are at present similar. Whether they should always be the same may depend on whether or not there are one or more qualitatively distinct, unique characteristics present in one group and absent in the other. Such qualitative differences have not appeared so far.

The broad classes of behavior are the same in machines and living organisms. Specific, narrow classes may be found exclusively in one or the other. Thus no machine is available yet that can write a Sanscrit-Mandarin dictionary. Thus, also, no living organism is known that rolls on wheels—imagine what the result would have been if engineers had insisted on copying living organisms and had therefore put legs and feet in their locomotives, instead of wheels.

While the behavioristic analysis of machines and living organisms is largely uniform, their functional study reveals deep differences. Structurally, organisms are mainly colloidal and include prominently protein molecules, large, complex, and anisotropic; machines are chiefly metallic and include mainly simple molecules. From the standpoint of their energetics, machines usually exhibit relatively large differences of potential, which permit rapid mobilization of energy; in organisms the energy is more uniformly distributed, it is not very mobile. Thus in electric machines conduction is mainly electronic, whereas in organisms electric changes are usually ionic.

Scope and flexibility are achieved in machines largely by temporal multiplication of effects; frequencies of one million per second or more are readily obtained and utilized. In organisms, spatial multiplication, rather than temporal, is the rule; the temporal achievements are poor—the fastest nerve fibers can conduct only about 1,000 impulses per second; spatial multiplication is, on the other hand, abundant and admirable in its compactness. This difference is well illustrated by the comparison of a television receiver and the eye. The television receiver may be described as a single cone retina; the images are formed by scanning, by orderly successive detection of the signal with a rate of about 20 million per second. Scanning is a process which seldom or never occurs in

27

organisms, since it requires fast frequencies for effective performance. The eye uses a spatial, rather than a temporal, multiplier. Instead of the one cone of the television receiver, a human eye has about 6.5 million cones and about 115 million rods.

If an engineer were to design a robot roughly similar in behavior to an animal organism, he would not attempt at present to make it out of proteins and other colloids. He would probably build it out of metallic parts, some dielectrics and many vacuum tubes. The movements of the robot could readily be much faster and more powerful than those of the original organism. Learning and memory, however, would be quite rudimentary. In future years, as the knowledge of colloids and proteins increases, future engineers may attempt the design of robots not only with a behavior, but also with a structure similar to that of a mammal. The ultimate model of a cat is of course another cat, whether it be born of still another cat or synthesized in a laboratory.

In classifying behavior the term *teleology* was used as being synonymous with "purpose controlled by feedback." Teleology has been interpreted in the past to imply purpose, and the vague concept of a "final cause" has been often added. This concept of final causes has led to the opposition of teleology to determinism. A discussion of causality, determinism, and final causes is beyond the scope of this essay. It may be pointed out, however, that purposefulness, as defined here, is quite independent of causality, initial or final. Teleology has been discredited chiefly because it was defined to imply a cause subsequent in time to a given effect. When this aspect of teleology was dismissed, however, the associated recognition of the importance of purpose was also unfortunately discarded. Since we consider purposefulness a concept necessary for the understanding of certain modes of behavior we suggest that a teleological study is useful if it avoids problems of causality and concerns itself merely with an investigation of purpose.

We have restricted the connotation of teleological behavior by applying this designation only to purposeful reactions which are controlled by the error of the reaction, that is, by the difference between the state of the behaving object at any time and the final state interpreted as the purpose. Teleological behavior thus becomes synonymous with behavior controlled by negative feedback and gains therefore in precision by a sufficiently restricted connotation.

According to this limited definition, teleology is not opposed to determinism, but to nonteleology. Both teleological and nonteleological systems are deterministic when the behavior considered belongs to the realm where determinism applies. The concept of teleology shares only one thing with the concept of causality: a time axis. But causality implies a one-way, relatively irreversible, functional relationship, whereas teleology is concerned with behavior, not with functional relationships.

COMMENTS ON A MECHANISTIC CONCEPTION OF PURPOSEFULNESS*

Richard Taylor

In a highly original and provocative essay entitled "Behavior, Purpose, and Teleology," published a few years ago, Professors Arturo Rosenblueth, Norbert Wiener, and Julian Bigelow attempt to indicate the scientific importance and usefulness of the concepts of purpose and teleology. Since this essay appeared, the suggestions it contains seem to have acquired a significance which was not wholly apparent at that time. This is due primarily to the fact that a somewhat novel and, it appears to some, revolutionary approach to certain problems has arisen in the sciences, an approach which is more or less loosely referred to as "cybernetics" and among whose outstanding spokesmen are to be found the very authors of this essay—particularly Professor Wiener, whose recently published *Cybernetics* has been claiming the attention of an increasing number of scientists and nonscientists alike. In this book, it may be noted, Professor Wiener, in tracing the development of cybernetics over the past few years, gives a good indication of the importance he attaches to the earlier essay. He writes, with reference to it: "The three of us [Rosenblueth, Wiener, and Bigelow] felt that this new point of view merited a paper, which we wrote up and published. Dr. Rosenblueth and I foresaw that the paper could only be a statement of program for a large body of experimental work, and we decided that if we could ever bring our plan for an interscientific institute to fruition, this topic would furnish an almost ideal center for our activity." It would seem, then, that an examination of the contents of this essay should not be without interest at this time.

---

* From Richard Taylor, "Comments on a Mechanistic Conception of Purposefulness," *Philosophy of Science*, 17 (1950), 310 –17. Copyright © 1950, The Williams & Wilkins Co. Reproduced by permission.

29

My objective in this paper will be to elicit what appears to be a gross confusion underlying these authors' main contention. This contention is that the notions of purpose and teleology, "although rather discredited at present," are in fact not only useful and important but unavoidable and necessary for the interpretation of certain kinds of behavior, both animate and inanimate. I shall maintain, on the contrary, that the concepts, as they are defined and illustrated by these authors, cannot possibly serve the ends for which they are invoked. This conclusion will be indicated, I believe, if it can be shown (1) that purposive behavior, as they describe it, is indistinguishable from any other kind of active behavior, and (2) that the term *purpose,* as thus used, bears no similarity whatever to the meaning which is ordinarily attached to it. This second point might seem to be largely a verbal matter, and indeed it is; but it would be a mistake to conclude from this that it is therefore of slight significance.

The concept of purposiveness is applied by these authors only to certain kinds of *active* behavior, that is to say, to that kind of behavior "in which the object is the source of the output energy involved in a given specific reaction." And the term *behavior* itself is taken to mean "any change of an entity with respect to its surroundings,"[1] or, "any modification of an object, detectable externally." Thus examples of active behavior would be, as I understand the definition, such things as a clock which is running, an automobile in operation, an exploding bomb, as well as the active behavior of living organisms generally. On the other hand, passive behavior, that is, behavior in which "the object is not a source of energy" and in which "all the energy in the output can be traced to the immediate input" would be exemplified by such things as a falling stone, melting ice, and a revolving water wheel. The terms *active* and *passive* are themselves quite unambiguous and serve to convey, I believe, the distinction intended. But it needs particularly to be noted at this point that active behavior is taken to characterize certain inanimate objects, no less than living ones.

With these distinctions in mind, we can consider now the discussion of purposefulness itself. The authors define purposeful and nonpurposeful behavior in these words: "The term purposeful is meant to denote that the act or behavior may be interpreted as directed to the attainment of a goal—that is, to a final condition in which the behaving object reaches a definite correlation in time or in space with respect to another object or event. Purposeless behavior then is that which is not interpreted as directed to a goal."

Now the writers concede that the words "may be interpreted" are vague, but, insist that "the recognition that behavior may sometimes be purposeful is unavoidable and useful." I do not see that the expression "may be interpreted" is really vague; the words themselves seem to have reasonably precise meanings, and I think there is little danger of their being mistaken. What the writers probably have in mind is that the definition itself is rather *general*—and in this, I should certainly concur. Indeed, the definition is so broad that it not only fails to distinguish, even in some general way, the feature which it is intended to describe, but it makes any behavior whatever, whether active *or* passive, a case of purposiveness. One or two examples will show this to be the case.

Imagine, for instance, a clock which runs properly for many years and then breaks down at 12 o'clock, New Year's Eve—such behavior admirably fits every requirement of purposiveness. Or again, consider a more humble example, such as a stone which falls from a rooftop, and kills a passerby, or more simply still, one that just makes a dent in the ground. Now such behavior not only *may* be interpreted as that in which the behaving object "reaches a definite correlation in time or in space with respect to another object or event," but such an interpretation is precisely the one which constitutes a simple and, as far as it goes, accurate description of just what has taken place. It seems hardly necessary to multiply examples here, for a very little reflection will show that any instance of behavior one might choose will necessarily be a case of "purposefulness," whether one considers active or passive behavior. And the reason for this is very apparent: it is simply that any behavior culminates, at whatever point we choose to call its culmination, in a definite correlation in time or space between the behaving object and other objects or events.[2]

Of course the definition specifies that purposeful behavior is that active behavior which may be interpreted as being *directed* toward such a goal. But this, so far as I can discern, can only mean either (a) that such behavior is directed by some purposeful being *other* than the behaving object itself—by a human being, for example; or (b) that the behaving object directs *itself* toward some correlation. Now the first meaning is clearly not what the authors intend, for in that case the purposiveness would reside, not in the object itself, but in the being who directs it; a hammer does not itself become purposeful by being used *for* the purpose of driving nails. But if we consider the second meaning, which is the only other possible one, innumerable difficulties arise. In the first place, it presupposes the as yet unjustified assumption that some mechanisms other than living organisms *are* "intrinsically purposeful" in the distinctive sense of directing themselves toward the attainment of "goals." But even if this assumption were granted, then it is at once clear that *any* correlation in time or space between the behaving objects and other objects or events can be taken at precisely the one toward which the supposedly purposeful object "directs" itself. For it is at all times in some such state of correlation, and so long as we leave distinctively human purposes out of account, as these authors try rigorously to do, then there is no conceivable way of selecting *some* particular reciprocal relationship between the object and some state of affairs as being the "goal" toward which that object was directing itself. Of course it might be suggested that we select as the goal of the object some *final* correlation; indeed, this seems to be exactly what the authors have in mind in reiterating the expression *final condition*. But this is of little help, because (a) unless the behaving object is destroyed, there *is* no such final condition; so long as it exists, it exists in a state of reciprocal relationship with other objects and events; and (b) such a criterion is wholly arbitrary. It obliges us to assert that whenever a supposedly purposeful mechanism culminates in such a "final condition" (however this "culmination" might be determined), then that final condition is, ipso facto, the very "goal" toward which it was directing itself. So if the behavior of an organism, say, culminates in some such final condition as death, then we shall be required to conclude that precisely this was, by definition, its purpose, that is, the "goal" toward which it directed itself. And this seems palpably incorrect; it would render such an expression as "accidental death" quite meaningless, for example.

Clearly, then, we cannot expect much light from such descriptions as these; they appear arbitrary, and so general as to make purposiveness a ubiquitous phenomenon. Therefore let us turn now to the actual examples which the writers submit of both purposeful and nonpurposeful behavior, to see whether these will serve any better to elicit the distinction intended.

It is a mistake, they contend, to regard all machines as purposeful, and in this they are doubtless correct; it seems to be a mistake which none but the overly superstitious would be likely to make, however. As examples of mechanical devices which are *not* purposeful, they suggest a roulette wheel, a clock, and a gun. A roulette, it is pointed out, is "designed precisely for purposelessness." And a clock, although it is designed to serve a purpose, is not in itself purposeful—because there is, again, no "final condition" toward which it "strives." The same consideration applies to the example of a gun; it can, to be sure, be used for a purpose, but purposiveness itself "is not intrinsic to the performance of the gun," because it can also be shot at random.

As contrasted with these mechanisms, on the other hand, the authors cite the example of a torpedo containing a target-seeking device as being an instance of a machine which is "intrinsically purposeful." Indeed, they single out an entire class of mechanical devices as possessing intrinsic purposiveness, namely, "servomechanisms," or machines which are controlled by negative feedback.[3] "The term servomechanisms," they note, "has been coined precisely to designate machines with intrinsic purposeful behavior." Those who are acquainted with Professor Wiener's recent book are aware of the importance he and his colleagues attach to these mechanisms. Before examining the discussion of these, however, a few remarks suggest themselves concerning the examples already referred to.

In the first place, it is difficult to see, from the descriptions given, in what sense roulettes, clocks, and guns are "purposeless," as contrasted with other mechanisms in which purposefulness is "intrinsic." A gun, it is pointed out, may be used for a purpose, but it can also be shot at random; therefore, "the attainment of a goal is not intrinsic to the performance of the gun." It would seem, however, that whether the gun is "used for a deliberate purpose (for example, shooting a duck) or simply shot at random, in either case it serves a purpose—if only the amusement of the gunner. Moreover, even target-seeking missiles, which are classed as "intrinsically purposeful," *can* be used for random shooting or even left to rust away in an ammunition dump; why does this not indicate a parallel conclusion in their case? Apparently the authors are utilizing here an unnamed criterion of purposiveness.

The remarks concerning the behavior of clocks are similarly puzzling. A clock is denied the attribute of "intrinsic" purposefulness because "there is no specific final condition toward which the movement of the clock strives." But if mechanical devices are once granted the power of "striving" toward some goal or "final condition," then how are we to know that the final condition which a clock ultimately attains—say, breakdown at a particular time and place—was not the very one toward which it was "striving"? The difficulty in such a supposition is no greater than in the case of target-seeking missiles, however great it may be in either case.

Finally, a roulette wheel is said to be "designed precisely for purposelessness." By this the authors apparently have in mind that this device is designed in a manner such that it will not, in the long run, turn up any specific number, or order of numbers, more frequently than any other. Such, at any rate, is the distinguishing characteristic of an ideal roulette. How, then, should one describe a number wheel which has a weight affixed to its circumference, in a way so as to determine the wheel always to stop on the number six? Such a mechanism satisfies perfectly every condition of intrinsic purposefulness which the writers set down; unlike the clock, for example, there *is* here a "specific final condition toward which the movement of the [wheel] strives"—provided, again, that "striving" may without incongruity be attributed to mechanical devices.

I question whether anyone would undertake to defend such a conclusion as this; first, because it seems prima facie bizarre to maintain that a wheel becomes a purposeful object by the mere addition to it of a weight, and second, because if it were maintained that such behavior as this is purposive, then it would be difficult to find an instance of behavior which is not. Yet, I submit, this conclusion is absolutely forced by the descriptions and criteria which the authors adduce. Now I should suppose that the only relevant distinction to be drawn between an honest roulette and a weighted one is that in the case of the second, we can usually predict its "final condition," whereas in the case of the first, we cannot. But the reason for this is not that the one is purposeless while the other is not, but rather that we know and can measure the causal factors involved in the behavior of the loaded wheel, whereas we do not have such knowledge of the other. If, on the other hand, we *did* know all of the causal factors (force, mass, friction, etc.) involved in the behavior of an honest roulette, then we *could,* within the limits of accuracy of our measuring instruments, predict its final condition, that is, the number on which it will stop; at least, this ability is universally taken for granted in the sciences so long as we are dealing with such relatively macroscopic objects as wheels and the like. In what sense, then, is a roulette wheel a purposeless machine? So far as I can discern, the distinction to be made regarding purposiveness is simply this and this only: If a purposive *being,* that is, a man, spins a roulette with the *purpose* of turning up a specific number, then he will be less likely to succeed if he uses an honest wheel than if he uses one which is weighted properly; and the only reason for this is, again, that his knowledge of the causal factors involved in the behavior of the first wheel is insufficient to enable him to predict. And if this is a correct description, then, I submit, neither purposefulness nor purposelessness is appropriately attributable to the wheel, of whichever kind, but only to the being who uses it *for* a purpose.

The objective of the examples we have been considering was to elicit the distinction between purposeful and purposeless behavior—a distinction which the writers believe, correctly, is not made sufficiently clear by their definition. The distinction which is apparently intended is simply this: that although such objects as roulette wheels, clocks, and guns can be made to *serve* a purpose, they do not have any purposes of their own; while a target-seeking missile, on the other hand, not only serves a purpose but *does* have a purposiveness of its own; it is, in the words of the authors, an "intrinsically purposeful" object. At least, so far as the notion of "purpose" is concerned, this is the only distinction I can discern between machines which only serve a purpose, on one hand, and those which are "intrinsically purposeful," on the other. As soon as this distinction is made clear and precise, however, instead of simply hovering vaguely in the background, then, I believe, its dubious status becomes quite apparent.

Let us consider, finally, that class of machines which are distinguished by the possession of "intrinsic purposeful behavior," namely, servomechanisms. The term "servomechanisms" is used to denote such objects as thermostats, target-seeking missiles, ship steering devices, radar-controlled guns, and so on, the distinguishing characteristic of which is that the behavior of all such objects is controlled by negative feedback. That is to say, such a mechanism is so designed that the *effects* of its behavior themselves enter as causal factors *on* its behavior, the objective being to have a device that will maintain itself in a certain desired correlation with other objects or events, which also operate upon it as causal factors. This is doubtless an overly simple description, but I think it will do for our purposes. Thus a thermostat controls and is in turn controlled by temperature; a target-seeking missile is directed at, and is in turn directed by, its target, and so on. In the case of all such mechanisms, then, the objects or events which they operate upon, in turn operate upon them, in such a manner as to maintain a constant reciprocal relationship. The governor of a steam engine was, I believe, one of the earliest of such manmade devices.

Professor Wiener and his colleagues regard these mechanisms as exhibiting a kind of purposiveness par excellence, namely, *teleological* purposefulness;[4] they maintain, in fact, that the concepts of purpose and teleology are not only useful, but necessary for the understanding of this class of machines. It seems significant to note, however, that what is here called "teleological purposeful behavior" is by no means limited to higher organisms and servomechanisms, but is exhibited as well by some of the most ordinary objects of our daily experience—a fact which these authors entirely neglect to point out. The leaves of many green plants, for example, follow the course of the sun and thus exhibit a behavior pattern which is precisely the same, so far as teleology is concerned, as that of a machine which is designed to impinge upon a moving luminous object—a servomechanism which is cited by the writers as clearly exemplifying teleological behavior. Again, consider the needle of an ordinary magnetic compass. If it is diverted from its alignment with the magnetic forces of its locus, it vacillates momentarily and finally resumes its former correlation. The behavior of the compass thus fits precisely the description of a "purposeful reaction," as being that which is exhibited by an object whose behavior "is controlled by the margin of error at which the object stands at a given time with reference to a relatively specific goal," assuming that we can designate its final correlation with the magnetic forces as its "goal." Other examples, such as the behavior of a pendulum or of a vibrating cord, come readily to mind; if servomechanisms differ in any way, other than that of mere mechanical complexity, from such everyday phenomena as these, then the writers have at any rate failed to give any hint as to what this difference might be. The behavior of servomechanisms does, to be sure, satisfy perfectly the criteria of purposiveness which the authors adduce, but the behavior of these other objects seems to satisfy them equally well.

I should maintain, therefore, that the notions of purpose and teleology are not only useless for the understanding of this sort of mechanical behavior, but are wholly incongruous as thus applied; this conclusion follows, I believe, from the fact that such behavior is describable in terms of, and only in terms of, the same fundamental categories as are employed for the description of any other physical process.

A single example should make this last point clear. Consider the illustration used by the authors, that of a torpedo with a target-seeking mechanism. Now if such a machine is so designed as to be guided by, say, sound waves proceeding from the ship's engines or propellers, then its behavior is describable, in general, as follows. The sound waves emanating from the target act causally on the sonic mechanism of the torpedo, and the behavior of this device in turn acts (through intermediary devices) as a cause on the steering mechanism of the missile. Accordingly, if the torpedo is diverted from its course, the resulting change in the sound waves, relative to the sonic device, suffices to reorient the torpedo, that is, it causes it to resume its course relative to the target. Similarly, if the target itself moves, the correlation between sound waves and missile is likewise upset, and this, again, suffices to alter the course of the torpedo, relative to the target, through the complex nexus of causes and effects obtaining between the sound

35

waves and the torpedo's rudders and vanes. Of course an accurate description of this process is much less simple than this, but, I submit, such further description consists only in the addition of details to this general picture. One point to note here is that the torpedo is guided, *not* by the target itself, but by the sound waves impinging on the sonic mechanism; it does not literally "seek" the target, for its behavior would be the same even if no target were there, provided only that sound waves or certain other immediate causes obtained. The expression "target-seeking missile" is, in fact, metaphorical.

Is there, then, any room in such a description for the notion of *intrinsic* purposefulness on the part of the torpedo? I think not; and to illustrate this, we need only to alter the example in one respect. Let us suppose that the missile, instead of being governed by sound waves, is propelled along a cable, attached to the target. Now the behavior of this missile is precisely analogous to the first, the only relevant difference being that whereas the first was guided by sound waves between itself and the target, this one is guided by the much simpler means of a cable. If this second torpedo is diverted from its path, the change in its alignment, relative to the cable, suffices to reorient it; and the same is true if the target itself moves. In short, the analogy seems complete, the *only* difference being in the degree of mechanical complexity—and I doubt whether anyone would contend that complexity by itself is a criterion of a purposive object. Accordingly, if the first missile is to be characterized as "intrinsically purposeful," then we are obliged to conclude that the second one must be similarly described. But from this concession it would follow that a vast number of other machines become "intrinsically purposeful" objects, even though no one has ever suspected them of being such; trains, for example, or elevators, in fact, almost any machine one might choose.

My conclusion with respect to servomechanisms is, therefore, the same as before; namely, that Professors Rosenblueth, Wiener, and Bigelow (a) use criteria which render purposeful behavior a ubiquitous phenomenon, and (b) thereby endow the word "purpose" with a meaning having no similarity to any meaning it has customarily been taken to possess. Of course it might be claimed that one is entitled to assign to his terms any meaning he chooses, and in a sense this is true; it must be added, however, that if this is what these writers have done, then their discussion sacrifices any interest and significance which it may have been intended to have. For it is exactly as if one were to announce the discovery that $2 + 3 = 6$, only to add later that the term "+" is taken by him to have the meaning which has traditionally been assigned to the symbol "x". His claim would be entirely correct, but scarcely significant.

NOTES

1. On this definition, it may be noted, a perfectly static object surrounded by others in motion exhibits "behavior."

2. The word "correlation" is not defined by these writers, and in fact they use it only once. I therefore assume it to have no special or technical meaning in their usage. Ordinarily, to say of two objects or events that they are correlated, is simply to say that they stand in some reciprocal or mutual relationship, that is, that they are co-related. The word is also used more precisely to indicate a constant relationship between kinds of objects or events or to indicate that one is a universal accompaniment of the other, as when we speak of mental states being correlated with brain processes or of the hands of a clock being correlated with each other, and so on. The more general meaning is what the authors seem to have in mind in their definition, although the more precise one would not alter their argument.

3. The expression "negative feedback" is a technical one of physics and engineering. The authors point out that they are using it "to signify that the behavior of an object is controlled by the margin of error at which the object stands at a given time with reference to a relatively specific goal." The same idea could be expressed by saying that an object is controlled by *negative* feedback when the effects of its behavior, in turn, act indirectly on the object itself to *oppose* whatever it is doing (cf. *Cybernetics*, p. 115).

4. This expression may appear as a redundancy, but the authors qualify as "teleological" only those purposeful objects which are controlled by negative feedback.

INFORMATION PROCESSING IN COMPUTER AND MAN *

Herbert A. Simon and Allen Newell

Organizing a computer to perform complex tasks depends very much more on the characteristics of the task environment than on the "hardware"—the specific physical means for realizing the processing in the computer. Thus all past and present digital computers perform basically the same kinds of symbol manipulations.

In programing a computer it is substantially irrelevant what physical processes and devices—electromagnetic, electronic, or what not—accomplish the manipulations. A program, written in one of the symbolic programing languages, like ALGOL or FORTRAN, will produce the same symbolic output on a machine that uses electron tubes for processing and storing symbols, one that incorporates magnetic drums, one with a magnetic core memory, or one with completely transistorized circuitry. The program, the organization of symbol-manipulating processes, is what determines the transformation of input into output. In fact, provided with only the program output and without information about the processing speed, one cannot determine what kinds of physical devices accomplished the transformations, whether the program was executed by a solid-state computer, an electron-tube device, an electrical relay machine, or a room full of statistical clerks! Only the organization of the processes is determinate. Out of this observation arises the possiblity of an independent science of information processing.

By the same token, since the thinking human being is also an information processor, it should be possible to study his processes and their organization independently on the details of the biological mechanisms—the "hardware"—that

---

* Reprinted by permission, *American Scientist,* journal of Sigma Yi, the Scientific Research Society of North America, Inc.

implement them. The output of the processes, the behavior of *Homo cogitans,* should reveal how the information processing is organized without necessarily providing much information about the protoplasmic structures or biochemical processes that implement it. From this observation follows the possiblity of constructing and testing psychological theories to explain human thinking in terms of the organization of information processes and of accomplishing this without waiting until the neurophysiological foundations at the next lower level of explanation have been constructed.

Finally, there is a growing body of evidence that the elementary information processes used by the human brain in thinking are highly similar to a subset of the elementary information processes that are incorporated in the instruction codes of present-day computers. As a consequence it has been found possible to test information-processing theories of human thinking by formulating these theories as computer programs—organizations of the elementary information processes—and examining the outputs of computers so programed. The procedure assumes no similarity between computer and brain at the "hardware" level, only similarity in their capacities for executing and organizing elementary information processes. From this hypothesis has grown up a fruitful collaboration between research in "artificial intelligence" aimed at enlarging the capabilities of computers and research in human cognitive psychology.

These, then, are the three propositions on which this discussion rests:

(1) A science of information processing can be constructed that is substantially independent of the specific properties of particular information-processing mechanisms.

(2) Human thinking can be explained in information-processing terms without waiting for a theory of the underlying neurological mechanisms.

(3) Information-processing theories of human thinking can be formulated in computer programing languages and can be tested by simulating the predicted behavior with computers.

LEVELS OF EXPLANATION

No apology is needed for carrying explanation only to an intermediate level, leaving further reduction to the future progress of science. The other sciences provide numerous precedents, perhaps the most relevant being nineteenth-century chemistry. The atomic theory and the theory of chemical combination were invented and developed rapidly and, fruitfully during the first three quarters of the nineteenth century—from Dalton, through Kekulé, to Mendeleev—without any direct physical evidence for or description of atoms, molecules, or valences. To quote Pauling:

> Most of the general principles of molecular structure and the nature of the chemical bond were formulated long ago by chemists by induction from the great body of chemical facts. . . .
> The study of the structure of molecules was originally carried on by chemists using methods of investigation that were essentially chemical in nature, relating to the chemical composition of substances, the existence of isomers, the nature of the chemical reactions in which a substance takes part, and so on. From the consideration of facts of this kind Frankland, Kekulé, Couper, and Butlerov were led a century ago to formulate the theory of valence and to write the first structural formulas for molecules, van't Hoff and le Bel were led to bring classical organic stereochemistry into its final form by their brilliant postulate of the tetrahedral orientation of the four valence bonds of the carbon atom, and Werner was led to his development of the theory of the stereochemistry of complex inorganic substances.[1]

The history this passage outlines is worth pondering, because the last generation of psychologists has engaged in so much methodological dispute about the nature, utility, and even propriety of theory. The vocal, methodologically self-conscious behaviorist wing of experimental psychology has expressed its scepticism of "unobserved entities" and "intermediate constructs."[2] Sometimes it has seemed to object to filling the thinking head with anything whatsoever. Psychologists who rejected the empty-head viewpoint, but who were sensitive to the demand for operational constructs, tended to counter the behaviorist objections by couching their theories in physiological language.[3]

The example of atomic theory in chemistry shows that neither horn of this dilemma need be seized. On the one hand, hypothetical entities, postulated because they were powerful and fruitful for organizing experimental evidence, proved exceedingly valuable in that science and did not produce objectionable metaphysics. Indeed, they were ultimately legitimized in the present century by "direct" physical evidence.

On the other hand, the hypothetical entities of atomic theory initially had no *physical* properties (other than weight) that could explain why they behaved as they did. While an electrical theory of atomic attraction predated valence theory, the former hypothesis actually impeded the development of the latter and had to be discredited before the experimental facts could fall into place. The valence of the mid-century chemist was a "chemical affinity" without any underlying physical mechanisms. So it remained for more than half a century until the electron-shell theory was developed by Lewis and others to explain it.

Paralleling this example from chemistry, information-processing theories of human thinking employ unobserved entities—symbols—and unobserved processes

—elementary information processes. The theories provide explanations of behavior that are mechanistic without being physiological. That they are mechanistic, that they postulate only processes capable of being effected by mechanism, is guaranteed by simulating the behavior predicted on ordinary digital computers. (See the Appendix, "Computer Programs as Theories.") Simulation provides a basis for testing the predictions of the theories, but it does not imply that the protoplasm in the brain resembles the electronic components of the computer.

A SPECIFIC INFORMATION-PROCESSING THEORY: PROBLEM SOLVING IN CHESS

Information-processing theories have been constructed for several kinds of behavior; they undertake to explain behavior in varying degrees of detail. As a first example, we consider a theory that deals with a rather narrow and special range of human problem-solving skill, attempting to explain the macroscopic organization of thought in a particular task environment.

Good chess players often detect strategies—called in chess, "combinations" —that impose a loss of a piece or a checkmate on the opponent over a series of moves, no matter what the latter does in reply. In actual game positions where a checkmating possibility exists, a strong player may spend a quarter hour or more discovering it and verifying the correctness of his strategy. In doing so, he may have to look ahead four or five moves, or even more.[4] If the combination is deep, weaker players may not be able to discover it at all, even after protracted search. How do good players solve such problems? How do they find combinations?

A theory now exists that answers these questions in some detail. First, I shall describe what it asserts about the processes going on in the mind of the chess player as he studies the position before him and what it predicts about his progress in discovering an effective strategy. Then we can see to what extent it accounts for the observed facts. The actual theory is a computer program couched in a list-processing language, called Information Processing Language V (IPL-V). Our account of the theory will be an English-language translation of the main features of the program.[5]

The statement of the theory has five main parts. The first two of these specify the way in which the chess player stores in memory his representation of the chess position and his representation of the moves he is considering, respectively. The remaining parts of the theory specify the processes he has available for extracting information from these representations and using that information, processes for discovering relations among the pieces and squares of the chess position, for synthesizing chess moves for consideration, and for organizing his search among alternative move sequences. We will describe briefly each of these five parts of the theory.

41

The theory asserts, first of all, that *the human chess player has means for storing internally, in his brain, encoded representations of the stimuli presented to him.* In the case of a highly schematized stimulus like a chess position, the internal symbolic structure representing it can be visualized as being similar to the printed diagram used to represent it in a chess book. The internal representation employs symbols that name the squares and the pieces, and symbolizes the relations among squares, among pieces, and between squares and pieces.

For example, the internal representation symbolizes rather explicitly that a piece on the king's squares is a knight's-move away, in a SSW direction, from a piece on the third rank of the queen's file. Similarly, if the king's knight is on the king's bishop's third square (KB3), the representation associates the symbol designating the knight with the symbol designating the KB3 square and the symbol designating the square with that designating the knight. On the other hand, the representation does not symbolize directly that two pieces stand on the same diagonal. Relations like this must be discovered or inferred from the representation by the processes to be discussed below.

Asserting that a position is symbolized internally in this way does not mean that the internal representations are verbal (any more than the diagrams in a chess book are verbal). It would be more appropriate, in fact, to describe the representations as a "visual image," provided that this phrase is not taken to imply that the chess player has any conscious explicit image of the entire board in his "mind's eye."

The chess player also has means for representing in memory the moves he is considering. He has symbol-manipulating processes that enable him, from his representations of a position and of a move, to use the latter to modify the former—the symbolic structure that describes the position—into a new structure that represents what the position would be *after* the move. The same processes enable him to "unmake" a move, to symbolize the position as it was before the move was considered. Thus if the move that transfers the king's knight from his original square (KN1) to the king's bishop's third square (KB3) is stored in memory, the processes in question can alter the representation of the board by changing the name of the square associated with knight from KN1 to KB3, and conversely for unmaking the move.

The chess player has processes that enable him to discover new relations in a position, to symbolize these, and to store the information in memory. For example, in a position he is studying (whether the actual one on the board or one he has produced by considering moves), he can discover whether his king is in check (attacked by an enemy man) or whether a specified piece can move to a specified square or whether a specified man is defended. The processes for detecting such relations are usually called perceptual processes. They are characterized by the fact that they are relatively direct; they obtain the desired information from the representation with a relatively small amount of manipulation.

42

The chess player has processes, making use of the perceptual processes, that permit him to generate or synthesize for his consideration moves with specified properties—for example, to generate all moves that will check the enemy king. To generate moves having desired characteristics may require a considerable amount of processing. If this were not so, if any kind of move could be discovered effortlessly, the entire checkmating program would consist of the single elementary process: *discover checkmating moves.*

An example of these more complex, indirect processes is a procedure that would discover certain forking moves (moves that attack two pieces simultaneously) somewhat as follows:

Find the square of the opposing queen. Find all squares that lie a knight's-move from this square. Determine for each of these squares whether it is defended (whether an opposing piece can move to it). If not, test all squares a knight's-move away from it to see if any of them has a piece that is undefended or that is more valuable than a knight.

Finally, the chess player has processes for organizing a search for mating combinations through the "tree" of possible move sequences. This search makes use of the processes already enumerated and proceeds as follows:

The player generates all the checking moves available to him in the given position, and for each checking move, generates the legal replies open to his opponent. If there are no checking moves, he concludes that no checkmating combination can be discovered in the position, and stops his search. If, for one of the checking moves, he discovers there are no legal replies, he concludes that the checking move in question is a checkmate. If, for one of the checking moves, he discovers that the opponent has more than four replies, he concludes that this checking move is unpromising, and does not explore it further.

Next, the player considers all the checking moves (a) that he has not yet explored and (b) that he has not yet evaluated as "checkmate" or "no mate." He selects the move that is most promising, by criteria to be mentioned presently, and pushes his analysis of that move one move deeper. That is, he considers each of its replies in turn, generates the checking moves available after those replies, and the replies to those checking moves. He applies the criteria of the previous paragraph to attach "checkmate" or "no mate" labels to the moves when he can. He also "propagates" these labels to antecedent moves. For example, a reply is labeled checkmate if at least one of its derivative checking moves is checkmate; it is labeled no mate if all the consequent checking moves are so labeled. A checking move is labeled checkmate if all of the replies are so labeled; it is labeled no mate if at least one reply is so labeled.

The most promising checking move for further exploration is selected by these criteria: that checking move to which there are the fewest replies receives first priority.[6] If two or more checking moves are tied on this criterion, a double check (check with two pieces) is given priority over a single check. If there is still a tie, a check that does not permit a recapture by the opponent is given priority over one that does. Any remaining ties are resolved by selecting the check generated most recently.

A number of details have been omitted from this description, but it indicates the theory's general structure and the kinds of processes incorporated. The theory predicts, for any chess position that is presented to it, whether a chess player will discover a mating combination in that position, what moves he will consider and explore in his search for the combination, and which combination (if there are several alternatives, as there often are) he will discover. These predictions can be compared directly with published analyses of historical chess positions or tape recordings of the thinking-aloud behavior of human chess players to whom the same position is presented.

Now it is unlikely that, if a chess position were presented to a large number of players, all of them would explore it in exactly the same way. Certainly strong players would behave differently from weak players. Hence, the information-processing theory, if it is a correct theory at all, must be a theory only for players of a certain strength. On the other hand, we would not regard its explanation of chess playing as very satisfactory if we had to construct an entirely new theory for each player we studied.

Matters are not so bad, however. First, the interpersonal variations in search for chess moves in middle-game positions appear to be quite small for players at a common level of strength, as we shall see in a moment. Second, some of the differences that are unrelated to playing strength appear to correspond to quite simple variants of the program—altering, for example, the criteria that are used to select the most promising checking move for exploration. Other differences, on the other hand, have major effects on the efficacy of the search, and some of these, also, can be represented quite simply by variants of the program organization. Thus the basic structure of the program and the assumptions it incorporates about human information-processing capacities provides a general explanation for the behavior, while particular variants of this basic program allow specific predictions to be made of the behavioral consequences of individual differences in program organization and content.

The kinds of information the theory provides and the ways in which it has been tested can be illustrated by a pair of examples. Adrian de Groot[7] has gathered and analyzed a substantial number of thinking-aloud protocols, some of them from grandmasters. He uniformly finds that, even in complicated positions, a player seldom generates a "tree" of more than 50 or 75 positions before he chooses his move. Moreover, the size of the tree does not depend on the player's strength. The thinking-aloud technique probably underestimates the size of the search tree somewhat, for a player may fail to mention some variations he has seen, but the whole tree is probably not an order of magnitude greater than that reported.

In 40 positions from a standard published work on mating combinations where the information-processing theory predicted that a player would find mating strategies, the median size of its search tree ranged from 13 positions for two-move mates to 53 for five-move mates. A six-move mate was found with a tree of 95 positions and an eight-move mate with a tree of 108. (The last two mates, as well as a number of the others, were from historically celebrated games between grandmasters and are among the most "brilliant" on record.) Hence, we can conclude that the predictions of the theory on amount of search are quite consistent with de Groot's empirical findings on the behavior of highly skilled human chess players.

The second example tests a much more detailed feature of the theory. In the eight-move mate mentioned above, it had been known that by following a different strategy the mate could have been achieved in seven moves. Both the human grandmaster (Edward Lasker in the game of Lasker-Thomas, 1912) and the program found the eight-move mate. Examination of the exploration shows that the shorter sequence could only have been discovered by exploring a branch of the tree that permitted the defender two replies before exploring a branch that permitted a single reply. The historical evidence here confirms the postulate of the theory that players use the "fewest replies" heuristic to guide their search. (The evidence was discovered after the theory was constructed.) A second piece of evidence of the same sort has been found in a recent game between experts reported in *Chess Life* (December 1963). The winner discovered a seven-move mate but overlooked the fact that he could have mated in three moves. The annotator of the game, a master, also overlooked the shorter sequence. Again, it could only have been found by exploring a check with two replies before exploring one with a single reply.

The "fewest replies" heuristic is not a superficial aspect of the players' search, nor is its relevance limited to the game of chess. Most problem-solving tasks—for example, discovering proofs of mathematical theorems—require a search through a branching "tree" of possibilities. Since the tree branches geometrically, solving a problem of any difficulty would call for a search of completely unmanageable scope (numbers like 10^{120} arise frequently in estimating the magnitude of such searches), if there were not at hand powerful heuristics, or rules of thumb, for selecting the promising branches for exploration. Such heuristics permit the discovery of proofs for theorems (and mating combinations) with the limited explorations reported here.

The "fewest replies" heuristic is powerful because it combines two functions: It points search in those directions that are most restrictive for the opponent, giving him the least opportunity to solve his problem; at the same time, it limits the growth of the search tree by keeping its rate of branching as low as possible. The "fewest replies" heuristic is the basis for the idea of retaining the initiative in military strategy and in competitive activities generally; it is also a central heuristic in decision making in the face of uncertainty. Hence, its appearance in the chess-playing theory and in the behavior of the human players is not fortuitous.

PARSIMONIOUS AND GARRULOUS THEORIES

Granting its success in predicting both some general and some very specific aspects of human behavior in chess playing, like the examples just described, the theory might be confronted with several kinds of questions and objections. It somehow fails to conform to our usual notions of generality and parsimony in theory. First, it is highly specific—the checkmating theory purports to provide an explanation only of how good chess players behave when they are confronted with a position on the board that calls for a vigorous mating attack. If we were to try to explain the whole range of human behavior, over all the enormous variety of tasks that particular human beings perform, we would have to compound the explanations from thousands of specific theories like the checkmate program. The final product would be an enormous compendium of "recipes" for human behavior at specific levels of skill in specific task environments.[8]

Second, the individual theories comprising this compendium would hardly be parsimonious, judged by ordinary standards. We used about a thousand words above to provide an approximate description of the checkmate program. The actual program—the formal theory—consists of about 3,000 computer instructions in a list-processing language, equivalent in information content to about the same number of English words. (It should be mentioned that the program includes a complete statement of the rules of chess, so that only a small part of the total is given over to the description of the player's selection rules and their organization.)

Before we recoil from this unwieldy compendium as too unpleasant and unesthetic to contemplate, let us see how it compares in bulk with theories in the other sciences. With the simplicity of Newtonian mechanics (why is this always the first example to which we turn?), there is, of course, no comparison. If classical mechanics is the model, then a theory should consist of three sentences or a couple of differential equations.[9]

But chemistry, and particularly organic chemistry, presents a different picture. It is perhaps not completely misleading to compare the question "How does a chess player find a checkmating combination?" with a question like "How do photoreceptors in the human eye operate?" or "How is the carbohydrate and oxygen intake of a rabbit transformed into energy usable in muscular contraction?"

The theory of plant metabolism provides a striking example of an explanation of phenomena in terms of a substantial number of complex mechanisms. Calvin and Bassham, in their book, *The Photosynthesis of Carbon Compounds*[10] introduce a figure entitled "carbon reduction pathways in photosynthesis" with the statement: "We believe the *principal* pathways for photosynthesis of simple organic compounds from CO_2 to be those shown in Figure 2" (italics ours). The figure referred to represents more than 40 distinct chemical reactions and a corresponding number of compounds. This diagram, of course, is far from representing the whole theory. Not only does it omit much of the detail, it contains none of the quantitative considerations for predicting reaction rates, energy balances, and so on. The verbal description accompanying the figure, which also has little to say about the quantitative aspects, or the energetics, is over two pages long—almost as long as our description of the chess-playing program. Here we have a clear-cut example of a theory of fundamental importance that has none of the parsimony we commonly associate with scientific theorizing.

The answer to the question of how photosynthesis proceeds is decidedly longwinded, as is the answer to the question of how chess players find mating combinations. We are often satisfied with longwinded answers because we believe that the phenomena are intrinsically complex and that no brief theory will explain them in detail. We must adjust our expectations about the character of information-processing theories of human thinking to a similar level. Such theories, to the extent that they account for the details of the phenomena, will be highly specific and highly complex. We might call them "garrulous theories" in contrast with our more common models of parsimonious theories.

ELEMENTARY INFORMATION PROCESSES

We would like to carry the analogy with chemistry a step further. Part of our knowledge in chemistry—and a very important part for the experimental chemist—consists of vast catalogs of substances and reactions, not dissimilar in bulk to the compendium of information processes we are proposing. But as we come to understand these substances and their reactions more fully, a second level of theory emerges which explains them (at least their general features) in a more parsimonious way. The substances, at this more basic level, become geometrical arrangements of particles from a small set of more fundamental substances—atoms and submolecules—held together by a variety of known forces whose effects can be estimated qualitatively and, in simple cases, quantitatively.

If we examine an information-processing theory like the checkmating program more closely, we find that it too is organized from a limited number of building blocks—a set of elementary information processes—and some composite processes that are compounded from the more elementary ones in a few characteristic ways. Let us try to describe these buildings blocks in general terms. First, we will characterize the way in which symbols and structures of symbols are represented internally and held in memory. Then, we shall mention some of the principal elementary processes that alter these symbol structures.[11]

Symbols, Lists, and Descriptions:

The smallest units of manipulable information in memory are *symbol tokens,*[12] or symbol occurrences. It is postulated that tokens can be compared and that comparison determines that the tokens are occurrences of the same symbol (*symbols type*) or that they are different.

Symbol tokens are arranged in larger structures, called *lists.* A list is an ordered set, a sequence of tokens. Hence, with every token on a list, except the last, there is associated a unique *next* token. Associated with the list as a whole is a symbol, its *name.* Thus a list may be a sequence of symbols that are themselves names of lists—a list of lists. A familiar example of a list of symbols that all of us carry in memory is the alphabet. (Its name is "alphabet.") Another is the list of days of the week, in order—Monday is next to Sunday, and so on.

Associations also exist between symbol types. An association is a two-termed relation involving three symbols, one of which names the relation, the other two its arguments. "The color of the apple is red" specifies an association between "apple" and "red" with the relation "color." A symbol's associations *describe* that symbol.

Some Elementary Processes:

A symbol, a list, and an association are abstract objects. Their properties are defined by the elementary information processes that operate on them. One important class of such processes are the *discrimination* processes. The basic discrimination process, which compares symbols to determine whether or not they are identical, has already been mentioned. Pairs of compound structures—lists and sets of associations—are discriminated from each other by matching processes that apply the basic tests for symbol identity to symbols in corresponding positions in the two structures. For example, two chess positions can be discriminated by a matching process that compares the pieces standing on corresponding squares in the two positions. The outcome of the match might be a statement that "the two positions are identical except that the white king is on his knight's square in the first but on his rook's square in the second."

Other classes of elementary information processes are those capable of *creating* or *copying* symbols, lists, and associations. These processes are involved, for example, in fixating or memorizing symbolic materials presented to the sense organs—learning a tune. Somewhat similar information processes are capable of modifying existing symbolic structures by *inserting a symbol* into a list, by *changing a term of an association* (from "its color is red" to "its color is green"), or by *deleting a symbol* from a list.

Still another class of elementary information processes *finds* information that is in structures stored in memory. We can think of such a process schematically as follows: to answer the question, "What letter follows 'g' in the alphabet?" a process must find the list in memory named "alphabet." Then another process must search down that list until (using the match for identity of symbols) it finds a "g." Finally, a third process must find the symbol *next* to "g" in the list. Similarly, to answer the question, "What color is the apple?" there must be a process capable of finding the second term of an association, given the first term and the name of the relation. Thus there must be processes for finding named objects, for finding symbols on a list, for finding the next symbol on a list, and for finding the value of an attribute of an object.

This list of elementary information processes is modest, yet it provides an adequate collection of building blocks to implement the chess-playing theory as well as the other information-processing theories of thinking that have been constructed to date, including a general problem-solving theory, a theory of rote verbal learning, and several theories of concept formation and pattern recognition.[13]

Elementary Processes in the Chess Theory:

A few examples will show how the mechanisms employed in the chess-playing theory can be realized by symbols, lists, associations, and elementary information processes. The player's representation of the chess board is assumed to be a collection of associations: with each square is associated the symbol representing the man on that square and symbols representing the adjoining squares in the several directions. Moves are similarly represented as symbols with which are associated the names of the squares from which and to which the move was made, the name of the piece moved, the name of the piece captured, if any, and so on.

Similarly, the processes for manipulating these representations are compounded from the elementary processes already described. To make a move, for example, is to modify the internal representation of the board by deleting the association of the man to be moved with the square on which he previously stood and by creating the new association of that man with the square to which he moved, and, in case of a capture, by also deleting the association of the captured man with the square on which he stood. Another example: testing whether the king is in check involves finding the square associated with the king, finding adjoining squares along ranks, files, and diagonals, and testing these squares for the presence of enemy men who are able to attack in the appropriate direction. (The latter is determined by associating each man with his *type* and associating with each type of man the directions in which such men can legally be moved.)

We see that, although the chess-playing theory contains several thousand program instructions, these are comprised of only a small number of elementary processes (far less than the number of elements in the periodic table). The elementary processes combine in a few simple ways into compound processes and operate on structures (lists and descriptions) that are constructed, combinatorially, from a single kind of building block—the symbol. There are two levels of theory: an "atomic" level, common to all the information-processing theories, of symbols, lists, associations, and elementary processes, and a "macromolecular" level, which is peculiar to each type of specialized human performance, of representations in the form of list structures and webs of associations, and of compound processes for manipulating these representations.

Processes in Serial Pattern Recognition:

A second example of how programs compounded from the elementary processes explain behavior is provided by an information-processing theory of serial pattern recognition.

Consider a sequence like:

ABMCDMEFM——.

An experimental subject in the laboratory, asked to extrapolate the series will, after a little thought, continue:

GHM, etc.

To see how he achieves this result, we examine the original sequence. First, it makes use of letters of the Roman alphabet. We can assume that the subject holds this alphabet in memory stored as a list, so that the elementary list process for finding the *next* item on a list can find B, given A, or find S, given R, and so on. Now we note that any letter in the sequence, after the first three, is related to previous letters by the relations *next* and *same*. Specifically, if we organize the series into periods of three letters each:

ABM   CDM   EFM

we see that:

(1) The first letter in each period is *next* in the alphabet to the second letter in the previous period.

(2) The second letter in each period is *next* in the alphabet to the first letter in that period.

(3) The third letter in each period is the *same* as the corresponding letter in the previous period.

50

The relations of *same* and *next* also suffice for a series like:

AAA   CCC   EEE . . .

or for a number series like:

1 7 2 8 3 9 4 0 . . .

In the last case, the "alphabet" to which the relation of *next* is applied is the list of digits, 0 to 9, and *next* is applied circularly, that is, after 9 comes 0 and then 1 again.

Several closely related information-processing theories of human pattern recognition have been constructed using elementary processes for finding and generating the next item in a list.[14] These theories have succeeded in explaining some of the main features of human behavior in a number of standard laboratory tasks, including so-called binary choice tasks, and series-completion and symbol-analogy tasks from intelligent tests.

The nature of the series-completion tasks has already been illustrated. In the binary choice experiment, the subject is confronted, one by one, with a sequence of tokens—each a "+" or "V," say. As each one is presented to him, he is asked what the next one will be. The actual sequence is, by construction, random. The evidence shows that, even when the subjects are told this, they rarely treat it as random. Instead, they behave as though they were trying to detect a serial pattern in the sequence and extrapolate it. They behave essentially like subjects faced by the series-completion task; basically similar information-processing theories using the same elementary processes can explain both behaviors.

A BROADER VIEW OF THINKING PROCESSES

A closer look at the principal examples of information-processing theories now extant suggests that another level of theory is rapidly emerging, intermediate between the "atomic" level common to all the theories and the "macromolecular" level idiosyncratic to each. It is clear that there is no prospect of eliminating all idiosyncratic elements from the individual theories. A theory to explain chess-playing performances must postulate memory structures and processes that are completely irrelevant to proving theorems in geometry, and vice versa.

On the other hand, it is entirely possible that human performances in different task environments may call on common components at more aggregative levels than the elementary processes. This, in fact, appears to be the case. The first information-processing theory that isolated some of these common components was called the General Problem Solver.[15]

Means-End Analysis:

The General Problem Solver is a program organized to keep separate (1) problem-solving processes that, according to the theory, are possessed and used by most human beings of average intelligence when they are confronted with any relatively unfamiliar task environment, from (2) specific information about each particular task environment.

The core of the General Problem Solver is an organization of process for *means-end analysis.* The problem is defined by specifying a *given situation* (*A*), and a *desired situation* (*B*). A discrimination process incorporated in the system of means-end analysis compares *A* with *B* and detects one or more *differences* (*D*) between them, if there are any. With each difference, there is associated in memory a set of *operators,* (*O$_D$*), or processes, that are possibly relevant to removing differences of that kind. The means-end analysis program proceeds to try to remove the difference by applying, in turn, the relevant operators.

Using a scheme of means-end analysis, a proof of a trigonometric identity like $\cos \theta \tan \theta = \sin \theta$ might proceed like this:

The right-hand side contains only the sine function, the left-hand side other trigonometric functions as well. The operator that replaces tan by sin/cos will eliminate one of these. Applying it, we get $\cos \theta (\sin \theta/\cos \theta) = \sin \theta$. The left-hand side still contains an extraneous function, cosine. The algebraic cancellation operator, applied to the two cosines, might remove this difference. We apply the operator, obtaining the identity $\sin \theta = \sin \theta$.

Planning Processes:

Another class of general processes discovered in human problem-solving performances and incorporated in the General Problem Solver are *planning* processes. The essential idea in planning is that the representation of the problem situation is simplified by deleting some of the detail. A solution is now sought for the new, simplified problem; if one is found, it is used as a plan to guide the solution of the original problem, with the detail reinserted.

Consider a simple problem in logic. Given: (1) "*A*," (2) "*not A or B,*" (3) "*if not C then not B*"; to prove "*C.*" To plan the proof, note that the first premise contains *A,* the second *A* and *B,* the third *B* and *C,* and the conclusion, *C.* The plan might be to obtain *B* by combining *A* with (*AB*), then to obtain *C* by combining *B* with (*BC*). The plan will in fact work, but it requires (2) to be transformed into "*A implies B*" and (3) "*B implies C,*" which transformations follow from the definitions of "or" and "if . . . then."

Problem-Solving Organization:

The processes for attempting subgoals in the problem-solving theories and the exploration processes in the chess-playing theory must be guided and controlled by executive processes that determine what goal will be attempted next. Common principles for the organization of the executive processes have begun to appear in several of the theories. The general idea has already been outlined above for the chess-playing exploration (*search*) phase and an evaluation (*scan*) phase. During the exploration phase, the available problem-solving processes are used to investigate subgoals. The information obtained through this investigation is stored in such a way as to be accessible to the executive. During the evaluation phase, the executive uses this information to determine which of the existing subgoals is the most promising and should be explored next. An executive program organized in this way may be called a search-scan scheme, for it searches an expanding tree of possibilities, which provides a common pool of information for scanning by its evaluative processes.[16]

The effectiveness of a problem-solving program appears to depend rather sensitively on the alternation of the search and scan phases. If search takes place in long sequences, interrupted only infrequently to scan for possible alternative directions of exploration, the problem solver suffers from stereotypy. Having initiated search in one direction, it tends to persist in that direction as long as the subroutines conducting the search determine, locally, that the possibilities for exploration have not been exhausted. These determinations are made in a very decentralized way and without benefit of the more global information that has been generated.

On the other hand, if search is too frequently interrupted to consider alternative goals to the one being pursued currently, the exploration takes on an uncoordinated appearance, wandering indecisively among a wide range of possibilities. In both theorem-proving and chess-playing programs, extremes of decentralized and centralized control of search have shown themselves ineffective in comparison with a balanced search-scan organization.

Discrimination Trees:

Common organizational principles are also emerging for the rote memory processes involved in almost all human performance. As a person tries to prove a theorem, say, certain expressions that he encounters along the way gradually become familiar to him, and his ability to discriminate among them gradually improves. An information-processing theory (EPAM) was constructed several years ago to account for this and similar human behavior in verbal learning experiments (for example, learning nonsense syllables by the serial anticipation or paired associate methods).[17] This theory is able to explain, for instance, how familiarity and similarity of materials affect rates of learning. The essential processes in EPAM include: (1) processes for discriminating among compound objects by sorting them in a "discrimination tree," (2) familiarization processes for associating pairs or short sequences of objects.

Discrimination processes operate by applying sequences of tests to the stimulus objects and sorting them on the basis of the test results—a sort of "20 questions" procedure. The result of discrimination is to find a memory location where information is stored about objects that are similar to the one sorted. *Familiarization processes* create new compound objects out of previously familiar elements. Thus, during the 1950s, the letter sequence "IPL" became a familiar word (to computer programers!), meaning "information processing language." The individual letters have been *associated* in this word. Similarly, the English alphabet, used by the serial pattern-recognizing processes, is a familiar object compounded from the letters arranged in a particular sequence. All sorts of additional information can be associated with an object, once familiarized. (For example, the fact that IPL's organize symbols in lists can be associated with "IPL.")

Because discrimination trees play a central role in EPAM, the program may also be viewed as a theory of pattern detection, and EPAM-like trees have been incorporated in certain information-processing theories of concept formation. It also now seems likely that the discrimination tree is an essential element in problem-solving theories like GPS, playing an important role in the gradual modification of the subject's behavior as he familiarizes himself with the problem material.

CONCLUSION

Our survey shows that a considerable range of human behaviors has been explained successfully by informtion-processing theories. We now know, for example, some of the central processes that are employed in solving problems, in detecting and extrapolating patterns, and in memorizing verbal materials.

Information-processing theories explain behavior at various levels of detail. In the theories now extant, at least three levels can be distinguished. At the most aggregative level are theories of complex behavior in specific problem domains: proving theorems in logic or geometry, discovering checkmating combinations in chess. These theories tend to contain very extensive assumptions about the knowledge and skills possessed by the human beings who perform these activities and about the way in which this knowledge and these skills are organized and represented internally. Hence, each of these theories incorporates a rather extensive set of assumptions and predicts behavior only in a narrow domain.

At the second level, similar or identical information-processing mechanisms are common to many of the aggregative theories. Means-end analysis, planning, the search-scan scheme, and discrimination trees are general-purpose organizations for processing that are usable over a wide range of tasks. As the nature of these mechanisms becomes better understood, they, in turn, begin to serve as basic building blocks for the aggregative theories, allowing the latter to be stated in more parsimonious form and exhibiting the large fraction of machinery that is common to all, rather than being idiosyncratic to individual tasks.

At the lowest, "atomic," level, all the information-processing theories postulate only a small set of basic forms of symbolic representation and a smaller number of elementary information processes. The construction and successful testing of large-scale programs that simulate complex human behaviors provide evidence that a small set of elements, similar to those now postulated in information-processing languages, is sufficient for the construction of a theory of human thinking.

Although none of the advances that have been described constitute explanations of human thought at the still more microscopic, physiological level, they open opportunities for new research strategies in physiological psychology. As the information-processing theories become more powerful and better validated, they disclose to the physiological psychologist the fundamental mechanisms and processes that he needs to explain. He need no longer face the task of building the whole long bridge from microscopic neurological and molecular structures to gross human behavior, but can instead concentrate on bridging the much shorter gap from physiology to elementary information processes.

The work of Lettvin, Maturana, McCulloch, and Pitts on information processing in the frog's eye[18] and the work of Hubel and Wiesel on processing of visual information by the cat[19] already provide some hints of the form this bridging operation may take.

APPENDIX: COMPUTER PROGRAMS AS THEORIES

Since the use of computer programs as formal theories, in the manner described in this paper, is still somewhat novel, this appendix sketches briefly the relation between this formalism and the formalisms that have been used more commonly in the physical sciences.

In the physical sciences, theories about dynamical systems usually take the form of systems of differential equations. This is the form of classical Newtonian mechanics, of Maxwell's electromagnetic theory, and of many other theories of central importance. In the classic dynamics of mass points, for example, it is assumed that the initial positions and velocities of a set of bodies (mass points) are given and that the forces acting on the bodies are known, instantaneous functions of the positions, say, of the bodies. Then, by Newton's Second Law, the acceleration (second derivative of position) of each body is proportional to the resultant force acting on it. The paths of the bodies over time are calculated by integrating twice the differential equations that express the Second Law.

More generally, a system of differential or difference equations is a set of conditional laws that determines the state of the system "a moment later" as a function of its state at a given time. Repeated application of the laws, equivalent to integrating the equations, then determines the path of the system over time.

A computer program is also literally a system of difference equations, albeit of a rather unorthodox kind, for it determines the behavior of the computer in the next instruction cycle as a function of the current contents of its memory. Executing the program is formally equivalent to integrating (numerically) the difference equations for a specified initial state of the computer. Thus information-processing theories, expressed as programs in computer languages, are not merely analogous to more familiar kinds of dynamical theories; formally, they are of an equivalent type.

Very simple systems of differential and integral equations can sometimes be integrated formally, so that general properties can be inferred about the paths of the systems they describe, independent of particular initial and boundary conditions. There are no known methods for integrating formally systems of difference equations such as those discussed in this paper. Hence, the principal means for making predictions about such systems is to simulate their behavior for particular initial and boundary conditions. This is the method of investigation that we have relied on here.

NOTES

1. *The Nature of the Chemical Bond,* Ithaca: Cornell Univ. Press, 1960, pp. 3–4.

2. The best-known exponent of this radical behaviorist position is B. F. Skinner. He has argued, for example, that "an explanation is the demonstration of a functional relationship between behavior and manipulable or controllable variables," in T. W. Wann, ed., *Behaviorism and Phenomenology,* Chicago: Univ. of Chicago Press, 1964, p. 102.

3. A distinguished example of such a theory is D. O. Hebb's formulation in terms of "cell assemblies." *The Organization of Behavior,* New York: Wiley, 1949. Hebb does not, however, insist on an exclusively physiological base for psychological theory, and his general methodological position is not inconsistent with that taken here. See his *Textbook of Psychology,* Philadelphia: Saunders, 1956, ch. 13.

4. A "move" means here a move by one player followed by a reply by his opponent. Hence to look ahead four or five moves is to consider sequences of eight or ten successive positions.

5. A general account of this program, with the results of some hand simulations, can be found in H. A. Simon and P. A. Simon, "Trial and Error Search in Solving Difficult Problems: Evidence from the Game of Chess," *Behavioral Science,* 7, 1962, pp. 425–29. The theory described there has subsequently been programmed and the hand-simulated findings confirmed on a computer.

6. This is perhaps the most important element in the strategy. It will be discussed further later.

7. *Thought and Choice in Chess,* The Hague, The Netherlands: Mouton & Company, 1964.

8. The beginnings of such a compendium have already appeared. A convenient source for descriptions of a number of the information-processing theories is the collection by E. A. Feigenbaum and J. Feldman, eds., *Computers and Thought,* New York: McGraw-Hill, 1964.

9. Of course, even Newtonian mechanics is not this simple in structure. See H. A. Simon, "The Axioms of Newtonian Mechanics," *Phil. Mag.,* Ser. 7, 38, 1947, pp. 888–905.

10. M. Calvin and J. A. Bassham, *The Photosynthesis of Carbon Compounds,* New York: W. A. Benjamin, 1962, pp. 8–11.

11. Only a few of the characteristics of list-processing systems can be mentioned here. For a fuller account, see A. Newell and H. A. Simon, "Computers in Psychology," in Luce, Bush, and Galanter, eds., *Handbook of Mathematical Psychology,* vol. 1, New York: Wiley, 1963, especially pp. 373–76, 380–84, 419–24.

12. Evidence as to how information is symbolized in the brain is almost nonexistent. If the reader is assisted by thinking of different symbols as different macromolecules, this metaphor is as good as any. A few physiologists think it may even be the correct explanation. See Holger Hyden, "Biochemical Aspects of Brain Activity," in S. M. Farber and R. H. Wilson, eds., *Control of the Mind,* New York: McGraw-Hill, 1961, pp. 18–39. Differing patterns of neural activity will do as well. See W. R. Adey, R. T. Kado, J. Didio, and W. J. Schindler, "Impedance Changes in Cerebral Tissue Accompanying a Learned Discriminative Performance in the Cat," *Experimental Physiology,* 7, 1963, pp. 259–81.

13. For examples, see Feignebaum and Feldman, *Computers and Thought,* part 2.

14. J. Feldman, F. Tonge, and H. Kanter, "Empirical Explorations of a Hypothesis-Testing Model of Binary Choice Behavior," in A. C. Hoggatt and F. E. Balderston, eds., *Symposium on Simulation Models,* Cincinnati: South-Western Publishing Company, 1964, pp. 55– 100; K. R. Laughery and L. W. Gregg, "Simulation of Human Problem-Solving Behavior," *Psychometrika,* 27, 1962, pp. 265–82; H. A. Simon and K. Kotovsky, "Human Acquisition of Concepts for Sequential Patterns," *Psychological Review,* 70, 1963, pp. 531–46.

15. A. Newell and H. A. Simon, "GPS, a Program that Simulates Human Thought," in Feigenbaum and Feldman, *Computers and Thought,* pp. 279–93.

16. Perhaps the earliest use of the search-scan scheme appeared in the Logic Theorist, the first heuristic theorem-proving program. See A. Newell and H. A. Simon, "Empirical Explorations with the Logic Theory Machine: A Case Study in Heuristics," in Feigenbaum and Feldman, *Computers and Thought,* pp. 153–63.

17. E. A. Feigenbaum, "The Simulation of Verbal Learning Behavior," in Feigenbaum and Feldman, *Computers and Thought,* pp. 297–309.

18. J. Y. Lettvin, H. R. Maturana, W. S. McCulloch, and W. H. Pitts, "What the Frog's Eye Tells the Frog's Brain," *Proceedings of the Institute of Radio Engineers,* 47, 1959, pp. 1,940–51.

19. D. H. Hubel and T. N. Wiesel, "Receptive Fields, Binocular Interaction and Functional Architecture in the Cat's Visual Cortex," *Journal of Physiology,* 160, 1962, pp. 106–54.

A CRITIQUE
OF
ARTIFICIAL
REASON*

Hubert L. Dreyfus

In a recent book on the mathematical theory of computers, Marvin Minsky, one of the leading workers in artificial intelligence, gave voice to the optimism guiding his research and that of others in the field: "Within a generation, I am convinced, few compartments of intellect will remain outside the machine's realm—the problem of creating "artificial intelligence" will be substantially solved."[1] Insofar as this is a prediction, one way to find out whether it is accurate is simply to wait a generation and see. But insofar as the prediction is presented as a conviction, we, as philosophers, may want to ask whether this conviction is well founded.

Minsky is typical of workers in the area in giving two sorts of arguments in support of his view: (1) empirical arguments based on progress achieved thus far, and (2) a priori arguments about what machines can, in principle, do. It might seem at first glance that these are two distinct sorts of arguments and that philosophers should concern themselves only with the a priori ones, but the truism that experimental data is meaningless until *interpreted* is especially applicable in this new, and barely scientific, area of inquiry. What we take the data to mean depends on our assumptions, so that the empirical arguments implicitly reflect the a priori ones. It will therefore be my contention that the optimism underlying work in artificial intelligence is unjustified *both* on empirical and a priori grounds. I will argue that the empirical arguments gain their plausibility only on the basis of an appeal to an implicit philosophical assumption and that this assumption, far from being justified, simply perpetuates a fundamental error of the Western philosophical tradition.

---

*From Hubert L. Dreyfus, "A Critique of Artificial Reason," *Thought,* vol. 43, no. 171 (Winter 1968), 507–522.

I

Language translation, or the use of computers to simulate the understanding of natural languages, offers the clearest illustration of how optimistic assumptions have enabled enthusiasts to interpret as promising, data which is ambiguous, to say the least. Minsky cites as encouraging evidence of progress the existence of "machines that handle abstract-nonmathematical problems and *deal with ordinary-language expressions.*"[2] Admittedly, "deal with" is rather vague, but in another article Minsky comes right out and says of a program for solving algebra word problems, Bobrow's STUDENT, that "it understands English."[3] In fact, this program embodies nothing one would ever want to call syntactic or semantic understanding. It simply breaks up the sentences into units on the basis of cues such as the words "times," "of," "equals," etc., equates these sentence chunks with x's and y's, and tries to set up simultaneous equations. If these equations cannot be solved, it appeals to further rules for breaking up the sentences into other units and tries again. The whole scheme works only because there is the constraint, not present in understanding ordinary discourse, that the pieces of the sentence, when represented by variables, will set up soluble equations. Such a program is so far from semantic understanding that, as Bobrow admits, it would interpret "the number of times I went to the movies" as the product of two variables: "the number of" and "I went to the movies," because "times" is always interpreted as an operator indicating multiplication.[4]

Why, then, does Minsky regard this program, which shows not the slightest sign of understanding, as progress toward the understanding of natural language? Presumably because he, like Bobrow, believes that the underlying "semantic theory of discourse can be used as a basis for a much more general language-processing system. . . ."[5] And why should they think, in the face of the peculiar restrictions necessary to the function of the program, that such a generalization must be possible? Nothing, I think, can justify or even explain their optimism concerning *this* approach. Their general optimism that *some* such computable approach must work, however, can be seen to follow from a fundamental metaphysical assumption concerning the nature of language and of human intelligent behavior, namely, that whatever orderly behavior people engage in can, in principle, be formalized and processed by digital computers. This leads them to shrug off all current difficulties as due to technological limitations such as the restricted size of the storage capacity of present machine memories.[6] If it were not for such an assumption, Bobrow's limited success, heralded by Minsky as the most promising work thus far, would be recognized as a trick which says nothing either for or against the possibility of machine understanding, and the fact that this is the best that an intelligent person like Bobrow could do would lead to discouragement.

59

II

The formalistic assumption which would lend plausibility to Minsky's optimistic interpretation of Bobrow's meager results is expressed in Minsky's motto: "There is no reason to suppose machines have any limitations not shared by man."[7] I think there *are* good reasons for attributing special limitations to machines, but that is beyond the scope of this paper.[8] Here I wish only to argue that, whatever the intrinsic capabilities of computers, they are limited in their performance by fundamental limitations on the kinds of programs human programmers are able to write for them. Before this can be shown, however, we must be clear what is meant by *machine,* for if a physical organism is to be counted as a machine, then man, too, would be a machine and the claim that machines have no limitations not shared by man would be vacuous.

A machine as defined by Minsky, who bases his definition on that of Turing, is a "rule-obeying mechanism." As Turing puts it: "The . . . computer is supposed to be following fixed rules. . . . It is the duty of the control to see that these instructions are obeyed correctly and in the right order. The control is so constructed that this necessarily happens."[9] So the machine in question is a very restricted but very fundamental sort of mechanism. It operates on determinate, unambiguous bits of data, according to strict rules which apply univocally to this data. The claim is made that this sort of machine—a Turing machine—which expresses the essence of a digital computer, can, in principle, do anything human beings can do, that is, it has no in-principle limitations not shared by man.

Minsky considers the antiformalist counterclaim that "Perhaps there are processes . . . which simply *cannot* be described in any formal language, but which can nevertheless be carried out, e.g., by minds."[10] Rather than answer this objection directly, he refers to Turing's "brilliant" article which, he asserts, contains arguments that "amount . . . to a satisfactory refutation of many such objections."[11] Turing does, indeed, take up this sort of objection. He states it as follows: "It is not possible to produce a set of rules purporting to describe what a man should do in every conceivable set of circumstances."[12] This is presumably Turing's generalization of the Wittgensteinian argument that one cannot make completely explicit the normative rules governing the correct use of a natural language. Turing's "refutation" is to make a distinction between "rules of conduct" and "laws of behavior" and then to assert that "we cannot so easily convince ourselves of the absence of complete laws of behavior as of complete rules of conduct."[13] Now as an answer to the Wittgenstein claim, this is well taken. Turing is, in effect, arguing that although we cannot formulate the normative rules for the correct application of a particular predicate, this does not show that we cannot formulate the rules which describe how, *in fact,* a particular individual applies such a predicate. In other words, while Turing is ready to admit that it may, in principle, be impossible to provide a set of rules determining what a person *should* do in every circumstance, he holds there is no reason to give up the supposition that one could in principle discover a set of rules determining what he *would* do. But why does this supposition seem so self-evident that the burden of proof is on those who call it into question? Why should we have to "convince ourselves of the *absence* of complete laws of behavior" rather than of their presence? Here we are face to face again with the formalist assumption. It is important to try to root out what lends this assumption its implied a priori plausibility.

To begin with, "laws of behavior" is ambiguous. In one sense human behavior is certainly lawful, if *lawful* simply means nonarbitrary. But the assumption that the laws in question are the sort that could be embodied in a computer program is a much stronger and more controversial claim, in need of further justification.

At this point the formalist presumably exploits the ambiguity of "laws of behavior." Human bodies are part of the physical world, and objects in the physical world have been shown to obey laws which can be expressed in a formalism manipulable on a digital computer. Thus, understood as motion, human behavior is presumably completely lawful in the sense the formalists require. But this in no way supports the formalist assumption as it appears in Minsky and Turing. When Minsky or Turing claim that man is a Turing machine, they cannot mean that a man is a physical system. Otherwise it would be appropriate to say that trees or rocks are Turing machines. These, too, obey mathematically formulable laws, and their behavior is no doubt capable of simulation to any degree of accuracy on a digital computer. When Minsky or Turing claim that man is a Turing machine, they must mean that man processes data received from the world, such as colors, shapes, sounds, etc., by means of logical operations that can be reduced to matching, classifying, and boolean operations. Workers in artificial intelligence are claiming that human *information processing* can be described in a digital formalism, while the considerations from physics show only that human motions, and presumably the neurological activity accompanying them, can, in principle, be described in this form.

All artificial intelligence is dedicated to using logical operations to manipulate data, not to solve physical equations. No one has tried, or hopes to try, to use the laws of physics to describe in detail the motion of human bodies. This would probably be physically impossible, for, according to the very laws of physics and information theory which such work would presuppose, such a calculation would seem to require a computer bigger than the universe.[14] Yet workers in the field of artificial intelligence, from Turing to Minsky, seem to take refuge in this confusion between physical laws and information-processing rules to convince themselves that there is reason to suppose that human behavior can be formalized, that the burden of proof is on those who claim that "there are processes . . . which simply cannot be described in a formal language but which can nevertheless be carried out by minds."

Once this ambiguity has been removed, what argument remains that human behavior, at what A.I. workers have called "the information-processing level," can be described in terms of strict rules? Here the discussion becomes genuinely philosophical because here A.I. theorists link up with an assumption characteristic of the Western philosophical tradition, an assumption which, if Heidegger is right, is, in fact, *definitive* of that tradition. The assumption begins as a moral demand. Socrates asks Euthyphro for what Turing and Minsky would call an "effective procedure." Minsky defines effective procedure as "a set of rules which tell us, from moment to moment, precisely how to behave."[15] In facing a moral dilemma, Socrates says: "I want to know what is characteristic of piety which makes all actions pious . . . that I may have it to turn to, and to use as a standard whereby to judge your actions and those of other men."[16]

Plato generalized this ethical demand for certainty into an epistemological demand. According to Plato, all knowledge must be stated in explicit definitions which anyone could apply. What could not be stated explicitly in such a definition—all areas of human thought which required skill, intuition, or a sense of tradition—were relegated to mere beliefs.

But Plato was not yet fully a cyberneticist, although according to Wiener he was the first to use the term, for Plato was looking for *semantic* rather than *syntactic* criteria. (He was operating on the fourth, rather than the third, level of his divided line.) His criteria could be applied by *man* but not by a machine, and this raises difficulties.

Minsky notes after introducing a commonsense notion of effective procedure: "This attempt at definition is subject to the criticism that the *interpretation* of the rules is left to depend on some person or agent."[17] Similarly Aristotle claimed that intuition was necessary to apply the Platonic rules:

> Yet it is not easy to find a formula by which we may determine how far and up to what point a man may go wrong before he incurs blame. But this difficulty of definition is inherent in every object of perception; such questions of degree are bound up with the circumstances of the individual case, where our only criterion *is* the perception.[18]

It requires one more move to remove all appeal to intuition and judgment. As Galileo discovered that, by ignoring secondary qualities and teleological considerations, one could find a pure formalism for describing physical motion, so, one might suppose, a Galileo of the mind might eliminate all semantic considerations (appeal to meanings) and introduce purely syntactic (formal) definitions.

The belief that such a final formalization must be possible came to dominate Western thought, both because it corresponded to a basic moral and intellectual demand and because the success of physical science seemed to imply to 16th-century philosophers, as it still seems to suggest to Turing and Minsky, that the demand could be satisfied. Hobbes was the first to make explicit this syntactic conception of thought as calculation: "When a man *reasons,* he does nothing else but conceive a sum total from addition of parcels. For REASON . . . is nothing but reckoning . . ."[19]

It only remained to work out the univocal parcels or bits on which this purely syntactic calculator could operate, and Leibnitz, the inventor of the binary system, dedicated himself to working out, unsuccessfully to be sure, a formal language of unambiguous terms in which all knowledge could be expressed.[20]

Leibnitz only had promises, but now it seems that the digital computer has realized his dream and thus Plato's demand. The computer operates according to syntactic rules, on uninterpreted, determinate bits of data, so that there is no question of rules for applying rules; no question of interpretation, no appeal to human intuition and judgment. It is thus entirely appropriate that in his UNESCO address Heidegger cites cybernetics (not, as formerly, the atom bomb) as the culmination of philosophy: "Philosphy has come to an end in the present epoch. It has found its place in the scientific view. . . . The fundamental characteristic of this scientific determination is that it is cybernetic, i.e., technological."[21]

We have now traced the history of the assumption that thinking is calculating. We have seen that its *attraction* harks back to the Platonic realization that moral life would be more bearable and knowledge more definitive if it were true. Its *plausibility,* however, rests only on a confusion between the mechanistic assumptions underlying the success of modern science and a correlative formalistic assumption underlying what would be a science of human behavior if such existed.

There seem to be no *arguments* for the formalistic assumption that all human behavior can be simulated by a Turing machine using syntactic operations without reduction to the laws of physics. (This would be unobjectionable if the assumption were put forward as an hypothesis, but, as we have seen, Turing and Minsky treat it rather as a postulate.) Can any arguments be given *against* the plausibility of this assumption?

III

Most striking evidence that such a limit to formalization does indeed exist and poses seemingly insurmountable difficulties can be found in analyzing current attempts to use digital computers to simulate the understanding of a natural language.

Yehoshua Bar-Hillel and Anthony Oettinger, two of the most respected and most informed workers in the field of automatic language translation, have each been led to pessimistic conclusions concerning the possibility of further progress in the field. They have each discovered that the order of the words in the sentence does not provide sufficient information to enable a machine to determine which of several possible parsings is the appropriate one, nor does the context of a word indicate which of several possible readings the author had in mind.

As Oettinger puts it:

[Work] to date has revealed a far higher degree of legitimate *syntactic* ambiguity in English and in Russian than has been anticipated. This, and a related fuzziness of the boundary between the grammatical and the nongrammatical, raises serious questions about the possibility of effective fully automatic manipulation of English or Russian for any purposes of translation or information retrieval.[22]

To understand this difficulty in its purest form we must distinguish between the *generation* of grammatical and meaningful sentences and the *understanding* of such sentences in actual instances of their use. For the sake of the argument we will grant that linguists will succeed in formulating rules for generating any sentences which native speakers recognize as grammatical and meaningful and excluding all sentences that native speakers reject as ungrammatical or meaningless. The remaining difficulty can then be stated as follows: In an instance of linguistic usage a native speaker is able to interpret univocally a sentence which, according to the rules, could have been generated in several different ways, and thus would have several different grammatical structures, that is, several legitimate meanings. (A famous example is the sentence: "Time flies like an arrow," which a computer would read as a statement that a certain kind of fly likes to eat arrows, and a command to rush out and clock flies, as well as a statement about the passage of time.)

In narrowing down this legitimate ambiguity the native speaker may be appealing either to specific information about the world, as, for example, when we recognize the sentence "the book is in the pen" means that the book is in a playpen or pig pen, not in a fountain pen, or to a sense of the situation as in the following example from Fodor and Katz: "An ambiguous sentence such as 'He follows Marx' occurring in a setting in which it is clear that the speaker is remarking about intellectual history cannot bear the reading 'he dogs the footsteps of Groucho.' "[23]

The appeal to context, moreover, is more fundamental than the appeal to facts, for the context determines the *significance* of the facts. Thus, in spite of our *general* knowledge about the relative size of pens and books, we might interpret "The book is in the pen," when uttered in a James Bond movie, as meaning just the opposite of what it means at home or on the farm. And, conversely, when no specifically odd context is specified, we assume a "normal" context and assign to the facts about relative size a "normal" significance.

It is such difficulties—specifically those concerning an appeal to facts—which make Oettinger and Bar-Hillel skeptical about the possibility of fully automatic, high-quality machine translation. Bar-Hillel claims that his "box-pen" argument from which mine is adapted "amounts to an almost full-fledged demonstration of the unattainability of fully automatic, high-quality translation, not only in the near future but altogether,"[24] if only because there would be no way of sorting through the enormous (Bar-Hillel says *infinite*)[25] quantity of information which might be relevant to determining the meaning of any specific utterance.

Katz and Fodor discuss this sort of difficulty in their article "The Structure of a Semantic Theory":

> Since a complete theory of setting selection must represent as part of the setting of an utterance any and every feature of the world which speakers need in order to determine the preferred reading of that utterance, and since . . . practically any item of information about the world is essential to some disambiguations, two conclusions follow. First, such a theory cannot, in principle, distinguish between the speaker's knowledge of his language and his knowledge of the world. . . . Second, since there is no serious possibility of systematizing all the knowledge about the world that speakers share . . . [such a theory] is not a serious model for linguistics.[26]

Katz and Fodor continue, "none of these considerations is intended to rule out the possibility that, by placing relatively strong limitations on the information about the world that a theory can represent in the characterization of a setting, a *limited* theory of selection by sociophysical setting can be constructed. What these considerations do show is that a *complete* theory of this kind is impossible."[27]

Thus Bar-Hillel claims we must appeal to specific *facts* such as the size of pens and books; Katz and Fodor assume we must appeal to the *sociophysical setting*. The difference between these views seems unimportant to the partisans of each, since both presumably assume that the setting is itself identified by features which are facts, and functions like a fact in disambiguation. We shall see, however, that disregarding the difference between fact and situation leads to an equivocation in both Bar-Hillel and Katz as to whether mechanical translation is impractical or impossible.

In Bar-Hillel's "demonstration" that since disambiguation depends on the use of facts, and the number of facts is "in a certain very pregnant sense infinite," fully automatic, high-quality mechanical translation is unattainable, it is unclear what is being claimed. If *unattainable* means that in terms of present computers and programs in operation or envisaged, no such massive storage and retrieval of information can be carried out, then the point is well made and is sufficient to cast serious doubt on claims that mechanical translation has been achieved or can be achieved in the foreseeable future. But if *unattainable* means theoretically impossible—which the appeal to infinity seems to imply—then Bar-Hillel is claiming too much. A machine would not have to store an infinite number of facts, for from a large number of facts and rules for concatenating them, it could produce further ones indefinitely. True, no machine could sort through such an endless amount of data. At present there exists no machine and no program capable of storing even a very large body of data so as to gain access to the relevant information in manageable time. There is work being done on what are called "associative memories" and ingenious tricks are used in programing, such as hash coding, which may in the distant future provide the means of storing and accessing vast bodies of information. Then information might be stored in such a way that in any given case only a finite number of relevant facts need be considered.

As long as Katz and Fodor accept the same implicit metaphysical premise as Bar-Hillel, that the world is the totality of facts, and speak of the setting in terms of "items of information," their argument is as equivocal as Bar-Hillel's. They have no right to pass from the claim that there is "no serious possibility" of systematizing the knowledge necessary for disambiguation, which seems to be a statement about our technological capabilities, to the claim that a complete theory of selection by sociophysical setting is "impossible." If a program for handling all knowledge is ever developed, and in their world there is no theoretical reason why it should not be, it will be such a theory.

Only if one refuses the traditional metaphysical assumption that the world can be analyzed as a set of facts—items of information—can one legitimately move beyond practical impossibility. We have already seen examples which suggest that the situation might be of a radically different order and fulfill a totally different function than any concatenation of facts. In the "Marx" example, the situation (academic) determines how to disambiguate "Marx" (Karl) and furthermore tells us which facts are relevant to disambiguate "follows" as ideological or chronological. (When was the follower born? what are his political views? etc.) In the book-pen example the size of the book and pen are clearly relevant since we are speaking of physical objects being "in" other physical objects, but here the situation, be it agricultural, domestic, or conspiratorial, determines the *significance* of the facts involved. Thus it is our sense of the situation which enables us to select from the potential infinity of facts the immediately relevant ones, and once these relevant facts are found, enables us to interpret them. This suggests that unless we can give the computer a way of recognizing situations, it will not be able to disambiguate them and thus, in principle, unable to understand utterances in a natural language.

But these considerations alone do not constitute a sufficient argument. The traditional metaphysician, reincarnated in the artificial intelligence researcher, can grant that facts used in disambiguation are selected and interpreted in terms of the situation and simply conclude that we need only first pick out and program the features which identify the situation.

But the same two problems which arose in disambiguation and necessitated

66

appeal to the situation arise again on the level of situation recognition. (1) If in disambiguation the number of simple facts is in some sense infinite, so that selection criteria must be applied before interpretation can begin, the number of facts that might be relevant to recognizing a situation is infinite too. How is the computer to consider all the features, such as how many people are present, the temperature, the pressure, the day of the week, etc., any one of which might be a defining feature of some context? (2) Even if the program provides rules for determining relevant facts, these facts would be ambiguous, that is, capable of defining several different situations, until they were interpreted. Evidently, a broader context will have to be used to determine which of the infinity of features is relevant and how each is to be understood. But if, in turn, the program must enable the machine to identify the broader context in terms of *its* relevant features—and this is the only way a computer could proceed—the programmer would seem to be faced with an infinite regress of contexts.

Such a regress would certainly be disastrous, but there still seems to be a ray of hope, for a computer programmer could plausibly claim that this regress might terminate in an ultimate context. In fact, there does seem to be such an ultimate context, though, as we shall see, this is equally disastrous to those working toward machine intelligence.

We have seen that in order to identify which facts are relevant for recognizing an academic or a conspiratorial situation, and to interpret these facts, one must appeal to a broader context. Thus it is only in the broader context of social intercourse that we see we must normally take into account what people are wearing and what they are doing, but not how many insects there are in the room or the cloud formations at noon or a minute later. Only this broader context enables us to determine whether these facts will have their normal significance.

Moreover, even the facts necessary to recognize social intercourse can be singled out only because social intercourse is a subcase of human activity, which also includes working alone or studying a primitive tribe. And finally, human activity itself is only a subclass of some even broader situation—call it the human life-world—which would have to include even those situations where no human beings were directly involved. But what facts would be relevant to recognizing this broadest context? Or does it make sense to speak of "recognizing" the life-world at all? It seems we simply take for granted this broadest context in being people. As Wittgenstein puts it: "If I have exhausted the justifications I have reached bedrock, and my spade is turned. Then I am inclined to say: 'This is simply what I do.' "[28] or: "What has to be accepted, the given is—someone could say—*forms of life*."[29]

Well then, why not make explicit the significant features of the human form of life from within it? Indeed, this has been the implicit goal of philosophers for 2,000 years, and it should be no surprise that nothing short of a formalization of the human form of life can ever give us artificial intelligence. But how are we to proceed? Everything we experience in some way, immediate or remote, reflects our human concerns. Everything and nothing is relevant. Everything is significant and insignificant. Without some *particular* interest, without some *particular* inquiry to help us select and interpret, we are back confronting the infinity of meaningless facts we were trying to avoid.

It seems that, given the artificial intelligence worker's conception of reason as calculation and thus his need to formalize the ultimate context of human life, his attempt to produce intelligent behavior leads to an antinomy. On one hand, we have the thesis: There must always be a broader context in which to work out our formalization, otherwise we have no way to distinguish relevant from irrelevant facts. On the other hand, we have the antithesis: There must be an ultimate context which we can make completely explicit, otherwise there will be an infinite regress of contexts, and we can never begin our formalization.

As Kant noted, the resolution of such an antinomy requires giving up the assumption that these are the only possible alternatives. They are, indeed, the only alternatives open to someone trying to construct *artificial* reason, for a digital computer program must always proceed from the elements to the whole and thus treat the world as a set of facts. But *human* reason is able to avoid this antinomy by operating within a context or horizon which gives to facts their significance but need not itself be analyzed in terms of facts.

IV

In the face of this antinomy, it seems reasonable to claim that, on the information-processing level, as opposed to the level of the laws of physics, we cannot analyze human behavior in terms of explicit rules. And since we have seen no argument brought forward by the A.I. theorists for the formalist assumption that human behavior *must be* simulateable by a digital computer operating with strict rules on determinate bits, we would seem to have good philosophical grounds for rejecting this assumption.

If we do abandon this assumption, then the empirical data available to date would take on different significance. The persistent difficulties which have plagued all areas of A.I. would then need to be reinterpreted as failures, and these failures, interpreted as empirical evidence against the formalist's assumption that one can treat the situation or context as if it were an object. In Heideggerian terms, this is to say that Western metaphysics reaches its culmination in cybernetics, and the recent difficulties in A.I., rather than reflecting technological limitations, may reveal the limitations of technology.

NOTES

1. Marvin Minsky, *Computation, Finite and Infinite Machines,* Englewood Cliffs, N.J.: Prentice-Hall, 1967, p. 2.

2. *Ibid.,* p. 2.

3. Marvin Minsky, "Artificial Intelligence," *Scientific American,* 215 (September 1966), 257.

4. Daniel G. Bobrow, *Natural Language Input for a Computer Problem-Solving System,* Project MAC report MAC-TR-1, p. 102.

5. *Ibid.* Minsky makes even more surprising and misleading claims in his introduction to *Semantic Information Processing,* Cambridge, Mass.: M.I.T. Press, 1968. There, in discussing Bobrow's program, he acclaims its "enormous 'learning potential.' "

Consider the colossal effect, upon future performance of Bobrow's STUDENT, of telling it that "distance equals speed times time." That one experience enables it to then handle a very large new portion of "high-school algebra"—all the linear physical position-velocity-time problems. We don't consider it "learning" perhaps only because it is too intelligent! We become muddled by our associations with the psychologist's image of learning as a slow-improvement-attendant-upon sickeningly-often-repeated experience!

Again, it is easy to show that what has been acquired by the machine can in no way be called "understanding." The machine has indeed been given another *equation,* but it does not understand it as a *formula.* That is, the program can now plug one distance, one rate, and one time into the equation d = rt, but that it does not understand anything is clear from the fact that it cannot use this equation twice in one problem, for it has no way of determining which quantities should be used in which equation.

6. For example, in his *Scientific American* article, Minsky asks: "Why are the programs not more intelligent than they are?" and responds: " . . . until recently resources—in people, time and computer capacity—have been quite limited. A number of the more careful and serious attempts have come close to their goal . . . others have been limited by core memory capacity; still others encountered programing difficulties." (p. 258).

7. Minsky, *Computation,* p. vii.

8. Cf. my forthcoming book, *A Critique of Artificial Reason,* New York: Harper & Row, 1969.

9. A. H. Turing, "Computing Machinery and Intelligence," in *Minds and Machines,* ed. Alan Ross Anderson, Englewood Cliffs, N.J.: Prentice-Hall, 1964, p. 8.

10. Minsky, *Computation,* p. 107.

11. *Ibid.*

12. Turing, "Computing Machinery and Intelligence," p. 23.

13. *Ibid.*

14. Cf. H. J. Bremermann, "Optimization through Evolution and Recombination," in *Self-Organizing Systems,* ed. M. C. Yonts, G. T. Jacobi, and G. D. Goldstein, Washington, D.C.: Spartan, 1962, pp. 93–106. In this article Bremermann demonstrated that "No data processing system whether artificial or living can process more than (2×10^{47}) bits per second per gram of its mass." He goes on to draw the following conclusions:

There are $\pi \times 10^7$ seconds in a year. The age of the earth is about 10^9 years, its mass less than 6×10^{27} grams. Hence even a computer of the size of the earth could not process more than 10^{93} bits during a time equal to the age of the earth. [Not to mention the fact, one might add, that the bigger the computer, the more the speed of light would be a factor in slowing down its operations.] . . . Theorem proving and problem solving . . . lead to exponentially growing problem trees. If our conjecture is true, then it seems that the difficulties that are currently encountered in the field of pattern recognition and theorem proving will not be resolved by sheer speed of data processing by some future supercomputers.

15. Minsky, *Computation,* p. 106. Of course, Minsky is thinking of computation, not moral action.

16. Plato, *Euthyphro,* New York: Library of Liberal Arts, 1948.

17. Minsky, *Computation,* p. 106.

18. Aristotle, *Nicomachean Ethics,* Baltimore: Penguin Books, 1953, p. 75.

19. Hobbes, *Leviathan,* New York: Library of Liberal Arts, 1958, p. 45.

20. This is not the only reason Leibnitz deserves to be called the first cyberneticist. His sketchy general descriptions of his "universal characteristic," coupled with his promise that given enough money and time he could easily work out the details, makes him the father of modern grant proposals.

21. Martin Heidegger, "La fin de la philosophie et la tache de la pensée," in *Kierkegaard Vivant,* Colloque organise par L'Unesco à Paris du 21 au 23 avril 1964, Paris: Gallimard, 1966, pp. 178–79.

22. Anthony G. Oettinger, "The State of the Art of Automatic Language Translation: An Appraisal," *Beitraege zur Sprachkunde und Information Verarbeitung,* vol. 1, Heft 2, Munich, 1963, p. 27.

23. Jerrold Katz and Jerry Fodor, "The Structure of a Semantic Theory," in *The Structure of Language,* ed. Jerrold Katz and Jerry Fodor, Englewood Cliffs, N.J.: Prentice-Hall, 1964, p. 487.

24. Yehoshua Bar-Hillel, "The Present Status of Automatic Translation of Languages," in *Advances in Computers,* vol. 1, New York: Academic Press, 1960, p. 94.

25. *Ibid.,* p. 160.

26. Katz and Fodor, "Structure of a Semantic Theory," p. 489.

27. *Ibid.,* p. 179.

28. Ludwig Wittgenstein, *Philosophical Investigations,* New York: Macmillan, 1953, Article 217.

29. *Ibid.,* Article 226.

2

BEHAVIORISM

"Thou canst not touch the freedom of my mind."

— John Milton, *Comus*, line 663

"Come quick Mulvaney, I've discovered something remarkable—a sensation identical to a nerve ending."

— Christopher Norgood
The Philosopher's Dilemma

INTRODUCTION

Everything is either matter or made of matter. This is the doctrine of *materialism.* It is a thesis that scientists find plausible. But human beings are often quite reluctant to think of themselves simply as bits of matter organized in complicated ways. There is the ancient doctrine of the soul, of course, in which the gross physical realities of a body subject to decay and eventual destruction are juxtaposed against some immortal and intangible substance or stuff. Descartes, the greatest of early modern philosophers, wrote that the world was divided into two substances, the one material, the other mental. How two such distinct substances could interact, Descartes never explained; still, Cartesian *dualism* does give voice to the instinctive and common suspicion that the human mind and the body to which it is associated are items of a fundamentally different kind. This blotches the clean sweep of things that materialists believe materialism affords. It has thus become important in both 20th century philosophy and psychology to show that appearances and common inclinations notwithstanding, the machine that we inhabit and which carries on with such dubious success as strictly a physical object has no soullike ghost; those mental properties that provoked Descartes to name a separate substance are, when everything is properly understood, merely aspects of the way in which a material body is arranged in space and time.

Behaviorism is the doctrine that psychology need concern itself only with the observable responses that an organism makes in response to sensed stimuli. It is thus a science concerned only with behavior and not with any of the mental states that human subjects might insist go along with items in a behavioral repertoire. Materialists have always felt congenially toward behaviorists, and with good reasons. The behaviorist need not avow that there are no minds but he can, he often reports, make do without them. Behaviorism, then, is *methodological* materialism, a stern doctrine. And a doctrine of some slipperiness. If it turns out in the end that there really are no minds, the behaviorist has credentials made impeccable by virtue of a long standing commitment to their inexistence; and if, on the other hand, the various behavioral strategies all fail, the behaviorist can remind his audience that his was merely methodological materialism, adopted only as a scruple of Science.

Behaviorism has been part of the American psychological orthodoxy for 60 years. For almost that long, B. F. Skinner has argued tirelessly in its behalf. In his essay, Professor Skinner sets out the main points of the behaviorist charge in the context of a critique of Freudian psychology—an irrestible target, of course, for any fastidious behaviorist. Between stimulus and response, Freud interposed a system rich in belief, memory and desire. Although Freud wrote approvingly of materialism, his own work depicted a universe (filled as it was with unconscious drives, instinctual processes, implacable needs and hidden motives) that can at first blush be understood *only* in mentalistic terms. Skinner is by no means insensitive to the scope of Freud's insights; but the method by which they were achieved, he insists, involves a systematic deformation of the scientific procedure. What should be an account strictly of behavior appears as the description of some intermediate mental construction which, when the plain facts are soberly considered, does not happen even to exist.

For what seemed a great many years, behaviorists in America succeeded in depicting opposition to behaviorism as a sign of intellectual weak headedness. This period of self-satisfaction has come to an end. Philosophers and psychologists who for the longest time remarked merely that the details of the behaviorist program might require alteration now argue that theirs was a passionate and deeply held opposition to virtually all of the chief behavioral principles. Professor Scriven teaches philosophy at the University of California in Berkeley. He is known for his wide ranging interests in the philosophy of science and an intellectual air that his admirers describe as self-assured and his detractors as wrong-headed. "A Study of Radical Behaviorism" is an important paper in the philosophy of psychology, for it marks, I think, the first sustained effort to evaluate that haughty methodological chauvinism that has characterized behaviorism since the time of Watson and points before. Although it is obviously contraposed to Skinner's "Critique of Psychoanalytic Concepts and Theories," Scriven appeals now and then to other books and articles by Skinner so the careful reader should not succumb to feelings of discombobulation when he finds in Scriven an argument attributed to Skinner that he cannot track down to Skinner's article on Freud. The two papers, read together, will give the impression of a unified whole.

Behaviorism is in many respects a methodological position. Hence, my caricature of it as methodological materialism. To the question whether sensations, feelings, desires, wishes and beliefs really exist, the behaviorist may reply calmly that ontological assurances are quite beyond his ken. Philosophers though have felt that even if behaviorism yielded a science of some content, the basic issue raised by Cartesian dualism would nonetheless remain. And in this respect, they are clearly right. If a man tells you that there is nothing in the world save for matter or bits of matter, then, if his case is to be persuasive, he must also be prepared to show you that what you naturally think of as something really unlike matter turns out (when properly analyzed) to be matter after all. In the 1930s analytic philosophers undertook to show that the language by which we habitually describe our mental and emotional states is identical in meaning to language which says nothing about sensations, thoughts, wishes, desires or dreams and refers instead only to the gross or subtle motions of the body. When I remark that I feel giddy, although I may move my body in certain characteristic ways, I do not mean just that I am moving my body in those ways.

This is an oversimplification of an interesting chapter in the development of modern philosophy; I indulge myself only to set the stage somewhat for J. J. C. Smart. "Sensations and Brain Processes" has, I think redefined the problems of Cartesian dualism by simplifying them radically. Many philosophers had concluded from the fact that the language of mental events was not identical in meaning to the language of physical events, that mental events were not identical to physical events. Smart observed that this is a non-sequitur. What the linguistic evidence showed, if anything, was only that mental events and physical events were not necessarily identical. It is still possible that when I have a pain what I report is *as a matter of contingent fact* identical to a particular state of my brain, much as it is a matter of contingent fact that the evening star is identical to Venus.

This is the *identity* thesis. Materialists dismayed by the crushing difficulties facing an earlier if purer positivism look on it as a divinely inspired oblation. Norman Malcolm teaches philosophy at Cornell University. Although deeply influenced by Ludwig Wittgenstein, who was in some sense a philosopher intrigued by behaviorism, Malcolm here takes issue with Smart on a point-by-point basis. Although both essays read smoothly, they are deceptively difficult in philosophically characteristic ways. Thus theses that are simply stated turn out to hinge upon such deep concepts as *identity, strict identity* and the nature of necessity.

A large literature exists both on behaviorism, considered simply as a psychological movement and on the identity thesis. Berlinski and Bever have edited a collection of the most important objections to behaviorism under the title *Against Behaviorism* (to be published, Aldine). B. F. Skinner has expressed his most recent methodological thoughts in *Beyond Freedom and Dignity* (Random House). Other references and an interesting account of behaviorism as a movement in philosophy and psychology may be found in Arnold Kaufman's article in Vol. 1 of *The Encyclopedia of Philosophy,* edited by Paul Edwards (Macmillan & Co.). A good collection of essays on the identity theory is anthologized in *The Philosophy of Mind,* edited by V. C. Chappel (Prentice-Hall); another collection covering similar ground is D. F. Gustafson's essays in *Philosophical Psychology* (Doubleday). A very nifty refutation of the identity thesis is briefly advanced in Gilbert Harman's *Thought* (Princeton University Press).

CRITIQUE
OF PSYCHOANALYTIC
CONCEPTS
AND THEORIES*

B. F. Skinner

Freud's great contribution to Western thought has been described as the application of the principle of cause and effect to human behavior. Freud demonstrated that many features of behavior hitherto unexplained—and often dismissed as hopelessly complex or obscure—could be shown to be the product of circumstances in the history of the individual. Many of the causal relationships he so convincingly demonstrated had been wholly unsuspected—unsuspected, in particular, by the very individuals whose behavior they controlled. Freud greatly reduced the sphere of accident and caprice in our considerations of human conduct. His achievement in this respect appears all the more impressive when we recall that he was never able to appeal to the quantitative proofs characteristic of other sciences. He carried the day with sheer persuasion—with the massing of instances and the delineation of surprising parallels and analogies among seemingly diverse materials.

This was not, however, Freud's own view of the matter. At the age of seventy he summed up his achievement in this way: "My life has been aimed at one goal only: to infer or guess how the mental apparatus is constructed and what forces interplay and counteract in it."[1] It is difficult to describe the mental apparatus he refers to in noncontroversial terms, partly because Freud's conception changed from time to time and partly because its very nature encouraged misinterpretation and misunderstanding. But it is perhaps not too wide of the mark to indicate its principal features as follows: Freud conceived of some realm of the mind, not necessarily having physical extent, but nevertheless capable of topographic description and of subdivision into regions of the conscious, co-conscious, and

*Reprinted by permission from B. F. Skinner, "Critique of Psychoanalytic Concepts and Theories," *Scientific Monthly,* 79, pp. 300-305, November 1954.

unconscious. Within this space, various mental events—ideas, wishes, memories, emotions, instinctive tendencies, and so on—interacted and combined in many complex ways. Systems of these mental events came to be conceived of almost as subsidiary personalities and were given proper names: the id, the ego, and the superego. These systems divided among themselves a limited store of psychic energy. There were, of course, many other details.

No matter what logicians may eventually make of this mental apparatus, there is little doubt that Freud accepted it as real rather than as a scientific construct or theory. One does not at the age of seventy define the goals of one's life as the exploration of an explanatory fiction. Freud did not use his "mental apparatus" as a postulate system from which he deduced theorems to be submitted to empirical check. If there was any interaction between the mental apparatus and empirical observations, such interaction took the form of modifying the apparatus to account for newly discovered facts. To many followers of Freud the mental apparatus appears to be equally as real as the newly discovered facts, and the exploration of such an apparatus is similarly accepted as the goal of a science of behavior. There is an alternative view, however, which holds that Freud did not discover the mental apparatus but rather invented it, borrowing part of its structure from a traditional philosophy of human conduct but adding many novel features of his own devising.

There are those who will concede that Freud's mental apparatus was a scientific construct rather than an observable empirical system but who, nevertheless, attempt to justify it in the light of scientific method. One may take the line that metaphorical devices are inevitable in the early stages of any science and that although we may look with amusement today upon the "essences," "forces," "phlogistons," and "ethers" of the science of yesterday, these nevertheless were essential to the historical process. It would be difficult to prove or disprove this. However, if we have learned anything about the nature of scientific thinking, if mathematical and logical researches have improved our capacity to represent and analyze empirical data, it is possible that we can avoid some of the mistakes of adolescence. Whether Freud could have done so is past demonstrating, but whether we need similar constructs in the future prosecution of a science of behavior is a question worth considering.

Constructs are convenient and perhaps even necessary in dealing with certain complicated subject matters. As Frenkel-Brunswik shows,[2] Freud was aware of the problems of scientific methodology and even of the metaphorical nature of some of his own constructs. When this was the case, he justified the constructs as necessary or at least highly convenient. But awareness of the nature of the metaphor is no defense of it, and if modern science is still occasionally metaphorical, we must remember that, theorywise, it is also still in trouble. The point is not that metaphor or construct is objectionable but that particular metaphors and constructs have caused trouble and are continuing to do so. Freud recognized the damage worked by his own metaphorical thinking, but he felt that it could not be avoided and that the damage must be put up with. There is reason to disagree with him on this point.

Freud's explanatory scheme followed a traditional pattern of looking for a cause of human behavior inside the organism. His medical training supplied him with powerful supporting analogies. The parallel between the excision of a tumor, for example, and the release of a repressed wish from the unconscious is quite compelling and must have affected Freud's thinking. Now, the pattern of an inner explanation of behavior is best exemplified by doctrines of animism, which are primarily concerned with explaining the spontaneity and evident capriciousness of behavior. The living organism is an extremely complicated system behaving in an extremely complicated way. Much of its behavior appears at first blush to be absolutely unpredictable. The traditional procedure has been to invent an inner determiner, a "demon," "spirit," "homunculus," or "personality" capable of spontaneous change of course or of origination of action. Such an inner determiner offers only a momentary explanation of the behavior of the outer organism, because it must, of course, be accounted for also, but it is commonly used to put the matter beyond further inquiry and to bring the study of a causal series of events to a dead end.

Freud, himself, however, did not appeal to the inner apparatus to account for spontaneity or caprice because he was a thoroughgoing determinist. He accepted the responsibility of explaining, in turn, the behavior of the inner determiner. He did this by pointing to hitherto unnoticed external causes in the environmental and genetic history of the individual. He did not, therefore, need the traditional explanatory system for traditional purposes; but he was unable to eliminate the pattern from his thinking. It led him to represent each of the causal relationships he had discovered as a series of three events. Some environmental condition, very often in the early life of the individual, leaves an effect upon the inner mental apparatus, and this in turn produces the behavioral manifestation or symptom. Environmental event, mental state or process, behavioral symptom—these are the three links in Freud's causal chain. He made no appeal to the middle link to explain spontaneity or caprice. Instead he used it to bridge the gap in space and time between the events he had proved to be causally related.

A possible alternative, which would have had no quarrel with established science, would have been to argue that the environmental variables leave *physiological* effects that may be inferred from the behavior of the individual, perhaps at a much later date. In one sense, too little is known at the moment of these physiological processes to make them useful in a legitimate way for this purpose. On the other hand, too much is known of them, at least in a negative way. Enough is known of the nervous system to place certain dimensional limits upon speculation and to clip the wings of explanatory fiction. Freud accepted, therefore, the traditional fiction of a mental life, avoiding an out-and-out dualism by arguing that eventually physiological counterparts would be discovered. Quite apart from the question of the existence of mental events, let us observe the damage that resulted from this maneuver.

We may touch only briefly upon two classical problems that arise once the conception of a mental life has been adopted. The first of these is to explain how such a life is to be observed. The introspective psychologists had already tried to solve this problem by arguing that introspection is only a special case of the observation upon which all science rests and that man's experience necessarily stands between him and the physical world with which science purports to deal. But it was Freud himself who pointed out that not all of one's mental life was accessible to direct observation, that many events in the mental apparatus were necessarily inferred. Great as this discovery was, it would have been still greater if Freud had taken the next step, advocated a little later by the American movement called Behaviorism, and insisted that conscious, as well as unconscious, events were inferences from the facts. By arguing that the individual organism simply reacts to its environment, rather than to some inner experience of that environment, the bifurcation of nature into physical and psychic can be avoided.[3]

A second classical problem is how the mental life can be manipulated. In the process of therapy, the analyst necessarily acts upon the patient only through physical means. He manipulates variables occupying a position in the first link of Freud's causal chain. Nevertheless, it is commonly assumed that the mental apparatus is being directly manipulated. Sometimes it is argued that processes are initiated within the individual himself, such as those of free association and transference, and that these in turn act directly upon the mental apparatus. But how are these mental processes initiated by physical means? The clarification of such a causal connection places a heavy and often unwelcome burden of proof upon the shoulders of the dualist.

The important disadvantages of Freud's conception of mental life can be described somewhat more specifically. The first of these concerns the environmental variables to which Freud so convincingly pointed. The cogency of these variables was frequently missed because the variables were transformed and obscured in the course of being represented in mental life. The physical world of the organism was converted into conscious and unconscious experience, and these experiences were further transmuted as they combined and changed in mental processes. For example, early punishment of sexual behavior is an observable fact that undoubtedly leaves behind a changed organism. But when this change is represented as a state of conscious or unconscious anxiety or guilt, specific details of the punishment are lost. When, in turn, some unusual characteristic of the sexual behavior of the adult individual is related to the supposed guilt, many specific features of the relationship may be missed that would have been obvious if the same features of behavior had been related to the punishing

80

episode. Insofar as the mental life of the individual is used as Freud used it to represent and to carry an environmental history, it is inadequate and misleading.

Freud's theory of the mental apparatus had an equally damaging effect on his study of behavior as a dependent variable. Inevitably, it stole the show. Little attention was left to behavior per se. Behavior was relegated to the position of a mere mode of expression of the activities of the mental apparatus or the symptoms of an underlying disturbance. Among the problems not specifically treated in the manner that was their due, we may note five.

1. The nature of the act as a unit of behavior was never clarified. The simple *occurrence* of behavior was never well represented. "Thoughts" could "occur" to an individual; he could "have" ideas according to the traditional model; but he could "have" behavior only in giving expression to these inner events. We are much more likely to say that "the thought occurred to me to ask him his name" than that "the act of asking him his name occurred to me." It is in the nature of thoughts and ideas that they occur to people, but we have never come to be at home in describing the emission of behavior in a comparable way. This is especially true of verbal behavior. In spite of Freud's valuable analysis of verbal slips and of the techniques of wit and verbal art, he rejected the possibility of an analysis of verbal behavior in its own right rather than as the expression of ideas, feelings, or other inner events, and therefore missed the importance of this field for the analysis of units of behavior and the conditions of their occurrence.

The behavioral nature of perception was also slighted. To see an object as an object is not mere passing sensing; it is an act, and something very much like it occurs when we see an object although no object is present. Fantasy and dreams were for Freud not the perceptual *behavior* of the individual but pictures painted by an inner artist in some atelier of the mind which the individual then contemplated and perhaps then reported. This division of labor is not essential when the behavioral component of the act of seeing is emphasized.

2. The dimensions of behavior, particularly its dynamic properties, were never adequately represented. We are all familiar with the fact that some of our acts are more likely to occur upon a given occasion than others. But this likelihood is hard to represent and harder to evaluate. The dynamic changes in behavior that are the first concern of the psychoanalyst are primarily changes in probability of action. But Freud chose to deal with this aspect of behavior in other terms—as a question of "libido," "cathexis," "volume of excitation," "instinctive or emotional tendencies," "available quantities of psychic energy," and so on. The delicate question of how probability of action is to be quantified was never answered, because these constructs suggested dimensions to which the quantitative practices of science in general could not be applied.

3. In his emphasis on the genesis of behavior, Freud made extensive use of processes of learning. These were never treated operationally in terms of changes in behavior but rather as the acquisition of ideas, feelings, and emotions later to

be expressed by, or manifested in, behavior. Consider, for example, Freud's own suggestion that sibling rivalry in his own early history played an important part in his theoretical considerations as well as in his personal relationships as an adult.

An infant brother died when Freud himself was only one and a half years old, and as a young child Freud played with a boy somewhat older than himself and presumably more powerful, yet who was, strangely enough, in the nominally subordinate position of being his nephew. To classify such a set of circumstances as sibling rivalry obscures, as we have seen, the many specific properties of the circumstances themselves regarded as independent variables in a science of behavior. To argue that what was learned was the effect of these circumstances on unconscious or conscious aggressive tendencies or feelings of guilt works a similar misrepresentation of the dependent variable. An emphasis on behavior would lead us to inquire into the specific acts plausibly assumed to be engendered by these childhood episodes. In very specific terms, how was the behavior of the young Freud shaped by the special reinforcing contingencies arising from the presence of a younger child in the family, by the death of that child, and by later association with an older playmate who nevertheless occupied a subordinate family position? What did the young Freud learn to do to achieve parental attention under these difficult circumstances? How did he avoid aversive consequences? Did he exaggerate any illness? Did he feign illness? Did he make a conspicuous display of behavior that brought commendation? Was such behavior to be found in the field of physical prowess or intellectual endeavor? Did he learn to engage in behavior that would in turn increase the repertoires available to him to achieve commendation? Did he strike or otherwise injure young children? Did he learn to injure them verbally by teasing? Was he punished for this, and if so, did he discover other forms of behavior that had the same damaging effect but were immune to punishment?

We cannot, of course, adequately answer questions of this sort at so late a date, but they suggest the kind of inquiry that would be prompted by a concern for the explicit shaping of behavioral repertoires under childhood circumstances. What has survived through the years is not aggression and guilt, later to be manifested in behavior, but rather patterns of behavior themselves. It is not enough to say that this is "all that is meant" by sibling rivalry or by its effects on the mental apparatus. Such an expression obscures, rather than illuminates, the nature of the behavioral changes taking place in the childhood learning process. A similar analysis could be made of processes in the fields of motivation and emotion.

4. An explicit treatment of behavior as a datum, of probability of response as the principal quantifiable property of behavior, and of learning and other processes in terms of changes of probability is usually enough to avoid another pitfall into which Freud, in common with his contemporaries, fell. There are many words in the layman's vocabulary that suggest the activity of an organism

yet are not descriptive of behavior in the narrower sense. Freud used many of these freely; for example, the individual is said to discriminate, remember, infer, repress, decide, and so on. Such terms do not refer to specific acts. We say that a man discriminates between two objects when he behaves differently with respect to them; but discriminating is not itself behavior. We say that he represses behavior which has been punished when he engages in other behavior just because it displaces the punished behavior; but repressing is not action. We say that he decides upon a course of conduct either when he enters upon one course to the exclusion of another, or when he alters some of the variables affecting his own behavior in order to bring this about; but there is no other "act of deciding." The difficulty is that when one uses terms which suggest an activity, one feels it necessary to invent an actor, and the subordinate personalities in the Freudian mental apparatus do, indeed, participate in just these activities rather than in the more specific behavior of the observable organism.

Among these activities are conspicuous instances involving the process of self-control—the so-called "Freudian mechanisms." These need not be regarded as activities of the individual or any subdivision thereof—they are not, for example, what happens when a skillful wish evades a censor—but simply as ways of representing relationships among responses and controlling variables. I have elsewhere tried to demonstrate this by restating the Freudian mechanisms without reference to Freudian theory.[4]

5. Since Freud never developed a clear conception of the behavior of the organism and never approached many of the scientific problems peculiar to that subject matter, it is not surprising that he misinterpreted the nature of the observation of one's own behavior. This is admittedly a delicate subject, which presents problems that no one, perhaps, has adequately solved. But the act of self-observation can be represented within the framework of physical science. This involves questioning the reality of sensations, ideas, feelings, and other states of consciousness which many people regard as among the most immediate experiences of their life. Freud himself prepared us for this change. There is, perhaps, no experience more powerful than that which the mystic reports of his awareness of the presence of God. The psychoanalyst explains this in other ways. He himself, however, may insist upon the reality of certain experiences that others wish to question. There are other ways of describing what is actually seen or felt under such circumstances.

Each of us is in particularly close contact with a small part of the universe enclosed within his own skin. Under certain limited circumstances, we may come to react to that part of the universe in unusual ways. But it does not follow that that particular part has any special physical or nonphysical properties or that our observations of it differ in any fundamental respect from our observations of the rest of the world. I have tried to show elsewhere how self-knowledge of this sort arises and why it is likely to be subject to limitations that are troublesome from the point of view of physical science. Freud's representation of these events was a particular personal contribution influenced by his own cultural history. It is possible that science can now move on to a different description of them. If it is impossible to be wholly nonmetaphorical, at least we may improve upon our metaphors.

The crucial issue here is the Freudian distinction between the conscious and unconscious mind. Freud's contribution has been widely misunderstood. The important point was not that the individual was often unable to describe important aspects of his own behavior or identify important causal relationships, but that his ability to describe them was irrelevant to the occurrence of the behavior or to the effectiveness of the causes. We begin by attributing the behavior of the individual to events in his genetic and environmental history. We then note that because of certain cultural practices, the individual may come to describe some of that behavior and some of those causal relationships. We may say that he is conscious of the parts he can describe and unconscious of the rest. But the act of self-description, as of self-observation, plays no part in the determination of action. It is superimposed on behavior. Freud's argument that we need not be aware of important causes of conduct leads naturally to the broader conclusion that awareness of cause has nothing to do with causal effectiveness.

In addition to these specific consequences of Freud's mental apparatus in obscuring important details among the variables of which human behavior is a function and in leading to the neglect of important problems in the analysis of behavior as a primary datum, we have to note the most unfortunate effect of all. Freud's methodological strategy has prevented the incorporation of psychoanalysis into the body of science proper. It was inherent in the nature of such an explanatory system that its key entities would be unquantifiable in the sense in which entities in science are generally quantifiable, but the spatial and temporal dimensions of these entities have caused other kinds of trouble.

One can sense a certain embarrassment among psychoanalytic writers with respect to the primary entities of the mental apparatus. There is a predilection for terms that avoid the embarrassing question of the spatial dimensions, physical or otherwise, of terms at the primary level. Although it is occasionally necessary to refer to mental events and their qualities and to states of consciousness, the analyst usually moves on in some haste to less committal terms such as *forces, processes, organizations, tensions, systems,* and *mechanisms.* But all these imply terms at a lower level. The notion of a conscious or unconscious "force" may be a useful metaphor, but if this is analogous to force in physics, what is the analogous mass that is analogously accelerated? Human behavior is in a state of flux and undergoing changes that we call "processes," but what is changing in what direction when we speak of, for example, an affective process? Psychological "organizations," "mental systems," "motivational interaction"—these all imply arrangements or relationships among *things,* but what are the things so related or arranged? Until this question has been answered the problem of the dimensions of the mental apparatus can scarcely be approached. It is not likely that the problem can be solved by working out independent units appropriate to the mental apparatus, although it has been proposed that such a step be undertaken in an attempt to place psychoanalysis on a scientific footing.

Before one attempts to work out units of transference, or scales of anxiety, or systems of mensuration appropriate to the regions of consciousness, it is worth asking whether there is not an alternative program for a *rapprochement* with physical science that would make such a task unnecessary. Freud could hope for an eventual union with physics or physiology only through the discovery of neurological mechanisms that would be the analogues of, or possibly only other aspects of, the features of his mental apparatus. Since this depended on the prosecution of a science of neurology far beyond its current state of knowledge, it was not an attractive future. Freud appears never to have considered the possibility of bringing the concepts and theories of a psychological science into contact with the rest of physical and biological science by the simple expedient of an operational definition of terms. This would have placed the mental apparatus in jeopardy as a life goal, but it would have brought him back to the observable, manipulable, and preeminently physical variables with which, in the last analysis, he was dealing.

NOTES

1. Jones, E. *Life and Work of Sigmund Freud,* Vol. 1. New York: Basic Books, 1953.

2. Frenkel-Brunswick, Else. "Meaning of Psychoanalytic Concepts and Confirmation of Psychoanalytic Theories," *Scientific Monthly,* 79: 293–300 (1954).

3. Although it was Freud himself who taught us to doubt the face value of introspection, he appears to have been responsible for the view that another sort of direct experience is required if certain activities in the mental apparatus are to be comprehended. Such a requirement is implied in the modern assertion that only those who have been psychoanalyzed can fully understand the meaning of transference or the release of a repressed fear.

4. Skinner, B. F. *Science and Human Behavior.* New York: Macmillan, 1953.

A STUDY
OF
RADICAL
BEHAVIORISM*

Michael Scriven

Those who cry "No politics" often thereby support bad politics, and those in whose prefaces philosphy is abjured often proceed to expound bad philosophy. In this paper, I want to examine the views of a man who has recommended the abolition of theories: Professor B. F. Skinner.

But I shall not be trying to show that Skinner's theories are bad; I wish to show only that he does employ them, and that his general arguments against the adoption of theories (or at least certain kinds of theory) are not altogether satisfactory. It is, indeed, only because I regard his work so highly and his arguments as so persuasive that I hope to compensate a little for his influence in the methodological sphere. I shall be especially concerned with his 1954 article "Critique of Psychoanalytic Concepts and Theories" (CPCT; 10) in the *Scientific Monthly,* but also with his amplification of certain of these points in his 1953 book, *Science and Human Behavior* (SHB; 9) and in the 1950 article "Are Theories of Learning Necessary?" (ATLN; 8).

The general point I hope to make is this: Skinner's position on almost every issue admits of two interpretations—one of them exciting, controversial, and practically indefensible; the other moderately interesting, rather widely accepted, and very plausible—and Skinner's views quite often appear to be stated in the first form but defended in the second. Specifically, I wish to suggest that:

1. Skinner's idea of the relationship between the "pure" molar behavior approach and neurological, mentalistic, or conceptual theories is seriously oversimplified in a way that, if corrected, renders untenable most of his objections to the latter.

---

*Scriven, Michael, "A Study of Radical Behaviorism," in Minnesota Studies in the Philosophy of Science, vol. I, *The Foundations of Science and the Concepts of Psychology and Psychoanalysis,* ed. Herbert Feigl and Michael Scriven, University of Minnesota Press, Minneapolis, © Copyright 1956 by the University of Minnesota.

2. Skinner's analysis of causation, explanation, and classification is subject to correction in the same way.

Imagine that, as a trained psychologist, you are a member of the first survey team sent out to the Alpha Centauri system, and that an inhabited planet is discovered there. On landing, you find that the atmosphere is unbreathable and that you have to remain in a space suit. The first sight you get of the inhabitants raises the question whether they are actually indigenous, since they also appear to be wearing space suits. You might think of the alternative possibilities that severe changes in the atmosphere have required them to devise these garments in order to survive, or that they come from a more hospitable part of the planet, perhaps underground. These hypotheses are not theories or parts of theories in Skinner's sense. Suppose that, after a long period of study, you discover a large number of laws concerning their habits, needs, and social structuring, and you organize these into various categories so that you can predict and control and understand the behavior of the Centaurians (who exhibit, in particular, a remarkable power of memory and a great fondness for aniseed); moreover, you can converse with them and exchange technological data with them. Thus fortified, you consider publishing some of this material in a paper called "A Theory of Social Behavior Among the Centaurians." Skinner would prefer that you refrain from using that title, because he would not wish you to imagine that he was opposing that sort of an activity. But suppose that one day it occurred to you that the extraordinary success exhibited by the Centaurians in recognizing people apparently on the basis of descriptions alone might be due to small television signal receivers in their suits feeding direct into their optic nerves: then you have a theory ("any explanation of an observed fact which appeals to events . . . at some other level of observation" [ATLN, p. 193]). As a matter of fact even a complex mathematical formalization of your data would count as a theory, at least in a sense (ATLN, p. 216); and certainly, if you introduced such concepts as "excitatory potential of a habit" in organizing your thought about Centaurian dispositions, let alone "the significance of the Terran landing in the eyes of the Centaurian Council," you would indeed be guilty of theorizing (ATLN, p. 195; SHB, p. 89).

Now Skinner has two approaches to theories in his sense of "theories."-At the very least, he wants to argue that bothering with them is pragmatically unjustifiable (ATLN, p. 194). This is, of course, not the same as saying that such theories do not produce practically useful results: it is to say that there is a better way to obtain these results. *In view of this better way,* theories are, pragmatically speaking, a luxury. Professor Ginsberg cannot, therefore, get very far by calling on Skinner "to account for [the] fabulous success [of micro-theories] in physics" (ODT, p. 241) since Skinner would not have to deny this success, although he would, at the very least, suggest that other methods might have been preferable. ("It would be foolhardy to deny the achievements of theories of this sort in the history of science. The question of whether they are necessary, how-ever, has other implications . . ." [ATLN, p. 194].)

But Skinner will, on occasion, go considerably further than this. He regards it as distinctly possible that the attempt to theorize has resulted in a net absolute loss in the history of science—not a relative loss compared to the alternative he prefers, but an over-all loss. It would appear that this position could be seriously supported only if we can establish that there are more unsolved problems or pseudo-solutions in science today than there have been successes. Now it is clear that in terms of Skinner's favorite criterion, the possibility of control, we have advanced enormously since, say, 1300. How can we evaluate the losses? Certainly, more scientists are working on more problems than ever before, and in that very positivistic sense the area of darkness is larger; but even under Skinner's direction the same situation would of course arise, so this will not support the relative point he makes, let alone the absolute one. If we are not going to appeal to the number of problems known to be unsolved for evidence of retrogression, then we must insist that many of the solutions in which we commonly believe are, in fact, unsound. Clearly, this alternative is more consistent with Skinner's general position. Throughout his work runs the trail of the debunker, the cry of a man who is by no means afraid to say that what we have always known to be true is, in fact, false—for example, our belief in what he calls "the traditional fiction of the mental life" (CPCT, p. 302). Could he really point out enough pseudo-explanations to show that the progress of modern science has been ap-parent, not real? To do so, he would certainly have to pass very adverse judg-ment on many fields other than his own. I think we should conclude that, on the whole, when adopting this extreme position, he is trying to bring us up short, make us worry whether the approach we have taken for granted can really be justified, rather than trying to convince us of a literal truth. One of the reasons why it would be so difficult to show that there has been a net absolute loss from the use of theories in the history of science is the curious disanalogy between net progress in science and net profit on a balance sheet. If at time t_2 we definitely have certain laws which predict with some reliability and which we did not have at t_1 ($t_1 < t_2$), and we have not lost any laws which we did have at t_1, then there is a straightforward sense in which it can be definitely said that our science has progressed—no matter whether we have also adopted large numbers of useless theories or misleading explanations. We cannot regard an inaccurate belief as cancelling out an accurate one in the way that a loss cancels out a profit. Of course, it is certainly possible that progress has been slowed up by such para-phernalia, but this is a comparative point, a more moderate point. Relative to other methods, we may have done poorly. We shall certainly consider this inter-pretation of Skinner's position.

But there is a more subtle point involved, one which does not fall naturally into the two categories we have established—reasons supporting the relative loss position and those supporting the absolute loss position. While Skinner would not be able to support a claim of actual error in other sciences, he would, as I understand him, be more inclined to argue that the theoretical approach has stultified or prevented research into certain important and actually open questions. These questions concern the correlation between the supposed theoretical event or state that is said by the theorist to explain the observed phenomena (in our case, the minute television receiver is said to explain the hyper-recognition pheonomenon) and its own antecedent causes (in our case, the action of the Centaurians when they inserted the apparatus). According to Skinner, the basic fallacy of the theoretical approach is the idea that a proper explanation of the observed pheonomena can be given in terms of the theoretical event alone. For Skinner, the essential question would still remain. What are the causes of the theoretical event? Referring to learning theory, he says, "When we assert that an animal acts in a given way because it expects to receive food, then what began as the task of accounting for learned behavior becomes the task of accounting for expectancy" (ATLN, p. 194). My justification for believing that Skinner at least suspects that this criticism applies to science in general stems not only from hearing him say it but also from the fact that he always avoids denying it in print, even when it would greatly simplify his argument, and that he regards it as closely analogous to metaphorical thinking, of which he says ". . . if modern science is still occasionally metaphorical, we must remember that theorywise it is also still in trouble" (CPCT, p. 101).

Yet, would he really deny that the discovery of a television receiver in the Centaurian cranial enclosure constitutes an adequate explanation of the observed phenomenon? In an attempt to answer this, we may ask what he says about the corresponding explanations in the field of human behavior. He is willing to concede (in CPCT) that a neurophysiological account of neurosis may one day provide a useful accessory to, or translation of, a science of behavior (p. 302). But the tone of ATLN is less compromising; although he does not wish to deny that neural events may "actually occur or be studied by appropriate sciences" (p. 194), he does not concede that they will ever be in the least useful for a science of behavior—and the same goes for conceptual and mentalistic theories. In SHB, he again makes clear that he thinks neurology, at best, a different subject (p. 28) and, at worst, a misleading fantasy when he suggests that shock treatment or medical treatment of psychiatric disorders is based on a conception "not far removed from the view—which large numbers of people still hold—that neurotic behavior arises because the Devil or some other intruding personality is in temporary 'possession' of the body" (p. 374). Here, again, we have an example of one of Skinner's extreme positions emerging for a moment—a position which, in the three years since SHB was written, has become much less tenable. As he himself has said, "Advance estimates of the limits of science have generally proved inaccurate" (SHB, p. 20). But Skinner's extreme position in this issue is not merely a matter of pessimism about certain lines of research. It springs from a methodological point. He is not merely arguing that reference to theoretical, for example, neural, events will stultify our thinking, "create a false sense of security, an unwarranted satisfaction with the status quo" (ATLN, p. 194); he wants to suggest that it is, in some sense, a logical error to suppose that such an analysis can solve our problems in a science of behavior.

> Eventually a science of the nervous system based upon direct observation rather than inference will describe the neural states and events which immediately precede, say, the response, "No, thank you." These events in turn will be found to be preceded by other neurological events, and these in turn by others. This series will lead us back to events outside the nervous system and, eventually, outside the organism. (SHB, p. 28)

Thus the basic question is only postponed: What are the relations between these original independent environmental variables and the eventual behavior? Neurology has not really advanced the inquiry.

It is worth pausing for a moment in our survey to note that we have already discovered an extreme and a moderate interpretation of Skinner's position on (1) the role of neural theories in a science of behavior (either methodological mistakes, or merely pragmatically worthless); (2) the extent of the role of theories in various fields (unnecessary in any science; unnecessary in a science of behavior); and (3) the success of theories (more harm than good; more harm than the functional approach). The combinations of these points alone provide him with eight alternatives, and I make no excuse for trying to simplify the issue by making some judgments as to the foundation stones of this methodological analysis and concentrating on these points.

Let us begin by distilling out of ATLN Skinner's actual answer to the theoretical question comprising the title, but using the term "theory" in its ordinary sense. I take Skinner to be saying, "Theories that are very abstract are premature; theories involving neural, mentalistic, or postulationally defined concepts are (a) misleading, (b) possibly based on a logical error, and (c) certainly unnecessary, since theories involving terms defined operationally by reference to observable behavior are perfectly adequate."

I am not interested in the merely verbal question whether we attach the label of "theory" to Skinner's position, but I am interested in the underlying analyses which have led him to reject it, and me to favor it. There must be, if there is any logic to his position, certain reasons why Skinner thinks that the gap between his methods of prediction and control and those of Hull is more significant than the gap between Hull and, say, Allport. I wish to examine those reasons a little further and see whether we cannot come to some conclusion about their validity and the validity of their extrapolations as criticisms of psychoanalytic theory in particular.

Certainly, we can agree that Skinner's position is *less* theoretical than even Tolman's; the question is whether it is nontheoretical. I shall argue that it is not, and that Skinner has elevated the relatively untheoretical nature of his approach into a sterile purity that his approach fortunately lacks, thereby illicitly obtaining the semantically somewhat shocking slogan, "The science of human behavior requires no theories."

"Theory" is ordinarily taken in a wider sense than Skinner's. Webster gives as the two most relevant senses, "A more or less plausible or scientifically acceptable general principle offered to explain phenomena" and "The general or abstract principles of any body of facts"; and defines "abstract" as "considered apart from any relation to a particular object." An abstract principle is, hence, one which involves concepts that refer to a class rather than to an individual. Ginsberg starts with a very similar definition (ODT, p. 233), but later goes on to tighten the notion up in a way that is clearly related to a particular philosophical analysis (originally that of N. Campbell), although it, too, would cover Skinner's account of behavior. Feigl has argued (especially in his article "Some Remarks on the Meaning of Scientific Explanation") that a distinguishing characteristic of the set of propositions comprising a theory T of domain D is that we can deduce ("explain") *all* the empirical laws L of D from any proper T of D; whereas from any L, he says, we can only deduce particular facts F of D or other L's of D. Thus $(T \rightarrow L \rightarrow F)$ D, where " $\rightarrow$ " represents entailment. Skinner's position would then be expressed by saying that there is no need to go beyond the L level, except for purposes of guessing at further possible L's—and such guessing has no place in a scientific report, which should contain only the results of the tests performed on the putative L's. The appropriate reply is that this procedure does not answer the perfectly proper question, "Why do these particular L's hold in this particular D?" Skinner's response could take several forms:

a. The question is not proper because it is not within the province of science to ask why the world is the way it is, only to describe how it is. But Chapter 3 of SHB is entitled "Why Organisms Behave," so Skinner does not reject such questions; however, the answers he offers do not apply to the basic laws—e.g., the Law of Effect in his system. Clearly, it would be unsatisfactory to reject such a question in connection with any law (unless an illegitimate type of teleological answer is expected); we can give a perfectly respectable scientific answer to the question, Why do rarefied gases at normal temperatures obey Boyle's Law? in terms of the kinetic theory and gas molecules.

b. The question is not proper within a science of behavior. If a science of behavior is concerned to "clarify these uniformities [the ones noticed by everyone in the course of their ordinary social contacts] and make them explicit" (SHB, p. 16), then its task does not extend to explaining the basic laws themselves. Yet it is quite obviously appropriate for some part of the scientific enterprise to be devoted to such questions, and they do concern behavior. This answer

91

is, therefore, in part a persuasive definition of the term "science of behavior"; it is as though I were to say, "Chemistry is concerned to describe the composition and the interaction properties of all substances." Then a man who tried to find out why an acid combines with a base to produce a salt would not be doing chemistry. Well, we could call him a physicist or a physical chemist instead, but there's nothing illegitimate about his activity; and we may reasonably expect his discoveries to be very useful to chemists, for example, in predicting ways in which substances with only some of the properties of an acid may be expected to react with bases. Here too, of course, it might be possible to answer this question without recourse to the micro-level.

c. Skinner could simply reply that nobody knows why these particular L's hold yet, so the only practical way to do a science of behavior is to find out more L's. For example, he says, "At the moment we have no way of directly altering neural processes . . ."; hence, reference to neurophysiology "is useless in the control of behavior" (SHB, p. 34). (Although this section begins by dealing with explanation rather than control, he does not make any comments about the possibility that neural processes might have explanatory power even if we could not manipulate them; compare the possibility of explaining death as due to an inoperable cancer.) Again, he says, "The objection to inner states is not that they do not exist, but that they are not relevant in a functional analysis. We cannot account for the behavior of a system while staying wholly inside it . . ." (SHB, p. 35). This is a somewhat stronger position than saying we can't do it yet, though not as strong as saying that inner states are completely irrelevant (position b.), since, at the end of the same paragraph he says, "Valid information about [inner states] . . . may throw light upon this relationship [between antecedent environmental conditions and eventual behavior] but can in no way alter it." Superfluous certainly—"we may avoid many tiresome and exhausting digressions" by examining the relationship directly without reference to inner states— but not quite irrelevant.

The only difficulty inherent in Skinner's position with respect to this point, then, is that he cannot offer an explanation of his basic laws within what he regards as the limits of a science of behavior, and he can offer only one rather restricted type of explanation of the other laws, although he suggests that the functional approach can provide a complete account of behavior. It is most important to realize that he does provide an explanation of many observed laws of behavior—by deducing them from more basic laws together with some particular information—and it is partly for this reason that I think it appropriate to say that Skinner has a theory of behavior. For, although theories of domain D often do refer to events that are micro-with-respect-to D, and I would go so far as to say that it is almost always the case that there is, or should be, one or more such T for any D, there are some T, in the ordinary sense, which are exceptions. The theory of evolution, for example, seeks to explain the origin of species, among other phenomena, in terms of observable small differences between individuals of the same species and the differential survival value of these variations in a complex environment. The theory of gravitation, with the basic law formulated in terms of acceleration rather than force, is another possible candidate.

Looking at the Webster definition again, we can see that Feigl might be inclined to feel it included too much, even mere laws, since there is a sense in which they could fall under the heading of "general or abstract principles of any body of facts" and could each be regarded individually as a "general principle offered to explain phenomena." But the law by itself would not, I think, be regarded as providing the whole set of "abstract principles" of D nor, usually, as providing a complete "explanation" of D. A matter of emphasis, perhaps, and the theory of gravitation is little more than a law. It is chiefly the existence of a selected ordered set of basic laws, carefully chosen so that the entire range of empirically observed laws can be derived, that turns Skinner's system into a theory; though, as I shall argue below, other important aspects of it would suffice, especially the terminology. Yet I have used the qualification "usually" above, because there are certain borderline cases in which we talk of a theory without undertaking to go further than (though we do more than) stating the law, for example, the "theory of gravitation." I think there are certain special reasons why we do not regard it as necessary in these cases to go beyond the law (cf. Skinner's inability to derive the Law of Effect itself), and I would regard them as showing that Feigl's criterion is too narrowly drawn. For reasons that will be expounded in the next volume of this series, I think the basis for Feigl's criterion can be shown to be a comparatively unimportant formal truth; and its general, but not inevitable, applicability is due to an empirical fact, namely, that we very rarely get to the point of isolating a particular D from other D's without having discovered some L's of D. That we sometimes do is illustrated by the cases above.

But the fact remains, and we shall need to remember it below, that Skinner's system offers no explanation of its basic laws. Describing a demonstration of the Law of Effect, Skinner says, "Anyone who has seen such a demonstration knows that the Law of Effect is no theory" (ATLN, p. 200). Anyone who has seen an Eötvös balance give a direct reading of the gravitational pull of a block of lead might be tempted to say something similar. But just as the law of gravitation forms the foundation of the theory of gravitation, the Law of Effect forms the foundation of the theory of behavior. It is even more obvious that a system based explicitly on probability of response ("The business of a science of behavior is to evaluate this probability and explore the conditions that determine it" [ATLN, p. 198]) cannot explain every response individually with more than a probability determinable only by prior manifest behavior. There is a limit to the resolving power of the molar approach, and Skinner takes it to be a certain level of probability in explaining the individual response. It is a perfectly respectable

93

scientific enterprise to examine the proximate (neural) causes of a response in order to increase this probability, whether or not we can do it now or prefer never to call it part of a science of behavior.

In understanding the role of theory in psychology, the most important single point is that in this subject, unlike every other scientific subject as it now stands, a considerable proportion of the highly inferential knowledge (or supposed knowledge) is embodied in our everyday talk; and there is a great deal there. It took many thousands of years after man devised a language for him to produce a satisfactory science of dynamics; but common sense had long since incorporated a "theory" of motion according to which certain norms were defined such that only deviations from these norms required explanation, and a very comprehensive pattern of explanations was available. Perhaps we could call it an early application of "pre-Aristotelian dynamics" when Egyptian bird-hunters blamed the wind for their inability to cast a throwing stick the usual distance, but we might as well call it common sense—a commonsense theory. Today, the theory of dynamics is very far removed from the everyday language. In the same sense, the language of "possession" in the history of psychopathology and that of "humours" in psychology were as much part of the theoretical activity as appeal to "reinforcement" or "reserve strength" have been recently. The difference is that both are far less abstract than terms from current dynamics. The mistake is to imagine that they are not past the logical threshold for the application of the term "theory."

To much of this, Skinner would agree. ("We all know thousands of facts about behavior. . . . We may make plausible generalizations about the conduct of people in general. But very few of these will survive careful analysis. . . . The next step is the discovery of some sort of uniformity. . . . Any plausible guess about what a friend will do or say in a given circumstance is a prediction based upon some such uniformity" [SHB, pp. 14-16].) I am more struck than Skinner is, apparently, by the extent to which we successfully predict the behavior of our friends. Now, the language which reflects these uniformities is the sophisticated language of character traits, of attitudes, needs, beliefs, of degrees of intelligence and carelessness. It is not the naive observation language of acts, colors, sounds, shapes, and sensations. Whether one calls this vast conceptual apparatus a theory or merely the commonsense language of behavior analysis is unimportant. It is important that this language is an enormously long way from the naive observation language: it tells us a great deal about the probabilities of certain responses, though not with the accuracy we would like; if it did not, indeed "we could scarcely be effective in dealing with human affairs" (SHB, p. 16). What militates against calling it a theory in a scientific sense is its lack of organization and of explicit formulation, the absence of a sufficient number of basic experiments whose results can be predicted with extreme accuracy and of knowledge about the results of cross-validation checks, inter-judge reliability, and so on. It is precisely these objections that Hull and Allport were seeking to overcome and which make us all, including Skinner, willing to call their systems "theories." But it is also these remaining (scientific) imperfections in the commonsense language about behavior which Skinner himself has sought to overcome by the careful choice of carefully defined categories, by the careful organization of the laws which he has discovered, and by the standards of explanation that he attempts to meet. Let us now examine the nature of the terms, as opposed to the laws, of theories.

There are two dimensions to the dichotomy "theoretical term-observational term." The one Skinner is conscious of is that along which the appropriate dimensions of measurement change, means of or possibility of observation alters, and technique of definition varies (from postulational "implicit definition" to "ostensive definition," presumably via operational definition as he sees it). But the other dimension is just as important. This we might call the teleological as opposed to the ontological dimension, although, of course, both are methodological in the general sense. Whereas one can invent or select one's terms (that is, entities) according to either of the two positions Skinner would distinguish as the theoretical and the functional points of view—that is, according to one's ontological assumptions, presupposing the purpose of explanation-prediction—so along the other axis one introduces or adopts one's terms according to different purposes, ranging from the sense datum or visual-field neutral-description vocabulary to the explanation-prediction, that is, the theoretical language, presupposing some ontological position. On this axis, Skinner is fairly and squarely a theorist. He selects the segments of behavior to label as a result of theoretical considerations, that is, considerations of predictive power, experimental verifiability, etc. Naturally, the psychology of learning being in the state of development described above, where even the most highly theoretical terms of any "plausible or scientifically acceptable" account are comparatively close to commonsense language, we can often just as well talk of these considerations as being those of common sense rather than of theory. But common sense is what makes us obey speed limits, at least when a patrol car is behind us, and what leads us to fill our gas tanks at the second or third "Last Stop" before crossing the Nevada desert. These are not very theoretical activities; they involve very rudimentary induction and merely hedonistic evaluation. The particular type of common sense we need in picking out the categories for a science of behavior incorporates, according to Skinner, the belief that we should so choose them as to obtain data "showing orderly changes characteristic of the the learning process" (ATLN, p. 215). But, *ex hypothesi,* we have no reliable account of the learning process at this point. What makes Skinner think that the changes "characteristic of the learning process" are really "orderly"? This is an excellent example of a theoretical conclusion already embedded in the commonsense language. We can call it a theorem of the background theory, to use Professor Wilfrid Sellar's term, which guides our continuing attempts to provide a more powerful and further-reaching theory. Skinner fully recognizes the existence of this background theory—except that he does not apply the wicked term itself—both in the above quotation and later, when he instructs the psychologist to discover his independent variables "through a *commonsense* exploration of the field" (ATLN, p. 215; italics mine). For the reasons given, it seems sensible to recognize that this is a very special part of common sense—that part concerned with the explanation-prediction-control approach to the field of learning—and we can better call it a background-theoretical "exploration of the field." After all, Skinner would hardly wish to insist that common sense could not be radically mistaken.

Let us look more carefully at Skinner's practice and see if we can detect other cases where the background theory is affecting his choice of, or definition of, terms, remembering that "beyond the collection of uniform relationships lies the need for a formal representation of the data reduced to a minimum number of terms"—as long as it does not "refer to another dimensional system" (ATLN, pp. 215-16).

Skinner has always had one rather imprecise notion in his vocabulary, one which occupies a key position: the idea of *topographically differentiable* responses. The way in which this term is treated is characteristic of the interplay between background theory and the current working vocabulary of the developing theory. We begin with the observation that certain instrumental or motor activities are associated with certain objects in the world: we pick up and chew bananas; we throw stones; we embrace our parents; etc. We wish to produce a general account of the development of all these associations, since we have observed certain similarities in the developmental process. We want our generalization to extend, not only over two successive movements of the jaw, but also over all these activities. Now the most promising-looking lever in our background theory derives from our longitudinal S-R studies in everyday life, and we wish to retain a link with them; so the word "response" is appropriate. The sense in which the various responses mentioned above are different from each other appears pretty straightforward, so we talk of "topographically different responses." Then the troubles begin: Is the response of raising the hand "topographically different" from that of raising the arm? Background knowledge makes it obvious that these two could not be conditioned wholly independently; indeed, it leads us to believe that there will be certain types of relationship between the times required to successfully condition first the hand and then the arm. How are we to cut the pie of past and future experiments? Vast reservoirs of evidence to aid our choice are already in the history of scientific theory-building. We select as the basic term "topographically wholly independent responses" and include "induction," "reinforcement," and "latency" as three other useful-looking bricks with which to construct our account. Notice the powerful background-theoretical content that has been built into each of those extra bricks by their previous existences in other theory structures, including the background theory, that is, the commonsense explanation systems. This makes them far more useful, though, of course, when we have begun to see exactly how this building will have to be shaped, they may have their dangers for the new bricklayer who has not yet caught up on their latest connotations; he may tend to treat them in a previously but no longer appropriate way. Thus the word "response," which began in Pavlov's day as a fairly simple-to-use brick, in Skinner's system has to cover not just "striking-a-key" but "changing-to-the-other-key-and-striking" as opposed to "striking-the-same-key-a-second-time" (ATLN, p. 211); and it begins to become less readily distinguishable from what previously would have been identified as a series of responses. But if we regarded it in that way, we would find it quite impossible to uncover those very desirable "orderly changes characteristic of the learning process" which the background theory very much prefers to have at the expense of a little redefinition of the term "response." The operant versus respondent distinction can be woven into the system here to tighten up the incipient fraying.

Meehl and MacCorquodale provide (5, pp. 218-21) an extremely thorough analysis of the maze through which any psychological theorist must guide his definition of the term "response." It is clear, as they point out, that defining the response in terms of achievement is a very easy way to build one's theory into one's definitions with deplorable consequences for the interpretation of the experiments said to be confirmatory of the theory. They recommend the elimination, in the definition of "response," of "language which refers even implicitly to the properties of other intervals or to stimulation not present to the organism at the time the response is being admitted" (p. 231). This is an excellent prophylactic with respect to the disease of defining responses in terms of goals. But I am not sure that, in the process, it does not make life awkward for Skinner and others who refer to the past in defining some of their responses, for example, changing keys. In such a simple case, perhaps we can suppose stimulation to be still present from the past behavior without trouble. But more complex cases referring to organisms responding and reinforced at a very low rate—for example, to visual stimuli by differential blinking—would render progressively more theoretical the assertion that the response of "changing response" refers only to stimulation present at the time the response is completed[1] ("emitted" will hardly do: an organism can't "emit" a change—it emits a response which is, in fact, a change). The possiblity of entering into a jungle like the one in which the fractional anticipatory goal response was last reported begins to appear. One can read the latent learning controversy directly as a battle over the workability of various definitions of "response," including implicitly Skinner's. Kendler's paper (4, pp. 269-77) illustrates the connection well.

This process of redefining in order to save the regularities is a very important, legitimate, and useful part of the procedure of theory-building. The history of the concepts of "temperature," "intelligence," and, more recently, "anxiety" affords some striking examples of this point. Why did we abandon the definition of temperature in terms of the ideal gas scale? Principally because we came to see that the behavior of no physical gas could possibly give us that smooth monotonic curve, which the background theory insisted on for a base line, in the regions to which thermodynamics had turned. It is significant of an inadequate realization of this redefinition maneuver that, in his attack on mentalistic and psychoanalytic explanation, Skinner twice produces what he takes to be terms dating from early animistic explanations, both of which have been transformed as the general theory incorporating them has been transformed. Both "force" and "vis viva" have been respectively redefined as the product of mass and acceleration and twice the kinetic energy, and the view that their original use involved explicit animism is as speculative as the view that Skinner's use of the term strength (of a response) involves the same commitment.[2] It is not even true that Skinner's terms are, in any sense, operationally definable, as we shall see later.

Skinner starves his pigeons to 80 percent of their *ad lib* weight; he is fortunate that such a simple procedure yields workable results. We may expect, with some confidence, that with higher organisms this regimen will not yield quite such high intraspecies predictability. The pigeons show greatly different response rates but the same *type* of learning behavior under these conditions; apes may display basically different learning behavior in the same circumstances. Skinner would be ready to introduce new qualifications to the laws (perhaps by widening his "emotional behavior" escape valve) or so to extend the meaning of his terms as to provide the greatest generality. It is instructive to consider the differences between *SHB* and *The Behavior of Organisms* published 15 years earlier, in 1938. For an author who, in the earlier book, considered himself to be almost above producing explanations or hypotheses (p. 44), there have been substantial changes in the description of behavior. They are not due solely to early error, but rather to a present preference for a different formulation—for theoretical reasons, ones which were by no means wholly absent in the 1938 discussion (see W. S. Verplanck's chapter on Skinner [11]). This is the theoretical approach. Hull was supposedly operating in the same way, Hebb and Tolman too, and, as we shall see, Freud. It is comparatively unimportant methodologically that some of them start by trying, or talking about, a more ambitious goal than Skinner's— that is, a tie-in with neurology; it is a matter of practical interest if, by so doing, they fail to achieve the primary goal. What is important is that Skinner's terms are defined and redefined for purposes of optimizing their value in a systematic account of behavior, that his observations are referred back to a hierarchy of laws for explanation in an orderly way with the Law of Effect forming the keystone, and that his intentions are of a certain kind, namely, the discovery of causal (functional) laws. These are the marks of the theorist. I repeat that I am not here saying anything about the more moderate Skinnerian claim that the neural, mentalistic, and conceptual theorizers have not done as well in discussing learning theory as Skinner has. I am stressing the fact that this is a dispute between proponents of various theories, albeit theories of different levels of abstraction, strictly comparable to that between the proponents of classical and statistical thermodynamics, between macrochemistry and the valence theorists, and to a dozen other disputes in the history of science. I wish to argue that there is no logical or methodological error involved in the approach to behavior through the C.N.S. (whether the "C" stands for "Conceptual" or "Central") or the drive-reduction model, unless we wish to argue that trying to run before we can walk is (a) a relevant criticism and (b) a methodological error. Even there, especially in view of the latent learning experiments, it is difficult to establish conclusively that the time for running is so far away that expectancy theory never got moving.[3]

Before I conclude this discussion of learning theory, it is perhaps worth commenting on the very casual way that the term *learning* itself is defined by the theorists. Skinner, an environmentalist to the end, says, "We may define learning as a change in probability of response . . ." (ATLN, p. 199). No account of learning which is part of a Skinnerian science of human behavior will ever accomplish this, since the changes in the probability of a response following a disease infection such as chicken pox (increased strength of the scratching response, etc.), an injury, involutional changes, and genetic changes are all forever beyond the reach of a molar theory of psychology, although it is by no means easy to exclude them by a watertight definition. Indeed, from this difficulty springs another justification for a subcutaneous rounding out of the theory of learning—via the attempt to explain variations (intra- or inter-individual) in the capacity to learn or in the basic laws—just as the difficulty of excluding genetics from evolutionary theory makes the attempt arbitrary and costly. As Skinner admits, in a revealing passage with which I shall conclude my discussion of his approach to learning,

> A biological explanation of reinforcing power is perhaps as far as we can go in saying why an event is reinforcing. Such an explanation is probably of little help in a functional analysis for it does not provide us with any way of identifying a reinforcing stimulus as such before we have tested its reinforcing power upon a given organism (SHB, p. 84).

This implies that appropriate developments in biochemistry and physiology could even make them useful for a functional approach; that is, Skinner is here conceding that there are no methodological errors involved in microtheorizing.

Skinner's critique of psychoanalytic theories and concepts, to which I now wish to direct my arguments, is based on certain extensions of the basic position considered above.

One can understand his approach better if one bears in mind two points which are already pretty clear in his discussion of learning theories. First, he is almost exclusively concerned with the applications of a study of behavior, the control aspect, and he is consequently somewhat intolerant of considerations which do not at the moment display signs of giving us more control over behavior. Second, the self-application of the first point makes it very important to him to state his arguments as forcefully as possible—to convince people to change the way they spend their research hours, the way they think. I shall argue that the first of these points makes Skinner too impatient with psychoanalytic theory and that the second makes him overstate his case, leads him to put it in terms that suggest logical error rather than lack of practical consequences. And, surely, it takes a man strongly affected by both these considerations to say, "When the individual is wholly out of control, it is difficult to find effective therapeutic techniques. Such an individual is called psychotic" (SHB, p. 380). Psychoanalytic terminology has its defects indeed, but it is surely not quite so outcome-oriented.

My specific contentions will be that Skinner, in general, underestimates (a) the empirical content and (b) the practical utility of propositions about "mental states," including unconscious ones, and that he overestimates the commitments of psychoanalytic theory and hence the deleterious effects of Freud's influence.

Let us consider some of Skinner's proffered analyses of "mental-state" ascriptions. At a very general level, he considers descriptions of purpose to be open to the same objections, and I shall begin by taking one such example.

> . . . we ask him what he is doing and he says, "I am looking for my glasses." This is not a further description of his behavior but of the variables of which his behavior is a function; it is equivalent to "I have lost my glasses," "I shall stop what I am doing when I find my glasses," or "When I have done this in the past, I have found my glasses." These translations may seem unnecessarily roundabout, but only because expressions involving goals and purposes are abbreviations (SHB, p. 90).

Without agreeing or disagreeing with the thesis that "expressions involving goals and purposes are abbreviations," we may show that such expressions involve (that is, are equivalent to, or imply) a great deal more than any one of Skinner's suggested "translations." If a man correctly describes himself or another as "looking for his glasses," then we can infer *all* of the following:

(1) He owns glasses or believes he does.

(2) He does not now know where they are.

(3) He is engaging in operant behavior of a type that has previously led him or others of whom he knows to find objects of this kind (Skinner's restriction to the man's *own* experience with lost glasses is clearly too narrow).

(4) The aspect of his behavior described under (3) will cease when he discovers his glasses.

100

There are certain "mental-state" references in (1), (2), and (3). These in turn, may be reduced to Skinnerian terminology (with or without loss—I am not now passing judgment on that aspect of the issue). To say that the man believes he owns glasses is necessary, since one could not correctly describe someone as "looking for his glasses" unless he believed that he possessed glasses. It is too strong a condition to require that he actually own glasses since they may, in fact, have fallen into the wastebasket and been long since consumed. But we do not have to imagine that beliefs are mysterious states of the man's forever unobservable mind; we can, in turn, reduce "X believes Y" to a series of statements, at least some of which are conditional and all of which involve probability of specified observable responses. We can, in fact, avoid the conditional element (again, perhaps, at some cost) by restricting the type of prediction we make. Without going to this extreme (the arguments for so doing are entirely philosophical, since the conditional has an extremely respectable place in the logical vocabulary of science and mathematics), we can expect the analysis of "X believes Y" to involve a series of statements such as the following.

(a) If X is asked, "Do you believe Y?" under standard conditions, he will reply "Yes" or "Indeed" or "Of course" with 80 percent probability.

(b) If X is hypnotized or injected with specified amounts of sodium ethyl thiobarbiturate, he will respond as in (a) with 75 percent probability.

In the same way, we can analyze statements (2) and (3), in which the word "know" occurs.

Two comments on these subsidiary analyses should be made. In the first place, each of the samples given contains arbitrary probability figures, presumably not based on research. How could one give a more precise analysis? Secondly, giving a complete list of the stimulus-response patterns that would be relevant is clearly a problem of equal difficulty. It is in the face of the peculiar intransigence of these problems that Skinner, among others, is led to abandon the entire vocabulary of "mental-state" descriptions. Why not, he says, stick to the unambiguous observation language in view of the remarkable achievements possible within its boundaries (the moderate position) and the eventual necessity of returning to it, assuming that one could successfully complete the analysis of "believe," "know," etc. (the extreme position). The reply is that, if we are seeking to analyze any purpose, goal, desire, intention, or mentalistic language, we can succeed only by doing the analysis, not by considering another problem; it should be clear from the discussion above that Skinner's suggested "translations" are thoroughly inadequate.

This is not to deny that Skinner can do a great deal, much of it related to this problem, without actually solving the problem. One might ask whether the original problem is really worth troubling with, when we come to see the extreme vagueness of ordinary language. But the original problem and its relatives make up the problem of analyzing purposive behavior, that is, what we ordinarily call purposive behavior (or mentalistic language of the other varieties mentioned); we can't palm off an analysis of something that our intuition suggests is the "essential behavioral component" instead, because intuition isn't objective argument and people have widely varying intuitions on this matter. In fact, the subtleties involved in ordinary language are considerable and, as I shall later argue, highly functional. The arguments so far given are intended to support the thesis that Skinner's analysis is much too simple and that a complete reduction to Skinnerian language ("operationally" definable terms in response probability statements) is extremely difficult. Now, before we conclude that some simplified reduction will have to be made if any scientific investigation is ever to be possible, let us examine some of Skinner's own "operationally definable" language and see whether it is really free of what we can call (after Waismann) the "open texture" of the ordinary language of intending, knowing, and believing, and a fortiori of unconscious attitudes. If it is not, we shall have to decide whether the gain involved in the "simplification" is actually sufficient to compensate for the confusion involved in changing the meaning of many familiar terms. After all, we could not get very far by defining *intelligence* as "the average rating on a 1-10 scale scored by three friends"; the proposed operational definition corresponds very poorly to our background notion of intelligence since it will not be at all constant for each individual—and it doesn't analyze the notion itself, merely referring it to others for analysis. Furthermore, it is spuriously operational since there is no one such rating, and it is a spurious improvement for all these reasons. Are Skinner's "reductions" substantially better than the original terms? He makes a poor start with "intelligent," of which he says it "appears to describe properties of behavior but in reality refers to its controlling relations" (SHB, p. 36). The reality is that it describes a property of behavior, which does not at all prevent its analysis from involving reference to its controlling relations. Skinner's belief in the incompatibility of these alternatives presages an unsound analysis of the permissible and useful modes of definition.

Consider another example: in CPCT Skinner refers to

. . . another pitfall into which Freud, in common with his contemporaries, fell. There are many words in the layman's vocabulary that suggest the activity of an organism yet are not descriptive of behavior in the narrower sense. Freud used many of these freely—for example, the individual is said to discriminate, remember, infer, repress, decide, and so on. Such terms do not refer to specific acts. We say that a man discriminates between two objects when he behaves differently with respect to them; but discriminating is not itself behavior. We say that he represses behavior which has been punished when he engages in other behavior just because it displaces the punished behavior; but repressing is not action. We say that he decides upon a course of conduct either when he enters upon one course to the exclusion of another, or, when he alters some of the variables affecting his own behavior in order to bring this about; but there is no other "act of deciding" (p. 304).

Looking at this example of Skinnerian analysis, we can again ask (a) whether or how nearly the products of the analysis are equivalent to the original, and (b) whether they are really acceptable for Skinner's purpose, that is, operationally pure. In this instance, I wish to concentrate attention on the second question. Skinner's analytic base here includes the following crucial terms: "behaves"; "behaves differently with respect to X and Y"; "behavior segment X displaces behavior segment Y"; "enters upon X to the exclusion of Y"; "alters variables affecting own behavior." Elsewhere in this paper, we find him using (not quoting from Freud) such terms as "reinforces," "verbally injures," "pattern of behavior," etc. Now we all know pretty well what these terms mean. But it must be noted that to say an organism "behaves" is not to describe its behavior in Skinner's "narrower sense"; and to say that some of its behavior "displaces" other behavior is no more to describe behavior in Skinner's sense than to say that one course of action was decided on rather than another (unless one makes the erroneous assumption that the latter necessarily refers to some inaccessible inner activity, which Skinner would scarcely wish to do). It appears that one could reply to this complaint by giving a list of actions or activities of an organism such that the disjunction of them all is equivalent to "behaves." But, clearly, one could never complete such a list. Alternatively, then, could one not equate "behaves" with some concatenation of anatomically-physiologically defined movements? But this is a very awkward alternative, since there are clearly certain movements, like the patellar reflex, PGR, epileptic frenzies, paretic and aphasic behavior, which cannot be explained at all within molar psychology; and there are many "motionless" states, ranging from the catatonic to the reflective, which Skinner thinks are susceptible to his type of explanation. It is significant that Skinner never attempts to define *behavior* in his book *Science and Human Behavior*. After all, the anatomical-physiological definition would be likely to create great difficulties in excluding physiological explanatory theories; and the alternative of a long-list definition would, equally clearly, be interminable, especially since the progress of a science of behavior will itself bring about the extension of the list. Even more serious difficulties arise over the term "displaces." Deeply embedded as it is in a spatial analogy, it has in addition all the problems involved in defining its range of application, namely, segments of behavior.

Skinner constantly reiterates his complaints about certain metaphors and their awful effects ("When one uses terms which describe an activity, one feels it necessary to invent an actor . . ." [CPCT, p. 304] ; qualified by "The point is not that metaphor or construct is objectionable but that particular metaphors and constructs have caused trouble and are continuing to do so" [CPCT, p. 301—the rest of the paper makes it fairly clear that he doubts the utility of *any* metaphors or constructs in a science of *behavior*]). It is as well to remember that the whole language of reinforcement, displacement, satiation, etc., used by Skinner is loaded with metaphorical meaning, and meaning to which serious objections can be raised (especially if one takes the very tough line that Skinner does about metaphors—for example, he objects to "motivational interaction" on the grounds that it implies "arrangements or relationships among *things,* but what are the things so related or arranged?" [CPCT, p. 305]). I have discussed earlier in this paper the utility and legitimacy of using such concepts on a trial basis; their success and that of their subsequent partial redefinition is a matter for scientific appraisal. I want to stress the fact that, although Skinner raises the ghost of his extreme position in CPCT ("It would be difficult to prove or disprove . . . that metaphorical devices are inevitable in the early stages of any science" [p. 301] certainly suggests their superfluity in later stages), he could not possibly avoid these charges against his own system. Among "metaphorical devices" he includes the use of terms such as "force" and "essence," on which he says we "look with amusement [as part of the] science of yesterday" (CPCT, p. 301; he elsewhere, as previously mentioned, gives "vis viva" as an example [SHB, p. 27]). It is clear that these terms, which came into the scientific language with some metaphorical connotations, are now entirely respectable terms in mechanics, oleo-chemistry, and dynamics ("vis viva" = twice the kinetic energy) and retain the greater part of their original connotations. For example, Skinner says, "The motion of a rolling stone was once attributed to its vis viva" (SHB, p. 27); it still is. As far as I know, the ancients never imagined the stone was actually alive; they merely attached a name to the hypothesized property which would explain the motion—the property which turned out to be a multiple of kinetic energy. They chose a word which would carry some connotation of "explanatory of motion" from the field which they best understood, where motion distinguished living things. They were saying, in effect, "Moving inanimate objects have some of the properties of living things; let us name the concept that explains this aspect of their behavior *their* type of 'life-force.' " It was exactly this line of thought which led to the introduction of the term *response;* there may have been, or still be, people so stupid as to feel it "necessary to invent an actor" who gives the response, but it seems unlikely.

It may be the case that so many people have been misled by the use of terms such as "repress," "sublimate," and "project" that the contribution of psychoanalytic theory has been neutralized, but at least the introduction of these terms was as legitimate as that of Skinner's terms. Certainly at the level of criticism which Skinner introduces, he is no better off; for example, he says, "The notion of a conscious or unconscious 'force' may be a useful metaphor, but if this is analogous to force in physics, what is the analogous mass that is analogously accellerated?" (CPCT, p. 305). Analogies are defined as incomplete parallels: the "force" analogy comes not from mechanics, where the term has been partially redefined, but from the same place that mechanics got it, ordinary usage—and force is not defined as the product of mass and acceleration in ordinary usage but as "strength or energy; vigor" (Webster). Now, if no fundamental logical error is involved in using "metaphorical devices," as I have tried to show, then we should consider the possibility of redefining or reconstructing the theory rather than rejecting it. In fact, both Skinner, in SHB, and Ellis make serious attempts to do this.

Skinner's objections on this point—the use of "metaphorical devices"—are now, I think, boiled down to the claim that the ones he uses are less misleading than Freud's. This ties in with his complaints about "Freud's explanatory scheme," to which I shall return in a moment. I hope to suggest that Skinner's explanatory scheme applied to psychoanalysis often provides an interpretation rather than an alternative.

The discussion of metaphor was introduced in the course of analyzing Skinner's own terminology for conformity to Skinner's standards. I hope that I have shown that its success in meeting these standards is different at most only in degree from that of the terms to which Skinner takes exception. His own terms still retain the property of open texture; that is, there is the same type of difficulty about categorically defining *behavior* or *displacement* as there is about *purpose* or *belief.*

Yet there hangs above us the pall of smoke from the battle over introspection.[4] "How can one deny that 'purpose' and 'belief' are words with an inner reference, and sometimes with no external manifestations?" say the introspectionists, while the radical behaviorists fidget at this metaphysics ("the traditional fiction of a mental life" [CPCT, p. 302]). Here I wish only to argue that Skinner's analysis is unsound, *even for a behaviorist,* and does not achieve what he thinks it will achieve. It is not a special feature of mentalistic concepts that they cannot be given an explicit unambiguous definition in basic observation language ("the left hand was raised three inches, the head turned to the right about 45°, eye fixation remained constant, etc."); but it is a feature of all useful scientific concepts, including Skinner's own. This point is fundamental, and it is difficult to accept because the whole trend of thought since scientists really became self-conscious about their definitions, say with Mach, has been in the opposite direction. Indeed, it sounds reasonable and admissible to insist on terms that can be explicitly and unambiguously defined in terms of basic observations. It is, in fact, a valuable exercise to attempt this at any stage in the development of a science; but, if successful, one is merely taking a still photograph of a changing scene, and the motion, not the snapshot, shows progress. Both the philosopher and the scientist can learn from the snapshots, but they will not understand the changes without a great many snapshots and a good deal of inference. So it is with the changing meaning of scientific concepts: at any stage it is possible to give their cash value in terms of observations, but to understand them properly one must also know their role in the theory and have some idea of their future movements given certain contingencies. A term is fruitful only if it encourages changes in its own meaning; and, to some considerable extent, this is incompatible with operational definition. It is sometimes easier to learn how to use terms than to learn how to work out their cash value in a certain currency, and sometimes the reverse. We all know very well how to use terms such as "purpose" and "belief" and we can teach someone who doesn't speak the language how to use them (child or foreigner), but it's not easy to reduce them to Skinner's currency (and, some suspect, not possible). But Skinner won't pay in other currency, which he views with suspicion; and, if we want to collect the real value of our investment from him, we must compromise: collect a good deal from him on his terms and talk him around on the rest, perhaps by showing him some defects in his own coinage.

On Skinner's own terms, his analyses are not satisfactory; and, when we look at the currency itself, it seems to have the same weaknesses as the promissory notes that he won't negotiate.

There were two difficulties about our original analysis of "belief," which sprang from an attempt to improve Skinner's analysis of "looking for his glasses." The first, into which we have now gone at some length, stems from the impossibility of completely itemizing the units of behavior to which "belief" (in some way) refers, and is a difficulty which some of Skinner's basic terms share. The second was the difficulty of giving precise estimates of the response-probability in *any* of the component statements. He would, I think, be the first to agree that the corresponding statements in his own system—that is, dispositional statements involving response induction or stimulus discrimination and generalization—could not contain exact values except by arbitrary redefinition. Corresponding to "S believes p" would be "S discriminates red keys from green keys in a Skinner-box." We had difficulty in giving a cutting frequency for affirmative responses (to the question "Do you believe p?" put to S as a stimulus) which would differentiate a state of belief in p from one of uncertainty about p. Similarly, Skinner could not guarantee in advance the response frequency or, indeed, the existence of discrimination, if we set up conditions different from those under which the S was trained—for example, there is the possibility of what he terms "emotional behavior."

A great deal more could be said about the comparison here with reference to the behaviorist's philosophical thesis, but I wish to avoid direct engagements with this and instead bring the above points to bear on Skinner's account of Freud's "explanatory scheme." I would conclude this examination of Skinner's attack on purposive and mentalistic terminology by saying that the substitute he offers is not obviously required, is not as good as it could be, and, even if it were improved to its natural limits, would be insufficiently distinguishable from the original to justify the effort. Skinner is practically allergic to even the most harmless references to the "mental life." I think this prevents him from seeing that, if his translations were really satisfactory, there would be a "mind" in his system, too. Consider, for example, this quotation: "One who readily engages in a given activity is not showing an interest, he is showing the effect of reinforcement" (SHB, p. 72). But a very special type of effect, one which is extremely important to distinguish from the readiness to engage in a given activity springing from severe punishment for failure to do so. One can no more deny that Skinner has shown an interest in psychology during much of his academic life—the propriety of the phrase "showing an interest" in this case—than one can deny that this book has pages (that is, since standard conditions obtain, the propriety of the phrase "books have pages") even if it does suggest ownership. We shall see how this hypersensitivity to one interpretation (quite possibly an unfortunate or unproductive one) leads him to underestimate the utility of psychoanalytic theory. It is by no means necessary to interpret these phrases in this way; and, in fact, we can improve Skinner's suggested behavioral analysis to the point where it provides a good scientific substitute for the original phrase. This could be described as "translating the mind into behavioral terms"; or, equally well, it could be said to show that the reference to mind was not objectionable in the first place. To say that such phrases as "making up one's mind," "having an idea," etc., are "obvious" cases in which the mind and ideas are "being invented on the spot to provide spurious explanations" (SHB, p. 30) is to miss the point that these are genuine explanations but do not involve reference to some scientifically inaccessible realm. No one, without stretching an etymological point, reads into such phrases what Skinner objects to in them; they are invariably used as shorthand for a set of descriptive plus dispositional propositions, just as "believe," "behave," and "beta-particle" are.

Taking the bull by the horns, I shall argue that Skinner, partly because of errors of translation of the kind just discussed, underestimates the practical value and logical validity of explanations of behavior in terms of "mental events." Basic to all his arguments is the belief that any reference to inner states is an unnecessary complication, since eventually one has to explain them in terms of environmental variables. The counterargument, that the egg comes before the chicken and that we must, therefore, get back inside the skin to the organism's inherited genetic composition in order to achieve a complete explanation, would presumably cut no ice because, Skinner would say, we can't control the genes (or neurons). But we mustn't be misled by the combination of Skinner's use of the word *control* and his analyses of familiar processes. For example, he argues that "awareness of cause [of one's actions] has nothing to do with causal effectiveness" (CPCT, p. 305). But this is a verbal trick. He is not really denying (as he appears to) that the patient who attains insight into his aggressive remarks to his brother will often abandon them subsequently. He is (essentially) arguing that, since both insight and behavior improvement are due to changes in other environmental variables, it is wrong to say that one of them causes the other; that is, it is wrong to say that it is the awareness of the hostile impulses that reduces their effectiveness. He is not denying that the first might always be followed by the second or that the second might never occur without the first, that is, that the process of bringing about the insight produces the remission of the symptoms. Analysts, including Freud, have long stressed the fact that mere enunciation of the relation between unconscious hostility and aggressive remarks will not bring an end to the latter. Thus the analyst believes:

(1) The hostile feelings (C_1) cause the aggressive behavior (E_1).

(2) Getting the patient to the stage where he volunteers the interpretation—getting-him-to-achieve-insight-in-this-respect (C_2)—causes the symptoms' disappearance (E_2).

Achieving insight is the standard psychoanalytic case of "awareness of cause"; it is followed by the termination of the causal relation (1). Moreover, the process of achieving insight actually causes the improvement (as stated in (2)). It is, therefore, extremely misleading of Skinner to say "awareness of cause has nothing to do with causal effectiveness." It is trivially true that if A causes B under conditions C, and C does not contain a provision excluding an observer, then A will still cause B even if there is an observer. The analytic discovery was that, in certain cases of caused behavior, C does include such a prohibition and A no longer produces B in a patient P when P has learned about the connection (this schema oversimplifies in certain respects). It might appear that Skinner is making a more substantial point, that he is suggesting something empirically distinguishable from Freud. I am not clear that he is. The following quotation suggests there is no such tangible difference, but only a difference of emphasis: "Therapy consists, not in getting the patient to discover the solution to his problem, but in changing him in such a way that he is able to discover it" (SHB, p. 382). But on other occasions this is not clear: "The parallel between the excision of a tumor, for example, and the release of a repressed wish from the unconscious is quite compelling and must have affected Freud's thinking" (CPCT, p. 301)—and Skinner has made clear to me in conversation that he regards this as perhaps Freud's most serious error. Now what is the pattern of explanation here? We have:

1. The tumor (C_1) causes illness (E_1).
2. Removal-of-the-tumor (C_2) causes recovery (E_2).

and the analogy, which Skinner disputes, would be

1'. The repressed wish (C'_1) causes, say, stuttering (E'_1).
2'. Release-of-the-wish (C'_2) causes cure (E'_2).

If Freud thought that the "releasing of a suppressed wish from the unconscious" meant the mere uttering of the words, perhaps even parrot-wise, after the analyst, and was in itself curative, then Skinner is disagreeing with Freud on empirical grounds. It seems clear enough that this was not Freud's view. But if Freud thought that the mere verbalization had little or no therapeutic value, whereas the "spontaneous" release of a wish marked the penultimate stage of therapy for this symptom (culminated by the application of this insight), then I am not sure that Skinner would disagree, in view of the fact that he is presenting no new evidence. After all, discovering the wish makes it possible for P and the analyst to reorient P's behavior accordingly, and the fact that it has been voluntarily produced makes it likely the behavior will be successfully reoriented. If the re-orientation is successful, could one not then say that producing the wish produced the cure under these circumstances? The hard work goes into achieving C'_2, but if we define cure as the actual vanishing of symptoms, then it is the release of the wish that produces it. Thus we might agree with Skinner that therapy consists in changing the patient until he can achieve C'_2, but that the (proximate) cause of the cure is C'_2. And Freud would not, as far as I can see, disagree with this. I do not think this position justifies such strong statements as the following:

> Freud's contribution . . . [was] . . . not that the individual was often unable to describe important aspects of his own behavior, or identify important caus-al relationships but that his ability to describe them *was irrelevant* to the oc-currence of the behavior or the effectiveness of the causes (CPCT, p. 304; my italics).

I have gone into this point in detail because I think it well illustrates the difficulty of dealing with Skinner's criticisms of Freud. An attempt to wholly disentangle his ideas about the formal status of psychoanalytic theory would be unrewarding, but I think it important to show that it rests on an erroneous dichotomy, which explains a great deal about the rest of his approach. He says: "No matter what logicians may eventually make of this mental apparatus, there is little doubt that Freud accepted it as real *rather than* as a scientific construct or theory" (CPCT, p. 301; my italics).

Skinner is here reaping the whirlwind of early positivism, and this eddy affects his position more seriously than his other philosophical inheritances from the same source.[5] The idea that scientific constructs are not "real" but are mere "explanatory fictions," as he goes on to describe them, is untenable. But if one believes it, one will not be encouraged to invent many. It is a little misleading to insist that scientific constructs are real, although it is certainly better than the alternative (I have never heard anyone arguing whether theories are real: what would an unreal theory be like?). The issue is a spurious one; such constructs should always be said to be real in such-and-such a respect, but unreal—that is, unlike such earthily real things as platypuses—in such-and-such another respect, etc., etc. Few are observable like animals, but many have observable consequences, like the neutrino, and their existence is said to be confirmed when these consequences eventuate. Philosophy has outgrown such questions as "Do groups exist over and above their members?" "Do electrons really exist?" though it learned much from answering them. The answer must always be, "In a certain sense, yes, and in a certain sense, no." The important point is that a theory can and does proceed without having to distinguish each construct as "real" or "explanatory fiction." There are other rules to be obeyed (those of factor-analysis in certain cases, for example) but not this rule. We may have grave reservations about the meaning, if any, of *libido*, which we may awkwardly express by asking whether there really is a libido; but if a satisfactory answer can be given, it does not show that *libido* is *not* a scientific concept, that it is an observable: it would be a scientific construct, it would "exist," but it need not be actually observable as long as it has effects we can observe. The libido has to undergo the same examinations as Spearman's g, the concept of isostasy, and cultural lag. If they are satisfactory constructs, they may figure in explanations in a way we shall consider, although they are not observables and not all operationally definable in terms of observables. But that does not make them "fictions." Indeed, "explanatory fiction" is a contradiction in terms: abbreviatory devices are not normally explanatory, and explanatory devices are never fictitious.

There is no obligation on the libido to be located in the brain, or to have spatial location at all. The rules are flexible; they require only that we be able to make some objective distinction between cases in which the term can be properly applied and the rest. The same applies to Skinner's use of "reserve" (of responses—ATLN, p. 203) or the physicist's concept of entropy. But Skinner believes in the "observable-or-explanatory-fiction dichotomy," so he is at great pains in SHB to show that introspection is not a form of observation and, hence, that "conscious, as well as unconscious events [are] inferences from the facts" (CPCT, p. 302)—hence, are constructs and hence unreal. On one occasion, he puts it in this way: ". . . the act of self-observation [sic] can be represented within the framework of physical science. This involves questioning the reality of sensations, ideas, feelings, and other states of consciousness . . ." (CPCT, p. 304). The example which follows shows, as one might expect, that he is not going to question the *reality* of these things but the *reliability* of reports on them: the mystic's religious experience is not unreal but (according to Skinner's hypothesized psychoanalyst) incorrectly described as communion with a supernatural being. One can often show that someone's description of his sensations is inaccurate; it does not follow that he had none. Having arrived at the conclusion that mental events are unreal, Skinner feeds it back into the argument and attacks explanations in terms of mental states as circular and/or superfluous. Only in this way, as he sees it, can one get past the Scylla of explaining how the mind and body interact and the Charybdis of explaining how we can know the contents of another's mind. Union rules prevent me from divulging the secret of the problems which provide a guaranteed annual wage for philosophers; but it is not difficult to show some very important ways in which mental states can figure in extremely respectable explanations, in whose company, indeed, no behaviorist should feel ashamed to be seen.

Suppose that we accept the behaviorist analysis of mental states that Skinner is anxious to sell us, making some modifications to the actual model he is vending, along the lines suggested in our account of "He's looking for his glasses" and "He's showing an interest in this activity." Ignore, for the moment, the twin difficulties of inexhaustibility and inaccuracy in specifying the exact propositions in behavior-language to which we reduce the mental state. Then, taking a simple case,

"X is in mental-state M." = "If X is in circumstances Y, he will (with probability P) do Z."

Now, there will normally be many other circumstances $(Y', Y'', \ldots)$ under which X will also do Z. For example, he will drink a glass of water (Z) not only when thirsty (M)—that is, when he has been deprived of water for some time, etc.(Y)—but also when there is a gun at his back even if he is satiated (Y'), when he has been deprived of food and no food is now present (Y''), etc. Suppose that X is in an observation room, taking part in an experiment of whose purposes you are ignorant. You do not know whether he is being paid, deprived, or intellectually stimulated. At 3:00 p.m. he looks at the clock, takes up a glass of water, and drinks it. You ask, having these other possibilities in mind: Why did he drink? A perfectly proper and informative explanation is "Because he is thirsty." It is informative because you now know (always assuming the behaviorsit analysis to be correct) that this means circumstances Y must obtain, as opposed to $Y', Y''\ldots$

This type of request for an explanation is perhaps the most common of all. Skinner would describe it as a request for information about "the external variables of which behavior is a function" because he thinks that "inner-state" language is really translatable into descriptions of external variables. But if it is, then explanations in terms of inner states are perfectly legitimate. Even if it is not, even if there is something more involved in reports on inner states, it is still true that they are connected with external variables, that is, whatever "X is thirsty" may refer to, we know it is probabilistically connected with hours of deprivation, aversive preconditioning, etc., so that the *worst* charge that Skinner can lay is vagueness. Of course, he may not like the obscurity of the connection between a state of thirst and behavior; we can help him by accepting tentatively the identification of the two. Thus, one does not have to solve the mind-body problem in order to find out what independent variables are related to subjective reports of feelings of thirst, actual drinking without such reports, etc. Even the decision that thirst is not *wholly* reducible to behavioral criteria does not imply that it is not a good basis for explanation, since it clearly has many behavioral consequences. It is not important to a public health officer in charge of mosquito control whether we define DDT in terms of its entomological effects or whether we define it chemically, as long as we don't deny its entomological effects. Similarly, whether we say that thirst is or is not something more than a certain pattern of behavior is unimportant, as long as we agree that it is the psychologist who studies the whole behavioral aspect. The presence of vagueness not only affects his own more general concepts (notice the difficulties in distinguishing operant from response conditioning under certain circumstances) but also has certain virtues for a scientific concept in the field of behavior, a fact which will be further elaborated below.

The first point made, then, is that, on a radical behaviorist analysis of inner states, explanations in such terms are vital and legitimate. I did not say "on Skinner's analysis" because we have already made a number of improvements on that without abandoning radical behaviorism. To uncover some more of the very serious difficulties in Skinner's own analysis, I am going to examine one or two further instances of it, still on his own standards. Then I shall consider the results of our suggested changes in the radical behaviorist analysis of mental-state terminology, in an attempt to show that one can produce a fully scientific account that is much closer to being an analysis of the actual mental concepts we ordinarily employ, which Skinner views with such suspicion.

But what is Skinner's position?

> To what extent is it helpful to be told "He drinks because he is thirsty"? If to be thirsty means nothing more than to have a tendency to drink, this is mere redundancy. If it means that he drinks because of a state of thirst, an inner causal event is invoked. If this state is purely inferential—if no dimensions are assigned to it which would make direct observation possible—it cannot serve as an explanation (SHB, p. 33).

All these conclusions are erroneous. Even if "to be thirsty means nothing more than to have a tendency to drink," it is by no means merely redundant to be told that on this occasion he drank because of that tendency rather than under compulsion or because of a tendency to eat or etc. To have a tendency is to have a certain disposition, and everyone has some disposition to drink, but it is not always that disposition which explains our drinking. When we are satiated, for example, we have a short-term disposition not to drink; and, in such a case, the statement that we drank because we were thirsty would not, even on Skinner's final analysis, be redundant; it would be false. It follows that Skinner does not see the importance of dispositions, nor does he see the nature of what I shall call "discrimination-explanations," that is, explanations of event E as due to antecedents A rather than A' or A", all of which we realize are capable of producing E.

Of course, there are occasions on which pseudo-explanations—looking rather similar to this one—are offered. If we explain someone's frequent sleepy appearance by saying he is a soporific type, we may well be deceiving ourselves. But to chastise the ordinary explanations of individual events by reference to dispositions, on the grounds that some explanations of patterns of behavior by reference to dispositions are redundant, is manifestly unfair. Skinner's failure to distinguish these is clearly shown in the following quotation:

> When we say that a man eats because he is hungry, smokes a great deal because he has the tobacco habit, fights because of the instinct of pugnacity, behaves brilliantly because of his intelligence, or plays the piano well because of his musical ability, we seem to be referring to causes. But on analysis these phrases prove to be merely redundant descriptions. A single set of facts is described by the two statements: "He eats" and "He is hungry." A single set of facts is described by the two statements: "He smokes a great deal" and "He has the smoking habit.". . . (SHB, p. 31).

This is guilt by association! Every one of these examples except the first is susceptible to Skinner's criticism; but the first is the vital one for his attack on mental states, partly because we don't introspect "having a smoking habit" whereas we do introspect "being hungry." It is a logical error, *even for a radical behaviorist,* to imagine that the same "set of facts" is described by "He eats" and "He is hungry" since, for a radical behaviorist, the second statement is equivalent to "He has a disposition to eat," that is, "Under specifiable conditions it is P percent probable that he will eat," which neither implies nor is implied by "He eats."

Skinner's third conclusion—that if thirst is a purely inferential state not susceptible to direct observation, it cannot serve as an explanation—is also in my view mistaken. I have argued above that it is only necessary for the hypothesis embodying scientific concepts to be susceptible to confirmation, not observation—or else temperature, inertial mass, and the spin of the electron would be illicit—and the argument applies here. Furthermore, it is possible to construct an example which will demonstrate this and, at the same time, answer any doubts that may have arisen in the reader's mind as to the propriety of explaining one observed drinking event in terms of a disposition if the latter is interpreted as a construct out of drinking events.

Suppose that we introduce the symbol Ω into psychological discourse in the following way: if an organism O is such that variable $v_1 > N_1$, while $v_2, v_3, \ldots v_n < N_2$, we shall say that O is in state Ω (Ω(O)). Further, if $v_1 \leq N_1$ while $v_2 + v_3$ or $v_2 + v_4$ or $v_3 + v_4$ or $\ldots > 2N_1$ and $v_1, v_2, v_3, \ldots v_n < N_2$, we shall also say that $\Omega(O)$. And if some one of $v_2, v_3, \ldots v_n \geq N_2$, we shall say that it is not the case that $\Omega(O)$. Notice that we have not said anything about the case $v_1, v_2, v_3, \ldots v_n \leq N_1$, except under certain conditions on the ratio N_1/N_2 between the constants. This example is a rough model of a personality or pathology category, interpreted operationally. Now, we have not in any sense assigned dimension to Ω, any more than we do to schizophrenia. According to Skinner, then, "it cannot serve as an explanation" since no direct observation is possible. But it may provide a most useful means of classifying organisms, such that laws can be stated in simpler forms; that is, it can be a step toward a sort of theory which Skinner approves of ("a formal representation of the data reduced to a minimal number of terms" [ATLN, p. 216]), and it can certainly figure in discrimination explanations. What can Skinner say to resolve this contradiction? The necessary compromise seems obvious: Ω is satisfactory because it at least is defined in terms of observables. So it appears. And yet the word "state" occurs. Can we really infer from any formal considerations that O is in a certain state? Indeed not: one could not introduce a state defined by reference to the number of people within a one-mile circle with center 50 miles south of O without changing the present meaning of *state*. *State* is a word that needs a great deal of unpacking; it is appropriate only when we are sure that a causal account of the phenomena that differentiate *states* can be given in terms of actual physical changes in the organism corresponding to changes of *state* in the proposed sense.

This simple fact makes the language of states at once more complex and more useful than Skinner allows and partially explains how the tie-in of psychoanalysis or psychology with neurology is so strong. As it stands, Ω can give us discrimination explanations of the fact that certain variables have certain values (for example, that X drinks or stutters or produces neologisms) insofar as it contains a reference to other variables which are causally related to those observed, and it can only do that by referring to a current state. Even the thirst case, which appears as the simplest possible example, where v_1 is the only variable on which Ω depends as well as being that which is explained, is less simple than it appears since, for the explanation to be valid, it must be the case that the earlier history of v_1 variation has causally effected the present state of O. It is immaterial that we cannot demonstrate this physiologically. As long as we have no direct evidence against it and it works as an explanation, then we have evidence for it, indirect evidence. But it must be true. Moreover, it is not incumbent on us to say how the matter could be tested by direct observation at all. We may believe that this will be possible, for example, by identification with some neural and intestinal configuration; but we may also believe it will never be possible, as long as we are prepared to give (a) the conditions which will count as confirming evidence for and against the use of the construct, and (b) reasons for believing that some causal connection is possible between the independent environmental variables and the behavioral output variables. Thus one could not, in the world as it now is, argue that an Ω defined by reference to the past population density of an area geographically distant from O could explain either the present drinking behavior or indeed almost any other behavior of O, since one can give no reasons for thinking that it could produce any present effects on O at all.

It is this basic process in science—the process of ascribing states to substances and organisms—which forms the first level of theory-building. It is one that Skinner cannot avoid himself, for example, when he describes an organism as "satiated." This term would have to be abandoned even if Skinner's data were still accepted, if we did not believe that the gratification had produced an effect on the organism that, in fact, persisted. Our reason for thinking this is true is the change in response frequency after unrestricted eating (for example) is allowed, when the reinforcement is food. This striking result, we would argue, shows clearly that an effect has persisted on the organism. Let us call this effect "satiation"; it is a state of the organism. Now, Skinner overlooks the theoretical element in this analysis and imagines he can define the word without any reference to state: he views it as a summary of past history. I have already shown that he gives a bad summary; now I am arguing that he is committed to more than a summary. The reason is that one cannot believe the past history to affect the present behavior except via a present state—and science as a whole (not molar psychology) must explain how this is justified. It is a rare explanation which does not produce new discoveries—and one need give no further justification for neurologically oriented behavior research. Skinner is misled by the argument that neural states are dispensable and inaccessible (for molar psychology) into behaving as though they are scientifically dispensable, which they are not, even if inaccessible, and into imagining that he does not use them. So, states may be "purely inferential" and yet "serve as an explanation." It is psychologically unfortunate if other people are really misled by talking about states—conscious or unconscious—into imagining that science should not be concerned with discovering the antecedents, but the sin is no worse than that of imagining states to be dispensable.

Skinner is seriously in error on this whole issue, and understandably so, for if he too often acknowledges this implicit and necessary belief in the state differences brought about by various schedules, he would have to face the question, What sort of state differences do you have in mind? The reply that he means no more by the state than "that which is produced by the past reinforcement schedule and which produces the future responses" would, of course, be open to his own objection that it is an "explanatory fiction," unless he can give directly observable properties to it. Certainly it is obvious that if the organism reacts differently, it is in a different state; but insofar as its reactions are physically determined by its neurology, so far it is obvious that neurology must provide the foundations for this basic assumption of molar psychology. Now it becomes clear why Skinner prefers to talk of functional dependency rather than causal dependency: because causal dependency is necessarily mediated by a state of the

organism about which Skinner can say nothing. We cannot object to what Skinner does positively; but in his criticism, he implies that the supplementary activities are unnecessary and invalid, and in this he is surely wrong. Of repression
and the other defense mechanisms, he says in CPCT that they should not be regarded "as activities of the individual or any subdivision thereof . . . but simply
as ways of representing relationships among responses and controlling variables."
But they are activities (successions of states) of the individual, the very ones
necessary to link the controlling variables to the responses; and we can still agree
that they are to be distinguished by study of the functional relationships they
mediate. Skinner does not hold the only alternative position—that the childhood
trauma itself directly causes (across space and time) the neurotic behavior—but
at times he sounds very like it. The state of anxiety, he says, "is of no functional
significance, either in a theoretical analysis or in the practical control of behavior"
(SHB, p. 181). Well, it is an absolute necessity in the total scientific study of behavior to have such states, and the anxiety-reducing drugs show that this one has
considerable functional significance in the control of behavior, somewhat contrary to the implications of this passage or of the even more dogmatic statement
preceding it—"Any therapeutic attempt to reduce the 'effects of anxiety' must
operate upon these [controlling] circumstances, not upon any intervening state."

I want now to suggest that the psychoanalytic or group dynamic or historical or sociological approach is an alternative (to molar psychology) of a most
respectable kind for dealing with certain areas of behavior. From a certain
point of view, these approaches are simply examples of molar approaches: they
are molar approaches to molar behavior in certain areas—they are branches of
molar behavior science. The psychoanalyst is taking a particular pattern of
behavior as his unit—say the deprivation-desire-deed pattern in analyzing defenses—which to the molar psychologist is quite a complex structure. I think
that Skinner is in the position of a man who is asked for his suggestions at a
research conference in the chemistry department, where they are tackling the
problem of yeast assessment for bread-making. He says, "Find out all the physical properties of enzyme molecules and you'll have the answer." True, but only
if old age is conquered in the meantime. Physics will some day perhaps be able
to account for all chemical reactions, but today we have to evolve a selective
approach via the chemical properties. It *may* not work, it may be necessary to
get down to bedrock before a solid foundation can be laid; but it's well worth
trying—and in chemistry it has paid off for a long time. Similarly in the social
sciences, we can build up from the bricks of individual psychology or try to
make a useful building with the large blocks of stones lying around with just a
little chipping and perhaps a little more quarrying. And in psychology, we can
work up from physiology or neurology, or tackle the issues more directly.
Skinner is defending an approach to psychology which he rejects as an approach
to psychopathology.

116

It is useless to complain that this is only a part of psychology; such an assumption is (a) extremely speculative and (b) even if true, no more effective than the argument that chemistry is only part of physics, which has hardly prevented chemists from discovering useful concepts at their own level. Skinner's extreme aversion to anything that looks like animistic talk leads him to miss the great wealth that can be mined from a logically sophisticated behavioristic analysis (not reduction—this is unnecessary and begs the philosophical question) of mental-state talk.

In particular, we can return to the two oversimplifications we made when beginning the discussion of "psychic states." A behavioristic analysis of "know" or "believe" has these two dimensions of flexibility (a better word than "vagueness," whose negative connotations spring from a failure to appreciate the necessity and utility of open texture in scientific language). How can this be useful in a science of behavior? How can it be anything but a drawback? The questions are immensely vain: for they presuppose that psychology is appropriate for or capable of answering such questions as What is knowledge? And, on the other hand, they are overly modest; for they presuppose that we have no idea how to shape the lists or estimate the probabilities.

Psychology should, of course, not be mainly concerned with epistemological questions, even though (a) its results may sometimes be relevant to them, and (b) the inspiration and description of research should not be independent of epistemological thought. Thus, psychologists concerned with "knowledge" characteristically ask such questions as these: What do seventh-grade math pupils know that sixth-graders do not? What does a man know about his childhood that he cannot immediately recall? Does a nondirective discussion result in the absorption of more knowledge than a lecture on the same topic? Does the teacher really know which of his pupils are the most intelligent? etc. There are endless experiments of this kind done, none of which fall into difficulties over the term "know," though, of course, some others do, just as in physics some experiments are doomed from the beginning, owing to faulty logical analysis. Only the crypto-philosophical psychologist inflates his experimental results into epistomological conclusions, and he is usually somewhat short on logical training. Even though some important questions are not properly answered by experiment—among them legal, literary, and logical ones—it is not necessary to reject as nonexperimental all problems involving mentalistic concepts, as Skinner does, for every man who can speak a language understands very well how to use these words and can almost always tell a proper question from a nonsense statement involving them. The fact that we can all use this language with great efficiency shows that one cannot judge the utility of a language by the test of whether it is reducible to a specific list of specific statements in the observation language. Nor even its scientific utility, for the language of many sciences has this feature. Thus for proper psychological questions, we shall, I suggest, no more frequently find ourselves in difficulty understanding or formulating a problem about knowledge or belief in ordinary language than if we invent some vaguely related and still imprecise (if still useful) language of our own. Inventing new terms is too frequently a substitute for analyzing the old ones and a move which only postpones the difficulties, for at some stage we try to relate the discoveries formulated in the new language to the problems formulated in the old. We can have our Taylor Scale on which we define a psychological concept of anxiety, but we can't avoid the question, "Does this give a good measure of anxiety as we ordinarily use the term?" Because if it doesn't, we can't use it to find out whether students are made more anxious by subjective than objective examinations, or patients less anxious by piped music in the waiting room. The background concept and theory cannot be ignored, though they can nearly always be improved; they have to be studied. A similar study of scientific terms reveals, below that surface sheen of operationism, the same open texture or flexibility. The difference lies in the purpose, not the nature, of the definitions employed, or employable except for some variations of degree (which are not all in one direction).

The language of psychoanalysis, in particular, is very open-textured; it is a first approach. Being so, it runs the risk of becoming empirically meaningless, a ritual form of mental alchemy. But the *approach* is fully justifiable, and it is as wrong to suggest that Freud should have pinned his terms down to infant neurology (CPCT, p. 302) or, by the "simple expedient of an operational definition," to physical and biological science (CPCT, p. 305), as it would be to insist that the founders of radio astronomy should have early said whether a radio star was a solid body or a region of space. They introduced the term as a name for the hypothesized origin of short-wave electromagnetic radiation. It now appears they were justified in using a name (that is, spatial location is well supported), but we cannot yet tell exactly what radio stars (physically speaking) are, what the name stands for. Freud introduced the concept of the ego-ideal or superego as the hypothesized repository of the learned censoring activities of the personality. It is less certain that he was justified in using a name and quite unclear what, if any, physical reference it will have. It certainly need have no observable or measurable referent (". . . the most unfortunate effect of all" those due to Freud's use of a "mental apparatus" approach [CPCT, p. 305]) to be respectable, though the hypothesis of its existence or operation must have observable consequences that are reliably identifiable. It was obvious to Freud that these consequences will have their neural counterpart if they exist and that the superego will thus, at least indirectly, have a neural counterpart; no one knew more than that. But everyone knew, or thought they knew, a great deal about conscience, anxiety, and guilt; and Freud discovered a great deal more, just as a psychologist might discover a great deal more about knowledge by an extension of the experiments described above. And just as the psychologist might quite accurately sum up some of his discoveries by distinguishing two types of knowledge (say kinesthetic and verbal), so Freud could distinguish two stages in the development of the superego. Should we argue whether both types of knowledge exist or are real? We can, and we know how to do it in terms of correlation coefficients and chi^2 values—but it's an odd way to put the question. Does the superego exist? is it real? Well, we can deal with those questions, too, by pointing out certain undeniable features of behavior and arguing for their correlation and common subsumption under this heading. This doesn't show that the superego is observable, nor does it show that it is an explanatory fiction: Skinner's dichotomy is unsound. But—if it can be done—it justifies talking about the superego, which is as near as we can get to showing that it's real. It isn't real like a brain tumor, but it is real rather like an electric field; and it's certainly not unreal or a "fiction" or a "myth" like the ether—unless the arguments for it can be met, as those for the ether were met, on their own ground.

The other way of throwing over a theory, and a common one in the history of science, is to produce a better one. This Skinner would not be anxious to describe himself as doing. But his account of psychotherapy in SHB is an illuminating one, and it is theoretical. It is still far from being capable of dealing with the strange complexities of neurosis at an explanatory level, and it has no therapeutic success to support any claims for its practical efficiency. In fact, we have argued that while Skinner belabors Freud (somewhat unfairly, I think) for failing to give "an explicit treatment of behavior as a datum, of probability of response as the principal quantifiable property of behavior . . ." (CPCT, p. 304), in short, for being too theoretical, Skinner is himself a little too upset by the idea of explanations involving mental states to do them justice, even in his own operational terms. It is sometimes these errors of emphasis, rather than of fact, that lead us to abandon an approach. In his discussion of early psychological theories, Skinner comments on the simple reflex approach with these words: "It is neither plausible nor expedient to conceive of the organism as a complicated jack-in-the-box with a long list of tricks, each of which may be evoked by pressing the proper button" (SHB, p. 49). Reading Skinner, one sometimes wonders whether it is any more plausible or expedient to conceive of the organism as a complicated (but transparent) marionette with a long list of tricks, each of which may be evoked by pulling the proper string.

NOTES

1. See Skinner's comments on the great difference between 60-second and 15-second intervals in producing "superstitious" behavior in pigeons (SHB, p. 85).

2. For a further discussion of this point, see the discussion of "metaphorical devices" below.

119

3. Perhaps I should add the comment, quite irrelevant to the methodological discussion in which this paper consists, that, in my view, the practical achievements of the Skinner-box (and the teaching machine) and the theoretical analyses of their inventor will rank as more lasting contributions to learning theory than his methodological arguments. But if Skinner's methodology is unsound, it is in part a needed reaction against the colossal failure of Hull's theory-building attempts. In his review of "Principles of Behavior" (7) Skinner presents some insuperable criticisms, that only in their later overgeneralization become invalid (ATLN, SHB, CPCT).

4. Skinner's logical maneuvers in his skirmishes with introspection repay careful study. His case depends on a crucial misuse of perception language, for example, a systematically ambiguous use of "see" (SHB, pp. 273–78). It is further weakened in CPCT by his argument that Freud's evidence for self-deception in introspection shows introspection not to be like observation. On the contrary, it shows how very much it is like observation (itself fallible), though it is not the observation of logically inaccessible inner states, but of states some of whose aspects are sometimes not externally displayed.

5. E.g., "Certain basic assumptions, essential to any scientific activity, are sometimes called theories. That nature as orderly rather than capricious is an example" (ATLN, p. 193).

REFERENCES

1. Feigl, Herbert. "Some Remarks on the Meaning of Scientific Explanation," in H. Feigl and W. Sellars (eds.), *Readings in Philosophical Analysis,* pp. 510–14. New York: Appleton-Century-Crofts, 1949.

2. Feigl, Herbert. "Principles and Problems of Theory Construction in Psychology," in W. Dennis (ed.), *Current Trends in Psychological Theory,* pp. 179–213. Pittsburgh: University of Pittsburgh Press, 1951.

3. Ginsberg, Arthur. "Operational Definitions and Theories," *Journal of General Psychology,* 52:223–45 (1955).

4. Kendler, H. H. "What Is Learned—A Theoretical Blind Alley," *Psychological Review,* 59:269–77 (1952).

5. Meehl, P. E., and Kenneth MacCorquodale. "Edward C. Tolman," in William K. Estes et al. (eds.), *Modern Learning Theory,* pp. 177–266. New York: Appleton-Century-Crofts, 1954.

6. Skinner, B. F. *The Behavior of Organisms.* New York: Appleton-Century-Crofts, 1938.

7. Skinner, B. F. Review of Hull's "Principles of Behavior," *American Journal of Psychology,* 57:276–81 (1944).

8. Skinner, B. F. "Are Theories of Learning Necessary?" *Psychological Review,* 57: 193–216 (1950).

9. Skinner, B. F. *Science and Human Behavior.* New York: Macmillan, 1953.

10. Skinner, B. F. "Critique of Psychoanalytic Concepts and Theories," *Scientific Monthly,* 79:300–5 (1954).

11. Verplanck, W. S. "Burrhus F. Skinner," in William K. Estes et al. (eds.) *Modern Learning Theory,* pp. 267–316. New York: Appleton-Century-Crofts, 1954.

SENSATIONS
AND
BRAIN
PROCESSES*
J. J. C. Smart

Suppose that I report that I have at this moment a roundish, blurry-edged after-image which is yellowish toward its edge and is orange toward its center. What is it that I am reporting?[1] One answer to this question might be that I am not reporting anything, that when I say that it looks to me as though there is a roundish yellow orange patch of light on the wall I am expressing some sort of *temptation,* the temptation to say that there *is* a roundish yellowy orange patch on the wall (though I may know that there is not such a patch on the wall). This is perhaps Wittgenstein's view in the *Philosophical Investigations* (see paragraphs 367, 370). Similarly, when I "report" a pain, I am not really reporting anything (or, if you like, I am reporting in a queer sense of "reporting"), but am doing a sophisticated sort of wince. (See paragraph 244: "The verbal expression of pain replaces crying and does not describe it." Nor does it describe anything else?[2]) I prefer most of the time to discuss an after-image rather than a pain, because the word "pain" brings in something which is irrelevant to my purpose: the notion of "distress." I think that "he is in pain" entails "he is in distress," that is, that he is in a certain agitation-condition.[3] Similarly, to say "I am in pain" may be to do more than "replace pain behavior": it may be partly to report something, though this something is quite nonmysterious, being an agitation-condition, and so susceptible of behavioristic analysis. The suggestion I wish if possible to avoid is a different one, namely that "I am in pain" is a genuine report and that what it reports is an irreducibly psychical something. And similarly the suggestion I wish to resist is also that to say "I have a yellowish orange after-image" is to report something irreducibly psychical.

*Reprinted by permission, J.J.C. Smart, "Sensations and Brain Processes," *The Philosophical Review,* 68 (1959).

Why do I wish to resist this suggestion? Mainly because of Occam's razor. It seems to me that science is increasingly giving us a viewpoint whereby organisms are able to be seen as physicochemical mechanisms;[4] it seems that even the behavior of man himself will one day be explicable in mechanistic terms. There does seem to be, so far as science is concerned, nothing in the world but increasingly complex arrangements of physical constituents. All except for one place: in consciousness. That is, for a full description of what is going on in a man you would have to mention not only the physical processes in his tissue, glands, nervous system, and so forth, but also his states of consciousness: his visual, auditory, and tactual sensations, his aches and pains. That these should be *correlated* with brain processes does not help, for to say that they are *correlated* is to say that they are something "over and above." You cannot correlate something with itself. You correlate footprints with burglars, but not Bill Sikes the burglar with Bill Sikes the burglar. So sensations, states of consciousness, do seem to be the one sort of thing left outside the physicalist picture, and for various reasons I just cannot believe that this can be so. That everything should be explicable in terms of physics (together of course with descriptions of the ways in which the parts are put together—roughly, biology is to physics as radio engineering is to electromagnetism) except the occurrence of sensations seems to me to be frankly unbelievable. Such sensations would be "nomological danglers," to use Feigl's expression.[5] It is not often realized how odd would be the laws whereby those nomological danglers would dangle. It is sometimes asked, "Why can't there be psychophysical laws which are of a novel sort, just as the laws of electricity and magnetism were novelties from the standpoint of Newtonian mechanics?" Certainly we are pretty sure in the future to come across new ultimate laws of a novel type, but I expect them to relate simple constituents—for example, whatever ultimate particles are then in vogue. I cannot believe that ultimate laws of nature could relate simple constituents to configurations consisting of perhaps billions of neurons (and goodness knows how many billion billions of ultimate particles) all put together for all the world as though their main purpose in life was to be a negative feedback mechanism of a complicated sort. Such ultimate laws would be like nothing so far known in science. They have a queer "smell" to them. I am just unable to believe in the nomological danglers themselves or in the laws whereby they would dangle. If any philosophical arguments seemed to compel us to believe in such things, I would suspect a catch in the argument. In any case it is the object of this paper to show that there are no philosophical arguments which compel us to be dualists.

The above is largely a confession of faith, but it explains why I find Wittgenstein's position (as I construe it) so congenial. For on this view there are, in a sense, no sensations. A man is a vast arrangement of physical particles, but there are not, over and above this, sensations or states of consciousness. There are just behavioral facts about this vast mechanism, such as that it expresses a temptation (behavior disposition) to say "there is a yellowish-red patch on the wall" or that it goes through a sophisticated sort of wince, that is, says "I am in pain." Admittedly Wittgenstein says that though the sensation "is not a something," it is nevertheless "not a nothing either" (paragraph 304), but this need only mean that the word "ache" has a use. An ache is a thing, but only in the innocuous sense in which the plain man, in the first paragraph of Frege's *Foundations of Arithmetic,* answers the question "what is the number one?" by "a thing." It should be noted that when I assert that to say "I have a yellowish-orange after-image" is to express a temptation to assert the physical-object statement "there is a yellowish-orange patch on the wall," I mean that saying "I have a yellowish-orange after-image" is (partly) the exercise of the disposition[6] which is the temptation. It is not to *report* that I have the temptation, any more than is "I love you" normally a report that I love someone. Saying "I love you" is just part of the behavior which is the exercise of the disposition of loving someone.

Though, for the reasons given above, I am very receptive to the above "expressive" account of sensation statements, I do not feel that it will quite do the trick. Maybe this is because I have not thought it out sufficiently, but it does seem to me as though, when a person says "I have an after-image," he *is* making a genuine report, and that when he says "I have a pain," he *is* doing more than "replace pain-behavior," and that "this more" is not just to say that he is in distress. I am not so sure, however, that to admit this is to admit that there are nonphysical correlates of brain processes. Why should not sensations just be brain processes of a certain sort? There are, of course, well-known (as well as lesser-known) philosophical objections to the view that reports of sensations are reports of brain processes, but I shall try to argue that these arguments are by no means as cogent as is commonly thought to be the case.

Let me first try to state more accurately the thesis that sensations are brain processes. It is not the thesis that, for example, "after-image" or "ache" means the same as "brain process of sort X" (where X is replaced by a description of a certain sort of brain process). It is that, insofar as "after-image" or "ache" is a report of a process, it is a report of a process that *happens to be* a brain process. It follows that the thesis does not claim that sensation statements can be *translated* into statements about brain processes.[7] Nor does it claim that the logic of a sensation statement is the same as that of a brain-process statement. All it claims is that insofar as a sensation statement is a report of something, that something is, in fact, a brain process. Sensations are nothing over and above brain processes. Nations are nothing "over and above" citizens, but this does not prevent the logic of nation statements being very different from the logic of citizen statements, nor does it insure the translatability of nation statements into citizen statements. (I do not, however, wish to assert that the relation

123

of sensation statements to brain-process statements is very like that of nation statements to citizen statements. Nations do not just *happen to be* nothing over and above citizens, for example. I bring in the "nations" example merely to make a negative point: that the fact that the logic of A-statements is different from that of B-statements does not insure that A's are anything over and above B's.)

Remarks on Identity

When I say that a sensation is a brain process or that lightning is an electric discharge, I am using *is* in the sense of strict identity. (Just as in the—in this case necessary—proposition "7 is identical with the smallest prime number greater than 5.") When I say that a sensation is a brain process or that lightning is an electric discharge, I do not mean just that the sensation is somehow spatially or temporally continuous with the brain process or that the lightning is just spatially or temporally continuous with the discharge. When, on the other hand, I say that the successful general is the same person as the small boy who stole the apples, I mean only that the successful general I see before me is a time slice[8] of the same four-dimensional object of which the small boy stealing apples is an earlier time slice. However, the four-dimensional object which has the general-I-see-before-me for its late time slice is identical in the strict sense with the four-dimensional object which has the small-boy-stealing-apples for an early time slice. I distinguish these two senses of "is identical with" because I wish to make it clear that the brain-process doctrine asserts identity in the *strict* sense.

I shall now discuss various possible objections to the view that the processes reported in sensation statements are, in fact, processes in the brain. Most of us have met some of these objections in our first year as philosophy students. All the more reason to take a good look at them. Others of the objections will be more recondite and subtle.

Objection 1

Any illiterate peasant can talk perfectly well about his after-images or how things look or feel to him or about his aches and pains; yet he may know nothing whatever about neurophysiology. A man may, like Aristotle, believe that the brain is an organ for cooling the body without any impairment of his ability to make true statements about his sensations. Hence the things we are talking about when we describe our sensations cannot be processes in the brain.

124

Reply

You might as well say that a nation of slug-abeds, who never saw the morning star or knew of its existence, or who had never thought of the expression "the morning star," but who used the expression "the evening star" perfectly well, could not use this expression to refer to the same entity as we refer to (and describe as) "the morning star."[9]

You may object that the morning star is, in a sense, not the very same thing as the evening star, but only something spatiotemporally continuous with it. That is, you may say that the morning star is not the evening star in the strict sense of *identity* that I distinguished earlier. I can perhaps forestall this objection by considering the slug-abeds to be New Zealanders and the early risers to be Englishmen. Then the thing the New Zealanders describe as "the morning star" could be the very same thing (in the strict sense) as the Englishmen describe as "the evening star." Yet they could be ignorant of this fact.

There is, however, a more plausible example. Consider lightning.[10] Modern physical science tells us that lightning is a certain kind of electrical discharge due to ionization of clouds of water vapor in the atmosphere. This, it is now believed, is what the true nature of lightning is. Note that there are not two things, a flash of lightning and an electrical discharge; there is one thing, a flash of lighting, which is described scientifically an an electrical discharge to the earth from a cloud of ionized water molecules. The case is not at all like that of explaining a footprint by reference to a burglar. We say that what lightning really is, what its true nature as revealed by science is, is an electric discharge. (It is not the true nature of a footprint to be a burglar.)

To forestall irrelevant objections, I should like to make it clear that by "lightning" I mean the publicly observable physical object, lightning, not a visual sense-datum of lightning. I say that the publicly observable physical object lightning is in fact the electric discharge, not just a correlate of it. The sense-datum, or at least the having of the sense-datum, the "look" of lightning, may well in my view be a correlate of the electric discharge. For in my view, it is a brain state *caused* by the lightning. But we should no more confuse sensations of lightning with lightning than we confuse sensations of a table with the table.

In short, the reply to Objection 1 is that there can be contingent statements of the form "A is identical with B," and a person may well know that something is an A without knowing that it is a B. An illiterate peasant might well be able to talk about his sensations without knowing about his brain processes, just as he can talk about lightning though he knows nothing of electricity.

Objection 2

It is only a contingent fact (if it is a fact) that when we have a certain kind of sensation there is a certain kind of process in our brain. Indeed, it is possible, though perhaps in the highest degree unlikely, that our present physiological theories will be as out of date as the ancient theory connecting mental processes with goings on in the heart. It follows that when we report a sensation, we are not reporting a brain process.

Reply

The objection certainly proves that when we say "I have an after-image" we cannot *mean* something of the form "I have such and such a brain-process." But this does not show that what we report (having an after-image) is not *in fact* a brain process. "I see lightning" does not *mean* "I see an electric discharge." Indeed, it is logically possible (though highly unlikely) that the electrical discharge account of lightning might one day be given up. Again, "I see the evening star" does not *mean* the same as "I see the morning star," and yet "the evening star and the morning star are one and the same thing" is a contingent proposition. Possibly Objection 2 derives some of its apparent strength from a "Fido"—Fido theory of meaning. If the meaning of an expression were what the expression names, then of course it *would* follow from the fact that "sensation" and "brain process" have different meanings that they cannot name one and the same thing.

Objection 3[11]

Even if Objections 1 and 2 do not prove that sensations are something over and above brain processes, they do prove that the qualities of sensations are something over and above the qualities of brain processes. That is, it may be possible to get out of asserting the existence of irreducibly psychic processes but not out of asserting the existence of irreducibly psychic *properties.* Suppose we identify the morning star with the evening star. Then there must be some properties which logically imply that of being the morning star and quite distinct properties which entail that of being the evening star. Again, there must be some properties (for example, that of being a yellow flash) which are logically distinct from those in the physicalist story.

Indeed, it might be thought that the objection succeeds at one jump, for consider the property of "being a yellow flash." It might seem that this property lies inevitably outside the physicalist framework within which I am trying to work (either by "yellow" being an objective emergent property of physical objects, or else by being a power to produce yellow sense-data, where "yellow," is this second instantiation of the word, refers to a purely phenomenal or introspectible quality). I must therefore digress for a moment and indicate how I deal with secondary qualities. I shall concentrate on color.

First, let me introduce the concept of a normal percipient. One person is more a normal percipient than another if he can make color discriminations that the other cannot. For example, if A can pick a lettuce leaf out of a heap of cabbage leaves, whereas B cannot though he can pick a lettuce leaf out of a heap of beetroot leaves, then A is more normal than B. (I am assuming that A and B are not given time to distinguish the leaves by their slight difference in shape, and so forth.) From the concept of "more normal than" it is easy to see how we can introduce the concept of "normal." Of course, Eskimos may make the finest discriminations at the blue end of the spectrum, Hottentots at the red end. In this case the concept of a normal percipient is a slightly idealized one, rather like that of "the mean sun" in astronomical chronology. There is no need to go into such subtleties now. I say that "This is red" means something roughly like "A normal percipient would not easily pick this out of a clump of geranium petals, though he would pick it out of a clump of lettuce leaves." Of course, it does not exactly mean this: a person might know the meaning of "red" without knowing anything about geraniums, or even about normal percipients. But the point is that a person can be *trained* to say "This is red" of objects which would not easily be picked out of geranium petals by a normal percipient, and so on. (Note that even a colorblind person can reasonably assert that something is red, though, of course, he needs to use another human being, not just himself, as his "color meter.") This account of secondary qualities explains their unimportance in physics, for obviously the discriminations and lack of discriminations made by a very complex neurophysiological mechanism are hardly likely to correspond to simple and nonarbitrary distinctions in nature.

I therefore elucidate colors as powers, in Locke's sense, to evoke certain sorts of discriminatory responses in human beings. They are also, of course, powers to cause sensations in human beings (an account still nearer Locke's). But these sensations, I am arguing, are identifiable with brain processes.

Now, how do I get over the objection that a sensation can be identified with a brain process only if it has some phenomenal property not possessed by brain processes, whereby one-half of the identification may be, so to speak, pinned down?

My suggestion is as follows. When a persons says, "I see a yellowish-orange after-image," he is saying something like this: "*There is something going on which is like what is going on when* I have my eyes open, am awake, and there is an orange illuminated in good light in front of me, that is, when I really see an orange." (And there is no reason why a person should not say the same thing when he is having a veridical sense-datum, so long as we construe "like" in the last sentence in such a sense that something can be like itself.) Notice that the italicized words, namely "there is something going on which is like what is going on when," are all quasi-logical or topic-neutral words. This explains why the ancient Greek peasant's reports about his sensations can be neutral between

127

dualistic metaphysics or my materialistic metaphysics. It explains how sensations can be brain processes and yet how those who report them need know nothing about brain processes. For he reports them only very abstractly as "something going on which is like what is going on when. . . ." Similarly, a person may say "someone is in the room," thus reporting truly that the doctor is in the room, even though he has never heard of doctors. (There are not two people in the room: "someone" *and* the doctor.) This account of sensation statements also explains the singular elusiveness of "raw feels"—why no one seems to be able to pin any properties on them.[12] Raw feels, in my view, are colorless for the very same reason that *something* is colorless. This does not mean that sensations do not have properties, for if they are brain processes they certainly have properties. It only means that in speaking of them as being like or unlike one another we need not know or mention these properties.

This, then, is how I would reply to Objection 3. The strength of my reply depends on the possiblity of our being able to report that one thing is like another without being able to state the respect in which it is like. I am not sure whether this is so or not, and that is why I regard Objection 3 as the strongest with which I have to deal.

Objection 4

The after-image is not in physical space. The brain process is. So the after-image is not a brain process.

Reply

This is an *ignoratio elenchi*. I am not arguing that the after-image is a brain process, but that the experience of having an after-image is a brain process. It is the *experience* which is reported in the introspective report. Similarly, if it is objected that the after-image is yellowy orange but that a surgeon looking into your brain would see nothing yellowy orange, my reply is that it is the experience of seeing yellowy orange that is being described, and this experience is not a yellowy orange something. So to say that a brain process cannot be yellowy orange is not to say that a brain process cannot, in fact, be the experience of having a yellowy orange after-image. There is, in a sense, no such thing as an after-image or a sense-datum, though there is such a thing as the experience of having an image, and this experience is described indirectly in material object language, not in phenomenal language, for there is no such thing.[13] We describe the experience by saying, in effect, that it is like the experience we have when, for example, we really see a yellowy orange patch on the wall. Trees and wallpaper can be green, but not the experience of seeing or imagining a tree or wallpaper. (Or if they are described as green or yellow this can only be in a derived sense.)

Objection 5

It would make sense to say of a molecular movement in the brain that it is swift or slow, straight or circular, but it makes no sense to say this of the experience of seeing something yellow.

Reply

So far we have not given sense to talk of experiences as swift or slow, straight or circular. But I am not claiming that "experience" and "brain process" mean the same or even that they have the same logic. "Somebody" and "the doctor" do not have the same logic, but this does not lead us to suppose that talking about somebody telephoning is talking about someone over and above, say, the doctor. The ordinary man, when he reports an experience, is reporting that something is going on, but he leaves it open as to what sort of thing is going on, whether in a material solid medium, or perhaps in some sort of gaseous medium, or even perhaps in some sort of nonspatial medium (if this makes sense). All that I am saying is that "experience" and "brain process" may, in fact, refer to the same thing; if so, we may easily adopt a convention (which is not a change in our present rules for the use of experience words but an addition to them) whereby it would make sense to talk of an experience in terms appropriate to physical processes.

Objection 6

Sensations are private, brain processes are *public.* If I sincerely say, "I see a yellowish-orange after image" and I am not making a verbal mistake, then I cannot be wrong. But I can be wrong about a brain process. The scientist looking into my brain might be having an illusion. Moreover, it makes sense to say that two or more people are observing the same brain process but not that two or more people are reporting the same inner experience.

Reply

This shows that the language of introspective reports has a different logic from the language of material processes. It is obvious that until the brain-process theory is much improved and widely accepted there will be no *criteria* for saying "Smith has an experience of such-and-such a sort" *except* Smith's introspective reports. So we have adopted a rule of language that (normally) what Smith says goes.

Objection 7

I can imagine myself turned to stone and yet having images, aches, pains, and so on.

Reply

I can imagine that the electrical theory of lightning is false, that lightning is some sort of purely optical phenomenon. I can imagine that lightning is not an electrical discharge. I can imagine that the evening star is not the morning star. But it is. All the objection shows is that "experience" and "brain process" do not have the same meaning. It does not show that an experience is not, in fact, a brain process.

This objection is perhaps much the same as one which can be summed up by the slogan: "What can be composed of nothing cannot be composed of anything."[14] The argument goes as follows: on the brain process thesis the identity between the brain process and the experience is a contingent one. So it is logically possible that there should be no brain process and no process of any other sort, either (no heart process, no kidney process, no liver process). There would be the experience but no "corresponding" physiological process with which we might be able to identify it empirically.

I suspect that the objector is thinking of the experience as a ghostly entity. So it is composed of something, not of nothing, after all. On his view it is composed of ghost stuff, and on mine it is composed of brain stuff. Perhaps the counter-reply will be[15] that the experience is simple and uncompounded; so it is not composed of anything after all. This seems to be a quibble, for, if it were taken seriously, the remark "What can be composed of nothing cannot be composed of anything" could be recast as an a priori argument against Democritus and atomism and for Descartes and infinite divisibility. And it seems odd that a question of this sort could be settled a priori. We must, therefore, construe the word "composed" in a very weak sense, which would allow us to say that even an indivisible atom is composed of something (namely, itself). The dualist cannot really say that an experience can be composed of nothing, for he holds that experiences are something over and above material processes, that is, that they are a sort of ghost stuff (or perhaps ripples in an underlying ghost stuff). I say that the dualist's hypothesis is a perfectly intelligible one. But I say that experiences are not to be identified with ghost stuff but with brain stuff. This is another hypothesis, and in my view a very plausible one. The present argument cannot knock it down a priori.

Objection 8

The "beetle in the box" objection (see Wittgenstein, *Philosophical Investigations,* paragraph 293). How could descriptions of experiences, if these are genuine reports, get a foothold in language? For any rule of language must have public criteria for its correct application.

Reply

The change from describing how things are to describing how we feel is just a change from uninhibitedly saying "this is so" to saying "this looks so." That is, when the naive person might be tempted to say, "There is a patch of light on the wall which moves whenever I move my eyes" or "A pin is being stuck into me," we have learned how to resist this temptation and say "It *looks as though* there is a patch of light on the wallpaper" or "It *feels as though* someone were sticking a pin into me." The introspective account tells us about the individual's state of consciousness in the same way as does "I see a patch of light" or "I feel a pin being stuck into me": it differs from the corresponding perception statement insofar as (a) in the perception statement the individual "goes beyond the evidence of his senses" in describing his environment and (b) in the introspective report he withholds descriptive epithets he is inclined to ascribe to the environment, perhaps because he suspects that they may not be appropriate to the actual state of affairs. Psychologically speaking, the change from talking about the environment to talking about one's state of consciousness is simply a matter of inhibiting descriptive reactions not justified by appearances alone and of disinhibiting descriptive reactions which are normally inhibited because the individual has learned that they are unlikely to provide a reliable guide to the state of the environment in the prevailing circumstances.[16] To say that something looks green, to me, is to say that my experience is like the experience I get when I see something that really is green. In my reply to Objection 3, I pointed out the extreme openness or generality of statements which report experiences. This explains why there is no language of private qualities (just as "someone," unlike "the doctor," is a colorless word).[17]

If it is asked what is the difference between those brain processes which, in my view, are experiences and those brain processes which are not, I can only reply that this is at present unknown. But it does not seem to me altogether fanciful to conjecture that the difference may in part be that between perception and reception (in Dr. D. M. MacKay's terminology) and that the type of brain process which is an experience might be identifiable with MacKay's active "matching response."[18]

I have now considered a number of objections to the brain-process thesis. I wish now to conclude with some remarks on the logical status of the thesis itself. U. T. Place seems to hold that it is a straight-out scientific hypothesis.[19] If so, he is partly right and partly wrong. If the issue is between, say, a brain-process thesis and a heart thesis, or a liver thesis, or a kidney thesis, then the issue is a purely empirical one, and the verdict is overwhelmingly in favor of the brain. The right sorts of things don't go on in the heart, liver, or kidney, nor do these organs possess the right sort of complexity of structure. On the other hand, if the issue is between a brain-or-heart-or-liver-or-kidney thesis (that is, some form of materialism), on one hand, and epiphenomenalism, on the other, then the issue is not an empirical one, for there is no conceivable equipment which could decide between materialism and epiphenomenalism. This latter issue is not like the average straightforward empirical issue in science, but like the issue between the 19th century English naturalist Philip Gosse[20] and the orthodox geologists and paleontologists of his day. According to Gosse, the earth was created about 4000 B.C. exactly as described in *Genesis,* with twisted rock strata, "evidence" of erosion, and so forth, and all sorts of fossils, all in their appropriate strata, just as if the usual evolutionist story had been true. Clearly this theory is in a sense irrefutable: no evidence can possibly tell against it. Let us ignore the theological setting in which Philip Gosse's hypothesis had been placed, thus ruling out objections of a theological kind, such as "what a queer God who would go to such elaborate lengths to deceive us." Let us suppose that it is held that the universe just *began* in 4004 B.C. with the initial conditions just everywhere as they were in 4004 B.C., and in particular that our own planet began with sediment in the rivers, eroded cliffs, fossils in the rocks, and so on. No scientist would ever entertain this as a serious hypothesis, consistent though it is with all possible evidence. The hypothesis offends against the principles of parsimony and simplicity. There would be far too many brute and inexplicable facts. Why are pterodactyl bones just as they are? No explanation in terms of the evolution of pterodactyls from earlier forms of life would any longer be possible. We would have millions of facts about the world as it was in 4004 B.C. that just have to be *accepted.*

The issue between the brain-process theory and epiphenomenalism seems to be of the above sort (assuming that a behavioristic reduction of introspective reports is not possible). If it is agreed that there are no cogent philosophical arguments which force us into accepting dualism and if the brain-process theory and dualism are equally consistent with the facts, then the principles of parsimony and simplicity seem to decide overwhelmingly in favor of the brain-process theory. As I pointed out earlier, dualism involves a large number of irreducible psychophysical laws (whereby the "nomological danglers" dangle) of a queer sort, that just have to be taken on trust, and are just as difficult to swallow as the irreducible facts about the paleontology of the earth with which we are faced on Philip Gosse's theory.

NOTES

1. This paper takes its departure from arguments to be found in U. T. Place's "Is Consciousness a Brain Process?" (*British Journal of Psychology*, XLVII, 1956, 44-50). I have had the benefit of discussing Place's thesis in a good many universities in the United States and Australia, and I hope that the present paper answers objections to his thesis which Place has not considered, and presents his thesis in a more nearly unobjectionable form. This paper is meant also to supplement "The 'Mental' and the 'Physical'," by H. Feigl (in *Minnesota Studies in the Philosophy of Science*, II, 370-497), which argues for much the same thesis as Place's.

2. Some philosophers of my acquaintance, who have the advantage over me in having known Wittgenstein, would say that this interpretation of him is too behavioristic. However, it seems to me a very natural interpretation of his printed words, and whether or not it is Wittgenstein's real view it is certainly an interesting and important one. I wish to consider it here as a possible rival both to the "brain-process" thesis and to straight-out old-fashioned dualism.

3. See Ryle, *Concept of Mind* (New York, 1949), p. 93.

4. On this point see Paul Oppenheim and Hilary Putnam, "Unity of Science as a Working Hypothesis," in *Minnesota Studies in the Philosophy of Science*, II, 3-36; also my note "Plausible Reasoning in Philosophy," *Mind*, LXVI (1957), 75-78.

5. Feigl, *op. cit.*, p. 428.

6. Wittgenstein did not like the word "disposition." I am using it to put in a nutshell (and perhaps inaccurately) the view which I am attributing to Wittgenstein. I should like to repeat that I do not wish to claim that my interpretation of Wittgenstein is correct. Some of those who knew him do not interpret him in this way. It is merely a view which I find myself extracting from his printed words and which I think is important and worth discussing for its own sake.

7. See Place, *op. cit.*, p. 45, near top, and Feigl, *op. cit.*, p. 390, near top.

8. See J. H. Woodger, *Theory Construction* (Chicago, 1939), p. 38 (International Encyclopedia of Unified Science, Vol. 2, No. 5). I here permit myself to speak loosely. For warnings against possible ways of going wrong with this sort of talk, see my note "Spatialising Time," *Mind*, LXIV (1955), 239-41.

9. Cf. Feigl, *op. cit.*, p. 439.

10. See Place, *op. cit.*, p. 47; also Feigl, *op. cit.*, p. 438.

11. I think this objection was first put to me by Professor Max Black. I think it is the most subtle of any of those I have considered, and the one which I am least confident of having satisfactorily met.

12. See B. A. Farrell, "Experience," *Mind*, LIX (1950), especially 174.

13. Dr. J. R. Smythies claims that a sense-datum language could be taught independently of the material object language ("A Note on the Fallacy of the 'Phenomenological Fallacy,'" *British Journal of Psychology*, XLVIII, 1957, (141-144.) I am not so sure of this; there must be some public criteria for a person having got a rule wrong before we can teach him the rule. I suppose someone might *accidentally* learn color words by Dr. Smythies' procedure. I am not, of course, denying that we can learn a sense-datum language in the sense that we can learn to report our experience. Nor would Place deny it.

14. I owe this objection to Mr. C. B. Martin. I gather that he no longer wishes to maintain this objection, at any rate in its present form.

15. Martin did not make this reply, but one of his students did.

16. I owe this point to Place, in correspondence.

17. The "beetle in the box" objection is, *if it is sound,* an objection to any view, and in particular the Cartesian one, that introspective reports are genuine reports. So it is no objection to a weaker thesis that I would be concerned to uphold, namely, that if introspective reports of "experiences" are genuinely reports, then the things they are reports of are in fact brain processes.

18. See his article "Towards an Information-Flow model of Human Behaviour," *British Journal of Psychology,* XLVII (1956), 30-43.

19. *Op. cit.*

20. See the entertaining account of Gosse's book *Omphalos* by Martin Gardner in *Fads and Fallacies in the Name of Science* (2nd ed., New York, 1957).

SCIENTIFIC MATERIALISM AND THE IDENTITY THEORY*

Norman Malcolm

I

My main topic will be, roughly speaking, the claim that mental events or conscious experiences or inner experiences are brain processes. I hasten to say, however, that I am not going to talk about "mental events" or "conscious experiences" or "inner experiences." These expressions are almost exclusively philosophers' terms, and I am not sure that I have got the hang of any of them. Philosophers are not in agreement in their use of these terms. One philosopher will say, for example, that a pain in the foot is a mental event, whereas another will say that a pain *in the foot* certainly is not a *mental* event.

I will avoid these expressions, and concentrate on the particular example of *sudden thoughts.* Suddenly remembering an engagement would be an example of suddenly thinking of something. Suddenly realizing, in a chess game, that moving this pawn would endanger one's queen would be another example of a sudden thought. Professor Smart says that he wishes to "elucidate thought as an inner process,"[1] and he adds that he wants to identify "such inner processes with brain processes." He surely holds, therefore, that thinking and thoughts, including sudden thoughts, are brain processes. He holds also that conscious experiences (pp. 656 and 657), illusions (p. 659), and aches and pains (p. 654) are brain processes, and that love (p. 652) is a brain state. I will restrict my discussion, however, to sudden thoughts.

My first inclination, when I began to think about this topic, was to believe that Smart's view is false—that a sudden thought certainly is not a brain process. But now I think that I do not know what it *means* to say that a sudden thought

*Reprinted by permission of the author and of *Dialogue: Canadian Philosophical Review,* vol. 3 (1964), pp. 115-25.

is a brain process. In saying this I imply, of course, that the proponents of this view also do not know what it means. This implication is risky, for it might turn out, to my surprise and gratification, that Smart will explain his view with great clarity.

In trying to show that there is real difficulty in seeing what his view means, I will turn to Smart's article "Sensations and Brain Processes."[2] He says there that in holding that a sensation is a brain process he is "using 'is' in the sense of strict identity" (p. 163). "I wish to make it clear," he says, "that the brain process doctrine asserts identity in the *strict* sense" (p. 164). I assume that he wishes to say the same about the claimed identity of a thought with a brain process. Unfortunately he does not attempt to define this "strict sense of identity," and so we have to study his examples.

One of his examples of a "strict identity" is this: 7 is identical with the smallest prime number greater than 5 (p. 163). We must remember, however, that one feature of the "identity theory," as I shall call it, is that the alleged identity between thoughts, sensations, etc., and brain processes, is held to be *contingent*. Since the identity of 7 with the smallest prime greater than 5 is a priori and relates to timeless objects, it does not provide me with any clue as to how I am to apply the notion of "strict identity" to temporal events that are *contingently* related. The example is unsatisfactory, therefore, for the purpose of helping me to deal with the question of whether thoughts are or are not "strictly identical" with certain brain processes.

Let us move to another example. Smart tells us that the sense in which the small boy who stole apples is the same person as the victorious general is *not* the "strict" sense of "identity" (p. 164). He thinks there is a mere spatiotemporal continuity between the apple-stealing boy and the general who won the war. From this nonexample of "strict identity" I think I obtain a clue as to what he means by it. Consider the following two sentences: "General De Gaulle is the tallest Frenchman"; "The victorious general is the small boy who stole apples." Each of these sentences might be said to express an identity, yet we can see a difference between the two cases. Even though the victorious general *is* the small boy who stole apples, it is possible for the victorious general to be in this room at a time where there is *no* small boy here. In contrast, if General De Gaulle *is* the tallest Frenchman, then General De Gaulle is not in this room unless the tallest Frenchman is here. It would be quite natural to say that this latter identity (if it holds) is a *strict* identity and that the other one is not. I believe that Smart would say this. This suggests to me the following rule for his "strict identity": If something, x, is in a certain place at a certain time, then something, y, is strictly identical with x only if y is in that same place at that same time.

If we assume that Smart's use of the expression "strict identity" is governed by the necessary condition I have stated, we can possibly understand why he is somewhat hesitant about whether to say that the morning star is strictly identical with the evening star. Smart says to an imaginary opponent: "You may object that the morning star is in a sense not the very same thing as the evening star, but only something spatiotemporally continuous with it. That is, you may say that the morning star is not the evening star in the strict sense of 'identity' that I distinguished earlier" (p. 164). Instead of rebutting this objection, Smart moves on to what he calls "a more plausible example" of strict identity. This suggests to me that Smart is not entirely happy with the case of the stars as an example of strict identity. Why not? Perhaps he has some inclination to feel that the planet that is both the morning and evening star, is not the morning star *at the same time* it is the evening star. If this were so, the suggested necessary condition for "strict identity" would not be satisfied. Smart's hesitation is thus a further indication that he wants his use of the expression "strict identity" to be governed by the rule I have stated.

Let us turn to what Smart calls his "more plausible" example of strict identity. It is this: Lightning is an electric discharge. Smart avows that this is truly a strict identity (pp. 163, 164-65). This example provides additional evidence that he wants to follow the stated rule. If an electrical discharge occurred in one region of the sky and a flash of lightning occurred simultaneously in a different region of the sky, Smart would, I think, have no inclination to assert that the lightning was strictly identical with the electric discharge. Or if electrical discharges and corresponding lightning flashes occurred in the same region of the sky, but not at the same time, there normally being a perceptible interval of time between a discharge and a flash, then Smart, I believe, would not wish to hold that there was anything more strict than a systematic correlation (perhaps causal) between electric discharges and lightning.[3]

I proceed now to take up Smart's claim that a sudden thought is strictly identical with some brain process. It is clear that a brain process has spatial location. A brain process would be a mechanical, chemical or electrical process in the brain substance, or an electric discharge from the brain mass, or something of the sort. As Smart puts it, brain processes take place "inside our skulls."[4]

Let us consider an example of a sudden thought. Suppose that when I am in my house I hear the sound of a truck coming up the driveway and it suddenly occurs to me that I have not put out the milk bottles. Now is this sudden thought (which is also a sudden memory) literally inside my skull? I think that in our ordinary use of the terms *thought* and *thinking,* we attach no meaning to the notion of determining the bodily location of a thought. We do not seriously debate whether someone's sudden thought occurred in his heart, throat, or brain. Indeed, we should not know what the question meant. We should have no idea what to look for to settle this "question." We do say such a thing as "He can't get the thought out of his head"; but this is not taken as giving the location of a thought, any more than the remark "He still has that girl on the brain," is taken as giving the location of a girl.

137

In might be replied that *as things are,* the bodily location of thoughts is not a meaningful notion; but if massive correlations were discovered between thoughts and brain processes, then we might *begin* to locate thoughts in the head. To this I must answer that our philosophical problem *is* about how things are. It is a question about our *present* concepts of thinking and thought, not about some conjectured future concepts.[5]

The difficulty I have in understanding Smart's identity theory is the following. Smart wants to use a concept of "strict identity." Since there are a multitude of uses of the word *is* from the mere fact that he tells us that he means *is* in the sense of "strict identity," it does not follow that he has explained which use of *is* he intends. From his examples and nonexamples, I surmise that his "strict identity" is governed by the necessary condition that if *x* occurs in a certain place at a certain time, then *y* is strictly identical with *x* only if *y* occurs in the same place at the same time. But if *x* is a brain process and *y* is a sudden thought, then this condition for strict identity is not (and cannot be) satisfied. Indeed, it does not even make sense to set up a test for it. Suppose we had determined by means of some instrument that a certain process occurred inside my skull at the exact moment I had the sudden thought about the milk bottles. How do we make the further test of whether my *thought* occurred inside my skull? For it would have to be a *further* test: it would have to be logically independent of the test for the presence of the brain process, because Smart's thesis is that the identity is *contingent.* But no one has any notion of what it would mean to test for the occurrence of the thought inside my skull *independently* of testing for a brain process. The idea of such a test is not intelligible. Smart's thesis, as I understand it, requires this unintelligible idea, for he is not satisfied with holding that there is a systematic correlation between sudden thoughts and certain brain processes. He wants to take the additional step of holding that there is a "strict identity." His concept of strict identity either embodies the necessary condition I stated previously or it does not. If it does not, then I do not know what he means by "strict identity," over and above systematic correlation. If his concept of strict identity does embody that necessary condition, then his concept of strict identity cannot be meaningfully applied to the relationship between sudden thoughts and brain processes. My conclusion is what I said in the beginning: the identity theory has no clear meaning.

II

I turn now to a different consideration. A thought requires circumstances or, in Wittgenstein's word, "surroundings" (Umgebung). Putting a crown on a man's head is a coronation only in certain circumstances.[6] The behavior of exclaiming, "Oh, I have not put out the milk bottles," or the behavior of suddenly jumping up, rushing to the kitchen, collecting the bottles and carrying them outside—such behavior expresses the thought that one has not put out the milk bottles, *only in certain circumstances.*

The circumstances necessary for this simple thought are complex. They include the existence of an organized community, of a practice of collecting and distributing milk, of a rule that empty bottles will not be collected unless placed outside the door, and so on. These practices, arrangements, and rules could exist only if there was a common language, and this, in turn, would presuppose shared activities and agreement in the use of language. The thought about the milk bottles requires a background of mutual purpose, activity and understanding.

I assume that if a certain brain process were strictly identical with a certain thought, the occurrence of that brain process would be an absolutely sufficient condition for the occurrence of that thought. If this assumption is incorrect, then my understanding of what Smart means by "strict identity" is even *less* than I have believed. In support of this assumption I will point out that Smart has never stated his identity theory in the following way: *In certain circumstances* a particular brain process is identical with a particular thought. His thesis has not carried such a qualification. I believe his thesis is the following: A particular brain process is, *without qualification,* strictly identical with a particular thought. If this thesis were true it would appear to follow that the occurrence of that brain process would be an absolutely sufficient condition for the occurrence of that thought.

I have remarked that a necessary condition for the occurrence of my sudden thought about the milk bottles is the previous existence of various practices, rules, and agreements. If the identity theory were true, then the surroundings that are necessary for the existence of my sudden thought would also be necessary for the existence of the brain process with which it is identical.[7] That brain process would not have occurred unless, for example, there was or had been a practice of delivering milk.

This consequence creates a difficulty for those philosophers who, like Smart, hold both to the identity theory and also to the viewpoint that I shall call "scientific materialism." According to the latter viewpoint, the furniture of the world "in the last resort" consists of "the ultimate entities of physics."[8] Smart holds that everything in the world is "explicable in terms of physics."[9] It does not seem to me that this can be true. My sudden thought about the milk bottles was an occurrence in the world. That thought required a background of common practices, purposes and agreements. But a reference to a practice of, for example, delivering milk could not appear in a proposition of physics. The word *electron* is a term of physics, but the phrase "a practice of delivering milk" is not. There could not be an explanation of the occurrence of my

139

thought (an explanation taking account of all the necessary circumstances) which was stated solely in terms of the entities and laws of physics.

My sudden thought about the milk bottles is not unique in requiring surroundings. The same holds for any other thought. No thought would be explicable wholly in the terms of physics (and/or biology) because the circumstances that form the "stage setting" for a thought cannot be described in terms of physics.

If I am right on this point, and if the identity theory were true, it would follow that none of those *brain processes* that are identical with thoughts could be given a purely physical explanation. A philosopher who holds both to the identity theory and to scientific materialism is forced, I think, into the self-defeating position of conceding that many brain processes are not explicable solely in terms of physics.[10] The position is self-defeating because such a philosopher regards a brain process as a *paradigm* of something wholly explicable in terms of physics.

A defender of these two positions might try to avoid this outcome by claiming that the circumstances required for the occurrence of a thought, do themselves consist of configurations of ultimate particles (or of their statistical properties, or something of the sort). I doubt, however, that anyone knows what it would mean to say, for example, that the *rule* that milk bottles will not be collected unless placed outside the door, is a configuration of ultimate particles. At the very least, this defense would have to assume a heavy burden of explanation.

III

There is a further point connected with the one just stated. At the foundation of Smart's monism there is, I believe, the desire for a homogeneous system of explanation. Everything in the world, he feels, should be capable of the same *kind* of explanation, namely, one in terms of the entities and laws of physics. He thinks we advance toward this goal when we see that sensations, thoughts, etc., are identical with brain processes.

Smart has rendered a service to the profession by warning us against a special type of fallacy. An illustration of this fallacy would be to argue that a sensation is not a brain process because a person can be talking about a sensation and yet not be talking about a brain process.[11] The verb "to talk about" might be called an "intentional" verb, and this fallacy committed with it might be called the "intentional fallacy." Other intentional verbs would be "to mean," "to intend," "to know," "to predict," "to describe," "to notice," and so on.

It is easy to commit the intentional fallacy, and I suspect that Smart himself has done so. The verb "to explain" is also an intentional verb and one must beware of using it to produce a fallacy. Suppose that the Prime Minister of Ireland is the ugliest Irishman. A man might argue that this cannot be so, because someone might be explaining the presence of the Irish Prime Minister in New York and yet not be explaining the presence in New York of the ugliest Irishman. It would be equally fallacious to argue that since the Irish Prime Minister and the ugliest Irishman *are* one and the same person, therefore, to explain the presence of the Prime Minister *is* to explain the presence of the ugliest Irishman.

I wonder if Smart has not reasoned fallaciously, somewhat as follows: If a sudden thought *is* a certain brain process, then to *explain* the occurrence of the brain process *is* to explain the occurrence of the thought. Thus there will be just one kind of explanation for both thoughts and brain processes.

The intentional fallacy here is transparent. If a thought is identical with a brain process, it does not follow that to explain the occurrence of the brain process is to explain the occurrence of the thought. In fact, an explanation of the one differs in *kind* from an explanation of the other. The explanation of why someone *thought* such and such, involves different assumptions and principles and is guided by different interests than is an explanation of why this or that process occurred in his brain. These explanations belong to different *systems* of explanation.

I conclude that even if Smart were right in holding that thoughts are strictly identical with brain processes (a claim that I do not yet find intelligible), he would not have established that there is one and the same explanation for the occurrence of the thoughts and for the occurrence of the brain processes. If he were to appreciate this fact, then, I suspect, he would no longer have any *motive* for espousing the identity theory, for this theory, even if true, would not advance us one whit toward the single, homogeneous system of explanation that is the goal of Smart's materialism.

IV

I shall close by taking note of Smart's conceptual experiment with a human brain kept alive *in vitro*.[12] What is supposed to be proved by this experiment? That for thinking, pain, and "mental experience" in general, what goes on in the brain is more "important" or "essential" than behavior. How is this proved? By the supposed fact that the experimental brain has thoughts, illusions, pains, and so on, although separated from a human body.

Could this supposed fact be a fact? Could a *brain* have thoughts, illusions, or pains? The senselessness of the supposition seems so obvious that I find it hard to take it seriously. No experiment could establish this result for a brain. Why not? The fundamental reason is that a brain does not sufficiently resemble a human being.[13]

What can have led Smart to suppose that a brain can have thoughts? The only explanation which occurs to me is that he thinks that if my thought is in my brain, then my brain has a thought. This would be like thinking that if my invitation to dinner is in my pocket, then my pocket has an invitation to dinner. One bad joke deserves another.

NOTES

1. J. J. C. Smart, "Materialism" in *The Journal of Philosophy,* vol. LX, No. 22: October 1963, p. 657.

2. J. J. C. Smart, "Sensations and Brain Processes," *The Philosophical Review,* April 1959; republished in *The Philosophy of Mind,* ed. V. C. Chappell, Prentice-Hall 1962. Page references will be to the latter.

3. Mr. U. T. Place, in his article "Is Consciousness A Brain Process?" (*The Philosophy of Mind,* V. C. Chappell, ed., Prentice-Hall 1962) also defends the identity theory. An example that he uses to illustrate the sense of identity in which, according to him, "consciousness" could turn out to be a brain process is this: "A cloud is a mass of water droplets or other particles in suspension" (*loc. cit.,* pp. 103 and 105). I believe that Place would not be ready to hold that this is a genuine identity, *as contrasted with* a systematic and/or causal correlation, if he did not assume that in the very same region of space occupied by a cloud there is, at the very same time, a mass of particles in suspension.

4. "Materialism," *loc. cit.,* p. 654.

5. Mr. Jerome Shaffer proposes an ingenious solution to our problem ("Could Mental States Be Brain Processes?", *Journal of Philosophy,* Vol. LVIII, No. 26: December 21, 1961). He allows that at present we do not attach any meaning to a bodily location of thoughts. As he puts it, we have no "rules" for asserting or denying that a particular thought occurred in a certain part of the body. But how could we not *adopt* a rule, he asks? Supposing that there was discovered to be a one-to-one correspondence between thoughts and brain processes, we could *stipulate* that a thought is located where the corresponding brain process is located. Nothing would then stand in the way of saying that thoughts are *identical* with those brain processes! Although filled with admiration for this philosophical technique, I disagree with Shaffer when he says (*ibid.,* p. 818) that the adopted convention for the location of thoughts would not have to be merely an elliptical way of speaking of the location of the corresponding brain processes. Considering the origin of the convention, how could it amount to anything else?

6. *Investigations,* Sec. 584.

7. It is easy to commit a fallacy here. The circumstances that I have mentioned are *conceptually* necessary for the occurrence of my thought. If the identity theory were true it would not follow that they were *conceptually* necessary for the occurrence of the brain process that is identical with that thought. But it would follow that those circumstances were necessary for the occurrence of the brain process *in the sense* that the brain process *would not* have occurred in the absence of those circumstances.

8. "Materialism," *loc. cit.,* p. 651.

9. "Sensations and Brain Processes," *loc. cit.,* p. 161.

10. I believe this argument is pretty similar to a point made by J. T. Stevenson, in his "Sensations and Brain Processes: A Reply to J. J. C. Smart," *The Philosophical Review,* October 1960, p. 507. Smart's view, roughly speaking, is that unless sensations are identical with brain processes they are "nomological danglers." Stevenson's retort is that by insisting that sensations are identical with brain processes we have not got rid of any nomological danglers. He says "Indeed, on Smart's thesis it turns out that brain processes are danglers, for now brain processes have all those properties that made sensations danglers."

11. Smart, "Sensations and Brain Processes," *loc. cit.,* p. 164.
12. "Materialism," *loc. cit.,* pp. 659-660.
13. Cf. Wittgenstein, *Investigations,* sections 281 and 283.

3
THE SAGAS OF EMPIRICISM

"Contrariwise," continued Tweedledee, "if it was so, it might be; and if it were so, it would be; but as it isn't, it ain't. That's logic."

— Lewis Carroll, *Through the Looking Glass,* Chapter 2

"Anecdote after anecdote testifies to Johnson's distaste for speculative philosophy. The best known concerns Bishop Berkeley's Three Dialogues between Hylas and Philonous *(1713), which subtly argues the case for 'subjective idealism' against the common sense view that our perceptions bring us into contact with a world of objects that exist independently of our perceiving them. Asked how he would set about refuting such a view, Johnson went up to a large stone, kicked it hard, and said 'I refute Berkeley thus.' "*

— John Wain

INTRODUCTION

Empiricism is the theory that knowledge is derived from experience. The empiricist thus believes that what he knows he knows as the result of a series of sensory stimulations along the edges and surfaces of the human body. Historically, empiricism has been juxtaposed against *rationalism,* the doctrine that the human intellect comes to ordinary perceptual experiences stocked like a trout pool with a set of accessible truths. Such are the *innate ideas* and empiricists have been steadfast in maintaining that they do not exist. To the flux and fleen of things, the mind brings to bear only an information processing device with limited powers of association and storage. There is an obvious and unforced point of contact between empiricism and behaviorism, and between both and materialism.

To many modern philosophers, empiricism has seemed inextricably bound to the methods of science itself; they have rejected out of hand arguments impugning the whole of the empiricist position. This no doubt reflects some of the innocence of a dogma deeply held, and it gives to the exchanges of this section the character of internal controversy with philosophers who agree on little else except at least that they are jointly empiricists.

Edmund Gettier, who teaches philosophy at the University of Rochester, brings to his work a reputation as a distinctive philosophical miniaturist. His essay "Is Justified True Belief Knowledge?" shows some of the strengths associated with smallness of scale. For a long time philosophers in the United States and in England rested easy with the immemorial assumption that knowledge could be analyzed as justified true belief. By means of a stunning and persuasive counter-example, Gettier shows quite simply that they were wrong.

The exchange between A. J. Ayer and J. L. Austin, by way of contrast, involves grand issues such as the nature of perception. Professor Ayer is presently the Grote Professor of Mind and Logic at the University of London. He is the elegant and considerable author of *Language, Truth and Logic* (a book which outlined the details of modern positivism in the 1930s) and a philosopher given to a certain cultivated scepticism about philosophical passions and positions. At issue in his essay, "The Argument from Illusion," is the adequacy of a position espoused by a hypothetical *naive realist*. To the naive realist's way of thinking, what justifies our ordinary perceptual claims—reports that say X is F—are just the experiences one has in seeing X; experiences, he goes on to claim, that put a man directly in perceptual touch with the ordinary world of enduring objects. There seems to be no arguing with a man who takes as his epistemological credo a fancy version of the doctrine that seeing is believing; but against the naive realist's bluff optimism the *argument from illusion* is widely considered a powerful corrosive. Just the experiences that the naive realist has, run the refutation, he might have had even if X were not F.

The argument from illusion having been accepted, a gulf opens between the objects of perception and objects in the real world. Thus arises an interesting deformation in the history of thought with philosophers invoking as the true objects of perception a class of markedly suspicious entities, such as *sense data* or *appearances*—items of such resolute peculiarity that philosophers of J. L. Austin's irrefragable good sense find themselves moved toward the defense of what seemed the hopelessly naive realism of the naive realist. Professor Austin, who died in 1961, was a major force in contemporary philosophy. The phrase, *the linguistic turn,* suggests something of the direction of modern philosophical thought. If Ludwig Wittgenstein gave to the analysis of grammar a kind of brooding fashionability, Austin subsequently gave to the same subject his immense powers of meticulous observation and analysis. His basic position was one of conservative appreciation for the stock of distinctions and nuances built into the vernacular. Attend to them carefully enough and some, but not necessarily all, philosophical disputes will turn out to involve nothing more than crudeness of thought and perception. It is just such crudeness and contempt for the subtleties of ordinary language that mark Ayer's exposition of the argument from illusion, Austin claims. When first published, Austin's seemed an irresistible voice. More recently there have been second thoughts, with Ayer's article gaining retrospective luster, as the force of the argument from illusion continues to impress.

That pattern of sceptical doubt that has a shattering effect on naive realism, shatters too ordinary expectations concerning other minds. The existence of other minds is hardly a matter that promises much by way of direct inspection—at least not if by direct inspection I mean anything like that inward look that regularly convinces me that *I* at least have a mind. There is, of course, the *argument from analogy*, a philosophical standby that seems to discharge spontaneously from time to time. I can reckon that you have a mind and correspondingly suffer the same sensations that I myself do by reading into the activities of your body, as it grimaces (in pain) or breaks into a wide smile (in happiness), just those same mental processes and powers that I might have were my body carrying on as yours is. I know there is a relationship between what I do and what I feel; by analogy there is some similar relationship between what you do and what you feel.

I infer; but do I know? This is the question that philosophers have traditionally urged against the argument from analogy and it is a question of some force since the inference that was to have established the existence of other minds can never be checked.

Stuart Hampshire teaches philosophy at Oxford University and his work is marked by the influence of J. L. Austin. In his difficult and demanding paper "The Analogy of Feeling," Hampshire argues for the resuscitation of the argument from analogy thus going roughly against the common view that our knowledge of other minds is based on nothing like analogy. It is this negative view that is in turn defended against Hampshire by Norman Malcolm in his paper "Knowledge of Other Minds." Here Malcolm sets out the argument *against* the argument from analogy, savaging Hampshire as he goes and critizing too H. H. Price, whose essay is not reprinted here.

Perhaps the most pressing and inescapable difficulty for empiricism as a theory of knowledge comes on contemplating our knowledge of mathematical truths. For surely we have such knowledge and although J. S. Mill argued gamely that mathematical truths are in fact generalizations from experience, he argued alone. The line that gained favor early in 20th century discussions of empiricism was one of brilliant simplicity—the truths of mathematics and of logic are true in virtue of their meaning. They do not describe the external world at all and consequently the question of how they are derived from ordinary perceptual experiences does not arise. Every sentence, the empiricist observes, splits its truth two ways. "Snow is white," to take an obvious case, would not be true if snow were black; nor would it be true if the word "snow" happened to mean grass. In sentences that are true in virtue of their meaning alone we have the limiting case—sentences that are all form and no content. Thus, the empiricist sees the sentences subject to uniform division with a line separating those that are true strictly in virtue of their meaning—the *analytic* sentences—from all the rest.

It is a division that Professor Quine believes does not exist. Philosophers who appeal to it are in the service of a variety of philosophical misconceptions—most notably the thought that any intelligible case can be made for the concept of a sentence being true strictly in virtue of its meaning. Quine is the most important American philosopher of the 20th century. His essay is tough going. Portions are technical, other stretches are allusive or incompletely argued. Still, it is a commanding essay and one on which an era of intellectual history turns.

Philosophers who aspire to themes that are plainly counterintuitive, as Quine does, find themselves reading in response, essays that simply repeat deeply held convictions with ever increasing stridency. This is by no means an ineffective strategy of argument. It leads, if carried on long enough, to rather a formalistic and measured kind of debate, marked mainly by the periodic publication of unchanging positions. The history of controversy over the issue of analyticity has had something of this hieratic character: pairs of matched pieces seem indistinguishable. Professors Grice and Strawson are both Oxford-trained philosophers, students in some sense of J. L. Austin, and in any case susceptible to the lures and attractions of what has come to be called ordinary language philosophy.

Theirs was an early and attentive reply to Quine and the arguments as they are set out here have the force at least of historical novelty.

The literature dealing with contemporary empiricism is of course vast. C. D. Broad's *The Mind and its Place in Nature* (K. Paul, Trench, Trubner & Co.) is one of the great works of contemporary philosophy; it is no longer widely read and while this is not decisive in its favor, the evidence is very hard to ignore. A. J. Ayer's *Language, Truth, and Logic* (V. Gollancz) offers a brilliantly readable account of empiricism under the influence of the doctrine that only empiricism is meaningful. Wilfred Sellars has issued some of his opinions in a volume entitled *Science, Perception and Reality* (Routledge & Kegan Paul). His essays, "Empiricism and the Philosophy of Mind" and "Phenomenalism," both of which are reprinted in that collection, have had considerable influence. W. V. Quine's *From a Logical Point of View* contains a batch of essays that taken together express a fashionable and sophisticated point of view. It is not possible to read anything by Bertrand Russell without profit. Good places to start are either, *An Inquiry into Meaning and Truth* (Norton & Co.) or *Our Knowledge of the External World* (George Allen & Unwin, Ltd.). D. M. Armstrong's *Perception and the Physical World* (London, Routledge & Kegan Paul) has the merit of clarity. *Words and Objections,* edited by Donald Davidson and Jakko Hintikka (Synthese Library) contains a group of important papers given over to a discussion of Quine's work. *Perceiving, Sensing and Knowing,* edited by Robert J. Swartz (Doubleday Anchor) is a good collection of essays attached to an excellent bibliography. Finally, the entry under "Empiricism" in *The Encyclopedia of Philosophy,* edited by Paul Edwards (Macmillan & Co.) finishes off with an excellent general guide to the literature of empiricism.

IS
JUSTIFIED
TRUE BELIEF
KNOWLEDGE?*

Edmund L. Gettier

Various attempts have been made in recent years to state necessary and sufficient conditions for someone's knowing a given proposition. The attempts have often been such that they can be stated in a form similar to the following.[1]

(a) S knows that P   *IFF*   (1) P is true,
                                             (2) S believes that P, and
                                             (3) S is justified in believing that P.

For example, Chisholm has held that the following gives the necessary and sufficient conditions for knowledge:[2]

(b) S knows that P   *IFF*   (1) S accepts P,
                                             (2) S has adequate evidence for P, and
                                             (3) P is true.

Ayer has stated the necessary and sufficient conditions for knowledge as follows:[3]

(c) S knows that P   *IFF*   (1) P is true,
                                             (2) S is sure that P is true, and
                                             (3) S has the right to be sure that P is true.

I shall argue that (a) is false, in that the conditions stated therein do not constitute a *sufficient* condition for the truth of the proposition that S knows that P. The same argument will show that (b) and (c) fail if "has adequate evidence for" or "has the right to be sure that" is substituted for "is justified in believing that" throughout.

---

* From *Analysis,* vol. 23 (Blackwell, 1963), pp. 121–23; reprinted by permission of the author, *Analysis,* and Basil Blackwell.

I shall begin by noting two points. First, in that sense of "justified" in which S's being justified in believing P is a necessary condition of S's knowing that P, it is possible for a person to be justified in believing a proposition that is in fact false. Secondly, for any proposition P, if S is justified in believing P, and P entails Q, and S deduces Q from P and accepts Q as a result of this deduction, then S is justified in believing Q. Keeping these two points in mind, I shall now present two cases in which the conditions stated in (a) are true for some proposition, though it is at the same time false that the person in question knows that proposition.

Case I:

Suppose that Smith and Jones have applied for a certain job. And suppose that Smith has strong evidence for the following conjunctive proposition:

(d) Jones is the man who will get the job, and Jones has 10 coins in his pocket.

Smith's evidence for (d) might be that the president of the company assured him that Jones would in the end be selected and that he, Smith, had counted the coins in Jones's pocket 10 minutes ago. Proposition (d) entails:

(e) The man who will get the job has 10 coins in his pocket. Let us suppose that Smith sees the entailment from (d) to (e) and accepts (e) on the grounds of (d), for which he has strong evidence. In this case, Smith is clearly justified in believing that (e) is true.

But imagine, further, that unknown to Smith, he himself, not Jones, will get the job. And, also, unknown to Smith, he himself has 10 coins in his pocket. Proposition (e) is then true, though proposition (d), from which Smith inferred (e), is false. In our example, then, all of the following are true: (1) (e) is true, (2) Smith believes that (e) is true, and (3) Smith is justified in believing that (e) is true. But it is equally clear that Smith does not *know* that (e) is true; for (e) is true in virtue of the number of coins in Smith's pocket, while Smith does not know how many coins are in Smith's pocket, and bases his belief in (e) on a count of the coins in Jones's pocket, whom he falsely believes to be the man who will get the job.

Case II:

Let us suppose that Smith has strong evidence for the following proposition:
(f) Jones owns a Ford.

Smith's evidence might be that Jones has at all times in the past within Smith's memory owned a car and always a Ford, and that Jones has just offered Smith a ride while driving a Ford. Let us imagine, now, that Smith has another friend, Brown, of whose whereabouts he is totally ignorant. Smith selects three place names quite at random, and constructs the following three propositions:

(g) either Jones owns a Ford or Brown is in Boston
(h) either Jones owns a Ford or Brown is in Barcelona
(i) either Jones owns a Ford or Brown is in Brest-Litovsk.

Each of these propositions is entailed by (f). Imagine that Smith realizes the entailment of each of these propositions he has constructed by (f) and proceeds to accept (g), (h), and (i) on the basis of (f). Smith has correctly inferred (g), (h), and (i) from a proposition for which he has strong evidence. Smith is therefore completely justified in believing each of these three propositions. Smith, of course, has no idea where Brown is.

But imagine now that two further conditions hold. First, Jones does *not* own a Ford but is at present driving a rented car. Second, by the sheerest coincidence and entirely unknown to Smith, the place mentioned in proposition (h) happens really to be the place where Brown is. If these two conditions hold, then, Smith does *not* know that (h) is true, even though (1) (h) *is* true, (2) Smith does believe that (h) is true, and (3) Smith is justified in believing that (h) is true.

These two examples show that definition (a) does not state a *sufficient* condition for someone's knowing a given proposition. The same case, with appropriate changes, will suffice to show that neither definition (b) nor definition (c) do so either.

NOTES

1. Plato seems to be considering some such definition at *Theaetetus* 201 and perhaps accepting one at *Meno* 98.

2. Roderick M. Chisholm, *Perceiving: A Philosophical Study,* Ithaca: Cornell Univ. Press, 1957, p. 16.

3. A. J. Ayer, *The Problem of Knowledge,* London: Macmillan, 1956, p. 34.

THE
ARGUMENT
FROM
ILLUSION*
A. J. Ayer

Why may we not say that we are directly aware of material things? The answer is provided by what is known as the argument from illusion. This argument, as it is ordinarily stated, is based on the fact that material things may present different appearances to different observers or to the same observer in different conditions and that the character of these appearances is to some extent causally determined by the state of the conditions and the observer. For instance, it is remarked that a coin which looks circular from one point of view may look elliptical from another, or that a stick which normally appears straight looks bent when it is seen in water, or that to people who take drugs such as mescal, things appear to change their colors. The familiar cases of mirror images, double vision, and complete hallucinations such as the mirage are further examples. Nor is this a peculiarity of visual appearances. The same things occur in the domains of the other senses, including the sense of touch. It may be pointed out, for example, that the taste that a thing appears to have may vary with the condition of the palate or that a liquid will seem to have a different temperature according to whether the hand that is feeling it is itself hot or cold, or that a coin seems larger when it is placed on the tongue than when it is held in the palm of the hand, or, to take a case of complete hallucination, that people who have had limbs amputated may still continue to feel pain in them.

Let us now consider one of these examples, say, that of the stick which is refracted in water, and see what is to be inferred. For the present it must be assumed that the stick does not really change its shape when it is placed in water. (I shall discuss the meaning and validity of this assumption later on.) Then it

* From A. J. Ayer, in *Foundations of Empirical Knowledge,* London: Macmillan, 1940; by permission of the author and Macmillan.

follows that at least one of the visual appearances of the stick is delusive, for it cannot be both crooked and straight. Nevertheless, even in the case where what we see is not the real quality of a material thing, it is supposed that we are still seeing something and that it is convenient to give it a name. It is for this purpose that philosophers have recourse to the term "sense-datum." By using it, they are able to give what seems to them a satisfactory answer to the question: What is the object of which we are directly aware, in perception, if it is not part of any material thing? Thus when a man sees a mirage in the desert, he is not thereby perceiving any material thing, for the oasis which he thinks he is perceiving does not exist. At the same time, it is argued, his experience is not an experience of nothing; it has a definite content. Accordingly, it is said that he is experiencing sense-data which are similar in character to what he would be experiencing if he were seeing a real oasis but which are delusive in the sense that the material thing which they appear to present is not actually there. Or again, when I look at myself in the glass, my body appears to be some distance behind the glass; but other observations indicate that it is in front of it. Since it is impossible for my body to be in both these places at once, these perceptions cannot all be veridical. I believe, in fact, that the ones that are delusive are those in which my body appears to be behind the glass. But can it be denied that when one looks at oneself in the glass, one is seeing something? And if, in this case, there really is no such material thing as my body in the place where it appears to be, what is it that I am seeing? Once again, the answer we are invited to give is that it is a sense-datum. The same conclusion may be reached by taking any other of my examples.

If anything is established by this, it can be only that there are some cases in which the character of our perceptions makes it necessary for us to say that what we are directly experiencing is not a material thing but a sense-datum. It has not been shown that this is so in all cases. It has not been denied, but rather assumed, that there are some perceptions that do present material things to us as they really are; in their case there at first seems to be no ground for saying that we directly experience sense-data rather than material things. But as I have already remarked, there is general agreement among the philosophers who make use of the term sense-datum or some equivalent term that what we immediately experience is always a sense-datum and never a material thing, and for this they give further arguments which I shall now examine.

In the first place, it is pointed out that there is no intrinsic difference in kind between those of our perceptions that are veridical in their presentation of material things and those that are delusive.[1] When I look at a straight stick which is refracted in water and so appears crooked, my experience is qualitatively the same as if I were looking at a stick that really was crooked. When as the result of my putting on green spectacles, the white walls of my room appear to me to be green, my experience is qualitatively the same as if I were perceiving walls that really were green. When people whose legs have been amputated continue to feel pressure on them, their experience is qualitatively the same as if pressure really were being exerted on their legs. But it is argued that, if, when our perceptions were delusive, we were always perceiving something of a different kind from what we perceived when they were veridical, we should expect our experience to be qualitatively different in the two cases. We should expect to be able to tell from the intrinsic character of a perception whether it was a perception of a sense-datum or of a material thing. But this is not possible, as the examples that I have given have shown. In some cases there is indeed a distinction with respect to the beliefs to which the experiences give rise, as can be illustrated by my original example. For when, in normal conditions, we have the experience of seeing a straight stick, we believe that there really is a straight stick there; but when the stick appears crooked, through being refracted in water, we do not believe that it really is crooked; we do not regard the fact that it looks crooked in water as evidence against its being really straight. It must, however, be remarked that this difference in the beliefs which accompany our perceptions is not grounded in the nature of the perceptions themselves, but depends on our past experience. We do not believe that the stick which appears crooked when it stands in water really is crooked because we know from past experience that under normal conditions it looks straight. But a child who had not learned that refraction was a means of distortion would naturally believe that the stick really was crooked as he saw it. The fact, therefore, that there is this distinction between the beliefs that accompany veridical and delusive perceptions does not justify the view that these are perceptions of generically different objects, especially as the distinction by no means applies to all cases. For it sometimes happens that a delusive experience is not only qualitatively indistinguishable from one that is veridical but is also itself believed to be veridical, as in the example of the mirage; conversely, there are cases in which experiences that are actually veridical are believed to be delusive, as when we see something so strange or unexpected that we say to ourselves that we must be dreaming. The fact is that from the character of a perception considered by itself, that is, apart from its relation to further sense-experience, it is not possible to tell whether it is veridical or delusive. But whether we are entitled to infer from this that what we immediately experience is always a sense-datum remains to be seen.

Another fact which is supposed to show that even in the case of veridical perceptions we are not directly aware of material things is that veridical and delusive perceptions may form a continuous series, both with respect to their qualities and with respect to the conditions in which they are obtained.[2] Thus if I gradually approach an object from a distance, I may begin by having a series of perceptions which are delusive in the sense that the object appears to be smaller than it really is. Let us assume that this series terminates in a veridical perception. Then the difference in quality between this perception and its immediate predecessor will be of the same order as the difference between any two delusive perceptions that are next to one another in the series; on the assumption that I am walking at a uniform pace, the same will be true of the difference in the conditions on which the generation of the series depends. A similar example would be that of the continuous alteration in the apparent color of an object which was seen in a gradually changing light. Here again, the relation between a veridical perception and the delusive perception that next comes to it in the series is the same as that which obtains between neighboring delusive perceptions, both with respect to the difference in quality and to the change in the conditions. These are differences of degree, not of kind. But this, it is argued, is not what we should expect if the veridical perception were a perception of an object of a different sort, a material thing as opposed to a sense-datum. Does not the fact that veridical and delusive perceptions shade into one another in the way that is indicated by these examples show that the objects that are perceived in either case are generically the same? And from this it would follow, if it was acknowledged that the delusive perceptions were perceptions of sense-data, that what we directly experienced was always a sense-datum and never a material thing.

The final argument that has to be considered in this context is based on the fact that all our perceptions, whether veridical or delusive, are to some extent causally dependent, both on external conditions such as the character of the light and on our own physiological and psychological states. In the case of perceptions that we take to be delusive, this is a fact that we habitually recognize. We say, for example, that the stick looks crooked because it is seen in water, that the white walls appear green to me because I am wearing green spectacles, that the water feels cool because my hand is hot, that the murderer sees the ghost of his victim because of his bad conscience or because he has been taking drugs. In the case of perceptions that we take to be veridical we are apt not to notice such causal dependencies, since, as a rule, it is only the occurrence of the unexpected or the abnormal that induces us to look for a cause. But in this matter, also, there is no essential difference between veridical and delusive perceptions. When, for example, I look at the piece of paper on which I am writing, I may claim that I am seeing it as it really is. But I must admit that in order that I should have this experience it is not sufficient that there should actually be such a piece of paper there. Many other factors are necessary, such as the condition of the light, the distance at which I am from the paper, the nature of the background, the state of my nervous system and of my eyes. A proof that they are necessary is that if I vary them I find that I have altered the character of my perception. Thus if I screw up my eyes I see two pieces of paper instead of one; if I grow dizzy the appearance of the paper becomes blurred; if I alter my position sufficiently it appears to have a different shape and size; if the light is extinguished or another object is interposed, I cease to see it altogether. On the other hand, the converse does not hold. If the paper is removed I will cease to see it; but the state of the light or of my nervous system or any other of the factors that were relevant to the occurrence of my perception may still remain the same. From this it may be inferred that the relation between my perception and these accompanying conditions is such that, while they are not causally dependent on it, it is causally dependent on them. The same would apply to any other instance of a veridical perception that one cared to choose.

This point being established, the argument proceeds as follows. It is held to be characteristic of material things that their existence and their essential properties are independent of any particular observer. For they are supposed to continue the same whether they are observed by one person or another or not observed at all. But this, it is argued, has been shown not to be true of the object we immediately experience. So the conclusion is reached that what we immediately experience is in no case a material thing. According to this reasoning, if some perceptions are rightly held to be veridical and others delusive, it is because of the different relations in which their objects stand to material things, and it is a philosophical problem to discover what these relations are. We may be allowed to have indirect knowledge of the properties of material things, but this knowledge, it is held, must be obtained through the medium of sense-data, since they are the only objects of which, in sense-perception, we are immediately aware.

NOTES

1. Cf. H. H. Price, *Perception*, p. 31.
2. *Ibid.*, p. 32.

A REFUTATION
OF THE
ARGUMENT
FROM ILLUSION*

J. L. Austin

I want to call attention, first of all, to the name of this argument—the "argument from *illusion*," and to the fact that it is produced as establishing the conclusion that at least some of our "perceptions" are *delusive*. For in this there are two clear implications: (a) that all the cases cited in the argument are cases of *illusions*, and (b) that *illusion* and *delusion* are the same thing. But both of these implications, of course, are quite wrong; it is by no means unimportant to point this out, for, as we shall see, the argument trades on confusion at just this point.

What, then, would be some genuine examples of illusion? (The fact is, hardly any of the cases cited by Ayer are at any rate without stretching things, a case of illusion at all.) First, there are some quite clear cases of *optical* illusion— for instance, the case in which, of two lines of equal length, one is made to look longer than the other. Then again, there are illusions produced by professional "illusionists," conjurors—for example, the Headless Woman on the stage, who is made to look headless, or the ventriloquist's dummy which is made to appear to be talking. Rather different—not (usually) produced on purpose—is the case where wheels rotating rapidly enough in one direction may look as if they were rotating quite slowly in the opposite direction. Delusions, on the other hand, are something altogether different from this. Typical cases are delusions of persecution and delusions of grandeur. These are primarily a matter of grossly disordered beliefs (and so, probably, behavior) and may well have nothing in particular to do with perception.[1] But I think we might also say that the patient who sees

---

* From J. L. Austin, *Sense and Sensibilia,* Oxford: The Clarendon Press, 1962, pp. 22-32, 46-54.

pink rats has (suffers from) delusions—particularly, no doubt, if, as would probably be the case, he is not clearly aware that his pink rats aren't real rats.[2]

The most important differences here are that the term "illusion" (in a perceptual context) does not suggest that something totally unreal is *conjured up*—on the contrary, there is just the arrangement of lines and arrows on the page, the woman on the stage with her head in a black bag, the rotating wheels, whereas the term "delusion" *does* suggest something totally unreal, not really there at all. (The convictions of the man who has delusions of persecution can be *completely* without foundation.) For this reason, delusions are a much more serious matter. Something is really wrong, and what's more, wrong *with* the person who has them. But when I see an optical illusion, however well it comes off, there is nothing wrong with me personally, the illusion is not a little (or a large) peculiarity or idiosyncrasy of my own; it is quite public, anyone can see it, and in many cases standard procedures can be laid down for producing it. Furthermore, if we are not actually to be taken in, we need to be *on our guard;* but it is no use to tell the sufferer from delusions to be on his guard. He needs to be cured.

Why is it that we tend—if we do—to confuse illusions with delusions? Partly, no doubt, the terms are often used loosely. But there is also the point that people may have, without making this explicit, different views or theories about the facts of some cases. Take the case of seeing a ghost, for example. It is not generally known, or agreed, what seeing ghosts *is*. Some people think of seeing ghosts as a case of something being conjured up, perhaps by the disordered nervous system of the victim; so in their view, seeing ghosts is a case of delusion. But other people have the idea that what is called seeing ghosts is a case of being taken in by shadows perhaps or reflections or a trick of the light; that is, they assimilate the case in their minds to illusion. In this way, seeing ghosts, for example, may come to be labeled sometimes as "delusion" and sometimes as "illusion." It may not be noticed that it makes a difference which label we use. Rather, similarly, there seem to be different doctrines in the field as to what mirages are. Some seem to take a mirage to be a vision conjured up by the crazed brain of the thirsty and exhausted traveler (delusion), while in other accounts it is a case of atmospheric refraction whereby something below the horizon is made to appear above it (illusion). (Ayer, you may remember, takes the delusion view, although he cites it along with the rest as a case of illusion. He says not that the oasis appears to be where it is not, but roundly that "it does not exist.")

The way in which the "argument from illusion" positively trades on not distinguishing illusions from delusions is, I think, this. So long as it is being suggested that the cases paraded for our attention are cases of *illusion,* there is the implication (from the ordinary use of the word) that there really is something there that we perceive. But then, when these cases begin to be quietly called delusive, there comes in the very different suggestion of something being conjured up, something unreal or at any rate "immaterial." These two implications taken together may then subtly insinuate that in the cases cited, there really is something that we are perceiving but that this is an immaterial something, and this insinuation, even if not conclusive by itself, is certainly well calculated to edge us a little closer toward just the position where the sense-datum theorist wants to have us.

So much then (though certainly there could be a good deal more), for the differences between illusions and delusions and the reasons for not obscuring them. Now let us look briefly at some of the other cases Ayer lists. Reflections, for instance. No doubt you *can,* if you are so disposed, produce illusions with mirrors. But is just *any* case of seeing something in a mirror an illusion, as he implies? Quite obviously not. For seeing things in mirrors is a perfectly *normal* occurrence, completely familiar, and there is usually no question of anyone being taken in. No doubt, if you're an infant or an aborigine and have never come across a mirror before, you may be pretty baffled, even visibly perturbed, when you do. But is that a reason why the rest of us should speak of illusion here? And just the same goes for the phenomena of perspective—again, one *can* play tricks with perspective, but in the ordinary case there is no question of illusion. That a round coin should "look elliptical" (in one sense) from some points of view is exactly what we expect and what we normally find; indeed, we should be badly put out if we ever found this not to be so. Refraction again—the stick that looks bent in water—is far too familiar a case to be properly called a case of illusion. We may perhaps be prepared to agree that the stick looks bent, but then we can see that it's partly submerged in water, so that is exactly how we should expect it to look.

It is important to realize here how familiarity, so to speak, takes the edge off illusion. Is the cinema a case of illusion? Just possibly the first man who ever saw moving pictures felt inclined to say that here was a case of illusion. But, in fact, it's pretty unlikely that even he, even momentarily, was actually taken in; by now the whole thing is so ordinary a part of our lives that it never occurs to us even to raise the question. One might as well ask whether producing a photograph is producing an illusion—which would obviously be just silly.

Then we must not overlook, in all this talk about illusions and delusions, that there are plenty of more or less unusual cases, not yet mentioned, which certainly aren't either. Suppose that a proofreader makes a mistake—he fails to notice that what ought to be "causal" is printed as "casual"; does he have a delusion? Or is there an illusion before him? Neither, of course; he simply *misreads.* Seeing after-images, too, though not a particularly frequent occurence and not just an ordinary case of seeing, is neither seeing illusions nor having delusions. And what about dreams? Does the dreamer see illusions? Does he have delusions? Neither; dreams are *dreams.*

Let us turn for a moment to what Price has to say about illusions. He produces,[3] by way of saying "what the term 'illusion' means," the following "provisional definition": "An illusory sense-datum of sight or touch is a sense-datum which is such that we tend to take it to be part of the surface of a material object, but if we take it so, we are wrong." It is by no means clear, of course, what this dictum itself means; but still, it seems fairly clear that the definition doesn't actually fit all the cases of illusion. Consider the two lines again. Is there anything here which we tend to take, wrongly, to be part of the surface of a material object? It doesn't seem so. We just see the two lines, we don't think or even tend to think that we see anything else, we aren't even raising the question whether anything is or isn't "part of the surface" of—what, anyway? the lines? the page?—the trouble is just that one line looks longer than the other, though it isn't. Nor surely, in the case of the Headless Woman, is it a question whether anything is or isn't part of her surface; the trouble is just that she looks as if she had no head.

It is noteworthy, of course, that, before he even begins to consider the "argument from illusion," Price has already incorporated in this "definition" the idea that in such cases there is something to be seen *in addition to* the ordinary things—which is part of what the argument is commonly used, and not uncommonly taken, to *prove*. But this idea surely has no place in an attempt to say what "illusion" *means*. It comes in again, improperly I think, in his account of perspective (which, incidently, he also cites as a species of illusion)—"a distant hillside which is full of protuberances, and slopes upwards at quite a gentle angle, will appear flat and vertical. . . . This means that the sense-datum, the color-expanse which we sense, actually *is* flat and vertical." But why should we accept this account of the matter? Why should we say that there is *anything* we see which *is* flat and vertical, though not "part of the surface" of any material object? To speak thus is to assimilate all such cases to cases of delusion, where there *is* something not "part of any material thing." But we have already discussed the undesirability of this assimilation.

Next, let us have a look at the account Ayer himself gives of at least some of the cases he cites. (In fairness, we must remember here that Ayer has a number of quite substantial reservations of his own about the merits and efficacy of the argument from illusion, so that it is not easy to tell just how seriously he intends his exposition of it to be taken; but this is a point we shall come back to.)

First, then, the familiar case of the stick in water. Of this case Ayer says (a) that since the stick looks bent but is straight, "at least one of the visual appearances of the stick is *delusive*"; and (b) that "what we see [directly anyway] is not the real quality of [a few lines later, not part of] a material thing." Well now: does the stick "look bent" to begin with? I think we can agree that it does, we have no better way of describing it. But of course it does *not* look *exactly* like a bent stick, a bent stick out of water—at most, it may be said to look rather like a bent stick partly immersed *in* water. After all, we can't help seeing the water the stick is partly immersed in. So exactly what in this case is supposed to be *delusive?* What is wrong, what is even faintly surprising, in the idea of a stick's being straight but looking bent sometimes? Does anyone suppose that if something is straight, then it jolly well has to *look* straight at all times and in all circumstances? Obviously no one seriously supposes this. So what mess are we supposed to get into here, what is the difficulty? For, of course, it has to be suggested that there *is* a difficulty—a difficulty, furthermore, which calls for a pretty radical solution, the introduction of sense-data. But what is the problem we are invited to solve in this way?

Well, we are told, in this case you are seeing *something,* and what is this something "if it is not part of any material thing"? But this question is, really, completely mad. The straight part of the stick, the bit not under water, is presumably part of a material thing; don't we see that? And what about the bit *under* water?—we can see that too. We can see, come to that, the water itself. In fact, what we see is *a stick partly immersed in water.* It is particularly extraordinary that this should appear to be called into question—that a question should be raised about *what* we are seeing—since this, after all, is simply the description of the situation with which we started. It was, that is to say, agreed at the start that we were looking at a stick, a "material thing," part of which was under water. If, to take a rather different case, a church were cunningly camouflaged so that it looked like a barn, how could any serious question be raised about what we see when we look at it? We see, of course, *a church* that now *looks like a barn.* We do *not* see an immaterial barn, an immaterial church, or an immaterial anything else. And what in this case could seriously tempt us to say that we do?

Notice, incidentally, that in Ayer's description of the stick-in-water case, which is supposed to be prior to the drawing of any philosophical conclusions, there has already crept in the unheralded but important expression "visual appearances." It is, of course, ultimately to be suggested that all we *ever* get when we see is a visual appearance (whatever that may be).

Consider next the case of my reflection in a mirror. My body, Ayer says, "appears to be some distance behind the glass"; but as it's in front, it can't really be behind the glass. So what am I seeing? A sense-datum. What about this? Well, once again, although there is no objection to saying that my body "appears to be some distance behind the glass," in saying this we must remember what sort of situation we are dealing with. It does not "appear to be" there in a way which might tempt me (though it might tempt a baby or a savage) to go round the back and look for it, and be astonished when this enterprise proved a failure. (To say that A is *in* B doesn't always mean that if you open B you will find A, just as to say that A is *on* B doesn't always mean that you could pick it off—consider "I saw my face in the mirror"; "There's a pain in my toe"; "I heard him on the radio"; "I saw the image on the screen," etc. Seeing something in a mirror is not like seeing a bun in a shop window.) But does it follow that, since my body is not actually located behind the mirror, I am not seeing a material thing? Plainly not. For one thing, I can see the mirror (nearly always, anyway). I can see my own body "indirectly," in the mirror. I can also see the reflection of my own body or, as some would say, a mirror image. And a mirror image (if we choose this answer) is not a "sense-datum"; it can be photographed, seen by any number of people, and so on. (Of course, there is no question here of either illusion or delusion.) If the question is pressed, what actually *is* some distance, five feet say, behind the mirror, the answer is, not a sense-datum, but some region of the adjoining room.

The mirage case—at least if we take the view, as Ayer does, that the oasis the traveller thinks he can see "does not exist"—is significantly more amenable to the treatment it is given. For here we are supposing the man to be genuinely deluded, he is *not* "seeing a material thing."[4] We don't actually have to say, however, even here that he is "experiencing sense-data"; for though, as Ayer says above, "it is convenient to give a name" to what he is experiencing, the fact is that it already has a name—a *mirage*. Again, we should be wise not to accept too readily the statement that what he is experiencing is "*similar in character* to what he would be experiencing if he were seeing a real oasis." For is it at all likely, really, to be very similar? And, looking ahead, if we were to concede this point we should find the concession being used against us at a later state—namely, at the stage where we shall be invited to agree that we see sense-data always, in normal cases too.

[Austin now proceeds to discuss the second stage of the argument, which seeks to show that what we (directly) perceive is always a sense-datum. Ayer's version is given in S.9 above. Price's version, also criticised, is found on pp. 31-32 of his *Perception;* he makes the same point about the indistinguishability of normal and abnormal sense-data: "The abnormal crooked sense-datum of a straight stick standing in water is qualitatively indistinguishable from a normal sense-datum of a crooked stick. Again a mirror image of a right-hand glove 'looks exactly like' a real left-hand glove; i.e. the two sense-data are indistinguishable, though one is abnormal, the other normal. Is it not incredible that two entities so similar in all these qualities should really be so utterly different: that the one should be a real constituent of a material object, wholly independent of the observer's mind and organism, while the other is merely the fleeting product of his cerebral processes?" He also emphasizes the continuity between abnormal and normal sense-data as one moves toward or away from an object. N.B. (1) While he talks of "normal and abnormal sense-data," Ayer talks of "veridical and delusive perception"; the two are not quite parallel in that by "perception" Ayer seems to mean the experience or awareness of an object not the object or datum itself. (2) Austin admittedly does not discuss Ayer's "final argument".]

1. It is pretty obvious, for a start, that the terms in which the argument is stated by Ayer are grossly tendentious. Price, you remember, is not producing the argument as a proof that we are always aware of sense-data; in his view that question has already been settled, and he conceives himself to be faced here only with the question whether any sense-data are "parts of the surfaces of material objects." But in Ayer's exposition the argument *is* put forward as a ground for the conclusion that what we are (directly) aware of in perception is always a sense-datum; and if so, it seems a rather serious defect that this conclusion is practically assumed from the very first sentence of the statement of the argument itself. In that sentence Ayer uses, not indeed for the first time, the term "perceptions" (which incidentally has never been defined or explained), and takes it for granted, here and throughout, that there is at any rate some kind of entities of which we are aware in absolutely all cases—namely, "perceptions," delusive or veridical. But of course, if one has already been induced to swallow the idea that every case, whether "delusive" or "veridical," supplies us with "perceptions," one is only too easily going to be made to feel that it would be straining at a gnat not to swallow sense-data in an equally comprehensive style. But in fact one has not even been told what "perceptions" *are;* and the assumption of their ubiquity has been slipped in without any explanation or argument whatever. But if those to whom the argument is ostensibly addressed were not thus made to concede the essential point from the beginning, would the statement of the argument be quite such plain sailing?

2. Of course we shall also want to enter a protest against the argument's bland assumption of a simple dichotomy between "veridical and delusive experiences." There is, as we have already seen, *no* justification at all *either* for lumping all so-called "delusive" experiences together, *or* for lumping together all so-called "veridical" experiences. But again, could the argument run quite so smoothly without this assumption? It would certainly—and this, incidentally, would be all to the good—take rather longer to state.

3. But now let us look at what the argument actually says. It begins, you will remember, with an alleged statement of fact—namely, that "there is no intrinsic difference in kind between those of our perceptions that are veridical in their presentation of material things and those that are delusive" (Ayer), that "there is no qualitative difference between normal sense-data as such and abnormal sense-data as such" (Price). Now, waiving so far as possible the numerous obscurities in and objections to this manner of speaking, let us ask whether what is being alleged here is actually true. Is it the case that "delusive and veridical experiences" are not "qualitatively different"? Well, at least it seems perfectly extraordinary to say so in this sweeping way. Consider a few examples. I may have the experience (dubbed "delusive" presumably) of dreaming that I am being presented to the Pope. Could it be seriously suggested that having this dream is "qualitatively indistinguishable" from *actually being* presented to the

167

Pope? Quite obviously not. After all, we have the phrase "a dream-like quality"; some waking experiences are said to have this dream-like quality, and some artists and writers occasionally try to impart it, usually with scant success, to their works. But of course, if the fact here alleged *were* a fact, the phrase would be perfectly meaningless, because applicable to everything. If dreams were not "qualitatively" different from waking experiences, then *every* waking experience would be like a dream; the dream-like quality would be, not difficult to capture, but impossible to avoid.[5] It is true, to repeat, that dreams are *narrated* in the same terms as waking experiences: these terms, after all, are the best terms we have; but it would be wildly wrong to conclude from this that what is narrated in the two cases is *exactly alike*. When we are hit on the head we sometimes say that we "see stars"; but for all that, seeing stars when you are hit on the head is *not* "qualitatively" indistinguishable from seeing stars when you look at the sky.

Again, it is simply not true to say that seeing a bright green after-image against a white wall is exactly like seeing a bright green patch actually on the wall; or that seeing a white wall through blue spectacles is exactly like seeing a blue wall; or that seeing pink rats in D.T.s is exactly like really seeing pink rats; or (once again) that seeing a stick refracted in water is exactly like seeing a bent stick. In all these cases we may *say* the same things ("It looks blue," "It looks bent," etc.), but this is no reason at all for denying the obvious fact that the "experiences" are *different*.

4. Next, one may well wish at least to ask for the credentials of a curious general principle on which both Ayer and Price seem to rely,[6] to the effect that, if two things are not "generically the same," the same "in nature," then they can't be alike, or even very nearly alike. If it were true, Ayer says, that from time to time we perceived things of two different kinds, then "we should expect" them to be qualitatively different. But why on earth should we?—particularly if, as he suggests would be the case, we never actually found such a thing to be true. It is not at all easy to discuss this point sensibly, because of the initial absurdity in the hypothesis that we perceive just *two* kinds of things. But if, for example, I had never seen a mirror, but were told (a) that in mirrors one sees reflections of things, and (b) that reflections of things are not "generically the same" as things, is there any reason why I should forthwith *expect* there to be some whacking big "qualitative" difference between seeing things and seeing their reflections? Plainly not; if I were prudent, I should simply wait and see what seeing reflections was like. If I am told that a lemon is generically different from a piece of soap, do I "expect" that no piece of soap could look just like a lemon? Why should I?

(It is worth noting that Price helps the argument along at this point by a bold stroke of rhetoric: how *could* two entities be "qualitatively indistinguishable," he asks, if one is a "real constituent of a material object," the other "a fleeting product of his cerebral processes"? But how in fact are we supposed to have been persuaded that sense-data are *ever* fleeting products of cerebral processes? Does this colorful description fit, for instance, the reflection of my face in a mirror?)

5. Another erroneous principle which the argument here seems to rely on is this: that it *must* be the case that "delusive and veridical experiences" are not (as such) "qualitatively" or "intrinsically" distinguishable—for if they were distinguishable, we should never be "deluded." But of course this is not so. From the fact that I am sometimes "deluded," mistaken, taken in through failing to distinguish A from B, it does not follow at all that A and B must be *indistinguishable*. Perhaps I should have noticed the difference if I had been more careful or attentive; perhaps I am just bad at distinguishing things of this sort (e.g. vintages); perhaps, again, I have never learned to discriminate between them, or haven't had much practice at it. As Ayer observes, probably truly, "a child who had not learned that refraction was a means of distortion would naturally believe that the stick really was crooked as he saw it"; but how is the fact that an uninstructed child probably would not discriminate between *being refracted* and *being crooked* supposed to establish the allegation that there *is* no "qualitative" difference between the two cases? What sort of reception would I be likely to get from a professional tea-taster, if I were to say to him, "But there can't be any difference between the flavors of these two brands of tea, for I regularly fail to distinguish between them"? Again, when "the quickness of the hand deceives the eye," it is not that what the hand is really doing is *exactly like* what we are tricked into thinking it is doing, but simply that it is *impossible to tell* what it is really doing. In this case it may be true that we can't distinguish, and not merely that we don't; but even this doesn't mean that the two cases are exactly alike.

I do not, of course, wish to deny that there may be cases in which "delusive and veridical experiences" really are "qualitatively indistinguishable"; but I certainly do wish to deny (a) that such cases are anything like as *common* as both Ayer and Price seem to suppose, and (b) that there *have* to be such cases to accommodate the undoubted fact that we are sometimes "deceived by our senses." We are not, after all, quasi-infallible beings, who can be taken in only where the avoidance of mistake is completely impossible. But if we are prepared to admit that there may be, even that there are, *some* cases in which "delusive and veridical perceptions" really are indistinguishable, does this admission require us to drag in, or even let in, sense-data? No. For even if we were to make the prior admission (which we have so far found no reason to make) that in the "abnormal" cases we perceive sense-data, we should not be obliged to extend this admission to the "normal" cases too. For why on earth should it *not* be the case that, in some few instances, perceiving one sort of thing is exactly like perceiving another?

6. There is a further quite general difficulty in assessing the force of this

argument, which we (in common with the authors of our texts) have slurred over so far. The question which Ayer invites us to consider is whether two classes of "perceptions," the veridical and the delusive, are or are not "qualitatively different," "intrinsically different in kind"; but how are we supposed to set about even considering this question, when we are not told what "a perception" *is?* In particular, how many of the circumstances of a situation, as these would ordinarily be stated, are supposed to be included in "the perception"? For example, to take the stick in water again: it is a feature of this case that part of the stick is under water, and water, of course, is not invisible; is the water, then, part of "the perception"? It is difficult to conceive of any grounds for denying that it is; but *if* it is, surely this is a perfectly obvious respect in which "the perception" differs from, is distinguishable from, the "perception" we have when we look at a bent stick *not* in water. There is a sense, perhaps, in which the presence or absence of water is not the *main thing* in this case—we are supposed to be addressing ourselves primarily to questions about the stick. But in fact, as a great quantity of psychological investigation has shown, discrimination between one thing and another very frequently depends on such more or less extraneous concomitants of the main thing, even when such concomitants are not consciously taken note of. As I said, we are told nothing of what "a perception" is; but could any defensible account, if such an account were offered, completely exclude all these highly significant attendant circumstances? And if they *were* excluded—in some more or less arbitrary way—how much interest or importance would be left in the contention that "delusive" and "veridical" perceptions are indistinguishable? Inevitably, if you rule out the respects in which A and B differ, you may expect to be left with respects in which they are alike.

I conclude, then, that this part of the philosophical argument involves (though not in every case equally essentially) (a) acceptance of a quite bogus dichotomy of all "perceptions" into two groups, the "delusive" and the "veridical"—to say nothing of the unexplained introduction of "perceptions" themselves; (b) an implicit but grotesque exaggeration of the *frequency* of "delusive perceptions"; (c) a further grotesque exaggeration of the *similarity* between "delusive" perceptions and "veridical" ones; (d) the erroneous suggestion that there *must* be such similarity, or even qualitative *identity*; (e) the acceptance of the pretty gratuitous idea that things "generically different" could not be qualitatively alike; and (f)—which is really a corollary of (c) and (a)—the gratuitous neglect of those more or less subsidiary features which often make possible the discrimination of situations which, in other *broad* respects, may be roughly alike. These seem to be rather serious deficiencies.

NOTES

1. The latter point holds, of course, for *some* uses of "illusion" too; there are the illusions which some people (are said to) lose as they grow older and wiser.

2. Cp. the white rabbit in the play called *Harvey.*

3. Price, *Perception,* p. 27.

4. Not even "indirectly," no such thing is "presented." Doesn't this seem to make the case, though more amenable, a good deal less useful to the philosopher? It's hard to see how normal cases could be said to be *very like* this.

5. This is part, no doubt *only* part, of the absurdity in Descartes' toying with the notion that the whole of our experience might be a dream.

6. Ayer in fact expresses qualms later: see p. 12 of his book.

THE
ANALOGY
OF
FEELING*
Stuart Hampshire

1. I am concerned in this paper with only one source of one of the many puzzles associated with our knowledge of other minds. It is often said that statements about other people's feelings and sensations cannot be justified as being based upon inductive arguments of any ordinary pattern, that is, as being inferences from the observed to the unobserved of a familiar and accepted form; I shall argue that they can be so justified. I will not deny that such inferences are difficult; everyone has always known, apart altogether from philosophical theory, that they are difficult; but I will deny that they are *logically* peculiar or invalid when considered simply as inductive arguments. I believe that moaern philosophers have found something logically peculiar and problematical about our inferences to other minds, and have even denied the possibility of such inferences, at least in part because of an incomplete understanding of the functions of pronouns and of other contextual expressions in our language; in particular they have misunderstood the proper use of these expressions in combination with words like "know," "certain," "verify," "evidence." If I am right, it becomes easier to explain why what the solipsist wants to say cannot properly be said, why solipsism is a *linguistically* absurd thesis, and at the same time to explain why it is a thesis which tempts those who confuse epistemological distinctions with logical distinctions.

2. For reasons which will become clear later, I shall introduce two quasi-technical terms. As specimens of the type of sentence, the status of which, as normally used, is in dispute, I shall take the sentences, "I feel giddy," "you feel giddy," "he feels giddy," and so on through the other cases of the verb "feel."

---

* From Hampshire: "The Analogy of Feeling," *Mind,* 61, no. 241 (January 1952); reprinted by permission of the editor of *Mind*.

Any normal use of the sentence "I feel giddy" will be, in my invented terminology, a specimen of an autobiographical statement, where this phrase is simply shorthand for "a statement describing somebody's momentary feelings or sensations which is expressed in the first person singular." Any normal use of the sentences "he feels giddy," "you feel giddy," or "they feel giddy" will be specimens of heterobiographical statements—that is, statements describing somebody's feelings which are not expressed in the first person singular; "we feel giddy," as normally used, would be a statement which is partly autobiographical and partly heterobiographical in my sense. It may sometimes happen that someone chooses to tell the story of his own inner life, using not the first person singular, but the third person, or some fictitious or other name; it is actually possible to write one's own obituary notice, using the third person and including within it descriptions which are intended as descriptions of one's own feelings and sensations. But on such occasions the pronouns (or verb cases for an inflected language) are misleadingly used, and deliberately so. The ordinary function of the word "I" (or of the corresponding verb case in inflected languages) is to indicate explicitly that the author of the statement is also the designated subject of the statement; the exceptional, deliberately misleading uses mentioned above consciously take advantage of this fact. By "an autobiographical statement" I shall mean a statement describing someone's feelings or sensations which explicitly shows, in the actual form of its expression, that the author of the statement is also its designated subject. A statement, for example, in a novel about which we can argue, by reference to evidence external to the verbal form of the statement itself, whether it is, as a matter of fact, an autobiographical statement, will not therefore be an autobiographical statement in my artificial and restricted sense.

It has often been noticed that there are certain peculiarities about these first person singular statements about feelings and sensations, particularly when the main verb is in the present tense; these peculiarities have led some philosophers to characterize them as incorrigible statements and have led others to deny them the title of "statement" altogether; the peculiarities emerge in the use of words like "know," "believe," and "certain" in combination with these sentences, or rather in their lack of use. With regard to most statements, "I think that P is true but I may be mistaken" and "I have established that P is true beyond all reasonable doubt" are sentences having a normal use, whatever P may be; but there are no normal circumstances in which one would say "I think that I feel giddy but I may be mistaken" or "I have established beyond reasonable doubt that I feel giddy," and consequently there are no normal circumstances in which I would be in a position to say "I am absolutely certain that I feel giddy." By contrast, the sentences "you feel giddy" or "he feels giddy" do normally occur in statements of the form "I believe that he feels giddy but I am not certain" or "it is known that he feels giddy," and so on. But again, "he believes

173

that he feels giddy" or "he is certain that he feels giddy" have no normal use. It is the corollary of this that the questions "how do you know?" or "what is your evidence?" are out of place with respect to statements about momentary feelings and sensations, when addressed to the author of the statement, if he is also explicitly shown to be the designated subject of it.

One inference which might be drawn from these facts is that heterobiographical statements about feelings can never be known to be true directly, where "known directly" means that no question arises of how the statement is known to be true and no question arises of any evidence being required to support the statement. But this, as it stands, would be a plainly false conclusion, since the person who is the designated subject of such a heterobiographical statement does generally know directly, without need of evidence, whether the statement made about him is true or false. The proper conclusion is only that the *author* of a heterobiographical statement of this kind can never know directly, in the sense indicated, whether the statement he has made is true or false; the author can always properly be asked how he knows, or on what grounds he believes, his heterobiographical statement to be true; he is required to produce his evidence. So the so-called asymmetry is not a matter of statements expressed in the first person singular, *as such,* being different with respect to the evidence which they require from statements expressed in the second or third person singular. Both descriptions of feelings in the first person singular, and those in the second and third person, may be challenged either by reference to indirect evidence (for example, "I am sure you are lying; you have obvious motives for lying, and you show none of the symptoms which usually go with feeling giddy") or by a proper claim to direct knowledge (for example, "I can tell you quite definitely that I do feel giddy, in spite of the evidence to the contrary").

This point is obvious, but it is apt to be dangerously slurred over when philosophers talk in general of "statements about other minds," and then go on to inquire into *the* methods appropriate to confirming or confuting such statements. They may be thought to mean by "statements about other minds" what I have called heterobiographical statements—that is, statements describing feelings and sensations which are not expressed in the first person singular; but the so-called problem of other minds, which is sometimes presented as a problem of how a *certain kind of statement* can be tested, does not attach to *a class of statements of any one particular form;* it arises equally for first person singular statements if in this case the position of the audience is considered instead of that of the author. The problem of other minds is properly the problem of what tests and verifications are ever possible for anyone who is not in fact the designated subject of a statement about thoughts and feelings; it arises equally for any statement about feelings, whether the statement begins with the word "I" or with the word "you" or "we" or "they."

3. The commonsense answer to the question so reformulated seems obvious—indeed so obvious that simply to give it cannot possibly satisfy philosophers; something more is required to explain why it has been thought inadequate. The commonsense answer is: each one of us is sometimes the designated subject of an autobiographical statement and sometimes the subject of heterobiographical statements; each one of us sometimes makes, or is in a position to make, statements about feelings which are not inferential and do not require supporting evidence; each one of us also makes, or is in a position to make, statements about feelings which are inferential and do require supporting evidence. All that is required for testing the validity of any method of factual inference is that each one of us should sometimes be in a position to confront the conclusions of the doubtful method of inference with what is known by him to be true independently of the method of inference in question. Each one of us is certainly in this position with respect to our common methods of inference about the feelings of persons other than ourselves, in virtue of the fact that each one of us is constantly able to compare the results of this type of inference with what he knows to be true directly and noninferentially; each one of us is in the position to make this testing comparison, whenever he is the designated subject of a statement about feelings and sensations. I, Hampshire, know by what sort of signs I may be misled in inferring Jones' and Smith's feelings, because I have implicitly noticed (though probably not formulated) where Jones, Smith, and others generally go wrong in inferring my feelings. We all as children learn by experiment how to conceal and deceive, to pose and suppress; concurrently we are learning in this very process how to detect the poses and suppressions of others; we learn the signs and occasions of concealment at first hand, and we are constantly revising our canons of duplicity as our own direct experience of its forms and occasions widens.

These are the commonsense considerations which seem at first glance to allow us to regard any heterobiographical statement made by any one of us as the conclusion of a valid inductive inference, the reliability of the method of inference used in any particular case being in principle testable by each one of us in confrontation with direct experience, that is, with noninferential knowledge about the successes and failures of this particular method. I think that, as is usual in these questions, the third glance will confirm the first. But before going further, it is worth noticing how the argument from analogy, as stated by philosophers, approaches what I have called the commonsense position, but which also misrepresents and oversimplifies it. There is a sense of "analogy" in which it is true that I could justify my inference that Smith is now feeling giddy by an analogy between the particular method of inference which I am now using and other uses of the same methods of inference by other people in discussing my feelings and sensations; I know by direct experience how such feelings as giddiness are concealed and revealed; both I and Smith have been in a

175

position to test the reliability of those methods of indirect inference about giddiness and cognate sensations which we from time to time use in talking about other people. The argument from analogy, as commonly stated by philosophers, only fails because the analogy has been looked for in the wrong place. What is required is not some simple analogy between my feelings and my external symptoms, on the one hand, and someone else's external symptoms and so someone else's giddiness feeling, on the other; what is needed and is also available is an *analogy between different uses of the same methods of argument by different people on different occasions.* The inductive argument, the reliability of which is to be tested by each one of us, attaches both to the sentence "I feel giddy" and to the sentences "you feel giddy," "he feels giddy," etc.; it attaches to any sentence of the form "X feels giddy"; anyone hearing or using any sentence of this form, and anyone needing to test the statement conveyed on a particular occasion, can find such confirmation by looking for an analogy with occasions of its use when he was not in need of such inductive confirmation. To anyone entertaining a doubt about the justification of a particular method of inference about feelings and sensations, the reassuring analogy is between the different occasions of use of the sentence in question; for on some of these occasions the doubter, whoever he may be, was in a position to know non-inferentially that the method of inference now in question led to a correct or incorrect conclusion. Each of us is in a position to learn from his own experience that certain methods of inference to conclusions of the kind "X feels giddy" are generally successful. Of course, if I, Hampshire, have never felt giddy myself or had any sensation which is even remotely like this one, I would to that extent be at a loss to know whether other people are speaking the truth when they describe autobiographically this utterly unknown kind of sensation. In certain extreme cases this total failure of testability, and therefore failure of communication, does in fact happen; in such cases I am in fact content to admit that I personally have no means of knowing whether what is said by others is pure invention or not; I simply do not know what they are talking about. But over the normal range of statements about feelings and sensations of which I am either the author or audience, I can generally point to occasions on which I was the subject of the particular statement in question and other people had to use the now questionable method of inference. Suppose that Smith and I each suspect the other of deceiving and of encouraging the other to use unreliable methods of inference. This again is a testable and empirical doubt, because we each of us know how we ourselves proceed when we are trying to deceive in this particular manner. We each base our devices of deception on our observations of other people's methods of inference about us. We each know that there is something in common to our different methods of deception, since we each sometimes know that we have failed to deceive and so we each know from our own experience how such deception may be detected. But no common psychological language could be established with beings, outwardly human and sensitive, who never tried openly and in words to infer our feelings and who never acknowledged in words our success in inferring theirs, using the one to guide them in the other in a circle of mutual correction. We would have no good inductive grounds for speculating about the feelings of utterly silent people, or of people who did not betray themselves in speculating about us. It is merely a matter of natural history, and not of logic, that total failures of communication and understanding do not occur more frequently, and that in fact we are each generally in a position to reassure ourselves about our methods of inference to the feelings of others by confrontation with the successes and failures of others in talking about us.

It has been necessary, first, to insist on the truism that all statements about feelings and sensations, including such statements expressed in the first person singular, are "statements about other minds" for some people, but not "statements about other minds" for other people; for it is precisely this feature of them which allows any one of us to test in direct experience the reliability of the numerous specific methods of inference which he uses when talking about the feelings of others. The importance of the truism can be brought out in the analogous case of "statements about the past."

Philosophers have sometimes invented perplexities by writing as if they could pick out a class of statements as "statements about the past" and could then inquire how such statements can possibly be established as true by inductive argument; for how, it is asked, can we ever in principle confirm the validity of our inferences about the past? The mistakes which lead to this question are the same as in the "other minds" case. We cannot pick out a class of statements as statements about the past, unless we mean merely statements expressed in the past tenses. But the tenses, like the pronouns and cases of verbs, serve (among other functions) to relate a statement to the particular context or occasion of its utterance or of its consideration; clearly the *same* statement may be a statement about the past, present, or future when considered, accepted, or rejected by different people in different contexts. Similarly, the *same* statement may be made either heterobiographically or autobiographically. A statement in the present tense, which is in this artificial sense a statement about the present when verified and reaffirmed, may be reaffirmed as a statement about the past; equally, a statement about the future, when finally confirmed, may be reaffirmed as a statement about the present. *The very notion of confirmation involves this possibility of comparing the different contexts of utterance of the same statement.* It does not in general lie *within* the statement itself, or in its grammatical form of expression, that it is a statement about the mind of another or that it is a statement about the past. These are features of the circumstances of the utterance or consideration of the statement, features which are partially indicated (but not stated) by pronouns, by tenses, and by other contextual expressions,

177

whenever and by whomever the statement is asserted, reasserted or denied. Strictly speaking, there can be no class of statements about the past, standing in hopeless need of confirmation, any more than there can be a class of past events. Similarly, there can be no class of minds which are other minds or class of statements about them. This confusion of contextual idioms such as *other* and *past* with class terms has its roots in an unnoticed double use of the idioms, which must now be explained.

4. It is often suggested that the function of pronouns and other contextual expressions (*this, that, here, now,* etc.) is to designate or to refer uniquely to some person, thing, time, place, or event. Mr. Strawson (*Mind,* October 1950) has suggested the appropriate label, "uniquely referring expressions." Certainly one of the ways in which pronouns and these other contextual expressions are used is in this uniquely referring way—that is, to indicate, in a particular context of utterance, a particular person, thing, or event. But it is characteristic of the contextual expressions that they are not always or solely used to refer uniquely or to designate a particular person, thing, or event; they also have an important *generalized* use, in which they make no reference to a particular individual and in which they can be interpreted without any reference whatever to any particular context of utterance. Consider the slogan, "do it *now*" or "never put off till *tomorrow* what you can do *today*." In this use *now, today,* and *tomorrow* do not refer uniquely, but have a force in some (but not all) ways like that of a variable, and might be expanded into "now, to whatever moment 'now' may refer," or "today, whatever day 'today' may refer to." Another example: "The future is quite uncertain." As it stands, and without a context, this sentence is ambiguous and might be used to make two quite different statements or even two different kinds of statements. "The future" might be used in the uniquely referring way, so that we need to know the context of utterance in order to know what particular stretch of history is being referred to and described as uncertain; or "the future" might be used in the purely generalized way—"the future, at whatever point in history, is always uncertain." This familiar generalized, or quasi-variable, use is transferred to philosophy when we talk of "statements about *the past*," "statements about the *other* side of the moon," and "statements about *other* minds." Confusion between the two kinds of use arises when a transition is made within a single argument from the generalized to the uniquely referring use, or vice versa, without this transition being noticed; and just this is what generally happens in arguments about our knowledge of "other minds" and in formulations of the "*ego*centric" predicament. The solipsistic doubter will probably not put his question in the explicitly generalized form, but will ask: "How can *I* ever justify my inferences about what is going on in *your* mind, since *I* can have no independent means of checking *my* inferences about *your* feelings?" There may be a muddle in this: Does the "I" here mean "I, Hampshire"? Is it a lament about my, Hampshire's, peculiar isolation and the

peculiar inscrutability of you, Smith? Or does the "I" mean "whoever 'I' refers to" and the "you" "you, whoever 'you' may be"? If the latter is intended, and the pronoun is being used in the generalized way, the question becomes: "How can any one of us ever justify any inference to the feelings of someone other than himself, since no one of us, whoever he may be, has any means of checking any inference to the feelings of anyone other than himself?" And to this generalized form of the question the commonsense answer again suggests itself: each and every one of us, whoever he may be, has the means of independently checking the reliability of the methods of inference which he uses, although, naturally, on those occasions when he needs to use any particular method of inference, he cannot be independently checking the inference on the same occasion. When I, Hampshire, check in my own experience the reliability of the various particular methods of inference which I use when talking about the feelings of others, the statements which I make at the conclusion of these checks are *ex-hypothesi* not themselves the conclusions of an inference; but they are nonetheless efficient as checks to my methods of inference. The solipsistic problem, cleared of these confusions, can now be restated: whenever anyone uses the sentence "I feel giddy," one person and one person only is in a position to know directly and without need of inference whether the statement conveyed is true. Whenever anyone says "you feel giddy" or "he feels giddy" or "Smith feels giddy," one person and one person only is in a position to know without need of inference whether the statement is true. Whenever anyone says, "we both feel giddy" or "they feel giddy," no one can ever know directly and without need of inference whether the conjoint statements conveyed are true. So the solipsist may correctly say that it is a distinguishing characteristic of statements about feelings, as opposed to statements about physical things, that at most one person can ever properly claim to know directly, and without needing to give evidence or justification, whether such statements are true. But the solipsist originally wanted to separate, within the class of statement about minds, a class of statements about *other* minds, as being dubious and problematical, from autobiographical statements, which were held to be privileged and not dubious. It is this distinction which is untenable.

Suppose that, in talking about our feelings, we each solipsistically confined ourselves to statements which we may properly claim to know to be true directly and without appeal to evidence or to methods of inference. I, Hampshire, would be allowed to say "I feel giddy," and you, Smith, would be allowed to say "I feel giddy"; but since all uses of other cases of the verb require problematical inference, we would never be allowed to assent to or dissent from each other's statements or to place ourselves in the position of an audience discussing them. Under such conditions the pronouns and cases of the verb would have no further function, and all argument and the detection of lies would be excluded. Our psychological language would simply serve to convey a set of undiscussable announcements. Communication in the ordinary sense upon such topics would have ceased, for communication essentially involves the use of sentences to convey statements by an author to an actual or potential audience in such a way that all users of the language, in denying and confirming, may change from the position of audience to author in respect of any statement made. To compare the use of personal pronouns with the uses of tenses again: because those statements which refer to events long prior or subsequent to the moment of utterance are *pro tanto* relatively uncertain at the time they are made, it might be suggested that only statements in the present tense should be accepted as completely reliable. But unless we recognize the sense of "same statement" as something to be reaffirmed in different contexts, we remove the last possibility of correcting and denying statements, and with this we remove the possibility of all argument about them and testing of them and also the possibility of expressing belief or disbelief; we therefore remove the essential conditions or point of statement-making. This we would have done by failing to recognize the function of those devices which relate the same statement to the changing circumstances of its assertion. The formula often used, "I am in a position to judge of the truth of statements about my own feeling, but not about the feeling of others," has only succeeded in misleading, because of the two ways in which the expression "I" and "other" may be used, and the often unnoticed shift from one use to the other. It is this shift which suggests a solipsistic conclusion—for example, that one mind only can be known with certainty to exist and one set of feelings and sensations known with certainty to have occurred. But, of course, no such conclusion about *one* mind follows from the argument when correctly stated. The proper truism is, "No one of us, whoever he may be, is in need of inference to assure himself of the truth of statements about his own feelings, but he can never assure himself directly, and without needing to appeal to evidence, of the truth of statements about the feelings of others." Stated in this form, with a quasi-variable expression as the subject term, the truism cannot serve as a premise to any *solipsistic* conclusion.

5. The peculiarity of the word *know* and of its cognates—that the conditions of their proper use in combination with any type of statement vary with the indicated context of utterance—is not confined to discourse about minds and feelings; it applies over the whole range of application of words like *know, certain,* and *verify* with whatever kind of statement they are combined. Whatever may be the topic under discussion, whether a claim to knowledge or certainty is or is not in place, must always depend upon who makes the claim and when and under what conditions. It can never be solely a matter of the form of the statement itself or of its topic. Any empirical statement whatever is a matter of uncertain inference under some conditions of its use or consideration. There is no mystery in the fact that a statement which may be a matter of direct and certain knowledge for one person will always be a matter of uncertain inference

for another, any more than there is mystery in the fact that the same statement which may be known with certainty to be true at one time must be a matter of uncertain inference at other times. Philosophers (Plato, Descartes, Russell) have invented the mystery by writing as if being known to be true and being uncertain were intrinsic properties of statements, properties somehow adhering to them independently of the particular circumstances in which they were made or considered. It is proper and necessary that formal logicians who study patterns of transformations of sentence forms should disregard those features of statements which relate them to a context of utterance; but philosophers' questions about use and meaning hinge on the different contexts in which words like *know* and *certain* may occur in combination with sentences of different forms and different topics.

6. *Conclusion. Past, Present,* and *Other* are not class terms but contextual terms, and there can be no class of events which are past events and no class of minds which are other minds and no class of statements which are statements about either of these. "Statements about other minds" is either an incomplete expression, requiring knowledge of the particular circumstance of its use in order that it should be intelligible—for example, "minds other than mine, Hampshire's" or the contextual expression may be used in the generalized sense and mean "statements about minds other than the author's, whoever the author may be." If the latter is intended, then in raising the problem of other minds we are inquiring into the analogy which enables anyone to compare the situation in which he knows a statement about feelings to be true, independently of inference, with the situation in which he does not, and it is to this comparison that we refer when we talk of checking the reliability of any method of factual inference.

KNOWLEDGE
OF
OTHER
MINDS*
Norman Malcolm

I

I believe that the argument from analogy for the existence of other minds still enjoys more credit than it deserves, and my first aim will be to show that it leads nowhere. J. S. Mill is one of many who have accepted the argument and I take his statement of it as representative. He puts to himself the question, "By what evidence do I know, or by what considerations am I led to believe, that there exist other sentient creatures; that the walking and speaking figures which I see and hear, have sensations and thought, or in other words, possess minds?" His answer is the following.

I conclude that other human beings have feelings like mine, first, because they have bodies like mine, which I know, in my own case, to be the antecedent condition of feelings; and secondly, because they exhibit the acts, and other outward signs, which in my own case I know by experience to be caused by feelings. I am conscious in myself of a series of facts connected by a uniform sequence, of which the beginning is modifications of my body, the middle is feelings, the end is outward demeanor. In the case of other human beings I have the evidence of my senses for the first and last links of the series, but not for the intermediate link. I find, however, that the sequence between the first and last is as regular and constant in those other cases as it is in mine. In my own case I know that the first link produces the last through the intermediate link, and could not produce it without. Experience, therefore, obliges me to conclude that there must be an intermediate link, which must either be the same in others as in myself, or a

* From Norman Malcolm, "Knowledge of Other Minds," *Journal of Philosophy,* vol. 55, no. 23 (November 6, 1958); reprinted by permission of the author and the *Journal of Philosophy.*

different one. I must either believe them to be alive, or to be automatons; and by believing them to be alive, that is by supposing the link to be of the same nature as in the case of which I have experience, and which is in all other respects similar, I bring other human beings, as phenomena, under the same generalizations which I know by experience to be the true theory of my own existence.

I shall pass by the possible objection that this would be very weak inductive reasoning, based as it is on the observation of a single instance. More interesting is the following point. Suppose this reasoning could yield a conclusion of the sort "It is probable that that human figure" (pointing at some person other than oneself) "has thoughts and feelings." Then there is a question as to whether this conclusion can mean anything to the philosopher who draws it, because there is a question as to whether the sentence "That human figure has thoughts and feelings" can mean anything to him. Why should this be a question? Because the assumption from which Mill starts is that he has *no criterion* for determining whether another "walking and speaking figure" does or does not have thoughts and feelings. If he had a criterion he could apply it, establishing with certainty that this or that human figure does or does not have feelings (for the only plausible criterion would lie in behavior and circumstances that are open to view), and there would be no call to resort to tenuous analogical reasoning that yields at best a probability. If Mill has no criterion for the existence of feelings other than his own, then in that sense he does not understand the sentence "That human figure has feelings" and therefore does not understand the sentence "It is *probable* that that human figure has feelings."

There is a familiar inclination to make the following reply, "Although I have no criterion of verification still I understand, for example, the sentence 'He has a pain.' For I understand the meaning of 'I have a pain,' and 'He has a pain' means that he has the same thing I have when I have a pain." But this is a fruitless maneuver. If I do not know how to establish that someone has a pain then I do not know how to establish that he has the same as I have when I have a pain. You cannot improve my understanding of "He has a pain" by this recourse to the notion of "the same," unless you give me a criterion for saying that someone has the same as I have. If you can do this you will have no use for the argument from analogy; and if you cannot, then you do not understand the supposed conclusion of that argument. A philosopher who purports to rely on the analogical argument cannot, I think, escape this dilemma.

There have been various attempts to repair the argument from analogy. Stuart Hampshire has argued that its validity as a method of inference can be established in the following way: Others sometimes infer that I am feeling giddy from my behavior. Now I have direct, noninferential knowledge, says Hampshire, of my own feelings. So I can check inferences made about me against the facts, checking thereby the accuracy of the methods of inference. All that is required for testing the validity of any method of factual inference is that each one of us should sometimes be in a position to confront the conclusions of the doubtful method with what is known by him to be true independently of the method in question. Each one of us is certainly in this position with respect to our common methods of inference about the feelings of persons other than ourselves, because each one of us is constantly able to compare the results of this type of inference, directly and noninferentially, with what he knows to be true. Each one of us is in the position to make this testing comparison whenever he is the designated subject of a statement about feelings and sensations. I, Hampshire, know by what sort of signs I may be misled in inferring Jones' and Smith's feelings, because I have implicitly noticed (though probably not formulated) where Jones, Smith, and others generally go wrong in inferring my feelings. Presumably I can also note when the inferences of others about my feelings do not go wrong. Having ascertained the reliability of some inference procedures, I can use them myself in a guarded way to draw conclusions about the feelings of others, with a modest but justified confidence in the truth of those conclusions.

My first comment is that Hampshire has apparently forgotten the purpose of the argument from analogy, which is to provide some probability that "the walking and speaking figures which I see and hear, have sensations and thoughts" (Mill). For the reasoning that he describes involves the assumption that other human figures *do* have thoughts and sensations, for they are assumed to make inferences about me from observations of my behavior. But the philosophical problem of the existence of other minds *is* the problem of whether human figures other than oneself do, among other things, make observations, inferences, and assertions. Hampshire's supposed defense of the argument from analogy is an *ignoratio elenchi.*

If we struck from the reasoning described by Hampshire all assumption of thoughts and sensations in others we should be left with something roughly like this: "When my behavior is such and such there come from nearby human figures the sounds 'He feels giddy.' And generally I do feel giddy at the time. Therefore when another human figure exhibits the same behavior and I say 'He feels giddy,' it is probable that he does feel giddy." But the reference here to the sentence-like sounds coming from other human bodies is irrelevant, since I must not assume that those sounds express inferences. Thus the reasoning becomes simply the classical argument from analogy: "When my behavior is such and such I feel giddy; so probably when another human figure behaves the same way he feels the same way." This argument, again, is caught in the dilemma about the criterion of the *same.*

The version of analogical reasoning offered by Professor H. H. Price is more interesting. He suggests that "one's evidence for the existence of other minds is derived primarily from the understanding of language." His idea is that if another body gives forth noises one understands, like "There's the bus," and if these noises give one new information, this "provides some evidence that the foreign body which uttered the noises is animated by a mind like one's own. . . . Suppose I am often in its neighborhood and it repeatedly produces utterances which I can understand and which I then proceed to verify for myself. And suppose that this happens in many different kinds of situations. I think that my evidence for believing that this body is animated by a mind like my own would then become very strong." The body from which these informative sounds proceed need not be a human body. "If the rustling of the leaves of an oak formed intelligible words conveying new information to me, and if gorse bushes made intelligible gestures, I should have evidence that the oak or the gorse bush was animated by an intelligence like my own." Even if the intelligible and informative sounds did not proceed from a body they would provide evidence for the existence of a (disembodied) mind.

Although differing sharply from the classical analogical argument, the reasoning presented by Price is still analogical in form. I know by introspection that when certain combinations of sounds come from me, they are "symbols in acts of spontaneous thinking"; therefore similar combinations of sounds not produced by me "probably function as instruments to an act of spontaneous thinking, which in this case is not my own." Price says that the reasoning also provides an *explanation* of the otherwise mysterious occurrence of sounds which I understand but did not produce. He anticipates the objection that the hypothesis is nonsensical because unverifiable. "The hypothesis is a perfectly conceivable one," he says, "in the sense that I know very well what the world would have to be like if the hypothesis were true—what sorts of entities there must be in it and what sorts of events must occur in them. I know from introspection what acts of thinking and perceiving are, and I know what it is for such acts to be combined into the unity of a single mind . . ."

I wish to argue against Price that no amount of intelligible sounds coming from an oak tree or a kitchen table could create any probability that it has sensations and thoughts. The question to be asked is: What would show that a tree or table *understands* the sounds that come from it? We can imagine that useful warnings, true descriptions and predictions, even "replies" to questions, should emanate from a tree, so that it came to be of enormous value to its owner. How should we establish that it understood those sentences? Should we "question" it? Suppose that the tree "asked" it "What is a vixen? " and it "replied," "A vixen is a female fox." It might go on to do as well for "female" and "fox." This performance might incline us to say that the tree understood the words, in contrast to the possible case in which it answered "I don't know" or did not answer at all. But would it show that the tree understood the words in the same sense that a person could understand them? With a person such a performance would create a presumption that he could make correct *applications* of the word in question, but not so with a tree. To see this point, think of the normal teaching

185

of words (for example, "spoon," "dog," "red") to a child and how one decides whether he understands them. At a primitive stage of teaching one does not require or expect definitions, but rather that the child should *pick out* reds from blues, dogs from cats, spoons from forks. This involves his looking, pointing, reaching for and going to the right things and not the wrong ones. That a child says "red" when a red thing and "blue" when a blue thing is put before him is indicative of a mastery of those words *only* in conjunction with the other activities of looking, pointing, trying to get, fetching, and carrying. Try to suppose that he says the right words but looks at and reaches for the wrong things. Should we be tempted to say that he has mastered the use of those words? In the case of a tree there could be no disparity between its words and its "behavior" because it is logically incapable of behavior of the relevant kind.

Since it has nothing like the human face and body it makes no sense to say of a tree, or an electronic computer, that it is looking or pointing at or fetching something. (Of course one can always *invent* a sense for these expressions.) Therefore it would make no sense to say that it did or did not understand the above words. Trees and computers cannot either pass or fail the tests that a child is put through. They cannot take them. That an object was a source of intelligible sounds or other signs (no matter how sequential) would not be enough by itself to establish that it had thoughts or sensations. How informative sentences and valuable predictions could emanate from a gorse-bush might be a grave scientific problem, but the explanation could never be that the gorse-bush has a mind. Better no explanation than nonsense!

It might be thought that the above difficulty holds only for words whose meaning has a "perceptual content" and that if we imagined, for example, that our gorse-bush produced nothing but pure mathematical propositions we should be justified in attributing thought to it, although not sensation. But suppose there was a remarkable "calculating boy" who could give right answers to arithmetical problems but could not apply numerals to reality in empirical propositions, for example, he could not *count* any objects. I believe that everyone would be reluctant to say the he *understood* the mathematical signs and truths that he produced. If he could count in the normal way there would not be this reluctance. And "counting in the normal way" involves looking, pointing, reaching, fetching, and so on. That is, it requires the human face and body, and human behavior—or something similar. Things which do not have the human form or anything like it, not merely do not, but *cannot,* satisfy the criteria for thinking. I am trying to bring out part of what Wittgenstein meant when he said, "We only say of a human being and what is like one that it thinks" (*Investigations,* sec. 360), and "The human body is the best picture of the human soul" (*ibid,* p. 178).

I have not yet gone into the most fundamental error of the argument from analogy. It is present whether the argument is the classical one (the analogy between my body and other bodies) or Price's version (the analogy between my language and the noises and signs produced by other things). It is the mistaken assumption that *one learns from one's own case* what thinking and perceiving are . . ." It is the most natural assumption for a philosopher to make and indeed seems at first to be the only possibility. Yet Wittgenstein has made us see that it leads first to solipsism and then to nonsense. I shall try to state as briefly as possible how it produces those results.

A philosopher who believes that one must learn what thinking, fear, or pain is "from one's own case," does not believe that the thing to be observed is one's behavior, but rather something "inward." He considers behavior to be related to the inward states and occurrences merely as an accompaniment or possibly an effect. He cannot regard behavior as a *criterion* of psychological phenomena: for if he did he would have no use for the analogical argument (as was said before) and also the priority given to "one's own case" would be pointless. He believes that he notes something in himself that he calls "thinking" or "fear" or "pain," and then he tries to infer the presence of the *same* in others. He should then deal with the question of what his criterion of the *same* in others is. This he cannot do because it is of the essence of his viewpoint to reject circumstances and behavior as a criterion of mental phenomena in others. What else could serve as a criterion? He ought, therefore, to draw the conclusion that the notion of thinking, fear, or pain in others is in an important sense meaningless. He has no idea of what would count for or against it.[1] "That there should be thinking or pain other than my own is unintelligible," he ought to hold. This would be a rigorous solipsism, and a correct outcome of the assumption that one can know only from one's own case what the mental phenomena are. An equivalent way of putting it would be: "When I say 'I am in pain,' by 'pain' I mean a certain inward state. When I say '*He* is in pain,' by 'pain' I mean *behavior*. I cannot attribute pain to others *in the same sense* that I attribute it to myself."

Some philosophers before Wittgenstein may have seen the solipsistic result of starting from "one's own case." But I believe he is the first to have shown how that starting point destroys itself. This may be presented as follows: One supposes that one inwardly picks out something as thinking or pain and thereafter identifies it whenever it presents itself in the soul. But the question to be pressed is, Does one make *correct* identifications? The proponent of these "private" identifications has nothing to say here. He feels sure that he identifies correctly the occurrences in his soul; but feeling sure is no guarantee of being right. Indeed he has no idea of what being *right* could mean. He does not know how to distinguish between actually making correct identifications and being under the impression that he does. (See *Investigations*, secs. 258-9.) Suppose that he identified the emotion of anxiety as the sensation of pain? Neither he nor anyone else could know about this "mistake." Perhaps he makes a mistake *every* time! Perhaps all of us do! We ought to see now that we are talking nonsense.

We do not know what a *mistake* would be. We have no standard, no examples, no customary practice, with which to compare our inner recognitions. The inward identification cannot hit the bull's eye, or miss it either, because there is no bull's eye. When we see that the ideas of correct and incorrect have no application to the supposed inner identification, the latter notion loses its appearance of sense. Its collapse brings down both solipsism and the argument from analogy.

II

The destruction of the argument from analogy also destroys the *problem* for which it was supposed to provide a solution. A philosopher feels himself in a difficulty about other minds because he assumes that first of all he is acquainted with mental phenomena "from his own case." What troubles him is how to make the transition from his own case to the case of others. When his thinking is freed of the illusion of the priority of his own case, then he is able to look at the familiar facts and to acknowledge that the circumstances, behavior, and utterances of others actually are his *criteria* (not merely his evidence) for the existence of their mental states. Previously this had seemed impossible.

But now he is in danger of flying to the opposite extreme of behaviorism, which errs by believing that through observation of one's own circumstances, behavior, and utterances one can find out that one is thinking or angry. The philosophy of "from one's own case" and behaviorism, though in a sense opposites, make the common assumption that the first-person, present-tense psychological statements are verified by self-observation. According to the "one's own case" philosophy the self-observation cannot be checked by others; according to behaviorism the self-observation would be by means of outward criteria that are available to all. The first position becomes unintelligible; the second is false for at least many kinds of psychological statements. We are forced to conclude that the first-person psychological statements are not (or hardly ever) verified by self-observation. It follows that they have no verification at all, for if they had a verification it would have to be by self-observation.

But if sentences like "My head aches" or "I wonder where she is" do not express observations then what do they do? What is the relation between my declaration that my head aches and the fact that my head aches, if the former is not the report of an observation? The perplexity about the existence of *other* minds has, as the result of criticism, turned into a perplexity about the meaning of one's own psychological sentences about oneself. At our starting point it was the sentence "*His* head aches" that posed a problem; but now it is the sentence "*My* head aches" that puzzles us.

One way in which this problem can be put is by the question, "How does *one know when to say* the words 'My head aches'?" The inclination to ask this question can be made acute by imagining a fantastic but not impossible case of a person who has survived to adult years without ever experiencing pain. He is given various sorts of injections to correct this condition, and on receiving one of these one day, he jumps and exclaims, "Now I feel pain!" One wants to ask, "How did he *recognize* the new sensation as a *pain?*"

Let us note that if the man gives an answer (for example, "I knew it must be pain because of the way I jumped") then he proves by that very fact that he has not mastered the correct use of the words "I feel pain." They cannot be used to state a *conclusion*. In telling us *how* he did it he will convict himself of a misuse. Therefore the question "How did he recognize his sensation?" requests the impossible. The inclination to ask it is evidence of our inability to grasp the fact that the use of this psychological sentence has nothing to do with recognizing or identifying or observing a state of oneself.

The fact that this imagined case produces an especially strong temptation to ask the "How?" question shows that we have the idea that it must be more difficult to give the right name of one's sensation *the first time*. The implication would be that it is not so difficult *after* the first time. Why should this be? Are we thinking that then the man would have a paradigm of pain with which he could compare his sensations and so be in a position to know right off whether a certain sensation was or was not a pain? But the paradigm would be either something "outer" (behavior) or something "inner" (perhaps a memory impression of the sensation). If the former then he is misusing the first-person sentence. If the latter then the question of whether he compared *correctly* the present sensation with the inner paradigm of pain would be without sense. Thus the idea that the use of the first-person sentences can be governed by paradigms must be abandoned. It is another form of our insistent misconception of the first-person sentence as resting somehow on the identification of a psychological state.

These absurdities prove that we must conceive of the first-person psychological sentences in some entirely different light. Wittgenstein presents us with the suggestion that the first-person sentences are to be thought of as similar to the natural nonverbal, behavioral expressions of psychological states. "My leg hurts," for example, is to be assimilated to crying, limping, holding one's leg. This is a bewildering comparison and one's first thought is that two sorts of things could not be more unlike. By saying the sentence, one can make a *statement;* it has a *contradictory;* it is *true* or *false;* in saying it one *lies* or *tells the truth;* and so on. None of these things, exactly, can be said of crying, limping, holding one's leg. So how can there be any resemblance? But Wittgenstein knew this when he deliberately likened such a sentence to "the primitive, the natural, expressions" of pain, and said that it is "new pain-behavior" (*ibid.*, sec. 244). This analogy has at least two important merits: first, it breaks the hold on us of the question, "How does one *know when to say* 'My leg hurts'?", for in the light of the analogy this will be as nonsensical as the question "How does one know when to cry, limp, or

189

hold one's leg?"; second, it explains how the utterance of a first-person psycho-logical sentence by another person can have *importance* for us, although not as an identification—for in the light of the analogy it will have the same importance as the natural behavior which serves as our preverbal criterion of the psycho-logical states of others.

NOTES

1. One reason why philosophers have not commonly drawn this conclusion may be, as Wittgenstein acutely suggests, that they assume that they have "an infallible paradigm of identity in the identity of a thing with itself" (*Investigations*, sec. 215).

TWO
DOGMAS
OF
EMPIRICISM*
W. V. Quine

Modern empiricism has been conditioned in large part by two dogmas. One is a belief in some fundamental cleavage between truths which are *analytic,* or grounded in meanings independently of matters of fact, and truths which are *synthetic,* or grounded in fact. The other dogma is *reductionism:* the belief that each meaningful statement is equivalent to some logical construct upon terms which refer to immediate experience. Both dogmas, I shall argue, are ill founded. One effect of abandoning them is, as we shall see, a blurring of the supposed boundary between speculative metaphysics and natural science. Another effect is a shift toward pragmatism.

1. BACKGROUND FOR ANALYTICITY

Kant's cleavage between analytic and synthetic truths was foreshadowed in Hume's distinction between relations of ideas and matters of fact, and in Leibniz's distinction between truths of reason and truths of fact. Leibniz spoke of the truths of reason as true in all possible worlds. Picturesqueness aside, this is to say that the truths of reason are those which could not possibly be false. In the same vein we hear analytic statements defined as statements whose denials are self-contradictory. But this definition has small explanatory value, for the notion of self-contradictoriness, in the quite broad sense needed for this definition of analyticity, stands in exactly the same need of clarification as does the notion of analyticity itself. The two notions are the two sides of a single dubious coin.

---

*Reprinted by permission of the publishers from W. V. Quine, *From a Logical Point of View,* Cambridge, Mass.: Harvard University Press, © Copyright 1953, by the President and Fellows of Harvard College.

Kant conceived of an analytic statement as one that attributes to its subject no more than is already conceptually contained in the subject. This formulation has two shortcomings: it limits itself to statements of subject-predicate form, and it appeals to a notion of containment which is left at a metaphorical level. But Kant's intent, evident more from the use he makes of the notion of analyticity than from his definition of it, can be restated thus: a statement is analytic when it is true by virtue of meanings and independently of fact. Pursuing this line, let us examine the concept of *meaning* which is presupposed.

Meaning, let us remember, is not to be identified with naming. Frege's example of "Evening Star" and "Morning Star," and Russell's of "Scott" and "the author of *Waverley*" illustrate that terms can name the same thing but differ in meaning. The distinction between meaning and naming is no less important at the level of abstract terms. The terms "9" and "the number of the planets" name one and the same abstract entity but presumably must be regarded as unlike in meaning; for astronomical observation was needed, and not mere reflection on meanings, to determine the sameness of the entity in question.

The above examples consist of singular terms, concrete and abstract. With general terms, or predicates, the situation is somewhat different but parallel. Whereas a singular term purports to name an entity, abstract or concrete, a general term does not; but a general term is *true of* an entity or of each of many or of none. The class of all entities of which a general term is true is called the *extension* of the term. Now paralleling the contrast between the meaning of a singular term and the entity named, we must distinguish equally between the meaning of a general term and its extension. The general terms "creature with a heart" and "creature with kidneys," for example, are perhaps alike in extension but unlike in meaning.

Confusion of meaning with extension, in the case of general terms, is less common than confusion of meaning with naming in the case of singular terms. It is indeed a commonplace in philosophy to oppose intension (or meaning) to extension, or, in a variant vocabulary, connotation to denotation.

The Aristotelian notion of essence was the forerunner, no doubt, of the modern notion of intension or meaning. For Aristotle it was essential in men to be rational, accidental to be two-legged. But there is an important difference between this attitude and the doctrine of meaning. From the latter point of view it may indeed be conceded (if only for the sake of argument) that rationality is involved in the meaning of the word *man,* while two-leggedness is not; but two-leggedness may at the same time be viewed as involved in the meaning of *biped,* while rationality is not. Thus from the point of view of the doctrine of meaning, it makes no sense to say of the actual individual, who is at once a man and a biped, that his rationality is essential and his two-leggedness accidental, or vice versa. This had essences for Aristotle, but only linguistic forms

192

have meanings. Meaning is what essence becomes when it is divorced from the object of reference and wedded to the word.

For the theory of meaning a conspicuous question is the nature of its objects: what sort of things are meanings? A felt need for meant entities may derive from an earlier failure to appreciate that meaning and reference are distinct. Once the theory of meaning is sharply separated from the theory of reference, it is a short step to recognizing as the primary business of the theory of meaning simply the synonymy of linguistic forms and the analyticity of statements; meanings themselves, as obscure intermediary entities, may well be abandoned.

The problem of analyticity then confronts us anew. Statements which are analytic by general philosophical acclaim are not, indeed, far to seek. They fall into two classes. Those of the first class, which may be called *logically true,* are typified by:

(1)   No unmarried man is married.

The relevant feature of this example is that it not merely is true as it stands, but remains true under any and all reinterpretations of *man* and *married.* If we suppose a prior inventory of *logical* particles, comprising *no, un-, not, if, then, and,* etc., then in general a logical truth is a statement which is true and remains true under all reinterpretations of its components other than the logical particles.

But there is also a second class of analytic statements, typified by:

(2)   No bachelor is married.

The characteristic of such a statement is that it can be turned into a logical truth by putting synonyms for synonyms; thus (2) can be turned into (1) by putting *unmarried man* for its synonym *bachelor.* We still lack a proper characterization of this second class of analytic statements, and therewith of analyticity generally, inasmuch as we have had in the above description to lean on a notion of *synonymy* which is no less in need of clarification than analyticity itself.

In recent years Carnap has tended to explain analyticity by appeal to what he calls state-descriptions. A state-description is any exhaustive assignment of truth values to the atomic, or noncompound, statements of the language. All other statements of the language are, Carnap assumes, built up of their component clauses by means of the familiar logical devices, in such a way that the truth value of any complex statement is fixed for each state description by specifiable logical laws. A statement is then explained as analytic when it comes out true under every state description. This account is an adaptation of Leibniz's "true in all possible worlds." But note that this version of analyticity serves its purpose only if the atomic statements of the language are, unlike *John is a bachelor* and *John is married,* mutually independent. Otherwise there would be a state description which assigned truth to *John is a bachelor* and to John is married; consequently *No bachelors are married* would turn out synthetic rather than analytic under the proposed criterion. Thus the criterion of analyticity in terms of state descriptions serves only for languages devoid of extralogical synonym pairs such as *bachelor* and *unmarried man*—synonym pairs of the type which give rise to the "second class" of analytic statements. The criterion in terms of state descriptions is at best a reconstruction of logical truth, not of analyticity.

I do not mean to suggest that Carnap is under any illusions on this point. His simplified model language, with its state descriptions, is aimed primarily not at the general problem of analyticity but at another purpose, the clarification of probability and induction. Our problem, however, is analyticity, and here the major difficulty lies not in the first class of analytic statements, the logical truths, but rather in the second class, which depends on the notion of synonymy.

2. DEFINITION

There are those who find it soothing to say that the analytic statements of the second class reduce to those of the first class, the logical truths, by *definition; bachelor,* for example, is *defined* as *unmarried man.* But how do we find that bachelor is defined as *unmarried man?* Who defined it thus, and when? Are we to appeal to the nearest dictionary and accept the lexicographer's formulation as law? Clearly this would be to put the cart before the horse. The lexicographer is an empirical scientist whose business is the recording of antecedent facts; if he glosses *bachelor* as unmarried man, it is because of his belief that there is a relation of synonymy between those forms, implicit in general or preferred usage prior to his own work. The notion of synonymy presupposed here has still to be clarified, presumably in terms relating to linguistic behavior. Certainly the "definition" which is the lexicographer's report of an observed synonymy cannot be taken as the ground of the synonymy.

Definition is not, indeed, an activity exclusively of philologists. Philosophers and scientists frequently have occasion to "define" a recondite term by paraphrasing it into terms of a more familiar vocabulary. But ordinarily such a definition, like the philologist's, is pure lexicography, affirming a relation of synonymy antecedent to the exposition in hand.

Just what it means to affirm synonymy, just what the interconnections may be which are necessary and sufficient in order that two linguistic forms be properly describable as synonymous, is far from clear; but whatever these interconnections may be, ordinarily they are grounded in usage. Definitions reporting selected instances of synonymy come then as reports upon usage.

There is also, however, a variant type of definitional activity which does not limit itself to the reporting of preexisting synonymies. I have in mind what Carnap calls *explication*—an activity to which philosophers are given, and scientists also in their more philosophical moments. In explication the purpose is not merely to paraphrase the definiendum into an outright synonym, but actually to improve upon the definiendum by refining or supplementing its meaning. But even explication, though not merely reporting a preexisting synonymy between definiendum and definiens, does rest nevertheless on *other* preexisting synonymies. The matter may be viewed as follows. Any word worth explicating has some contexts which, as wholes, are clear and precise enough to be useful; and the purpose of explication is to preserve the usage of these favored contexts while sharpening the usage of other contexts. In order that a given definition be suitable for purposes of explication, therefore, what is required is not that the definiendum in its antecedent usage be synonymous with the definiens, but just that each of these favored contexts of the definiendum, taken as a whole in its antecedent usage, be synonymous with the corresponding context of the definiens.

Two alternative definientia may be equally appropriate for the purposes of a given task of explication and yet not be synonymous with each other, for they may serve interchangeably within the favored contexts but diverge elsewhere. By cleaving to one of these definientia rather than the other, a definition of explicative kind generates, by fiat, a relation of synonymy between definiendum and definiens which did not hold before. But such a definition still owes its explicative function, as seen, to preexisting synonymies.

There does, however, still remain an extreme sort of definition which does not hark back to prior synonymies at all: namely, the explicitly conventional introduction of novel notations for purposes of sheer abbreviation. Here the definiendum becomes synonymous with the definiens simply because it has been created expressly for the purpose of being synonymous with the definiens. Here we have a really transparent case of synonymy created by definition; would that all species of synonymy were as intelligible. For the rest, definition rests on synonymy rather than explaining it.

The word *definition* has come to have a dangerously reassuring sound, owing no doubt to its frequent occurrence in logical and mathematical writings. We shall do well to digress now into a brief appraisal of the role of definition in formal work.

In logical and mathematical systems either of two mutually antagonistic types of economy may be striven for, and each has its peculiar practical utility. On the one hand we may seek economy of practical expression—ease and brevity in the statement of multifarious relations. This sort of economy calls usually for distinctive concise notations for a wealth of concepts. Second, however, and oppositely, we may seek economy in grammar and vocabulary; we may try to find a minimum of basic concepts such that, once a distinctive notation has been appropriated to each of them, it becomes possible to express any desired further concept by mere combination and iteration of our basic notations. This second sort of economy is impractical in one way, since a poverty in basic idioms tends to a necessary lengthening of discourse. But it is practical in another way: it greatly simplifies theoretical discourse *about* the language, through minimizing the terms and the forms of construction wherein the language consists.

Both sorts of economy, though prima facie incompatible, are valuable in their separate ways. The custom has consequently arisen of combining both sorts of economy by forging, in effect, two languages, the one a part of the other. The inclusive language, though redundant in grammar and vocabulary, is economical in message lengths, while the part, called primitive notation, is economical in grammar and vocabulary. Whole and part are correlated by rules of translation whereby each idiom not in primitive notation is equated to some complex built up of primitive notation. These rules of translation are the so-called *definitions* which appear in formalized systems. They are best viewed not as adjuncts to one language but as correlations between two languages, the one a part of the other.

But these correlations are not arbitrary. They are supposed to show how the primitive notations can accomplish all purposes, save brevity and convenience, of the redundant language. Hence the definiendum and its definiens may be expected, in each case, to be related in one or another of the three ways lately noted. The definiens may be a faithful paraphrase of the definiendum into the narrower notation, preserving a direct synonymy as of antecedent usage; or the definiens may, in the spirit of explication, improve upon the antecedent usage of the definiendum; or finally, the definiendum may be a newly created notation, newly endowed with meaning here and now.

Thus, in formal and informal work alike, we find that definition—except in the extreme case of the explicitly conventional introduction of new notations—hinges on prior relations of synonymy. Recognizing, then, that the notion of definition does not hold the key to synonymy and analyticity, let us look further into synonymy and say no more of definition.

3. INTERCHANGEABILITY

A natural suggestion, deserving close examination, is that the synonymy of two linguistic forms consists simply in their interchangeability in all contexts without change of truth value—interchangeability, in Leibniz's phrase, *salva veritate*. Note that synonyms so conceived need not even be free from vagueness, as long as the vaguenesses match.

But it is not quite true that the synonyms *bachelor* and *unmarried man* are everywhere interchangeable *salva veritate*. Truths which become false under substitution of *unmarried man* for *bachelor* are easily constructed with the help of *bachelor of arts* or *bachelors buttons;* also with the help of quotations, thus:

> *Bachelor* has less than ten letters.

Such counterinstances can, however, perhaps be set aside by treating the phrases *bachelor of arts* and *bachelors buttons* and the quotation "bachelor" each as a single indivisible word and then stipulating that the interchangeability *salva veritate* which is to be the touchstone of synonymy is not supposed to apply to fragmentary occurrences inside of a word. This account of synonymy, supposing it acceptable on other counts, has indeed the drawback of appealing to a prior conception of *word* which can be counted on to present difficulties of formulation in its turn. Nevertheless, some progress might be claimed in having reduced the problem of synonymy to a problem of wordhood. Let us pursue this line a bit, taking *word* for granted.

The question remains whether interchangeability *salva veritate* (apart from occurrences within words) is a strong enough condition for synonymy, or whether, on the contrary, some heteronymous expressions might be thus interchangeable. Now let us be clear that we are not concerned here with synonymy in the sense of complete identity in psychological associations or poetic quality; indeed, no two expressions are synonymous in such a sense. We are concerned only with what may be called *cognitive* synonymy. Just what this is cannot be said without successfully finishing the present study; but we know something about it from the need which arose for it in connection with analyticity in §1. The sort of synonymy needed there was merely such that any analytic statement could be turned into a logical truth by putting synonyms for synonyms. Turning the tables and assuming analyticity, indeed, we could explain cognitive synonymy of terms as follows (keeping to the familiar example): to say that *bachelor* and *unmarried man* are cognitively synonymous is to say no more nor less than the statement:

(3)   All and only bachelors are unmarried men.

is analytic.

What we need is an account of cognitive synonymy not presupposing analyticity—if we are to explain analyticity conversely with help of cognitive synonymy as undertaken in §1. And, indeed, such an independent account of cognitive synonymy is at present up for consideration, namely, interchangeability *salva veritate* everywhere except within words. The question before us, to resume the thread at last, is whether such interchangeability is a sufficient condition for cognitive synonymy. We can quickly assure ourselves that it is by examples of the following sort. The statement:

(4)   Necessarily all and only bachelors are bachelors.

is evidently true, even supposing *necessarily* so narrowly construed as to be truly applicable only to analytic statements. Then, if *bachelor* and *unmarried man* are interchangeable *salva veritate,* the result:

(5)   Necessarily all and only bachelors are unmarried men.

of putting *unmarried man* for an occurrence of *bachelor* in (4) must, like (4), be true. But to say that (5) is true is to say that (3) is analytic, and hence that *bachelor* and *unmarried man* are cognitively synonymous.

Let us see what there is about the above argument that gives it its air of hocus-pocus. The condition of interchangeability *salva veritate* varies in its force with variations in the richness of the language at hand. The above argument supposes we are working with a language rich enough to contain the adverb *necessarily,* this adverb being so construed as to yield truth when and only when applied to an analytic statement. But can we condone a language which contains such an adverb? Does the adverb really make sense? To suppose that it does is to suppose that we have already made satisfactory sense of *analytic.* Then what are we so hard at work on right now?

Our argument is not flatly circular, but something like it. It has the form, figuratively speaking, of a closed curve in space.

Interchangeability *salva veritate* is meaningless until relativized to a language whose extent is specified in relevant respects. Suppose now we consider a language containing just the following materials. There is an indefinitely large stock of one-place predicates (for example, '*F*' where '*Fx*' means that *x* is a man) and many-place predicates (for example, '*G*' where '*Gxy*' means that *x* loves *y*), mostly having to do with extralogical subject matter. The rest of the language is logical. The atomic sentences consist each of a predicate followed by one or more variables '*x*', '*y*', etc.; and the complex sentences are built up of the atomic ones by truth functions ('not', 'and', 'or', etc.) and quantification. In effect, such a language also enjoys the benefits of descriptions and indeed singular terms generally, these being contextually definable in known ways. Even abstract singular terms naming classes, classes of classes, etc., are contextually definable in case the assumed stock of predicates includes the two-place predicate of class membership. Such a language can be adequate to classical mathematics and indeed to scientific discourse generally, except insofar as the latter involves debatable devices such as contrary-to-fact conditionals or modal adverbs like *necessarily.* Now a language of this type is extensional, in this sense: any two predicates which agree extensionally (that is, are true of the same objects) are interchangeable *salva veritate.*

In an extensional language, therefore, interchangeability *salva veritate* is no assurance of cognitive synonymy of the desired type. That *bachelor* and *unmarried man* are interchangeable *salva veritate* in an extensional language assures us of no more than that (3) is true. There is no assurance here that the extensional agreement of *bachelor* and *unmarried man* rests on meaning rather than merely on accidental matters of fact, as does the extensional agreement of *creature with a heart* and *creature with kidneys*.

For most purposes extensional agreement is the nearest approximation to synonymy we need care about. But the fact remains that extensional agreement falls far short of cognitive synonymy of the type required for explaining analyticity in the manner of §1. The type of cognitive synonymy required there is such as to equate the synonymy of *bachelor* and *unmarried man* with the analyticity of (3), not merely with the truth of (3).

So we must recognize that interchangeability *salva veritate,* if construed in relation to an extensional language, is not a sufficient condition of cognitive synonymy in the sense needed for deriving analyticity in the manner of §1. If a language contains an intensional adverb *necessarily* in the sense noted or other particles to the same effect, then interchangeability *salva veritate* in such a language does afford a sufficient condition of cognitive synonymy; but such a language is intelligible only insofar as the notion of analyticity is already understood in advance.

The effort to explain cognitive synonymy first, for the sake of deriving analyticity from it afterward as in §1, is perhaps the wrong approach. Instead we might try explaining analyticity somehow without appeal to cognitive synonymy. Afterward we could doubtless derive cognitive synonymy from analyticity satisfactorily enough if desired. We have seen that cognitive synonymy of *bachelor* and *unmarried man* can be explained as analyticity of (3). The same explanation works for any pair of one-place predicates, of course, and it can be extended in obvious fashion to many-place predicates. Other syntactical categories can also be accommodated in fairly parallel fashion. Singular terms may be said to be cognitively synonymous when the statement of identity formed by putting '=' between them is analytic. Statements may be said simply to be cognitively synonymous when their biconditional (the result of joining them by "if and only if") is analytic. If we care to lump all categories into a single formulation, at the expense of assuming again the notion of *word* which was appealed to early in this section, we can describe any two linguistic forms as cognitively synonymous when the two forms are interchangeable (apart from occurrences within *words*) *salve* (no longer *veritate* but) *analyticitate.* Certain technical questions arise, indeed, over cases of ambiguity or homonymy. Let us not pause for them, however, for we are already digressing. Let us, rather, turn our backs on the problem of synonymy and address ourselves anew to that of analyticity.

4. SEMANTICAL RULES

Analyticity at first seemed most naturally definable by appeal to a realm of meanings. On refinement, the appeal to meanings gave way to an appeal to synonymy of definition. But definition turned out to be a will-o'-the-wisp, and synonymy turned out to be best understood only by dint of a prior appeal to analyticity itself. So we are back at the problem of analyticity.

I do not know whether the statement "Everything green is extended" is analytic. Now does my indecision over this example really betray an incomplete understanding, an incomplete grasp of the "meanings" of *green* and *extended?* I think not. The trouble is not with *green* or *extended,* but with *analytic.*

It is often hinted that the difficulty in separating analytic statements from synthetic ones in ordinary language is due to the vagueness of ordinary language and that the distinction is clear when we have a precise artificial language with explicit "semantical rules." This, however, as I shall now attempt to show, is a confusion.

The notion of analyticity about which we are worrying is a purported relation between statements and languages: a statement S is said to be *analytic for* a language L. The problem is to make sense of this relation generally, that is, for variable S and L. The gravity of this problem is not perceptibly less for artificial languages than for natural ones. The problem of making sense of the idiom *S is analytic for L,* with variable S and L, retains its stubbornness even if we limit the range of the variable L to artificial languages. Let me now try to make this point evident.

For artificial languages and semantical rules we look naturally to the writings of Carnap. His semantical rules take various forms, and to make my point I shall have to distinguish certain of the forms. Let us suppose, to begin with, an artificial language L_0 whose semantical rules have the form explicitly of a specification, by recursion or otherwise, of all the analytic statements of L_0. The rules tell us that such and such statements, and only those, are the analytic statements of L_0. Now here the difficulty is simply that the rules contain the word *analytic,* which we do not understand! We understand what expressions the rules attribute analyticity to, but we do not understand what the rules attribute to those expressions. In short, before we can understand a rule which begins "A statement S is analytic for language L_0 if and only if . . . ," we must understand the general relative term *analytic for;* we must understand "S is analytic for L" where S and L are variables.

Alternatively we may, indeed, view the so-called rule as a conventional definition of a new simple symbol "analytic-for-L_0," which might better be written untendentiously as K so as not to seem to throw light on the interesting word *analytic.* Obviously any number of classes $K, M, N,$ etc. of statements of L_0 can be specified for various purposes or for no purpose; what does it mean to say that K, as against M, N, etc., is the class of the *analytic* statements of L_0?

By saying what statements are analytic for L_0 we explain "analytic-for-L_0" but not *analytic*, not *analytic for*. We do not begin to explain the idiom S is analytic for L with variable S and L, even if we are content to limit the range of L to the realm of artificial languages.

Actually we do know enough about the intended significance of *analytic* to know that analytic statements are supposed to be true. Let us then turn to a second form of semantical rule, which says not that such and such statements are analytic but simply that such and such statements are included among the truths. Such a rule is not subject to the criticism of containing the un-understood word *analytic;* we may grant for the sake of argument that there is no difficulty over the broader term *true*. A semantical rule of this second type, a rule of truth, is not supposed to specify all the truths of the language; it merely stipulates, recursively or otherwise, a certain multitude of statements which, along with others unspecified, are to count as true. Such a rule may be conceded to be quite clear. Derivatively, afterward, analyticity can be demarcated thus: a statement is analytic if it is (not merely true but) true according to the semantical rule.

Still there is really no progress. Instead of appealing to an unexplained word *analytic,* we are now appealing to an unexplained phrase *semantical rule.* Not every true statement which says that the statements of some class are true can count as a semantical rule—otherwise *all* truths would be *analytic* in the sense of being true according to semantical rules. Semantical rules are distinguishable, apparently, only by the fact of appearing on a page under the heading "Semantical Rules"; and this heading is itself then meaningless.

We can say, indeed, that a statement is *analytic-for-L_0* if and only if it is true according to such and such specifically appended "semantical rules," but then we find ourselves back at essentially the same case which was originally discussed: "S is analytic-for-L_0 if and only if. . . ." Once we seek to explain "S is analytic for L" generally for variable L (even allowing limitation of L to artificial languages), the explanation "true according to the semantical rules of L" is unavailing; for the relative term "semantical rule of" is as much in need of clarification, at least, as *analytic for*.

It may be instructive to compare the notion of semantical rule with that of postulate. Relative to a given set of postulates, it is easy to say what a postulate is: it is a member of the set. Relative to a given set of semantical rules, it is equally easy to say what a semantical rule is. But given simply a notation, mathematical or otherwise, and indeed as thoroughly understood a notation as you please in point of the translations or truth conditions of its statements, who can say which of its true statements rank as postulates? Obviously the question is meaningless—as meaningless as asking which points in Ohio are starting points. Any finite (or effectively specifiable infinite) selection of statements (preferably true ones, perhaps) is as much *a* set of postulates as any other. The word *postulate* is significant only relative to an act of inquiry; we apply the word to a set of statements just insofar as we happen, for the year or the moment, to be thinking of those statements in relation to the statements which can be reached from them by some set of transformations to which we have seen fit to direct our attention. Now the notion of semantical rule is as sensible and meaningful as that of postulate, if conceived in a similarly relative spirit—relative, this time, to one or another particular enterprise of schooling unconversant persons in sufficient conditions for truth of statements of some natural or artificial language *L*. But from this point of view no one signalization of a subclass of the truths of *L* is intrinsically more a semantical rule than another. If *analytic* means "true by semantical rules," no one truth of *L* is analytic to the exclusion of another.

It might conceivably be protested that an artificial language *L* (unlike a natural one) is a language in the ordinary sense *plus* a set of explicit semantical rules—the whole constituting, let us say, an ordered pair; and that the semantical rules of *L* then are specifiable simply as the second component of the pair *L*. But, by the same token and more simply, we might construe an artificial language *L* outright as an ordered pair whose second component is the class of its analytic statements. Then the analytic statements of *L* become specifiable simply as the statements in the second component of *L*. Or better still, we might just stop tugging at our bootstraps altogether.

Not all the explanations of analyticity known to Carnap and his readers have been covered explicitly in the above considerations, but the extension to other forms is not hard to see. Just one additional factor should be mentioned which sometimes enters: sometimes the semantical rules are, in effect, rules of translation into ordinary language, in which case the analytic statements of the artificial language are, in effect, recognized as such from the analyticity of their specified translations in ordinary language. Here certainly there can be no thought of an illumination of the problem of analyticity from the side of the artificial language.

From the point of view of the problem of analyticity, the notion of an artificial language with semantical rules is a *feu follet par excellence*. Semantical rules determining the analytic statements of an artificial language are of interest only insofar as we already understand the notion of analyticity; they are of no help in gaining this understanding.

Appeal to hypothetical languages of an artificially simple kind could conceivably be useful in clarifying analyticity, if the mental or behavioral or cultural factors relevant to analyticity—whatever they may be—were somehow sketched into the simplified model. But a model which takes analyticity merely as an irreducible character is unlikely to throw light on the problem of explicating analyticity.

It is obvious that truth in general depends on both language and extra-linguistic fact. The statement "Brutus killed Caesar" would be false if the world had been different in certain ways, but it would also be false if the word *killed* happened rather to have the sense of *begat*. Thus one is tempted to suppose in general that the truth of a statement is somehow analyzable into a linguistic component and a factual component. Given this supposition, it next seems reasonable that in some statements the factual component should be null; and these are the analytic statements. But, for all its a priori reasonableness, a boundary between analytic and synthetic statements simply has not been drawn. That there is such a distinction to be drawn at all is an unempirical dogma of empiricists, a metaphysical article of faith.

5. THE VERIFICATION THEORY AND REDUCTIONISM

In the course of these somber reflections we have taken a dim view first of the notion of meaning, then of the notion of cognitive synonymy, and finally of the notion of analyticity. But what, it may be asked, of the verification theory of meaning? This phrase has established itself so firmly as a catchword of empiricism that we should be very unscientific indeed not to look beneath it for a possible key to the problem of meaning and the associated problems.

The verification theory of meaning, which has been conspicuous in the literature from Peirce onward, is that the meaning of a statement is the method of empirically confirming or infirming it. An analytic statement is that limiting case which is confirmed no matter what.

As urged in §1, we can as well pass over the question of meanings as entities and move straight to sameness of meaning, or synonymy. Then what the verification theory says is that statements are synonymous if and only if they are alike in point of method of empirical confirmation or infirmation.

This is an account of cognitive synonymy not of linguistic forms generally, but of statements. However, from the concept of synonymy of statements we could derive the concept of synonymy for other linguistic forms by considerations somewhat similar to those at the end of §3. Assuming the notion of *word*, indeed, we could explain any two forms as synonymous when the putting of the one form for an occurrence of the other in any statement (apart from occurrences within "words") yields a synonymous statement. Finally, given the concept of synonymy thus for linguistic forms generally, we could define analyticity in terms of synonymy and logical truth as in §1. For that matter, we could define analyticity more simply in terms of just synonymy of statements together with logical truth; it is not necessary to appeal to synonymy of linguistic forms other than statements, for a statement may be described as analytic simply when it is synonymous with a logically true statement.

So if the verification theory can be accepted as an adequate account of statement synonymy, the notion of analyticity is saved after all. However, let us reflect. Statement synonymy is said to be likeness of method of empirical confirmation or infirmation. Just what are these methods which are to be compared for likeness? What, in other words, is the nature of the relation between a statement and the experiences which contribute to or detract from its confirmation?

The most naive view of the relation is that it is one of direct report. This is *radical reductionism.* Every meaningful statement is held to be translatable into a statement (true or false) about immediate experience. Radical reductionism, in one form or another, well antedates the verification theory of meaning explicitly so called. Thus Locke and Hume held that every idea must either originate directly in sense experience or else be compounded of ideas thus originating. Taking a hint from Tooke we might rephrase this doctrine in semantical jargon by saying that a term, to be significant at all, must be either a name of a sense datum or a compound of such names or an abbreviation of such a compound. So stated, the doctrine remains ambiguous as between sense data as sensory events and sense data as sensory qualities; and it remains vague as to the admissible ways of compounding. Moreover, the doctrine is unnecessarily and intolerably restrictive in the term-by-term critique which it imposes. More reasonably, and without yet exceeding the limits of what I have called radical reductionism, we may take full statements as our significant units—thus demanding that our statements as wholes be translatable into sense-datum language, but not that they be translatable term by term.

This emendation would unquestionably have been welcome to Locke and Hume and Tooke, but historically it had to await an important reorientation in semantics—the reorientation whereby the primary vehicle of meaning came to be seen no longer in the term but in the statement. This reorientation, seen in Bentham and Frege, underlies Russell's concept of incomplete symbols defined in use, also it is implicit in the verification theory of meaning, since the objects of verification are statements.

Radical reductionism, conceived now with statements as units, set itself the task of specifying a sense-datum language and showing how to translate the rest of significant discourse, statement by statement, into it. Carnap embarked on this project in the *Aufbau.*

The language which Carnap adopted as his starting point was not sense-datum language in the narrowest conceivable sense, for it included also the notations of logic, up through higher set theory. In effect, it included the whole language of pure mathematics. The ontology implicit in it (that is, the range of values of its variables) embraced not only sensory events but classes, classes of classes, and so on. Empiricists there are who would boggle at such prodigality. Carnap's starting point is very parsimonious, however, in its extralogical or sensory part. In a series of constructions in which he exploits the resources of modern logic with much ingenuity, Carnap succeeds in defining a wide array of important additional sensory concepts which, but for his constructions, one would not have dreamed were definable on so slender a basis. He was the first empiricist who, not content with asserting the reducibility of science to terms of immediate experience, took serious steps toward carrying out the reduction.

If Carnap's starting point is satisfactory, still his constructions were, as he himself stressed, only a fragment of the full program. The construction of even the simplest statements about the physical world was left in a sketchy state. Carnap's suggestions on this subject were, despite their sketchiness, very suggestive. He explained spatio-temporal point-instants as quadruples of real numbers and envisaged assignment of sense qualities to point-instants according to certain canons. Roughly summarized, the plan was that qualities should be assigned to point-instants in such a way as to achieve the laziest world compatible with our experience. The principle of least action was to be our guide in constructing a world from experience.

Carnap did not seem to recognize, however, that his treatment of physical objects fell short of reduction not merely through sketchiness, but in principle. Statements of the form "Quality q is at point-instant $x,y;z;t$" were, according to his canons, to be apportioned truth values in such a way as to maximize and minimize certain overall features, and with the growth of experience, the truth values were to be progressively revised in the same spirit. I think this is a good schematization (deliberately oversimplified, to be sure) of what science really does; but it provides no indication, not even the sketchiest, of how a statement of the form "Quality q is at $z,y;x;t$" could ever be translated into Carnap's initial language of sense data and logic. The connective *is at* remains an added undefined connective; the canons counsel us in its use but not in its elimination.

Carnap seems to have appreciated this point afterward, for in his later writings he abandoned all notion of the translatability of statements about the physical world into statements about immediate experience. Reductionism in its radical form has long since ceased to figure in his philosophy.

But the dogma of reductionism has, in a subtler and more tenuous form, continued to influence the thought of empiricists. The notion lingers that to each statement, or each synthetic statement, there is associated a unique range of possible sensory events such that the occurrence of any of them would add to the likelihood of truth of the statement, and that there is associated also another unique range of possible sensory events whose occurrence would detract from that likelihood. This notion is, of course, implicit in the verification theory of meaning.

The dogma of reductionism survives in the supposition that each statement, taken in isolation from its fellows, can admit of confirmation or infirmation at all. My countersuggestion, issuing essentially from Carnap's doctrine of the physical world in the *Aufbau,* is that our statements about the external world face the tribunal of sense experience not individually but only as a corporate body.

The dogma of reductionism, even in its attenuated form, is intimately connected with the other dogma, that there is a cleavage between the analytic and the synthetic. Indeed, we have found ourselves led from the latter problem to the former through the verification theory of meaning. More directly, the one dogma clearly supports the other in this way: as long as it is taken to be significant in general to speak of the confirmation and infirmation of a statement, it seems significant to speak also of a limiting kind of statement which is vacuously confirmed, ipso facto, come what may; and such a statement is analytic.

The two dogmas are, indeed, at root identical. We lately reflected that in general the truth of statements does obviously depend both on language and extralinguistic fact and noted that this obvious circumstance carries in its train, not logically but all too naturally, a feeling that the truth of a statement is somehow analyzable into a linguistic component and a factual component. The factual component must, if we are empiricists, boil down to a range of confirmatory experiences. In the extreme case where the linguistic component is all that matters, a true statement is analytic. But I hope we are now impressed with how stubbornly the distinction between analytic and synthetic has resisted any straightforward drawing. I am impressed also, apart from prefabricated examples of black and white balls in an urn, with how baffling the problem has always been of arriving at any explicit theory of the empirical confirmation of a synthetic statement. My present suggestion is that it is nonsense—and the root of much nonsense—to speak of a linguistic component and a factual component in the truth of any individual statement. Taken collectively, science has its double dependence upon language and experience; but this duality is not significantly traceable into the statements of science taken one by one.

The idea of defining a symbol in use was, as remarked, an advance over the impossible term-by-term empiricism of Locke and Hume. The statement, rather than the term, came with Bentham to be recognized as the unit accountable to an empiricist critique. But what I am now urging is that even in taking the statement as unit we have drawn our grid too finely. The unit of empirical significance is the whole of science.

6. EMPIRICISM WITHOUT THE DOGMAS

The totality of our so-called knowledge or beliefs, from the most casual matters of geography and history to the profoundest laws of atomic physics or even of pure mathematics and logic, is a manmade fabric which impinges on experience only along the edges. Or, to change the figure, total science is like a field of force whose boundary conditions are experience. A conflict with experience at the periphery occasions readjustments in the interior of the field. Truth values have to be redistributed over some of our statements. Reevaluation of some statements entails reevaluation of others, because of their logical interconnections—the logical laws being, in turn, simply certain further statements of the system, certain further elements of the field. Having reevaluated one statement we must reevaluate some others, which may be statements logically connected with the first or may be the statements of logical connections themselves. But the total field is so underdetermined by its boundary conditions, experience, that there is much latitude of choice as to what statements to reevaluate in the light of any single contrary experience. No particular experiences are linked with any particular statements in the interior of the field, except indirectly through considerations of equilibrium affecting the field as a whole.

If this view is right, it is misleading to speak of the empirical content of an individual statement—especially if it is a statement at all remote from the experiential periphery of the field. Furthermore it becomes folly to seek a boundary between synthetic statements, which hold contingently on experience, and analytic statements, which hold come what may. Any statement can be held true come what may, if we make drastic enough adjustments elsewhere in the system. Even a statement very close to the periphery can be held true in the face of recalcitrant experience by pleading hallucination or by amending certain statements of the kind called logical laws. Conversely, by the same token, no statement is immune to revision. Revision even of the logical law of the excluded middle has been proposed as a means of simplifying quantum mechanics; and what difference is there in principle between such a shift and the shift whereby Kepler superseded Ptolemy, or Einstein Newton, or Darwin Aristotle?

For vividness I have been speaking in terms of varying distances from a sensory periphery. Let me try now to clarify this notion without metaphor. Certain statements, though *about* physical objects and not sense experience, seem peculiarly germane to sense experience—and in a selective way: some statements to some experiences, others to others. Such statements, especially germane to particular experiences, I picture as near the periphery. But in this relation of "germaneness" I envisage nothing more than a loose association reflecting the relative likelihood, in practice, of our choosing one statement rather than another for revision in the event of recalcitrant experience. For example, we can imagine recalcitrant experiences to which we would surely be inclined to accommodate our system by reevaluating just the statement that there are brick houses on Elm Street, together with related statements on the same topic. We can imagine other recalcitrant experiences to which we would be inclined to accommodate our system by reevaluating just the statement that there are no centaurs, along with kindred statements. A recalcitrant experience can, I have urged, be accommodated by any of various alternative reevaluations in various alternative quarters of the total system; but, in the cases which we are now imagining, our natural tendency to disturb the total system as little as possible would lead us to focus our revisions upon these specific statements concerning brick houses or centaurs. These statements are felt, therefore, to have a sharper empirical reference than highly theoretical statements of physics or logic or ontology. The latter statements may be thought of as relatively centrally located within the total network, meaning merely that little preferential connection with any particular sense data obtrudes itself.

As an empiricist I continue to think of the conceptual scheme of science as a tool, ultimately, for predicting future experience in the light of past experience. Physical objects are conceptually imported into the situation as convenient intermediaries—not by definition in terms of experience, but simply as irreducible posits comparable, epistemologically, to the gods of Homer. For my part I do, qua lay physicist, believe in physical objects and not in Homer's gods; and I consider it a scientific error to believe otherwise. But in point of epistemological footing the physical objects and the gods differ only in degree and not in kind. Both sorts of entities enter our conception only as cultural posits. The myth of physical objects is epistemologically superior to most in that it has proved more efficacious than other myths as a device for working a manageable structure into the flux of experience.

Positing does not stop with macroscopic physical objects. Objects at the atomic level are posited to make the laws of macroscopic objects, and ultimately the laws of experience, simpler and more manageable; and we need not expect or demand full definition of atomic and subatomic entities in terms of macroscopic ones, any more than definition of macroscopic things in terms of sense data. Science is a continuation of common sense, and it continues the commonsense expedient of swelling ontology to simplify theory.

Physical objects, small and large, are not the only posits. Forces are another example; indeed we are told nowadays that the boundary between energy and matter is obsolete. Moreover, the abstract entities which are the substance of mathematics—ultimately classes and classes of classes and so on up—are another posit in the same spirit. Epistemologically these are myths on the same footing with physical objects and gods, neither better nor worse except for differences in the degree to which they expedite our dealings with sense experiences.

The overall algebra of rational and irrational numbers is underdetermined by the algebra of rational numbers, but is smoother and more convenient, and it includes the algebra of rational numbers as a jagged or gerrymandered part. Total science, mathematical and natural and human, is similarly but more extremely underdetermined by experience. The edge of the system must be kept squared with experience; the rest, with all its elaborate myths or fictions, has as its objective the simplicity of laws.

Ontological questions, under this view, are on a par with questions of natural science. Consider the question whether to countenance classes as entities. This, as I have argued elsewhere, is the question whether to quantify with respect to variables which take classes as values. Now Carnap [6] has maintained that this is a question not of matters of fact but of choosing a convenient language form, a convenient conceptual scheme or framework for science. With this I agree, but only on the proviso that the same be conceded regarding scientific hypotheses generally. Carnap ([6], p. 32n) has recognized that he is able to preserve a double standard for ontological questions and scientific hypotheses only by assuming an absolute distinction between the analytic and the synthetic. I need not say again that this is a distinction which I reject.

The issue over there being classes seems more a question of convenient conceptual scheme; the issue over there being centaurs, or brick houses on Elm Street, seems more a question of fact. But I have been urging that this difference is only one of degree, and that it turns upon our vaguely pragmatic inclination to adjust one strand of the fabric of science rather than another in accommodating some particular recalcitrant experience. Conservatism figures in such choices, and so does the quest for simplicity.

Carnap, Lewis, and others take a pragmatic stand on the question of choosing between language forms, scientific frameworks, but their pragmatism leaves off at the imagined boundary between the analytic and the synthetic. In repudiating such a boundary I espouse a more thorough pragmatism. Each man is given a scientific heritage plus a continuing barrage of sensory stimulation; and the considerations which guide him in warping his scientific heritage to fit his continuing sensory promptings are, where rational, pragmatic.

IN
DEFENSE
OF A
DOGMA*

H. P. Grice
and P. F. Strawson

In his article "Two Dogmas of Empiricism," Professor Quine advances a number of criticisms of the supposed distinction between analytic and synthetic statements, and of other associated notions. It is, as he says, a distinction which he rejects. We wish to show that his criticisms of the distinction do not justify his rejection of it.

There are many ways in which a distinction can be criticized, and more than one in which it can be rejected. It can be criticized for not being a sharp distinction (for admitting of cases which do not fall clearly on either side of it), or on the ground that the terms in which it is customarily drawn are ambiguous (have more than one meaning), or on the ground that it is confused (the different meanings being habitually conflated). Such criticisms alone would scarcely amount to a rejection of the distinction. They would, rather, be a prelude to clarification. It is not this sort of criticism which Quine makes.

Again, a distinction can be criticized on the ground that it is not useful. It can be said to be useless for certain purposes, or useless altogether, and, perhaps, pedantic. One who criticizes in this way may indeed be said to reject a distinction, but in a sense which also requires him to acknowledge its existence. He simply declares he can get on without it. But Quine's rejection of the analytic-synthetic distinction appears to be more radical than this. He would certainly say he could get on without the distinction, but not in a sense which would commit him to acknowledge its existence.

Or again, one could criticize the way or ways in which a distinction is customarily expounded or explained on the ground that these explanations did not

---

* From *The Philosophical Review,* vol. 65, 1956. Reprinted by permission of *The Philosophical Review* and the authors.

make it really clear. And Quine certainly makes such criticisms in the case of the analytic-synthetic distinction.

But he does, or seems to do, a great deal more. He declares, or seems to declare, not merely that the distinction is useless or inadequately clarified, but also that it is altogether illusory, that the belief in its existence is a philosophical mistake. "That there is such a distinction to be drawn at all," he says, "is an unempirical dogma of empiricists, a metaphysical article of faith." It is the existence of the distinction that he here calls in question, so his rejection of it would seem to amount to a denial of its existence.

Evidently such a position of extreme skepticism about a distinction is not, in general, justified merely by criticisms, however just in themselves, of philosophical attempts to clarify it. There are doubtless plenty of distinctions, drawn in philosophy and outside it, which still await adequate philosophical elucidation, but which few would want on this account to declare illusory. Quine's article, however, does not consist wholly, though it does consist largely, in criticizing attempts at elucidation. He does try also to diagnose the causes of the belief in the distinction, and he offers some positive doctrine, acceptance of which he represents as incompatible with this belief. If there is any general prior presumption in favor of the existence of the distinction, it seems that Quine's radical rejection of it must rest quite heavily on this part of his article, since the force of any such presumption is not even impaired by philosophical failures to clarify a distinction so supported.

Is there such a presumption in favor of the distinction's existence? Prima facie, it must be admitted that there is. An appeal to philosophical tradition is perhaps unimpressive and is certainly unnecessary. But it is worth pointing out that Quine's objection is not simply to the words "analytic" and "synthetic," but to a distinction which they are supposed to express, and which at different times philosophers have supposed themselves to be expressing by means of such pairs of words or phrases as "necessary" and "contingent," "a priori" and "empirical," "truth of reason" and "truth of fact"; so Quine is certainly at odds with a philosophical tradition which is long and not wholly disreputable. But there is no need to appeal only to tradition; for there is also present practice. We can appeal, that is, to the fact that those who use the terms "analytic" and "synthetic" do to a very considerable extent agree in the applications they make of them. They apply the term "analytic" to more or less the same cases, withhold it from more or less the same cases, and hesitate over more or less the same cases. This agreement extends not only to cases which they have been *taught* so to characterize, but to new cases. In short, "analytic" and "synthetic" have a more or less established philosophical *use*. This seems to suggest that it is absurd, even senseless, to say that there is no such distinction, for, in general, if a pair of contrasting expressions are habitually and generally used in application to the same cases, *where these cases do not form a closed list,* this is a sufficient

211

condition for saying that there are *kinds* of cases to which the expressions apply, and nothing more is needed for them to mark a distinction.

In view of the possibility of this kind of argument, one may begin to doubt whether Quine really holds the extreme thesis which his words encourage one to attribute to him. It is for this reason that we made the attribution tentative. For on at least one natural interpretation of this extreme thesis, when we say of something true that it is analytic and of another true thing that it is synthetic, it simply never is the case that we thereby mark a distinction between them. And this view seems terribly difficult to reconcile with the fact of an established philosophical usage (that is, of general agreement in application in an open class). For this reason, Quine's thesis might be better represented not as the thesis that there is *no difference at all* marked by the use of these expressions, but as the thesis that the nature of, and reasons for, the difference or differences are totally misunderstood by those who use the expressions, that the stories they tell themselves *about* the difference are full of illusion.

We think Quine might be prepared to accept this amendment. If so, it could, in the following way, be made the basis of something like an answer to the argument which prompted it. Philosophers are notoriously subject to illusion, and to mistaken theories. Suppose there were a particular mistaken theory about language or knowledge such that, seen in the light of this theory, some statements (or propositions or sentences) appeared to have a characterisitc which no statements really have, or even, perhaps, which it does not make sense to suppose that any statement has, and which no one who was not consciously or subconsciously influenced by this theory would ascribe to any statement. And suppose that there were other statements which, seen in this light, did not appear to have this characteristic, and others again which presented an uncertain appearance. Then philosophers who were under the influence of this theory would tend to mark the supposed presence or absence of this characteristic by a pair of contrasting expressions, say "analytic" and "synthetic." Now in these circumstances it still could not be said that there was no distinction at all being marked by the use of these expressions, for there would be at least the distinction we have just described (the distinction, namely, between those statements which appeared to have and those which appeared to lack a certain characteristic), and there might well be other assignable differences, too, which would account for the difference in appearance; but it certainly could be said that *the* difference these philosophers supposed themselves to be marking by the use of the expressions simply did not exist, and perhaps also (supposing the characteristic in question to be one which it was absurd to ascribe to any statement) that these expressions, as so used, were senseless or without meaning. We should only have to suppose that such a mistaken theory was very plausible and attractive, in order to reconcile the fact of an established philosophical usage for a pair of contrasting terms with the claim that *the* distinction which the terms purported to mark did not exist at all, though not with the claim that there simply did not exist a difference of any kind between the classes of statements so characterized. We think that the former claim would probably be sufficient for Quine's purposes. But to establish such a claim on the sorts of grounds we have indicated evidently requires a great deal more argument than is involved in showing that certain explanations of a term do not measure up to certain requirements of adequacy in philosophical clarification—and not only more argument, but argument of a very different kind. For it would surely be too harsh to maintain that the *general* presumption is that philosophical distinctions embody the kind of illusion we have described. On the whole, it seems that philosophers are prone to make too few distinctions rather than too many. It is their assimilations, rather than their distinctions, which tend to be spurious.

So far we have argued as if the prior presumption in favor of the existence of the distinction which Quine questions rested solely on the fact of an agreed *philosophical* usage for the terms "analytic" and "synthetic." A presumption with only this basis could no doubt be countered by a strategy such as we have just outlined. But, in fact, if we are to accept Quine's account of the matter, the presumption in question is not only so based. For among the notions which belong to the analyticity group is one which Quine calls "cognitive synonymy," and in terms of which he allows that the notion of analyticity could at any rate be formally explained. Unfortunately, he adds, the notion of cognitive synonymy is just as unclarified as that of analyticity. To say that two expressions x and y are cognitively synonymous seems to correspond, at any rate roughly, to what we should ordinarily express by saying that x and y have the same meaning or that x means the same as y. If Quine is to be consistent in his adherence to the extreme thesis, then it appears that he must maintain not only that the distinction we suppose ourselves to be marking by the use of the terms "analytic" and "synthetic" does not exist, but also that the distinction we suppose ourselves to be marking by the use of the expressions "means the same as," "does not mean the same as" does not exist either. At least, he must maintain this insofar as the notion of *meaning the same as,* in its application to predicate expressions, is supposed to differ from and go beyond the notion of *being true of just the same objects as.* (This latter notion—which we might call that of "coextensionality"—he is prepared to allow to be intelligible, though, as he rightly says, it is not sufficient for the explanation of analyticity.) Now since he cannot claim this time that the pair of expressions in question (namely, "means the same," "does not mean the same") is the special property of philosophers, the strategy outlined above, of countering the presumption in favor of their marking a genuine distinction, is not available here (or is at least enormously less plausible.) Yet the denial that the distinction (taken as different from the distinction between the coextensional and the noncoextensional) really exists, is extremely paradoxical. It involves saying, for example, that anyone who seriously remarks that "bachelor" means the same as "unmarried man" but that "creature with kidneys" does not mean the same as "creature with a heart"—supposing the last two expressions to be coextensional—*either* is not, in fact, drawing attention to any distinction at all between the relations between the members of each pair of expressions *or* is making a philosophical mistake about the nature of the distinction between them. In either case, what he says, taken as he intends it to be taken, is senseless or absurd. More generally, it involves saying that it is always senseless or absurd to make a statement of the form "Predicates *x* and *y,* in fact, apply to the same objects, but do not have the same meaning." But the paradox is more violent than this. For we frequently talk of the presence or absence of relations of synonymy between kinds of expressions—for example, conjunctions, particles of many kinds, whole sentences—where there does not appear to be any obvious substitute for the ordinary notion of synonymy, in the way in which coextensionality is said to be a substitute for synonymy of predicates. Is all such talk meaningless? Is all talk of correct or incorrect *translation* of sentences of one language into sentences of another meaningless? It is hard to believe that it is. But if we do successfully make the effort to believe it, we have still harder renunciations before us. If talk of sentence synonymy is meaningless, then it seems that talk of sentences having a meaning at all must be meaningless too. For if it made sense to talk of a sentence having a meaning, or meaning something, then presumably it would make sense to ask "What does it mean?" And if it made sense to ask "What does it mean?" of a sentence, then sentence synonymy could be roughly defined as follows: Two sentences are synonymous if and only if any true answer to the question "What does it mean?" asked of one of them, is a true answer to the same question, asked of the other. We do not, of course, claim any clarifying power for this definition. We want only to point out that if we are to give up the notion of sentence synonymy as senseless, we must give up the notion of sentence significance (of a sentence having meaning) as senseless too. But then perhaps we might as well give up the notion of sense. It seems clear that we have here a typical example of a philosopher's paradox. Instead of examining the actual use that we make of the notion of *meaning the same,* the philosopher measures it by some perhaps inappropriate standard (in this case some standard of clarifiability), and because it falls short of this standard, or seems to do so, denies its reality, declares it illusory.

We have argued so far that there is a strong presumption in favor of the existence of the distinction, or distinctions, which Quine challenges—a presumption resting both on philosophical and on ordinary usage—and that this presumption is not in the least shaken by the fact, if it is a fact, that the distinctions in question have not been, in some sense, adequately clarified. It is perhaps time to look at what Quine's notion of adequate clarification is.

The main theme of his article can be roughly summarized as follows. There is a certain circle or family of expressions, of which "analytic" is one, such that

214

if any one member of the circle could be taken to be satisfactorily understood or explained, then other members of the circle could be verbally, and hence satisfactorily, explained in terms of it. Other members of the family are: "self-contradictory" (in a broad sense), "necessary," "synonymous," "semantical rule," and perhaps (but again in a broad sense) "definition." The list could be added to. Unfortunately each member of the family is in as great need of explanation as any other. We give some sample quotations: "The notion of self-contradictoriness (in the required broad sense of inconsistency) stands in exactly the same need of clarification as does the notion of analyticity itself." Again, Quine speaks of "a notion of synonymy which is in no less need of clarification than anlyticity itself." Again, of the adverb "necessarily" as a candidate for use in the explanation of synonymy, he says, "Does the adverb *really make sense?* To suppose that it does is to suppose that we have already *made satisfactory sense of 'analytic.'* " To make "satisfactory sense" of one of these expressions would seem to involve two things. (1) It would seem to involve providing an explanation which does not incorporate any expression belonging to the family circle. (2) It would seem that the explanation provided must be of the same general character as those rejected explanations which do incorporate members of the family circle, (that is, it must specify some feature common and peculiar to all cases to which, for example, the word *analytic* is to be applied; it must have the same general form as an explanation beginning, "a statement is analytic if and only if . . ."). It is true that Quine does not explicitly state the second requirement; but since he does not even consider the question whether any other kind of explanation would be relevant, it seems reasonable to attribute it to him. If we take these two conditions together and generalize the result, it would seem that Quine requires of a satisfactory explanation of an expression that it should take the form of a pretty strict definition but should not make use of any member of a group of interdefinable terms to which the expression belongs. We may well begin to feel that a satisfactory explanation is hard to come by. The other element in Quine's position is one we have already commented on in general, before inquiring what (according to him) is to count as a satisfactory explanation. It is the step from "We have not made satisfactory sense (provided a satisfactory explanation) of *x*" to "*x* does not make sense."

It would seem fairly clearly unreasonable to insist *in general* that the availability of a satisfactory explanation in the sense sketched above is a necessary condition of an expression's making sense. It is perhaps dubious whether *any* such explanations can *ever* be given. (The hope that they can be is, or was, the hope of reductive analysis in general.) Even if such explanations can be given in some cases, it would be pretty generally agreed that there are other cases in which they cannot. One might think, for example, of the group of expressions which includes "morally wrong," "blameworthy," "breach of moral rules," and so on, or of the group which includes the propositional connectives and the

215

words "true" and "false," "statement," "fact," "denial," "assertion." Few people would want to say that the expressions belonging to either of these groups were senseless on the ground that they have not been formally defined (or even on the ground that it was impossible formally to define them) except in terms of members of the same group. It might, however, be said that while the unavailability of a satisfactory explanation in the special sense described was not a *generally* sufficient reason for declaring that a given expression was senseless, it was a sufficient reason in the case of the expressions of the analyticity group. But anyone who said this would have to advance a reason for discriminating in this way against the expressions of this group. The only plausible reason for being harder on these expressions than on others is a refinement on a consideration which we have already had before us. It starts from the point that "analytic" and "synthetic" themselves are technical philosophical expressions. To the rejoinder that other expressions of the family concerned, such as "means the same as" or "is inconsistent with" or "self-contradictory," are not at all technical expressions, but are common property, the reply would doubtless be that, to qualify for inclusion in the family circle, these expressions have to be used in specially adjusted and precise senses (or pseudo-senses) which they do not ordinarily possess. It is the fact, then, that all the terms belonging to the circle are *either* technical terms *or* ordinary terms used in specially adjusted senses that might be held to justify us in being particularly suspicious of the claims of members of the circle to have any sense at all and hence to justify us in requiring them to pass a test for significance which would admittedly be too stringent if generally applied. This point has some force, though we doubt if the special adjustments spoken of are in every case as considerable as it suggests. (This seems particularly doubtful in the case of the word "inconsistent"—a perfectly good member of the non-technician's meta-logical vocabulary.) But though the point has some force, it does not have whatever force would be required to justify us in insisting that the expressions concerned should pass exactly that test for significance which is in question. The fact, if it is a fact, that the expressions cannot be explained in precisely the way which Quine seems to require, does not mean that they cannot be explained at all. There is no need to try to pass them off as expressing innate ideas. They can be and are explained, though in other and less formal ways than that which Quine considers. (And the fact that they are so explained fits with the facts, first, that there is a generally agreed philosophical use for them, and second, that this use is technical or specially adjusted.) To illustrate the point briefly for one member of the analyticity family, let us suppose we are trying to explain to someone the notion of *logical impossibility* (a member of the family which Quine presumably regards as no clearer than any of the others), and we decide to do it by bringing out the contrast between logical and natural (or causal) impossibility. We might take as our examples the logical impossibility of a child of three being an adult, and the natural impossibility of a child of three understanding Russell's Theory of Types. We might instruct our pupil to imagine two conversations, one of which begins by someone (X) making the claim:

(1) "My neighbor's three-year-old child understands Russell's Theory of Types."

and the other of which begins by someone (Y) making the claim:

(1') "My neighbor's three-year-old child is an adult."

It would not be inappropriate to reply to X, taking the remark as a hyperbole:

(2) "You mean the child is a particularly bright lad."

If X were to say:

(3) "No, I mean what I say—he really does understand it."

one might be inclined to reply:

(4) "I don't believe you—the thing's impossible."

But if the child were then produced and did (as one knows he would not) expound the theory correctly, answer questions on it, criticize it, and so on, one would in the end be forced to acknowledge that the claim was literally true and that the child was a prodigy. Now consider one's reaction to Y's claim. To begin with, it might be somewhat similar to the previous case. One might say:

(2') "You mean he's uncommonly sensible or very advanced for his age."

If Y replies:

(3') "No, I mean what I say."

we might reply:

(4') "Perhaps you mean that he won't grow any more, or that he's a sort of freak, that he's already fully developed."

Y replies:

(5') "No, he's not a freak, he's just an adult."

At this stage—or possibly if we are patient, a little later—we shall be inclined to say that we just don't understand what Y is saying, and to suspect that he just

217

does not know the meaning of some of the words he is using. For unless he is prepared to admit that he is using words in a figurative or unusual sense, we shall say, not that we don't believe him, but that his words have *no* sense. And whatever kind of creature is ultimately produced for our inspection, it will not lead us to say that what Y said was literally true, but at most to say that we now see what he meant. As a summary of the difference between the two imaginary conversations, we might say that in both cases we would tend to begin by supposing that the other speaker was using words in a figurative or unusual or restricted way; but in the face of his repeated claim to be speaking literally, it would be appropriate in the first case to say that we did not believe him and in the second case to say that we did not understand him. If, like Pascal, we thought it prudent to prepare against very long chances, we should in the first case know what to prepare for; in the second, we should have no idea.

We give this as an example of just one type of informal explanation which we might have recourse to in the case of one notion of the analyticity group. (We do not wish to suggest it is the only type.) Further examples, with different though connected types of treatment, might be necessary to teach our pupil the use of the notion of logical impossibility in its application to more complicated cases—if indeed he did not pick it up from the one case. Now, of course, this type of explanation does not yield a formal statement of necessary and sufficient conditions for the application of the notion concerned. So it does not fulfill one of the conditions which Quine seems to require of a satisfactory explanation. On the other hand, it does appear to fulfill the other. It breaks out of the family circle. The distinction in which we ultimately come to rest is that between not believing something and not understanding something, or between incredulity yielding to conviction and incomprehension yielding to comprehension. It would be rash to maintain that *this* distinction does not need clarification; but it would be absurd to maintain that it does not exist. In the face of the availability of this informal type of explanation for the notions of the analyticity group, the fact that they have not received another type of explanation (which it is dubious whether *any* expressions *ever* receive) seems a wholly inadequate ground for the conclusion that the notions are pseudo-notions, that the expressions which purport to express them have no sense. To say this is not to deny that it would be philosophically desirable, and a proper object of philosophical endeavor, to find a more illuminating general characterization of the notions of this group than any that has been so far given. But the question of how, if at all, this can be done is quite irrelevant to the question of whether or not the expressions which belong to the circle have an intelligible use and mark genuine distinctions.

So far we have tried to show that sections 1 to 4 of Quine's article—the burden of which is that the notions of the analyticity group have not been satisfactorily explained—do not establish the extreme thesis for which he appears to be arguing. It remains to be seen whether sections 5 and 6, in which diagnosis and positive theory are offered, are any more successful. But before we turn to them, there are two further points worth making which arise out of the first two sections.

1. One concerns what Quine says about *definition* and *synonymy*. He remarks that definition does not, as some have supposed, "hold the key to synonymy and analyticity," since "definition, except in the extreme case of the explicitly conventional introduction of new notations, hinges on prior relations of synonymy." But now consider what he says of these extreme cases. He says: "Here the definiendum becomes synonymous with the definiens simply because it has been created expressly for the purpose of being synonymous with the definiens. Here we have a really transparent case of synonymy created by definition; would that all species of synonymy were as intelligible." Now if we are to take these words of Quine seriously, then his position *as a whole* is incoherent. It is like the position of a man to whom we are trying to explain, say, the idea of one thing fitting into another thing, or two things fitting together, and who says: "I can understand what it means to say that one thing fits into another, or that two things fit together, in the case where one was specially made to fit the other, but I cannot understand what it means to say this in any other case." Perhaps we should not take Quine's words here too seriously. But if not, then we have the right to ask him exactly what state of affairs he thinks *is* brought about by explicit definition, what relation between expressions *is* established by this procedure, and why he thinks it unintelligible to suggest that the same (or a closely analogous) state of affairs, or relation, should exist in the absence of this procedure. For our part, we should be inclined to take Quine's words (or some of them) seriously, and reverse his conclusions; and maintain that the notion of synonymy by explicit convention would be unintelligible if the notion of synonymy by usage were not presupposed. There cannot be law where there is not custom, or rules where there are not practices (though perhaps we can understand better what a practice is by looking at a rule).

2. The second point arises out of a paragraph on page 32 of Quine's book. We quote:

> I do not know whether the statement "Everything green is extended" is analytic. Now does my indecision over this example really betray an incomplete understanding, an incomplete grasp, of the "meanings" of "green" and "extended"? I think not. The trouble is not with "green" or "extended," but with "analytic."

If, as Quine says, the trouble is with "analytic," then the trouble should doubtless disappear when "analytic" is removed. So let us remove it and replace it with a word which Quine himself has contrasted favorably with "analytic" in respect of perspicuity—the word "true." Does the indecision at once disappear? We think not. The indecision over "analytic" (and equally, in this case, the indecision over "true") arises, of course, from a further indecision, that which we feel when confronted with such questions as "Should we count a *point* of green light as *extended* or not?" As is frequent enough in such cases, the hesitation arises from the fact that boundaries of application of words are not determined by usage in all possible directions. But the example Quine has chosen is particularly unfortunate for his thesis, in that it is only too evident that our hesitations are not *here* attributable to obscurities in "analytic." It would be possible to choose other examples in which we should hesitate between "analytic" and "synthetic" and have few qualms about "true." But no more in these cases than in the sample case does the hesitation necessarily imply any obscurity in the notion of analyticity; since the hesitation would be sufficiently accounted for by the same or similar kind of indeterminacy in the relations between the words occurring within the statement about which the question, whether it is analytic or synthetic, is raised.

Let us now consider briefly Quine's positive theory of the relations between the statements we accept as true or reject as false, on one hand, and the "experiences" in the light of which we do this accepting and rejecting on the other. This theory is boldly sketched rather than precisely stated. We shall merely extract from it two assertions, one of which Quine clearly takes to be incompatible with acceptance of the distinction between analytic and synthetic statements, and the other of which he regards as barring one way to an explanation of that distinction. We shall seek to show that the first assertion is not incompatible with acceptance of the distinction, but is, on the contrary, most intelligibly interpreted in a way quite consistent with it, and that the second assertion leaves the way open to just the kind of explanation which Quine thinks it precludes. The two assertions are the following:

(1) It is an illusion to suppose that there is any class of accepted statements the members of which are, in principle, "immune from revision" in the light of experience, for example, any that we accept as true and must continue to accept as true whatever happens.

(2) It is an illusion to suppose that an individual statement, taken in isolation from its fellows, can admit of confirmation or disconfirmation at all. There is no particular statement such that a particular experience or set of experiences decides once for all whether that statement is true or false, independently of our attitudes to all other statements.

The apparent connection between these two doctrines may be summed up as follows. Whatever our experience may be, it is, in principle, possible to hold on to or reject any particular statement we like so long as we are prepared to make extensive enough revisions elsewhere in our system of beliefs. In practice, our choices are governed largely by considerations of convenience: we wish our system to be as simple as possible, but we also wish disturbances to it, as it exists, to be as small as possible.

The apparent relevance of these doctrines to the analytic-synthetic distinction is obvious in the first case and less so in the second.

1. Since it is an illusion to suppose that the characteristic of immunity in principle from revision, come what may, belongs, or could belong, to any statement, it is an illusion to suppose that there is a distinction to be drawn between statements which possess this characteristic and statements which lack it. Yet, Quine suggests, this is precisely the distinction which those who use the terms *analytic* and *synthetic* suppose themselves to be drawing. Quine's view would perhaps also be (though he does not say this explicitly in the article under consideration) that those who believe in the distinction are inclined at least sometimes to mistake the characteristic of strongly resisting revision (which belongs to beliefs very centrally situated in the system) for the mythical characteristic of total immunity from revision.

2. The connection between the second doctrine and the analytic-synthetic distinction runs, according to Quine, through the verification theory of meaning. He says: "If the verification theory can be accepted as an adequate account of statement synonymy, the notion of analyticity is saved after all." In the first place, two statements might be said to be synonymous if and only if any experiences which contribute to, or detract from, the confirmation of one contribute to, or detract from, the confirmation of the other, to the same degree; and in the second place, synonymy could be used to explain analyticity. But, Quine seems to argue, acceptance of any such account of synonymy can rest only on the mistaken belief that individual statements, taken in isolation from their fellows, can admit of confirmation or disconfirmation at all. As soon as we give up the idea of a set of experiential truth conditions for each statement taken separately, we must give up the idea of explaining synonymy in terms of identity of such sets.

Now to show that the relations between these doctrines and the analytic-synthetic distinction are not as Quine supposes. Let us take the second doctrine first. It is easy to see that acceptance of the second doctrine would not compel one to abandon, but only to revise, the suggested explanation of synonymy. Quine does not deny that individual statements are regarded as confirmed or disconfirmed, are in fact rejected or accepted, in the light of experience. He denies only that these relations between single statements and experience hold independently of our attitudes to *other* statements. He means that experience can confirm or disconfirm an individual statement, only given certain assumptions about the truth or falsity of other statements. When we are faced with a "recalcitrant experience," he says, we always have a choice of what statements to amend. What we have to renounce is determined by what we are anxious to keep. This view, however, requires only a slight modification of the definition of statement synonymy in terms of confirmation and disconfirmation. All we have to say now is that two statements are synonymous if and only if any experiences which, *on certain assumptions about the truth values of other statements,* confirm or disconfirm one of the pair, also, *on the same assumptions,* confirm or disconfirm the other to the same degree. More generally, Quine wishes to substitute for what he conceives to be an overly simple picture of the confirmation relations between particular statements and particular experiences, the idea of a looser relation which he calls "germaneness." But however loosely *germaneness* is to be understood, it would apparently continue to make sense to speak of two statements as standing in the same germaneness relation to the same particular experiences. So Quine's views are not only consistent with, but even suggest, an amended account of statement synonymy along these lines. We are not, of course, concerned with defending such an account or even with stating it with any precision. We are only concerned with showing that acceptance of Quine's doctrine of empirical confirmation does not, as he says it does, entail giving up the attempt to define statement synonymy in terms of confirmation.

Now for the doctrine that there is no statement which is in principle immune from revision, no statement which might not be given up in the face of experience. Acceptance of this doctrine is quite consistent with adherence to the distinction between analytic and synthetic statements. Only, the adherent of *this* distinction must also insist on another; on the distinction between that kind of giving up which consists in merely admitting falsity, and that kind of giving up which involves changing or dropping a concept or set of concepts. Any form of words at one time held to express something true may, no doubt, at another time, come to be held to express something false. But it is not only philosophers who would distinguish between the case where this happens as the result of a change of opinion solely as to matters of fact, and the case where this happens at least partly as a result of a shift in the sense of the words. Where such a shift in the sense of the words is a necessary condition of the change in truth value, then the adherent of the distinction will say that the form of words in question changes from expressing an analytic statement to expressing a synthetic statement. We are not now concerned, or called upon, with elaborating an adequate theory of conceptual revision, any more than we were called upon, just now, to elaborate an adequate theory of synonymy. If we can make sense of the idea that the same form of words, taken in one way (or bearing one sense), may express something true, and taken in another way (or bearing another sense), may express something false, then we can make sense of the idea of conceptual revision. And if we can make sense of this idea, then we can perfectly well preserve the distinction between the analytic and the synthetic, while conceding to Quine the revisability-in-principle of everything we say. As for the idea that the same form of words taken in different ways may bear different senses and perhaps be used to say things with different truth values, the onus of showing that this is somehow a mistaken or confused idea rests squarely on Quine. The point of substance (or one of them) that Quine is making, by this emphasis on revisability, is that there is no absolute necessity about the adoption or use of any conceptual scheme whatever, or, more narrowly and in terms that he would reject, that there is no analytic proposition such that we *must* have linguistic forms bearing just the sense required to express that proposition. But it is one thing to admit this and quite another thing to say that there are no necessities within any conceptual scheme we adopt or use, or, more narrowly again, that there are no linguistic forms which do express analytic propositions.

The adherent of the analytic-synthetic distinction may go further and admit that there may be cases (particularly perhaps in the field of science) where it would be pointless to press the question whether a change in the attributed truth value of a statement represented a conceptual revision or not, and correspondingly pointless to press the analytic-synthetic distinction. We cannot quote such cases, but this inability may well be the result of ignorance of the sciences. In any case, the existence, if they do exist, of statements about which it is pointless to press the question of whether they are analytic or synthetic, does not entail the nonexistence of statements which are clearly classifiable in one or other of these ways and of statements our hesitation over which has different sources, such as the possibility of alternative interpretations of the linguistic forms in which they are expressed.

This concludes our examination of Quine's article. It will be evident that our purpose has been wholly negative. We have aimed to show merely that Quine's case against the existence of the analytic-synthetic distinction is not made out. His article has two parts. In one of them, the notions of the analyticity group are criticized on the ground that they had not been adequately explained. In the other, a positive theory of truth is outlined, purporting to be incompatible with views to which believers in the analytic-synthetic distinction either must be, or are likely to be, committed. In fact, we have contended, no single point is established which those who accept the notions of the analyticity group would feel any strain in accommodating in their own system of beliefs. This is not to deny that many of the points raised are of the first importance in connection with the problem of giving a satisfactory general account of analyticity and related concepts. We are criticizing here only the contention that these points justify the rejection, as illusory, of the analytic-synthetic distinction and the notions which belong to the same family.

4

GOD

"The reason all men do not obtain the true
Tâo is because their minds are perverted. Their
minds being perverted, their spirits become perturbed. Their spirits being perturbed, they are
attracted towards external things. Being
attracted toward external things, they begin to
seek for them greedily. This greedy quest leads
to perplexities and annoyances; and these again
result in disordered thoughts, which cause
anxiety and trouble to both body and mind. The
parties then meet with foul disgraces, flow
wildly on through the phases of life and death,
are liable to sink constantly in the sea of bitter-
ness, and for ever lose the true Tâo."

From the *Khing Kang King*

"We can act as if *there were a God; feel* as
if *we were free;* consider Nature as if *she were
full of special designs;* lay plans as if *we were
to be immortal;* and we find then that these
words do make a difference in our moral life."

— William James, *The Varieties of
Religious Experience*, Lecture 3

INTRODUCTION

Proofs for the existence of God have bulked large in the history of philosophy. To the modern ear however, the arguments seem arid, the result perhaps of a decline in the belief in personal immortality or perhaps more realistically the expression of distaste for rational analysis. Curiously, popular religious passions and enthusiasms seem to be waxing rather than waning. Innumerable plump Orientals criss-cross the country, apparently having been vouchsafed in their person with all the blessings of the Buddha. And students with no interest at all in arguments for the existence of God report with dismaying regularity that they too have seen Krishna and know at first hand the experiences of eternity. Among philosophers too there is some sense of reservation about purely philosophical theology. There is no shortage of papers on the classical arguments but no one, I dare say, cares deeply about the conclusions that result.

Within the analytic community the announcement by an otherwise respectable philosopher, Malcolm Strongwise, for example, that he has discovered an irrefutable argument for the existence of *The Evil One* is apt to draw little more than a few academic hear hear's from his colleagues. Their indifference to Strongwise rests on no theoretical foundation. The logical positivists thought that in the principle of verification they had an evaluative instrument of brilliant versatility, capable of sniffing out and rejecting all manner of philosophical nonsense, whether ethical, theological, existential or metaphysical. That principle (sticking now to the essentials) expressed the view that sentences whose truth conditions could not be fixed were meaningless. Theological statements were prime examples and positivists wasted no time at all in rejecting them out of hand. But the theory of meaning that made positivism possible is today merely a remembered embarrassment, so philosophers who think it their duty to make the case for the Deity can carry on with no *general* scruples whatsoever. But plainly the oomph has gone out of many arguments.

Carl Hempel teaches philosophy at Princeton University. His concern is chiefly with the philosophy of science but all his papers are composed with such stunning authority that each has become a fixed point of reference in contemporary philosophy. "The Empiricist Criterion of Meaning," which is reprinted here, is not altogether an essay in philosophical theology: it might be more appropriately fitted into the section devoted to the sagas of empiricism. I have included it here because the novel setting is pedagogically inspired. Although Hempel's essay is marvellously manicured, students who read it in intellectual isolation often react with irritated defiance, and they conclude after just a few pages that anything so dense has got to be dull. Place the same essay in the context of the charge that *theological language is meaningless*—the charge, after all, of the logical positivists—and precisely half the students to whom Hempel's essay is assigned will read it with furious concentration, hoping to discover that the claim is true, while precisely half the students again will attack it with no less zeal, hoping to discover that it is false. This is all to the good, for the segmentation of subjects within philosophy conceals the extent to which the various parts of the discipline affect each other.

For many years, Professor Paul Edwards has taught philosophy at Brooklyn College. He is the editor of *The Encyclopedia of Philosophy*. Now some philosophers plainly think of philosophy as an intellectually reckless pursuit. Only the metaphysician can take off after the ultimate nature of reality without knowing much in detail about any particular aspect of his subject matter and for minds of a certain cast the freedom that this chase affords more than makes up for the possibility that the experience it provides may be indistinguishable from mere bubbleheadedness. But then there is another and more sober philosophical character. Philosophers in whom this personality configuration predominates look upon themselves as performing workmanlike services; like a urologist. They see themselves involved chiefly in the discernment and diagnosis of conceptual confusion. They are at their best, and certainly their happiest, when given the opportunity to bring their analytical skills to bear on intellectual structures which, like the traditional principles of theology, are at once extravagant and soggy. It is in this spirit, I think, that Professor Edwards has composed his essay "Difficulties in the Idea of God." The most un-exhortative of men, Edwards is here concerned with nothing so relentless as the traditional proofs for the existence (or the inexistence) of the Deity; instead, his paper is composed according to principles that might govern a pathology report, with almost all of the attention being given over to the exhibition and dissection of what Edwards takes to be diseased conceptual tissue.

An exception to the observation that proofs of the existence of God have not been much at the forefront of contemporary philosophy is that curious construction of the ontological argument. The basic argument, as found say in Descartes, is simple to the point of triteness. God, it begins, surely numbers all perfections. But existence is a perfection since it is clearly better to be than not to be. But then God exists just in virtue of the fact that he has all perfections. Anselm, who formulated the argument for the first time in the 11th century, set it out in several more steps. God, he argued, was a being greater than which none other could be conceived. But then God surely exists in reality as well as in the understanding, since if He did not, a being greater than the being greater than which none other could be conceived could be conceived—namely one that did in fact exist in reality as well as in the Understanding. This is a contradiction. Thus God exists.

Now sketchiness aside, plainly something is wrong here. Or so our intuition runs. But such is the argument's intrinsic depth that philosophers thoughtfully arrange for its regular reappearance. Norman Malcolm, for example, offers a recent illustration of the argument's powers as he provides an outrageously skillful defense of a position that is known to be absurd. His piece has elicited many comments. Professor Plantinga, Malcolm's colleague, has prepared a refutation more compact but no less telling than most.

Alvin Plantinga's *The Ontological Argument* (Anchor Books) brings together papers that expound the ontological argument. Anthony Flew and Alasdair MacIntyre have edited an interesting collection of theological arguments in their volume *New Essays in Philosophical Theology* (SCM Press); the symposium "Theology and Falsification" has had some influence. Other useful texts are W. T. Blackstone's *The Problem of Religious Knowledge* (Prentice-Hall); John Hick's *Classical and Contemporary Readings in the Philosophy of Religion* (Prentice-Hall) and Sidney Hook's *Religious Experience and Truth* (New York University Press). John Wisdom's essay "Gods," which was printed originally in the *Proceedings of the Aristotelian Society for 1944-1945*, has been very widely reprinted.

MEMORIAL
SERVICE*

H. L. Mencken

Where is the grave-yard of dead gods? What lingering mourner waters their mounds? There was a day when Jupiter was the king of the gods, and any man who doubted his puissance was *ipso facto* a barbarian and an ignoramus. But where in all the world is there a man who worships Jupiter today? And what of Huitzilopochtli? In one year—and it is no more than five hundred years ago— 50,000 youths and maidens were slain in sacrifice to him. Today, if he is remembered at all, it is only by some vagrant savage in the depths of the Mexican forest. Huitzilopochtli, like many other gods, had no human father; his mother was a virtuous widow; he was born of an apparently innocent flirtation that she carried on with the sun. When he frowned, his father, the sun, stood still. When he roared with rage, earthquakes engulfed whole cities. When he thirsted he was watered with 10,000 gallons of human blood. But today Huitzilopochtli is as magnificently forgotten as Allen G. Thurman. Once the peer of Allah, Buddha and Wotan, he is now the peer of General Coxey, Richard P. Hobson, Nan Patterson, Alton G. Parker, Adelina Patti, General Weyler and Tom Sharkey.

Speaking of Huitzilopochtli recalls his brother, Tezcatilpoca. Tezcatilpoca was almost as powerful: he consumed 25,000 virgins a year. Lead me to his tomb: I would weep and hang a *couronne des perles.* But who knows where it is? Or where the grave of Quitzalcoatl is? Or Tialoc? Or Chalchihuitlicue? Or Xiehtecutli? Or Centeotl, that sweet one? Or Tlazolteotl, the goddess of love? Or Mictlan? Or Ixtlilton? Or Omacatl? Or Yacatecutli? Or Mixcoatl? Or Xipe? Or all the host of Tzitzimitles? Where are thier bones? Where is the willow on which they hung their harps? In what forlorn and unheard-of hell do

* From H. L. Mencken, *The Vintage Mencken,* New York: Random House, Inc., 1955. pp. 143–147; reprinted by permission of publisher.

231

they await the resurrection morn? Who enjoys their residuary estates? Or that of Dis, whom Caesar found to be the chief god of the Celts? Or that of Tarves, the bull? Or that of Moccos, the pig? Or that of Epona, the mare? Or that of Mullo, the celestial jack-ass? There was a time when the Irish revered all these gods as violently as they now hate the English. But today even the drunkest Irishman laughs at them.

But they have company in oblivion: the hell of dead gods is as crowded as the Presbyterian hell for babies. Damona is there, and Esus, and Drunemeton, and Silvana, and Dervones, and Adsalluta, and Deva, and Belisama, and Axona, and Vintios, and Taranuous, and Sulis, and Cocidius, and Adsmerius, and Dumiatis, and Caletos, and Moccus, and Ollovidius, and Albiorix, and Leucitius, and Vitucadrus, and Ogmios, and Uxellimus, and Borvo, and Grannos, and Mogons. All mighty gods in their day, worshiped by millions, full of demands and impositions, able to bind and loose—all gods of the first class, not dilettanti. Men labored for generations to build vast temples to them—temples with stones as large as hay-wagons. The business of interpreting their whims occupied thousands of priests, wizards, archdeacons, evangelists, haruspices, bishops, archbishops. To doubt them was to die, usually at the stake. Armies took to the field to defend them against infidels: villages were burned, women and children were butchered, cattle were driven off. Yet in the end they all withered and died, and today there is none so poor to do them reverence. Worse, the very tombs in which they lie are lost, and so even a respectful stranger is debarred from paying them the slightest and politest homage.

What has become of Sutekh, once the high god of the whole Nile Valley? What has become of:

Resheph	El	Isis	Sharrab
Anath	Nergal	Ptah	Yau
Ashtoreth	Nebo	Anubis	Amon-Re
Baal	Ninib	Addu	Osiris
Astarte	Melek	Shalem	Sebek
Hadad	Ahijah	Dagon	Molech?

All of these were once gods of the highest eminence. Many of them are mentioned with fear and trembling in the Old Testament. They ranked, five or six thousand years ago, with Jahveh himself; the worst of them stood far higher than Thor. Yet they have all gone down the chute, and with them the following:

Bilé	Gunfled	Pwyll	Nuada Argetlam
Lêr	Sokk-mimi	Ogyrvan	Tagd
Arianrod	Memetona	Dea Dia	Goibniu
Morrigu	Dagda	Gwydion	Odin
Govannon	Kerridwen	Manwyddan	Llaw Gyffes

Lleu	U-dimmer-an-kia	Vesta	Amurru
Ogma	Enurestu	Tilmun	Sin
Mider	U-sab-sib	Zer-panitu	AbilAddu
Rigantona	U-Mersi	Merodach	Apsu
Marzin	Tammuz	U-ki	Dagan
Mars	Venus	Dauke	Elali
Ceros	Bau	Gasan-abzu	Isum
Vaticanus	Mulu-hursang	Elum	Mami
Edulia	Anu	U-Tin-dir-ki	Nin-man
Adeona	Beltis	Marduk	Zaraqu
Iuno Lucina	Nusku	Nin-lil-la	Suqamunu
Saturn	Ni-zu	Nin	Zagaga
Furrina	Sahi	Persephone	Assur
Vediovis	Aa	Istar	Aku
Consus	Allatu	Lagas	Beltu
Cronos	Jupiter	U-urugal	Dumu-zi-abzu
Enki	Cunina	Sirtumu	Kuski-banda
Engurra	Potina	Ea	Kaawanu
Belus	Statilinus	Nirig	Nin-azu
Dimmer	Diana of Ephesus	Nebo	Lugal-Amarada
Mu-ul-lil	Robigus	Samas	Qarradu
Ubargisi	Pluto	Ma-banba-anna	Ura-gala
Ubilulu	Ops	En-Mersi	Ueras
Gasan-lil	Meditrina		

You may think I spoof. That I invent the names. I do not. Ask the rector to lend you any good treatise on comparative religion: you will find them all listed. They were gods of the highest standing and dignity—gods of civilized peoples—worshiped and believed in by millions. All were theoretically omnipotent, omniscient and immortal. And all are dead.

THE
EMPIRICIST
CRITERION
OF MEANING*
Carl. G. Hempel

1. INTRODUCTION

The fundamental tenet of modern empiricism is the view that all non-analytic knowledge is based on experience. Let us call this thesis the principle of empiricism.[1] Contemporary logical empiricism has added[2] to it the maxim that a sentence makes a cognitively meaningful assertion, and thus can be said to be either true or false, only if it is either (1) analytic or self-contradictory or (2) capable, at least in principle, of experiential test. According to this so-called *empiricist criterion of cognitive meaning, or of cognitive significance,* many of the formulations of traditional metaphysics and large parts of epistemology are devoid of cognitive significance—however rich some of them may be in non-cognitive import by virtue of their emotive appeal or the moral inspiration they offer. Similarly certain doctrines which have been, at one time or another, formulated within empirical science or its border disciplines are so contrived as to be incapable of test by any conceivable evidence; they are therefore qualified as pseudo-hypotheses which assert nothing and which therefore have no explanatory or predictive force whatever. This verdict applies, for example, to the neo-vitalist speculations about entelechies or vital forces, and to the "telefinalist hypothesis" propounded by Lecomte du Noüy.[3]

The preceding formulations of the principle of empiricism and of the empiricist meaning criterion provide no more, however, than a general and rather vague characterization of a basic point of view and need therefore to be elucidated and amplified. While in the earlier phases of its development, logical empiricism was to a large extent preoccupied with a critique of philosophic and

*From *Logical Positivism,* ed. A. J. Ayer, Glencoe, Ill.: Free Press, 1959; reprinted by permission of the author.

scientific formulations by means of those fundamental principles, there has been in recent years an increasing concern with the positive tasks of analyzing in detail the logic and methodology of empirical science and of clarifying and restating the basic ideas of empiricism in the light of the insights thus obtained. In this article, I propose to discuss some of the problems this search has raised and some of the results it seems to have established.

2. CHANGES IN THE TESTABILITY
CRITERION OF EMPIRICAL MEANING

As our formulation shows, the empiricist meaning criterion lays down the requirements of experiential testability for those among the cognitively meaningful sentences which are neither analytic nor contradictory; let us call them sentences with empirical meaning, or empirical significance. The concept of testability, which is to render precise the vague notion of being based—or rather baseable—on experience, has undergone several modifications which reflect an increasingly refined analysis of the structure of empirical knowledge. In the present section, let us examine the major stages of this development.

For convenience of exposition, we first introduce three auxiliary concepts, namely those of observable characteristic, of observation predicate, and of observation sentence. A property or a relation of physical objects will be called an *observable characteristic* if, under suitable circumstances, its presence or absence in a given instance can be ascertained through direct observation. Thus the terms "green," "soft," "liquid," "longer than," designate observable characteristics, while "bivalent," "radioactive," "better electric conductor," and "introvert" do not. Terms which designate observable characteristics will be called *observation predicates.* Finally, by an *observation sentence* we shall understand any sentence which—correctly or incorrectly asserts of one or more specifically named objects that they have, or that they lack, some specified observable characteristic. The following sentences, for example, meet this condition: "The Eiffel Tower is taller than the buildings in its vicinity," "The pointer of this instrument does not cover the point marked '3' on the scale," and even, "The largest dinosaur on exhibit in New York's Museum of Natural History had a blue tongue"; for this last sentence assigns to a specified object a characteristic—having a blue tongue—which is of such a kind that under suitable circumstances (for example, in the case of my Chow dog) its presence or absence can be ascertained by direct observation. Our concept of observation sentence is intended to provide a precise interpretation of the vague idea of a sentence asserting something that is "in principle" ascertainable by direct observation, even though it may happen to be actually incapable of being observed by myself, perhaps also by my contemporaries, and possibly even by any human being who ever lived or will live. Any evidence that might be adduced in the test of an empirical hypothesis may now be thought of as being expressed in observation sentences of this kind.[4]

We now turn to the changes in the conception of testability, and thus of empirical meaning. In the early days of the Vienna Circle, a sentence was said to have empirical meaning if it was capable, at least in principle, of complete verification by observational evidence, that is, if observational evidence could be described which, if actually obtained, would conclusively establish the truth of the sentence.[5] With the help of the concept of observation sentence, we can restate this requirement as follows: A sentence S has empirical meaning if and only if it is possible to indicate a finite set of observation sentences, O_1, O_2, ..., O_n, such that if these are true, then S is necessarily true, too. As stated, however, this condition is satisfied also if S is an analytic sentence or if the given observation sentences are logically incompatible with each other. By the following formulation, we rule these cases out and at the same time express the intended criterion more precisely:

(2.1) *Requirement of complete verifiability in principle:* A sentence has empirical meaning if and only if it is not analytic and follows logically from some finite and logically consistent class of observation sentences.[6]

This criterion, however, has several serious defects. The first of those here to be mentioned has been pointed out by various writers:

(*a*) The verifiability requirement rules out all sentences of universal form and thus all statements purporting to express general laws; for these cannot be conclusively verified by any finite set of observational data. And since sentences of this type constitute an integral part of scientific theories, the verifiability requirement must be regarded as overly restrictive in this respect. Similarly, the criterion disqualifies all sentences such as "For any substance these exists some solvent," which contain both universal and existential quantifiers (that is, occurrences of terms "all" and "some" or their equivalents); for no sentences of this kind can be logically deduced from any finite set of observation sentences.

Two further defects of the verifiability requirement do not seem to have been widely noticed:

(*b*) Suppose that S is a sentence which satisfies the proposed criterion, whereas N is a sentence such as "The absolute is perfect," to which the criterion attributes no empirical meaning. Then the alternation SvN (that is, the expression obtained by connecting the two sentences by the word "or"), likewise satisfies the criterion; for if S is a consequence of some finite class of observation sentences, then trivially SvN is a consequence of the same class. But clearly, the empiricist criterion of meaning is not intended to countenance sentences of this sort. In this respect, therefore, the requirement of complete verifiability is too inclusive.

(c) Let "P" be an observation predicate. Then the purely existential sentence "$(Ex)P(x)$" ("There exists at least one thing that has the property P") is completely verifiable, for it follows from any observation sentence asserting of some particular object that it has the property P. But its denial, being equivalent to the universal sentence "$(x) \sim P(x)$" ("Nothing has the property P") is clearly not completely verifiable, as follows from comment (a) above. Hence, under the criterion (2.1), the denials of certain empirically—and thus cognitively—significant sentences are empirically meaningless; and as they are neither analytic nor contradictory, they are cognitively meaningless. But however we may delimit the domain of significant discourse, we shall have to insist that if a sentence falls within that domain, then so must its denial. To put the matter more explicitly: The sentences to be qualified as cognitively meaningful are precisely those which can be significantly said to be either true or false. But then, adherence to (2.1) would engender a serious dilemma, as is shown by the consequence just mentioned. We would either have to give up the fundamental logical principle that if a sentence is true or false, then its denial is false or true, respectively (and thus cognitively significant); or else, we must deny, in a manner reminiscent of the intuitionistic conception of logic and mathematics, that "$(x) \sim P(x)$" is logically equivalent to the negation of "$(Ex) P (x)$." Clearly, the criterion (2.1), which has disqualified itself on several other counts, does not warrant such drastic measures for its preservation; hence, it has to be abandoned.[7]

Strictly analogous considerations apply to an alternative criterion, which makes complete falsifiability in principle the defining characteristic of empirical significance. Let us formulate this criterion as follows: A sentence has empirical meaning if and only if it is capable, in principle, of complete refutation by a finite number of observational data; or, more precisely:

(2.2) *Requirement of complete falsifiability in principle:* A sentence has empirical meaning if and only if its denial is not analytic and follows logically from some finite logically consistent class of observation sentences.[8]

This criterion qualifies a sentence as empirically meaningful if its denial satisfies the requirement of complete verifiability; as is to be expected, it is therefore inadequate on similar grounds as the latter:

(a) It rules out purely existential hypotheses, such as "There exists at least one unicorn," and all sentences whose formulation calls for mixed—that is, universal and existential—quantification; for none of these can possibly be conclusively falsified by a finite number of observation sentences.

(b) If a sentence S is completely falsifiable whereas N is a sentence which is not, then their conjunction, S.N. (that is, the expression obtained by connecting the two sentences by the word "and") is completely falsifiable; for if the denial of S is entailed by some class of observation sentences, then the denial of S.N. is, a fortiori, entailed by the same class. Thus, the criterion allows empirical significance to many sentences which an adequate empiricist criterion should rule out, such as, say "All swans are white and the absolute is perfect."

(c) If "P" is an observation predicate, then the assertion that all things have the property P is qualified as significant, but its denial, being equivalent to a purely existential hypothesis, is disqualified (cf. (a)). Hence, criterion (2.2) gives rise to the same dilemma as (2.1).

In sum, then, interpretations of the testability criterion in terms of complete verifiability or of complete falsifiability are inadequate because they are overly restrictive in one direction and overly inclusive in another, and because both of them require incisive changes in the fundamental principles of logic.

Several attempts have been made to avoid these difficulties by construing the testability criterion as demanding merely a partial and possibly indirect confirmability of empirical hypotheses by observational evidence.

(2.3) A formulation suggested by Ayer[9] is characteristic of these attempts to set up a clear and sufficiently comprehensive criterion of confirmability. It states, in effect, that a sentence S has empirical import if from S in conjunction with suitable subsidiary hypotheses it is possible to derive observation sentences which are not derivable from the subsidiary hypotheses alone.

This condition is suggested by a closer consideration of the logical structure of scientific testing; but it is much too liberal as it stands. Indeed, as Ayer himself has pointed out in the second edition of his book, *Language, Truth, and Logic*,[10] his criterion allows empirical import to any sentence whatever. Thus, for example, if S is the sentence "The absolute is perfect," it suffices to choose as a subsidiary hypothesis the sentence "If the absolute is perfect then this apple is red" in order to make possible the deduction of the observation sentence "This apple is red," which clearly does not follow from the subsidiary hypothesis alone.[11]

(2.4) To meet this objection, Ayer has recently proposed a modified version of his testability criterion. The modification restricts, in effect, the subsidiary hypotheses mentioned in (2.3) to sentences which are either analytic or can independently be shown to be testable in the sense of the modified criterion.[12]

But it can readily be shown that this new criterion, like the requirement of complete falsifiability, allows empirical significance to any conjunction S.N, where S satisfies Ayer's criterion while N is a sentence such as "The absolute is perfect," which is to be disqualified by that criterion. Indeed, whatever consequences can be deduced from S with the help of permissible subsidiary hypotheses can also be deduced from S.N. by means of the same subsidiary hypotheses, and as Ayer's new criterion is formulated essentially in terms of the deducibility of a certain type of consequence from the given sentence, it countenances S.N together with S. Another difficulty has been pointed out by Professor A. Church, who has shown[13] that if there are any three observation sentences none of which alone entails any of the others, then it follows for any sentence S whatsoever that either it or its denial has empirical import according to Ayer's revised criterion.

3. TRANSLATABILITY INTO AN EMPIRICIST LANGUAGE AS A NEW CRITERION OF COGNITIVE MEANING

I think it is useless to continue the search for an adequate criterion of testability in terms of deductive relationships to observation sentences. The past development of this search—of which we have considered the major stages—seems to warrant the expectation that as long as we try to set up a criterion of testability for individual sentences in a natural language, in terms of logical relationship to observation sentences, the result will be either too restrictive or too inclusive, or both. In particular it appears likely that such criteria would allow empirical import, in the manner of (2.1) (*b*) or of (2.2) (*b*), either to any alternation or to any conjunction of two sentences of which at least one is qualified as empirically meaningful; and this peculiarity has undesirable consequences because the liberal grammatical rules of English as of any other natural language countenance as sentences certain expressions ("The absolute is perfect" was our illustration) which even by the most liberal empiricist standards make no assertion whatever; and these would then have to be permitted as components of empirically significant statements.

The predicament would not arise, of course, in an artificial language whose vocabulary and grammar were so chosen as to preclude altogether the possibility of forming sentences of any kind which the empiricist meaning criterion is intended to rule out. Let us call any such language an *empiricist language*. This reflection suggests an entirely different approach to our problem: Give a general characterization of the kind of language that would qualify as empiricist, and then lay down the following.

(3.1) *Translatability criterion of cognitive meaning:* **A** sentence has cognitive meaning if and only if it is translatable into an empiricist language.

This conception of cognitive import, while perhaps not explicitly stated, seems to underlie much of the more recent work done by empiricist writers; as far as I can see it has its origin in Carnap's essay, "Testability and Meaning" (especially part IV).

As any language, so also any empiricist language can be characterized by indicating its vocabulary and the rules determining its logic; the latter include the syntactical rules according to which sentences may be formed by means of the given vocabulary. In effect, therefore, the translatability criterion proposes to characterize the cognitively meaningful sentences by the vocabulary out of which they may be constructed, and by the syntactical principles governing their construction. What sentences are singled out as cognitively significant will depend, accordingly, on the choice of the vocabulary and of the construction rules. Let us consider a specific possibility:

(3.2) We might qualify a language L as empiricist if it satisfies the following conditions:

(a) *The vocabulary of L* contains:

(1) The customary locutions of logic which are used in the formulation of sentences; including in particular the expressions "not," "and," "or," "if . . . then . . . ," "all," "some," "the class of all things such that . . . ," ". . . is an element of class . . .";

(2) Certain *observation predicates.* These will be said to constitute the basic empirical vocabulary of L;

(3) Any expression definable by means of those referred to under (1) and (2).

(b) *The rules of sentence formation for L* are those laid down in some contemporary logical system such as *Principia Mathematica.*

Since all defined terms can be eliminated in favor of primitives, these rules stipulate in effect that a language L is empiricist if all its sentences are expressible, with the help of the usual logical locutions, in terms of observable characteristics of physical objects. Let us call any language of this sort a thing-language in the narrower sense. Alternatively, the basic empirical vocabulary of an empiricist language might be construed as consisting of phenomenalistic terms, each of them referring to some aspect of the phenomena of perception or sensation. The construction of adequate phenomenalistic languages, however, presents considerable difficulties,[14] and in recent empiricism, attention has been focussed primarily on the potentialities of languages whose basic empirical vocabulary consists of observation predicates; for the latter lend themselves more directly to the description of that type of intersubjective evidence which is invoked in the test of scientific hypotheses.

If we construe empiricist languages in the sense of (3.2), then the translatability criterion (3.1) avoids all of the shortcomings pointed out in our discussion of earlier forms of the testability criterion:

(*a*) Our characterization of empiricist languages makes explicit provision for universal and existential quantification, that is, for the use of the terms "all" and "some"; hence, no type of quantified statement is generally excluded from the realm of cognitively significant discourse;

(*b*) Sentences such as "The absolute is perfect" cannot be formulated in an empiricist language (cf. (*d*) below); hence there is no danger that a conjunction or alternation containing a sentence of that kind as a component might be qualified as cognitively significant;

(*c*) In a language L with syntactical rules conforming to *Principia Mathematica,* the denial of a sentence is always again a sentence of L. Hence, the translatability criterion does not lead to the consequence, which is entailed by both (2.1) and (2.2), that the denials of certain significant sentences are non-significant;

(*d*) Despite its comprehensiveness, the new criterion does not attribute cognitive meaning to *all* sentences; thus, for example, the sentences "The absolute is perfect" and "Nothingness nothings" cannot be translated into an empiricist language because their key terms are not definable by means of purely logical expressions and observation terms.

4. THE PROBLEM OF DISPOSITION TERMS AND OF THEORETICAL CONSTRUCTS

Yet the new criterion is still too restrictive—as are, incidentally, also its predecessors—in an important respect which now calls for consideration. If empiricist languages are defined in accordance with (3.2), then, as we noted above, the translatability criterion (3.1) allows cognitive import to a sentence only if its constitutive empirical terms are explicitly definable by means of observation predicates. But as we shall argue presently, many terms even of the physical sciences are not so definable; hence the criterion would oblige us to reject, as devoid of cognitive import, all scientific hypotheses containing such terms—an altogether intolerable consequence.

The concept of temperature is a case in point. At first glance, it seems as though the phrase "Object x has a temperature of c degrees centigrade," or briefly "$T(x) = c$" could be defined by the following sentence, (D): $T(x) = c$ if and only if the following condition is satisfied: If a thermometer is in contact with x, then it registers c degrees on its scale.

Disregarding niceties, it may be granted that the definiens given here is formulated entirely in reference to observables. However, it has one highly questionable aspect. In *Principia Mathematica* and similar systems, the phrase "if p then q" is construed as being synonymous with "not p or q"; and under this so-called material interpretation of the conditional, a statement of the form "if p then q" is obviously true if (though not only if) the sentence standing in the place of "p" is false. If, therefore, the meaning of "if . . . then . . ." in the definiens of (D) is understood in the material sense, then that definiens is true if (though not only if) x is an object not in contact with a thermometer—no matter what numerical value we may give to c. And since the definiendum would be true under the same circumstances, the definition (D) would qualify as true the assignment of any temperature value whatsoever to any object not in contact with a thermometer! Analogous considerations apply to such terms as "electrically charged," "magnetic," "intelligent," "electric resistance," etc., in short to all disposition terms, that is, terms which express the disposition of one or

241

more objects to react in a determinate way under specified circumstances. A definition of such terms by means of observation predicates cannot be effected in the manner of (D), however natural and obvious in mode of definition this may at first seem to be.[15]

There are two main directions in which a resolution of the difficulty might be sought. On the one hand, it could be argued that the definition of disposition terms in the manner of (D) is perfectly adequate provided that the phrase "if . . . then . . ." in the definiens is construed in the sense it is obviously intended to have, namely as implying, in the case of (D), that even if x is not actually in contact with a thermometer, still if it *were* in such contact, then the thermometer *would* register c degrees. In sentences such as this, the phrase "if . . . then . . ." is said to be used counterfactually; and it is in this "strong" sense, which implies a counterfactual conditional, that the definiens of (D) would have to be construed. This suggestion would provide an answer to the problem of defining disposition terms if it were not for the fact that no entirely satisfactory account of the exact meaning of counterfactual conditionals seems to be available at present. Thus, the first way out of the difficulty has the status of a program rather than that of a solution. The lack of an adequate theory of counterfactual conditionals is all the more deplorable as such a theory is needed also for the analysis of the concept of general law in empirical science and of certain related ideas. A clarification of this cluster of problems constitutes at present one of the urgent desiderata in the logic and methodology of science.[16]

An alternative way of dealing with the definitional problems raised by disposition terms was suggested, and developed in detail, by Carnap. It consists in permitting the introduction of new terms, within an empiricist language, by means of so-called reduction sentences, which have the character of partial or conditional definitions.[17] Thus, for example, the concept of temperature in our last illustration might be introduced by means of the following reduction sentence, (R): If a thermometer is in contact with an object x, then $T(x) = c$ if and only if the thermometer registers c degrees.

This rule, in which the conditional may be construed in the material sense, specifies the meaning of "temperature," that is, of statements of the form "$T(x) = c$," only partially, namely in regard to those objects which are in contact with a thermometer; for all other objects, it simply leaves the meaning of "$T(x) = c$" undetermined. The specification of the meaning of "temperature" may then be gradually extended to cases not covered in (R) by laying down further reduction sentences, which reflect the measurement of temperature by devices other than thermometers.

Reduction sentences thus provide a means for the precise formulation of what is commonly referred to as operational definitions.[18] At the same time, they show that the latter are not definitions in the strict sense of the word, but rather partial specifications of meaning.

242

The preceding considerations suggest that in our characterization (3.2) of empiricist languages we broaden the provision *a* (3) by permitting in the vocabulary of L all those terms whose meaning can be specified in terms of the basic empirical vocabulary by means of definitions or reduction sentences. Languages satisfying this more inclusive criterion will be referred to as thing-languages in the wider sense.

If the concept of empiricist language is broadened in this manner, then the translatability criterion (3.1) covers—as it should—also all those statements whose constituent empirical terms include "empirical constructs," that is, terms which do not designate observables, but which can be introduced by reduction sentences on the basis of observation predicates.

Even in this generalized version, however, our criterion of cognitive meaning may not do justice to advanced scientific theories, which are formulated in terms of "theoretical constructs," such as the terms "absolute temperature," "gravitational potential," "electric field," "Ψ function," etc. There are reasons to think that neither definitions nor reduction sentences are adequate to introduce these terms on the basis of observation predicates. Thus, for example, if a system of reduction sentences for the concept of electric field were available, then—to oversimplify the point a little—it would be possible to describe, in terms of observable characteristics, some necessary and some sufficient conditions for the presence, in a given region, of an electric field of any mathematical description, however complex. Actually, however, such criteria can at best be given only for some sufficiently simple kinds of fields.

Now theories of the advanced type here referred to may be considered as hypothetico-deductive systems in which all statements are logical consequences of a set of fundamental assumptions. Fundamental as well as derived statements in such a system are formulated either in terms of certain theoretical constructs which are not defined within the system and thus play the role of primitives, or in terms of expressions defined by means of the latter. Thus, in their logical structure such systems equal the axiomatized uninterpreted systems studied in mathematics and logic. They acquire applicability to empirical subject matter, and thus the status of theories of empirical science, by virtue of an empirical interpretation. The latter is effected by a translation of some of the sentences of the theory—often derived rather than fundamental ones—into an empiricist language, which may contain both observation predicates and empirical constructs. And since the sentences which are thus given empirical meaning are logical consequences of the fundamental hypotheses of the theory, that translation effects, indirectly, a partial interpretation of the latter and of the constructs in terms of which they are formulated.[19]

In order to make translatability into an empiricist language an adequate criterion of cognitive import, we broaden therefore the concept of empiricist language so as to include thing-languages in the narrower and in the wider sense as well as all interpreted theoretical systems of the kind just referred to.[20] With this understanding, (3.1) may finally serve as a general criterion of cognitive meaning.

5. ON "THE MEANING" OF AN EMPIRICAL STATEMENT

In effect, the criterion thus arrived at qualifies a sentence as cognitively meaningful if its nonlogical constituents refer, directly or in certain specified indirect ways, to observables. But it does not make any pronouncement on what "the meaning" of a cognitively significant sentence is, and in particular it neither says nor implies that that meaning can be exhaustively characterized by what the totality of possible tests would reveal in terms of observable phenomena. Indeed, *the content of a statement with empirical import cannot, in general, be exhaustively expressed by means of any class of observation sentences.*

For consider first, among the statements permitted by our criterion, any purely existential hypothesis or any statement involving mixed quantification. As was pointed out earlier, under (2.2) (*a*), statements of these kinds entail no observation sentences whatever; hence their content cannot be expressed by means of a class of observation sentences.

And secondly, even most statements of purely universal form (such as "All flamingoes are pink") entail observation sentences (such as "That thing is pink") only when combined with suitable other observation sentences (such as "That thing is a flamingo").

This last remark can be generalized. The use of empirical hypotheses for the prediction of observable phenomena requires, in practically all cases, the use of subsidiary empirical hypotheses.[21] Thus, for example, the hypothesis that the agent of tuberculosis is rod-shaped does not by itself entail the consequence that upon looking at a tubercular sputum specimen through a microscope, rod-like shapes will be observed: a large number of subsidiary hypotheses, including the theory of the microscope, have to be used as additional premises in deducing that prediction.

Hence, what is sweepingly referred to as "the (cognitive) meaning" of a given scientific hypothesis cannot be adequately characterized in terms of potential observational evidence alone, nor can it be specified for the hypothesis taken in isolation. In order to understand "the meaning" of a hypothesis within an empiricist language, we have to know not merely what observation sentences it entails alone or in conjunction with subsidiary hypotheses, but also what other, non-observational, empirical sentences are entailed by it, what sentences in the given language would confirm or disconfirm it, and for what other hypotheses the given one would be confirmatory or disconfirmatory. In other

244

words, the cognitive meaning of a statement in an empiricist language is reflected in the totality of its logical relationships to all other statements in that language and not to the observation sentences alone. In this sense, the statements of empirical science have a surplus meaning over and above what can be expressed in terms of relevant observation sentences.[22]

6. THE LOGICAL STATUS OF THE EMPIRICIST CRITERION OF MEANING

What kind of a sentence, it has often been asked, is the empiricist meaning criterion itself? Plainly it is not an empirical hypothesis; but it is not analytic or self-contradictory either; hence, when judged by its own standard, is it not devoid of cognitive meaning? In that case, what claim of soundness or validity could possibly be made for it?

One might think of construing the criterion as a definition which indicates what empiricists propose to understand by a cognitively significant sentence; thus understood, it would not have the character of an assertion and would be neither true nor false. But this conception would attribute to the criterion a measure of arbitrariness which cannot be reconciled with the heated controversies it has engendered and even less with the fact, repeatedly illustrated in the present article, that the changes in its specific content have always been determined by the objective of making the criterion a more adequate index of cognitive import. And this very objective illuminates the character of the empiricist criterion of meaning: It is intended to provide a clarification and *explication* of the idea of a sentence which makes an intelligible assertion.[23] This idea is admittedly vague, and it is the task of philosophic explication to replace it by a more precise concept. In view of this difference of precision we cannot demand, of course, that the "new" concept, the explicatum, be strictly synonymous with the old one, the explicandum.[24] How, then, are we to judge the adequacy of a proposed explication, as expressed in some specific criterion of cognitive meaning?

First of all, these exists a large class of sentences which are rather generally recognized as making intelligible assertions, and another large class of which this is more or less generally denied. We shall have to demand of an adequate explication that it take into account these spheres of common usage; hence an explication which, let us say, denies cognitive import to descriptions of past events or to generalizations expressed in terms of observables has to be rejected as inadequate. As we have seen, this first requirement of adequacy has played an important role in the development of the empiricist meaning criterion.

But an adequate explication of the concept of cognitively significant statement must satisfy yet another, even more important, requirement: together with the explication of certain other concepts, such as those of confirmation and of probability, it has to provide the framework for a general theoretical account of the structure and the foundations of scientific knowledge. Explication, as here understood, is not a mere description of the accepted usages of the terms under consideration: it has to go beyond the limitations, ambiguities, and inconsistencies of common usage and has to show how we had better construe the meanings of those terms if we wish to arrive at a consistent and comprehensive theory of knowledge. This type of consideration, which has been largely influenced by a study of the structure of scientific theories, has prompted the more recent extensions of the empiricist meaning criterion. These extensions are designed to include in the realm of cognitive significance various types of sentences which might occur in advanced scientific theories, or which have to be admitted simply for the sake of systematic simplicity and uniformity,[25] but on whose cognitive significance or nonsignificance a study of what the term "intelligible assertion" means in everyday discourse could hardly shed any light at all.

As a consequence, the empiricist criterion of meaning, like the result of any other explication, represents a linguistic proposal which itself is neither true nor false, but for which adequacy is claimed in two respects: first in the sense that the explication provides a reasonably close *analysis* of the commonly accepted meaning of the explicandum—and this claim implies an empirical assertion; and secondly in the sense that the explication achieves a *rational reconstruction* of the explicandum, that is, that it provides, together perhaps with other explications, a general conceptual framework which permits a consistent and precise restatement and theoretical systematization of the contexts in which the explicandum is used—and this claim implies at least an assertion of a logical character.

Though a proposal in form, the empiricist criterion of meaning is therefore far from being an arbitrary definition; it is subject to revision if a violation of the requirements of adequacy, or even a way of satisfying those requirements more fully, should be discovered. Indeed, it is to be hoped that before long some of the open problems encountered in the analysis of cognitive significance will be clarified and that then our last version of the empiricist meaning criterion will be replaced by another, more adequate one.

NOTES

1. This term is used by Benjamin (2) in an examination of the foundations of empiricism. For a recent discussion of the basic ideas of empiricism see Russell (27), Part Six.

2. In his stimulating article, "Positivism," W. T. Stace argues, in effect, that the testability criterion of meaning is not logically entailed by the principle of empiricism. (See (29), especially section 11.) This is correct: according to the latter, a sentence expresses knowledge only if it is either analytic or corroborated by empirical evidence; the former goes further and identifies the domain of cognitively significant discourse with that of

potential knowledge; i.e., it grants cognitive import only to sentences for which—unless they are either analytic or contradictory—a test by empirical evidence is conceivable.

3. Cf. (19), Ch. XVI.

4. Observation sentences of this kind belong to what Carnap has called the thing-language (cf., e.g., (7), pp. 52-53). That they are adequate to formulate the data which serve as the basis for empirical tests is clear in particular for the intersubjective testing procedures used in science as well as in large areas of empirical inquiry on the common-sense level. In epistemological discussions, it is frequently assumed that the ultimate evidence for beliefs about empirical matters consists in perceptions and sensations whose description calls for a phenomenalistic type of language. The specific problems connected with the phenomenal-istic approach cannot be discussed here; but it should be mentioned that at any rate all the critical considerations presented in this article in regard to the testability criterion are applicable, *mutatis mutandis,* to the case of a phenomenalistic basis as well.

5. Originally, the permissible evidence was meant to be restricted to what is observable by the speaker and perhaps his fellow-beings during their lifetimes. Thus construed, the criterion rules out, as cognitively meaningless, all statements about the distant future or the remote past, as has been pointed out, among others, by Ayer in (1), Chapter I; by Pap in (21), Chapter 13, esp. pp. 333 ff.; and by Russell in (27), pp. 445-47. This difficulty is avoided, however, if we permit the evidence to consist of any finite set of "logically possible observation data," each of them formulated in an observation sentence. Thus, e.g., the sentence S_1, "The tongue of the largest dinosaur in New York's Museum of Natural History was blue or black" is completely verifiable in our sense; for it is a logical consequence of the Sentence S_2, "The tongue of the largest dinosaur in New York's Museum of Natural History was blue"; and this is an observation sentence, as has been shown above.

And if the concept of *verifiability in principle* and the more general concept of *confirmability in principle,* which will be considered later, are construed as referring to *logically possible evidence* as expressed by observation sentences, then it follows similarly that the class of statements which are verifiable, or at least confirmable, in principle includes such assertions as that the planet Neptune and the Antarctic Continent existed before they were discovered, and that atomic warfare, if not checked, may lead to the extermination of this planet. The objections which Russell (cf. (27), pp. 445 and 447) raises against the verifiability criterion by reference to those examples do not apply therefore if the criterion is understood in the manner here suggested. Incidentally, statements of the kind mentioned by Russell, which are not actually verifiable by any human being, were explicitly recognized as cognitively significant already by Schlick (in (28), Parv V), who argued that the impossi-bility of verifying them was "merely empirical." The characterization of verifiability with the help of the concept of observation sentences as suggested here might serve as a more explicit and rigorous statement of that conception.

6. As has frequently been emphasized in empiricist literature, the term "verifiability" is to indicate, of course, the conceivability, or better, the logical possibility of evidence of an observational kind which, if actually encountered, would constitute conclusive evidence for the given sentence; it is not intended to mean the technical possibility of performing the tests needed to obtain such evidence, and even less does it mean the possibility of actually finding directly observable phenomena which constitute conclusive evidence for that sentence—which would be tantamount to the actual existence of such evidence and would thus imply the truth of the given sentence. Analogous remarks apply to the terms "falsifi-ability" and "confirmability." This point has been disregarded in some recent critical discussions of the verifiability criterion. Thus, e.g., Russell (cf. (27), p. 448) construes verifiability as the actual existence of a set of conclusively verifying occurrences. This conception, which has never been advocated by any logical empiricist, must naturally turn out to be inadequate since according to it the empirical meaningfulness of a sentence could not be established without gathering empirical evidence, and moreover enough of it to permit a conclusive proof of the sentences in question! It is not surprising, therefore, that his extraordinary interpretation of verifiability leads Russell to the conclusion: "In fact, that a proposition is verifiable is itself not veriable" (*l. c.*). Actually, under the empiricist

interpretation of complete verifiability, any statement asserting the verifiability of some sentence S whose text is quoted, is either analytic or contradictory; for the decision whether there exists a class of observation sentences which entail S, i.e., whether such observation sentences can be formulated, no matter whether they are true or fale—that decision is a matter of pure logic and requires no factual information whatever.

A similar misunderstanding is in evidence in the following passage in which W. H. Werkmeister claims to characterize a view held by logical positivists: "A proposition is said to be 'true' when it is 'verifiable in principle'; i.e., when we know the conditions which, when realized, will make 'verification' possible (cf. Ayer)." (cf (31), p. 145). The quoted thesis, which, again, was never held by any logical positivist, including Ayer, is in fact logically absurd. For we can readily describe conditions which, if realized, would verify the sentence "The outside of the Chrysler Building is painted a bright yellow"; but similarly, we can describe verifying conditions for its denial; hence, according to the quoted principle, both the sentence and its denial would have to be considered true. Incidentally, the passage under discussion does not accord with Werkmeister's perfectly correct observation, *l. c.,* p. 40, that verifiability is intended to characterize the meaning of a sentence—which shows that verifiability is meant to be a criterion of cognitive significance rather than of truth.

7. The arguments here adduced against the verifiability criterion also prove the inadequacy of a view closely related to it, namely that two sentences have the same cognitive significance if any set of observation sentences which would verify one of them would also verify the other, and conversely. Thus, e.g., under this criterion, any two general laws would have to be assigned the same cognitive significance, for no general law is verified by any set of observation sentences. The view just referred to must be clearly distinguished from a position which Russell examines in his critical discussion of the positivistic meaning criterion. It is "the theory that two propositions whose verified consequences are identical have the same significance" ((27), p. 448). This view is untenable indeed, for what consequences of a statement have actually been verified at a given time is obviously a matter of historical accident which cannot possibly serve to establish identity of cognitive significance. But I am not aware that any logical positivist ever subscribed to that "theory."

8. The idea of using theoretical falsifiability by observational evidence as the "criterion of demarcation" separating empirical science from mathematics and logic on one hand and from metaphysics on the other is due to K. Popper (cf. (22), section 1-7 and 19-24; also see (23), vol. II, pp. 282-285). Whether Popper would subscribe to the proposed restatement of the falsifiability criterion, I do not know.

9. (1), Ch. I—The case against the requirements of verifiability and of falsifiability, and favor of a requirement of partial confirmability and disconfirmability is very clearly presented also by Pap in (21), Chapter 13.

10. (1), 2d ed., pp. 11-12.

11. According to Stace (cf. (29), p. 218), the criterion of partial and indirect testability, which he calls the positivist principle, presupposes (and thus logically entails) another principle, which he terms the *Principle of Observable Kinds*: "A sentence, in order to be significant, must assert or deny facts which are of a kind or class such that it is logically possible directly to observe some facts which are instances of that class or kind. And if a sentence purports to assert or deny facts which are of a class or kind such that it would be logically impossible directly to observe any instance of that class or kind, then the sentence is non-significant." I think the argument Stace offers to prove that this principle is entailed by the requirement of testability is inconclusive (mainly because of the incorrect tacit assumption that "on the transformation view of deduction," the premises of a valid deductive argument must be necessary conditions for the conclusion (*l. c.,* p. 225). Without pressing this point any further, I should like to add here a remark on the principle of observable kinds itself. Professor Stace does not say how we are to determine what "facts" a given sentence asserts or denies, or indeed whether it asserts or denies any "facts" at all. Hence, the exact import of the principle remains unclear. No matter, however, how one might choose the criteria for the factual reference of sentences, this much seems certain:

If a sentence expresses any fact at all, say f, then it satisfies the requirements laid down in the first sentence of the principle; for we can always form a class containing f together with the fact expressed by some observation sentence of our choice, which makes f a member of a class of facts at least one of which is capable, in principle, of direct observation. The first part of the principle of observable kinds is therefore all-inclusive, somewhat like Ayer's original formulation of the empiricist meaning criterion.

12. This restriction is expressed in recursive form and involves no vicious circle. For the full statement of Ayer's criterion, see (1), second edition, p. 13.

13. Church (11).

14. Important contributions to the problem have been made by Carnap (5) and by Goodman (15).

15. This difficulty in the definition of disposition terms was first pointed out and analyzed by Carnap (in (6); see esp. section 7).

16. The concept of strict implication as introduced by C. I. Lewis would be of no avail for the interpretation of the strong "if . . . then . . ." as here understood, for it refers to a purely logical relationship of entailment, whereas the concept under consideration will, in general, represent a nomological relationship, i.e., one based on empirical laws. For recent discussions of the problems of counterfactuals and laws, see Langford (18); Lewis (20), pp. 210-230; Chisholm (10); Goodman (14); Reichenbach (26), Chapter VIII; Hempel and Oppenheim (16), Part III; Popper (24).

17. Cf. Carnap (6); a brief elementary exposition of the central idea may be found in Carnap (7), Part III. The partial definition (R) formulated above for the expression "$T(x) = c$" illustrates only the simplest type of reduction sentence, the so-called bilateral reduction sentence.

18. On the concept of operational definition, which was developed by Bridgman, see, for example, Bridgman (3, 4) and Feigl (12).

19. The distinction between a formal deductive system and the empirical theory resulting from it by an interpretation has been elaborated in detail by Reichenbach in his penetrating studies on the relations between pure and physical geometry; c.f., e.g., Reichenbach (25). The method by means of which a formal system is given empirical content is characterized by Reichenbach as "coordinating definition" of the primitives in the theory by means of specific empirical concepts. As is suggested by our discussion of reduction and the interpretation of theoretical constructs, however, the process in question may have to be construed as a partial interpretation of the non-logical terms of the system rather than as a complete definition of the latter in terms of the concepts of a thing-language.

20. These systems have not been characterized here as fully and as precisely as would be desirable. Indeed, the exact character of the empirical interpretation of theoretical constructs and of the theories in which they function is in need of further investigation. Some problems which arise in this connection—such as whether, or in what sense, theoretical constructs may be said to denote—are obviously also of considerable epistemological interest. Some suggestions as to the interpretation of theoretical constructs may be found in Carnap (8), section 24, and in Kaplan (17); for an excellent discussion of the epistemological aspects of the problem, see Feigl (13).

21. This point is clearly taken into consideration in Ayer's criteria of cognitive significance, which were discussed in section 2.

22. For a fuller discussion of the issues here involved cf. Feigl (13) and the comments on Feigl's position which will be published together with that article.

23. In the preface to the second edition of his book, Ayer takes a very similar position: he holds that the testability criterion is a definition which, however, is not entirely arbitrary, because a sentence which did not satisfy the criterion "would not be capable of being understood in the sense in which either scientific hypotheses or commonsense statements are habitually understood" ((1), p. 16).

24. Cf. Carnap's characterization of explication in his article (9), which examines in outline the explication of the concept of probability. The Frege-Russell definition of integers as classes of equivalent classes, and the semantical definition of truth—cf. Tarski (30)—are outstanding examples of explication. For a lucid discussion of various aspects of logical analysis see Pap (21), Chapter 17.

25. Thus, for example, our criterion qualifies as significant certain statements containing, say, thousands of existential or universal quantifiers—even though such sentences may never occur in everyday nor perhaps even in scientific discourse. For indeed, from a systematic point of view it would be arbitrary and unjustifiable to limit the class of significant statements to those containing no more than some fixed number of quantifiers. For further discussion of this point, cf. Carnap (6), sections 17, 24, 25.

REFERENCES

1. Ayer, A. J., *Language, Truth and Logic*, Gollancz, London, 1936; 2nd ed., 1946.
2. Benjamin, A. C., "Is Empiricism Self-refuting?" (*Journal of Philos.*, Vol. 38, 1941).
3. Bridgman, P. W., *The Logic of Modern Physics*, The Macmillan Co., New York, 1927.
4. Bridgman, P. W., "Operational Analysis" (*Philos. of Science*, Vol. 5, 1938).
5. Carnap, R., *Der logische Aufbau der Welt*, Berlin, 1928.
6. Carnap, R., "Testability and Meaning" (*Philos. of Science*, Vol. 3, 1936, and Vol. 4, 1937).
7. Carnap, R., *Logical Foundations of the Unity of Science*, In: *Internat. Encyclopedia of Unified Science*, I, 1; Univ. of Chicago Press, 1938.
8. Carnap, R., *Foundations of Logic and Mathematics. Internat. Encyclopedia of Unified Science*, I, 3; Univ. of Chicago Press, 1939.
9. Carnap, R., "The Two Concepts of Probability" (*Philos. and Phenom. Research*, Vol. 5, 1945).
10. Chisholm, R. M., "The Contrary-to-Fact Conditional" (*Mind*, Vol. 55, 1946).
11. Church, A., Review of (1), 2nd ed. (*The Journal of Symb. Logic*, Vol. 14, 1949, pp. 52-53).
12. Feigl, H., "Operationism and Scientific Method" (*Psychol. Review*, Vol. 52, 1945). (Also reprinted in Feigl and Sellars, *Readings in Philosophical Analysis*, New York, 1949.)
13. Feigl, H., "Existential Hypotheses; Realistic vs. Phenomenalistic Interpretations," (*Philos. of Science*, Vol. 17, 1950).
14. Goodman, N., "The Problem of Counterfactual Conditionals" (*Journal of Philos.*, Vol. 44, 1947).
15. Goodman, N., *The Structure of Appearance*. Harvard University Press, 1951.
16. Hempel, C. G., and Oppenheim, P., "Studies in the Logic of Explanation" (*Philos. of Science*, Vol. 15, 1948).
17. Kaplan, A., "Definition and Specification of Meaning" (*Journal of Philos.*, Vol. 43, 1946).
18. Langford, C. H., Review in *The Journal of Symb. Logic*, Vol. 6 (1941), pp. 67-68.
19. Lecomte du Noüy, *Human Destiny*, New York, London, Toronto, 1947.
20. Lewis, C. I. *An Analysis of Knowledge and Valuation*, Open Court Publ., La Salle, Ill., 1946.
21. Pap, A. *Elements of Analytic Philosophy*, The Macmillan Co., New York, 1949.
22. Popper, K., *Logik der Forschung*, Springer, Vienna, 1935.
23. Popper, K., *The Open Society and Its Enemies*, 2 vols., Routledge, London, 1945.
24. Popper, K., "A Note on Natural Laws and So-called 'Contrary-to-Fact Conditionals' " (*Mind*, Vol. 58, 1949).
25. Reichenbach, H., *Philosophie der Raum-Zeit-Lehre*, Berlin, 1928.
26. Reichenbach, H., *Elements of Symbolic Logic*, The Macmillan Co., New York, 1947.

27. Russell, B., *Human Knowledge,* Simon and Schuster, New York, 1948.
28. Schlick, M., "Meaning and Verification" (*Philos. Review,* Vol. 45, 1936). (Also reprinted in Feigl and Sellars, *Readings in Philosophical Analysis,* New York, 1949.)
29. Stace, W. T., "Positivism" (*Mind,* Vol. 53, 1944).
30. Tarski, A., "The Semantic Conception of Truth and the Foundations of Semantics" (*Philos. and Phenom. Research,* Vol. 4, 1944). (Also reprinted in Feigl and Sellars, *Readings in Philosophical Analysis,* New York, 1949.)
31. Werkmeister, W. H., *The Basis and Structure of Knowledge,* Harper, New York and London, 1948.
32. Whitehead, A. N., and Russell, B., *Principia Mathematica,* 3 vols., 2nd ed., Cambridge, 1925-1927

DIFFICULTIES
IN THE
IDEA OF GOD*

Paul Edwards

The object of this paper is to set out briefly some of the main reasons why many contemporary philosophers reject belief in God in any of its familiar forms and shapes. Long experience has taught me that believers are, with few exceptions, remarkably ignorant of these reasons. Even when they are not ignorant, they rarely appreciate the full force of the objections in question and they tend to be satisfied with rejoinders that are incredibly weak. I know that many of the speakers at this convention are believers and I imagine that there are also a good many believers in the audience. My remarks are primarily addressed to them in the hope that they will come to appreciate a little better why thoughtful people have come to reject the basic tenet of their creeds. I would also like them to know that unbelievers like myself are just as seriously concerned with the issues as they are. The objections are not meant flippantly and if they can be answered, I am eager to hear the answers.

THREE KINDS OF BELIEF

It is notorious that the word *God* has been used in a great many different ways, and accordingly, different people, all of whom consider themselves believers in God (and often the same person at different moments), claim rather different things when they assert the existence, or in the case of some writers who eschew the word existence in this context, the "reality" or "actuality" of God. I propose to discuss the position of three types of believers here to whom I shall refer as *anthropomorphic, metaphysical* and *naturalistic* believers,

*From *The Idea of God,* ed. Edward Madden, Rollo Handy, and Marvin Faber, Springfield, Ill.: Charles C. Thomas, Publisher, 1968; by permission of the publisher.

respectively. I am at this stage using the expression *believer in God* in the extremely broad sense in which it refers to anybody who, in stating his position, uses the *words* "I believe in God." We shall see that, in the stricter senses which are more common, the people whom I call "naturalistic believers" are not really believers in God at all.

Both anthropomorphic and metaphysical believers would speak of God as a supreme personal being who is the creator or the ground of the universe and who, whatever his other attributes may be, is at the very least immensely powerful, highly intelligent and very good, loving and just. Anthropomorphic believers maintain that the predicates just mentioned—"powerful," "intelligent," "loving," and the rest—are used in a literal sense when applied to God. The philosophers to whom I refer as metaphysical believers would insist that, when applied to God, these predicates cannot be understood in any of their literal senses but must be employed in "metaphorical," "symbolic," or "analogical" senses. Among professional philosphers the metaphysical variety of belief has been very common. It is not implausible to regard Plato as the founder of this tradition. Whether Aquinas is to be classified as a metaphysical believer is a controversial question which we need not discuss here. There can be no doubt, however, that many of the outstanding Protestant theologians of the last 150 years were metaphysical believers. This is true of various Hegelian theologians, of the Hamiltonian school and its leading religious spokesman, Dean Mansel, and of the numerous contemporary Protestants who have been influenced by the philosophy of Heidegger. Most ordinary, philosophically unsophisticated believers can undoubtedly be classified as supporters of the anthropomorphic viewpoint, but such a position has also commanded the support of quite a number of eminent philosophers, especially believers who were also empiricists. Berkeley, Voltaire, and John Stuart Mill may be mentioned as illustrations; and many of the statements in the writings of William James suggest that, insofar as he believed at all, he believed in one or more Gods in the anthropomorphic sense of the word. Among recent philosophical defenders of belief in God, John Hick and A. C. Ewing, if I understand them correctly, favor the anthropomorphic view.

A naturalistic believer may be characterized as a person who says that he believes in God and who then identifies God with some feature of man's life and aspirations. John Dewey and various American philosophers influenced by him have championed views of this kind. Thus John Herman Randall, Jr., remarks that "the prophet and the saint . . . enable us to see and feel the religious dimension of our world better, the 'order of splendor,' and of man's experience in and with it. They teach us how to find the Divine; they show us visions of God."[1] But God, as conceived by Randall, is not to be regarded as the creator of the universe. The word *God,* as Randall uses it, stands for "our ideals, our controlling values, our 'ultimate concern' " and the religious dimension is simply "a quality to be discriminated in human experience of the world, the splendor of the vision that sees beyond the actual into the . . . realm of the imagination."[2] So far from being Christians, Dewey and Randall are for the most part highly critical of Christianity, but in more recent years exceedingly similar positions have been advocated by prominent members of Christian churches. Thus the Reverend Jack Mole, who seems to be a British counterpart to the American death-of-God "theologians," frankly asks the theologian to transform himself into a "mythologian." The word "god" should be retained but simply as a name for history rightly conceived; and history rightly conceived is nothing but "people in potential relationship." The proper study of theology is not any kind of transcendent being, either of the anthropomorphic or of the metaphysical variety, but "the comparative study of history and myth of man and imagination."[3] Similarly, Mr. John Wren-Lewis, a scientist and an influential Anglican layman, while calling himself a believer in God, makes it clear that he is nevertheless totally opposed to the view that "personal power of some kind is really in charge of the natural order behind the scenes."[4] "I believe in the Christian vision of God," writes Mr. Wren-Lewis, and this, he later explains, amounts to believing that "given enough hard work the natural order can be tamed and the world 'made a better place' in our efforts to realize the human values that are summed up in the word 'love.' "[5]

Among anthropomorphic believers it is necessary to distinguish between those who allow no limitations on the extent to which God possesses the various admirable characteristics—he is asserted to be *all*-powerful, *all*-knowing, *all*-loving, *infinitely good, perfectly* just, and so on—and those who allow that God is limited in one or more of these attributes. Professor Hick, who adopts the former of these positions and regards himself as standing for the Judaeo-Christian tradition, dismisses belief in a finite anthropomorphic God without much ado on the ground that it "abandons the basic premise of Hebrew/Christian monotheism" since it "amounts to rejecting belief in the infinity and sovereignty of God."[6] Similarly, Dr. Ewing remarks that the conception of a God who is limited by external obstacles is "very unsatisfying to the religious mind" and "seems to conflict with religious intuition."[7] Whether this is so or not—and apparently it is a position which does not conflict with the religious intuitions of *some* men, including a number who regard themselves as Christians—the belief in a finite anthropomorphic deity has seemed to a number of reasonably impartial students of the subject the only form of anthropomorphic belief that is not open to certain fatal objections. Mill spoke for many others when he accused traditional natural theologians of either "exhausting the resources of sophistry" or else "hardening their hearts" in their answers to the problem of evil. "The only admissible moral theory of Creation," he concluded, "is that the Principle of Good *cannot* at once and altogether subdue the powers of evil, either physical or moral. . . . Of all the religious explanations of the order

254

of nature, this alone is neither contradictory to itself, nor to the facts for which it attempts to account."[8]

THE SEMANTIC DIFFICULTIES OF ANTHROPOMORPHIC THEOLOGY

I now wish to discuss two momentous objections to anthropomorphic belief. The first of these equally bears on all forms of this position and it seems to me an absolutely decisive objection. Perhaps I can best explain it by first mentioning a familiar retort by believers to what they regard as a silly and superficial criticism. One of the Soviet astronauts remarked after his return that in his space trip he did not anywhere see traces of a deity. In this he echoed the statement attributed to Laplace that "in scanning the heavens with a telescope he found no God." Similarly, the Nineteenth Century German physiologist, Emil DuBois-Reymond, based his atheism on the contention that if there were a God one ought to be able to find a cosmic brain that would be suitable as bodily foundation of the divine consciousness, adding that in fact no such brain has ever been or is likely to be found in the future. The student of nature, in DuBois-Reymond's colorful language, before he can "allow a psychical principle to the universe," will demand to be shown "somewhere within it, embedded in neurine and fed with warm arterial blood under proper pressure, a convolution of ganglionic globules and nerve-tubes proportioned in size to the faculties of such a mind."[9]

Considerations of this kind are usually dismissed by believers as crude misunderstandings of their position. Etienne Borne speaks of such a challenge as "tritely positivist atheism" which "misses the point of the problem altogether."[10] Replying explicitly to Laplace and DuBois-Reymond, the 19th-century Unitarian theologian, James Martineau, observed that although the physiologist finds no soul when he opens up the brain, "we positively know" (by introspection) the existence of conscious thought. Similarly, that "the telescope misses all but the bodies of the universe and their light" has no tendency to prove "the absence of a Living Mind through all."[11] If you take the "wrong instrument" you will not find what you are looking for.

Let us, for the sake of argument, grant that Martineau and Borne are right— that since believers conceive of God as a purely spiritual being and not as a magnified man, the fact that we do not find any traces of a cosmic brain or body is irrelevant to the question of the existence of God. At the same time one feels constrained to raise the following questions: What is God like if he is not a grand consciousness tied to a grand body, if he is so completely nonphysical as to make any results of telescopic exploration antecedently irrelevant? If the telescope, as Martineau put it, is the "wrong instrument," what is the right

255

instrument? More specifically, what does it mean to speak of a pure spirit, a disembodied mind, as infinitely (or finitely) powerful, wise, good, just, and all the rest? We can understand these words when they are applied to human beings who have bodies and whose behavior is publicly observable; we could undoubtedly understand these words when they are applied to some hypothetical superhuman beings who also have bodies and whose behavior is in principle observable; but what do they mean when they are applied to a pure spirit? Do they then mean anything at all? What would it be like to be, for example, just, without a body? To be just, a person has to behave in certain ways. But how is it possible to perform these acts, to behave in the required ways, without a body? Similar remarks apply to the other divine attributes. These questions are of course inspired by the conviction, shared by many contemporary philosophers who have considered the subject at length, that it does not make any sense to talk about a disembodied consciousness, that psychological predicates are *logically* tied to the behavior of organisms. It should be observed that this is not the same as reductive materialism. It does not imply that a person is just his body, that there are no private experiences, or that feelings are simply ways of behaving. It makes the milder claim that however much more than a body a human being may be, one cannot sensibly talk about this "more" without presupposing (as part of what one means, and not as a mere contingent fact) that he is a living organism.

Believers and even unbelievers have a tendency not to see the seriousness of this problem, because, as far as their actual mental processes are concerned, they think of God as a being with a body regardless of the theoretical pronouncements to the contrary which they deliver in their more guarded moments. It is true that the images of most Western adults are not those of a big king on his heavenly throne, but it nevertheless seems to be the case that, when they think about God *unself-consciously* (and this is, incidentally, true of most unbelievers also), they vaguely think of him as possessing some kind of rather large body. The moment they assert or deny or question such statements as "God created the Universe" or "God will be a just judge when we come before him," they introduce a body into the background, if not into the foreground, of their mental picture. Adults differ from children not in having no images, but in having images that are less vivid and less definite.

Professor Hick is one of the few anthropomorphic believers who have tried to face the problem of how we can meaningfully apply such words as "loving" or "just" to a being without a body. "Love (whether *Eros* or *Agape*)," he writes, "is expressed in behavior, in the speaking of words of love, and in a range of actions from love-making to the various forms of practical and sacrificial caring. But God is said to be 'without body, parts or passion.' He has then, it would seem, no local existence or bodily presence through which to express love. But what is disembodied love; and how can we ever know that it exists? Parallel questions arise in relation to the other divine attributes."[12] Hick believes that this problem is at least partially solved by reference to the doctrine of the Incarnation. Following the traditional distinction between the metaphysical attributes of God (aseity, eternity, infinitey, etc.) and God's moral attributes (goodness, love, wisdom, etc.), Hick concedes that the Incarnation sheds no light on the metaphysical attributes, but he thinks that it shows us what is meant by moral attributes of God. The doctrine of the Incarnation involves the claim that the moral attributes of God:

> have been embodied, so far as this is possible, in a finite human life, namely, that of the Christ. This claim makes it possible to point to the person of Christ as showing what is meant by assertions such as, "God is good" and "God loves his human creatures." The moral attitudes of God toward mankind are held to have been incarnated in Jesus and expressed concretely in his dealings with men and women.[13]

> The Christian doctrine of the incarnation . . . points to the historical individual, Jesus of Nazareth, and regarding him from the special point of view of those who have received him as a divine Savior, it claims that the various attitudes which Jesus displayed toward the men and women whom he met in Palestine *were also God's attitudes toward those particular individuals.* Jesus' attitudes thus exhibit and reveal certain aspects of God's nature.[14]

> On the basis of this belief, the life of Christ as depicted in the New Testament records provides a foundation for statements about God. From God's attitudes in Christ toward a random assortment of men and women in First-Century Palestine, it is possible to affirm, for example, that God's love is *continuous in character* with that displayed in the life of Jesus.[15]

These considerations, Hick maintains, enable us to answer the question in what sense God can be said to be "loving." The answer is "in the sense in which Jesus can be seen to have exhibited this characteristic."[16]

At the outset of this paper I observed that believers have a tendency to be satisfied with rejoinders that are incredibly weak. I think that Hick's appeal to the Incarnation is a case in point. To begin with, if I understand him correctly, he implies that when anthropomorphic believers who do not accept the doctrine of Incarnation speak of God as good or loving, they, unlike believers in the Incarnation, are talking nonsense. This, it should be observed, would include all Jews, a great many people who call themselves Christians but who in varying degrees reject the Incarnation, all deists as well as philosophers like Mill and James. Such a consequence seems to me quite incredible. I have heard Jews and Christians remark that, although they differ on certain important matters, they, in opposition to atheists and agnostics, share the belief in a loving and just God. If Hick is right, the Jews who say this are talking nonsense while the Christians, provided they are sufficiently orthodox, are talking sense.

257

This objection, however, does not go to the root of the matter. The main trouble with Hick's answer may be stated very simply: Confining ourselves to the instance of love, the original problem was how one can meaningfully speak of God as loving his creatures when God does not possess a body. Hick proposes to solve this problem by pointing to loving acts on the part of Jesus. But this is a total evasion of the original difficulty. For, however, wonderful and over-whelming the love of Jesus may have been, it was the love of another person *with a body*. If God is conceived as having a body there is no semantic problem to begin with and reference to the loving acts of Jesus is not necessary—those of other human beings would then be quite sufficient to serve as a model. If, on the other hand, God is declared to be without a body, then reference to the char-acter and behavior of Jesus is no more helpful in explaining what it is for God to love his creatures than reference to the love of less illustrious embodied persons. When Hick remarks that Christ's acts make it "possible to affirm that God's love is continuous in character with that displayed in the life of Jesus" it is not at all clear what is meant by "continuous in character." I can understand what it means to say that the love of a dog for his master is "continuous in character" with the love of a child for its parents, but I can attach no meaning to the state-ment that the love of an embodied individual called Jesus is "continuous in character" with the love of a disembodied being called God. To be told that Jesus was the son of God, or in Hick's words, that "God the Son was incarnate in Jesus of Nazareth"[17] does not help in the least. For exactly the same problem arises in connection with the fatherhood of God. If God is taken to have a body we can understand what it means to say that Jesus was his son. But if God is said to be without a body the statement that Jesus was the son of God is as "problematic," as much in need of explanation as the statement that God loves his creatures.

Perhaps it is worth our while formulating this criticism in a slightly different way. The various attitudes which Jesus displayed toward his contemporaries, Hick remarks, "were also God's attitudes towards those particular individuals" and he adds that "Jesus' attitudes thus exhibit and reveal certain aspects of God's nature." As a genuine supernaturalist, Hick does not contend that the sentence "God loves his creatures" is just a way of referring to certain of the actions of Jesus. But if it is taken to assert more, then we must make a distinc-tion between two kinds of aspects or modes of God's love—those which are observable in the actions of Jesus and those which are distinct from anything done by Jesus and which are more directly or immediately part of God's nature or character. The puzzle arises in connection with the latter aspects or modes of love of a disembodied being, and our observation or knowledge of the modes or aspects that are identical with the acts of Jesus does not help us to understand what the latter aspects or modes are. It should be pointed out that Hick's use of the words *exhibit* and *reveal* in his statement that "Jesus' attitudes exhibit and reveal certain aspects of God's nature" is thoroughly misleading. Normally, when we say that something reveals certain features of something else, we imply that these features could in principle be independently identified or described. Thus we may say that a dental x-ray reveals an abscess or that a photograph reveals how much the person in question has aged. It is proper to use *reveal* in these statements only because we can independently explain what is meant by the word *abscess* and what it is to look older. Hick has not explained and as far as I can see, he cannot explain, independent of the attitudes of Jesus, what the aspects of God's nature are that are said to be revealed or exhibited in these attitudes.

I can now state the whole of what I regard as a fatal difficulty besetting all forms of anthropomorphic belief. It is best formulated as a dilemma: God must be conceived either as having or as not having a body. In the former case we do not have a semantic problem—words like "just," "good," "loving," can be meaningfully applied to God—but the Laplace-DuBois-Reymond objection becomes relevant: no appropriate bodily structure has been found and, as believers themselves acknowledge, no such structure is expected to be found. If, on the other hand, it is declared that God has no body, the believer escapes the Laplace-DuBois-Reymond objection only at the expense of depriving the predicates in question of their meaning. If God has a body what the believer asserts is intelligible but false or very likely to be false; if God is taken to be a disembodied spirit, the believer cannot be accused of asserting something false, but at the same time his position has ceased to be intelligible.

THE ESCHATOLOGICAL "SOLUTION" OF THE PROBLEM OF EVIL

The second of the two objections to the anthropomorphic position I wish to consider is much more familiar and it is one which has always disturbed sensitive and intelligent believers. This is the so-called argument from evil and it is directed only at the orthodox believers who assert that the universe is the creation of a being who is all-powerful, all-knowing, all-good and all-loving. The sufferings of animals could have been eliminated or greatly reduced by an all-powerful being. If there is such a being and he allowed the suffering although he could have prevented it, then he certainly is not all-good and not all-loving. Nor is the human scene much better. Rabbi Seymour Siegel, a Conservative theologian at the Jewish Theological Seminary—an unlikely source to quote in my support—recently asked the following question: "What does it mean after Auschwitz to say that God is working in the world?", adding, "This is an unanswered question on which no tradition has a monopoly."[18] Where was the all-powerful and the all-loving being in Auschwitz? Why did he not come to the help of the Jews? Granting that some of these Jews may have been wicked men, they scarcely deserved such a fate; and surely some of these Jews, at least the children, were not yet hopelessly depraved. Jean Jaurés and Karl Liebknecht and the late President Kennedy were men of good will, but the Almighty did nothing to deflect the path of the assassins' bullets. Hitler was not a man of good will, but between 1942 and 1944 he almost miraculously escaped numerous attempts on his life planned by men of courage and decency. When finally Count Stauffenberg succeeded in placing a time bomb in Hitler's headquarters, Hitler escaped with relatively minor injuries and it was Stauffenberg and his associates who were executed with the utmost cruelty. Occasionally one is told that what happened at Auschwitz and the untold sufferings of children at the hands of vicious parents and teachers is an inevitable consequence of the wonderful gift of free will. There is much that is objectionable in such a retort, but even if it were accepted, there would still remain all the terrible suffering that is in no way connected with free human choices. "For aught I know to the contrary," writes Bertrand Russell,

> there may be a Being of infinite power who chooses that children should die of meningitis, and older people of cancer; these things occur, and occur as the result of evolution. If, therefore, evolution embodies a Divine Plan, these occurrences must also have been planned. I have been informed that suffering is sent as a purification for sin, but I find it difficult to think that a child of four or five years old can be sunk in such black depths of iniquity as to deserve the punishment that befalls not a few of the children whom our optimistic divines might see any day, if they chose, suffering torments in children's hospitals. Again, I am told that though the child himself may not have sinned very deeply, he deserves to suffer on account of his parents' wickedness. I can only repeat that if this is the Divine sense of justice it differs from mine, and that I think mine superior. If indeed the world in which we live has been produced in accordance with a Plan, we shall have to reckon Nero a saint in comparison with the Author of that Plan.[19]

It is widely agreed today that various traditional answers to this challenge are hopelessly inadequate. Some believers, especially those influenced by Kierkegaard, content themselves with replying that their "Biblical faith" is unshakable no matter how dreadful the world may be. For "adherents of Biblical faith," writes Emil Fackenheim, "times of external or internal darkness" are not evidences against the existence of God, "but rather—to use Martin Buber's expression—evidence of an 'eclipse of God.' "[20] It is doubtful that these writers have fully understood the nature of the difficulty facing the anthropomorphic believer. If a person's belief is so strong that nothing can shake it, this in no way shows that certain of the facts which fail to shake his faith are not in fact inconsistent with *what* he believes.[21] Other believers are content to describe the existence of evil as "an ineffable mystery," but this seems to be simply an admission of defeat without saying so in so many words.

One of the few notable exceptions among contemporary believers who does not simply point to the unshakable nature of Biblical faith or concede that the evil in the world is nothing but "an ineffable mystery" is John Hick, whose views about the relation between God's love and the actions of Jesus we examined earlier in this paper. In a number of publications Hick has presented an elaborate theodicy or solution of the problem of evil.[22] Hick is also one of the few defenders of theology to be well informed of developments in analytic philosophy and he thus has some appreciation of difficulties (like that of giving any meaning to claims about disembodied survival) of which more old-fashioned believers are largely oblivious. It will be instructive to inquire whether his theodicy is any more plausible than those of earlier believers.

Hick is a fideist, and before presenting some of the highlights of his theodicy, something should be said about the nature of his fideism. Like other fideists, Hick concedes to the unbelievers that the existence of God cannot be proved or made probable by an appeal to evidence or arguments. It has to be accepted on faith. However, unlike Kierkegaardian fideists, Hick maintains that we have a right to believe something on faith only if it is intelligible and if it does not go against the observed facts. The fact that we cannot prove the existence of God is not an objection to belief in God, but if there were strong or decisive evidence against the existence of God, this would constitute a serious and perhaps even a fatal objection to the fideist's position. Accordingly, Hick is extremely concerned to show that the existence of evil is not incompatible with the belief in an all-powerful and all-loving God.

Hick begins by observing the customary distinction between "moral evil" and "the non-moral evil of suffering or pain."[23] He believes that the question "why does an all-good and all-powerful God permit moral evil?" can be at least partially answered by an appeal to human freedom, which Hick interprets along antideterministic lines. "We can never provide a complete causal explanation of a free act; if we could, it would not be a free act."[24] Hick brushes aside as quite untenable the view held by many contemporary philosophers that an action may well be "free" and at the same time completely caused and in principle predictable and that hence, in addition to giving us freedom, God could have provided us with the kind of character with which we would invariably choose the good. If God had given us such a character, we would, according to Hick, always "of necessity act in a certain way" and we would not be "genuinely independent persons in relation to him." The idea of "a person who can be infallibly guaranteed always to act rightly is self-contradictory."[25] However, although the appeal to freedom reconciles the *possibility* of moral evil with the perfect goodness of God, it does not explain the actuality of evil. Since freedom means absence of complete causation, free choices of evil (and I assume also of good) must "remain inexplicable." The origin of moral evil, we are told, "lies forever concealed within the mystery of human freedom."[26]

261

"Light" has now been thrown on "a great deal of suffering which afflicts mankind"—on all the evils that result from "the inhumanity or the culpable incompetence of mankind."[27] However, there remains all the nonmoral evil— "the sources of pain which are entirely independent of human will, for example, earthquakes, hurricanes, storm, flood, drought, and blight"; and there are also of course such phenomena as disease many of which cannot be attributed to "man's misuse" of his freedom. To reconcile these evils with belief in the reality of God, the latter must be considered "in its context of associated and corollary beliefs."[28] The first of these associated beliefs concerns the purpose of God's creation. God's purpose was *not* the perfect happiness of human beings but rather what Hick calls "soul-making." Hick usually gets lyrical when he tries to explain what we are to understand by "soul-making." Thus, on the first occasion when this phrase is introduced, we are told that a place of soul-making is one "in which free beings, grappling with the tasks and challenges of their existence in a common environment, may become 'children of God' and 'heirs of eternal life.' "[29] However, it seems fairly clear that Hick means by "soul-making" much the same as what old-fashioned educators used to call "character training," that is, the development of such qualities as courage, honesty, patience, "loving sympathy," "self-giving for others," loyalty to friends, etc.—qualities whose possession, he implies, does not necessarily make a person any happier but may on the contrary result in a great deal of pain and suffering. If God, in creating the world, had aimed at the establishment of a "permanent hedonistic paradise," then the problem of evil would indeed be insoluble, since the environment in which we find ourselves is "so manifestly not designed for the maximization of human pleasure and the minimization of human pain." In relation to the purpose of soul-making, on the other hand, our world "may be rather well adapted." Courage and fortitude, for example, "would have no point in an environment in which there is no danger or difficulty."[30] Sometimes at least we can see "sin ending in repentence" and "calamities producing patience and moral steadfastness."[31] "Even tragedy, though truly tragic," can have desirable consequences from the point of view of soul-making.

The second associated belief to which we must appeal in order to reconcile the goodness of God with the evil in the world is the belief in a future life of bliss and fulfillment. Hick concedes that "although there are many striking instances of good being triumphantly brought out of evil through a man's or a woman's reaction to it, there are many other cases in which the opposite has happened."[32] There are also many instances in which suffering, so far from producing strength, courage and unselfishness, leads instead to "resentment, fear, grasping, selfishness and disintegration of character." We are therefore obliged to conclude that "any divine purpose of soul-making which is at work in earthly history must continue beyond this life if it is ever to achieve more than a very partial and fragmentary success."[33] Furthermore, although the goal of

262

God's creation is not conceived as the establishment of a hedonistic paradise, pain and sorrow *as such* remain evils, and in order to reconcile their existence with the goodness of God, they must be justified in terms of a "future good" which is "great enough."[34] If the soul-making purpose fails—and "so far as we can see it does in fact fail in our own world at least as often as it succeeds"[35] — there could be no justification for "the heavy and weary weight of all this unintelligible world."

In order to present a satisfactory answer to the problem of evil we must accordingly advocate the doctrine that "beyond death God will resurrect or re-create or reconstitute the human personality in both its inner and its outer aspects."[36] The life beyond death has to be conceived as a "state of exultant and blissful happiness" symbolized in the teaching of Jesus as "a joyous banquet in which all and sundry, having accepted God's gracious invitation, rejoice together."[37] Only such a "triumphant resolution," only "this infinite future good" can "render worthwhile all the pain and travail and wickedness that has occurred on the way to it." Hick is most emphatic that unless one supports these eschatological predictions it would not be possible "to believe in the perfect goodness of God and in His unlimited capacity to perform His will. For if there are finally wasted lives and finally unredeemed sufferings, either God is not perfect in love or He is not sovereign in rule over His creation."[38] Hick is well aware of the weakness of the arguments in support of theories of "natural immortality" and he frankly rests this portion of this theodicy on hope and faith.[39]

There is a great deal in all this that I find objectionable but since my time is limited I will confine my criticisms to the eschatological aspects of Hick's theory. I should, however, remark in passing that one may legitimately question whether a loving God would really prefer soul-making to happiness as the goal of his creation and whether he might not perhaps have simultaneously aimed at both. I also find almost all of Hick's statements on the subject of freedom exceedingly dubious. He implies, at least as far as human actions are concerned, that determinism is false; but it seems to me that all the evidence indicates that in this area determinism is true. Hick also implies that an action would not be free if it were in principle predictable, but in fact it seems to me that in any ordinary sense in which we use the word *free,* most emphatically including situations in which we hold people morally accountable for their actions, a person is not deprived of his freedom if his action is seen to be in principle predictable. However, these are big questions which cannot be pursued here, and in any case it will be seen that Hick's theodicy would not work even if he were right on all the issues just mentioned.

It seems to me that there are two fatal objections to the eschatological parts of Hick's solution. First, regardless of how wonderful the joyous banquet at God's table may be, regardless of the infinite duration of the future good, regardless of the "triumphant" nature of the "eventual perfect fulfillment of God's purpose," *what happened happened and cannot be undone.* The infinite future good will not undo what Hitler and Stalin and their predecessors and associates did to countless human beings. It will not undo the dreadful tortures and sufferings of animals and children. Nobody has stated this point more movingly than Dostevski, who was not an atheist but a puzzled believer, and who was too honest and too sensitive to be satisfied with nebulous promises about triumphant resolutions. In *The Brothers Karamozov,* Ivan relates the tortures of some innocent children—actual, not fictional events—and then explains why an eschatological theodicy will not satisfy him.

> I took the case of children only to make my case clearer. Of the other tears of humanity with which the earth is soaked from its crust to its center, I will say nothing.
>
> . . . . .
>
> I've only taken the children, because in their case what I mean is so unanswerably clear. Listen! If all must suffer to pay for the eternal harmony, what have children to do with it, tell me please? It's beyond all comprehension why they should suffer, and why they should pay for the harmony. Why should they, too, furnish material to enrich the soil for the harmony of the future?
>
> . . . . .
>
> Oh, Alyosha, I am not blaspheming! I understand, of course what an upheaval of the universe it will be, when everything in heaven and earth blends in one hymn of praise and everything that lives and has lived cries aloud: "Thou art just, O Lord, for Thy ways are revealed."
>
> . . . . .
>
> It really may happen that if I live to that moment, or rise again to see it, I, too, perhaps, may cry aloud with the rest, looking at the mother embracing the child's torturer, "Thou art just, O Lord!" but I don't want to cry aloud then. While there is still time, I hasten to protect myself and so I renounce the higher harmony altogether. It's not worth the tears of that one tortured child who beat itself on the breast with its little fist and prayed in its stinking outhouse with an unexpiated tear to "dear, kind God!!' It's not worth it, because those tears are unatoned for. They must be atoned for, or there can be no harmony. But how? How are you going to atone for them? It is possible? By their being avenged? But what do I care for avenging them? What do I care for a hell for oppressors? What good can hell do, since those children have already been tortured?
>
> . . . . .
>
> Imagine that you are creating a fabric of human destiny with the object of making men happy in the end, giving them peace and rest at last, but that it was essential and inevitable to torture to death only one tiny creature—that baby beating its breast with its fist, for instance—and to found that edifice on its unavenged tears, would you consent to be the architect on those conditions? Tell me, and tell the truth. No. I wouldn't consent, said Alyosha softly . . .[40]

Dostoevski here speaks of the object of "making men happy in the end" and this, as we saw, is not part of Hick's theodicy; but if we substitute "soul-making" for happiness, the objection does not lose any of its sting. Soul-making, here or in the hereafter, is not promoted by the cruel murder of children.

Hick refers to Dostoevski and he has some slight awareness of this difficulty, but in effect his answer amounts to a lame evasion. "Could even an endless heavenly joy," he asks, "ever heal the scars of deep human suffering?" He admits that "it is very difficult to resolve such a question; for we do not know what is possible, let alone what is probable in realms of being so far beyond our present experience."[41] However, there are some possible ways of meeting the difficulty:

> It may be that the personal scars and memories of evil remain forever, but are transfigured in the light of the universal mutual forgiveness and reconciliation on which the life of heaven is based. Or it may be that the journey to the heavenly Kingdom is so long, and traverses such varied spheres of existence, involving so many new and transforming experiences, that in the end the memory of our earthly life is dimmed to the point of extinction.[42]

Such "possibilities" suggest that, "although not at present soluble," the puzzle is "not such as to overthrow the theodicy that we have been developing."

As elsewhere, Hick makes things too easy for himself. He asks the wrong question when he inquires whether endless heavenly joy can heal deep scars. Scars may heal, even deep ones, but this does not mean that the events which brought about the scars did not take place or that they were not evil—and that is the point at issue. Again, "new and transforming experiences" may extinguish the memory of our earthly life; but this does not wipe out what happened. Trotsky, in his heavenly life, may forget what Stalin did to him and to his family here on earth, but this will not undo the fact that Stalin did what he did. I should add that I also have some misgivings about the moral rightness of the orgy of "mutual forgiveness" which, according to Hick, will take place in our heavenly lives. I think it would be wrong for Trotsky to forgive Stalin, it would be wrong for Thomas Paine to forgive George Washington's treachery, it would be wrong for Bertrand Russell to forgive Judge McGeehan, and it would most certainly be wrong for Jewish children to forgive their Nazi exterminators. It is one thing to refrain from seeking vengeance, but it is quite another to forgive cruelty and injustice. People who can forgive this kind of thing are usually as much lacking in a sense of what is right and wrong as those who perpetrated the acts in question.

There are, however, even more serious objections. These are an immediate consequence of the resort to eschatology. Hick insists that an intelligent Christian will want his position to be judged as a whole and that the doctrine of eternal bliss is an essential part of his position. "This eschatological element," he writes, "is quite inseparable from any conception of God and the universe which is to be recognizably Christian."[43] In the light of such statements it would be unfair to judge the ability of Hick's system to withstand the problem of evil without a consideration of his claims about the life beyond death. At the same time, however, any objections to the immortality theory will now ipso facto be objections to the system as a whole. If the goodness of God can be vindicated only by assuming that people live beyond death in a permanent state of bliss, then anything that might show that this latter doctrine is meaningless or false or highly improbable will at the same time undermine the theory that there is an all-powerful and all-loving God.

Hick writes as if the immortality-question were a perfectly open one—that while there is no good evidence for the theory, there is equally no good evidence against it. In fact the situation seems to be radically different from this. There are extremely strong grounds for dismissing belief in survival as either meaningless or false, depending on how it is construed. If it is construed as survival without a body, it is difficult to see, for reasons explained earlier in connection with the logic of psychological predicates, what this could mean and Hick himself regards such talk as unintelligible. If it is construed as survival of a person with his resurrected body, then all the evidence—and it is overwhelming evidence—indicates that no such resurrection takes place. Hick himself is satisfied[44]—as most other people are, whether they believe in God or not—that the bodies of plants and animals are not resurrected. We have exactly the same kind of evidence for concluding that the bodies of human beings are also not resurrected: no matter where we have looked, we have never witnessed such resurrections; and, more important, we frequently know what happens to the particles of dead human bodies and what happens is not participation in the reconstitution of the original body.

In a chapter entitled "Human Destiny,"[45] Hick shows some appreciation of these problems. He tries to resolve them by interpreting "resurrection" in a very special way. The resurrection that he, Hick, is talking about "has nothing to do with the resurrection of corpses in a cemetery."[46] The "resurrection replicas" of our earthly bodies which figure in Hick's eschatology are to be located in a "different world altogether, a resurrection world inhabited only by resurrection persons."[47] This world, Hick further remarks,

> occupies its own space distinct from that with which we are now familiar. That is to say, an object in the resurrection world is not situated at any distance or in any direction from the objects in our present world, although each object in either world is spatially related to every other object in the same world.[48]

As now interpreted, the objections to the resurrection theory mentioned earlier would indeed be circumvented. The fact that we never observe resurrections is not due to there not being any, but to our inability, while alive in this world, to observe anything that goes on in the space of the resurrection world; and the fact that the particles of dead bodies in our world have a fate very different from that of being used as resurrection particles is irrelevant presumably because the resurrection replicas, in addition to occupying a different space, are also composed of numerically distinct though exactly similar particles. I fear I cannot attach any meaning to this sort of talk and I think Hick deludes himself into believing that it has some meaning because one does get various pictures of resurrections "somewhere in space" when one hears or reads Hick's sentences. I *can* attach meaning to claims about the resurrection of our bodies elsewhere in *our* space and then, as already observed, such claims are as fantastic as similar claims would be about the resurrection of plants and animals. Perhaps, rather than indulge in resurrection claims either in the obvious sense in which they are intelligible but utterly fantastic or in Hick's special "sense" in which they amount to picture-mongering and not to any genuine assertions, a believer in an anthropomorphic God would do well to move over into the camp of the "finitists" even if he thereby does some violence to his "religious intuitions."

Those who already strongly believe in an all-powerful and all-loving God are apt to misconceive the logic of the situation in which this belief is buttressed by the addition of the immortality assumption. They are apt to think that the immortality doctrine functions here much like an ad hoc hypothesis in science when this can be justified as a rational procedure. If we have a theory, *t*, which is based on a good deal of observed evidence and if then some fact, *F*, is observed which would disconfirm or falsify *t*, we are apt to introduce a special explanation of *F* so as to save *t*. We will do this although we do not actually have any evidence for this special explanation. Thus, if a certain drug has invariably been found to cure a certain disease and if it does not work in a new case, we may, rather than scrapping our theory about its universal potency, introduce the ad hoc assumption that something went wrong in the preparation of the drug or that the patient's disease had been wrongly diagnosed. However, this procedure is rational only because we do have strong evidence for the theory which we are interested in saving and because the ad hoc hypothesis is not itself absurd or extremely improbable. In Hick's case the theory to be saved is conceded to be unsupported by good evidence and the ad hoc assumption is open to the gravest objections. It should be added that at least the first of these criticisms would not apply to rationalistic believers like Aquinas or Descartes provided that their arguments for the existence of God are granted some logical force.

THE EMPTINESS OF METAPHYSICAL BELIEF

Whatever special difficulties there may be in the position of the metaphysical believers, the least that can be said for it is that it escapes the problem of evil with the greatest of ease. If one holds that God is all-powerful and all-good in the literal sense of these words, then indeed it follows that the world should not contain any evil or at least not all the kinds and quantities of evil that do exist; but if one avoids what Mansel calls a "vulgar Rationalism" or what Tillich castigates as a "disastrous literalism,"[49] no such consequence can be derived from the theological assertion and hence the problem of evil simply does not arise.

The "vulgar Rationalists," among whom Mansel would include all those whom we have called anthropomorphic believers, hold that

> all the excellences of which we are conscious in the creature, must necessarily exist in the same manner, though in a higher degree in the Creator. God is indeed more wise, more just, more merciful, than man; but for that very reason, his wisdom and justice and mercy must contain nothing that is incompatible with the corresponding attributes in their human character.[50]

This view that "the attributes of God differ from those of man in degree only and not in kind" and that "the mental and moral qualities of which we are conscious in ourselves" provide us with a "true image" of the "infinite perfections of God" is totally unfounded. Confining ourselves to the question of God's infinite goodness, it has to be stated that:

> the representation of God after the model of the highest human morality which we are capable of conceiving, is not sufficient to account for all the phenomena exhibited by the course of his natural Providence. The infliction of physical suffering, the permission of moral evil, the adversity of the good, the prosperity of the wicked, the crimes of the guilty involving the misery of the innocent, the tardy appearance and partial distribution of moral and religious knowledge in the world—these are facts which no doubt are reconcilable, we know not how, with the Infinite Goodness of God, but which certainly are not to be explained on the supposition that its sole and sufficient type is to be found in the finite goodness of man.[51]

We cannot conceive of God "as a whole composed of parts or a substance consisting of attributes, or a conscious subject in antithesis to an object,"[52] and indeed we cannot conceive or know any of God's essential attributes. For this reason we cannot judge what is or is not consistent with God's attributes and we cannot maintain that the evil in the world is inconsistent with God's goodness.

In our own day a very similar position has been advocated by various existentialist theologians, especially those who, under the influence of Heidegger, have identified God with "Being" or "Being-itself." Thus Professor John Macquarrie, a leading Protestant theologian and cotranslator of Heidegger's *Sein und Zeit,* criticizes the traditional anthropomorphic believers on the ground that by "God" they did not mean

> being but "some being" or "another being" in addition to the world; not, it may be, a "particular being," but still "*a* being," even if he is called the

ens realissimum and regarded as the most beingful of all beings. Even an almighty being of this sort is still *toto coelo* different from being itself, and is transcended by being.[53]

We must, Macquarrie goes on, "reconceive God, not as *a* being, however exalted, but as being, which must in any case be more ultimate than any being."[54] God reconsidered in this way "so far transcends" any of the objects of our experience that the "most positive characteristics" of these objects must "fall short and fail to reach him."[55]

Perhaps nobody in our century has championed metaphysical belief more vigorously than the late Paul Tillich. Repeatedly he attacked the position of the anthropomorphic believers in the most unqualified language. "A God," he writes in one place,

> about whose existence or nonexistence you can argue is a thing beside others within the universe of existing things. And the question is quite justified whether such a thing does exist, and the answer is equally justified that it does not exist.[56]

Theologians who regard God as "the highest being" treat God as an "individual substance" and "a cause alongside other causes."[57] They thereby transform "the infinity of God into a finiteness which is merely an extension of the categories of finitude."[58] The naturalists who oppose this kind of theology are quite in the right. In fact, those advocating anthropomorphic belief "are more dangerous for religion than the so-called atheistic scientists."[59]

No, God is not a being. He is Being-itself and there is an "infinite distance" between God so conceived and "the whole of finite things."[60] Like Macquarrie, Tillich emphasizes that "God transcends every being and also the totality of beings—the world." Between Being-itself and finite beings, "there is an absolute break, 'an infinite jump' "—there is "no proportion or graduation between the finite and the infinite."[61] It is a direct consequence of this position that words like "good" and "loving" and "caring" which are introduced in connection with "segments of finite experience" cannot be used literally when applied to God. Tillich is not opposed to the retention of traditional religious language so long as it is realized that the words in question are used symbolically or metaphorically and not literally. "Everything religion has to say about God, including his qualities, actions, and manifestations, has a symbolic character and . . . the meaning of 'God' is completely missed if one takes the symbolic language literally."[62] It is true that "everything finite participates in being itself and its infinity,"[63] but Being-itself or the infinite cannot be an object of anybody's secular or mystical experience. "Unconditioned transcendence as such is not perceptible."[64] It can only be talked about in "mythical conceptions" and not even "mysticism eliminates the myth."[65] God, rightly conceived, "transcends

269

both mysticism and the person-to-person encounter."[66] The reality referred to by religious symbols "is absolutely beyond human comprehension."[67]

We saw that, according to Macquarrie, God—reconceived as being—is "more ultimate than any being." What Macquarrie means is I think explained by Tillich when he insists that, unlike the God of the anthropomorphic believers whose existence can be as legitimately questioned as the existence of any other thing or being, God conceived as Being-itself is not a contingent entity. The idea of God, in the metaphysical sense, is not the idea of "some*thing* or some*one* who might or might not exist."[68] From various of his discussions it is clear that Tillich— and the same is probably true of Macquarrie—regards the ontological argument as fundamentally sound. It does not, as some of its supporters may have thought, prove the existence of the anthropomorphic God and it is not really a "proof" at all, but it embodies the insight that Being is not a contingent entity and that its reality cannot be meaningfully questioned.

Granting that the position of the metaphysical believers is immune to the problem of evil, this immunity appears to be purchased at a very steep price. In protecting themselves against any possible counterevidence, the metaphysical believers have made their theology *compatible with anything whatsoever*; and normally we regard a statement as empty or devoid of any assertive force if it is retained no matter what the world is like. In order to make a genuine factual assertion, we must exclude some conceivable state of affairs, but it is clear that the theology of Mansel, Tillich, and Macquarrie excludes no conceivable state of the universe. If the world became very much worse, even if there were a future life in which all just and kind people are subjected to horrible and unending tortures, we could not regard this as incompatible with the goodness of Mansel's Infinite, since that goodness is inconceivable and the Being championed by Tillich and Macquarrie would still be "actual." We saw that the latter was so "ultimate" that it cannot not be and that its actuality is completely independent of the detailed characteristics of the world. It should be observed that the anthropomorphic believer is not open to this objection. Whatever the difficulties besetting his position, it is *not* compatible with anything whatsoever. Hick, for example, is committed to abandoning his theology if there were no afterlife or if there were another life which is no better than the present one. He also appears to imply that his position would be falsified or at least seriously weakened if it could be shown that all human actions are completely caused or alternatively that the only intelligible sense in which a person can be said to be free is one in which this presupposes the complete causation of his action. Although I am myself inclined to verificationism, I wish to emphasize that the above criticism of metaphysical theology does not rest on acceptance of the Verification Principle. I am here allowing, for the sake of argument, that there may be aspects of the world which are in principle unobservable and I am also allowing, what most verificationists would deny, that it makes sense to talk about happiness or suffering in "the next world."

270

Mr. Michael Novak, in a recent article in which he asserts that I fail to understand Tillich because of my "limited equipment," has offered a rebuttal to the kind of criticism just advanced:

> God does not make a difference *within* the universe of science or *within* the universe of ordinary experience; the fact that God is does not interrupt the probabilities and/or necessities of scientific laws, nor obtrude into our ordinary conscious experience. *Within* the world of our experience the actuality of being-itself is, as Edwards puts it, "compatible with anything whatsoever." Such a concession, Edwards argues, shows that the term "God" fails to have a referent; but to Tillich it shows that God is not an object in our experience but transcendent. The question that has arrested Tillich's attention, but not that of Edwards, is why anything should exist at all. The word "being-itself" does not refer to a power that is discovered by its interventions *within* the universe known to science or *within* the universe known to ordinary experience. It refers, rather, to a power that has determined that the universes of science and ordinary experience, whatever their successive state of affairs, should *be* rather than *not be*.[69]

To this question "Why should anything exist at all?" which, according to Novak, has not arrested my attention, Tillich offers the following answer:

> Because the ultimate point to which our minds can penetrate is that being-itself prevails; there could have been nothing at all, but there are things.

> There are atheists and agnostics who search for God but do not find Him. Tillich, in archaic language, tells them that God is not to be found *among* things; they are looking with the wrong focus. The fruitful focus is one that does not look for a God who is needed to manipulate the states of affairs within the world, but one who is present in any and all states of affairs, present wherever things, events, and persons are, present by the fact that things are, rather than by the characteristics that things have.[70]

Mr. Novak compliments me on my effort to understand Tillich, but with the best will in the world I cannot see that he has answered my objection. In the first part of his rejoinder he tells us what we already knew, namely, that according to Tillich God or Being-itself is "transcendent" though he fails to mention that God "infinitely transcends every finite being." This, however, only tells us what the word God does *not* mean for Tillich. It does not tell us what it does mean. In the second part of his rejoinder God's transcendence is forgotten and we are told that He "is present in any and all states of affairs . . . present by the fact that things are" rather than by their characteristics. If I understand this, the actuality of God is now identified with the fact that there are things and not nothing. I do not wish to dispute this fact, but it surely does nothing to give meaning to Tillich's metaphysical theology which, in claiming God's infinite transcendence, claims a great deal more than that things are. This last assertion

271

is not denied by agnostics, atheists, or any of the other people opposed to existentialist theology. Furthermore I really do not see that Tillich, as here represented by Mr. Novak, has answered the question "why does anything at all exist?" If I ask a hostess "why are you serving tea and not coffee?" no sane person would suppose that she had answered my question by saying "I am serving tea and not coffee." Similarly, Tillich and Novak, in telling us that there are things although there could have been nothing at all, are not answering the question "why are there things and not nothing?" As for the question itself, I assure Mr. Novak that it has arrested my attention, but there is another logically more basic question which has also arrested my attention and which, I gather, has not arrested his—namely: *what is meant* by "Why is there something and not nothing?" I have tried to show in some detail that, as asked by Heidegger and Heideggerian theologians, it is a senseless question.[71]

What is in effect the same objection may also be expressed in the following way: In disclaiming that predicates like "good" and "loving" are used literally when applied to God, the metaphysical believers have not thereby told us in what sense they *are* to be understood. At the same time, various of their statements about the uncharacterizability of the ultimate reality makes it impossible for them to supply a new sense to these words. Mansel told us that the goodness of God is different in kind from human goodness, but what the divine goodness is he never told us. Nor is it possible for him to do so in view of his general position that God's essential attributes are inconceivable. There is a story about two New York salesmen having a "deep" conversation while drinking tea at the Governor Cafeteria. "You see this cup of tea," remarks the first, "Life is like a cup of tea." "What do you mean—life is like a cup of tea?" asks the other man. "How should I know?" replies the first, "I am not a philosopher." Mansel is really in no better position than this salesman. If he does not know what he means, the salesman should not have exclaimed that life is like a cup of tea, and if he does not know what "good" means when applied to God, Mansel should not have asserted that there is a good God.

Very similar comments may be made about various of the declarations by Tillich, Macquarrie, and other Heideggerian theologians that, when applied to Being, words like "good" and "loving" must be understood symbolically or metaphorically and not literally. Such declarations tell us that the words in question do not here mean what they normally mean—they do not tell us what the words do mean and in fact Tillich (to confine ourselves to one such writer) does not, and given his initial position, he cannot succeed in explaining what they mean. Tillich evidently does not appreciate the difference between translatable and untranslatable metaphors and he does not see that *his* metaphors are of the latter kind. Frequently indeed, when words are used metaphorically, the context or certain special conventions make it clear what is asserted. Thus, a few months ago when Cassius Clay refused to be inducted into the army, although he knew that this action was going to cost him his heavyweight title and that it would in all likelihood result in his imprisonment for several years, I remarked to a friend that I was taking my hat off to this man. I said this although I never wear a hat. I used the expression "taking one's hat off" metaphorically and yet what I said was quite intelligible. Why? Because the metaphor was translatable—because it is possible, and in this instance quite easy, to specify in non-metaphorical terms what the sentence was intended to assert. If it were impossible to eliminate the metaphor, I would not have succeeded in making any assertion. In Tillich's case no statements literally characterizing Being-itself are available and hence the metaphors cannot be eliminated. Tillich apparently believes that he can eliminate the metaphors, but whenever he makes an attempt in this direction what we get is a new metaphor and literal significance is never achieved. Thus, to give one example, he proposes to translate the sentence "God is his own destiny." By means of this "symbolic" statement, we "point to . . . the participation of God in becoming and in history."[72] A little earlier, however, we had been informed that "God's participation is not a spatial or temporal presence," and twice in the same paragraph we had been given to understand that when we speak of God, participation "is meant not categorically but symbolically."[73]

I know of only one place in his voluminous writings where Tillich shows some awareness of this problem. It appears that objections along the lines just described were brought to Tillich's attention at some time after the publication of the first volume of *Systematic Theology*. He briefly takes note of them in the early pages of volume II. "The question arises (and has arisen in public discussion)," he writes there, "as to whether there is a point at which a nonsymbolic assertion about God must be made." Tillich confidently and breezily disposes of this question. "There is such a point" [at which a nonsymbolic assertion about God can be made], namely, "the statement that everything we say about God is symbolic. Such a statement is an assertion about God which itself is not symbolic. Otherwise we would fall into a circular argument."[74] This answer is surely based on a misconception of the problem. What is needed to break out of the circle of expressions lacking literal significance is a nonsymbolic or literal statement about God or Being-itself, not a literal statement about the class of theological statements. If we distinguish between theological statements—those in which the word "God" or the word "being" is *used* or which the believer would describe as referring to God or being—and metatheological statements—statements saying something about theological statements in which therefore the words "God" or "being" are *mentioned* and not used—we may say that what Tillich needs is a nonsymbolic *theological* statement and what he gives us instead is a nonsymbolic *metatheological* statement.

NATURALISTIC "THEOLOGY" AND
VERBAL DECEPTION

In conclusion I turn to what I earlier called "naturalistic believers" and for the sake of brevity I shall concentrate on the views of Mr. Wren-Lewis. It will be remembered that, in calling himself a believer in God, Mr. Wren-Lewis does not endorse the position of the anthropomorphic believers and he also does not support what we have been calling metaphysical theology. He merely asserts that "given enough hard work, the natural order can be tamed and the world made a better place in our efforts to realize the human values that are summed up in the word 'love.' " I find this statement somewhat vague, but I agree that the "natural order" can be tamed and that in striving for various goals the world can be made a better place. This naturalistic "theology" is certainly not unintelligible, and since we do not have a categorical prediction, it is also very likely to be true. Nevertheless, I have a serious objection to any talk of this kind. It seems to me a flagrant case of verbal deception. By all accepted criteria, Mr. Wren-Lewis is an atheist who has, however, retained the *word* "God." What Mill said about Mansel's retention of the word "good" when he did not mean what we normally mean by "good" applies just as much to Mr. Wren-Lewis: "to assert in words what we do not think in meaning, is as suitable a definition as can be given of a moral falsehood."[75] The fact that Mr. Wren-Lewis is not a member of some antireligious society but a distinguished layman in the Church of England is an indication of the troubled state of that venerable institution— apparently anybody is admitted regardless of what he believes or does not believe so long as he *says* some of the right things. I myself greatly welcome the disintegration of Christianity which we are witnessing all around us, but, because of the dishonesty that is involved, I cannot approve of this particular symptom of dissolution.

NOTES

I wish to thank my friend Donald Levy for reading a draft of this paper and for offering valuable suggestions.

1. *The Role of Knowledge in Western Religion.* Boston, Beacon Press, 1958, pp. 128-9.

2. *Op. cit.,* p. 119.

3. After the death of God. *The Listener,* May 11, 1967, pp. 615-616.

4. Ayer, A. J., *et al.: What I Believe,* London, Allen & Unwin, 1966, p. 233.

5. *Op. Cit.,* p. 231.

6. *Philosophy of Religion.* New York, Prentice-Hall, 1962, from now on abbreviated as PR, p. 40.

7. *The Fundamental Questions of Philosophy.* New York, Collier, 1962, p. 264.

8. *Three Essays on Religion.* London, Longmans, 1874, pp. 36-39.

9. *Uber die Grenzen des Naturerkennens.* Berlin, 1873, p. 37.

10. *Modern Atheism.* London, Burns & Oates, 1961, p. 145.

11. *Modern Materialism and Its Relation to Religion and Theology.* London, 1876, p. 184.

12. PR, p. 79.

13. PR, p. 84.

14. Meaning and truth in theology (from now on abbreviated at MTT). In *Religious Experience and Truth,* S. Hook (Ed.). New York, New York U.P., 1961, pp. 205-206 (my italics).

15 PR, p. 84 (my italics).

16. MTT, p. 206.

17. *Ibid.*

18. *The New York Times,* May 21, 1967.

19. *The Scientific Outlook.* New York, Norton & Co., 1931, pp. 130-131.

20. On the eclipse of God. *Commentary, 40:* 56, 1964.

21. For a detailed discussion of the confusions contained in his kind of rejoinder see my article: Is fideistic theology irrefutable? *The Rationalist Annual, 83:* 43-44, 1966.

22. The fullest statement is found in Hick's *Evil and the God of Love.* New York, Harper & Row, 1966 (from now on referred to as EGL). There are briefer and in some respects more easily discussable statements in Chapter 3 of PR and in Hick's article on "Evil, the Problem of," in *The Encyclopedia of Philosophy.* New York, Macmillan & Free Press, 1967, Vol. III, pp. 136-141.

23. PR, p. 41.

24. PR, p. 43.

25. PR, p. 41.

26. PR, p. 43. In EGL there is an attempt to remove some of this mystery and to provide an account of freedom as contracausal and yet distinct from randomness.

27. PR, p. 43.

28. Skeptics and believers (from now on referred to as SB). In J. Hick (Ed.): *Faith and the Philosophers.* London, Macmillan, 1964, p. 249.

29. PR, p. 44.

30. PR, pp. 45-46.

31. EGL, p. 375.

32. PR, pp. 46-47.

33. *Ibid.*

34. *Ibid.*

35. EGL, p. 372.

36. EGL, p. 376.

37. *Ibid.*

38. *Ibid.*

39. *Id.,* pp. 376-377.

40. Book V, Ch. 4, Garnett translation.

41. EGL, p. 386.

42. *Id.,* pp. 386-387.

43. SB, p. 249.

44. EGL, p. 352.

45. PR, Ch. 4.

46. *Id.*, p. 51.

47. *Id.*, p. 52.

48. *Ibid.*

49. Existential analyses and religious symbols. Reprinted in *Classical and Contemporary Readings in the Philosophy of Religion*, J. Hick (Ed.). New York, Prentice-Hall, 1964, p. 409.

50. *Limits of Religious Thought*. London, 1858, p. 28.

51. *Op. cit.*, p. 13.

52. *Id.*, p. 33.

53. *Principles of Christian Theology*. New York, Scribner's, 1966, pp. 105-106.

54. *Ibid.*

55. *Id.*, p. 109.

56. *Theology of Culture*. New York, Oxford U. P., 1964, p. 5.

57. *Systematic Theology*, Vol. II (from now on abbreviated as ST II). Chicago, U. of Chicago, 1957, p. 5.

58. *Ibid.*

59. *Theology of Culture, op. cit.*, p. 5.

60. ST II, p. 7.

61. *Systematic Theology*, Vol. I (from now on abbreviated as ST I). Chicago, U. of Chicago, 1951, p. 237.

62. ST II, p. 9.

63. ST I, p. 237. See also p. 263: "The infinite is present in everything finite, in the stone as well as in the genius."

64. The religious symbol (from now on abbreviated as RS). In S. Hook (Ed.): *Religious Experiences and Truth, op. cit.*, p. 310.

65. *Ibid.*

66. *The Courage to Be*. New Haven, Yale U. P., 1959, p. 178.

67. RS, p. 316.

68. ST I, p. 205, Tillich's italics.

69. The Religion of Paul Tillich. *Commentary, 43*: 56, 1967, Novak's italics.

70. *Ibid.*

71. See my article: Why. *The Encyclopedia of Philosophy, op. cit.*, Vol. 8, pp. 296-302.

72. ST I, p. 249.

73. ST 1, p. 245. For a fuller discussion of Tillich's practice of offering such circular "translations" see my article: Professor Tillich's confusions. *Mind, LXXIV*: 203-205, 1965. For an excellent discussion of the general problem besetting metaphysical believers, see R. W. Hepburn: The gospel and the claims of logic. *The Listener, LXIX*: 619-621, 1963.

74. ST II, p. 10.

75. *An Examination of Sir William Hamilton's Philosophy*, 4th ed., London, Longmans, 1872, p. 128.

COMMENTARY ON PAUL EDWARDS'S PAPER*

Donald Evans

Professor Edwards' stimulating paper is monumental and complex, but it is perhaps possible to summarize it in terms of the three main conclusions:

I. Naturalistic theology, which identifies God with some feature of man's life or aspirations, is misleading.

II. Theodicies, which purport to reconcile evil with a God of unlimited power and love, do not succeed.

III. Propositions in anthropomorphic theology and metaphysical theology are meaningless pseudo-assertions.

I am in general agreement with the first two conclusions, but I reject the third.

I. NATURALISTIC THEOLOGY

This, I agree, is a misleading way of talking about various human attitudes and activities. Where an honest atheist might say, "Human love is what matters most in life," a naturalistic theologian says, "God is love" but means the same thing as the honest atheist. The disguised atheism is deceptive, since the word "God" is not used by believers merely to describe or to commend a human attitude or activity.

Why is a naturalistic theologian tolerated within some Christian communions? Edwards has suggested a cynical explanation, that Christians only care whether a man *says* some of the right things, still using the word "God." This may sometimes be the reason, but there are also two good reasons. These

*From *The Idea of God,* ed. Edward Madden, Rollo Handy, and Marvin Faber, Springfield, Ill.: Charles C. Thomas, Publisher, 1968, by permission of the publisher.

good reasons apply, however, to many honest atheists as well. One reason arises from the conviction that what matters most is not a man's intellectual position but his basic attitudes and activities in relation to his fellow men. This conviction may include the theological belief that God is at work in many muddled naturalistic theologians and in many honest atheists. The second reason arises from an account of theological assertions as having a meaning only in *relation* to such attitudes and activities while not being *reducible* to them. On such an account many atheists, whether disguised or undisguised, have a better basis for personal understanding of talk about God than many professed believers. As a heresy, theological naturalism is less remote from Christian truth as I understand it than many forms of theological supernaturalism are. I shall return to this briefly at the end of my commentary.

Here I wish only to express my agreement with Edwards' basic criticism of naturalistic theology. If talk about God is reducible without remainder to talk about men, then we ought to stop talking about God. Naturalistic theology is at worst a dishonest apologetic and at best a mistaken muddle.

II. THEODICIES

Edwards' passionate and lucid attack on Christian theodicies includes many of the considerations which have forced me to abandon an unqualified affirmation of divine omnipotence. His attack is not against a Christian straw man, but against the clearest and most sensitive theodicy that I know, John Hick's *Evil and the God of Love.* It seems to me that Hick, at best, leads us by logically dubious arguments to a morally dubious deity. Other theodicies end up with a God worse than Stalin, sacrificing millions to the future, or punishing millions because of their fathers. In discussions of theodicy, the moral sensitivity of atheists is often, paradoxically, much more genuinely Christian than the efforts of Christian apologists to defend the indefensible.

Having said this, however, I should note one general area where I disagree with Edwards, so that his objection to theodicy has in this respect less weight for me. He questions the rightness of forgiving wrongs done to oneself, he omits[1] the Christian punch line in the Dostoevski passage quoted (Alyosha affirms the right of the crucified Christ to forgive wrongs done to *others*), and he implies that nothing happening after the occurrence of evil can make it a good thing that the evil happened. In each case my disagreement does not mean I think I can clearly establish the possibility of a final, means-justifying harmony; but I would not accept Edwards' rigid position on the matter. In this commentary, however, I want to move immediately to his third main claim, that theological utterances are meaningless, pseudo-assertions.

III. PROPOSITIONS IN ANTHROPOMORPHIC THEOLOGY AND METAPHYSICAL THEOLOGY

Edwards' charge of meaninglessness is made on the basis of several verificationist dogmas. I shall challenge these. In doing so, I am not claiming that I thereby eliminate fundamental problems concerning the meaning of talk about God. But I am claiming that unless they are challenged, we do not even begin to see what the fundamental problems really are. Edwards' crude verificationism is easily dismissed by theologians because it so obviously rests on the questionable dogmas of a positivist world-view. This is a pity, for theology can greatly benefit from criticism by empirically minded philosophers. The price of an "absolutely decisive" attack is that it misses the target, since it is merely the expression of an alternative world-view.

I find four dogmas in Edwards' paper and also in some of his other writings:[2]

1. *Literal/nonliteral dichotomy:* There is a clear distinction between literal and nonliteral (metaphorical, symbolic, analogical) senses of a word.
2. *Cognitive/nonliteral dichtomy:* Sentences can have cognitive meaning as assertions only if they contain no nonliteral expressions or if any such expressions can be reduced to literal expressions. Irreducible metaphor is merely pictorial in meaning.
3. *Verificationist theory of meaning:* The cognitive meaning of an assertion is exhaustively given in its method of verification.
4. *Verificationist test of meaningfulness:* The cognitive meaning of an assertion, while not necessarily being exhaustively given in its method of verification, cannot be abstracted from this method of verification. Any such abstraction produces meaninglessness.

Let us have a brief look at each of these dogmas:

1. First, the dichtomy between literal and nonliteral senses of a word. Even in the philosophy of science there are difficulties in formulating a clear distinction between literal and nonliteral, especially in the case of half-dead metaphors such as "electric *current*." In philosophical analysis of the everyday language on which religious language depends, the literal-nonliteral dichotomy is even less tenable and the notion of "literal" even less clear. So when Tillich denies that any expression except "being-itself" can be used *literally* of God, or when Edwards insists that some other expression must be used *literally* if anything is to be asserted, I am not clear as to what either man is saying.

Moreover, since Edwards' way of distinguishing between metaphysical and anthropomorphic theology depends on his literal-nonliteral distinction, the difference between the two alleged kinds of theology is not very clear. Indeed, some predicates can have no nonliteral use—for example "good," "unified,"

279

and "true." Other predicates are applied to God in a nonmetaphorical way ("God is wise" is not logically on a par with "God is a fountain"), yet in a way which differs from their normal use. Does "alive" mean exactly the same thing when applied to an amoeba and a man? To a man and God? There are no simple answers to such questions, and the literal-nonliteral dichotomy is not very illuminating.

It is possible to distinguish in another way between "anthropomorphic" and "metaphysical" elements in theology; but then all main-line Christian theology, including Tillich's, includes *both* elements. A theology is "anthropomorphic" in that God is understood as the perfection of various human attributes. Tillich even asserts deficiency (pompously labeled "non-being") in God, since human virtue involves overcoming of deficiencies. A theology is also "metaphysical" in that it includes some second-order comment on the first-order anthropomorphic language, denying its adequacy, denying that any of it can be strictly true of God when understood as *we* humans must understand it. Some of the crucial problems of meaningfulness arise for theologians in this attempt to combine anthropomorphic and metaphysical elements. This is the context where trenchant philosophical criticisms would be most relevant and illuminating—and perhaps most devastating.

2. The second dogma, you recall, was the restriction of cognitive meaning to literal meaning. This dogma depends on a prior distinction between literal and nonliteral. It insists that metaphors and other nonliteral expressions either are translatable into literal expressions or are merely pictorial in meaning. The dogma has been challenged not only by religious apologists and literary critics but also by such down-to-earth philosophers as Max Black.[3]

Once we grant the possibility that irreducible metaphors may be used to make meaningful assertions about the real world, a vast area is opened up for philosophical analysis. But the cognitive meaningfulness of religious language is not thereby assured. Even if men experience elusive, mysterious realities which can only be obscurely hinted at in successions of poetic metaphors, this does not of itself eliminate basic problems for traditional theology. Indeed, it may provide an aesthetic *alternative* to traditional religious belief. Edwards' dogma, however, does not allow us even to pose such an issue, since both sides are in the black realm of meaninglessness.

3. The third dogma is the verificationist theory of meaning. Edwards uses this dogma when believers attempt to explain what they mean by referring to observables. Hick points to the loving activity of the man Jesus, and Novak point to the fact that there are things (rather than no things); in each case Edwards argues that all the believer *can* mean is given exhaustively in the observables to which they refer. If Hick talks about God "expressing" moral attitudes in Jesus' activities or Novak talks about God as the "power present" by the fact that things are, neither is allowed to mean anything beyond Jesus' activities or the fact that things are.

The verificationist theory of meaning is today carefully hedged and qualified even in neo-positivist philosophy of science. Why it should remain in its pure form for Edwards, I do not know. Of course, if we reject it, we do not thereby guarantee to Hick or Novak the meaningfulness which they claim for their religious utterances. But the possibility is open for exploration. I share much of Edwards' distaste for what he has elsewhere called "bombastic redescriptions of empirical facts,"[4] but not his assurance that all assertions which are verified or explicated by reference to empirical facts must be merely redescriptions—bombastic or otherwise—of those facts.

Indeed, Edwards' use of the fourth dogma involves him in a position which is in conflict with his use of the verificationist theory of meaning.

4. A verificationist test of meaningfulness is at work in the following passage:

> It does not make any sense to talk about a disembodied consciousness . . . psychological predicates are *logically* tied to the behavior of organisms. It should be observed that this is not the same as reductive materialism. It does not imply that a person is just his body, that there are no private experiences or that feelings are simply ways of behaving. It makes the milder claim that however much more than a body a human being may be, one cannot sensibly talk about this "more" without presupposing (as part of what one means, and not as a mere contingent fact) that he is a living organism.

On such a view, talk about the attitudes or decisions of men, though verified by reference to their observable behavior, is not merely a redescription of that behavior, for it involves a reference to something more. This something more cannot be independently identified by us, the observers, though it is revealed in the behavior. In spite of this, Edwards insists that when Hick talks about God being *revealed* in Jesus, Hick has to be talking about an alleged something which is independently identifiable by us. Yet the point of Edwards' remarks about the meaning of psychological predicates is that the relation between human behavior and inner mental state is *not* like that between a dental X-ray and an abscess which can be independently identified. So the relation between human behavior and *God* need not fit this model either, though whether or not it is intelligible is still left an open question.

Nor on such a view is it obviously meaningless to talk about bodiless agencies—poltergeists, for example. Where what is observed has considerable similarity to the results of familiar human actions, we can meaningfully apply predicates which normally apply to human beings. Whether or not there are poltergeists, I do not know. But I have no trouble in understanding talk about them: for example, "The poltergeist got angry." This statement is not exhaustively analyzed in terms of observables such as flying cutlery, nor do I need to picture, surreptitiously, an embodied consciousness in order to understand what is being said. It is true that we *learn* to use such predicates as "angry" in relation to bodily behavior, but this does not mean that talk about a bodiless consciousness is unintelligible.

But having said this, I have not thereby opened the door to an obviously meaningful theology. The really difficult problems still remain. For me, the central problem arises when observable human behavior is interpreted theologically as not only revelatory of an unobservable human attitude and initiative but also of the attitude and initiative of a hidden personal being called "God." This problem is central for me both because it is basic in my own religious experience and because it seems to me that Christian theology should start with the claim that God reveals Himself in human love. One possible conceptual model with which to begin reflection concerning this is the alleged phenomenon of telepathic influence. Other theologians may suggest a different model. Whatever is suggested should be subjected to rigorous philosophical scrutiny both by believers and by unbelievers. Here, I would suggest, is an arena for useful intellectual combat concerning the possibility of theology.

If I have misinterpreted Edwards, I can only hope that in spite of his reservations about forgiveness, he will forgive me. If his reply is devastating, I may regret that I rashly implied a forgiveness in advance!

NOTES

1. So does Nelson Pike (Ed.): *God and Evil.* New York, Prentice-Hall, 1964.

2. Professor Tillich's confusions. *Mind,* April, 1965; Some notes on anthropomorphic theology. *Religious Experience and Truth,* Sidney Hook (Ed.). New York U. P., 1961.

3. *Models and Metaphors.* Ithaca, Cornell U. P., 1962, ch. 3.

4. Professor Tillich's confusions. *op. cit.,* p. 206.

THE ONTOLOGICAL ARGUMENT*

Norman Malcolm

ANSELM'S ONTOLOGICAL ARGUMENTS

I believe that in Anselm's *Proslogion* and *Responsio editoris* there are two different pieces of reasoning which he did not distinguish from one another, and that a good deal of light may be shed on the philosophical problem of "the ontological argument" if we do distinguish them. In Chapter 2 of the *Proslogion*[1] Anselm says that we believe that God is *something a greater than which cannot be conceived*. (The Latin is *aliquid quo nihil maius cogitari possit*. Anselm sometimes uses the alternative expressions *aliquid quo maius nihil cogitari potest, id quo maius cogitari nequit, aliquid quo maius cogitari non valet*.) Even the fool of the Psalm who says in his heart there is no God, when he hears this very thing that Anselm says, namely "something a greater than which cannot be conceived," understands what he hears, and what he understands is in his understanding though he does not understand that it exists.

Apparently Anselm regards it as tautological to say that whatever is understood is in the understanding (*quidquid intelligitur in intellectu est*): he uses *intelligitur* and *in intellectu est* as interchangeable locutions. The same holds for another formula of his: whatever is thought is in thought (*quidquid cogitatur in cogitatione est*).[2]

Of course many things may exist in the understanding that do not exist in reality; for example, elves. Now, says Anselm, something a greater than which cannot be conceived exists in the understanding. But it cannot exist *only* in the understanding, for to exist in reality is greater. Therefore that thing a greater than which cannot be conceived cannot exist only in the understanding, for

---

*From *The Philosophical Review,* vol. 69 (1960); reprinted by permission of *The Philosophical Review*.

for then a greater thing could be conceived: namely, one that exists both in the understanding and in reality.[3]

Here I have a question. It is not clear to me whether Anselm means that (a) existence in reality by itself is greater than existence in the understanding, or that (b) existence in reality and existence in the understanding together are greater than existence in the understanding alone. Certainly he accepts (b). But he might also accept (a), as Descartes apparently does in *Meditation III* when he suggests that the mode of being by which a thing is "objectively in the understanding" is *imperfect*.[4] Of course Anselm might accept both (a) and (b). He might hold that in general something is greater if it has both of these "modes of existence" than if it has either one alone, but also that existence in reality is a more perfect mode of existence than existence in the understanding.

In any case, Anselm holds that something is greater if it exists both in the understanding and in reality than if it exists merely in the understanding. An equivalent way of putting this interesting proposition, in a more current terminology, is: something is greater if it is both conceived of and exists than if it is merely conceived of. Anselm's reasoning can be expressed as follows: *id quo maius cogitari nequit* cannot be merely conceived of and not exist, for then it would not be *id quo maius cogitari nequit*. The doctrine that something is greater if it exists in addition to being conceived of, than if it is only conceived of, could be called the doctrine that *existence is a perfection*. Descartes maintained, in so many words, that existence is a perfection,[5] and presumably he was holding Anselm's doctrine, although he does not, in *Meditation V* or elsewhere, argue in the way that Anselm does in *Proslogion* 2.

When Anselm says, "And certainly, that than which nothing greater can be conceived cannot exist merely in the understanding. For suppose it exists merely in the understanding, then it can be conceived to exist in reality, which is greater,"[6] he is claiming that if I conceived of a being of great excellence, that being would be *greater* (more excellent, more perfect) if it existed than if it did not exist. His supposition that "it exists merely in the understanding" is the supposition that it is conceived of but does not exist. Anselm repeated this claim in his reply to the criticism of the monk Gaunilo. Speaking of the being a greater than which cannot be conceived, he says:

> I have said that if it exists merely in the understanding it can be conceived to exist in reality, which is greater. Therefore, if it exists merely in the understanding obviously the very being a greater than which cannot be conceived, is one a greater than which can be conceived. What, I ask, can follow better than that? For if it exists merely in the understanding, can it not be conceived to exist in reality? And if it can be so conceived does not he who conceives of this conceive of a thing greater than it, if it does exist merely in the understanding? Can anything follow better than this: that if a being a greater than which cannot be conceived exists merely in the understanding, it is something a greater than which can be conceived? What could be plainer?[7]

He is implying, in the first sentence, that if I conceive of something which does not exist then it is possible for it to exist, and *it will be greater if it exists than if it does not exist.*

The doctrine that existence is a perfection is remarkably queer. It makes sense and is true to say that my future house will be a better one if it is insulated than if it is not insulated; but what could it mean to say that it will be a better house if it exists than if it does not? My future child will be a better man if he is honest than if he is not; but who would understand the saying that he will be a better man if he exists than if he does not? Or who understands the saying that if God exists He is more perfect than if He does not exist? One might say, with some intelligibility, that it would be better (for oneself or for mankind) if God exists than if He does not—but that is a different matter.

A king might desire that his next chancellor should have knowledge, wit, and resolution; but it is ludicrous to add that the king's desire is to have a chancellor who exists. Suppose that two royal councilors, A and B, were asked to draw up separately descriptions of the most perfect chancellor they could conceive, and that the descriptions they produced were identical except that A included existence in his list of attributes of a perfect chancellor and B did not. (I do not mean that B put nonexistence in his list.) One and the same person could satisfy both descriptions. More to the point, any person who satisfied A's description would *necessarily* satisfy B's description and vice versa! This is to say that A and B did not produce descriptions that differed in any way but rather one and the same description of necessary and desirable qualities in a chancellor. A only made a show of putting down a desirable quality that B had failed to include.

I believe I am merely restating an observation that Kant made in attacking the notion that "existence" or "being" is a "real predicate." He says:

> By whatever and by however many predicates we may think a thing—even if we completely determine it—we do not make the least addition to the thing when we further declare that this thing *is*. Otherwise, it would not be exactly the same thing that exists, but something more than we had thought in the concept; and we could not therefore, say that the exact object of my concept exists.[8]

Anselm's ontological proof of *Prosolgion* 2 is fallacious because it rests on the false doctrine that existence is a perfection (and therefore that "existence" is a "real predicate"). It would be desirable to have a rigorous refutation of the doctrine but I have not been able to provide one. I am compelled to leave the matter at the more or less intuitive level of Kant's observation. In any case, I believe that the doctrine does not belong to Anselm's other formulation of the ontological argument. It is worth noting that Gassendi anticipated Kant's criticism when he said, against Descartes:

Existence is a perfection neither in God nor in anything else; it is rather that in the absence of which there is no perfection. . . . Hence neither is existence held to exist in a thing in the way that perfections do, nor if the thing lacks existence is it said to be imperfect (or deprived of a perfection), so much as to be nothing.[9]

II

I take up now the consideration of the second ontological proof, which Anselm presents in the very next chapter of the *Proslogion*. (There is no evidence that he thought of himself as offering two different proofs.) Speaking of the being a greater than which cannot be conceived, he says:

And it so truly exists that it cannot be conceived not to exist. For it is possible to conceive of a being which cannot be conceived not to exist; and this is greater than one which can be conceived not to exist. Hence, if that, than which nothing greater can be conceived, can be conceived not to exist, it is not that than which nothing greater can be conceived. But this is a contradiction. So truly, therefore, is there something than which nothing greater can be conceived, that it cannot even be conceived not to exist. And this being thou art, O Lord, our God.[10]

Anselm is saying two things: first, that a being whose nonexistence is logically impossible is "greater" than a being whose nonexistence is logically possible (and therefore that a being a greater than which cannot be conceived must be one whose nonexistence is logically impossible); second, that *God* is a being than which a greater cannot be conceived.

In regard to the second of these assertions, there certainly is *a* use of the word "God," and I think far the more common use, in accordance with which the statements "God is the greatest of all beings," "God is the most perfect being," "God is the supreme being," are *logically* necessary truths, in the same sense that the statement "A square has four sides" is a logically necessary truth. If there is a man named "Jones" who is the tallest man in the world, the statement "Jones is the tallest man in the world" is merely true and not a logically necessary truth. It is a virtue of Anselm's unusual phrase, "a being a greater than which cannot be conceived,"[11] to make it explicit that the sentence "God is the greatest of all beings" expresses a logically necessary truth and not a mere matter of fact such as the one we imagined about Jones.

With regard to Anselm's first assertion (namely, that a being whose nonexistence is logically impossible is greater than a being whose nonexistence is logically possible) perhaps the most puzzling thing about it is the use of the word "greater." It appears to mean exactly the same as "superior," "more excellent," "more perfect." This equivalence by itself is of no help to us, however, since the latter expressions would be equally puzzling here. What is required is some explanation of their use.

We do think of *knowledge,* say, as an excellence, a good thing. If A has more knowledge of algebra than B we express this in common language by saying that A has a *better* knowledge of algebra than B, or that A's knowledge of algebra is *superior* to B's, whereas we should not say that B has a better or superior *ignorance* of algebra than A. We do say "greater ignorance," but here the word "greater" is used purely quantitatively.

Previously I rejected *existence* as a perfection. Anselm is maintaining in the remarks last quoted, not that existence is a perfection, but that *theological impossibility of nonexistence is a perfection.* In other words, *necessary existence* is a perfection. His first ontological proof uses the principle that a thing is greater if it exists than if it does not exist. His second proof employs the different principle that a thing is greater if it necessarily exists than if it does not necessarily exist.

Some remarks about the notion of *dependence* may help to make this latter principle intelligible. Many things depend for their existence on other things and events. My house was built by a carpenter: its coming into existence was dependent on a certain creative activity. Its continued existence is dependent on many things: that a tree does not crush it, that it is not consumed by fire, and so on. If we reflect on the common meaning of the word "God" (no matter how vague and confused this is), we realize that it is incompatible with this meaning that God's existence should *depend* on anything. Whether we believe in Him or not we must admit that the "almighty and everlasting God" (as several ancient prayers begin), the "Maker of heaven and earth, and of all things visible and invisible" (as is said in the Nicene Creed), cannot be thought of as being brought into existence by anything or as depending for His continued existence on anything. To conceive of anything as dependent upon something else for its existence is to conceive of it as a lesser being than God.

If a housewife has a set of extremely fragile dishes, then as dishes they are *inferior* to those of another set like them in all respects except that they are *not* fragile. Those of the first set are *dependent* for their continued existence on gentle handling; those of the second set are not. There is a definite connection in common language between the notions of dependency and inferiority, and independence and superiority. To say that something which was dependent on nothing whatever was superior to ("greater than") anything that was dependent in any way upon anything is quite in keeping with the everyday use of the terms "superior" and "greater." Correlative with the notions of dependence and independence are the notions of *limited* and *unlimited.* An engine requires fuel and this is a limitation. It is the same thing to say that an engine's operation is *dependent* on as that it is *limited* by its fuel supply. An engine that could

287

accomplish the same work in the same time and was in other respects satisfactory, but did not require fuel, would be a *superior* engine.

God is usually conceived of as an *unlimited* being. He is conceived of as a being who *could not* be limited, that is, as an absolutely unlimited being. This is no less than to conceive of Him as *something a greater than which cannot be conceived*. If God is conceived to be an absolutely unlimited being He must be conceived to be unlimited in regard to His existence as well as His operation. In this conception it will not make sense to say that He depends on anything for coming into or continuing in existence. Nor, as Spinoza observed, will it make sense to say that something could *prevent* Him from existing.[12] Lack of moisture can prevent trees from existing in a certain region of the earth. But it would be contrary to the concept of God as an unlimited being to suppose that anything other than God Himself could prevent Him from existing, and it would be self-contradictory to suppose that He Himself could do it.

Some may be inclined to object that although nothing could prevent God's existence, still it might just *happen* that He did not exist. And if He did exist that too would be by chance. I think, however, that from the supposition that it could happen that God did not exist it would follow that, if He existed, He would have mere duration and not eternity. It would make sense to ask, "How long has He existed?" "Will He still exist next week?" "He was in existence yesterday but how about today?" and so on. It seems absurd to make God the subject of such questions. According to our ordinary conception of Him, He is an eternal being. And eternity does not mean endless duration, as Spinoza noted. To ascribe eternity to something is to exclude as senseless all sentences that imply that it has duration. If a thing has duration then it would be merely a *contingent* fact, if it was a fact, that its duration was endless. The moon could have endless duration but not eternity. If something has endless duration it will *make sense* (although it will be false) to say that it will cease to exist, and it will make sense (although it will be false) to say that something will *cause* it to cease to exist. A being with endless duration is not, therefore, an absolutely unlimited being. That God is conceived to be eternal follows from the fact that He is conceived to be an absolutely unlimited being.

I have been trying to expand the argument of *Proslogion* 3. In *Responsio* 1 Anselm adds the following acute point: if you can conceive of a certain thing and this thing does not exist then if it *were* to exist its nonexistence would be *possible*. It follows, I believe, that if the thing were to exist it would depend on other things both for coming into and continuing in existence, and also that it would have duration and not eternity. Therefore it would not be, either in reality or in conception, an unlimited being, *aliquid quo nihil maius cogitari possit*.

Anselm states his argument as follows:

If it [the thing a greater than which cannot be conceived] can be conceived at all it must exist. For no one who denies or doubts the existence of a being a greater than which is inconceivable, denies or doubts that if it did exist its nonexistence, either in reality or in understanding, would be impossible. For otherwise it would not be a being a greater than which cannot be conceived. But as to whatever can be conceived but does not exist: if it were to exist its non-existence either in reality or in the understanding would be possible. Therefore, if a being a greater than which cannot be conceived, can even be conceived, it must exist.[13]

What Anselm has proved is that the notion of contingent existence or of contingent nonexistence cannot have any application to God. His existence must either be logically necessary or logically impossible. The only intelligible way of rejecting Anselm's claim that God's existence is necessary is to maintain that the concept of God, as a being a greater than which cannot be conceived, is self-contradictory or nonsensical.[14] Supposing that this is false, Anselm is right to deduce God's necessary existence from his characterization of Him as a being a greater than which cannot be conceived.

Let me summarize the proof. If God, a being a greater than which cannot be conceived, does not exist then He cannot *come* into existence. For if He did He would either have been *caused* to come into existence or have *happened* to come into existence, and in either case He would be a limited being, which by our conception of Him He is not. Since He cannot come into existence, if He does not exist His existence is impossible. If He does exist He cannot have come into existence (for the reasons given), nor can He cease to exist, for nothing could cause Him to cease to exist nor could it just happen that He ceased to exist. So if God exists His existence is necessary. Thus God's existence is either impossible or necessary. It can be the former only if the concept of such a being is self-contradictory or in some way logically absurd. Assuming that this is not so, it follows that He necessarily exists.

It may be helpful to express ourselves in the following way: to say, not that *omnipotence* is a property of God, but rather that *necessary omnipotence* is; and to say, not that omniscience is a property of God, but rather that *necessary omniscience* is. We have criteria for determining that a man knows this and that and can do this and that, and for determining that one man has greater knowledge and abilities in a certain subject than another. We could think of various tests to give them. But there is nothing we should wish to describe, seriously and literally, as "testing" God's knowledge and powers. That God is omniscient and omnipotent has not been determined by the application of criteria: rather these are requirements of our conception of Him. They are internal properties of the concept, although they are also rightly said to be properties of God. *Necessary existence* is a property of God in the *same sense* that *necessary omnipotence* and *necessary omniscience* are His properties. And we are not to think that "God necessarily exists" means that it follows necessarily from something that God exists *contingently*. The a priori proposition "God necessarily exists" entails the proposition "God exists," if and only if the latter also is understood as an a priori proposition: in which case the two propositions are equivalent. In this sense Anselm's proof is a proof of God's existence.

Descartes was somewhat hazy on the question of whether existence is a property of things that exist, but at the same time he saw clearly enough that *necessary existence* is a property of God. Both points are illustrated in his reply to Gassendi's remark, which I quoted above:

> I do not see what class of reality you wish to assign existence, nor do I see why it may not be said to be a property as well as omnipotence, taking the word property as equivalent to any attribute or anything which can be predicated of a thing, as in the present case it should be by all means regarded. Nay, necessary existence in the case of God is also a true property in the strictest sense of the word, because it belongs to Him and forms part of His essence alone.[15]

Elsewhere he speaks of "the necessity of existence" as being "that crown of perfections without which we cannot comprehend God."[16] He is emphatic on the point that necessary existence applies solely to "an absolutely perfect Being."[17]

III

I wish to consider now a part of Kant's criticism of the ontological argument which I believe to be wrong. He says:

> If, in an identical proposition, I reject the predicate while retaining the subject, contradiction results; and I therefore say that the former belongs necessarily to the latter. But if we reject subject and predicate alike, there is no contradiction; for nothing is then left that can be contradicted. To posit a triangle, and yet to reject its three angles, is self-contradictory; but there is no contradiction in rejecting the triangle together with its three angles. The same holds true of the concept of an absolutely necessary being. If its existence is rejected, we reject the thing itself with all its predicates; and no question of contradiction can then arise. There is nothing outside it that would then be contradicted, since the necessity of the thing is not supposed to be derived from anything external; nor is there anything internal that would be contradicted, since in rejecting the thing itself we have at the same time rejected all its internal properties. "God is omnipotent" is a necessary judgment. The omnipotence cannot be rejected if we posit a Deity, that is, an infinite being; for the two concepts are identical. But if we say, "There is no God," neither the omnipotence nor any other of its predicates is given; they are one and all rejected together with the subject, and there is therefore not the least contradiction in such a judgment.[18]

To these remarks the reply is that when the concept of God is correctly understood one sees that one cannot "reject the subject." "There is no God" is seen to be a necessarily false statement. Anselm's demonstration proves that the proposition "God exists" has the same a priori footing as the proposition "God is omnipotent."

Many present-day philosophers, in agreement with Kant, declare that existence is not a property and think that this overthrows the ontological argument. Although it is an error to regard existence as a property of things that have contingent existence, it does not follow that it is an error to regard necessary existence as a property of God. A recent writer says, against Anselm, that a proof of God's existence "based on the necessities of thought" is "universally regarded as fallacious: it is not thought possible to build bridges between mere abstractions and concrete existence."[19] But this way of putting the matter obscures the distinction we need to make. Does "concrete existence" mean contingent existence? Then to build bridges between concrete existence and mere abstractions would be like inferring the existence of an island from the concept of a perfect island, which both Anselm and Descartes regarded as absurd. What Anselm did was to give a demonstration that the proposition "God necessarily exists" is entailed by the proposition "God is a being a greater than which cannot be conceived" (which is equivalent to "God is an absolutely unlimited being"). Kant declares that when "I think a being as the supreme reality, without any defect, the question still remains whether it exists or not."[20] But once one has grasped Anselm's proof of the necessary existence of a being a greater than which cannot be conceived, no question remains as to whether it exists or not, just as Euclid's demonstration of the existence of an infinity of prime numbers leaves no question on that issue.

Kant says that "every reasonable person" must admit that "all existential propositions are synthetic."[21] Part of the perplexity one has about the ontological argument is in deciding whether or not the proposition "God necessarily exists" is or is not an "existential proposition." But let us look around. Is the Euclidean theorem in number theory, "There exists an infinite number of prime numbers," an "existential proposition"? Do we not want to say that *in some sense* it asserts the existence of something? Cannot we say, with equal justification, that the proposition "God necessarily exists" asserts the existence of something, *in some sense*? What we need to understand, in each case, is the particular sense of the assertion. Neither proposition has the same sort of sense as do the propositions, "A low pressure area exists over the Great Lakes," "There still exists some possibility that he will survive," "The pain continues to exist in his abdomen." One good way of seeing the difference in sense of these various propositions is to see the variously different ways in which they are proved or supported. It is wrong to think that all assertions of existence have the same kind of meaning. There are as many kinds of existential propositions as there are kinds of subjects of discourse.

291

Closely related to Kant's view that all existential propositions are "synthetic" is the contemporary dogma that all existential propositions are contingent. Professor Gilbert Ryle tells us that "Any assertion of the existence of something, like any assertion of the occurrence of something, can be denied without logical absurdity."[22] "All existential statements are contingent," says Mr. I. M. Crombie.[23] Professor J. J. C. Smart remarks that "Existence is not a property" and then goes on to assert that "There can never be any *logical contradiction* in denying that God exists."[24] He declares that "The concept of a logically necessary being is a self-contradictory concept, like the concept of a round square. . . . No existential proposition can be logically necessary," he maintains, for "the truth of a logically necessary proposition depends only on our symbolism, or to put the same things in another way, on the relation of concepts" (p. 38). Professor K. E. M. Baier says, "It is no longer seriously in dispute that the notion of a logically necessary being is self-contradictory. Whatever can be conceived of as existing can equally be conceived of as not existing."[25] This is a repetition of Hume's assertion, "Whatever we conceive as existent, we can also conceive as nonexistent. There is no being, therefore, whose nonesistence implies a contradiction."[26]

Professor J. N. Findlay ingeniously constructs an ontological *dis*proof of God's existence, based on a "modern" view of the nature of "necessity in propositions": the view, namely, that necessity in propositions "merely reflects our use of words, the arbitrary conventions of our language."[27] Findlay undertakes to characterize what he calls "religious attitude," and here there is a striking agreement between his observations and some of the things I have said in expounding Anselm's proof. Religious attitude, he says, presumes *superiority* in its object and superiority so great that the worshiper is in comparison as nothing. Religious attitude finds it "anomalous to worship anything *limited* in any thinkable manner. . . . And hence we are led on irresistibly to demand that our religious object should have an *unsurpassable* supremacy along all avenues, that it should tower *infinitely* above all other objects" (p. 51). We cannot help feeling that "the worthy object of our worship can never be a thing that merely *happens* to exist, nor one on which all other objects merely *happen* to depend. The true object of religious reverence must not be one, merely, to which no *actual* independent realities stand opposed: it must be one to which such opposition is totally *inconceivable*. . . . And not only must the existence of *other* things be unthinkable without him, but his own nonexistence must be wholly unthinkable in any circumstances" (p. 52). And now, says Findlay, when we add up these various requirements, what they entail is "not only that there isn't a God, but that the Divine Existence is either senseless or impossible" (p. 54). For on the one hand, "If God is to satisfy religious claims and needs, He must be a being in every way inescapable, One whose existence and whose possession of certain excellences we cannot possibly conceive away." On the other hand, "modern views make it self-evidently absurd (if they don't make it ungram-matical) to speak of such a Being and attribute existence to Him. It was indeed an ill day for Anselm when he hit upon his famous proof. For on that day he not only laid bare something that is of the essence of an adequate religious object, but also something that entails its necessary nonexistence" (p. 55).

Now I am inclined to hold the "modern" view that logically necessary truth "merely reflects our use of words" (although I do not believe that the conven-tions of language are always *arbitrary*). But I confess that I am unable to see how that view is supposed to lead to the conclusion that "the Divine existence is either senseless or impossible." Findlay does not explain how this result comes about. Surely he cannot mean that this view entails that nothing can have necessary properties: for this would imply that mathematics is "senseless or impossible," which no one wants to hold. Trying to fill in the argument that is missing from his article, the most plausible conjecture I can make is the following: Findlay thinks that the view that logical necessity "reflects the use of words" implies, not that nothing has necessary properties, but that *existence* cannot be a necessary property of anything. That is to say, every proposition of the form "*x* exists," including the proposition "God exists," must be *contingent.*[28] At the same time, our concept of God requires that His existence be *necessary*, that is, that "God exists" be a necessary truth. Therefore, the modern view of necessity proves that what the concept of God requires *cannot* be fulfilled. It proves that God *cannot* exist.

The correct reply is that the view that logical necessity merely reflects the use of words cannot possibly have the implication that every existential proposi-tion must be contingent. That view requires us to *look at* the use of words and not manufacture a priori theses about it. In the Ninetieth Psalm it is said: "Before the mountains were brought forth, or ever thou hadst formed the earth and the world, even from everlasting to everlasting, thou art God." Here is expressed the idea of the necessary existence and eternity of God, an idea that is essential to the Jewish and Christian religions. In those complex systems of thought, those "languages-games," God has the status of a necessary being. Who can doubt that? Here we must say with Wittgenstein, "This language-game is played!"[29] I believe we may rightly take the existence of those religious systems of thought in which God figures as a necessary being to be a disproof of the dogma, affirmed by Hume and others, that no existential proposition can be necessary.

Another way of criticizing the ontological argument is the following. "Granted that the concept of necessary existence follows from the concept of a being a greater than which cannot be conceived, this amounts to no more than granting the a priori truth of the *conditional* proposition, 'If such a being exists then it necessarily exists.' This proposition, however, does not entail the *existence of anything,* and one can deny its antecedent without contradiction."

Kant, for example, compares the proposition (or "judgment," as he calls it) "A triangle has three angles" with the proposition "God is a necessary being." He allows that the former is "absolutely necessary" and goes on to say:

> The absolute necessity of the judgment is only a conditional necessity of the thing, or of the predicate in the judgment. The above proposition does not declare that three angles are absolutely necessary, but that, under the condition that there is a triangle (that is, that a triangle is given), three angles will necessarily be found in it.[30]

He is saying, quite correctly, that the proposition about triangles is equivalent to the conditional proposition, "If a triangle exists, it has three angles." He then makes the comment that there is no contradiction "in rejecting the triangle together with its three angles." He proceeds to draw the alleged parallel: "The same holds true of the concept of an absolutely necessary being. If its existence is rejected, we reject the thing itself with all its predicates; and no question of contradiction can then arise."[31] The priest, Caterus, made the same objection to Descartes when he said:

> Though it be conceded that an entity of the highest perfection implies its existence by its very name, yet it does not follow that that very existence is anything actual in the real world, but merely that the concept of existence is inseparably united with the concept of highest being. Hence you cannot infer that the existence of God is anything actual, unless you assume that that highest being actually exists; for then it will actually contain all its perfections, together with this perfection of real existence.[32]

I think that Caterus, Kant, and numerous other philosophers have been mistaken in supposing that the proposition "God is a necessary being" (or "God necessarily exists") is equivalent to the conditional proposition "If God exists then He necessarily exists."[33] For how do they want the antecedent clause, "*If* God exists," to be understood? Clearly they want it to imply that it is *possible* that God does *not* exist.[34] The whole point of Kant's analysis is to try to show that it is possible to "reject the subject." Let us make this implication explicit in the conditional proposition, so that it reads: "If God exists (and it is possible that He does not) then He necessarily exists." But now it is apparent, I think, that these philosophers have arrived at a self-contradictory position. I do not mean that this conditional proposition, taken alone, is self-contradictory. Their position is self-contradictory in the following way. On the one hand, they agree that the proposition "God necessarily exists" is an a priori truth; Kant implies that it is "absolutely necessary," and Caterus says that God's existence is implied by His very name. On the other hand, they think that it is correct to analyze this proposition in such a way that it will entail the proposition "It is possible that God does not exist." But so far from its being the case that the proposition

"God necessarily exists" entails the proposition "It is possible that God does not exist," it is rather the case that they are *incompatible* with one another! Can anything be clearer than that the conjunction "God necessarily exists but it is possible that He does not exist" is self-contradictory? Is it not just as plainly self-contradictory as the conjunction "A square necessarily has four sides but it is possible for a square not to have four sides"? In short, this familiar criticism of the ontological argument is self-contradictory, because it accepts *both* of two incompatible propositions.[35]

One conclusion we may draw from our examination of this criticism is that (contrary to Kant) there is a lack of symmetry, in an important respect, between the propositions "A triangle has three angles" and "God has necessary existence," although both are a priori. The former can be expressed in the conditional assertion "If a triangle exists (and it is possible that none does) it has three angles." The latter cannot be expressed in the corresponding conditional assertion without contradiction.

IV

I turn to the question of whether the idea of a being a greater than which cannot be conceived is self-contradictory. Here Leibniz made a contribution to the discussion of the ontological argument. He remarked that the argument of Anselm and Descartes

is not a paralogism, but it is an imperfect demonstration, which assumes something that must still be proved in order to render it mathematically evident; that is, it is tacitly assumed that this idea of the all-great or all-perfect being is possible, and implies no contradiction. And it is already something that by this remark it is proved that, assuming that God is possible, he exists, which is the privilege of divinity alone.[36]

Leibniz undertook to give a proof that God is possible. He defined a *perfection* as a simple, positive quality in the highest degree.[37] He argued that since perfections are *simple* qualities they must be compatible with one another. Therefore the concept of a being possessing all perfections is consistent.

I will not review his argument because I do not find his definition of a perfection intelligible. For one thing, it assumes that certain qualities or attributes are "positive" in their intrinsic nature, and others "negative" or "privative," and I have not been able clearly to understand that. For another thing, it assumes that some qualities are intrinsically simple. I believe that Wittgenstein has shown in the *Investigations* that nothing is *intrinsically* simple, but that whatever has the status of a simple, an indefinable, in one system of concepts, may have the status of a complex thing, a definable thing, in another system of concepts.

295

I do not know how to demonstrate that the concept of God—that is, of a being a greater than which cannot be conceived—is not self-contradictory. But I do not think that it is legitimate to demand such a demonstration. I also do not know how to demonstrate that either the concept of a material thing or the concept of *seeing* a material thing is not self-contradictory, and philosophers have argued that both of them are. With respect to any particular reasoning that is offered for holding that the concept of seeing a material thing, for example, is self-contradictory, one may try to show the invalidity of the reasoning and thus free the concept from the charge of being self-contradictory *on that ground.* But I do not understand what it would mean to demonstrate *in general,* and not in respect to any particular reasoning, that the concept is not self-contradictory. So it is with the concept of God. I should think there is no more of a presumption that it is self-contradictory than is the concept of seeing a material thing. Both concepts have a place in the thinking and the lives of human beings.

But even if one allows that Anselm's phrase may be free of self-contradiction, one wants to know how it can have any *meaning* for anyone. Why is it that human beings have even *formed* the concept of an infinite being, a being a greater than which cannot be conceived? This is a legitimate and important question. I am sure there cannot be a deep understanding of that concept without an understanding of the phenomena of human life that give rise to it. To give an account of the latter is beyond my ability. I wish, however, to make one suggestion (which should not be understood as autobiographical).

There is the phenomenon of feeling guilt for something that one has done or thought or felt or for a disposition that one has. One wants to be free of this guilt. But sometimes the guilt is felt to be so great that one is sure that nothing one could do oneself, nor any forgiveness by another human being, would remove it. One feels a guilt that is beyond all measure, a guilt "a greater than which cannot be conceived." Paradoxically, it would seem, one nevertheless has an intense desire to have this incomparable guilt removed. One requires a forgiveness that is beyond all measure, a forgiveness "a greater than which cannot be conceived." Out of such a storm in the soul, I am suggesting, there arises the conception of a forgiving mercy that is limitless, beyond all measure. This is one important feature of the Jewish and Christian conception of God.

I wish to relate this thought to a remark made by Kierkegaard, who was speaking about belief in Christianity but whose remark may have a wider application. He says:

> There is only one proof of the truth of Christianity and that, quite rightly, is from the emotions, when the dread of sin and a heavy conscience torture a man into crossing the narrow line between despair bordering upon madness—and Christendom.[38]

One may think it absurd for a human being to feel a guilt of such magnitude, and even more absurd that, if he feels it, he should *desire* its removal. I have nothing to say about that. It may also be absurd for people to fall in love, but they do it. I wish only to say that there *is* that human phenomenon of an unbearably heavy conscience and that it is importantly connected with the genesis of the concept of God, that is, with the formation of the "grammar" of the word "God." I am sure that this concept is related to human experience in other ways. If one had the acuteness and depth to perceive these connections one could grasp the *sense* of the concept. When we encounter this concept as a problem in philosophy, we do not consider the human phenomena that lie behind it. It is not surprising that many philosophers believe that the idea of a necessary being is an arbitrary and absurd construction.

What is the relation of Anselm's ontological argument to religious belief? This is a difficult question. I can imagine an atheist going through the argument, becoming convinced of its validity, acutely defending it against objections, yet remaining an atheist. The only effect it could have on the fool of the Psalm would be that he stopped saying in his heart "There is no God," because he would now realize that this is something he cannot meaningfully say or think. It is hardly to be expected that a demonstrative argument should, in addition, produce in him a living faith. Surely there is a level at which one can view the argument as a piece of logic, following the deductive moves but not being touched religiously? I think so. But even at this level the argument may not be without religious value, for it may help to remove some philosophical scruples that stand in the way of faith. At a deeper level, I suspect that the argument can be thoroughly understood only by one who has a view of that human "form of life" that gives rise to the idea of an infinitely great being, who views it from the *inside* not just from the outside and who has, therefore, at least some inclination to *partake* in that religious form of life. This inclination, in Kierkegaard's words, is "from the emotions." This inclination can hardly be an *effect* of Anselm's argument, but is rather presupposed in the fullest understanding of it. It would be unreasonable to require that the recognition of Anselm's demonstration as valid must produce a conversion.

NOTES

1. I have consulted the Latin text of the *Proslogion,* of *Gaunilonis Pro Insipiente,* and of the *Responsio editoris,* in S. Anselmi, *Opera Omnia,* edited by F. C. Schmitt (Secovii, 1938), vol. I. With numerous modifications, I have used the English translation by S. N. Deane: *St. Anselm* (LaSalle, Illinois, 1948).

2. See *Proslogion* 1 and *Responsio* 2.

3. Anselm's actual words are: "Et certe id quo maius cogitari nequit, non potest esse in solo intellectu. Si enim vel in solo intellectu est, potest cogitari esse et in re, quod

maius est. Si ergo id quo maius cogitari non potest, est in solo intellectu: id ipsum quo maius cogitari non potest, est quo maius cogitari potest. Sed certe hoc esse non potest." *Proslogion* 2.

4. Haldane and Ross, *The Philosophical Works of Descartes,* 2 vols. (Cambridge, 1931), I, 163.

5. *Op. cit.,* p. 182.

6. *Proslogion* 2; Deane, p. 8.

7. *Responsio* 2; Deane, pp. 157-158.

8. *The Critique of Pure Reason,* tr. by Norman Kemp Smith (London, 1929), p. 505.

9. Haldane and Ross, II, 186.

10. *Proslogion* 3; Deane, pp. 8-9.

11. Professor Robert Calhoun has pointed out to me that a similar locution had been used by Augustine. In *De moribus Manichaeorum* (Bk. II, ch. xi, sec. 24), he says that God is a being *quo esse aut cogitari melius nihil possit* (*Patrologiae Patrum Latinorum,* ed. by J. P. Migne, Paris, 1841-1845, vol. 32; *Augustinus,* vol. 1).

12. *Ethics,* pt. I, prop. 11.

13. *Responsio* 1; Deane, pp. 154-155.

14. Gaunilo attacked Anselm's argument on this very point. He would not concede that a being a greater than which cannot be conceived existed in his understanding (*Gaunilonis Pro Insipiente,* secs. 4 and 5; Deane, pp. 148-150). Anselm's reply is: "I call on your faith and conscience to attest that this is most false" (*Responsio* 1; Deane, p. 154). Gaunilo's faith and conscience will attest that it is false that "God is not a being a greater than which is inconceivable," and false that "He is not understood (*intelligitur*) or conceived (*cogitatur*)" (*ibid.*). Descartes also remarks that one would go to "strange extremes" who denied that we understand the words "*that thing which is the most perfect that we conceive;* for that is what all men call God" (Haldane and Ross, II, 129).

15. Haldane and Ross, II, 228.

16. *Ibid.,* I, 445.

17. E.g., *ibid.,* Principle 15, p. 225.

18. *Op. cit.,* p. 502.

19. J. N. Findlay, "Can God's Existence Be Disproved?," *New Essays in Philosophical Theology,* ed. by A. N. Flew and A. MacIntyre (London, 1955), p. 47.

20. *Op. cit.,* pp. 505-506.

21. *Ibid.,* p. 504.

22. *The Nature of Metaphysics,* ed. by D. F. Pears (New York, 1957), p. 150.

23. *New Essays in Philosophical Theology,* p. 114.

24. *Ibid.,* p. 34.

25. *The Meaning of Life,* Inaugural Lecture, Canberra University College (Canberra, 1957), p. 8.

26. *Dialogues Concerning Natural Religion,* pt. IX.

27. Findlay, *op. cit.,* p. 154.

28. The other philosophers I have just cited may be led to this opinion by the same thinking. Smart, for example, says that "the truth of a logically necessary proposition depends only on our symbolism, or to put the same thing in another way, on the relationship of concepts" (*supra*). This is very similar to saying that it "reflects our use of words."

29. *Philosophical Investigations* (New York, 1953), sec. 654.

30. *Op. cit.,* pp. 501-502.

31. *Ibid.,* p. 502.

32. Haldane and Ross, II, 7.

33. I have heard it said by more than one person in discussion that Kant's view was that it is really a misuse of language to speak of a "necessary being," on the grounds that necessity is properly predicated only of propositions (judgments) not of *things*. This is not a correct account of Kant. (See his discussion of "The Postulates of Empirical Thought in General," *op. cit.*, pp. 239-256, esp. p. 239 and pp. 247-248.) But if he had held this, as perhaps the above philosophers think he should have, then presumably his view would not have been that the pseudo-proposition "God is a necessary being" is equivalent to the conditional "If God exists then He necessarily exists." Rather his view would have been that the genuine proposition " 'God exists' is necessarily true" is equivalent to the conditional "If God exists then He exists" (*not* "If God exists then He *necessarily* exists," which would be an illegitimate formulation, on the view imaginatively attributed to Kant.)

"If God exists then He exists" is a foolish tautology which says nothing different from the tautology "If a new earth satellite exists then it exists." If "If God exists then He exists" were a correct analysis of " 'God exists' is necessarily true," then "If a new earth satellite exists then it exists" would be a correct analysis of " 'A new earth satellite exists' is necessarily true." If the *analysans* is necessarily true then the *analysandum* must be necessarily true, provided the analysis is correct. If this proposed Kantian analysis of " 'God exists' is necessarily true" were correct, we should be presented with the consequence that not only is it necessarily true that God exists, but also it is necessarily true that a new earth satellite exists: which is absurd.

34. When summarizing Anselm's proof (in part II, *supra*) I said: "If God exists He necessarily exists." But there I was merely stating an entailment. "If God exists" did not have the implication that it is possible He does not exist. And of course I was not regarding the conditional as *equivalent* to "God necessarily exists."

35. This fallacious criticism of Anselm is implied in the following remarks by Gilson: "To show that the affirmation of necessary existence is analytically implied in the idea of God, would be . . . to show that God is necessary if He exists, but would not prove that He does exist" (E. Gilson, *The Spirit of Medieval Philosophy*, New York, 1940, p. 62).

36. *New Essays Concerning the Human Understanding*, Bk. IV, ch. 10; ed. by A. G. Langley (LaSalle, Illinois, 1949), p. 504.

37. See *Ibid.*, Appendix X, p. 714.

38. *The Journals*, tr. by A. Dru (Oxford, 1938), sec. 926.

A VALID
ONTOLOGICAL
ARGUMENT?
A REPLY*
Alvin Plantinga

I wish to discuss Professor Malcolm's absorbingly powerful defense of a version of Anselm's ontological proof for the existence of God. Professor Malcolm believes "that in Anselm's *Proslogion* and *Responsio editoris* there are two different pieces of reasoning which he did not distinguish from one another, and that a good deal of light may be shed on the philosophical problem of 'the ontological argument' if we do distinguish them." One of these pieces of reasoning is what is usually referred to as Anselm's· ontological argument; Malcolm agrees with a tradition beginning with Gaunilo in rejecting that argument. But it is the other argument with which Malcolm is particularly concerned; this one, he believes, is a perfectly sound argument for the existence of God.

I shall not be concerned with the question whether Malcolm has interpreted Anselm correctly, nor shall I discuss his criticism of Kant's refutation of the ontological argument, though I believe that his criticism is mistaken. Instead I shall stick to Malcolm's exposition of this hitherto unnoticed version of the ontological argument, hoping to show that the argument is invalid and that its conclusion (that God's existence is logically necessary) is false. In essence, the proof is an attempt to deduce God's necessary existence from our conception of Him as a being than which none greater can be conceived by showing "that the notion of contingent existence or of contingent nonexistence cannot have any application to God." Malcolm's account of the proof falls into two parts: an exposition and expansion of Anselm's argument and a summary of it. In order to get the argument in its entirety before us, I shall begin by examining the summary.

*From *The Philosophical Review,* vol. 70 (1961); reprinted by permission of *The Philosophical Review.*

Let me summarize the proof. If God, a being a greater than which cannot be conceived, does not exist then He cannot *come* into existence. For if He did He would either have been *caused* to come into existence or have *happened* to come into existence, and in either case He would be a limited being, which by our concept of Him He is not. Since He cannot come into existence, *if He does not exist His existence is impossible* [my italics]. If He does exist He cannot have come into existence (for the reasons given), nor can He cease to exist, for nothing could cause Him to cease to exist nor could it just happen that he ceased to exist. So *if God exists His existence is necessary* [italics mine]. Thus God's existence is either impossible or necessary. It can be the former only if the concept of such a being is self-contradictory or in some way logically absurd. Assuming that this is not so, it follows that He necessarily exists.

The structure of the main argument here seems to be the following:

(1) If God does not exist, His existence is logically impossible.
(2) If God does exist, His existence is logically necessary.
(3) Hence either God's existence is logically impossible or it is logically necessary.
(4) If God's existence is logically impossible, the concept of God is contradictory.
(5) The concept of God is not contradictory.
(6) Therefore God's existence is logically necessary.

(3), I take it, is equivalent to the assertion that "the notion of contingent existence or of contingent nonexistence cannot have any application to God"; in fact (3) follows from (1) and (2). Before examining the argument for (1) and (2), however, I wish to consider the intended meaning of the phrase "logically necessary" as it occurs in the proof. A normal inclination would be to understand the assertion "God's existence is logically necessary" as equivalent to the assertion "The proposition 'God exists' is logically necessary." I think this is Malcolm's intention:

> It may be helpful to express ourselves in the following way: to say, not that *omnipotence* is a property of God, but rather that *necessary omnipotence* is; and to say, not that omniscience is a property of God, but rather that *necessary omniscience* is. We have criteria for determining that a man knows this and that and can do this and that, and for determining that one man has greater knowledge and abilities in a certain subject than another.... That God is omniscient and omnipotent has not been determined by the application of criteria: rather these are requirements of our conception of Him. They are internal properties of the concept, although they are also rightly said to be properties of God. *Necessary existence* is a property of God in the *same sense* that *necessary omnipotence* and *necessary omniscience* are His properties.

It is a requirement of our conception of God that He is omnipotent; it is merely putting this point a different way, I believe, to say that the proposition "God is omnipotent" is logically necessary. The sense in which necessary omnipotence is a property of God is that the proposition "God is omnipotent" is necessary. And necessary existence, says Malcolm, is a property of God in the same sense in which necessary omnipotence and necessary omniscience are. To say "God necessarily exists," then, is to say the same as " 'God exists' is a necessary proposition." This interpretation receives confirmation from the following sentence: "The a priori proposition 'God necessarily exists' entails the proposition 'God exists,' if and only if the latter also is understood as an a priori proposition: in which case the two propositions are equivalent." Taking "logically necessary" and "a priori" as synonyms here, this passage seems to mean that "God necessarily exists" is equivalent to " 'God exists' is necessary." I am assuming further that for Malcolm a proposition is logically necessary if and only if its contradictory is self-contradictory. If Malcolm's reconstruction of Anselm's argument is correct, therefore, the proposition "God does not exist" is self-contradictory.

I turn now to premises (1) and (2) of the argument as outlined above. The first step in the argument given in the summary for (1) is to show that from the conception of God as the greatest conceivable being it follows that it is logically impossible for God to come (or to have come) into existence. For if He had either been caused to come into existence, or merely happend to come into existence, He would be a limited being. This inference seems quite correct; it follows from our conception of God that:

(a) N^1 (God never has and never will come into existence).

In the summary Malcolm apparently deduces (1) from (a). But this seems to be a mistake; for (a) does not entail (1) although it entails a proposition similar in some respect to the latter. Taking (a) and the antecedent of (1) as premises and the consequent of (1) as the conclusion, the deduction of (1) from (a) is equivalent to the following argument:

(a) N (God never has and never will come into existence).
(1a) God does not exist—antecedent of (1).

Therefore

(1c) N (God does not exist)—consequent of (1).

But (1c) does not follow from (a) and (1a). What does follow is (1c'): God never will exist. That is, the proposition "It is logically necessary that God never comes into existence" entails:

(1′) N (If there is a time at which God does not exist, then there is no subsequent time at which He does exist).

But (1′), of course, cannot play the role assigned to (1) in Malcolm's argument, for (1′) cannot help to show that the notion of contingent existence does not apply to God. The argument for (1) in the summary seems invalid, then.

In the exposition of the proof there seem to be two different though related arguments whose conclusions entail (1). I believe that Malcolm's reply to the above criticism would be to appeal to one of these arguments. The one I am referring to runs along the following lines: if God did not exist, and if the fact that He did not were merely contingent, then either He is prevented from existing or He merely happens not to exist. But it is contrary to the concept of God to suppose that anything could prevent Him from existing; and if the supposition that He merely happens not to exist is consistent, then if He did exist He would have "mere duration rather than eternity." But it is a requirement of our concept of God that He is an eternal Being; hence it cannot be true both that God does not exist and that the proposition "God does not exist" is logically contingent. I shall consider this argument after examining the argument in the summary for premise (2) of the proof.

(2) is deduced from (a) (see above) together with (b):
    (b) N (God never has and never will cease to exist).

(b), like (a), is deduced from the proposition that God is a being than which no greater can be conceived. Taking (a) and (b) together with the antecedent of (2) as premises and the consequent of (2) as conclusion we get the following inference:

    (a) N (God never has and never will begin to exist).
    (b) N (God never has and never will cease to exist).
    (2a) God exists—antecedent of (2).

Therefore

    (2c) N (God exists)—consequent of (2).

Once again it is apparent that (2c) does not follow from (a), (b), and (2a). What does follow is:

    (2c′) God always has existed and always will exist.

To put it differently, (a) and (b) together entail the following necessary conditional:

303

(2′) N (If at *any* time God exists, then at *every* time God exists).

If God cannot (logically) come into or go out of existence, it is a necessary truth that if He ever exists, He always exists. But it does not follow that if He exists, the proposition "God exists" is necessary. The correct definition of "God" might contain or entail that He never comes into or goes out of existence, in which case it would be a necessary truth that He never has and never will either begin or cease to exist. But nothing has been said to show that the fact, if it is a fact, that there is a being so defined is a necessary fact. The argument given in the summary for (2), then, is also invalid.

Allow me to venture a guess as to the origin of the confusion here. One way of advertising the necessary truth of a conditional, in English, is to inject some modal term into the consequent. We might say, for example, "If Jones is a bachelor, he can't be married"; and in so saying, of course, we do not mean to assert that if Jones is a bachelor, the proposition "Jones is unmarried" is necessary. What we do mean is that "If Jones is a bachelor, he is unmarried" is necessary. Similarly here: it is a necessary truth that if God exists, He always has and always will. A normal though misleading way of putting this is to say: if God exists, He cannot fail to exist eternally. But the assertion which is equivalent to my (2′) above, and which does follow from (a) and (b), should not be confused with (2) which does not so follow.

Now the argument given in the summary for (1) and (2) contains an omission. Malcolm argues that God cannot merely happen to begin to exist nor merely happen to cease to exist, and also that He cannot have been caused either to begin to exist or to cease to exist. But he does not consider the possibility that it just happens that God always has and always will exist (and so happens neither to begin nor cease existing, nor is caused either to begin or cease existing), nor does he consider the possibility that it just happens that God never has existed and never will exist. Malcolm's reply, as I have intimated, is that if either of these were the case, then if God exists, He has mere duration rather than eternity. After arguing that it is contrary to the concept of God to suppose that He depends upon anything for existence or that He could be prevented from existing, Malcolm considers the possibility that God just happens to exist:

> Some may be inclined to object that although nothing could prevent God's existence, still it might just *happen* that He did not exist. And if He did exist that too would be by chance. I think, however, that from the supposition that it could happen that God did not exist it would follow that, if He existed, He would have mere duration and not eternity. It would make sense to ask, "How long has He existed?" "Will He still exist next week?" "He was in existence yesterday but how about today?" and so on. It seems absurd to make God the subject of such questions. According to our ordinary conception of Him, He is an eternal being. And eternity does not mean endless duration, as Spinoza noted. To ascribe eternity to something is to exclude as senseless all sentences that imply that it has duration.

The principle of this argument seems to be the contention that if God merely happened to exist He would have duration rather than eternity. In order to see whether the argument holds up we must ask what it is to "happen to exist" and what it is to have mere duration rather than eternity. Now Malcolm appears to be using the locution "happens to exist" in such a way that the proposition "God just happens to exist" is equivalent to the conjunction of the following four propositions.

God just happens to exist ≡ (a) God exists.
                                      (b) "God exists" is logically contingent.
                                      (c) God is not caused to exist.
                                      (d) "God is not caused to exist" is logically necessary.

I am not sure about the inclusion of (d), but my argument will hold without it. The situation with respect to the terms "duration" and "eternity" is not quite so clear, unfortunately. But at any rate the last sentence of the above quotation makes it apparent that if something has eternity, it does not have duration. We must therefore inquire what it is to have duration. First of all it appears that if God had duration it would make sense to ask "How long has He existed?" "He was in existence yesterday, but how about today?" and so forth. Now Malcolm is quite correct, surely, in holding that such questions cannot sensibly be asked about God. But he seems mistaken in inferring the sensibility of these questions from the proposition that God just happens to exist. Let us agree that our normal conception of God includes or entails that He is not caused to exist and that His existence has neither beginning nor end. It will then be true and necessarily true that:

(7) If God exists, then there is a being whose existence is not caused and who has neither beginning nor end.

The whole conditional is necessary, but we have no reason so far for supposing that either its antecedent or its consequent is. It may be a logically contingent truth, if it is a truth, that there actually is a being so conceived. And if God, so defined, does exist, the four conditions I suggested as constituting the meaning of "God happens to exist" will all be fulfilled. But the question "How long has God existed?" will not "make sense." For in asking the question one implies that He does exist. And the assertion that God exists entails the assertion that He has always existed. Hence anyone who understands the question already knows the answer; to ask that question seriously is to betray misapprehension of the concept of God. Similarly the question "Will He still exist next week?" will be absurd. For it also implies that He does exist, but in the conception suggested above the conjunction "He does exist now, but next week He will no longer exist" is contradictory. Hence I conclude that "God merely happens to exist" does not entail that God has duration in any sense involving the logical propriety of questions of the sort Malcolm mentions.

Further on in the same passage, however, there seems to be a slightly different sense of "duration" introduced:

> If a thing has duration then it would be merely a *contingent* fact, if it was a fact, that its duration was endless. The moon could have endless duration but not eternity. If something has endless duration it will *make sense* (although it will be false) to say that it will cease to exist, and it will make sense (although it will be false) to say that something will *cause* it to cease to exist. A being with endless duration is not, therefore, an absolutely unlimited being.

Here it is suggested that the assertion "God has duration" has three components. That assertion entails (a) that any statement specifying the temporal limits of God's existence is contingent, (b) that "God will cease to exist" is sensible, and (c) that "God will be caused to cease to exist" is sensible. (c) appears to entail (b); perhaps it is also meant to entail (a), but I leave that question on one side. Now it seems clear that the proposition "God merely happens to exist," understood as above, does not entail (b). If an adequate definition of "God" includes or entails that He never comes into or goes out of existence, it obviously will not "make sense" to suppose that God will cease to exist. For "God will cease to exist" entails "There is a time at which God exists and a later time at which He does not." But under the definition in question that proposition is contradictory. Hence the supposition that God merely happens to exist does not entail (b). Nor does it entail (c), since (c) entails (b).

The situation with respect to (a) is a bit more complicated. Suppose we take the assertion:

(8) God has neither beginning nor end

as a specification of God's temporal limits in the somewhat Pickwickian sense that it denies any such limits to His existence. There are two possible interpretations of this proposition:

(8a) If God exists, then He has always existed and will always exist; and
(8b) God does exist and He always has existed and always will exist.

On the interpretation I have been suggesting, (8a) is logically necessary; (8b) is contingent, though each of its conjuncts entails the remaining two. Accepting the second interpretation of (8), then, we might say that the proposition "God

306

merely happens to exist" entails that God has duration. But this is a weak sense indeed of "duration"; in fact to say that God has duration in that sense is to say no more than that "God exists" is logically contingent—which, after all, was the essential component of the contention that God merely happens to exist. In particular this in no way implies that questions of the sort Malcolm mentions are legitimate; nor does having duration in this sense constitute a limitation. It is a mistake, therefore, to suppose that God's happening to exist is inconsistent with His being "that than which none greater can be conceived."

Malcolm supports the argument I have just criticized by an exegesis of a passage in Anselm's *Responsio I:*

> In *Responsio I* Anselm adds the following acute point: if you can conceive of a certain thing and this thing does not exist then if it *were* to exist its nonexistence would be *possible*. It follows, I believe, that if the thing were to exist it would depend on other things both for coming into and continuing in existence, and also that it would have duration and not eternity. Therefore it would not be, either in reality or in conception, an unlimited being.

The first point here seems to be that the proposition "God can be conceived but does not exist" entails the proposition "If God existed, His nonexistence would be possible." This seems correct. But Malcolm draws the further inference that if God were to exist, then He would "depend upon other things" and would have mere duration rather than eternity. This argument comes to the following:

(9) If the existence of God were logically contingent, God would depend upon other beings both for coming into existence and for continuing in existence, and God would have duration rather than eternity.

I believe I have already shown that from the supposition that God's existence is logically contingent it does not follow that He has duration rather than eternity, except in the trivial sense in which predicating duration of God is saying no more than that the proposition "God exists" is logically contingent. But it seems equally clear that God's dependence upon other things does not follow from the supposition that His existence is logically contingent. Malcolm states his argument in such a way that any statement of contingent existence entails that the subject of the statement depends upon other things both for coming into and for continuing in existence. But this is surely a mistake. For all we know, certain elementary physical particles—for example, electrons—may always have existed, in which case they surely don't depend upon anything for coming into existence. And for all we know there may be nothing upon which they depend for their continued existence. But of course it would not follow from the truth of these suppositions that the statement "Electrons don't exist" is self-contradictory, or that the existence of electrons is logically necessary.

307

Perhaps Malcolm had the following in mind here: even if electrons depend upon nothing at all for coming into or continuing in existence the assertion that they do not so depend is contingent. But the assertion that God does not depend upon anything is necessary. And it is inconsistent to hold both that God's existence is contingent and that it is a necessary truth that He depends upon nothing at all either for coming into or for continuing in existence. I think this is the heart of Malcolm's argument. But I must confess inability to see the inconsistency. Malcolm is entirely correct in taking it that the proposition "God does not depend upon anything for coming into or continuing in existence" is logically necessary. As he says, the necessity of this proposition follows from the fact that God is conceived, in the Hebraic-Christian tradition, as a being than which nothing greater can be conceived. And hence an adequate definition of the word "God" must include or entail that He is dependent upon nothing whatever. But the assertion that a being so defined exists, that the definition actually applies to something, may well be, for all that Malcolm and Anselm have said, a contingent assertion. It is a necessary truth that if God exists, then there is a being who neither comes into nor goes out of existence and who is in no way dependent on anything else. But from this it does not follow, contrary to Malcolm's argument, that the proposition "There is a being who neither comes into nor goes out of existence and who depends upon nothing" is necessary; nor does it follow that "God exists" is necessary. Malcolm's reconstruction of the ontological argument therefore fails.

NOTES

1. The letter "N" before a proposition signifies that the proposition is logically necessary.

5

THE GOOD,
THE BAD,
AND THE UGLY

"The teaching of virtue, Socrates, they said, is our principal occupation, and we believe we can impart it quicker and better than any man."

— Plato, *Euthydemus*, 273

"Crito, I owe a cock to Asclepius; will you remember to pay the debt?"

From Plato, *Phaedo* (Socrates' last words)

INTRODUCTION

There comes a time, Professor Prichard remarks at the very beginning of his essay, when the student of moral philosophy comes to doubt the worthwhileness of his study. That time comes rather early for most students. And it comes as the average undergraduate—Richard Bludweiss, say, to give him a name and fix him as a character—issues his first and most deeply felt disclaimer with respect to the possibilities of moral philosophy at all. The principles that guide conduct are all of them relative, Bludweiss believes. If I choose to amuse myself by leading a life of splendid dissoluteness and perpetual cruelty to others, well, that is my business and those are my values and one set of values has all the dignity of another. What is involved in a dispute between those who affirm and those who deny that it is wrong to eat babies is not an adjudicable principle but a taste, and while tastes may be cultivated, in the end there is nothing to be said to the man who relentlessly indulges a fondness for Mountain Dew when he might be drinking Chateau Lafite.

Here are a medley of themes that taken together comprise Bludweiss's lament. Each part will seem familiar to anyone arguing for the prospects of moral philosophy in the face of an instinctive moral relativism.

General principles in the form that Bludweiss espouses them do not spring to mind in anything like a philosophical vacuum. It is a pity that in his callowness Bludweiss let moral philosophy pass him by, for the chief principle after which he ought to grope involves

311

the affirmation of an unbridgeable gap between the world of value and the realm of fact; and this principle, in one fashion or another, has been variously championed by philosophers looking after ethics since the time of G. E. Moore. While proclamations of the autonomy of ethics need not inevitably commit the philosopher to Bludweiss's gargling vulgarity and relativism, plainly there is a stock of sympathy in moral philosophy that Bludweiss might have exploited had he been so disposed.

Some of that sympathy is available in H. A. Prichard's elegant and important paper. Prichard was an Oxford philosopher. His paper was composed in 1912, but the influence of G. E. Moore's *Principia Ethica* is strong throughout. It was Moore who argued the thesis that goodness was not the name of a natural property. By a natural property Moore meant something that could be grasped by the sensory modalities. Philosophers who confused the two were committing the *naturalistic fallacy.* Now Moore left much of what he said in a state of splendid ambiguity; and he commenced more-over a long tradition in British moral philosophy of assertion under-taken without argument. Still, the effect of his doctrines was all in the direction of enforcing a stern segregation between moral and factual discourse. But philosophers who insisted too boldly on just this distinction found themselves confronted with a pair of obvious questions. First, if moral discourse stands quite apart from factual discourse, what then is it really about? And, second, if the usual methods for inquiring into factual states of affairs lapse with respect to moral inquiry, what faculty must we use to obtain moral knowl-edge? Moore and Prichard were both passionately moral men. In answer to the first question, they insisted that moral language was legitimately about something quite palpable—an autonomous moral realm. And Prichard took the case still further by arguing specifically for a cognitive capacity, something like a truffle pig, specially geared to the sensing of moral properties. It is this capacity that he dubs intuition. The promptness and inevitability with which it acts shows that it is a mistake to imagine that the judgements delivered by intuition can be strengthened or supported by something as prosaic as mere argument, especially when the evidence supplied by argu-ment generally strikes us as less persuasive than the judgements they were meant to support.

This is *intuitionism,* then, at least as Prichard saw it, and quite

312

clearly any doctrine at once so vague and presumptuous constitutes a polemicist's dream. P. F. Strawson's essay constitutes just such an indulgent attack upon intuitionism. Strawson has couched his piece as a dialogue, the victim no doubt, of the inexpungable belief among philosophers that if Plato could manage the dialogue form with some literary effect so in fact could they. Although his essay is quite general, it is Prichard as much as any of the other intuitionists who figures as the critical object.

The intuitionist is a man who believes that moral discourse is objective, (in the sense of being either true or false) and yet not distinctly factual, (in the sense of being about such aspects of the world as a man might notice in using his eyes, ears or even his nose). This is a difficult synthesis and one that philosophers have historically proved incapable of maintaining. The central and unfailing property by which sentences or assertions are judged is *truth*. And in the concept of truth one also has the means to evaluate arguments, since the sound ones are those valid arguments with true premises, and validity can be defined in terms of truth. Now the philosopher who holds that ethical assertions are not about matters of fact, runs the very great risk of concluding shortly thereafter that neither are they true. Statements about the empirically accessible world, together with the propositions of mathematics seem to exhaust the category of sentences that can be either true or false.

Classical intuitionism thus embodied a difficult and sophisticated compromise. Emotivism followed intuitionism in the course of 20th century philosophy, both historically, as a movement, and intellectually, as a phase of thought. The intuitionists insisted on the autonomy of ethical language; and the emotivists took this doctrine to its outer limits, arguing that moral discourse was so unlike factual language that it failed completely to be about anything at all. By this the emotivists meant quite bluntly that moral language lacked cognitive significance. This was always a chain of thought that was implicit in the intuitionist's decision to sever moral discourse from central standards of appraisal and evaluation. In the emotivists' writings, this tendency came to prominence.

But if moral language is (strictly speaking) language without content, how does one explain the extraordinary vehemence with which moral positions are held? Philosophers such as A. J. Ayer and Charles Stevenson answered this question by forging an extraordinary conceptual link between *expressive* and ethical language. While moral language is factually quite without significance, they argued, nonetheless such language functions to express the attitudes and emotions of the man who uses it; And generally such language is used with the aim of persuading others to share the sentiments of the moral agent.

This is emotivism in full cry; and the doctrine received, I think, its most sophisticated exposition in the writings of the American philosopher Charles Stevenson. His essay "The Quasi-Imperative Function of Ethical Terms" develops in some detail the leading theme of the emotivist position. We use moral language to *express* our attitudes and to get others to share them; for this, imperative forms of speech are appropriate, and it is this form of speech, Stevenson holds, that is distinctively ethical.

Emotivism is, I should judge, the ethical doctrine that at first reading seems most natural to contemporary students. My own feeling is that Bludweiss and his crowd see in Stevenson their own doctrines writ large and made respectable. These are doctrines of course, that simply swarm with logical and philosophical difficulties. Some of them Professor Baier tracks down in his critical essay "Difficulties in the Emotive-Imperative Theory." But the Dialectic moves in mysterious fashion and the most telling commentary on emotivism has come about in the context of the ethical theory that in a certain sense extends and even supplants it. The cardinal weakness of emotivism is the flabbiness with which it outlined a theory of moral inference or reasoning. It is difficult to have a theory of moral reasoning if one thinks antecedently that moral discourse is not genuinely about anything save the expression of emotion. It has been R. M. Hare's writings, as much as anything, that have made good this defect and thus given the basic structure of emotivism intellectual depth and sophistication. Hare shares with Stevenson the insight that moral language is essentially imperative. We utter morally in order to commend our moral positions to others. But he goes considerably beyond Stevenson in his theory of moral judgement, and especially in his analysis of the relationship between the descriptive and purely evaluative functions of moral language.

For all that, however, Hare is in the Bludweissian tradition. Those ultimate principles on which conduct is based and to which we appeal in moral discourse are not themselves subject to anything like objective justification. This follows from the thesis that factual and moral language are distinct. On this point Philippa Foot has been especially sharp. Foot has remained steadily uninterested in the grand theory, arguing instead that views such as Hare's, for all their overall self-satisfaction, fail to come to grips with the character of some very simple moral judgements. Interestingly enough, these moral judgements suggest that the severance between moral and factual discourse is itself not quite so clean as theorists such as Hare, Stevenson, and even Prichard and Bludweiss might suggest. With this line of thought, the circle of convergence in moral philosophy comes to something like a natural point of closure.

Modern ethical theory begins with G. E. Moore's *Principia Ethica* (Cambridge University Press), a book whose riveting persuasiveness is certainly not accounted for by the quality of its argument. W. D. Ross's *The Right and the Good* (Oxford: The Clarendon Press) discusses ethics from the intuitionist point of view, while Charles Stevenson's *Ethics and Languages* and A. J. Ayer's *Language, Truth and Logic* (Yale University Press and Dover Books) set out the emotivist theory. R. M. Hare's *The Language of Morals* (Oxford: The Clarendon Press) is the book that begins the most recent episode of ethical theory. A comparable text is Stephen Toulmin's *The Place of Reason in Ethics* (Cambridge University Press); and there is also Patrick Nowell-Smith's *Ethics* (Penguin books). An excellent collection of papers has been edited by Wildrid Sellars and John Hospers under the title *Readings in Ethical Theory* (Appleton-Century-Crofts). Another good collection is George Nakhnikian and Hector-Neri Castaneda's *Morality and the Language of Conduct* (Wayne State University Press).

DOES
MORAL
PHILOSOPHY
REST ON A
MISTAKE?*

H. A. Prichard

Probably to most students of moral philosophy there comes a time when they feel a vague sense of dissatisfaction with the whole subject, and the sense of dissatisfaction tends to grow rather than to diminish. It is not so much that the positions, and still more the arguments, of particular thinkers seem unconvincing, though this is true; it is rather that the aim of the subject becomes increasingly obscure. "What," it is asked, "are we really going to learn by moral philosophy?" "What are books on moral philosophy really trying to show, and when their aim is clear, why are they so unconvincing and artificial?" And again: "Why is it so difficult to substitute anything better?" I have been led by growing dissatisfaction of this kind to wonder whether the reason may not be that the subject, at any rate as it is usually understood, consists in the attempt to answer an improper question. And in this article I will venture to contend that the existence of the whole subject, as usually understood, rests on a mistake and on a mistake parallel to that on which rests, as I think, the subject usually called the Theory of Knowledge.

If we reflect on our own mental history or on the history of the subject, we feel no doubt about the nature of the demand which originates the subject. Anyone who, stimulated by education, has come to feel the force of various obligations in life, at some time or other comes to feel the irksomeness of carrying them out and to recognize the sacrifice of interest involved. If thoughtful, he inevitably puts to himself the question: "Is there really a reason why I should act in the ways in which hitherto I have thought I ought to act? May I not have been all the time under an illusion in so thinking? Shouldn't I really be justified in simply trying to have a good time?" Yet, like Gaucon,

*Reprinted from *Mind*, 21, 1912. by kind permission of the publisher, Basil Blackwell, Oxford.

feeling that somehow he ought after all to act in these ways, he asks for a *proof* that his feeling is justified. In other words, he asks, "*Why* should I do these things?" and his and other people's moral philosophizing is an attempt to supply the answer, that is, to supply by a process of reflection a proof of the truth of what he and they have prior to reflection believed immediately or without proof. This frame of mind seems to present a close parallel to the frame of mind which originates the theory of knowledge. Just as the recognition that the doing of our duty often vitally interferes with the satisfaction of our inclinations leads us to wonder whether we really ought to do what we usually call our duty, so the recognition that we and others are liable to mistakes in knowledge generally leads us, as it did Descartes, to wonder whether hitherto we may not have been always mistaken. Just as we try to find a proof, based on the general consideration of action and of human life, that we ought to act in the ways usually called moral, so we, like Descartes, propose by a process of reflection on our thinking to find a test of knowledge, that is, a principle by applying which we can show that a certain condition of mind was really knowledge, a condition which *ex hypothesi* existed independently of the process of reflection.

How has the moral question been answered? As far as I can see, the answers all fall, and fall from the necessities of the case, into one of two species. *Either* they state that we ought to do such and such because, as we see when we fully apprehend the facts, doing so will be for our good, that is, really, as I would rather say, for our advantage, or better still, for our happiness; *or* they state that we ought to do such and such because something realized either in or by the action is good. In other words, the reason *why* is stated in terms either of the agent's happiness or of the goodness of something involved in the action.

To see the prevalence of the former species of answer, we have only to consider the history of moral philosophy. To take obvious instances, Plato, Butler, Hutcheson, Paley, Mill, each in his own way seeks to convince the individual that he ought to act in "moral" ways by showing that to do so will really be for his happiness. Plato is perhaps the most significant instance, because of all philosophers he is the one to whom we are least willing to ascribe a mistake on such matters, and a mistake on his part would be evidence of the deeprootedness of the tendency to make it. To show that Plato really justifies morality by its profitableness, it is only necessary to point out (1) that the very formulation of the thesis to be met, namely, that justice is ἀλλότριον ἀγαθόν,* implies that any refutation must consist in showing that justice is οἰκεῖον ἀγαθόν, that is, as the context shows, one's own advantage, and (2) that the term λυσιτελεῖν** supplies the key not only to the problem but also to its solution.

The tendency to justify acting on moral rules in this way is natural, for if,

---

*[Someone else's good, that is, advantage.—Ed.]
**[To profit (someone), that is, to be to someone's advantage.—Ed.]

as often happens, we put to ourselves the question, "Why should we do such and such?" we are satisfied by being convinced either that doing so will lead to something which we want (for example, that taking certain medicine will cure our disease) or that doing so itself, as we see when we appreciate its nature, is something that we want or should like, for example, playing golf. The formulation of the question implies a state of unwillingness or indifference toward the action, and we are brought into a condition of willingness by the answer. This process seems to be precisely what we desire when we ask, for example, "Why should we keep our engagements to our own loss?", for it is precisely the fact that the keeping of our engagements runs counter to the satisfaction of our desires which produced the question.

The answer is, of course, not an answer, for it fails to convince us that we ought to keep our engagements; even if successful on its own lines, it only makes us *want* to keep them. Kant was really only pointing out this fact when he distinguished hypothetical and categorical imperatives, even though he obscured the nature of the fact by wrongly describing his "hypothetical imperatives" as imperatives. But if this answer is no answer, what other can be offered? Only, it seems, an answer which bases the obligation to do something on the *goodness* either of something to which the act leads or of the act itself. Suppose, when wondering whether we really ought to act in the ways usually called moral, we are told as a means of resolving our doubt that those acts are right which produce happiness. We at once ask, "Whose happiness?" If we are told, "Our own happiness," then, though we will lose our hesitation to act in these ways, we will not recover our sense that we ought to do so. But how can this result be avoided? Apparently, only by being told one of two things, *either* that anyone's happiness is a thing good in itself, and that *therefore* we ought to do whatever will produce it, *or* that working for happiness is itself good, and that the intrinsic goodness of such an action is the reason why we ought to do it. The advantage of this appeal to the goodness of something consists in the fact that it avoids reference to desire, and instead, refers to something impersonal and objective. In this way it seems possible to avoid the resolution of obligation into inclination. But just for this reason it is of the essence of the answer, that to be effective it must neither include nor involve the view that the apprehension of the goodness of anything necessarily arouses the desire for it. Otherwise the answer resolves itself into a form of the former answer by substituting desire or inclination for the sense of obligation, and in this way it loses what seems its special advantage.

It seems to me that both forms of this answer break down, though each for a different reason.

Consider the first form. It is what may be called utilitarianism in the generic sense, in which what is good is not limited to pleasure. It takes its stand on the distinction between something which is not itself an action, but which can be produced by an action, and the action which will produce it, and contends that if something which is not an action is good, then we *ought* to undertake the action which will, directly or indirectly, originate it.[1]

But this argument, if it is to restore the sense of obligation to act, must presuppose an intermediate link, namely, the further thesis that what is good ought to be.[2] The necessity of this link is obvious. An "ought," if it is to be derived at all, can only be derived from another "ought." Moreover, this link tacitly presupposes another, namely, that the apprehension that something good which is not an action ought to be involves just the feeling of imperativeness or obligation which is to be aroused by the thought of the action which will originate it. Otherwise the argument will not lead us to feel the obligation to produce it by the action. Surely both this link and its implication are false.[3] The word *ought* refers to actions and to actions alone. The proper language is never "so and so ought to be," but "I ought to do so and so." Even if we are sometimes moved to say that the world or something in it is not what it ought to be, what we really mean is that God or some human being has not made something what he ought to have made it. And it is merely stating another side of this fact to urge that we can only feel the imperativeness upon us of something which is in our power; for it is actions and actions alone which, directly at least, are in our power.

Perhaps the best way to see the failure of this view is to see its failure to correspond to our actual moral convictions. Suppose we ask ourselves whether our sense that we ought to pay our debts or to tell the truth arises from our recognition that in doing so we should be originating something good, for example, material comfort in A or true belief in B, that is suppose we ask ourselves whether it is this aspect of the action which leads to our recognition that we ought to do it. We at once and without hesitation answer No. Again, if we take as our illustration our sense that we ought to act justly as between two parties, we have, if possible, even less hesitation in giving a similar answer, for the balance of resulting good may be and often is, not on the side of justice.

At best it can only be maintained that there is this element of truth in the utilitarian view, that unless we recognized that something which an act will originate is good, we should not recognize that we ought to do the action. Unless we thought knowledge a good thing, it may be urged, we should not think that we ought to tell the truth; unless we thought pain a bad thing, we should not think the infliction of it, without special reason, wrong. But this is not to imply that the badness of error is the reason why it is wrong to lie, or the badness of pain the reason why we ought not to inflict it without special cause.[4]

It is, I think, just because this form of the view is so plainly at variance with our moral consciousness that we are driven to adopt the other form of the view, namely, that the act is good in itself and that its intrinsic goodness is the reason why it ought to be done. It is this form which has always made the most serious appeal, for the goodness of the act itself seems more closely related to the obligation to do it than that of its mere consequences or results; therefore, if obligation is to be based on the goodness of something, it would seem that this goodness should be that of the act itself. Moreover, the view gains plausibility from the fact that moral actions are most conspicuously those to which the term "intrinsically good" is applicable.

Nevertheless, this view, though perhaps less superficial, is equally untenable, for it leads to precisely the dilemma which faces everyone who tries to solve the problem raised by Kant's theory of the good will. To see this, we need only consider the nature of the acts to which we apply the term "intrinsically good."

There is, of course, no doubt that we approve and even admire certain actions and also that we should describe them as good, as good in themselves. But it is, I think, equally unquestionable that our approval and our use of the term *good* is always with regard to the motive and refers to actions that have been actually done and of which we think we know the motive. Further, the actions of which we approve and which we should describe as intrinsically good are of two and only two kinds. They are either actions in which the agent did what he did because he thought he ought to do it, or actions of which the motive was a desire prompted by some good emotion such as gratitude, affection, family feeling, or public spirit. In books on moral philosophy the most prominent of such desires are ascribed to what is vaguely called benevolence. For the sake of simplicity I omit the case of actions done partly from some such desire and partly from a sense of duty, for even if all good actions are done from a combination of these motives, the argument will not be affected. The dilemma is this: if the motive with regard to which we think an action good is the sense of obligation, then far from the sense that we ought to do it being derived from our apprehension of its goodness, our apprehension of its goodness will presuppose the sense that we ought to do it. In other words, in this case the recognition that the act is good will plainly *presuppose* the recognition that the act is right, whereas the view under consideration is that the recognition of the goodness of the act *gives rise* to the recognition of rightness. On the other hand, if the motive with regard to which we think an action good is some intrinsically good desire, such as the desire to help a friend, the recognition of the goodness of the act will equally fail to give rise to the sense of obligation to do it. We cannot feel that we ought to do that, the doing of which is *ex hypothesi* prompted by the desire to do it.[5]

The fallacy underlying the view is that while to base the rightness of an act on its intrinsic goodness implies that the goodness in question is that of the motive, in reality the rightness or wrongness of an act has nothing to do with any question of motives at all. For, as any instance will show, the rightness of an action concerns an action not in the fuller sense of the term in which we include the motive in the action, but in the narrower and commoner sense in which we distinguish an action from its motive and mean by an action merely the conscious origination of something, an origination which on different occasions or in different people may be prompted by different motives. The question, "Ought I to pay my bills?" really means simply, "Ought I to bring about my tradesmen's possession of what by my previous acts I explicitly or implicitly promised them?" There is, and can be, no question of whether I ought to pay my debts from a particular motive. No doubt we know that if we pay our bills we shall pay them with a motive, but in considering whether we ought to pay them we inevitably think of the act in abstraction from the motive. Even if we knew what our motive would be if we did the act, we should not be any nearer an answer to the question.

Moreover, if we eventually pay our bills from fear of the county court, we shall still have done *what* we ought, even though we shall not have done it *as* we ought. The attempt to bring in the motive involves a mistake similar to that involved in supposing that we can will to will. To feel that I ought to pay my bills is to be *moved toward* paying them. But what I can be moved toward must always be an action and not an action in which I am moved in a particular way, that is, an action from a particular motive. Otherwise I should be moved toward being moved, which is impossible. Yet the view under consideration involves this impossibility, for it really resolves the sense that I ought to do so and so, into the sense that I ought to be moved to do it in a particular way.[6]

So far my contentions have been mainly negative, but they form, I think, a useful, if not a necessary, introduction to what I take to be the truth. This I will now endeavor to state, first formulating what I think is the real nature of our apprehension or appreciation of moral obligations and then applying the result to elucidate the question of the existence of moral philosophy.

The sense of obligation to do, or of the rightness of, an action of a particular kind is absolutely underivative or immediate. The rightness of an action consists in its being the origination of something of a certain kind A in a situation of a certain kind, a situation consisting of a certain relation B of the agent to others or to his own nature. To appreciate its rightness, two preliminaries may be necessary. We may have to follow out the consequences of the proposed action more fully than we have hitherto done in order to realize that in the action we should originate A. Thus we may not appreciate the wrongness of telling a certain story until we realize that we should thereby be hurting the feelings of one of our audience. Again, we may have to take into account the relation B involved in the situation, which we had hitherto failed to notice. For instance, we may not appreciate the obligation to give X a present until we remember that he has done us an act of kindness. But, given that by a process which is, of course, merely a process of general and not of moral thinking we come to recognize that the proposed act is one by which we shall originate A in a relation B, then we appreciate the obligation immediately or directly, the appreciation being an activity of *moral* thinking. We recognize, for instance, that this performance of a service to X, who has done us a service, just in virtue of its being the performance of a service to one who has rendered a service to the would-be agent, ought to be done by us. This apprehension is immediate, in precisely the sense in which a mathematical apprehension is immediate, for example, the apprehension that this three-sided figure, in virtue of its being three-sided, must have three angles. Both apprehensions are immediate in the sense that in both insight into the nature of the subject directly leads us to recognize its possession of the predicate. It is only stating this fact from the other side to say that in both cases the fact apprehended is self-evident.

The plausibility of the view that obligations are not self-evident but need proof lies in the fact that an act which is referred to as an obligation may be incompletely stated, what I have called the preliminaries to appreciating the obligation being incomplete. If, for example, we refer to the act of repaying X by a present merely as giving X a present, it appears, and indeed is, necessary to give a reason. In other words, wherever a moral act is regarded in this incomplete way the question "*Why* should I do it?" is perfectly legitimate. This fact suggests, but suggests wrongly, that even if the nature of the act is completely stated, it is still necessary to give a reason, or, in other words, to supply a proof.

The relations involved in obligations of various kinds are, of course, very different. In certain cases the relation is a relation of others due to a past act of theirs or ours. The obligation to repay a benefit involves a relation due to a past act of the benefactor. The obligation to pay a bill involves a relation due to a past act of ours in which we have either said or implied that we would make a certain return for something which we have asked for and received. On the other hand, the obligation to speak the truth implies no such definite act; it involves a relation consisting in the fact that others are trusting us to speak the truth, a relation the apprehension of which gives rise to the sense that communication of the truth is something owing by us to them. Again, the obligation not to hurt the feelings of another involves no special relation of us to that other, that is, no relation other than that involved in our both being men, and men in one and the same world. Moreover, it seems that the relation involved in an obligation need not be a relation to another at all. Thus we should admit that there is an obligation to overcome our natural timidity or greediness, and that this involves no relations to others. Still there is a relation involved, namely, a relation to our own disposition. It is simply because we can and because others cannot directly modify our disposition that it is our business to improve it, and that it is not theirs, or, at least, not theirs to the same extent.

The negative side of all this is, of course, that we do not come to appreciate an obligation by an *argument,* that is, by a process of nonmoral thinking, and that, in particular, we do not do so by an argument of which a premiss is the ethical but not moral activity of appreciating the goodness either of the act or of a consequence of the act, that is, that our sense of the rightness of an act is not a conclusion from our appreciation of the goodness either of it or of anything else.

It will probably be urged that on this view our various obligations form, like Aristotle's categories, an unrelated chaos in which it is impossible to acquiesce. According to it, the obligation to repay a benefit, pay a debt, keep a promise presupposes a previous act of another, whereas the obligation to speak the truth or not to harm another does not. Again, the obligation to remove our timidity involves no relations to others at all, yet an effective *argumentum ad hominem* is at hand in the fact that the various qualities which we recognize as good are equally unrelated; for example, courage, humility, and interest in knowledge. If, as is plainly the case, ἀγαθά [goods] differ ᾗ ἀγαθά [qua goods], why should not obligations equally differ *qua* their obligatoriness? Moreover, if this were not so there could in the end be only one obligation which is palpably contrary to fact.[7]

Certain observations will help to make the view clearer.

In the first place, it may seem that the view, being—as it is—avowedly put forward in opposition to the view that what is right is derived from what is good, must itself involve the opposite of this, namely, the Kantian position that what is good is based on what is right, that is, that an act, if it be good, is good because it is right. But this is not so, for on the view put forward, the rightness of a right action lies solely in the origination in which the act consists, whereas the intrinsic goodness of an action lies solely in its motive. This implies that a morally good action is morally good not simply because it is a right action but because it is a right action done because it is right, that is, from a sense of obligation, and this implication, it may be remarked incidentally, seems plainly true.

In the second place, the view involves that when, or rather so far as, we act from a sense of obligation, we have no purpose or end. By a "purpose" or "end," we mean really something the existence of which we desire, and desire of the existence of which leads us to act. Usually our purpose is something which the act will originate, as when we turn around in order to look at a picture. But it may be the action itself, that is, the origination of something, as when we hit a golf ball into a hole or kill someone out of revenge.[8] If by a purpose, we mean something the existence of which we desire and desire for which leads us to act, then plainly, so far as we act from a sense of obligation, we have no purpose consisting either in the action or in anything which it will produce. This is so obvious that it scarcely seems worth pointing out, but I do so for two reasons: (1) If we fail to scrutinize the meaning of the terms *end* and *purpose*, we are apt to assume uncritically that all deliberate action, that is, action proper, must have a purpose; we then become puzzled both when we look for the purpose of an action done from a sense of obligation, and when we try to apply to such an action the distinction of means and end, the truth all the time being that since there is no end, there is no means either; (2) The attempt to base the sense of obligation on the recognition of the goodness of something is really an attempt to find a purpose in a moral action in the shape of something good which, as good, we want. And the expectation that the goodness of something underlies an obligation disappears as soon as we cease to look for a purpose.

The thesis, however, that, so far as we act from a sense of obligation we have no purpose, must not be misunderstood. It must not be taken either to mean or to imply that so far as we so act we have no *motive*. No doubt, in ordinary speech the words *motive* and *purpose* are usually treated as correlatives, *motive* standing for the desire which induces us to act and *purpose* standing for the object of this desire. But this is only because, when we are looking for the motive of the action, say, of some crime, we are usually presupposing that the act in question is prompted by a desire and not by the sense of obligation. At bottom we mean by a motive what moves us to act; a sense of obligation does sometimes move us to act; and in our ordinary consciousness we should not hesitate to allow that the action we were considering might have had as its motive a sense of obligation. Desire and the sense of obligation are coordinate forms or species of motive.

In the third place, if the view put forward is right, we must sharply distinguish morality and virtue as independent, though related, species of goodness, neither being an aspect of something of which the other is an aspect, nor again a form or species of the other, nor again something deducible from the other. We must, at the same time, allow that it is possible to do the same act either virtuously or morally or in both ways at once. Surely this is true. An act, to be virtuous, must, as Aristotle saw, be done willingly or with pleasure. As such, it is done not just from a sense of obligation but from some desire which is intrinsically good emotion. Thus, in an act of generosity the motive is the desire to help another arising from sympathy with that other. In an act which is courageous and no more, that is, in an act which is not at the same time an act of public spirit or family affection or the like, we prevent ourselves from being dominated by a feeling of terror, desiring to do so from a sense of shame at being terrified. The goodness of such an act is different from the goodness of an act to which we apply the term moral in the strict and narrow sense, namely, an act done from a sense of obligation. Its goodness lies in the intrinsic goodness of the emotion and of the consequent desire under which we act, the goodness of this motive being different from the goodness of the moral motive proper, the sense of duty or obligation. Nevertheless, in certain cases, an act can be done either virtuously or morally or in both ways at once. It is possible to repay a benefit either from desire to repay it or from the feeling that we ought to do so, or from both motives combined. A doctor may tend his patients either from a desire arising out of interest in his patients or in the exercise of skill, or from a sense of duty, or from a desire and a sense of duty combined. Further, although we recognize that in each case the act possesses an intrinsic goodness, we regard that action as the best in which both motives are combined. In other words, we regard as the really best man the man in whom virtue and morality are united.

It may be objected that the distinction between the two kinds of motive is untenable, on the ground that the *desire* to repay a benefit, for example, is only the manifestation of that which manifests itself as the *sense of obligation* to repay whenever we think of something in the action which is other than the repayment and which we should not like, such as the loss or pain involved. Yet I think the distinction can easily be shown to be tenable, for in the analogous case of revenge, the desire to return the injury and the sense that we ought not to do so, leading as they do in opposite directions, are plainly distinct. The obviousness of the distinction here seems to remove any difficulty in admitting the existence of a parallel distinction between the desire to return a benefit and the sense that we ought to return it.[9]

Further, the view implies that an obligation can no more be based on or derived from a virtue than a virtue can be derived from an obligation, in which latter case a virtue would consist in carrying out an obligation. The implication is surely true and important. Take courage. It is untrue to urge that, since courage is a virtue, we ought to act courageously. It is and must be untrue, because, as we see in the end, to feel an obligation to act courageously would involve a contradiction. I have urged before, we can only feel an obligation to *act*; we cannot feel an obligation to *act from a certain desire*, in this case the desire to conquer one's feelings of terror arising from the sense of shame which they arouse. Moreover, if the sense of obligation to act in a particular way leads to an action, the action will be an action done from a sense of obligation and not (if the above analysis of virtue is right) an act of courage.

The mistake of supposing that there can be an obligation to act courageously seems to arise from two causes. First, there is often an obligation to do that which involves the conquering or controlling of our fear in the doing of it, for example, the obligation to walk along the side of a precipice to fetch a doctor for a member of our family. Here acting on the obligation is externally, though only externally, the same as an act of courage proper. Second, there is an obligation to acquire courage, to do things that will enable us afterwards to act courageously, and this may be mistaken for an obligation to act courageously. The same considerations can, of course, be applied, *mutatis mutandis*, to the other virtues.

The fact (if it is a fact) that virtue is no basis for morality will explain what otherwise it is difficult to account for, namely, the extreme sense of dissatisfaction produced by a close reading of Aristotle's *Ethics*. Why is the *Ethics* so disappointing? Not, I think, because it really answers two radically different questions as if they were one: (1) "What is the happy life?" (2) "What is the virtuous life?" It is, rather, because Aristotle does not do what we as moral philosophers want him to do: convince us that we really ought to do what in our nonreflective consciousness we have hitherto believed we ought to do, or if not, to tell us what, if any, are the other things which we really ought to do and to prove to us that he is right. If what I have just been contending is true, a systematic account of the virtuous character cannot possibly satisfy this demand. At best it can make clear to us the details of one of our obligations, the obligation to make ourselves better men. But the achievement of this does not help us to discover what we ought to do in life as a whole, and why. To think that it did would be to think that our only business in life was self-improvement, hence it is not surprising that Aristotle's account of the good man strikes us as almost wholly of academic value, with little relation to our real demand, which is formulated in Plato's words: οὐ γὰρ περὶ τοῦ ἐπιτυχόντος ὁ λόγος, ἀλλὰ περὶ τοῦ ὄντινα τρόπον χρὴ ζῆν.*

I am not, of course, *criticizing* Aristotle for failing to satisfy this demand, except so far as here and there he leads us to think that he intends to satisfy it. My main contention is that the demand cannot be satisfied; it cannot be satisfied because it is illegitimate. Thus we are brought to the question: "Is there really such a thing as moral philosophy, and, if there is, in what sense?"

We should first consider the parallel case—as it appears to be—of the theory of knowledge. As I urged before, at some time or other in the history of all of us, if we are thoughtful, the frequency of our own and of others' mistakes is bound to lead to the reflection that possibly we and others have *always* been mistaken because of some radical defect of our faculties. Consequently, certain things which previously we should have said without hesitation that we *knew*, as for example, that $4 \times 7 = 28$, become subject to doubt; we become able only to say that we thought we knew these things. We inevitably go on to look for some general procedure by which we can ascertain that a given condition of mind is really one of knowledge, and this involves the search for a criterion of knowledge, that is, for a principle by applying which we can settle that a given state of mind is really knowledge. The search for this criterion and the application of it, when found, is what is called the theory of knowledge. The search implies that instead of its being the fact that the knowledge that A is B is obtained directly by consideration of the nature of A and B, the knowledge that A is B, in the full or complete sense, can only be obtained by first knowing that A is B and then knowing that we knew it by applying a criterion, such as Descartes' principle that what we clearly and distinctly conceive is true.

It is easy to show that the doubt whether A is B, based on this speculative

---

*[For no light matter is at stake; the question concerns the very manner in which human life is to be lived (*Republic*, Bk. I, 352D)—Ed.].

or general ground, could, if genuine, never be set at rest. For if, in order really to know that *A* is *B*, we must first know that we knew it, then really, to know that we knew it, we must first know that we knew that we knew it. But—what is more important—it is also easy to show that this doubt is not a genuine doubt but rests on a confusion the exposure of which removes the doubt. For when we *say* we doubt whether our previous condition was one of knowledge, what we *mean*, if we mean anything at all, is that we doubt whether our previous *belief* was *true*, a belief which we should express as the *thinking* that *A* is *B*. In order to doubt whether our previous condition was one of knowledge, we have to think of it not as knowledge but as only belief, and our only question can be "Was this belief true?" But as soon as we see that we are thinking of our previous condition as only one of belief, we see that what we are now doubting is not what we first *said* we were doubting, namely, whether a previous condition of knowledge was really knowledge. Hence, to remove the doubt, it is only necessary to appreciate the real nature of our consciousness in apprehending, for example, that $7 \times 4 = 28$ and thereby see that it was no mere condition of believing but a condition of knowing, and then to notice that in our subsequent doubt what we are really doubting is not whether this consciousness was really knowledge, but whether a consciousness of another kind—a belief that $7 \times 4 = 28$—was true. We thereby see that though a doubt based on speculative grounds is possible, it is not a doubt concerning what we believed the doubt concerned, and that a doubt concerning this latter is impossible.

Two results follow. In the first place, if, as is usually the case, we mean by the "theory of knowledge" the knowledge which supplies the answer to the question "Is what we have hitherto thought knowledge really knowledge?" there is and can be no such thing, and the supposition that there can is simply due to a confusion. There can be no answer to an illegitimate question, except that the question is illegitimate. Nevertheless, the question is one which we continue to put until we realize the inevitable immediacy of knowledge. It is positive knowledge that knowledge is immediate and neither can be, nor needs to be, improved or vindicated by the further knowledge that it was knowledge. This positive knowledge sets at rest the inevitable doubt, and, so far as by the "theory of knowledge" is meant this knowledge, then even though this knowledge is the knowledge that there is no theory of knowledge in the former sense, to that extent the theory of knowledge exists.

In the second place, suppose we come genuinely to doubt whether $7 \times 4 = 28$, owing to a genuine doubt whether we were right in believing yesterday that $7 \times 4 = 28$, a doubt which can in fact only arise if we have lost our hold of, that is, no longer remember, the real nature of our consciousness of yesterday and so think of it as consisting in believing. Plainly, the only remedy is to do the sum again, or, to put the matter generally, if we do come to doubt whether it is true that *A* is *B*, as we once thought, the remedy lies not in any process of reflection but in such a reconsideration of the nature of A and B as leads to the knowledge that A is B.

With these considerations in mind, consider the parallel which, as it seems to me, is presented—though with certain differences—by moral philosophy. The sense that we ought to do certain things arises in our unreflective consciousness, being an activity of moral thinking occasioned by the various situations in which we find ourselves. At this stage our attitude to these obligations is one of unquestioning confidence. But inevitably the appreciation of the degree to which the execution of these obligations is contrary to our interest raises the doubt whether after all these obligations are really obligatory, that is, whether our sense that we ought not to do certain things is not illusion. We then want to have it *proved* to us that we ought to do so, that is, to be convinced of this by a process which, as an argument, is different in kind from our original and unreflective appreciation of it. This demand is, as I have argued, illegitimate.

In the first place, if, as is almost universally the case, by moral philosophy is meant the knowledge which would satisfy this demand, there is no such knowledge, and all attempts to attain it are doomed to failure because they rest on a mistake, the mistake of supposing the possibility of proving what can only be apprehended directly by an act of moral thinking. Nevertheless the demand, though illegitimate, is inevitable until we have carried the process of reflection far enough to realize the self-evidence of our obligations, that is, the immediacy of our apprehension of them. This realization of their self-evidence is positive knowledge, and so far, and so far only, as the term Moral Philosophy is confined to this knowledge and to the knowledge of the parallel immediacy of the apprehension of the goodness of the various virtues and of good dispositions generally, is there such a thing as Moral Philosophy. But since this knowledge may allay doubts which often affect the whole conduct of life, it is, though not extensive, important and even vitally important.

In the second place, suppose we come genuinely to doubt whether we ought, for example, to pay our debts, owing to a genuine doubt whether our previous conviction that we ought to do so is true, a doubt which can, in fact, only arise if we fail to remember the real nature of what we now call our past conviction. The only remedy lies in actually getting into a situation which occasions the obligation, or—if our imagination is strong enough—in imagining ourselves in that situation, and then letting our moral capacities of thinking do their work. Or, to put the matter generally, if we do doubt whether there is really an obligation to originate A in a situation B, the remedy lies not in any process of general thinking, but in getting face to face with a particular instance of the situation B, and then directly appreciating the obligation to originate A in that situation.

NOTES

1. Cf. Dr. Rashdall's *Theory of Good and Evil,* vol. i, p. 138.

2. Dr. Rashdall, if I understand him rightly, supplies this link (cf. ibid., pp. 135-6).

3. When we speak of anything, for example, of some emotion or of some quality of a human being, as good, we never dream in our ordinary consciousness of going on to say that therefore it ought to be.

4. It may be noted that if the badness of pain were the reason why we ought not to inflict pain on another, it would equally be a reason why we ought not to inflict pain on ourselves; yet, though we should allow the wanton infliction of pain on ourselves to be foolish, we should not think of describing it as wrong.

5. It is, I think, on this latter horn of the dilemma that Martineau's view falls; cf. *Types of Ethical Theory,* part ii, book i.

6. It is of course not denied here that an action done from a particular motive may be *good*; it is only denied that the *rightness* of an action depends on its being done with a particular motive.

7. Two other objections may be anticipated: (1) that obligations cannot be self-evident, since many actions regarded as obligations by some are not so regarded by others, and (2) that if obligations are self-evident, the problem of how we ought to act in the presence of conflicting obligations is insoluble.

To the first I should reply:

(*a*) That the appreciation of an obligation is, of course, only possible for a developed moral being, and that different degrees of development are possible.

(*b*) That the failure to recognize some particular obligations is usually due to the fact that, owing to a lack of thoughtfulness, what I have called the preliminaries to this recognition are incomplete.

(*c*) That the view put forward is consistent with the admission that, owing to a lack of thoughtfulness, even the best men are blind to many of their obligations, and that in the end our obligations are seen to be co-extensive with almost the whole of our life.

To the second objection I should reply that obligation admits of degrees, and that where obligations conflict, the decision of what we ought to do turns not on the question "Which of the alternative courses of action will originate the greater good?" but on the question "Which is the greater obligation?"

8. It is no objection to urge that an action cannot be its own purpose, since the purpose of something cannot be the thing itself. For, speaking strictly, the purpose is not the *action's* purpose but *our* purpose, and there is no contradiction in holding that our purpose in acting may be the action.

9. This sharp distinction of virtue and morality as co-ordinate and independent forms of goodness will explain a fact which otherwise it is difficult to account for. If we turn from books on Moral Philosophy to any vivid account of human life and action such as we find in Shakespeare, nothing strikes us more than the comparative remoteness of the discussions of Moral Philosophy from the facts of actual life. Is not this largely because, while Moral Philosophy has, quite rightly, concentrated its attention on the fact of obligation, in the case of many of those whom we admire most and whose lives are of the greatest interest, the sense of obligation, though it may be an important, is not a dominating factor in their lives?

ETHICAL
INTUITIONISM*
P. F. Strawson

North

What is the trouble about moral facts? When someone denies that there is an objective moral order, or asserts that ethical propositions are pseudo-propositions, cannot I refute him (rather as Moore refuted those who denied the existence of the external world) by saying: "You know very well that Brown did wrong in beating his wife. You know very well that you ought to keep promises. You know very well that human affection is good and cruelty bad, that many actions are wrong and some are right"?

West

Isn't the trouble about moral facts another case of trouble about knowing, about learning? We find out facts about the external world by looking and listening; about ourselves, by feeling; about other people, by looking and listening *and* feeling. When this is noticed, there arises a wish to say that the facts *are* what is seen, what is heard, what is felt; and consequently, that moral facts fall into one of these classes. So those who have denied that there are "objective moral characteristics" have not wanted to deny that Brown's action was wrong or that keeping promises is right. They have wanted to point out that rightness and wrongness are a matter of what is felt in the heart, not of what is seen with the eyes or heard with the ears. They have wanted to emphasize the way in which "Promise-keeping is right" resembles "Going abroad is exciting," "Stories about mothers-in-law are comic," "Bombs are terrifying";

*Reprinted from P. F. Strawson, "Ethical Intuitionism," *Philosophy*, 24 (1949).

and differs from "Roses are red" and "Seawater is salt." This does not prevent you from talking about the moral order, or the moral world, if you want to; but it warns you not to forget that the only access to the moral world is through remorse and approval and so on; just as the only access to the world of comedy is through laughter; and the only access to the coward's world is through fear.

North

I agree, of course, that we cannot see the goodness of something as we see its color, or identify rightness by the sense of touch, though I think you should add that the senses are indispensable as a means of our becoming aware of those characteristics on which moral characteristics depend. You may be partly right, too, in saying that access to the moral world is obtained through experience of the moral emotions; for it may be that only when our moral feelings have been strongly stirred do we first become clearly aware of the characteristics which evoke these feelings. But these feelings are not identical with that awareness. "Goodness" does not stand to "feeling approval," "guilt" to "feeling guilty," "obligation" to "feeling bound," as "excitingness" stands to "being excited" and "humorousness" to "feeling amused." To use the jargon for a moment: moral characteristics and relations are nonempirical, and awareness of them is neither sensory nor introspectual. It is a different kind of awareness, which the specialists call "intuition": and it is only empiricist prejudice which prevents your acknowledging its existence. Once acknowledged, it solves our problems: and we see that while "Promise-keeping is right" differs from "The sea is salt," this is not because it resembles "Detective-stories are exciting"; it differs from *both* in being the report neither of a sensible nor an introspectible experience, but of an intuition. We may, perhaps, know some moral characteristics mediately, through others. ("Obligation" is, perhaps, definable in terms of "goodness.") But at least one such characteristic—rightness or goodness—is unanalysable, and known by intuition alone. The fundamental cognitive situation in morals is that in which we intuit the rightness of a particular action or the goodness of a particular state of affairs. We see this moral characteristic as present in virtue of some other characteristics, themselves capable of being described in empirical terms, which the action or state of affairs possesses. (This is why I said that sense-perception is a necessary, though not a sufficient, condition of obtaining information about the moral order.) Our intuition, then, is not a bare intuition of the moral characteristic, but also the intuition of its dependence on some others: so that this fundamental situation yields us, by intuitive induction, knowledge of moral rules, generalizations regarding the right and the good, which we can apply in other cases, even when an actual intuition is lacking. So much do these rules become taken for granted, a part of our habitual moral life, that most of our everyday moral judgments involve merely an implicit reference to them:[1] a reference which becomes explicit only if the judgment is challenged or queried. Moral emotions, too, assume the character of habitual reactions. But emotions and judgments alike are grounded upon intuitions. Emotion may be the gatekeeper to the moral world; but intuition is the gate.

West

Not so fast. I understand you to say that at least one fundamental moral characteristic—rightness or goodness—is unanalysable. Perhaps both are. The experts are divided. In any case, the fundamental characteristic (or characteristics) can be known only by intuitive awareness of its presence in some particular contemplated action or state of affairs. There is, then, a kind of analogy between the word "right" (or "good") and the name of some simple sensible characteristic such as "red."[2] Just as everybody who understands the word "red" has seen some red things, so everybody who understands the word "right" or the word "good" has intuited the character, rightness, in some actions, or the character, goodness, in some states of affairs; and nobody who has not intuited these characters understands the words "right" or "good." But this is not quite enough, is it? In order for me to know *now* the meaning of an indefinable word, it is not enough that a certain perceptual or intuitional event should have occurred at some particular point in my history; for I might not only have forgotten the details of that event, I might have forgotten what *kind* of an event it was; I might not know *now* what it would be like for such an event to occur. If the word "red" expresses an indefinable visual concept, then it is self-contradictory to say: "I know what the word 'red' means, but I can't remember ever *seeing* red and I don't know what it would be *like* to see red." Similarly, if the word "right," or the word "good," expresses an indefinable intuitive concept, then it is self-contradictory to say: "I know what the word 'right' or the word 'good' means, but I can't remember ever *intuiting* rightness or goodness, and I don't know what it would be *like* to intuit rightness or goodness." If your theory is true, then this statement is a contradiction.

But it is not at all obvious to me that it is a contradiction. I should be quite prepared to assert that I understood the words "right" and "good," but that I couldn't remember ever intuiting rightness or goodness and that I couldn't imagine what it would be like to do so. And I think it is quite certain that I am not alone in this, but that there are a large number of people who are to be presumed capable of accurate reporting of their own cognitive experience, and who would find nothing self-contradictory in saying what I say. And if this is so, you are presented with a choice of two possibilities. The first is that the words "right" and "good" have quite a different meaning for one set of people from the meaning which they have for another set. But neither of us believes this. The second is that the intuitionist theory is a mistake; that the phrase "intuitional event having a moral characteristic as its object (or a part of its object)" is a phrase which describes nothing at all; or describes misleadingly the kind of emotional experience we both admit. There is no third possibility. It is no good saying: "All people who succeed in learning the meaning of moral words do as a matter of fact have moral intuitions, but unfortunately many people are inclined to forget them, to be quite unable to remember what they are like." True, there would be nothing self-contradictory in saying this: but it would simply be a variant of the first possibility; for I cannot be said to know *now* the meaning of a word expressing an intuitive concept unless I know now what it would be like to intuit the characteristic of which it is a concept. The trouble with your intuitionist theory is that, if true, it should be a truism. There should be no doubt about the occurrence of the distinctive experience of intuiting rightness (or goodness), and about its being the only way to learn the meaning of the primary moral words; just as there is no doubt about the occurrence of seeing red (or blue), and about this being the only way to learn the meaning of the primary color words. But there *is* doubt; and over against this doubt there rises a certainty: the certainty that we all know what it is to *feel* guilty, to *feel* bound, to *feel* approving.

North

What I have said *is* a truism; and that is its strength. It is not I who am inventing a mythical faculty, but you, irritated, perhaps, by the language of intuitionism, who are denying the obvious. When you said that you couldn't *imagine* what it would be like to have moral intuitions, isn't it clear that you wanted "intuiting a moral characteristic" to be like seeing a color or hearing a sound? Naturally you couldn't *imagine* anything of the sort. But I have already pointed out that moral characteristics are dependent on others of which the presence *is* ascertainable by looking and listening. You do not intuit rightness or goodness independently of the other features of the situation. You intuit *that* an action is (or would be) right, a state of affairs good, *because* it has (or would have) certain other empirically ascertainable qualities. The total content of your intuition includes the "because" clause. Of course, our ordinary moral judgments register unreflective reactions. Nevertheless "This act is right (or this state of affairs is good) because it has P, Q, R"—where "P, Q, R" stands for such empirically ascertainable qualities—expresses the type of fundamental cognitive situation in ethics, of which our normal judgments are copies, mediated by habit, but readily, if challenged, to become explicit as their original. Consider what happens when someone dissents from your opinion. You produce reasons. And this is not a matter of accounting for an emotional condition; but of bringing evidence in support of a verdict.

West

When the jury brings in a verdict of guilty on a charge of murder, they do so because the facts adduced in evidence are of the kind covered by the definition of "murder." When the chemical analyst concludes that the material submitted for analysis is a salt, he does so because it exhibits the defining properties of a salt. The evidence is the sort of thing that is *meant* by "murder," by "salt." But the fundamental moral word, or words, you say, cannot be defined; their concepts are unanalysable. So it cannot be in this way that the "because" clause of your ethical sentence functions as evidence. "X is a right action because it is a case of promise-keeping" does not work like "X is a salt because it is a compound of basic and acid radicals"; for, if "right" is indefinable, "X is right" does not *mean* "X is an act of promise-keeping or of relieving distress or of telling the truth or . . ."

When I say "It will be fine in the morning; for the evening sky is red," the evidence is of a different sort. For I might observe the fine morning without having noticed the state of the evening sky. But you have rightly stressed the point that there is no *independent* awareness of *moral* qualities: that they are always "seen" as dependent on those other features mentioned in the "because" clause. So it is not in this way, either, that the "because" clause of your ethical sentence functions as evidence. And there is no other way. Generally, we may say that whenever q is evidence for p, *either* q is the sort of thing we mean by "p" ("p" is definable in terms of "q") *or* we can have knowledge of the state of affairs described by "p" independently of knowledge of the state of affairs described by "q." But neither of these conditions is satisfied by the q, the "because" clause, of your ethical sentence.

The "because" clause, then, does not, as you said it did, constitute evidence for the ethical judgment. And this, it seems to me, should be a serious matter for you. For where is such evidence to be found? It is no good saying that, after all, the ethical judgments of other people (or your own at other times) may corroborate your own present judgment. They may agree with it; but their agreement strengthens the probability of your judgment only on the assumption that their moral intuitions tend on the whole to be correct. But the only possible evidence for the existence of a *tendency* to have correct intuitions is the correctness of *actual* intuitions. And it is precisely the correctness of actual intuitions for which we are seeking evidence, and failing to find it.

And evidence you must have, if your account of the matter is correct. You will scarcely say that ethical intuitions are infallible; for ethical disagreements may survive the resolution of factual disagreements. (You might, of course, say that *genuine* intuitions were infallible: then the problem becomes one of finding a criterion for distinguishing between the genuine ones and those false claimants that carry the same inner conviction.) So your use of the language of "unanalysable predicates ascribed in moral judgment to particular actions and states of affairs" leads to contradiction. For to call such a judgment "non-infallible" would be meaningless unless there were some way of checking it; of confirming or confuting it, by producing evidence for or against it. But I have just shown that your account of these judgments is incompatible with the possibility of producing evidence for or against them. So, if your account is true, these judgments are both corrigible and incorrigible; and this is absurd.

But the absurdity points to the solution. Of course these judgments are corrigible: but not in the way in which the diagnosis of a doctor is corrigible; rather in the way in which the musical taste of a child is corrigible. Correcting them is not a matter of *producing evidence* for them or their contraries, though it is (partly) a matter of *giving reasons* for them or their contraries. We say, warningly, that ethical judgments are corrigible, because ethical disagreement sometimes survives the resolution of factual disagreement. We say, encouragingly, that ethical judgments are corrigible, because the resolution of factual disagreement sometimes leads to the resolution of ethical disagreement. But the one kind of agreement leads (when it *does* lead) to the other, not in the way in which agreed evidence leads to an agreed conclusion, but in the way in which common experience leads to sympathy. The two kinds of agreement, the two kinds of judgment, are as different as chalk from cheese. Ordinary language can accommodate the difference without strain: it is the pseudo-precise philosophical use of "judgment" which slurs over the difference and raises the difficulty. Is it not clear, then, what people have meant when they said that ethical disagreements were like disagreements in taste, in choice, in practical attitude?[3] Of course, as you said, when we produce our reasons, we are not often simply giving the causes of our emotional condition. But neither are we producing evidence for a verdict, for a moral diagnosis. We are using the facts to back our attitudes, to appeal to the capacity of others to feel as we feel, to respond as we respond.

North

I think I see now what you have been leaving out all the time. First, you accused me of inventing a mythical faculty to give us ethical knowledge. Then, when I pointed out that ethical qualities are not intuited out of all relation to other empirically ascertainable features of actions and states of affairs, but are intuited as dependent upon these, you twisted this dependence out of all recognition. You wanted to make it like the causal dependence of a psychological disposition upon some empirical feature of its object: as a child's fondness for strawberries depends upon their sweetness. But the connection between wrongness and giving pain to others is not an accident of our constitution; nor does its perception require any special faculty—but *simply that which we use in all our reasoning.* From the fact that an action involves inflicting needless pain upon others, *it follows* necessarily that the action is wrong, just as, from the fact that a triangle is equilateral, it follows necessarily that its angles are equal. This is the kind of dependence that we intuit; not an analytic dependence, but a synthetic entailment; and this is why the "because" clause of my ethical sentence does, after all, constitute evidence for the ascription of the moral characteristic.

I can anticipate the obvious objection. No moral rule, you will say, no moral generalization concerning the rightness of acts or the goodness of conditions, holds without exception. It is always possible to envisage circumstances in which the generalization breaks down. Or, if the generalization is so wide that no counter-example can be found, if it can be so interpreted as to cover every case, then it has become too wide: it has become tautologous, like "It is always right to do that which will have the best results on the whole," or intolerably vague, like "It is always right to treat people as ends in themselves" or "The greatest good is the greatest general welfare." It is plainly not with the help of such recipes as these that we find out what is right, what is good, in a particular case. There are no criteria for the meaning of "treating a man as an end," for "the greatest general welfare," which do not presuppose the narrower criteria of rightness and goodness of which I spoke and which seem always to have exceptions. All this is true. But it calls only for a trifling amendment to those narrower criteria. We cannot, for example, assert, as a necessary synthetic proposition, "All acts of promise-keeping are right" or "All states of aesthetic enjoyment are good." But we *can* assert, as a necessary synthetic proposition, "All acts of promise-keeping *tend as such* to be right (or have *prima facie* rightness)"[4] or "All states of aesthetic enjoyment *tend as such* to be good." And we derive our knowledge of such general necessary connections from seeing, in particular cases, that the rightness of an action, the goodness of a state, *follows from* its being an action or state of a certain kind.

West

Your "trifling amendment" is a destructive one. When we say of swans that they tend to be white, we are not ascribing a certain quality, namely "tending to be white," to each individual swan. We are saying that the number of swans which are white exceeds the number of those which are not, that if anything is a swan, the chances are that it will be white. When we say "Welshmen tend to be good singers," we mean that most Welshmen sing well; and when we say, of an *individual* Welshman, that *he* tends to sing well, we mean that he sings well more often than not. In all such cases, we are talking of a *class* of things or occasions or events; and saying, not that *all* members of the class have the property of *tending to have* a certain characteristic, but that *most* members of the class do in fact have that characteristic. Nobody would accept the claim that a sentence of the form *"Most* As are Bs" expresses a necessary proposition. Is the claim made more plausible by rewriting the proposition in the form *"All* As *tend to be* Bs"?

But, waiving this point, there remains the difficulty that the need for such an amendment to our moral generalizations is incompatible with the account you gave of the way in which we come to know both the moral characteristics of individual actions and states, and the moral generalizations themselves. You said that we intuited the moral characteristic as *following from* some empirically ascertainable features of the action or state. True, if we did so, we should have implicitly learned a moral generalization: but it would be one asserting *without qualification* the entailment of the moral characteristic by these other features of the case. In other words, and to take your instance, if it *ever* follows, from the fact that an act has the empirically ascertainable features described by the phrase "being an act of promise-keeping," that the act is right, then it *always* follows, from the fact that an act is of this kind, that it has this moral quality. If, then, it is true that we intuit moral characteristics as thus "following from" others, it is false that the implied generalizations require the "trifling amendment"; and if it is true that they require the amendment, it is false that we so intuit moral characteristics.[5]

And this is all that need be said of that rationalist superstition according to which a quasi-logical necessity binds moral predicates to others. "Le coeur a ses raisons, que la raison ne connait pas": this is the whole truth of the matter: but your attention was so riveted to the first half of it that you forgot the second.

Looking for a logical nexus where there was none to be found, you overlooked the logical relations of the ethical words among themselves. And so you forgot what has often been pointed out: that for every expression containing the words "right" or "good," used in their ethical senses, it is always possible to find an expression with the same meaning, but containing, instead of these, the word "ought." The equivalences are various, and the variations subtle; but they are always to be found. For one to say, for example, "I know where the good lies, I know what the right course is; but I don't know the end I *ought* to aim at, the course I *ought* to follow" would be self-contradictory. "Right"-sentences, "good"-sentences, are shorthand for "ought"-sentences.

And this is enough in itself to explode the myth of unanalysable characteristics designated by the indefinable predicates, "right" and "good." For "ought" is a *relational* word; whereas "right" and "good" are *predicative*. The simplest sentences containing "ought" are syntactically more complicated than the simplest sentences containing "right" or "good." And hence, since the equivalences of meaning hold, the various ethical usages of "right" and "good" *are all definable*: variously definable in terms of "ought."

Of course this last consideration alone is not decisive against intuitionism. If this were all, you could still re-form the ranks: taking your stand on an intuited unanalysable nonnatural *relation* of obligation, and admitting the definability of the ethical predicates in terms of this relation. But the objections I have already raised apply with equal force against this modified position; and, in other ways, its weakness is more obvious.[6]

North

Well, then, suppose we agree to bury intuitionism. What have you to offer in its place? Has any analysis of moral judgments in terms of feeling ever been suggested which was not monstrously paradoxical or artificial? Even the simplest ethical sentence obstinately resists translation: and not in the way in which "Life, like a dome of many-colored glass, Stains the white radiance of eternity" resists translation. For the ethical language is not the language of the poets, but the language of all the world. Somehow justice must be done both to this irreducible element of significance in ethical sentences, and to the community of knowledge of their correct, their appropriate, use. Intuitionism, at any rate, was a way of attempting to do this.

West

Yes, intuitionism was a way of attempting to do this. It started from the fact that thousands and thousands of people can say, with perfect propriety: "I know that this is right, that is good"; and ended, as we have seen, by making it inexplicable how anybody could ever say such a thing. This was because of a failure to notice that the whole sentence, including the "I know," and not just the last word in the subordinate clause, is a unit of the ethical language; and, following upon this failure, a feverish ransacking of the drawers of a Theory of Knowledge for an "I know" which would fit. (Do I, perhaps, work it out like the answer to a sum?)

The man who attempts to provide a translation sees more than this. He sees, at any rate, that the sentence must be treated as a unit. His error is to think

339

that he can find a substitute, in a different language, which will serve the same purpose. So long as he confines himself to describing how, in what sort of circumstances, the sentence is used, he does valuable work. He errs when he talks as if to say how a sentence is used is the same as to use it. The man who says he can translate ethical sentences into feeling sentences makes the same sort of mistake as some who said they could (if they had time) translate material-object sentences into sentences about actual and possible sense experiences. What they *mean*—the commentary they are making on the use of the ethical language or the material-object language—is correct. And it is precisely because the commentary would be incorrect as a translation that it is useful as a commentary. For it brings out the fact that the irreducibility of these languages arises from the systematic vagueness of the notation they use in comparison with that of the commentary languages, and not from their being used to talk of, to describe, different things from those of which the commentary languages talk. This descriptive vagueness is no defect: it is what makes these languages useful for the kinds of communication (and persuasion) for which they are severally required. But by being mistaken for something more than it is, it leads to one kind of metaphysics: the metaphysics of substance (the thing-in-itself), or of intuited unanalysable ethical characteristics. And by being ignored altogether, it leads to another kind of metaphysics: the tough metaphysics of translation, the brutal suggestion that we could get along just as well without the ethical language. Neither metaphysics—neither the tender metaphysics of ultimacy, nor the tough metaphysics of reduction[7]—does justice to the facts: but the latter does them less injustice; for it doesn't seek to supplement them with a fairy tale.

And so the alternative to intuitionism is not the provision of translations. For the communication and sharing of our moral experience, we must use the tools, the ethical language, we have. No sentences provided by the philosopher will take their place. His task is not to supply a new set of tools, but to describe what it is that is communicated and shared, and how the tools are used to do the work. And though the experience he describes is emotional experience, his descriptions are not like those of the psychologist. The psychologist is concerned with the relation of these experiences to others of a different sort; the philosopher is concerned with their relation to the ordinary use of ethical language. Of course, then, it would be absurd for the philosopher to deny that some actions are right (fair, legitimate, etc.) and others wrong (unfair, illegitimate, etc.), and that we know this; and absurd to claim that we can say what such sentences say without using such words. For this *is* the language we use in sharing and shaping our moral experience; and the occurrence of experience so shared, so shaped, is not brought into question.

We are in the position of the careful phenomenalist; who, for all his emphasis on sense experience, neither denies that there is a table in the dining room, nor claims to be able to assert this without using such words as "dining

340

room" and "table." A phenomenalism as careful as this has been said to forfeit the right to be called a "philosophical doctrine."[8] Then let the title be reserved for the productions of those who rest in myth or paradox, and fail to complete that journey, from the familiar to the familiar,[9] which is philosophical analysis.

NOTES

1. Cf. D. Daiches Raphael, *The Moral Sense,* chs. 5 and 6.

2. Cf. G. E. Moore, *Principia Ethica,* p. 7 *et seq.*

3. Cf. Charles Stevenson, *Ethics and Language,* chap. 1. See also his paper, "The Emotive Meaning of Ethical Terms."

4. Ross, *Foundations of Ethics,* pp. 83-86; Broad, "Something of the Main Problems of Ethics," *Philosophy,* 1946, p. 117. [Reprinted in Herbert Feigl and Wilfrid Sellars, eds., *Reading in Philosophical Analysis,* Appleton-Century-Crofts, Inc., 1949.]

5. One desperate expedient might occur to North. He might say that it is not the bare presence of the promise-keeping feature that entails the rightness of the act, but the presence of this feature, coupled with the absence of any features which would entail its wrongness. His general rules would then be, not of the form " 'x has ϕ' entails 'x is right,' " but of the form " 'x had ϕ and x has no ψ such that "x has ψ" entails "x is wrong" ' entails 'x is right.' " But the suggestion is inadmissible, since (i) the establishment of the general proposition "x has no ψ, etc." would require the enumeration of all those features which would make it wrong to keep a promise, and (ii) any rule of the form " 'x has ψ' entails 'x is wrong' " would require expansion in exactly the same way as the "right-making" rule; which would involve an infinite regress of such expansions. Besides having this *theoretical* defect, the suggested model is, of course, *practically* absurd.

6. E.g. There was a certain plausibility in saying "My feeling morally obliged to pursue such a course (or end) presupposes my believing that it is right (or good)," and thence concluding that this belief cannot be "reduced to" the feeling which it arouses. (For examples of this sort of argument, see Ross, *op. cit.,* pp. 216-262, and Broad, *op. cit.,* p. 115.) But the weakness of this reasoning is more clearly exposed when the sentence is re-written as "My feeling morally obliged to pursue such a course presupposes my believing that I *am* morally obliged to pursue it." The point is that "presupposes" and "believing" are both ambiguous. If "presupposes" means "causally requires" and "believing" is used in its ordinary sense, then it is obviously false that the beliefs which *occasion* such a feeling invariably include some belief which would be correctly described in these terms. (Compare: "My feeling frightened presupposes my believing that I am frightened.") But the argument begins to have weight against the "analysability" of beliefs correctly so described only if they are invariably present as occasioning factors. If, on the other hand, "presupposes" means "logically requires," then "believing" might be used in a queer sense such that the sentence is *tautologically* true. But this result is secured only by defining "believing" (used in this sense) in terms of feeling (compare the sense in which "thinking x funny" means "being amused by x"): and this was precisely the result with North sought to avoid.

7. Cf. Wisdom, "Metaphysics and Verification," *Mind,* 1938.

8. Hardie, "The Paradox of Phenomenalism," *Proceedings of the Aristotelian Society,* 1945-46, p. 150.

9. Wisdom.

THE QUASI-IMPERATIVE FUNCTION OF ETHICAL TERMS*
C. L. Stevenson

Our first question, though seemingly peripheral, will prove to be of central importance:

What is the nature of ethical *agreement* and *disagreement*? Is it parallel to that found in the natural sciences, differing only with regard to the relevant subject matter; or is it of some broadly different sort?

If we can answer the question, we shall obtain a general understanding of what constitutes a normative *problem*; and our study of terms and methods, which must explain how this kind of problem becomes articulate and how it is open to argument or inquiry, will be properly oriented. There are certain normative problems, of course, to which the question is not directly relevant—those which arise in personal deliberation, rather than in interpersonal discourse, and which involve not disagreement or agreement but simply uncertainty or growing conviction. But ... the question is indirectly relevant even to them; and meanwhile there is a convenience in looking chiefly to the interpersonal problems, where the use of terms and methods is most clearly evidenced.

For simplicity let us limit our explicit attention to "disagreement," treating the positive term by implication. And let us begin by distinguishing two broad kinds of disagreement. We can do this in a wholly general way, temporarily suspending any decision about which kind is most typical of normative ethics, and drawing our examples from other fields.

The disagreements that occur in science, history, biography, and their counterparts in everyday life, will require only brief attention. Questions about the nature of light transmission, the voyages of Leif Ericsson, and the date on which Jones was last in to tea, are all similar in that they may involve an opposi-

*Reprinted by permission of Yale University Press from *Ethics and Language,* by Charles L. Stevenson, pp. 2-31. Copyright © 1944 by Yale University Press.

tion that is primarily of beliefs. (The term "beliefs" must not, at least for the moment, include reference to ethical convictions; for whether or not the latter are "beliefs" in the present sense is largely the point that is to be discussed.) In such cases one man believes that p is the answer and another that not p, or some proposition incompatible with p, is the answer; and in the course of discussion each tries to give some manner of proof for his view, or revise it in the light of further information. Let us call this "disagreement in belief."

There are other cases, differing sharply from these, which may yet be called "disagreements" with equal propriety. They involve an opposition, sometimes tentative and gentle, sometimes strong, which is not of beliefs, but rather of attitudes—that is to say, an opposition of purposes, aspirations, wants, preferences, desires, and so on.[1] Since it is tempting to overintellectualize these situations, giving too much attention to beliefs, it will be helpful to examine them with care.

Suppose that two people have decided to dine together. One suggests a restaurant where there is music; another expresses his disinclination to hear music, and suggests some other restaurant. It may then happen, as we commonly put it, that they "cannot easily agree on which restaurant to choose." The disagreement springs more from divergent preferences than from divergent beliefs, and will end whey they both *wish* to go to the same place. It will be a mild, temporary disagreement for this simple case—a disagreement in miniature; yet it will be a "disagreement" in a wholly familiar sense.

Further examples are easily found. Mrs. A has social aspirations, and wants to move with the elite. Mr. A is easygoing, and loyal to his old friends. They accordingly disagree about what guests they will invite to their party. The curator of the museum wants to buy pictures by contemporary artists; some of his advisers prefer the purchase of old masters. They disagree. John's mother is concerned about the dangers of playing football, and doesn't want him to play. John, even though he agrees (in belief) about the dangers, wants to play anyhow. Again, they disagree. These examples, like the previous one, involve an opposition of attitudes, and differ only in that the attitudes in question are a little stronger, and are likely to be defended more seriously. Let us refer to disagreement of this sort as "disagreement in attitude."[2] Two men will be said to disagree in attitude when they have opposed attitudes to the same object—one approving of it, for instance, and the other disapproving of it—and when at least one of them has a motive for altering or calling into question the attitude of the other. Let us be careful to observe, however, that when one man is seeking to alter another's attitudes, he may at the same time be preparing to alter his own attitudes in the light of what the other may say. Disagreement in attitude, like disagreement in belief, need not be an occasion for forensic rivalry; it may be an occasion for an interchange of aims, with a reciprocal influence that both parties find to be beneficial.

343

The two kinds of disagreement differ mainly in this respect: the former is concerned with how matters are truthfully to be described and explained; the latter is concerned with how they are to be favored or disfavored, and hence with how they are to be shaped by human efforts.

It is by no means the case that every argument represents one sort of disagreement to the exclusion of the other. There is often disagreement of both sorts. This is to say little more than that our beliefs and attitudes must not be compartmentalized. Our attitudes, as many have pointed out, often affect our beliefs, not only by causing us to indulge in wishful thinking, but also by leading us to develop and check such beliefs as point out the means of getting what we want. And conversely, our beliefs often affect our attitudes; for we may alter our form of approval of something when we change our beliefs about its nature. The causal connection between beliefs and attitudes is usually not only intimate but reciprocal. To ask whether beliefs in general direct attitudes in general, or whether the causal connection goes rather in the opposite direction is simply a misleading question. It is like asking, "Do popular writers influence public taste, or does public taste influence them?" Any implication that the alternatives are mutually exclusive can only be rejected. The influence goes both ways, although at times only one direction of influence may predominate.

There is accordingly a close relationship between the sorts of disagreement that have been distinguished. Indeed, in some cases the existence of one may wholly depend on the existence of the other. Suppose that A and B have convergent attitudes toward the *kind* of thing that X *actually* is, but indicate divergent attitudes to X itself simply because A has erroneous beliefs about it, whereas B has not. Discussion or inquiry, correcting A's errors, may resolve the disagreement in belief; and this in turn may be sufficient to resolve the disagreement in attitude. X was an occasion for the latter sort of disagreement *only* because it was an occasion for the former.

In cases of this sort one might be inclined to reject the expression, "Both kinds of disagreement were intially present, the one depending on the other," and say instead, "Only disagreement in belief was intially present, the disagreement in attitude with regard to X being simply apparent." If X was designated without ambiguity, however, so that the same X could be *recognized* by both parties regardless of their divergent beliefs about it, then the latter idiom would be seriously misleading. One man was definitely striving for X, and the other definitely striving to oppose it; and if this involved ignorance, where one of the men was acting to defeat his broader aims, it remains altogether appropriate to say that the initial divergence in attitude, so far as X was concerned, was genuine. It is convenient to restrict the term "apparent" disagreement to cases which involve ambiguity—to cases where the term that seems to designate X for both parties actually designates Y for one of them.

The relationship between the two sorts of disagreement, whenever it occurs, is always factual, never logical. So far as the logical possibilities are concerned, there may be disagreement in belief without disagreement in attitude; for even if an argument must always be motivated, and to that extent involve attitudes, it does not follow that the attitudes which attend opposed beliefs must themselves be opposed. People may share the ideals and aims which guide their scientific theorizing, for instance, and still reach divergent beliefs. Similarly, there may be disagreement in attitude without disagreement in belief. Perhaps every attitude must be accompanied by some belief about its object; but the beliefs which attend opposed attitudes need not be incompatible. A and B may both believe that X has Q, for instance, and have divergent attitudes to X *on that very account*, A approving of objects that have Q and B disapproving of them. Since it may also happen that both sorts of disagreement occur conjointly, or that neither should occur, the logical possibilities are all open. Hence one must appeal to experience to determine which of the possibilities, in any given case or class of cases, is in fact realized. But experience clearly shows that the cases which involve *both* sorts of disagreement (or agreement) are extremely numerous.

Our conclusions about disagreement have prepared the way for a study of the ethical terms, and the characteristic features of ethical methodology. The present chapter will deal with both of these topics, but in a manner that is deliberately oversimplified. In place of a detailed analysis of ethical judgments, it will provide only "working models" for analysis—definitions which approximate to ethical meanings with sufficient accuracy to be of temporary help. Methods of proving or supporting ethical judgments will be considered only to the extent that the working models suggest them.

Let us begin with some remarks about meaning. Any definition which seeks to identify the meaning of ethical terms with that of scientific ones, and which does so without further explanation or qualification, is extremely likely to be misleading. It will suggest that the questions of normative ethics, like those of science, give rise to an agreement or disagreement that is exclusively in *belief*. In this way, ignoring disagreement in attitude, it will lead to only a half-picture, at best, of the situations in which the ethical terms are actually used.

This conclusion must not be pressed insensitively, without regard to the ambiguities and flexibilities of language. It may well be that at *some* times *all* of the effective meaning of ethical terms is scientific, and that at *all* times *some* of it is; but there remain multitudes of familiar cases in which the ethical terms are used in a way that is *not exclusively* scientific, and we must recognize a meaning which suits them to their additional function.

What is the nature of this extrascientific meaning? Let us proceed by analogy, comparing ethical sentences with others that are less perplexing but have a similar use.

Interesting analogues can be found in ordinary imperatives. Is there not a ready passage from "You ought to defend your country" to "Defend your country"? Or more prosaically, is not the expression, "You oughtn't to cry," as said to children, roughly interchangeable with "Stop crying"? There are many differences, unquestionably; but there are likewise these similarities: Both imperative and ethical sentences are used more for encouraging, altering, or redirecting people's aims and conduct than for simply describing them. Both differ in this respect from the sentences of science. And in arguments that involve disagreement in attitude, it is obvious that imperatives, like ethical judgments, have an important place. The example about the restaurant, for instance, by which the conception of disagreement in attitude was introduced, might begin with the use of imperatives exclusively:

A: Meet me at the Glenwood for dinner at 7:00.
B: Don't let's go to a restaurant with music. Meet me at the Ambassador instead.
A: But do make it the Glenwood . . . etc.

So the argument might begin, disagreement in attitude being indicated either by the ordinary second person form of the imperative, or by the first person plural form that begins with "Let's."

On account of this similar function of imperative and ethical sentences, it will be useful to consider some definitions that *in part* identify them. These definitions will not be adequate to the subtleties of common usage; they will be markedly inaccurate. But they will preserve in rough form much that is essential to ethical analysis, and on that account will be instructive approximations. It is they which will constitute the "working models" that have previously been mentioned.

There are many ways in which working models can be devised, but those which follow are perhaps the most serviceable:

(1) "This is wrong" means *I disapprove of this; do so as well.*
(2) "He ought to do this" means *I disapprove of his leaving this undone; do so as well.*
(3) "This is good" means *I approve of this; do so as well.*

It will be noted that the definiens in each case has two parts: first a declarative statement, "I approve" or "I disapprove," which describes the attitudes of the speaker, and secondly an imperative statement, "do so as well," which is addressed to changing or intensifying the attitudes of the hearer. These components, acting together, readily provide for agreement or disagreement in attitude. The following examples will illustrate how this is so:

A: This is good.
B: I fully agree. It is indeed good.

346

Freely translated in accordance with mode (3) above, this becomes:

A: I approve of this, do so as well.
B: I fully concur in approving of it; (continue to) do so as well.

Here the declarative parts of the remarks, testifying to convergent attitudes, are sufficient to imply the agreement. But if taken alone, they hint too much at a bare description of attitudes. They do not evidence the *contagion* of warmly expressed approval—the interaction of attitudes that makes each man's favorable evaluation strengthen and invigorate the other's. This latter effect is highly characteristic of an articulate ethical agreement; and the imperatives in our translated version of the example do something (though in a most imperfect way) to make it evident.

Let us consider an example of disagreement:

A: This is good.
B: No, it is bad.

Translated in accordance with the working models, this becomes:

A: I approve of this, do so as well.
B: No, I disapprove of it; do so as well.

The declarative parts of the remarks show that the men have opposed attitudes, one approving and the other disapproving. The imperative parts show that each man is suggesting that the other redirect his attitudes. Since "disagreement in attitude" has been defined with exclusive reference to an opposition of attitudes and efforts to redirect them or call them into question, it will be clear that a place for this sort of disagreement is retained (though again only in an imperfect way) by the working models that have been suggested.

But if the models are to help us more than they hinder us, they must be used with extreme caution. Although they give a needed emphasis to agreement and disagreement in attitude, they give no emphasis to agreement and disagreement in belief. Hence the *dual* source of ethical problems is not made evident. If traditional theory too often lost sight of attitudes in its concern with beliefs, we must not make the opposite error of losing sight of beliefs in our concern with attitudes. The latter error, which would give ethics the appearance of being cut off from reasoned argument and inquiry, would be even more serious than the former.

It is possible to avoid this error, however, and at the same time to retain the working models as rough approximations. Although it may at first seem that the full nature of ethical issues, and the relative importance of their component factors, should be made evident from the definitions of the ethical terms alone,

347

this requirement is not an inviolable one. It may be dispensed with provided that the proper weight of emphasis is established elsewhere. The central requirement for a definition, then, is simply that it *prepare the way* for a complete account. Now if the models had accentuated beliefs at the expense of attitudes, the emphasis could not easily have been corrected by subsequent remarks; and for that reason it has been necessary to deviate from definitions of the traditional sort. But when the models accentuate attitudes at the expense of beliefs, the correct emphasis can easily be reestablished. We shall later turn to a study of methodology, where in the nature of the case there must be close attention to the cognitive aspects of ethics. If we are careful, in that connection, to restore beliefs to their proper place, recognizing their great complexity and variety, we shall preserve a proper weighting of the factors involved.

In the meanwhile, every care must be taken to prevent the discussion of meaning, whenever it proceeds in temporary isolation from the rest of analysis, from suggesting that beliefs have only an inconsequential, secondary role in ethics. Such a view is wholly foreign to the present work, and foreign to the most obvious facts of daily experience.

If we avoid this confusion, we shall find that the working models are often instructive. The imperative sentence, which is one of their constituents, has a function that is of no little interest. To understand this, let us compare (3), the working model for "good," with one that is closely parallel to it:

(4) "This is good" means *I approve of this and I want you to do so as well.*

This differs from (3) only in that the imperative sentence, "Do so as well," gives place to the declarative sentence "I want you to do so as well." The change *seems* trivial, for it is often the case that "Do so and so" and "I want you to do so and so" have the same practical use. "I want you to open the window," for instance, has much the same imperative effect, usually, as "Open the window." The imperative function is not confined to the imperative mood. And *if* the declarative sentence which occurs in (4) is taken to have an imperative function, then to belabor the distinction between (3) and (4) is indeed trivial. It remains the case, however, that (4) is likely to be confusing. Although "I want you to do so as well" may be taken to have an imperative function, it also may not. It may be taken as a bare introspective report of the speaker's state of mind, used to describe his wants, to communicate beliefs about them for cognitive purposes, rather than to secure their satisfaction. (If such an interpretation is unlikely to occur in common life, it may easily occur amid the perplexing abstractions of philosophical theory.) In particular, (4) may suggest that "This is good" is used primarily, or even exclusively, to express *beliefs about* attitudes. It may accentuate agreement or disagreement in belief to the exclusion of agreement or disagreement in attitude. Definition (3) is preferable to (4) because it is not open to this misinterpretation. Its component imperative, being never used *merely* as an introspective report, renders unambiguously explicit the fact that "good" is used not only in expressing beliefs about attitudes, but in strengthening, altering, and guiding the attitudes themselves.

The misleading character of definition (4) can be shown by a continuation of the second example on page 133. Translated after the manner of (4), rather than (3), this becomes:

A: I approve of this, and want you to do so as well.
B: No. ' disapprove of this, and want you to do so as well.

Taken purely as introspective reports, these statements are logically compatible. Each man is describing his state of mind, and since their states of mind may be different, each may be correct. Now remembering that the statements purport to be translations, respectively, of "This is good" and "No, it is bad," one may be inclined to conclude: "Then according to definition (4) people don't really disagree about what is good or bad. They may think that they do, but only because of an elementary confusion in the use of pronouns." G. E. Moore has actually used this as a reductio ad absurdum of any definition which makes "good" refer wholly to the speaker's own attitudes; and granted the tacit assumptions on which he works, his point is well taken. But if "I want you to do so as well" is interpreted as having an imperative function, supplementing its descriptive one—or better, if this declarative sentence is replaced by an imperative one, following definition (3)—and if ethical controversy is recognized to involve disagreement in attitude, then the preposterous consequence that "people don't really disagree in ethics" becomes a consequence, it is suggested, not of neglecting Moore's indefinable quality of goodness, but of insisting that ethical controversy centers *entirely* on beliefs—and indeed, beliefs which are to be found by scrutinizing ethical sentences in themselves, isolated from the many other sentences that form a part of their living context.

The nature of the working models has now been indicated. To the question, "What distinguishes ethical statements from scientific ones?" it has been answered: Ethical statements have a meaning that is approximately, and in part, imperative. This imperative meaning explains why ethical judgments are so intimately related to agreement and disagreement in attitude, and helps to indicate how normative ethics can be distinguished from psychology and the natural sciences.

We must now turn to questions about method. When people argue about evaluative matters, by what sort of reasoning can they hope to reach agreement? The answer can as yet be presented only in a schematic form. It will presuppose that the working models can be accepted without further criticism; and since that is manifestly not the case, only rough approximations will be possible.

349

The model for "This is good" consists of the conjunction of (a) "I approve of this," and (b) "Do so as well." If a proof is possible for (a) and (b) taken separately, then and only then will it be possible for their conjunction. So let us see what can be done with the sentences separately.

Sentence (a) offers no trouble. It makes an assertion about the speaker's state of mind, and like any psychological statement, is open to empirical confirmation or disconfirmation, whether introspective or behavioristic.

Sentence (b), however, raises a question. Since it is an imperative, it is not open to proof at all. What is it like to prove a command? If we told a person to close the door, and received the reply, "Prove it!" should we not to speak mildly, grow somewhat impatient?

Thus it would seem that ethical judgments are amenable only to a partial proof. So far as "This is good" includes the meaning of (a) a proof is possible, but so far as it includes the meaning of (b) the very request for a proof is nonsensical. We seem forced to a distressingly meager conclusion: If a man says "X is good," and if he can prove that he really approves of X, then he has all the proof that can be demanded of him.

So, indeed, it now *seems*. But it does so only because we have tacitly assumed that a proof in ethics must be exactly like a proof in science. The possibility that ethical judgments may have a *different sort* of proof has not been considered. Or rather, since "proof" may be a misleading term, let us put it this way: It has yet to be considered whether there is some "substitute for a proof" in ethics, some support or reasoned argument which, although different from a proof in science, will be equally serviceable in removing the hesitations that usually prompt people to ask for a proof.

If there is some such analogue to proof, it must unquestionably be considered in the present study of methodology. Otherwise the study will be open to a gross misunderstanding. It may lead people to suppose that the meagerness of proof *in the strict sense* deprives ethics of a "rational foundation" or "intersubjective validity" that is sorely needed; whereas all that is needed may in fact be provided for by the analogue mentioned.

To develop this point, let us return to imperatives, which have presented a methodological perplexity. Although imperatives cannot be "proved," are there not reasons or arguments which may at least "support" them?

The question is by no means difficult. An imperative may be met by the question "Why?" and this "Why?" asks for a *reason*. For instance: If told to close the door, one may ask "Why?" and receive some such reason as "It is too drafty," or "The noise is distracting." Or again, if a person is told to work harder, he may ask "Why?" and receive some such reply as "If you don't you will become an unhappy sort of dilettante." These reasons cannot be called "proofs" in any but a dangerously extended sense, nor are they demonstratively or inductively related to an imperative; but they manifestly do *support* an imperative. They "back it up," or "establish it," or "base it on concrete references to fact." And they are analogous to proofs in that they may remove the doubts or hesitations that prevent the imperative from being accepted.

The *way* in which the reasons support the imperative is simply this: The imperative is used to alter the hearer's attitudes or actions. In asking "Why?" the hearer indicates his hesitancy to comply. He will not do it "just because he is told to." The supporting reason then describes the situation which the imperative seeks to alter, or the new situation which the imperative seeks to bring about; and if these facts disclose that the new situation will satisfy a preponderance of the hearer's desires, he will hesitate to obey no longer. More generally, reasons support imperatives by altering such beliefs as may in turn alter an unwillingness to obey.

But do these remarks require elaboration? A moment's consideration will show that they do not; for they coincide with the remarks about agreement that have [already] been made. We saw that since attitudes tend to alter with altered beliefs, agreement in attitude may often be obtained by securing agreement in belief. Here we need only apply this general principle to a special type of case. The connection becomes apparent when the above paragraph is stated in different terminology:

An imperative is used to secure the satisfaction of the speaker's desire. The question "Why?" expressing the hearer's hesitation to comply, indicates an actual or incipient counter-desire. There is accordingly a disagreement in attitude. The reason, supporting the imperative, locates a possible source of disagreement in belief; and if the latter is settled, then, since beliefs and attitudes stand in intimate causal relationship, the disagreement in attitude may be caused to vanish in a way that makes the imperative willingly obeyed.

The "substitute proofs" or "supporting reasons" that we have been seeking can thus be recognized as familiar acquaintances under a new name: they are the expressions of belief that so often play an important, if indirect, role in situations that involve disagreement in attitude. Nor are these supporting reasons peculiar to imperatives. They may be used wherever disagreement in attitude occurs, whether it is indicated by laudatory or derogatory words, rhetorical questions, metaphors, animated inflections of voice, and so on.

With regard to the judgment that here particularly concerns us—"This is good" as schematically analyzed by definition (3)—the relevance of the supporting reasons will be obvious. Although the imperative component of the definiens, "Approve as well," is inadequate to the subtleties of ethics, it is doubly marked for use in disagreement in attitude; the very fact that it is an imperative at all so marks it, and it is marked again by its direct mention of the hearer's approval. Since reasons may support any statement that leads to agreement or disagreement in attitude, they clearly may support this one.

Supporting reasons are particularly important in ethics—far more so than the narrow proof that was mentioned above. When a man says "X is good" he is seldom called upon to prove that he now approves of X. He is called on, rather, to adduce considerations which will make his attitudes acceptable to his opponent, and to show that they are not directed to situations of whose nature he is ignorant. This more important procedure, typical of ethical issues, always requires supporting reasons.

The following example, with comments interspersed, will serve to show more concretely how supporting reasons may occur in an argument that is characteristically ethical:

A: *Jones is fundamentally a good man.*
This judgment (a) asserts that A approves of Jones, and (b) acts (quasi-) imperatively to make B, the hearer, have a similar attitude.

B: *Why do you say that?*
B indicates his hesitancy or unwillingness to concur in approving of Jones. Disagreement in attitude is thus apparent.

A: *His harsh manner is only a pose. Underneath, he has the kindest of hearts.*
A reason is now given, describing a characteristic of Jones that B may not know about, and which is likely to elicit B's favor.

B: *That would be interesting, if true. But does he ever express this kind heart of his in actions?*
The reason is acknowledged to be relevant, but its truth is questioned. Disagreement in belief now comes to play an important part in the argument. It is closely related to the disagreement in attitude previously noted; for if A and B can agree in belief about Jones' kindness, they are likely to agree on whether or not to approve of him.

A: *He does. His old servant told me that Jones never uttered an unkind word to her, and recently provided her with a luxurious pension. And there are many such instances. I was actually present when . . . etc.*
A here provides an empirical proof—not a direct proof of his initial judgment, but of the reason which supports it.

B: *Well, I confess I do not know him intimately. Perhaps he is a good man.*
B here complies with the (quasi-) imperative component of A's initial judgment, by indicating his approval. His reluctance has been altered by A's well-proved reason. Agreement in belief has brought about agreement in attitude.

This example shows in miniature how ethical judgments (the working models remaining essentially uncriticized) may be supported by reasons of an important kind, and just how the reasons become relevant. It shows as well how very naturally these reasons serve some of the purposes of a proof. They lead the hearer to accept the judgment willingly, without any feeling that it is "dogmatic" or "arbitrary" or "unfounded."

Before leaving this provisional, introductory account of methods, there is a further question which must receive attention. At the beginning of this section, it will be remembered, ethical proofs were found to be distressingly meager. To supplement them, "substitute proofs" were sought, which might serve the purposes of a proof, even though they were not exactly like scientific proofs. Such substitutes were readily found in the "supporting reasons" for the judgments—reasons which may bring about agreement in attitude by securing agreement in belief. But it has yet to be asked whether reasons of this sort are sufficient to provide ethics with an adequate "foundation." That is to say: Theories of ethics which stress attitudes have often been accused of "building morality on shifting sands," providing no check for the caprices and fads to which human attitudes are subject. Or they have been accused of sanctioning a vicious tolerance, tantamount to chaos, by implying that "Anything which a person feels to be good, *is* good, for him." Does the present account of method-ology, once support by reasons is acknowledged, become free from such charges? Or is it rather the case that the present account is still too meager, and that some further method must be sought, even though it be sought blindly and despairingly, if ever moral codes are to have their needed authority?

Clearly, the present account of methodology will fail to content the great number of theorists who are embarked on the "the quest for certainty." The supporting reasons here mentioned have no sort of *logical* compulsion. Persons who make opposed ethical judgments may (so far as theoretical possibility is concerned) continue to do so in the face of all manner of reasons that their argument includes, even though neither makes any logical or empirical error. Supporting reasons have only to do with beliefs; and in so far as they in turn are proved by demonstrative or empirical methods, only agreement in belief will, in the first instance, be secured. Ethical agreement, however, requires more than agreement in belief; it requires agreement in attitude. Accordingly, unless some further method can be found, a reasoned agreement in ethics is theoreti-cally possible only to the extent that agreement in belief will cause people to agree in attitude.

How serious is this requirement? To what extent *will* agreement in belief cause people to agree in attitude? If the answer is to be grounded not on hopes but on facts, it must inescapably run thus: We usually *do not know,* before the outcome of any argument, whether the requirement holds true for it or not; and although it is often convenient to assume that it does, to prolong enlighten-ing argument and delay hortatory efforts to secure ethical agreement, the assumption can be only heuristic, without a proper basis of confirmation. Those who seek an absolutely definitive method for normative ethics, and who want to rule out the possibility of rival moral codes, each equally well supported by reasons, will find that the present account gives them less than they want.

But the serious question concerns not what people now want; for in this connection people want, and have always wanted, what they cannot clearly articulate, and perhaps want an absurdity. The serious question concerns what people *would* want if they thought more clearly. If confusions about ethical methodology were swept away—confusions which are often more serious in ethical theory than in ethical practice—and if the psychological mechanisms which these confusions have fostered were accordingly readjusted, would people *then* feel that some more "objective" conception is required? To this question the present work will answer with a definite negative.

NOTES

1. The term "attitude" is here used in much the same broad sense that R. B. Perry gives to "interest." See his *General Theory of Value* (Longmans, Green & Co., Inc., 1926), particularly p. 115.

2. In all of the examples given there may be a *latent* disagreement in belief, in addition to the disagreement in attitude. This is likely to be true of any example that is not painfully artificial; but the present examples are serviceable enough for their introductory purpose.

DIFFICULTIES
IN THE
EMOTIVE-IMPERATIVE
THEORY*
Kurt Baier

It is plain enough that moral judgments are not verifiable by looking in the way that color judgments are. It may even be true that they are not correctly describable as true or false. Nevertheless, a person saying that there is nothing morally wrong with murder may be making a moral judgment which is faulty, whereas a man who says that murder is morally wrong is making one which is not. If we can so distinguish between two contradictory moral judgments, then there is an epistemological problem (or a problem exactly analogous to an epistemological one), namely, how can we characterize this distinction, what are the criteria of the distinction, and what are the methods of eliminating mistakes.

The *impact theory*[1] maintains that, in ethics, no epistemological problem exists, because there can be no moral questions, properly speaking, and because, where there is nothing to ask, there is nothing to answer hence nothing to know.

Why, on this view, can there be no moral questions? When I ask, "Has Joan blue eyes?" I demand an utterance which would constitute an answer, namely, "Joan has blue eyes" or "Joan does not have blue eyes." Hence I am raising a genuine question, for both these remarks are factual assertions that can be verified or shown false. Factual questions are genuine since they are requests for factual assertions. But when I ask a moral question, I am not requesting a factual assertion. "Jones' conduct was wrong" is not a factual assertion; it is merely the expression of my feelings or attitudes, with the aim and the effect of arousing similar feelings and attitudes in my listener. Accordingly, if I ask "Was Jones' action wrong?" I am not asking a genuine question. For the "answer" to this "question" would have to be either "Yes, Jones' conduct was wrong" or "No, Jones' conduct was not wrong," neither of which is a factual assertion. In asking a moral question, I request merely a moral reply, that is, the expression by my

*From Kurt Baier, *The Moral Point of View*, Ithaca: Cornell Univer. Press, 1958, chap. 1.

listener of his feelings or attitudes. I ask for this in order to be influenced by my listener's feelings and attitudes. Why? Because I myself have as yet no feelings or attitudes, or only conflicting ones. The impact theory thus maintains that moral "questions" can be "asked" only when the speaker has no clear feeling or attitude toward a certain course of action (either because he has none at all or because he has conflicting ones), that such "questions" express the speaker's indecision and request the listener to express his feelings and attitudes in order thereby correspondingly to influence the speaker and to terminate his indecision.

It must be admitted that the impact theory emphasizes an important feature of moral judgments: their tendency to influence hearers in certain comparatively uniform ways. It must also be admitted that certain other types of utterance, such as descriptive or narrative or scientific utterances, do not have this tendency. However, it does not follow from this that while the function of descriptive utterances is to say something, to make assertions or claims, to say what can be true or false, correct or incorrect, and so on, the function of moral judgments is none of these, but merely to produce in others certain effects, namely, to arouse certain feelings and attitudes.

This distinction between the functions of descriptive and of moral utterances would be plausible if it were the case that factual remarks only made assertions, but did not have any effects on hearers, did not arouse feelings and attitudes in them. However, factual remarks also tend to influence hearers. If I tell someone that the forecast is for rain, he will be disposed to take his raincoat or his umbrella, or to stay home, or to cancel his weekend trip.

Stevenson admits that both descriptive and moral utterances have an influence on hearers but attempts to overcome this difficulty by distinguishing between two different kinds of influence, "cognitive" and "affective-conative." He claims that descriptive utterances are characterized by descriptive meaning, that is, by their tendency to arouse in hearers certain cognitive dispositions, whereas moral utterances are characterized by emotive meaning, that is, their tendency to arouse in hearers affective-conative dispositions. Both cognitive and dynamic dispositions consist, on Stevenson's view, in dispositions to behave and feel in certain ways. But Stevenson is quite unable to point to any distinguishing marks between them.

This is not surprising, for the distinction is bogus. It is not true that the function of some kinds of remark is to produce a certain influence on hearers while the function of others is to say something; or of some kinds of remark to produce cognitive, and of others to produce emotive, dispositions in the hearer. The truth is that both kinds of remark have a meaning, that in as far as they can be said to have a function at all it is their function to convey that meaning, and that both kinds of remark produce certain effects, but what effects they produce will vary from person to person and from situation to situation.

356

We must in all cases distinguish between *what* I say or mean, *why* I said it, and *what effect* it will have on my listener. In mentioning the forecast, I may merely wish to tell my listener, or I may wish to achieve a certain effect which I expect the telling will have. "The forecast is for rain" always has the same sense, whether I merely aimed at giving him my opinion or whether perhaps I hoped it would cause him to cancel his weekend trip, and whether or not it had the intended effect. Similarly, the remark "Joan's conduct was wicked" always has the same sense, whether I merely intend to give him my opinion, or whether I desire to cause my friend to break off his engagement with Joan, and whether or not my remark has the intended effect.

The facts emphasized by the impact theory are important, but while they may show that moral judgments tend to influence hearers more often and in a more uniform way than do other types of remark, they do not show that, in addition to "What was the effect of Robert's moral judgment on Jones?" we may not ask the further question "Was *what* Robert said correct?" I conclude that the impact theory cannot make good its main contention that no epistemological problem exists in ethics. It cannot prove that the function of moral judgments is not to *say something* but merely to evince emotions and feelings and thereby to influence hearers. Hence it can offer no reason for saying that in ethics there is nothing to ask and nothing to answer, hence nothing to know, and therefore no epistemological problem.

The *imperatival theory* reiterates the claim that the function of moral judgments is not to describe things or state facts or say anything capable of being true or false.[2] However, it correctly distinguishes between what a remark means or says and the influence it has or tends to have on those who hear it. Instead of distinguishing between conveying information and influencing hearers, as does the impact theory, it distinguishes between *what* a persons says (the content) and the effect which his saying it has on a hearer, on the one hand; and on the other, between two ways of saying something, between telling someone what is the case and telling someone to do something. On the imperatival theory, moral remarks are not merely ways of *influencing someone;* they are characteristic ways of *saying something,* though not ways of conveying information (of telling someone certain facts) but of commanding or requesting someone, of telling him to act in a certain way. Therefore, there are genuine moral questions and they are of the same kind as the question "What shall I do?" and moral judgments are of the same kind as answers to that question, namely, commands such as "Do this."

Even if this analysis were correct, it could not be used to solve our epistemological problem. For the admission of genuine moral questions poses a dilemma for the imperatival theory, namely, whether or not to allow the existence of moral reasons bearing on the answers to moral questions. If such moral reasons are disallowed, then the imperativalist analysis of moral questions

357

renders them meaningless, thereby making the imperatival indistinguishable from the impact theory. If, on the other hand, we admit the existence of such moral reasons, then the old epistemological problem arises again.

Embracing the first horn of the dilemma, let us say that there are no moral reasons that bear on the answers to moral questions. When I say, "Jones' conduct was wrong," then, on the imperatival theory, I am expressing my disapproval and am "prescribing" to my listener to do the same. But what is Roberts doing when he asks Richards a moral question, let us say, "Was Jones' conduct wrong?" A question is always a request for an answer, that is, for a remark which would constitute an answer. In our case, this would be either "Jones' conduct was wrong" or "Jones' conduct was not wrong," that is to say, Richards' expression of his disapproval or approval of Jones' conduct together with Richards' command to Roberts to do the same as he, Richards. But this would turn Roberts' moral question into a request addressed to Richards to express his approval or disapproval and to command Roberts to do the same as Richards. In other words, the questioner is commanding the listener to command the questioner to do the same as the listener. But if no listener can give reasons for his command, why should any questioner wish to be commanded? What point could there be in asking anyone for such a service? Why should a man rather wish to obey the command of a man whom he had commanded to command him something than simply to make up his own mind? Asking a moral question in that case would be no different from tossing a coin, for in tossing a coin I resolve to obey "the command" of the coin which I have forced to give me "a command." But this is to do what the impact theory does: it is to make moral questions into requests to be helped to terminate one's indecision. We have already seen reason to reject this view.

Even odder than the above is the analysis of Roberts' question "Was Jones' conduct wrong?" when addressed to himself. For when addressed to himself it becomes a command to himself to command himself to do the same as himself. But what can one make of this? If Roberts does not yet approve or disapprove of Jones' conduct, he cannot ask himself whether his conduct was wrong, for if he does not yet have a feeling or attitude he cannot command himself to command himself to do the same. But surely a person will often ask himself the question "Was Jones' conduct wrong?" when he has not yet got an opinion. And if a person already has an opinion, then the question "Was Jones' conduct wrong?" can never lead to a truer view than he already has because, in asking it, he is merely commanding himself to command himself to do the same as himself. Surely this is all nonsense.

Let us then try the other horn of the dilemma, and let us say that there are moral reasons relevant to the answers to moral questions. But this fatally weakens the case for saying that there is no epistemological problem in ethics. For if reasons are admitted at all, there can and will be cases of sufficient or conclusive reasons. Where there are conclusive reasons, there are knowledge and error. If, for example, there are conclusive reasons for saying that Jones killed his wife, then he who has them can and does know that Jones killed his wife. And if there are conclusive reasons for saying that Jones' action was wrong, then he who has them can know that Jones' action was wrong. If I can adduce reasons for having a feeling of disapproval of what Jones did, it becomes at least possible for me to have conclusive reasons for my feeling. And if so, then I have conclusive reasons for saying that what Jones did was wrong. But then I can and do *know* that what he did was wrong.

It might be objected that the emotive theory uses the word "reason" in a special sense, namely, the sense in which a command can be supported by reasons, and that, therefore, this conclusion does not follow. Stevenson, for instance, claims that a reason for or against a moral judgment is "*any* statement about *any* matter of fact which *any* speaker considers likely to alter attitudes,"[3] whether or not this statement will actually make any difference to the attitudes of the hearer. So defined, "reasons" which support or controvert moral judgments are related to them psychologically, but not logically. It follows that by whatever combination of reasons a moral judgment is supported, a person rejecting that moral judgment need never be guilty of an error of fact or of logic. The giving of such "reasons" does not serve the same purpose as the giving of proofs or disproofs. Its only function is to intensify and render more permanent the influence on attitudes which the emotive meaning of words can often no more than begin. Giving reasons is one way of imparting the speaker's attitude to someone else. The use of moral and other words with emotive meaning is another way of achieving the same end. On this view, giving reasons is mentioning facts which *one thinks* will move the listeners. Giving conclusive reasons is giving reasons which *actually will* move the person in the desired way.

From this special sense of "reason," none of the conclusions follow which I have drawn above. For to say in this special sense that I have "conclusive reason" for my opinion that Jones' conduct was morally wrong is not to imply that it is thereby proved that Jones' conduct was morally wrong, that I now know that it was wrong, that anyone rejecting this would be guilty of an error of fact or of logic. It only means that I am in possession of facts which I know will move a certain person or persons to agree with me.

It is perhaps worth pointing out that this is not the ordinary use of "reason." As we normally use the word, we may have, and offer to someone, conclusive reasons for holding an opinion, and yet that person might not be convinced. The mere fact that a person is not convinced does not prove, as Stevenson maintains it does, that the reason was not conclusive. But, contrary to what Stevenson says, it does follow that if a hearer does not accept a proposition that is supported by conclusive reasons, then he is in the wrong, "is guilty of an error of logic."

NOTES

1. This is Professor Baier's name for what I have called the emotive theory [Ed. note.]

2. This claim was also made by the impact theory.

3. Stevenson, *Ethics and Language,* p. 114. For further statements on this point see also *ibid.,* pp. 30-31, 36, 113.

DESCRIPTIVISM*

R. M. Hare

I

The term "Descriptivism" was first suggested to me by a phrase of the late Professor Austin's. He refers in two places to what he calls the "descriptive fallacy" of supposing that some utterance is descriptive when it is not;[1] and, although I agree with him that the word might mislead, it will serve. "Descriptivism," then, can perhaps be used as a generic name for philosophical theories which fall into this fallacy. I shall, however, be discussing, not descriptivism in general, but the particular variety of it which is at present fashionable in ethics; and I shall not attempt to discuss all forms even of ethical descriptivism, nor, even, all the arguments of those descriptivists whom I shall consider. A sample will be all that there is time for. I cannot claim that my own arguments are original—I am in particularly heavy debt to Mr. Urmson and Professor Nowell-Smith; but if old mistakes are resuscitated, it is often impossible to do more than restate, in as clear a way as possible, the old arguments against them. Philosophical mistakes are like dandelions in the garden; however carefully one eradicates them there are sure to be some more next year, and it is difficult to think of novel ways of getting rid of their familiar faces. "Naturalistas expellas furca, tamen usque recurrent." But in fact the best implement is still the old fork invented by Hume.

An essential condition for the use of this tool is that there should be a distinction between description and evaluation; and, since the more sophisticated of modern descriptivists sometimes seek to impugn this distinction, I must start by establishing its existence, though I shall not have time to add to what I have said elsewhere about its nature.[2] This problem is very like that

---

*From Proceedings of the British Academy, London: 1963; reprinted by permission of the publisher.

concerning the distinction between analytic and synthetic (indeed, it is an offshoot of that problem). Both distinctions are useful—indeed essential—tools of the philosopher, and it is no bar to their use that we have not yet achieved a completely clear formal elucidation of their nature.

The fundamental distinction is not that between descriptive and evaluative *terms*, but that between the descriptive and evaluative meaning which a single term may have in a certain context. In order to establish that there is a distinction between descriptive and evaluative meaning, it is not necessary to deny the existence of cases in which it is difficult to say whether a term is being used evaluatively or not. There is a clear distinction between a heap of corn and no corn at all, even though it is hard to say just when the corn that I am piling up has become a heap.[3] The descriptive and evaluative meaning of a term in a given context may be tied to it with varying degrees of tightness (we may be more, or less, sure that one or other of them, would or would not get detached if we were faced with varying instances of its use: for example, if the cause to which a man was contributing large sums of money were one which I considered not good but pernicious, would I still say that he was generous?). But for all that, the distinction between descriptive and evaluative meaning may be a perfectly sustainable one.

II

We can show that such a distinction exists, at any rate, if we can isolate one of these two sorts of meaning in a given context, and show that it does not exhaust the meaning of the term in that context. Suppose, for example, that we can show that in a certain context a term has descriptive meaning; and suppose that we can isolate this descriptive meaning by producing another term which could be used in the same context with the same descriptive meaning, but such that the two terms differ in that one has evaluative meaning and the other not; then we shall have established that there can be these two different components in a term's meaning.

Let us suppose that somebody says that a certain wine (let us call it "Colombey-les-deux-églises 1972") is a good wine. I think it will be obvious that he says that it is a good wine *because* it has a certain taste, bouquet, body, strength, &c. (I shall say "taste" for short). But it is equally clear that we do not have a name for precisely the taste which this wine has. A descriptivist might therefore argue as follows (thereby committing the fashionable fallacy of *nullum nomen nullum nominandum*): there is nothing more we can say about this wine, by way of telling somebody what is good about it, or what makes us call it good (which would be to give the descriptive meaning of "good" in this context); we can only repeat that it is good. It is good because it tastes as it does, admittedly;

but this is like saying that a thing is red because it looks as it does. How else could we describe the way it tastes than by saying that it is good? Therefore the description cannot be detached from the evaluation, and the distinction is rendered ineffective.

In this instance, such an argument would not carry conviction. If a descriptivist tried to show, by this means, that the descriptive meaning of "good" in this context could not be isolated, we should no doubt answer that the difficulty lies only in the non-existence of a *word* for the quality that we are seeking to isolate. But this does not matter, provided that it is possible to coin a word and give it a meaning. This I shall now show how to do. I may point out in passing that, if we did not have the words "sweet," "juicy," "red," "large," and a few more, it would be impossible, without inventing words, to isolate the descriptive meaning of "good" in the phrase "good strawberry"; but this would not stop us saying that the phrase has a descriptive meaning distinct from its evaluative meaning. We should just have to coin a word meaning "like this strawberry in respect of taste, texture, size, &c."; and this is what I am now going to do in the "wine" case.

Let us invent a word, "ϕ," to stand for that quality of the wine which makes us call it a good wine. The quality is, as I have explained, a complex one. Will you allow me to suppose, also, that (as is not improbable) by the time 1972 wines of this sort begin to be good, the science of aromatics (if that is the right name) will have advanced enough to put the wine-snobs out of business; that is to say, that it will have become possible to manufacture by chemical means additives which, put into cheap wines, will give to them tastes indistinguishable by any human palate from those of expensive wines. We should then have a chemical recipe for producing liquid tasting ϕ. This would make it easy (though even without such a scientific advance it would be perfectly possible) to teach somebody to recognize the ϕ taste by lining up samples of liquids tasting ϕ, and others having different tastes, and getting him to taste them, telling him in each case whether the sample tasted ϕ or not. It is worth noticing that I could do this whether or not he was himself disposed to think that these liquids tasted good, or that, if they were wines, they were good wines. He could, that is to say, learn the meaning of "ϕ" quite independently of his own estimation of the merit of wines having that taste.

It is possible, indeed, that, if he did think that wines having that taste were good wines, he might mistake my meaning; he might think that "ϕ wine" (the expression whose meaning I was trying to explain to him) meant the same as "good wine." It is always possible to make mistakes when a person is trying to explain to one the meaning of a word. But the mistake could be guarded against. I might say to him, "I want you to understand that, in calling a wine ϕ, I am not thereby commending it or praising it in any way, any more than it is commending it or praising it to say that it is produced by this chemical recipe;

I am indeed (for such is my preference) disposed to commend wines which have this taste; but in simply saying that a wine is ϕ I am not hereby commending it any more than I should be if I said that it tasted like vinegar or like water. If my preference (and for that matter everybody else's) changed in such a way that a wine tasting like this was no longer thought any good, and we could do nothing with it but pour it down the drain, we could still go on describing it as ϕ."

Now it seems to me that the descriptivist argument which we are considering depends on what I have just said being quite unintelligible. If a man can understand the explanation of the meaning of "ϕ," he must reject the descriptivist argument. For if the explanation works, then it is possible to explain the meaning of "ϕ" ostensively as a descriptive expression; and when this has been done, we can separate out the descriptive from the evaluative meaning of the expression "good wine" in the sentence "Colombey 1972 is a good wine." For it will be possible for two people to agree that Colombey 1972 tastes ϕ, but disagree about whether it is a good wine; and this shows (which is all that I am trying to show) that there is more to the statement that Colombey 1972 is a good wine than to the the statement that Colombey 1972 is a wine which tastes ϕ. The more is, of course, the commendation; but I shall not in this lecture try to explain what this is, since I have done my best elsewhere.

This answer to the descriptivist argument is not, as might be thought at first hearing, circular. It is true that I introduced into it the distinction between commendation and description, which was what I was trying to establish; but I did not merely assume it as a premiss in my argument—I produced a clear example in which we could not do without it. What I did was to ask, "Was it possible to understand what I was saying when I explained to the man that to call a thing ϕ is not thereby to commend or praise it, any more than it is praise or commendation to say that it tastes like the product of a certain chemical recipe, or that it tastes like vinegar or water?" And the premiss which I put into the argument was that this was perfectly intelligible. A determined descriptivist might at this point protest "It isn't intelligible to me"; but I can only ask you whether, if he said this, he would not be professing to find unintelligible a distinction which we all know perfectly well how to operate (a familiar habit of philosophers). This distinction has, indeed, to be elucidated, and this is the task of moral philosophy; but it exists.

III

This "wine" case is one where the difficulty arises because there is no word available having the descriptive meaning of "good" in a certain context without its evaluative meaning. But a very similar difficulty arises when, as in most moral and aesthetic cases, there is no *one* word which has just the descriptive meaning that we want, but a multitude of possible ways of describing, in greater or less detail, the sort of thing that we have in mind. Here what is required is not ostensive definition (though that may help) but a long story. It is, for example, very hard to say what it is about a particular picture which makes us call it a good one; but nevertheless what makes us call it a good one is a series of describable characteristics combined in just this way. We can see this quite clearly if we think of the painter himself building up the picture—putting in features and then perhaps painting them out again and trying something else. There is no doubt whatever that what makes him satisfied or dissatisfied is something there on the canvas which is certainly describable in neutral terms (e.g. he has a lot of things round the edge of the picture which draw the eye, but no feature in the middle which does so). Or, to take a simpler example, let us suppose that the painter is somebody like Kandinsky, and that the only thing that dissatisfies him about the picture is the precise colour of one of the exactly-drawn circular patches near the top right-hand corner. Suppose then that the painter is suddenly and incurably paralysed, but wants to finish the picture; can he not get a pupil to alter the colour for him, telling him, in neutral descriptive terms, just what paints to mix in what proportions and where to put the resulting mixture in order to make it a better picture? The paralysed painter would not have to say "Make the picture better" or "Make the circular patch in the top right-hand corner a better colour"; he could tell the pupil just how to do these things.

If, instead of asking what makes a man call *this* picture a good one, we ask what in general makes him call pictures (or wines or men) good ones, the position becomes even more complicated. But in principle it remains true that the descriptive meaning which the man attaches to the expression "good picture" could be elicited, as a very complex conjunction and disjunction of characteristics, by questioning him sufficiently closely about a sufficiently large number of pictures.[4] For to have a settled taste in pictures is to be disposed to think pictures good which have certain characteristics. That such a process would reveal a good deal about his taste to the man himself does not affect the argument; the process of rendering articulate the grounds of evaluation is always a revealing one. If his evaluations have been made on vague or uncertain grounds, as will be the case with a man whose taste is not well developed, the process of trying to explain the grounds may well cause the evaluations themselves to change in the course of being made articulate. This again is irrelevant to the argument; for nobody wants to maintain that the descriptive meaning attached to people's evaluations is in all cases precise or cut-and-dried.

Lest you should think that I have been talking about pictures simply in order to make a logical point about value-judgements, I should like to say that there seems to me to be a lesson, in all this, about how to improve one's

365

appreciation of works of art. In so far as I have attained to any articulate appreciation of any sorts of works of art—or of anything else which has aesthetic merit—it has been by trying to formulate to myself what I find good or bad about particular works, or about the works of a particular style or period. This is, of course, no substitute for the completely inarticulate absorption in a work—say a piece of music—which alone makes art worth while; but analysis does undoubtedly help. I have derived much more profit from looking at pictures and buildings, listening to music, &c., and asking myself what it is about them that I find worth while, than I have from reading the works of critics; and when critics have helped me, it has been by doing the same sort of thing, i.e. drawing attention to and characterizing particular features of works of art which contribute to their excellence. I think that many descriptivists would agree with me about this. But unless what I have said is true (viz. that the descriptive meaning of "good" in a given context can always in principle be given) critics would be unable to tell us why they think certain works of art good; they would just have to go on repeating that they are good.

IV

Morality is in these respects quite like aesthetics. There are certain ways of behaving, describable in perfectly neutral terms, which make us commend people as, for example, courageous. Citations for medals do not simply say that the recipient behaved courageously; they give descriptive details; and though these, for reasons of brevity, often themselves contain evaluative terms, this need not be the case, and in a good citation it is the neutral descriptions which impress. They impress us because we already have the standards of values according to which to do *that* sort of thing is to display outstanding merit.

A descriptivist might object to this argument that in some of my examples, although it is perfectly easy to say what the *descriptive* meaning of the term in question is, there is no separately discernible *evaluative* meaning. For example, it might be claimed that if we have said that the man has done what he has done, then we have said, implicitly, that he has been courageous; and if "courageous" is a term of commendation, we have commended him. The commendation is simply the description. This I think to be false. With the standards of values that we have, and which it is natural for us to have in our historical circumstances (or perhaps in any likely historical circumstances), we shall be disposed to commend such a man. But the commendation is a further step which we are not logically compelled to take. A man who said that such behaviour did not make a man any better would be morally eccentric, but not logically at fault. I have argued this point elsewhere.[5]

It follows that it is possible for two people without logical absurdity to agree about the description but disagree about the evaluation—though it would not affect my argument if nobody ever actually disagreed. And therefore the distinction between evaluative and descriptive meanings is not impugned.

V

I have sought to establish that there is this distinction, because I shall need it later. I shall now go on to deal with some particular descriptivist arguments. Most of the arguments which I shall be discussing have a feature in common: namely that the descriptivism which they seek to establish is of a very minimal kind. That is to say, they seek to establish only that there are *some* logical restrictions upon what we can call good, right, &c. They fall far short of attempting to prove anything that could be helpful to us when faced with any serious moral problem, as will be at once apparent to anyone who tries to use the types of reasoning proposed in any actual moral perplexity. But in this lecture I shall address myself mainly to arguments for these very weak forms of descriptivism, because they might seem more difficult to refute.

Consider the following argument. It is not possible, it might be said, to think *anything* good, or good of its kind, just as it is not possible to want *anything*; it is possible to want or to think good only such things as are thought to be either the subjects of what have been called "desirability characterizations," or else means to attaining them. This expression "desirability characterizations" comes from Miss Anscombe's book *Intention,* pp. 66 ff.; but I hesitate to ascribe the argument itself to her, because, as I shall show, the expression admits of at least two quite different interpretations, and I am not sure in which sense, if either, she was using the term; and therefore I am not sure which of two possible versions of the argument, if either, she would support. Since, however, although both versions are perfectly valid, neither proves anything from which I wish to dissent, I shall not try to do more than clear up the ambiguity—an ambiguity which has, I think, led some people to suppose that the argument does prove something with which a prescriptivist like myself would have to disagree.

The first way of taking the expression "desirability characterization" is to take it as meaning "a description of that about the object which makes it an object of desire." If I may be allowed to revert to my previous example: suppose that I want some Colombey 1972, or think it is a good wine, because it tastes ϕ; then to say that it tastes ϕ is to give the required desirability characterization. If this is how the phrase is to be taken, then the argument shows that whenever we think something good, we do so because of something about it. Since I have often maintained the same position myself, nobody will expect me to demur.[6] It shows further that the "something about it" must be something thought desirable, or thought to be a means to something desirable. I do not think that I want to object to this either, provided that "desire" and "desirable" are taken in fairly wide senses, as translations of the Aristotelian *orexis* and *orekton*. So interpreted, the argument shows that, whenever we think something good, it must be, or be thought by us to be a means to, something to "try to get"[7] which (in actual or hypothetical circumstances) we have at least some disposition. This conclusion, which has, it may be noticed, marked non-descriptivist undertones, is one I can agree with. The crucial thing to notice, however, is that the argument does nothing to show what may or may not be the subject of a desirability characterization. It could, so far as this way of taking the argument goes, be anything you please. Thus, if our desires concerning wines were different, which they logically could be, "tasting ϕ" might be an "*un*desirability characterization"; and we should not be in the least put out if we found a man who wanted *not* to drink Colombey 1972 because it tasted like that.

The second way of taking the expression "desirability characterization" is as follows: we give a desirability characterization of an object if we say something about it which is *logically* tied in some way (weak or strong) to desiring. An example of this would be to say that something would be fun; others would be to call it pleasant, or interesting, or delightful. Notice that, in this sense of "desirability characterization," to say that the wine tasted ϕ would *not* be to give a desirability characterization of it; for there is no logical connexion between thinking that a thing tastes ϕ and desiring it. As I have said, a man might without logical fault say that he wanted *not* to drink Colombey 1972 because it tasted ϕ; and he might also say something less committal, namely that the fact that it tasted ϕ did not make him either want to drink it or want not to drink it—in short that he was indifferent to its tasting ϕ. But it would be logically odd for somebody to say that the fact that something would be pleasant, or fun, or interesting, or delightful, did not make him—to the smallest degree—disposed to do it (though of course he might not be disposed to do it when he considered the whole situation, including its consequences and the alternatives).

It may be that there is also a connexion in the reverse direction between being fun, &c., and being desired or thought good; though, if so, the nature of the connexion is obscure and tenuous. It may be, that is to say, that if we have said that we want something, or that we think it good, it is natural for us, if asked why, to say that it would be fun, or pleasant, or to give it some other characterization falling within an ill-defined class which includes these. It may even be true that it is logically compulsory, on pain of making ourselves incomprehensible, that we should be prepared to give such an explanation.

The difficulty with this suggestion is that it is not possible to rule out, *a priori*, additions to the list of desirability characterizations in this second sense. And it is a somewhat vacuous claim that an explanation falling within a certain class must be forthcoming, if the class itself is so easily expansible. "Exciting" is a desirability characterization—and in at least some uses a desirability characterization in the second of my two senses. Let us suppose, then, that there is a race of men who have not, up till now, valued the experience of danger (perhaps because their conditions of life have been such as to give them altogether too much of it), and have therefore not had the favourable characterization "exciting" in their vocabulary, but only such unfavourable characterizations as "frightening" and "terrifying." Then, when their life becomes less exposed to terrors, they begin to know what it is to be bored, and so come to value excitement for its own sake. There then comes to be a need for the favourable characterization "exciting," and they duly invent it. This is an example of what I mean by an addition to the list of desirability characterizations in the second sense.

One reason why it is easy to be confused by these two possible senses of the phrase "desirability characterization" is that words which are very commonly used as desirability characterizations in the first sense often end up by becoming desirability characterizations in the second sense. That is to say, they acquire a logical, as opposed to a merely contingent, connexion with being desired. The Latin word *virtus* underwent such a shift, owing to the contingent fact that the properties which are typical of the male sex are properties which the Romans desired people to have. Thus in particular cases it is sometimes hard to say whether a word is being used as a desirability characterization in the second sense. But this will not cause concern to anybody unless he is a victim of the "heap" fallacy to which I referred earlier.

A confusion between the two senses of "desirability characterization" might lead a careless descriptivist to suppose that descriptivism could be established in the following way. We should first establish that anything that is thought good must also be thought to be the subject of some desirability characterization, or a means to such (and here it does not matter for the argument in which sense the phrase is used; let us allow for the sake of argument that this premiss is true in both senses). We should then point out (correctly) that only some *words* can be desirability characterizations (sense two). Then we should assume that this proved that only some *things* can be the subjects of desirability characterizations (sense one). And so we should think that we had proved that only some things can be thought good. But the two connected fallacies in this argument should by now be obvious. The first is the equivocation on the phrase "desirability characterization." The second is the assumption that by proving that there are certain words that cannot be or that must be used in conjunction with the statement that something is good, we have proved that certain things cannot be thought good.

It must always be possible to want, or to think good, *new* sorts of thing (for example, new experiences); and therefore it can never be nonsense to *say* that we want them, or that they are good, provided that we are careful not to describe them in a way which is logically inconsistent with this. It is said that under the influence of mescaline people say things like "How simply marvellous that at the corner of the room three planes meet at a point!" So perhaps they might, on occasion, say (to use Miss Anscombe's example) "How simply marvellous to have this saucer of mud!" And if somebody asks what is marvellous about it, why should they not reply, with respectable precedent, "We can't tell you; you have to have the experience before any word for it would mean anything to you:

> Nec lingua valet dicere,
> Nec litera exprimere;
> Expertus potest credere"?

It may readily be admitted that whenever we desire something, it must be because of something about it; but if pressed to say what this something is, we may be tempted, since most of my opponents on this question are of the opposite sex, to rejoin with Wilbye's madrigal:

> Love me not for comely grace,
> For my pleasing eye or face,
> Nor for any outward part;
> No, nor for my constant heart;
> For those may fail or turn to ill,
> So thou and I shall sever.
> Keep therefore a true woman's eye,
> And love me still, but know not why,
> So has thou the same reason still
> To dote upon me ever.

Note that the poet does not here say that there is *no* reason for a woman's loving, but that she does not have to know (in the sense of "know how to say") what it is.

That logic cannot determine what we are going to be attracted by or averse from was well known to Shakespeare. He makes Shylock say, when challenged as to his motives for demanding the pound of flesh,

> Some men there are love not a gaping pig;
> Some, that are mad if they behold a cat;
> And others, when the bag-pipe sings i' th' nose,
> Cannot contain their urine; for affection,
> Mistress of passion, sways it to the mood
> Of what it likes or loaths.   (*M. of V.* iv. 1)

And he knew about love-potions, of one of which he says,

> The juice of it, on sleeping eyelids laid,
> Will make or man or woman madly dote
> Upon the next live creature that it sees . . .
> The next thing then she waking looks upon,
> (Be it on lion, bear, or wolf, or bull,
> On meddling monkey, or on busy ape,)
> She shall pursue it with the soul of love.
>
> (*M.N.D.* ii. I)

There are no logical limits (at least none relevant to the present issue)[8] to what such potions could make even a descriptivist philosopher desire; and therefore, if an argument about what can (logically) be thought good is based upon what can (logically) be desired, it is bound to fail. Logic tells us, indeed, that, if a man claims to desire a certain thing, there are certain *words* which he must not apply to it, and perhaps also that there are certain other words, some of which at least he must be prepared to apply to it. But the latter half of this logical restriction is rather indefinite and elusive, and I leave it to those who have a stake in it to make it more determinate than it is so far. The trouble is that, as Miss Anscombe rightly says, *bonum est multiplex*; and I can see no way of putting a logical limit to its multiplicity.

VI

The point that I have been making—or a closely related point—can be put in the following way. We can perhaps distinguish between objective properties of objects—i.e. those which they have, however a person is disposed towards them—and subjective properties, which an object has only if a person is disposed towards it in a certain way. I must confess that I do not like these words because they have been used in too many different senses; but perhaps, as so defined, they will serve our present purposes. In a similar way, we might distinguish between objective conditions which have to be satisfied before we can use a certain word of an object, and subjective conditions. The former consist in the possession by the object of objective properties; the latter in a person's being disposed in a certain way towards it. Now descriptivists often seem to be wanting to demonstrate to us that there are certain objective conditions for the use of words like "good." But the most that arguments like the foregoing can show is that there are certain subjective conditions.

Here, moreover, we must guard against another, related, ambiguity in the expression "conditions for the use of a word." It might mean "conditions" for a word being said to be used correctly to express what the speaker who calls a thing 'good' (for example) is wishing to convey"; or it might mean "conditions for a thing's being said to be good." This ambiguity is well illustrated on the first page of an article by Mrs. Foot.[9] In outlining a position which she is going to attack, she asks: "Is a connexion with the choices of the speaker ever a *sufficient* condition for the use of the word 'good,' as it would be if a man could ever call certain things (let us call them *A*s) good *A*s simply because these were the *A*s which he was thereafter ready to choose?" She goes on to argue that it is neither a sufficient nor a necessary condition; in this she deviates from Miss Anscombe, who thinks that if we call a thing good, we must attribute to it some desirability characteristic, and that "the primitive sign of wanting is trying to get."[10]

Now if here "a sufficient condition for the use of the word 'good' " meant "a sufficient condition for a thing's being said to be good," then it is, I think, quite plain that a connexion with choices is not a sufficient condition. At any rate, I have never thought that it was; indeed, though the view has sometimes been attributed to me that "So and so is a good *x*" means the same as "So and so is the *x* (or kind of *x*) that I would choose," this is a position which I have explicitly argued against.[11] Now there are indications in the article which might lead one to suppose that Mrs. Foot was taking the words "sufficient condition for the use of the word 'good' " to mean "sufficient condition for a thing's being said to be good." The chief indication is that few if any of her arguments are even plausible unless this were what she was trying to disprove. Also, her words in several places naturally bear this sense. For example, on p. 53 she says (referring to an example of a person playing a game with pebbles) "It is not by his readiness to pick up the pebbles that he *legitimizes his words*"; and she has just said that, on the contrary, "It is a plain matter of fact that the particular *A*s" (in this example pebbles) "*will be* good for his purposes, or from his point of view" (my italics). A similar kind of expression occurs earlier on p. 46, where she says, of a man talking about knives, "He could not say that a good knife was one which rusted quickly, *defending his use* of the word 'good' by showing that he picked out such knives for his own use." It certainly looks, at first sight, as if in both these instances, by "legitimize his words" and "defend his use" she means, not "show that he really does think that sort of knife or pebble good, and is therefore expressing correctly what he thinks," but rather "show that the knives or pebbles which he calls good *are* good." So it looked to me, when I first read the article, as if, when she was constructing these arguments, she had the purpose of attacking a position which I, at any rate, have never defended, and with which, therefore, I need not concern myself.

However, we must consider the other possible interpretation, in view of the fact that, unless my memory is deceiving me, and my notes incorrect (and I am not confident on either point), this was the interpretation which she authorized at the meeting at which her paper was discussed, after I had pointed out to her that on the first interpretation she was attacking a position which was not mine. If this second interpretation were what she meant, then in the "pebble" example she would be maintaining that, if a man were ready to pick up a certain kind of pebble for playing a game, and habitually did so, to point this out would not be a way of showing that those were the pebbles that he thought good for his purposes or from his point of view, and thus "legitimizing" the use of the word "good" by showing that it correctly expressed his thought (however preposterous the thought). But if so, she was maintaining something that is not very plausible. For if a man consistently and deliberately chose a certain kind of pebble, we *should* infer that he thought that kind of pebble good for his purposes or from his point of view; if we had doubts, they would be about what on earth the purposes or the point of view could be. I conclude that either she was attacking a position which I have never held, or else she was attacking one which I might, with certain explanations, accept, but attacking it in a way which could carry conviction only to somebody who confused the two possible interpretations of the phrase "condition for."

VII

This seems to be the best point at which to deal with another common descriptivist maneuvre. The maneuvre is rendered attractive by the following fact, which I think we can all admit. There are some things which, if wanted or thought good by somebody, seem to call for no explanation (for example, food, a certain degree of warmth, &c.). Other things, if wanted or thought good, require explanation. The explanation can perhaps be given: a man who wants a flat pebble may want it to play ducks and drakes with, and think it good for this purpose; but, as we progress to more and more bizarre examples, the explanation gets harder and harder to give. It therefore seems to be open to the descriptivist to take a very extraordinary imaginary example, and ask rhetorical questions about it, such as "Suppose that a man says that somebody is a good man because he clasps and unclasps his hands, and never turns NNE. after turning SSW.; could we understand him?"[12] It is implied that an anti-descriptivist has to claim that he can understand such an absurd statement, and this is treated as a *reductio ad absurdum* of his position.

This type of argument rests on a confusion between, on the one hand, logical absurdity and its various weaker analogues, and, on the other, various sorts of contingent improbability. That is why I said earlier that the problem about the distinction between descriptive and evaluative is an offshoot of the problem about the distinction between analytic and synthetic. It is contingently extremely unlikely, to say the least, that I should become able to lift a ton weight with my bare hands; but it is not logically impossible for this to happen, nor is it logically absurd, in any weaker way, to claim that it has happened. By this I mean that if a man claimed to be able to do this, there would be no ultimate obstacle to our understanding him. Admittedly, we might well think at first that we had misunderstood him; it is so improbable that anybody should even think that it had happened, that, if a person claimed that it had happened, we should think at first that he could not be meaning the words in their literal senses. We might think that he meant, for instance, that the weight in question was counter-balanced, so that he could put his hands underneath it and lift, and make it go up. That is to say, when a man says something which is sufficiently improbable (as we think the universe to be constituted), we tend to assume that he cannot mean it literally, and that therefore we have to search for some non-literal meaning if we are going to understand him. But for all that, what he says has in its literal sense nothing *logically* wrong with it. It follows that no conclusions whatever are to be drawn concerning the meanings or uses of words from the oddity of such a remark; what is odd is not the use of words, but that anybody should think such a thing.

The case before us is much the same. If a man said that somebody was a good man because he clasped and unclasped his hands, we should, indeed, at first find ourselves wondering whether we had understood him. But the reason is that, although what has been said is perfectly *comprehensible* in its literal sense, it is very odd indeed for anybody to think it. We should therefore look around for non-literal senses or contrived explanations, and should be baffled if we failed to find any. Why would it be odd for anybody to think this? For a reason which can, indeed, be gathered from the writings of descriptivists, who have given a tolerably correct account of it, vitiated only by their assumption that it can teach us anything about the uses or meanings of words, and that therefore it can support, or discredit, logical theses. The reason is that very few of us, if any, have the necessary "pro-attitude" to people who clasp and unclasp their hands; and the reason for this is that the pro-attitudes which we have do not just occur at random, but have explanations, albeit not (as the descriptivists whom I am discussing seem to think) explanations which logic alone could provide. To think something good of its kind is, let us say, to have at least some disposition to choose it when, or if, choosing things of that kind, in actual or hypothetical circumstances. After what I have said earlier, you will not, I know, confuse this thesis with the thesis that for something to *be* good is for us to have a disposition to choose it. Now we do not have, most of us, any disposition to choose, or to choose to be, men who clasp and unclasp their hands. We do not, accordingly, think that men who do this are good.

The explanation of our not thinking this is that such choices would hardly contribute to our survival, growth, procreation, &c.; if there have been any races of men or animals who have made the clasping and unclasping of hands a prime object of their pro-attitudes, to the exclusion of other more survival-promoting activities, they have gone under in the struggle for existence. I am, I know, being rather crude; but in general, to cut the matter short, we have the pro-attitudes that we have, and therefore call the things good which we do call good, because of their relevance to certain ends which are sometimes called "fundamental human needs."

To call them this, however, is already to make a *logical* connexion between them and what it is good for a man to have. This, indeed, is why descriptivists have fallen into the trap of supposing that, because the word "good" is logically tied in certain contexts to the *word* "needs," it is therefore logically tied to certain concrete *things* which are generally thought to be needs. But since this mistake is the same mistake as I discussed at length in connexion with desires, it need not detain us. The two words "desires" and "needs" have both misled descriptivists in the same way—and that because there is an intimate logical relation between what is needed and what is desired, so that in many contexts we could say that for a thing to be needed is for it to be a necessary condition for satisfying a desire. It follows that if "things desired" do not form a closed class, "things needed" will not either. If, as I said, logic does not prevent us from coming to desire new things, or ceasing to desire old ones, it cannot, either, determine what we do or do not need.

A man who used the word "good" of things which were unrelated to those ends which most of us call "needs" might, nevertheless, be using it, quite correctly, to express the thought which he had; but this might be (if a sufficiently crazy example were taken) a very extraordinary thought for a man to have, because most of us have a high regard for our survival, and for such other things as I mentioned, and our pro-attitudes are fairly consistently related to these. It is not, indeed, logically necessary that they should be. Those of some people are not. And it would not affect my argument (though it would obviously affect gravely that of the opposite party) if there were some things which some people just do, unaccountably, have a high regard for, like the music of Beethoven.

In short, our disposition to call only a certain range of things good (and to choose and desire them) can be explained—in so far as it can be explained—without bringing in logic; and therefore the explanation contributes nothing to logic either, and, specifically, tells us nothing about the meanings or uses of the evaluative words, except that they have certain common *descriptive* meanings.

VIII

I shall end this lecture with an attempt to clear up a quite simple confusion about the word "because"—a confusion which seems to me to lie at the root of a great many things which descriptivists say. If I am choosing between an ordinary mushroom and a poisonous toadstool to put in the dish that I am making for myself, I naturally choose, and prefer, and think it best to choose and that I ought to choose, the mushroom and not the toadstool; and I think this *because* the latter is poisonous (i.e. such as to cause death if eaten). That the toadstool is poisonous is my *reason* for rejecting it. Now it might be thought that, if I reject it *because* it is poisonous, there must be some logical connexion between the statement "It is poisonous" and the statements "It ought not to be chosen to eat" or "It is not good to eat"; or between my thought that it is poisonous and my disposition not to eat it. By "logical connexion" I mean that the *meanings* of the expressions are somehow linked (the precise nature of the link need not concern us; some descriptivists would make it a firmer one than others). Now to say this is to confuse logical entailment, together with its many weaker analogues, on the one hand, with the relation between choice and reasons for choice on the other. The relation between choice and reasons for choice is not a logical relation. There is no logical compulsion on me, or even any weaker logical constraint, to refrain from eating what I know will kill me. I refrain from eating it *because* I know it will kill me; but if I did the opposite, and *ate* it because I knew it would kill me, I should not be offending against any logical rule regulating the uses of words, however fashionably tenuous the rule is supposed to be.

There is, indeed, a logical inference that can be elicited from this situation. Given that the toadstool would kill me, I can infer that I ought not to eat it, if I also accept a further premiss that I ought not to eat what would kill me. To accept this other premiss is to have one of a class of things which I shall call, in Professor Braithwaite's phrase, "springs of action."[13] Desires belong to this class, as do convictions that something is better than something else. In fact anything belongs to it which can, as it were, turn a descriptive statement into a reason for doing something; or, more formally, the expression of which in language (though not, of course, its *description* in language), together with some descriptive statement, logically entails some prescription. But there is no logical link between the descriptive premiss, *by itself,* and the prescriptive conclusion.

A parallel from a quite distinct field of discourse, which has nothing to do with prescriptions, will perhaps make this point clear. There is a valid logical inference from the statement that cyanide is a poison, together with the statement that this dish contains cyanide, to the conclusion that this dish contains poison. But there is no logical connexion which can justify the inference from the statement, by itself, that the dish contains cyanide, to the conclusion that it contains poison. This is because the other premiss, that cyanide is a poison, is synthetic. Nevertheless, the dish is poisonous *because* it contains cyanide.

Now if anybody thinks that one can never say "*q* because *p*" unless there is a logical connexion between "*p*" and "*q*," he is likely to attempt to place opponents of descriptivism in the following dilemma. Either we have to admit that there is a logical connexion between statements of fact, taken by themselves, and evaluative conclusions (which is to surrender to at any rate a weak form of descriptivism); or else we must hold that evaluative judgements are never made *because* of anything—i.e. that they are quite irrational. It is to be hoped that if descriptivists reflect upon the falsity of this dilemma, they will abandon at least some of their arguments.

This lecture has been polemical. I felt it necessary to discuss certain mistaken views (as I think them to be); for it seems to me that, if we could put them behind us, we might liberate the subject for a real advance. In this sense my lecture has had a constructive purpose.

NOTES

1. *Philosophical Papers*, p. 71; cf. *How to do things with words*, p. 3.

2. *The Language of Morals* (*LM*), esp. chap. 7; *Freedom and Reason* (*FR*), pp. 22-27, 51, 56.

3. See Cicero, *Lucullus,* 16; Sextus Empiricus, *Adv. Math.* i. 69, 80 and *Hyp. Pyrrh.* ii. 253.

4. Though not competent to judge of such matters, I do not find the experiments described by Prof. H. J. Eysenck, *Sense and Nonsense in Psychology,* chap. 8, at all incredible, though I do not agree with his interpretation of them.

5. *FR,* pp. 187-9.

6. *FR,* p. 71; *LM,* p. 133.

7. See Anscombe, op. cit., p. 67; *FR,* p. 70.

8. For some restrictions which, though interesting, do not affect the present argument, see Anscombe, op cit., p. 66 and A. Kenny, *Action, Emotion and Will,* p. 112. Since states of affairs can be desired for their own sakes, the restriction that what is desired must be desired *for* something is a vacuous one.

9. *Ar. Soc. Supp. Vol.* xxxv (1961), 45.

10. Op. cit., p. 67; see above, p. 123.

11. *LM,* p. 107.

12. The example comes from Mrs. Foot's article in *Ar. Soc.,* 1958/9, 84.

13. *Ar. Soc. Supp. Vol.* xx (1946), 9. Aristotle's *orexeis* and Kenny's "volitions" (op. cit., p. 214) play similar roles.

MORAL ARGUMENTS*

Philippa Foot

Those who are influenced by the emotivist theory of ethics and yet wish to defend what Hare has called "the rationality of moral discourse" generally talk a lot about "giving reasons" for saying that one thing is right, and another wrong. The fact that moral judgements need defense seems to distinguish the impact of one man's moral views on others from mere persuasion or coercion and the judgements themselves from mere expressions of likes and dislikes. Yet the version of argument in morals currently accepted seems to say that while reasons must be given, no one need accept them unless he happens to hold particular moral views. It follows that disputes about what is right and wrong can be resolved only if certain contingent conditions are fulfilled. If they are not fulfilled, the argument breaks down, and the disputants are left face to face in an opposition which is merely an expression of attitude and will. Much energy is expended in trying to show that no sceptical conclusion can be drawn. It is suggested, for instance, that anyone who has considered all the facts which could bear on his moral position has ipso facto produced a "well-founded" moral judgement in spite of the fact that anyone else who has considered the same facts may well come to the opposite conclusion. How "x is good" can be a well-founded moral judgement when "x is bad" can be equally well founded it is not easy to see.

The statement that moral arguments "may always break down" is often thought of as something that has to be accepted. It is thought that those who deny it fail to take account of what was proved once and for all by Hume and elaborated by Stevenson, Ayer, and Hare. This article is an attempt to expose the assumptions which give the "breakdown" theory so tenacious a hold and to suggest an alternative view.

*Reprinted by permission of the publisher, Basil Blackwell, Oxford.

Looked at in one way, the assertion that moral arguments "may always break down" appears to make a large claim. What is meant is that they may break down in a way in which other arguments may not. We are therefore working on a model on which such factors as shortage of time or temper are not shown. The suggestion is not that A's argument with B may break down because B refuses for one reason or another to go on with it, but that their positions as such are irreconcilable. Now the question is, how can we assert that any disagreement about what is right and wrong may end like this? How do we know, without consulting the details of each argument, that there is always an impregnable position both for the man who says that X is right, or good, or what he ought to do, and for the man who denies it? How do we know that each is able to deal with every argument the other may bring?

Thus when Hare describes someone who listens to all his adversary has to say and then at the end simply rejects his conclusion, we want to ask, "How can he?" Hare clearly supposes that he can, for he says that at this point the objector can only be asked to make up his mind for himself.[1] No one would ever paint such a picture of other kinds of argument—suggesting, for instance, that a man might listen to all that could be said about the shape of the earth, and then ask why he should believe that it was round. We should want, in such a case, to know how he met the case put to him. It is remarkable that in ethics this question is thought not to be in place.

If a man making a moral judgement is to be invulnerable to criticism, he must be free from reproach on two scores: (a) he must have brought forward evidence, where evidence is needed, and (b) he must have disposed of any contrary evidence offered. It is worth showing why writers who insist that moral arguments may always break down assume, for both sides in a moral dispute, invulnerability on both counts. The critical assumption appears in different forms because different descriptions of moral arguments are given. I shall consider briefly what has been said by Stevenson and by Hare.

1. Stevenson sees the process of giving reasons for ethical conclusions as a special process of nondeductive inference in which statements expressing beliefs (R) form the premises and emotive (evaluative) utterances (E) the conclusion. There are no rules validating particular inferences, but only causal connections between the beliefs and attitudes concerned. "Suppose," he writes, "that a theorist should *tabulate* the 'valid' inferences from R's to E's. It is difficult to see how he could be doing anything more than specify what R's he thereby resolves to *accept* as supporting the various E's. . . . Under the name of 'validity' he will be selecting those inferences to which he is psychologically disposed to give assent, and perhaps inducing others to give a similar assent to them."[2] It follows that disputes in which each man backs up his moral judgement with "reasons" may always break down, and this is an implication on which Stevenson insists. So long as he does not contradict himself and gets his

facts right, a man may argue as he chooses or as he finds himself psychologically disposed. He alone says which facts are relevant to ethical conclusions, so that he is invulnerable on counts (a) and (b): he can simply assert that what he brings forward is evidence and can simply deny the relevance of any other. His argument may be ineffective, but it cannot be said to be wrong. Stevenson speaks of ethical "inference" and of giving "reasons," but the process which he describes is rather that of trying to produce a result, an attitude, by means of a special kind of adjustment, an alteration in belief. All that is needed for a breakdown is for different attitudes in different people to be causally connected to the same beliefs. Then even complete agreement in belief will not settle a moral dispute.

2. Hare gives a picture of moral reasoning which escapes the difficulties of a special form of inference without rules of validity. He regards an argument to a moral conclusion as a syllogistic inference, with the orginary rules. The facts, such as "this is stealing," which are to back up a moral judgement are to be stated in a "descriptive" minor premise, and their relevance is to be guaranteed by an "evaluative" major premise in which that kind of thing is said to be good or bad. There is thus no difficulty about the validity of the argument, but one does arise about the status of the major premise. We are supposed to say that a particular action is bad because it is a case of stealing and because stealing is wrong. But if we ask why stealing is wrong, we can only be presented with another argument of the same form, with another exposed moral principle as its major premise. In the end everyone is forced back to some moral principle which he simply asserts—and which someone else may simply deny. It can, therefore, be no reproach to anyone that he gives no reasons for a statement of moral principle since any moral argument must contain some undefended premise of this kind. Nor can he be accused of failing to meet arguments put forward by opponents arguing from different principles, for by denying their ultimate major premises he can successfully deny the relevance of anything they say.

Both of these accounts of moral argument are governed by the thought that there is no logical connection between statements of fact and statements of value, so that each man makes his own decision as to the facts about an action which are relevant to its evaluation. To oppose this view we should need to show that on the contrary, it is laid down that some things do, and some things do not, count in favor of a moral conclusion and that a man can no more decide for himself what is evidence for rightness and wrongness than he can decide what is evidence for monetary inflation or a tumor on the brain. If such objective relations between facts and values existed, they could be of two kinds: descriptive, or factual premises might *entail* evaluative conclusions, or they might count as *evidence* for them. It is the second possibility which chiefly concerns me, but I shall nevertheless consider the arguments which are supposed to show that the stronger relationship cannot exist, for I want to show that the arguments usually brought forward do not *even* prove this. I want to say that it has not even been proved that moral conclusions cannot be entailed by factual or descriptive premises.

It is often thought that Hume showed the impossibility of deducing "ought" from "is" but the form in which this view is now defended is, of course, that in which it was rediscovered by G. E. Moore at the beginning of the present century and developed by such other critics of "naturalistic" ethics as Stevenson, Ayer, and Hare. We therefore need to look into the case against naturalism to see exactly what was proved.

Moore tried to show that goodness was a nonnatural property and thus not to be defined in terms of natural properties. The problem was to explain the concept of a "natural property" and to prove that no ethical definition in terms of natural properties could be correct. As Frankena[3] and Prior[4] pointed out, the argument against naturalism was always in danger of degenerating into a truism. A natural property tended to become one not identical with goodness and the naturalistic fallacy that of identifying goodness with "some other thing."

What was needed to give the attack on naturalism new life was the identification of some deficiency common to the whole range of definitions rejected by Moore, a reason why they all failed. This was provided by the theory that value terms in general, and moral terms in particular, were used for a special function—variously identified as expressing feelings, expressing and inducing attitudes, or commending. It was said that words with emotive or commendatory force such as *good* were not to be defined by the use of words whose meaning was merely "descriptive." This discovery tended to appear greater than it was, because it looked as if the two categories of fact and value had been identified separately and found never to coincide, whereas, actually, the factual or descriptive was defined by exclusion from the realm of value. In the ordinary sense of "descriptive" the word *good* is a descriptive word, and in the ordinary sense of "fact," we say that it is a fact about so and so that he is a good man, so that the words must be used in a special sense in moral philosophy. But a special philosopher's sense of these words has never, so far as I know, been explained except by contrasting value and fact. A word or sentence seems to be called "descriptive" on account of the fact that it is *not* emotive, does *not* commend, does *not* entail an imperative, and so on according to the theory involved. This might seem to reduce the case against naturalism once more to an uninteresting tautology, but it does not do so. For if the nonnaturalist has discovered a special feature found in all value judgements, he can no longer be accused of saying merely that nothing is a definition of "good" unless it is a definition of *good* and not "some other thing." His part is now to insist that any definition which fails to allow for the special feature of value judgements must be rejected and to label as "naturalistic" all the definitions which fail to pass this test.

I shall suppose, for the sake of argument, that the nonnaturalist really has identified some characteristic (let us call it *f*) essential to evaluative words, that he is right in saying that evaluations involve emotions, attitudes, the acceptance of imperatives, or something of the kind. He is therefore justified in insisting that no word or statement which does not have the property *f* can be taken as equivalent to any evaluation and that no account of the use of an evaluative term can leave out *f* and yet be complete. What, if anything, follows about the relation between premises and conclusion in an argument designed to support an evaluation?

It is often said that what follows is that evaluative conclusions cannot be deduced from descriptive premises, but how is this to be shown? Of course, if a descriptive premise is redefined as one which does not entail an evaluative conclusion, the nonnaturalist will once more have bought security at the price of becoming a bore. He can once more improve his position by pointing to the characteristic *f* belonging to all evaluations and asserting that no set of premises which do not entail an *f* proposition can entail an evaluation. If he takes this course he will be more like the man who says that a proposition which entails a proposition about a dog must be one which entails a proposition about an animal. He is telling us what to look out for in checking the entailment. What he is not so far telling us is that we can test for the entailment by looking to see whether the premise itself has the characteristic *f*. For all that has yet been shown it might be possible for a premise which is not *f* to entail a conclusion which is *f*, and it is obviously this proposition which the nonnaturalist wants to deny.

It may seem obvious that a nonevaluative premise could not entail an evaluative conclusion, but it remains unclear how it is supposed to be proved.

In one form, the theory that an evaluative conclusion of a deductive argument needs evaluative premises is clearly unwarrantable; I mention this only to get it out of the way. We cannot possibly say that at least one of the premises must be evaluative if the conclusion is to be so, for there is nothing to tell us that whatever can truly be said of the conclusion of a deductive argument can truly be said of any one of the premises. It is not necessary that the evaluative element should "come in whole," so to speak. If *f* has to belong to the premises, it can only be necessary that it should belong to the premises *together*, and it may be no easy matter to see whether a set of propositions has the property *f*.

How, in any case, is it to be proved that if the conclusion is to have the characteristic *f* the premises taken together must also have it? Can it be said that unless this is so, it will always be possible to assert the premises and yet deny the conclusion? I will try to show that this at least is false; in order to do so, I will consider the case of arguments designed to show that a certain piece of behavior is or is not rude.

I think it will be agreed that in the wide sense in which philosophers speak of evaluation, *rude* is an evaluative word. At any rate, it has the kind of characteristics on which nonnaturalists fasten: it expresses disapproval, is meant to be used when action is to be discouraged, implies that other things being equal, the behavior to which it is applied will be avoided by the speaker, and so on. For the purpose of this argument I will ignore the cases in which it is admitted that there are reasons why something should be done in spite of, or even because of, the fact that it is rude. Clearly there are occasions when a little rudeness is in place, but this does not alter the fact that *rude* is a condemnatory word.

It is obvious that there is something else to be said about the word *rude* besides the fact that it expresses fairly mild condemnation; it can only be used where certain descriptions apply. The right account of the situation in which it is correct to say that behavior is rude is, I think, that this kind of behavior causes offense by indicating lack of respect. Sometimes it is merely conventional that such behavior does indicate lack of respect (for example, when a man keeps his hat on in someone else's house). Sometimes the behavior is naturally disrespectful, as when one man pushes another out of the way. (It should be mentioned that rudeness and the absence of rudeness do not exhaust the subject of etiquette; some things are not rude, yet are "not done." It is rude to wear flannels at a formal dinner party, but merely not done to wear a dinner jacket for tennis.)

Given that this reference to offense is to be included in any account of the concept of rudeness, we may ask what the relation is between the assertion that these conditions of offense are fulfilled—let us call it O—and the statement that behavior is rude—let us call it R. Can someone who accepts the proposition O (that this kind of offense is caused) deny the proposition R (that the behavior is rude)? I should have thought that this was just what he could not do, for if he says that it is not rude, we shall stare, and ask him what sort of behavior would be rude. What is he to say? Suppose that he were to answer, "a man is rude when he behaves conventionally" or "a man is rude when he walks slowly up to a front door," and this not because he believes that such behavior causes offense, but with the intention of leaving behind entirely the usual criteria of rudeness. It is evident that with the usual criteria of rudeness, he leaves behind the concept itself. He may say the words, "I think this rude," but it will not on that account be right to describe him as "thinking it rude." If I *say*, "I am sitting on a pile of hay" and present as evidence the fact that the object I am sitting on has four wooden legs and a hard wooden back, I will hardly be described as thinking, even mistakenly, that I am sitting on a pile of hay. All I am doing is to use the *words* "pile of hay."

It might be thought that the two cases were not parallel, for while the meaning of *pile of hay* is given by the characteristics which piles of hay must possess, the meaning of *rude* is given by the attitude it expresses. The answer is that if "thinking a thing rude" is to be described as having a particular attitude to it, then having an attitude presupposes, in this case, believing that certain conditions are fulfilled. If "attitudes" were solely a matter of reactions such as wrinkling the nose and tendencies to such things as making resolutions and scolding, then thinking something rude would not be describable solely in terms of attitudes. Either thinking something rude is not to be described in terms of attitudes or attitudes are not to be described in terms of such things. Even if we could suppose that a particular individual could react toward conventional behavior or to walking slowly up to an English front door, *exactly* as most people react to behavior which gives offense, this would not mean that he was to be described as thinking these things rude. In any case the supposition is nonsense. Although he could behave in some way as if he thought them rude, for example, by scolding conventional or slow-walking children but not turning daughters with these proclivities out of doors, his behavior could not be just as if he thought them rude. As the social reaction to conventional behavior is not the same as the social reaction to offensive behavior, he could not act in just the same way. He could not, for instance, apologize for what he would call his "rudeness," for he would have to admit that it had caused no offense.

I conclude that whether a man is speaking of behavior as rude or not rude, he must use the same criteria as anyone else, and that since the criteria are satisfied if O is true, it is impossible for him to assert O while denying R. It follows that if it is a sufficient condition of P's entailing Q that the assertion of P is inconsistent with the denial of Q, we have here an example of a non-evaluative premise from which an evaluative conclusion can be deduced.

It is, of course, possible to admit O while refusing to assert R, and this will not be like the refusal to say about prunes what one has already admitted about dried plums. Calling an action "rude" is using a concept which a man might want to reject, rejecting the whole practice of praising and blaming embodied in terms such as "polite" and "rude." Such a man would refuse to discuss points of etiquette, and arguments with him about what is rude would not so much break down as never begin. But once he did accept the question, "Is this rude?", he would have to abide by the rules of this kind of argument; he could not bring forward any evidence he liked, and he could not deny the relevance of any piece of evidence brought forward by his opponent. Nor could he say that he was unable to move from O to R on this occasion because the belief in O had not induced in him feelings or attitudes warranting the assertion of R. If he had agreed to discuss rudeness he had committed himself to accepting O as evidence for R, and evidence is not a sort of medicine which is taken in the hope that it will work. To suggest that he could refuse to admit that certain behavior was rude because the right psychological state had not been induced, is as odd as to suppose that one might refuse to speak of the world as round because in spite of the good evidence of roundness a feeling of confidence in the proposition had not been produced. When given good evidence, it is one's business to act on it, not to hang around waiting for the right state of mind. It follows that if a man is prepared to discuss questions of rudeness and hence to accept as evidence the fact that behavior causes a certain kind of offense, he cannot refuse to admit R when O has been proved.

The point of considering this example was to show that there may be the strictest rules of evidence even where an evaluative conclusion is concerned. Applying this principle to the case of moral judgements, we see that—for all that the nonnaturalist has proved to the contrary—Bentham, for instance, may be right in saying that when used in conjunction with the principle of utility, "the words *ought* and *right* and *wrong*, and others of that stamp, have meaning: when otherwise they have none."[5] Anyone who uses moral terms at all, whether to assert or deny a moral proposition, must abide by the rules for their use, including the rules about what shall count as evidence for or against the moral judgement concerned. For anything that has yet been shown to the contrary these rules could be entailment rules, forbidding the assertion of factual propositions. The only recourse of the man who refused to accept the things which counted in favor of a moral proposition as giving him a reason to do certain things or to take up a particular attitude would be to leave the moral discussion and abjure altogether the use of moral terms.

To say what Bentham said is not, then, to commit any sort of "naturalistic fallacy." It is open to us to inquire whether moral terms do lose their meaning when divorced from the pleasure principle or from some other set of criteria, as the word *rude* loses its meaning when the criterion of offensiveness is dropped. To me it seems that this is clearly the case; I do not know what could be meant by saying that it was someone's duty to do something unless there was an attempt to show why it mattered if this sort of thing was not done. How can questions such as "what does it matter?", "what harm does it do?", "what advantage is there in . . .?", "why is it important?", be set aside here? Is it even to be suggested that the harm done by a certain trait of character could be taken by some extreme moral eccentric to be just what made it a virtue? I suggest that such a man would not even be a moral eccentric any more than the man who used the word *rude* of conventional behavior was putting forward strange views about what was rude. Both descriptions have their proper application, but it is not here. How exactly the concepts of harm, advantage, benefit, importance, etc., are related to the different moral concepts such as rightness, obligation, goodness, duty, and virtue is something that needs the most patient investigation, but that they are so related seems undeniable, and it follows that a man cannot make his own personal decision about the considerations which are to count as evidence in morals.

Perhaps it will be argued that this kind of freedom of choice is not ruled out after all, because a man has to decide for himself what is to count as advantage, benefit, or harm. But is this really plausible? Consider the man described by Hare as thinking that torturing is morally permissible.[6] Apparently he is not supposed to be arguing that in spite of everything torture is justifiable as a means of extracting confessions from enemies of the state, for the argument is supposed to be at an end when he has said that torturing people is permissible, and his opponent has said that it is not. How is he supposed to have answered the objection that to inflict torture is to do harm? If he is supposed to have said that pain is good for a man in the long run, rather than bad, he will have to show the benefits involved, and he can no more choose what shall count as a benefit than he could have chosen what counted as harm. Is he perhaps supposed to count as harm only harm to himself? In this case he is guilty of *ignoratio elenchi.* By refusing to count as harm anything except harm to himself, he puts himself outside the pale of moral discussion and should have explained that this was his position. One might compare his case to that of a man who in some discussion of common policy says, "this will be the best thing to do," and announces afterwards that *he* meant best for himself. This is not what the word "best" does mean in the context of such a discussion.

It may be objected that these considerations about the evidence which must be brought for saying that one thing is good and another bad could not in any case be of the least importance; such rules of evidence, even if they exist, only reflecting the connection between our existing moral code and our existing moral terms. If there are no "free" moral terms in our language, it can always be supposed that some have been invented, as indeed they will have to be invented if we are to be able to argue with people who subscribe to a moral code entirely different from our own. This objection rests on a doubtful assumption about the concept of *morality.* It assumes that even if there are rules about the grounds on which actions can be called good, right, or obligatory, there are no rules about the grounds on which a principle which is to be called a moral principle may be asserted. Those who believe this must think it possible to identify an element of feeling or attitude which carries the meaning of the word "moral." It must be supposed, for instance, that if we describe a man as being for or against certain actions, bringing them under universal rules, adopting these rules for himself, and thinking himself bound to urge them on others, we shall be able to identify him as holding moral principles, whatever the content of the principle at which he stops. But why should it be supposed that the concept of morality is to be caught in this particular kind of net? The consequences of such an assumption are very hard to stomach, for it follows that a rule which was admitted by those who obeyed it to be completely pointless could yet be recognized as a moral rule. If people happened to insist that no one should run around trees left handed or look at hedgehogs in the light of the moon, this might count as a basic moral principle about which nothing more need be said.

I think that the main reason why this view is so often held in spite of these difficulties is that we fear the charge of making a verbal decision in favor of our own moral code. But those who bring that charge are merely begging the question against arguments such as those given above. Of course, if the rules we are refusing to call moral rules can really be given this name, then we are merely legislating against alien *moral codes*. But the suggestion which has been put forward is that this could not be the right description for rules of behavior for which an entirely different defense is offered from that which we offer for our moral beliefs. If this suggestion is right, the difference between ourselves and the people who have these rules is not to be described as a difference of moral outlook but rather as a difference between a moral and a nonmoral point of view. The example of etiquette is again useful here. No one is tempted to say that the ruling out, a priori, of rules of etiquette which each man decides on for himself when he feels so inclined, represents a mere verbal decision in favor of our kind of socially determined standards of etiquette. On what grounds could one call a rule which someone was allowed to invent for himself a rule of *etiquette*? It is not just a fact about the use of words "rude," "not done," etc., that they could not be applied in such a case; it is also a fact about etiquette that if terms in another language did appear in such situations they would not be terms of etiquette. We can make a similar point about the terms *legal* and *illegal* and the concept of law. If any individual were allowed to apply a certain pair of terms expressing approval and disapproval off his own bat, without taking notice of any recognized authority, such terms could not be legal terms. Similarly it is a fact about etiquette and law that they are both conventional as morality is not.

It may be that in attempting to state the rules which govern the assertion of moral propositions, we shall legislate against a moral system radically opposed to our own. But this is only to say that we may make a mistake. The remedy is to look more carefully at the rules of evidence, not to assume that there cannot be any at all. If a moral system such as Nietzsche's has been refused recognition as a moral system, then we have got the criteria wrong. The fact that Nietzsche was a moralist cannot, however, be quoted in favor of the private enterprise theory of moral criteria. Admittedly Nietzsche said, "You want to decrease suffering; I want precisely to increase it," but he did not *just* say this, nor did he offer as a justification the fact that suffering causes a tendency to absent mindedness or lines on the human face. We recognize Nietzsche as a moralist because he tries to justify an increase in suffering by connecting it with strength as opposed to weakness and individuality as opposed to conformity. That strength is a good thing can be denied only by someone who can show that the strong man overreaches himself or in some other way brings harm to himself or other people. That individuality is a good thing is something that has to be shown, but in a vague way we connect it with originality and with courage, hence there is no difficulty in conceiving of Nietzsche as a moralist when he appeals to such a thing.

In conclusion, it is worth remarking that moral arguments break down more often than philosophers tend to think, but that the breakdown is of a different kind. When people argue about what is right, good, or obligatory or whether a certain character trait is or is not a virtue, they do not confine their remarks to the adducing of facts which can be established by simple observation, or by some clear-cut technique. What is said may well be subtle or profound, and in this sort of discussion as in others, in the field of literary criticism for instance, or the discussion of character, much depends on experience and imagination. It is quite common for one man to be unable to see what the other is getting at. This sort of misunderstanding will not always be resolvable by anything which could be called argument in the ordinary sense.

NOTES

1. *The Language of Morals,* p. 69.
2. *Ethics and Language,* pp. 170-171.
3. W. K. Frankena, *"The Naturalistic Fallacy,"* Mind, 1939.
4. A. N. Prior, *Logic and the Basis of Ethics,* chap. I.
5. *Principles of Morals in Legislation,* chap. I, x.
6. *Universaliability, P.A.S.* 1954-1955, p. 304.

6
JUSTICE, UTILITY, RIGHTS

"Conscience is a coward, and those faults it has not strength enough to prevent it seldom has justice enough to accuse."

— Oliver Goldsmith,
The Vicar of Wakefield

"Nature has placed mankind under the governance of two sovereign masters, pain *and* pleasure. *It is for them alone to point out what we ought to do, as well as to determine what we shall do. On the one hand, the standard of right and wrong, on the other the chain of causes and effect, are fastened to their throne. They govern us in all we do, in all we say, in all we think: every effort we can make to throw off our subjection, will serve but to demonstrate and confirm it. In words a man may pretend to abjure their empire: but in reality he will remain subject to it all the while. The* principle of utility *recognizes this subjection, and assumes it for the foundation of that system, the object of which is to rear the fabric of felicity by the hands of reason and law. Systems which attempt to question it, deal in sounds instead of sense, in caprice instead of reason, in darkness instead of light."*

— Jeremy Bentham

389

INTRODUCTION

The typical questions of the last section deal mainly with the analysis of ethical language. Austere issues pertaining to the meaning of ethical terms and the way that they function in ethical discourse predominate. The utterances of analytic philosophers on moral philosophy are generally not calculated to do much for the man sunk in genuine moral perplexity. Having heard out the intuitionists, emotivists, descriptivists and their critics, Richard Bludweiss, for one, reports that they are of scant help in deciding between his moral options. Nor are they really meant to be. Still, the moral philosopher no less than his student has regularly got to face that galling and inexpungable question—What precisely ought I to do?

And it is usually not enough that he simply *face* the question. If he is like the rest of us the exigencies of life are such that he must answer it too. This calls for something like a system of moral rules. With the defense and elaboration of such systems, moral philosophy passes from meta-ethics—the study of ethical language or discourse—to ethics proper, which is really the study of moral choice. This gives to the readings of this section a certain robust quality; philosophers enjoy telling people what it is that they should do and how they should go about organizing their moral life, and their contentment shines through in their prose.

Utilitarianism is a system of ethics. Most simply put, which is the way it is often put, utilitarianism involves but a single principle by which moral choices are to be made. In choosing between A and B, the moral man should choose so as to promote the general net balance of pleasure over pain. Economists, who find the vernacular crude, have availed themselves of the term "utility" to avoid talking of happiness or general welfare; their usage has come to predominate and so the principle of utilitarianism is often cast simply as the injunction that that act is best which tends to maximize the general utility.

This is an ethical maxim that might well appeal to such students of moral philosophy as Richard Bludweiss. It has the considerable virtue of compressing what might well be a cumbersome system of rules into a single principle that is easily remembered and conveniently applied. What is more, the principle broadly understood seems to be an intuitively attractive and almost a straightforward generalization of the very principles that Bludweiss might recognize as giving voice to his own natural sense of obligation on those occasions when he means to please himself and no one else. Given some appreciation that the redoubtable Bludweiss places on a stock of goods or things, the rational choice, considering things now only from Bludweiss's point of view, will be to compute such satisfactions as his various options afford and then act in such a way as to get as much of what he wants as he possibly can. Acting under the pressures of this principle, Bludweiss is said to maximize or optimize his utility. The theory of decision making has gone some distance under the assumption that the essentials of rationality involve maximization of just this sort, although the theory contains many separate provisions for more complicated situations such as those that involve uncertainty about the future. Now generally the consequences of our ordinary acts have effects not only on the calculus of pleasure over pain that we keep for ourselves but on the calculus kept by others as well. In concluding that he ought to do what will maximize utility generally, with respect to everyone affected by his decisions, Bludweiss is taking the familiar principle of rationality one step further: he is acting as a utilitarian.

For a better part of a century, at least since the time of John Stuart Mill and Jeremy Bentham, utilitarianism has been part of the common philosophical consciousness in Great Britain and America. Nietzsche, it is true, sneered that only English shopkeepers desired happiness, but on the colder side of the English Channel his scruples were understood to suggest only his unquenchable enthusiasm for

Teutonic bombast, a response which in retrospect seems harsh but fair. Still, even the least romantic of utilitarian philosophers has on occasion succumbed to the gloomy conviction that utilitarianism is an ethical doctrine of irreducible fishiness. Outright inadequacy aside, there are surely many points at which the utilitarian doctrine seems unclear or uncertain—this despite its simplicity. The standard utilitarian injunction is to maximize; this requires not only an ordering of one's preferences but an ordering that computes them to a certain degree. Otherwise Bludweiss's sensible refusal to risk his life playing Russian roulette for high stakes would be largely inexplicable. Given that he vastly prefers being alive to being rich, his refusal makes sense but how many of his preferences admit of easy numerical construction? Worse, even if Bludweiss were to somehow blunder through to a completely quantified ordering of his tastes and predilections, how are we to compare the intensity measured on his scale with that exhibited on a comparable scale kept by someone altogether less fastidious than Bludweiss himself?

Criticism, and the rejection of a philosophical position in philosophy that it entails, is not always dramatic or prompt. A minor question is raised. A philosopher writing in an obscure journal formulates a stickly puzzle. A question emerges that those in a position to defend the faith find they cannot answer. They then tend to ignore the question supposing that those less knowledgeable than themselves will assume it answered. Graduate students make a name for themselves by proclaiming plangently that in fact the question has not been answered.

In the end a collection of cases builds up that the dominant position under attack cannot successfully discuss. Or so it comes to seem until either the position is given up or defended successfully. J. J. C. Smart's essay "Extreme and Restricted Utilitarianism" is entirely an effort at successful defense. Here the reader will find many of the contemporary objections to utilitarianism. These are by and large accounts of moral situations in which the ordinary judgements of our common moral intuitions and the judgements of the utilitarian appear to diverge. Physical scientists, when confronted with evidence that somehow manages not to fit the canons of a prevailing theory in which they have a vested interest, sometimes indulge in the natural temptation to say simply—so much the worse for the evidence. There is some of this too in Professor Smart's essay:

393

a feeling that if ordinary moral judgements and the determinations of utilitarianism conflict, the sensible man should have no false pride about giving up the first in order to rest easy with the second. But there is also a serious and altogether sober and sympathetic effort in this essay to discuss many of the classical objections to utilitarianism. Philosophers defending a position under attack are often convinced that their critics, in their callowness, have failed to perceive the largely hidden richness of the system they mean to discredit. Counterexamples arise, they will maintain, only because the central dogmas are formulated crudely. So it is with Professor Smart's essay, which in its overall form maintains the immemorial pattern of philosophical self-defense.

I have set Professor Smart's essay against "Justice as Fairness" by John Rawls even though neither piece refers directly to the other. In fact, Smart published his article after Rawls published his so one cannot even look for the appearance of direct conflict here. But in all but a superficial sense these are pieces diametrically in opposition. In philosophy as in physics the most effective critic of a system of thought is the man who proposes to replace it with another. Having in hand a rival system he is thus spared the indignity of hearing his criticisms dismissed as negative carping. Professor Rawls is an eminence of Harvard's department of philosophy, which in today's philosophical community comes tolerably close to being an eminence entirely. For twenty years or so he has been engaged in the creation of a system of ethical reasoning that might be set over and against the dominant tradition of utilitarianism. But it would be unfair to Rawls to suggest this his work is intended simply to offer a principle that might be substituted for the more familiar utilitarian doctrines. In fact, he has been employed in working out a fundamentally different system of moral justifications for the chief institutions of society, one that when fully deployed, as it is in his recent volume *A Theory of Justice,* will come to replace utilitarian rules of decision with rules that more deeply tap our moral intuitions. The dominant theme in his work has been the resuscitation of the *contractarian* tradition in political thought. Hobbes, for example, writing in the 17th century, justified the authority of the state by appealing to a hypothetical compact that men in the state of nature would make in order to evade the brutishness of natural life. It is this metaphor or image that Rawls deploys so brilliantly in *A Theory of Justice* but

394

many of the conclusions that are elaborately presented are in evidence already in "Justice as Fairness," published some twenty years before. There Rawls is concerned to show that a community of self-interested egotists, acting in substantial ignorance of the positions that they might occupy in society, would not be likely to opt for utilitarian principles. The principle that they would come to choose instead Rawls dubs justice as fairness. He has no quarrel with the usual budget of counterexamples to the principles of utility, but he takes them to show the need for an altogether richer system of principles. These he proposes to supply himself, together with an account of the manner in which they may be justified. Utilitarianism is really an invention of the 19th century; in re-creating contractarian traditions Rawls is making contact with the great work of the 17th century. But there is also something of Kant in Rawls's work so his work as a whole counts as something very much like a philosophical analogue to the phenomenon of double recessiveness.

The essays that remain in this section do not treat of utility directly, but there are obvious connections between the concerns of the first two essays and all the rest. In the days when the issue of abortion was raging in the state and federal courts and in various state legislatures, philosophers generally took the position that abortion was an issue of *moral obviousness.* That phrase itself I seem to recall figured in a resolution voted upon by one of the innumerable committees of the American Philosophical Association in its annual New York meetings. More recently, the courts seem to have arrived at a consensus on the issue of abortion. Displaying the imperturbable capacity for generalized irrelevance which is their distinguishing feature, philosophers renewed the debate just at that point when everyone else left it.

The results though have been worthwhile and there is some popular sense now that perhaps the underlying issues are not as obvious as they were once thought to be. Judith Jarvis Thompson teaches philosophy at the Massachusetts Institute of Technology. Her essay is remarkable, I think, in the amount it concedes to abortion's traditional opponents and critics. Not for her are niggling distinctions between viable and unviable creatures. She is quite prepared to accept the charge that at the time it is aborted, the human fetus looks remarkably like a human being and quite probably is one as well. Despite this, she argues, women bent on abortion may

395

argue their case; it is simply a moral untruth to claim that the rights to life of certain unoffending but inconvenient victims outweigh the rights to comfort or ease of mind of those women who mean to dispatch them.

It is against this alarmingly candid if well-argued point of view that Professor John Finis sets himself in his reply to Thompson. Finis is a British philosopher with an obvious interest in jurisprudence. It is interesting to compare the two essays simply as specimens of philosophical style. More interesting still is the nature of the arguments Finis brings to bear against Thompson. There are many fine distinctions drawn, it is true, (the result no doubt of an excessive exposure to the law), but there is also a measured and surprisingly effective use of what might be called the traditional Catholic wisdom on the subject of abortion, killing and the taking of life. This essay has provoked Professor Thompson to a riposte. The number of distinctions drawn in each of these essays would no doubt sustain defenses and counter-charges in numbers approaching the transcendental.

The remaining essays in this section, by Professors H. S. A. Hart and Isaiah Berlin are difficult and subtle essays by senior members of the British philosophical academy. Hart has written extensively on the concept of law and Isaiah Berlin has written extensively on everything.

If utilitarianism is the dominant if besieged ethical system in the Anglo-American countries, the system of ethical reasoning that it replaced was that of sonorous principles of natural law. This was largely a theological system of ethical reasoning, one in which moral acts were judged by reference to their position in a vast panorama of licit or illicit activity. A weakness of the system of natural law, of course, was that it floundered in the absence of a belief in a Deity who had thoughtfully arranged for the structure in the first place. But a corresponding strength of the doctrine lay in its capacity to reserve for an individual a stable system of rights and obligations which had in their essentials nothing to do with the powers of the State or the notions of propriety prevalent in a community. In this there was a comforting absoluteness. It is the strengths of this doctrine with none of its liabilities that Professor Hart wishes to resurrect. To the contemporary philosopher, theological arguments are, of course, simply embarrassing, so it is not surprising that Hart proposes to disinter very little of the ancient doctrine. Still, it comes as a surprise to see a philosopher devoting energies to any of it at all. In its essentials, Hart's very subtle argument is conditional: given that there exists a system of rights and obligations at all, he suggests, it follows that there is at least one *natural right*, which men enjoy strictly in virtue of their capacity as agents participating in moral life. This is a delicate point, and one that does not lend itself to easy summary. It is also, however, an important point since the natural right which Hart means to establish arises regardless of the particular configuration of special rights in which moral agents happen to find themselves enmeshed. It thus has the absolute character of rights established under the older tradition of natural law.

Professor Berlin's essay, "Equality as an Ideal," is devoted, by way of contrast, to an altogether more straightforward and accessible task—the analysis of the egalitarian doctrine, which figures conspicuously in the history of utilitarian thought and in recent social history, according to which all men are in some abstract sense equal and entitled therefore to be treated equally unless some specific reasons for treating them differently can be produced. Like so many moral principles, the saying of it is considerably easier than its analysis. Relevant differences, as Professor Berlin points out, are not hard to come by. I propose, for example, to treat you in a cavalier fashion because you are a woman. This, I am told, is the essence of reasoning advanced by the redoubtable Bludweiss and who can gainsay his conclusion that there is a difference between women and all the rest? Of course, it is by no means clear that such differences as there are between men and women, or between blacks and whites, or between the old and the young, should count as morally relevant differences. But this is just to bring out the complexity of the concept of a morally relevant difference. Nor is it really clear how the principle of equality, to which such avid service is regularly paid, should confront such facts that most men differ wildly in native gifts, talents, industry and capacity for work. Nor is it clear, for that matter, how far we would ordinarily wish to press the principle even assuming other questions to have been settled. Being equal in some fundamental respect to all other men, am I therefore entitled to share equally in whatever goods other men have even to the extent, for example, that on occasion I good-naturedly insist that you part with your eyes by donating them to an eye bank so that I may have the advantage for some period of time of your laser-sharp vision while you make do with my set of eyeballs which, while attractive, are as useless for seeing as a pair of stove lids?

Professor Berlin's paper appeared originally as part of a symposium and references to the ghostly Wohlheim, which crop up here and there, refer to his fellow panelist. Alone of the papers in this section, Berlin's is conceived and executed with no particular passion for a moral position. This gives it an easygoing and even a contemplative air, a relief one would think, after so much self-assured advocacy.

A Theory of Justice, by John Rawls (Harvard University Press) offers an account of the theory of justice from a contractarian rather than a utilitarian point of view. It is a magisterial and influential book. Alfred N. Page's *Utility Theory* (John Wiley & Sons) contains a number of interesting papers that bear on utilitarianism and welfare economics. Some of them are quite technical. Game Theoretic principles that have some relevance to the principle of utility are set out in Duncan Luce and Howard Raiffa's *Games and Decisions* (John Wiley & Sons). Two philosophical works of some recent influence are J. J. C. Smart's *An Outline of a System of Utilitarian Ethics* (Cambridge University Press) and David Lyons's *Forms and Limits of Utilitarianism* (Oxford University Press). Many of the important papers have appeared in the journals. There is, for example, R. F. Harrod's "Utilitarianism Revised," *Mind,* 1936; Jonathan Harrison's "Utilitarianism, Universalization and Our Duty to Be Just," *Proceedings of the Aristotelian Society,* 1952-1953; and J. O. Urmson's "The Interpretation of the Philosophy of J. S. Mill," *Philosophical Quarterly,* 1953.

ARE THERE ANY NATURAL RIGHTS?*[1]

H. L. A. Hart

I shall advance the thesis that if there are any moral rights at all, it follows that there is at least one natural right, the equal right of all men to be free. By saying that there is this right, I mean that in the absence of certain special conditions which are consistent with the right being an equal right, any adult human being capable of choice (1) has the right to forbearance on the part of all others from the use of coercion or restraint against him save to hinder coercion or restraint and (2) is at liberty to do (that is, is under no obligation to abstain from) any action which is not one coercing or restraining or designed to injure other persons.[2]

I have two reasons for describing the equal right of all men to be free as a *natural* right; both of them were always emphasized by the classical theorists of natural rights. (1) This right is one which all men have if they are capable of choice; they have it *qua* men and not only if they are members of some society or stand in some special relation to each other. (2) This right is not created or conferred by men's voluntary action; other moral rights are.[3] Of course, it is quite obvious that my thesis is not as ambitious as the traditional theories of natural rights; for although on my view all men are *equally* entitled to be free in the sense explained, no man has an absolute or unconditional right to do or not to do any particular thing or to be treated in any particular way; coercion or restraint of any action may be justified in special conditions consistently with the general principle. So my argument will not show that men have any right (save the equal right of all to be free) which is "absolute," "indefeasible," or "imprescriptible." This may for many reduce the importance of my contention, but I think that the principle that all men have an equal right to be

*Reprinted by permission from H. L. A. Hart, "Are There Any Natural Rights?", *Philosophical Review*, vol. 64, no. 2 (April 1955).

free, meager as it may seem, is probably all that the political philosophers of the liberal tradition need have claimed to support any program of action even if they have claimed more. But my contention that there is this one natural right may appear unsatisfying in another respect; it is only the conditional assertion that *if* there are any moral rights then there must be this one natural right. Perhaps few would now deny, as some have, that there are moral rights; for the point of that denial was usually to object to some philosophical claim as to the "ontological status" of rights, and this objection is now expressed not as a denial that there are any moral rights but as a denial of some assumed logical similarity between sentences used to assert the existence of rights and other kinds of sentences. But it is still important to remember that there may be codes of conduct quite properly termed moral codes (though we can of course say they are "imperfect") which do not employ the notion of *a* right, and there is nothing contradictory or otherwise absurd in a code or morality consisting wholly of prescriptions or in a code which prescribed only what should be done for the realization of happiness or some ideal of personal perfection.[4] Human actions in such systems would be evaluated or criticized as compliances with prescriptions or as *good* or *bad, right* or *wrong, wise* or *foolish, fitting* or *unfitting,* but no one in such a system would have, exercise, or claim rights, or violate or infringe them. So those who lived by such systems could not of course be committed to the recognition of the equal right of all to be free; nor, I think (and this is one respect in which the notion of a right differs from other moral notions), could any parallel argument be constructed to show that, from the bare fact that actions were recognized as ones which ought or ought not to be done, as right, wrong, good or bad, it followed that some specific kind of conduct fell under these categories.

I

(A) Lawyers have for their own purposes carried the dissection of the notion of a legal right some distance, and some of their results[5] are of value in the elucidation of statements of the form "X has a right to" outside legal contexts. There is, of course, no simple identification to be made between moral and legal rights, but there is an intimate connection between the two, and this itself is one feature which distinguishes a moral right from other fundamental moral concepts. It is not merely that as a matter of fact men speak of their moral rights mainly when advocating their incorporation in a legal system, but that the concept of a right belongs to that branch of morality which is specifically concerned to determine when one person's freedom may be limited by another's[6] and so to determine what actions may appropriately be made the subject of coercive legal rules. The words *droit, diritto,* and *Recht,* used by continental jurists, have no simple English translation and seem to English jurists to hover uncertainly between law and morals, but they do in fact mark off an area of morality (the morality of law) which has special characteristics. It is occupied by the concepts of justice, fairness, rights, and obligation (if this last is not used as it is by many moral philosophers as an obscuring general label to cover every action that morally we ought to do or forbear from doing). The most important common characteristic of this group of moral concepts is that there is no incongruity, but a special congruity in the use of force or the threat of force to secure that what is just or fair or someone's right to have done shall in fact be done; for it is in just these circumstances that coercion of another human being is legitimate. Kant, in the *Rechtslehre,* discusses the obligations which arise in this branch of morality under the title of *officia juris,* "which do not require that respect for duty shall be of itself the determining principle of the will," and contrasts them with *officia virtutis,* which have no moral worth unless done for the sake of the moral principle. His point is, I think, that we must distinguish from the rest of morality those principles regulating the proper distribution of human freedom which alone make it morally legitimate for one human being to determine by this choice how another should act; and a certain specific moral value is secured (to be distinguished from moral virtue in which the good will is manifested) if human relationships are conducted in accordance with these principles even though coercion has to be used to secure this, for only if these principles are regarded will freedom be distributed among human beings as it should be. And it is I think a very important feature of a moral right that the possessor of it is conceived as having a moral justification for limiting the freedom of another and that he has this justification not because the action he is entitled to require of another has some moral quality but simply because in the circumstances a certain distribution of human freedom will be maintained if he by his choice is allowed to determine how the other shall act.

(B) I can best exhibit this feature of a moral right by reconsidering the question whether moral rights and "duties"[7] are correlative. The contention that they are means, presumably, that every statement of the form "X has a right to" entails and is entailed by "Y has a duty (not) to," and at this stage we must not assume that the values of the name-variables X and Y must be different persons. Now there is certainly one sense of "a right" (which I have already mentioned) such that it does not follow from X's having a right that X or someone else has any duty. Jurists have isolated rights in this sense and have referred to them as "liberties" just to distinguish them from rights in the centrally important sense of "right" which has "duty" as a correlative. The former sense of "right" is needed to describe those areas of social life where competition is at least morally unobjectionable. Two people walking along both see a ten-dollar bill in the road 20 yards away, and there is no clue as to the owner. Neither of the two are under a "duty" to allow the other to pick it up;

each has in this sense a right to pick it up. Of course there may be many things which each has a "duty" not to do in the course of the race to the spot—neither may kill or wound the other—and corresponding to these "duties" there are rights to forbearances. The moral propriety of all economic competition implies the minimum sense of "a right" in which to say that "X has a right to" means merely that X is under no "duty" not to. Hobbes saw that the expression "a right" could have this sense but he was wrong if he thought that there is no sense in which it does follow from X's having a right that Y has a duty or at any rate an obligation.

(C) More important for our purpose is the question whether for all moral *duties* there are correlative moral rights, because those who have given an affirmative answer to this question have usually assumed without adequate scrutiny that to have a right is simply to be capable of benefiting by the performance of a *duty*, whereas, in fact, this is not a sufficient condition (and probably not a necessary condition) of having a right. Thus animals and babies who stand to benefit by our performance of our *duty* not to treat them ill are said *therefore* to have rights to proper treatment. The full consequence of this reasoning is not usually followed out; most have shrunk from saying that we have rights against ourselves because we stand to benefit from our performance of our duty to keep ourselves alive or develop our talents. But the moral situation which arises from a promise (where the legal-sounding terminology of rights and obligations is most appropriate) illustrates most clearly that the notion of having a right and that of benefiting by the performance of a duty are not identical. X promises Y in return for some favor that he will look after Y's aged mother in his absence. Rights arise out of this transaction, but it is surely Y to whom the promise has been made and not his mother who *has* or *possesses* these rights. Certainly Y's mother is a person concerning whom X has an obligation and a person who will benefit by its performance, but the person *to whom* he has an obligation to look after her is Y. This is something *due to* or *owed to* Y, so it is Y, not his mother, whose right X will disregard and to whom X will have done *wrong* if he fails to keep his promise, though the mother may be physically injured. And it is Y who has a moral *claim* upon X, is *entitled* to have his mother looked after, and who can *waive* the claim and *release* Y from the obligation. Y is, in other words, morally in a position to determine by his choice how X shall act and in this way to limit X's freedom of choice; and it is this fact, not the fact that he stands to benefit, that makes it appropriate to say that he has *a right.* Of course often the person to whom a promise has been made will be the only person who stands to benefit by its performance, but this does not justify the identification of "having a right" with "benefiting by the performance of a duty." It is important for the whole logic of rights that, while the person who stands to benefit by the performance of a duty is discovered by considering what will happen if the duty is not performed, the person who has a right (to whom performance is *owed* or *due*) is discovered by examining the transaction or antecedent situation or relations of the parties out of which the "duty" arises. These considerations should incline us not to extend to animals and babies whom it is wrong to ill treat the notion of a right to proper treatment, for the moral situation can be simply and adequately described here by saying that it is wrong or that we ought not to ill treat them or, in the philosopher's generalized sense of "duty," that we have a duty not to ill treat them.[8] If common usage sanctions talk of the rights of animals or babies, it makes an idle use of the expression "a right," which will confuse the situation with other different moral situations where the expression "a right" has a specific force and cannot be replaced by the other moral expressions which I have mentioned. Perhaps some clarity on this matter is to be gained by considering the force of the preposition "to" in the expression "having a duty to Y" or "being under an obligation to Y" (where "Y" is the name of a person); for it is significantly different from the meaning of "to" in "doing something to Y" or "doing harm to Y," where it indicates the person affected by some action. In the first pair of expressions, "to" obviously does not have this force, but indicates the person to whom the person morally bound is bound. This is an intelligible development of the figure of a bond (*vinculum juris: obligare*); the precise figure is not that of two persons bound by a chain, but of *one* person bound, the other end of the chain lying in the hands of another to use if he chooses.[9] So it appears absurd to speak of having duties or owing obligations to ourselves—of course we may have "duties" not to do harm to ourselves, but what could be meant (once the distinction between these different meanings of "to" has been grasped) by insisting that we have duties or obligations *to* ourselves not to do harm to ourselves?

(D) The essential connection between the notion of a right and the justified limitation of one person's freedom by another may be thrown into relief if we consider codes of behavior which do not purport to confer rights but only to prescribe what shall be done. Most natural law thinkers down to Hooker conceived of natural law in this way: there were natural duties compliance with which would certainly benefit man—things to be done to achieve man's natural end—but not natural rights. And there are of course many types of codes of behavior which only prescribe what is to be done, for example, those regulating certain ceremonies. It would be absurd to regard these codes as conferring rights, but illuminating to contrast them with rules of games, which often create rights, though not, of course, moral rights. But even a code which is plainly a moral code need not establish rights; the Decalogue is perhaps the most important example. Of course, quite apart from heavenly rewards human beings stand to benefit by general obedience to the Ten Commandments: disobedience is wrong and will certainly harm individuals. But it would be a surprising interpretation of them that treated them as conferring rights. In such an interpretation obedience to the Ten Commandments would have to be conceived as due to or owed to individuals, not merely to God, and disobedience not merely as wrong but as *a wrong to* (as well as harm to) individuals. The Commandments would cease to read like penal statutes designed only to rule out certain types of behavior and would have to be thought of as rules placed at the disposal of individuals and regulating the extent to which *they* may demand certain behavior from others. Rights are typically conceived of as *possessed* or *owned by* or *belonging to* individuals, and these expressions reflect the conception of moral rules as not only prescribing conduct but as forming a kind of moral property of individuals to which they are as individuals entitled; only when rules are conceived in this way can we speak of *rights* and *wrongs* as well as right and wrong actions.[10]

II

So far I have sought to establish that to have a right entails having a moral justification for limiting the freedom of another person and for determining how he should act; it is now important to see that the moral justification must be of a special kind if it is to constitute a right, and this will emerge most clearly from an examination of the circumstances in which rights are asserted with the typical expression "I have a right to." It is, I think, the case that this form of words is used in two main types of situations: (A) when the claimant has some special justification for interference with another's freedom which other persons do not have (*"I* have a right to be paid what you promised for my services"); (B) when the claimant is concerned to resist or object to some interference by another person as having no justification (*"I* have a right to say what I think").

(A) *Special rights.* When rights arise out of special transactions between individuals or out of some special relationship in which they stand to each other, both the persons who have the right and those who have the corresponding obligation are limited to the parties to the special transaction or relationship. I call such rights special rights to distinguish them from those moral rights which are thought of as rights against (that is, as imposing obligations upon)[11] everyone, such as those that are asserted when some unjustified interference is made or threatened as in (B) above.

(i) The most obvious cases of special rights are those that arise from promises. By promising to do or not to do something, we voluntarily incur obligations and create or confer rights on those to whom we promise; we alter the existing moral independence of the parties' freedom of choice in relation to some action and create a new moral relationship between them, so that it becomes morally legitimate for the person to whom the promise is given to determine how the promisor shall act. The promisee has a temporary authority or sovereignty in relation to some specific matter over the other's will which we

404

express by saying that the promisor is under an obligation *to* the promisee to do what he has promised. To some philosophers the notion that moral phenomena—rights and duties or obligations—can be brought into existence by the voluntary action of individuals has appeared utterly mysterious; but this, I think, has been so because they have not clearly seen how special the moral notions of a right and an obligation are, nor how peculiarly they are connected with the distribution of freedom of choice; it would indeed be mysterious if we could make actions morally good or bad by voluntary choice. The simplest case of promising illustrates two points characteristic of all special rights: (1) the right and obligation arise not because the promised action has itself any particular moral quality, but just because of the voluntary transaction between the parties; (2) the identity of the parties concerned is vital—only *this* person (the promisee) has the moral justification for determining how the promisor shall act. It is *his* right; only in relation to him is the promisor's freedom of choice diminished, so that if he chooses to release the promisor no one else can complain.

(ii) But a promise is not the only kind of transaction whereby rights are conferred. They may be *accorded* by a person consenting or authorizing another to interfere in matters which but for this consent or authorization he would be free to determine for himself. If I consent to your taking precautions for my health or happiness or authorize you to look after my interests, then you have a right which others have not, and I cannot complain of your interference if it is within the sphere of your authority. This is what is meant by a person surrendering his rights to another; and again the typical characteristics of a right are present in this situation: the person authorized has the right to interfere not because of its intrinsic character but because *these* persons have stood in *this* relationship. No one else (not similarly authorized) has any *right*[12] to interfere in theory even if the person authorized does not exercise his right.

(iii) Special rights are not only those created by the deliberate choice of the party on whom the obligation falls, as they are when they are accorded or spring from promises, and not all obligations to other persons are deliberately incurred, though I think it is true of all special rights that they arise from previous voluntary actions. A third very important source of special rights and obligations which we recognize in many spheres of life is what may be termed mutuality of restrictions, and I think political obligation is intelligible only if we see what precisely this is and how it differs from the other right-creating transactions (consent, promising) to which philosophers have assimilated it. In its bare schematic outline it is this: when a number of persons conduct any joint enterprise according to rules and thus restrict their liberty, those who have submitted to these restrictions when required have a right to a similar submission from those who have benefited by their submission. The rules may provide that officials should have authority to enforce obedience and make further rules, and this will create a structure of legal rights and duties, but the moral obligation to obey the rules in such circumstances is *due to* the cooperating members of the society, and they have the correlative moral right to obedience. In social situations of this sort (of which political society is the most complex example) the obligation to obey the rules is something distinct from whatever other moral reasons there may be for obedience in terms of good consequences (for example, the prevention of suffering); the obligation is due to the cooperating members of the society as such and not because they are human beings on whom it would be wrong to inflict suffering. The utilitarian explanation of political obligations fails to take account of this feature of the situation both in its simple version that the obligation exists because and only if the direct consequences of a particular act of disobedience are worse than obedience, and also in its more sophisticated version that the obligation exists even when this is not so, if disobedience increases the probability that the law in question or other laws will be disobeyed on other occasions when the direct consequences of obedience are better than those of disobedience.

Of course to say that there is such a moral obligation on those who have benefited by the submission of other members of society to restrictive rules to obey these rules in their turn does not entail either that this is the only kind of moral reason for obedience or that there can be no cases where disobedience will be morally justified. There is no contradiction or other impropriety in saying "I have an obligation to do X, someone has a right to ask me to, but I now see I ought not to do it." It will in painful situations sometimes be the lesser of two moral evils to disregard what really are people's rights and not perform our obligations to them. This seems to me particularly obvious from the case of promises: I may promise to do something and thereby incur an obligation just because that is one way in which obligations (to be distinguished from other forms of moral reasons for acting) are created; reflection may show that it would in the circumstances be wrong to keep this promise because of the suffering it might cause, and we can express this by saying "*I ought not* to do it though *I have an obligation to him* to do it" just because the italicized expressions are not synonyms but come from different dimensions of morality. The attempt to explain this situation by saying that our real obligation here is to avoid the suffering and that there is only a prima facie obligation to keep the promise seems to me to confuse two quite different kinds of moral reason, and in practice such a terminology obscures the precise character of what is at stake when "for some greater good" we infringe people's rights or do not perform our obligations to them.

The social-contract theorists rightly fastened on the fact that the obligation to obey the law is not merely a special case of benevolence (direct or indirect), but something which arises between members of a particular political society out of their mutual relationship. Their mistake was to identify *this* right-creating situation of mutual restrictions with the paradigm case of promising; there are of course important similarities, and these are just the points which all special rights have in common, namely, that they arise out of special relationships between human beings and not out of the character of the action to be done or its effects.

(iv) There remains a type of situation which may be thought of as creating rights and obligations: where the parties have a special natural relationship, as in the case of parent and child. The parent's moral right to obedience from his child would I suppose now be thought to terminate when the child reaches the age "of discretion," but the case is worth mentioning because some political philosophies have had recourse to analogies with this case as an explanation of political obligation, and also because even this case has some of the features we have distinguished in special rights, namely, the right arises out of the special relationship of the parties (though it is in this case a natural relationship) and not out of the character of the actions to the performance of which there is a right.

(v) To be distinguished from special rights, of course, are special liberties, where, exceptionally, one person is *exempted* from obligations to which most are subject but does not thereby acquire a *right* to which there is a correlative obligation. If you catch me reading your brother's diary, you say, "You have no right to read it." I say, "I have a right to read it—your brother said I might unless he told me not to, and he has not told me not to." Here I have been specially *licensed* by your brother who had a right to require me not to read his diary, so I am exempted from the moral obligation not to read it, but your brother is under no obligation to let me go on reading it. Cases where *rights,* not liberties, are accorded to manage or interfere with another person's affairs are those where the license is not revocable at will by the person according the right.

(B) *General rights.* In contrast with special rights, which constitute a justification peculiar to the holder of the right for interfering with another's freedom, are general rights, which are asserted defensively, when some unjustified interference is anticipated or threatened, in order to point out that the interference is unjustified. "I have the right to say what I think."[13] "I have the right to worship as I please." Such rights share two important characteristics with special rights. (1) To have them is to have a moral justification for determining how another shall act, namely that he shall not interfere.[14] (2) The moral justification does not arise from the character of the particular action to the performance of which the claimant has a right; what justifies the claim is simply—there being no special relation between him and those who are threatening to interfere to justify that interference—that this is a particular exemplification of the equal right to be free. But there are, of course, striking differences between such defensive general rights and special rights. (1) General rights do not arise out of any special relationship or transaction between men.

(2) They are not rights which are peculiar to those who have them but are rights which all men capable of choice have in the absence of those special conditions which give rise to special rights. (3) General rights have as correlatives obligations not to interfere to which everyone else is subject and not merely the parties to some special relationship or transaction, though of course they will often be asserted when some particular persons threaten to interfere as a moral objection to that interference. To assert a general right is to claim in relation to some particular action the equal right of all men to be free in the absence of any of those special conditions which constitute a special right to limit another's freedom; to assert a special right is to assert in relation to some particular action a right constituted by such special conditions to limit another's freedom. The assertion of general rights directly invokes the principle that all men equally have the right to be free; the assertion of a special right (as I attempt to show in Section III) invokes it indirectly.

III

It is, I hope, clear that unless it is recognized that interference with another's freedom requires a moral justification the notion of a right could have no place in morals; for to assert a right is to assert that there is such a justification. The characteristic function in moral discourse of those sentences in which the meaning of the expression "a right" is to be found—"I have a right to," "You have no right to," "What right have you to?"—is to bring to bear on interferences with another's freedom, or on claims to interfere, a type of moral evaluation or criticism specially appropriate to interference with freedom and characteristically different from the moral criticism of actions made with the use of expressions like *right, wrong, good,* and *bad.* And this is only one of many different types of moral ground for saying "You ought" or "You ought not." The use of the expression "What right have you to?" shows this more clearly, perhaps, than the others, for we use it, just at the point where interference is actual or threatened, to call for the moral *title* of the person addressed to interfere; and we do this often without any suggestion at all that what he proposes to do is otherwise wrong and sometimes with the implication that the same interference on the part of another person would be unobjectionable.

But though our use in moral discourse of a "right" does presuppose the recognition that interference with another's freedom requires a moral justification, this would not itself suffice to establish, except in a sense easily trivialized, that in the recognition of moral rights there is implied the recognition that all men have a right to equal freedom; for unless there is some restriction inherent in the meaning of "a right" on the type of moral justification for interference which can constitute a right, the principle could be made wholly vacuous. It would, for example, be possible to adopt the principle and then assert that some characteristic or behavior of some human beings (that they are improvident, or atheists, or Jews, or Negroes) constitutes a moral justification for interfering with their freedom; *any* differences between men could, so far as my argument has yet gone, be treated as a moral justification for interference and so constitute a right, so that the equal right of all men to be free would be compatible with gross inequality. It may well be that the expression "moral" itself imports some restriction on what can constitute a moral justification for interference which would avoid this consequence, but I cannot myself yet show that this is so. It is, on the other hand, clear to me that the moral justification for interference which is to constitute a *right* to interfere (as distinct from merely making it morally good or desirable to interfere) is restricted to certain special conditions and that this is inherent in the meaning of a "right" (unless this is used so loosely that it could be replaced by the other moral expressions mentioned). Claims to interfere with another's freedom based on the general character of the activities interfered with (for example, the folly or cruelty of "native" practices) or the general character of the parties ("We are Germans; they are Jews") even when well founded are not matters of moral right or obligation. Submission in such cases even where proper is not *due to* or *owed to* the individuals who interfere; it would be equally proper whoever of the same class of persons interfered. Hence other elements in our moral vocabulary suffice to describe this case, and it is confusing here to talk of rights. We saw in Section II that the types of justification for interference involved in special rights was independent of the character of the action to the performance of which there was a right but depended upon certain previous transactions and relations between individuals (such as promises, consent, authorization, submission to mutual restrictions). Two questions here suggest themselves: (1) On what intelligible principle could these bare forms of promising, consenting, submission to mutual restrictions, be either necessary or sufficient, irrespective of their content, to justify interference with another's freedom? (2) What characteristics have these types of transaction or relationship in common? The answer to both these questions is I think this: If we justify interference on such grounds as we give when we claim a moral right, we are in fact indirectly invoking as our justification the principle that all men have an equal right to be free. For we are in fact saying in the case of promises and consents or authorizations that this claim to interfere with another's freedom is justified because he has, in exercise of his equal right to be free, freely chosen to create this claim; and in the case of mutual restrictions we are in fact saying that this claim to interfere with another's freedom is justified because it is fair; and it is fair because only so will there be an equal distribution of restrictions and so of freedom among this group of men. So in the case of special rights as well as of general rights recognition of them implies the recognition of the equal right of all men to be free.

NOTES

1. I was first stimulated to think along these lines by Mr. Stuart Hampshire, and I have reached by different routes a conclusion similar to his.

2. Further explanation of the perplexing terminology of freedom is, I fear, necessary. *Coercion* includes, besides preventing a person from doing what he chooses, making his choice less eligible by threats; *restraint* includes any action designed to make the exercise of choice impossible and so includes killing or enslaving a person. But neither coercion nor restraint includes *competition*. In terms of the distinction between "having a right to" and "being at liberty to," used above and further discussed in Section I, B, all men may have, consistently with the obligation to forbear from coercion, the *liberty* to satisfy if they can such at least of their desires as are not designed to coerce or injure others, even though in fact, owing to scarcity, one man's satisfaction causes another's frustration. In conditions of extreme scarcity this distinction between competition and coercion will not be worth drawing; natural rights are only of importance "where peace is possible" (Locke). Further, freedom (the absence of coercion) can be *valueless* to those victims of unrestricted competition too poor to make use of it; so it will be pedantic to point out to them that though starving they are free. This is the truth exaggerated by the Marxists whose *identification* of poverty with lack of freedom confuses two different evils.

3. Save those general rights which are particular exemplifications of the right of all men to be free.

4. Is the notion of *a* right found in either Plato or Aristotle? There seems to be no Greek word for it as distinct from "right" or "just" (δικαιόν), though expressions like τά ἐμά δικαία are I believe fourth-century legal idioms. The natural expressions in Plato are τό ἐαύτου (ἔχειν) or τά τινι ὀφειλόμενα, but these seem confined to property or debts. There is no place for a moral right unless the moral value of individual freedom is recognized.

5. As W. D. Lamont has seen: cf. his *Principles of Moral Judgment* (Oxford, 1946); for the jurists, cf. Hohfeld's *Fundamental Legal Conceptions* (New Haven, 1923).

6. Here and subsequently I use "interfere with another's freedom," "limit another's freedom," "determine how another shall act," to mean either the use of coercion or demanding that a person shall do or not do some action. The connection between these two types of "interference" is too complex for discussion here; I think it is enough for present purposes to point out that having a justification for demanding that a person shall or shall not do some action is a necessary though not a sufficient condition for justifying coercion.

7. I write " 'duties' " here because one factor obscuring the nature of a right is the philosophical use of "duty" and "obligation" for all cases where there are moral reasons for saying an action ought to be done or not done. In fact "duty," "obligation," "right," and "good" come from different segments of morality, concern different types of conduct, and make different types of moral criticism or evaluation. Most important are the points (1) that obligations may be voluntarily incurred or created, (2) that they are *owed to* special persons (who have rights), (3) that they do not arise out of the character of the actions which are obligatory but out of the relationship of the parties. Language roughly though not consistently confines the use of "having an obligation" to such cases.

8. The use here of the generalized "duty" is apt to prejudice the question whether animals and babies have rights.

9. Cf. A. H. Campbell, *The Structure of Stair's Institutes* (Glasgow, 1954), p. 31.

10. Continental jurists distinguish between "*subjektives*" and "*objektives Recht,*" which corresponds very well to the distinction between *a* right, which an individual has, and what it is right to do.

11. Cf. Section (B) below.

12. Though it may be *better* (the lesser of two evils) that he should.

410

13. In speech the difference between general and special rights is often marked by stressing the pronoun where a special right is claimed or where the special right is denied. "You have no right to stop him reading that book" refers to the reader's general right. "*You* have no right to stop him reading that book" denies that the person addressed has a special right to interfere though others may have.

14. Strictly, in the assertion of a general right both the *right* to forbearance from coercion and the *liberty* to do the specified action are asserted, the first in the face of actual or threatened coercion, the second as an objection to an actual or anticipated demand that the action should not be done. The first has as its correlative an obligation upon everyone to forbear from coercion; the second the absence in any one of a justification for such a demand. Here, in Hohfeld's words, the correlative is not an obligation but a "no-right."

EXTREME
AND
RESTRICTED
UTILITARIANISM*
J. J. C. Smart

I

Utilitarianism is the doctrine that the rightness of actions is to be judged by their consequences. What do we mean by *actions* here? Do we mean particular actions or do we mean classes of actions? According to which way we interpret the word *actions* we get two different theories, both of which merit the appelation *utilitarian*.

(1) If by *actions* we mean particular individual actions, we get the sort of doctrine held by Bentham, Sidgwick, and Moore. According to this doctrine we test individual actions by their consequences, and general rules, like "keep promises," are mere rules of thumb which we use only to avoid the necessity of estimating the probable consequences of our actions at every step. The rightness or wrongness of keeping a promise on a particular occasion depends only on the goodness or badness of the consequences of keeping or of breaking the promise on that particular occasion. Of course part of the consequences of breaking the promise, and a part to which we will normally ascribe decisive importance, will be the weakening of faith in the institution of promising. However, if the goodness of the consequences of breaking the rule is in toto greater than the goodness of the consequences of keeping it, then we must break the rule, irrespective of whether the goodness of the consequences of *everybody's* obeying the rule is or is not greater than the consequences of *everybody's* breaking it. To put it

*From *The Philosophical Quarterly,* Vol. VI (1956), 344-354, with revisions. Reprinted by permission of the author and *The Philosophical Quarterly.* The major revision which Professor Smart has made occurs on pp. 351-2 of the original publication concerning a game theoretical solution of the act-utilitarian's problem. Since publication of this article Professor Smart has preferred to follow Brandt's terminology of "act-" and "rule-utilitarianism" instead of "extreme" and "restricted utilitarianism."

shortly, rules do not matter, save *per accidens* as rules of thumb and as de facto social institutions with which the utilitarian has to reckon when estimating consequences. I shall call this doctrine "extreme utilitarianism."

(2) A more modest form of utilitarianism has recently become fashionable. The doctrine is to be found in Toulmin's book *The Place of Reason in Ethics,* in Nowell-Smith's *Ethics* (though I think Nowell-Smith has qualms), in John Austin's *Lectures on Jurisprudence* (Lecture II), and even in J. S. Mill, if Urmson's interpretation of him is correct (*Philosophical Quarterly*, vol. 3, pp. 33-39, 1953). Part of its charm is that it appears to resolve the dispute in moral philosophy between intuitionists and utilitarians in a way which is very neat. The above philosophers hold, or seem to hold, that moral rules are more than rules of thumb. In general the rightness of an action is *not* to be tested by evaluating its consequences but only by considering whether or not it falls under a certain rule. Whether the rule is to be considered an acceptable moral rule, is, however, to be decided by considering the consequences of adopting the rule. Broadly, then, actions are to be tested by rules and rules by consequences. The only cases in which we must test an individual action directly by its consequences are (*a*) when the action comes under two different rules, one of which enjoins it and one of which forbids it, and (*b*) when there is no rule whatever that governs the given case. I shall call this doctrine "restricted utilitarianism."

It should be noticed that the distinction I am making cuts across, and is quite different from, the distinction commonly made between hedonistic and ideal utilitarianism. Bentham was an extreme hedonistic utilitarian and Moore an extreme ideal utilitarian, and Toulmin (perhaps) could be classified as a restricted ideal utilitarian. A hedonistic utilitarian holds that the goodness of the consequences of an action is a function only of their pleasurableness and an ideal utilitarian, like Moore, holds that pleasurableness is not even a necessary condition of goodness. Mill seems, if we are to take his remarks about higher and lower pleasures seriously, to be neither a pure hedonistic nor a pure ideal utilitarian. He seems to hold that pleasurableness is a necessary condition for goodness, but that goodness is a function of other qualities of mind as well. Perhaps we can call his a quasi-ideal utilitarian. When we say that a state of mind is good, I take it that we are expressing some sort of *rational preference*. When we say that it is pleasurable I take it that we are saying that it is enjoyable, and when we say that something is a higher pleasure I take it that we are saying that it is more truly, or more deeply, enjoyable. I am doubtful whether "more deeply enjoyable" does not just mean "more enjoyable, even though not more enjoyable on a first look," and so I am doubtful whether quasi-ideal utilitarianism, and possibly ideal utilitarianism too, would not collapse into hedonistic utilitarianism on a closer scrutiny of the logic of words like *preference, pleasure, enjoy, deeply enjoy,* and so on. However, it is beside the point of the present paper to go into these questions. I am here concerned only with the issue

413

between extreme and restricted utilitarianism and am ready to concede that both forms of utilitarianism can be either hedonistic or nonhedonistic.

The issue between extreme and restricted utilitarianism can be illustrated by considering the remark "But suppose everyone did the same." (Cf. A. K. Stout's article in *The Australasian Journal of Philosophy,* vol. 32, pp. 1-29.) Stout distinguishes two forms of the universalization principle, the causal form and the hypothetical form. To say that you ought not to do an action A because it would have bad results if everyone (or many people) did action A may be merely to point out that while the action A would otherwise be the optimific one, nevertheless when you take into account that doing A will probably cause other people to do A too, you can see that A is not, on a broad view, really optimific. If this causal influence could be avoided (as may happen in the case of a secret desert island promise) then we would disregard the universalization principle. This is the causal form of the principle. A person who accepted the universalization principle in its hypothetical form would be one who was concerned only with what would happen *if* everyone did the action A: he would be totally unconcerned with the question of whether in fact everyone would do the action A. That is, he might say that it would be wrong not to vote because it would have bad results if everyone took this attitude, and he would be totally unmoved by arguments purporting to show that my refusing to vote has no effect whatever on other people's propensity to vote. Making use of Stout's distinction, we can say that an extreme utilitarian would apply the universalization principle in the causal form, while a restricted utilitarian would apply it in the hypothetical form.

How are we to decide the issue between extreme and restricted utilitarianism? I wish to repudiate at the outset that milk-and-water approach which describes itself sometimes as "investigating what is implicit in the common moral consciousness" and sometimes as "investigating how people ordinarily talk about morality." We have only to read the newspaper correspondence about capital punishment or about what should be done with Formosa to realize that the common moral consciousness is in part made up of superstitious elements, of morally bad elements, and of logically confused elements. I address myself to good-hearted and benevolent people and so I hope that if we rid ourselves of the logical confusion the superstitious and morally bad elements will largely fall away. For even among good-hearted and benevolent people it is possible to find superstitious and morally bad reasons for moral beliefs. These superstitious and morally bad reasons hide behind the protective screen of logical confusion. With people who are not logically confused but who are openly superstitious or morally bad I can of course do nothing. That is, our ultimate pro-attitudes may be different. Nevertheless I propose to rely on *my own* moral consciousness and to appeal to *your* moral consciousness and to forget about what people ordinarily say. "The obligation to obey a rule," says Nowell-Smith (*Ethics,*

p. 239), "does not, *in the opinion of ordinary men*," (my italics), "rest on the beneficial consequences of obeying it in a particular case." What does this prove? Surely it is more than likely that ordinary men are confused here. Philosophers should be able to examine the question more rationally.

II

For an extreme utilitarian, moral rules are rules of thumb. In practice, the extreme utilitarian will mostly guide his conduct by appealing to the rules ("do not lie," "do not break promises," etc.) of commonsense morality. This is not because there is anything sacrosanct in the rules themselves but because he can argue that probably he will most often act in an extreme utilitarian way if he does not think as a utilitarian. For one thing, actions have frequently to be done in a hurry. Imagine a man seeing a person drowning. He jumps in and rescues him. There is no time to reason the matter out, but usually this will be the course of action which an extreme utilitarian would recommend if he did reason the matter out. If, however, the man drowning had been drowning in a river near Berchtesgaden in 1938, and if he had had the well-known black forelock and moustache of Adolf Hitler, an extreme utilitarian would, if he had time, work out the probability of the man's being the villainous dictator, and if the probability were high enough he would, on extreme utilitarian grounds, leave him to drown. The rescuer, however, has not time. He trusts to his instincts and dives in and rescues the man. And this trusting to instincts and to moral rules can be justified on extreme utilitarian grounds. Furthermore, an extreme utilitarian who knew that the drowning man was Hitler would nevertheless praise the rescuer, not condemn him, for by praising the man, he is strengthening a courageous and benevolent disposition of mind, and in general this disposition has great positive utility. We must never forget that an extreme utilitarian may praise actions which he knows to be wrong. Saving Hitler was wrong, but it was a member of a class of actions which are generally right, and the motive to do actions of this class is in general an optimific one. In considering questions of praise and blame it is not the expediency of the praised or blamed action that is at issue, but the expediency of the praise. It can be expedient to praise an inexpedient action and inexpedient to praise an expedient one.

Lack of time is not the only reason why an extreme utilitarian may, on extreme utilitarian principles, trust to roles of commonsense morality. He knows that in particular cases where his own interests are involved his calculations are likely to be biased in his own favor. Suppose that he is unhappily married and is deciding whether to get divorced. He will in all probability greatly exaggerate his own unhappiness (and possibly his wife's) and greatly underestimate the harm done to his children by the break-up of the

415

family. He will probably also underestimate the likely harm done by the weakening of the general faith in marriage vows. So probably he will come to the correct extreme utilitarian conclusion if he does not in this instance think as an extreme utilitarian but trusts to commonsense morality.

There are many more and subtle points that could be made in connection with the relation between extreme utilitarianism and the morality of common sense. All those that I have just made and many more will be found in Book IV, Chapters 3-5 of Sidgwick's *Methods of Ethics.* I think this book is the best book ever written on ethics, and that these chapters are the best chapters of the book. As they occur so near the end of a very long book, they are unduly neglected. I refer the reader, then, to Sidgwick for the classical exposition of the relation between (extreme) utilitarianism and the morality of common sense. One further point raised by Sidgwick in this connection is whether an (extreme) utilitarian ought on (extreme) utilitarian principles to propagate (extreme) utilitarianism among the public. As most people are not very philosophical and not good at empirical calculations, it is probable that they will most often act in an extreme utilitarian way if they do not try to think as extreme utilitarians. We have seen how easy it would be to misapply the extreme utilitarian criterion in the case of divorce. Sidgwick seems to think it quite probable that an extreme utilitarian should not propagate his doctrine too widely. However, the great danger to humanity comes nowadays on the plane of public morality—not private morality. There is a greater danger to humanity from the hydrogen bomb than from an increase of the divorce rate, regrettable though that might be, and there seems no doubt that extreme utilitarianism makes for good sense in international relations. When France walked out of the United Nations because she did not wish Morocco discussed, she said that she was within her rights because Morocco and Algiers are part of her metropolitan territory and nothing to do with the U.N. This was clearly a legalistic if not superstitious argument. We should not be concerned with the "rights" of France or any other country but with whether the cause of humanity would best be served by discussing Morocco in the U.N. (I am not saying that the answer to this is Yes. There are good grounds for supposing that more harm than good would come by such a discussion.) I myself have no hesitation in saying that on extreme utilitarian principles we ought to propagate extreme utilitarianism as widely as possible. But Sidgwick had respectable reasons for suspecting the opposite.

The extreme utilitarian, then, regards moral rules as rules of thumb and as sociological facts that have to be taken into account when deciding what to do, just as facts of any other sort have to be taken into account. But in themselves they do not justify any action.

III

The restricted utilitarian regards moral rules as more than rules of thumb for short-circuiting calculations of consequences. Generally, he argues, consequences are not relevant at all when we are deciding what to do in a particular case. In general, they are relevant only to deciding what rules are good reasons for acting in a certain way in particular cases. This doctrine is possibly a good account of how the modern unreflective twentieth-century Englishman often thinks about morality, but surely it is monstrous as an account of how it is most rational to think about morality. Suppose that there is a rule R and that in 99 percent of cases the best possible results are obtained by acting in accordance with R. Then clearly R is a useful rule of thumb; if we have not time or are not impartial enough to assess the consequences of an action it is an extremely good bet that the thing to do is to act in accordance with R. But is it not monstrous to suppose that if we *have* worked out the consequences and if we have perfect faith in the impartiality of our calculations, and if we *know* that in this instance to break R will have better results than to keep it, we should nevertheless obey the rule? Is it not to erect R into a sort of idol if we keep it when breaking it will prevent, say, some avoidable misery? Is not this a form of superstitious rule-worship (easily explicable psychologically) and not the rational thought of a philosopher?

The point may be made more clearly if we consider Mill's comparison of moral rules to the tables in the Nautical Almanack. (*Utilitarianism,* Everyman edition, pp. 22-23). This comparison of Mill's is adduced by Urmson as evidence that Mill was a restricted utilitarian, but I do not think that it will bear this interpretation at all. (Though I quite agree with Urmson that many other things said by Mill are in harmony with restricted rather than extreme utilitarianism. Probably Mill had never thought very much about the distinction and was arguing for utilitarianism, restricted or extreme, against other and quite non-utilitarian forms of moral argument.) Mill says: "Nobody argues that the art of navigation is not founded on astronomy, because sailors cannot wait to calculate the Nautical Almanack. Being rational creatures, they go out upon the sea of life with their minds made up on the common questions of right and wrong, as well as on many of the far more difficult questions of wise and foolish. . . . Whatever we adopt as the fundamental principle of morality, we require subordinate principles to apply it by." Notice that this is, as it stands, only an argument for subordinate principles as rules of thumb. The example of the Nautical Almanack is misleading because the information given in the almanack is in all cases the same as the information one would get if one made a long and laborious calculation from the original astronomical data on which the almanack is founded. Suppose, however, that astronomy were different. Suppose that the behavior of the sun, moon, and planets was very nearly as it is now, but that on rare occasions there were peculiar irregularities and discontinuities, so that the almanack gave us rules of the form "in 99 percent of cases where the observations are such and such you can deduce that your position is so and so." Furthermore, let us suppose that there were methods which enabled us, by direct and laborious calculation from the original astronomical data, not using the rough and ready tables of the almanack, to get our correct position in 100 percent of cases. Seafarers might use the almanack because they never had time for the long calculations and they were content with a 99 percent chance of success in calculating their positions. Would it not be absurd, however, if they *did* make the direct calculation, and finding that it disagreed with the almanack calculation, nevertheless they ignored it and stuck to the almanack conclusion? Of course the case would be altered if there were a high enough probability of making slips in the direct calculation: then we might stick to the almanack result, liable to error though we knew it to be, simply because the direct calculation would be open to error for a different reason, the fallibility of the computer. This would be analogous to the case of the extreme utilitarian who abides by the conventional rule against the dictates of his utilitarian calculations simply because he thinks that his calculations are probably affected by personal bias. But if the navigator were sure of his direct calculations would he not be foolish to abide by his almanack? I conclude, then, that if we change our suppositions about astronomy and the almanack (to which there are no exceptions) to bring the case into line with that of morality (to whose rules there are exceptions), Mill's example loses its appearance of supporting the restricted form of utilitarianism. Let me say once more that I am not here concerned with how ordinary men think about morality but with how they ought to think. We could quite well imagine a race of sailors who acquired a superstitious reverence for their alamanck, even though it was only right in 99 percent of cases, and who indignantly threw overboard any man who mentioned the possibility of a direct calculation. But would this behavior of the sailors be rational?

Let us consider a much discussed sort of case in which the extreme utilitarian might go against the conventional moral rule. I have promised to a friend, dying on a desert island from which I am subsequently rescued, that I will see that his fortune (over which I have control) is given to a jockey club. However, when I am rescued I decide that it would be better to give the money to a hospital, which can do more good with it. It may be argued that I am wrong to give the money to the hospital. But why? (*a*) The hospital can do more good with the money than the jockey club can. (*b*) The present case is unlike most cases of promising in that no one except me knows about the promise. In breaking the promise I am doing so with complete secrecy and am doing nothing to weaken the general faith in promises. That is, a factor, which would normally keep the extreme utilitarian from promise breaking even in otherwise unoptimific cases, does not at present operate. (*c*) There is no doubt a slight weakening in my own character as an habitual promise keeper, and moreover psychological tensions will be set up in me every time I am asked what the man made me promise him to do. For clearly I shall have to say that he made me promise to give the money to the hospital, and since I am an habitual truth teller, this will go very much against the grain with me. Indeed I am pretty sure that in practice I myself would keep the promise. But we are not discussing what my moral habits would probably make me do; we are discussing what I ought to do. Moreover, we must not forget that even if it would be most rational of me to give the money to the hospital it would also be most rational of you to punish or condemn me if you did, most improbably, find out the truth (for example, by finding a note washed ashore in a bottle). Furthermore, I would agree that though it was most rational of me to give the money to the hospital it would be most rational of you to condemn me for it. We revert again to Sidgwick's distinction between the utility of the action and the utility of the praise of it.

Many such issues are discussed by A. K. Stout in the article to which I have already referred. I do not wish to go over the same ground again, especially as I think that Stout's arguments support my own point of view. It will be useful, however, to consider one other example that he gives. Suppose that during hot weather there is an edict that no water must be used for watering gardens. I have a garden and I reason that most people are sure to obey the edict, and that as the amount of water that I use will be by itself negligible no harm will be done if I use the water secretly. So I do use the water, thus producing some lovely flowers which give happiness to various people. Still, you may say, though the action was perhaps optimific, it was unfair and wrong.

There are several matters to consider. Certainly my action should be condemned. We revert once more to Sidgwick's distinction. A right action may be rationally condemned. Furthermore, this sort of offense is normally found out. If I have a wonderful garden when everybody else's is dry and brown there is only one explanation. So if I water my garden I am weakening my respect for law and order, and as this leads to bad results an extreme utilitarian would agree that I was wrong to water the garden. Suppose now that the case is altered and that I can keep the thing secret: there is a secluded part of the garden where I grow flowers which I give away anonymously to a home for old ladies. Are you still so sure that I did the wrong thing by watering my garden? However, this is still a weaker case than that of the hospital and the jockey club. There will be tensions set up within myself: my secret knowledge that I have broken the rule will make it hard for me to exhort others to keep the rule. These psychological ill effects in myself may be not inconsiderable: directly and indirectly they may lead to harm which is at least of the same order as the happiness that the old ladies get from the flowers. You can see that on an extreme utilitarian view there are two sides to the question.

So far I have been considering the duty of an extreme utilitarian in a predominantly non-utilitarian society. The case is altered if we consider the extreme utilitarian who lives in a society every member, or most members, of which can be expected to reason as he does. Should he water his flowers now?

(Granting, what is doubtful, that in the case already considered he would have been right to water his flowers.) Clearly not. A simple argument, employing the game-theoretical concept of a mixed strategy, suggests that each extreme utilitarian should give himself a very small probability (say by tossing dice) of watering his garden. Suppose that there are m potential garden waterers and that $f(n)$ is the damage done by exactly n people watering their gardens. Now if each of them gives himself a probability p of watering his garden it is easy to calculate, in terms of p, the probability of $p_1, p_2, \ldots p_m$ of $1, 2, \ldots m$ persons respectively watering their gardens. Let a be the benefit to each gardener of watering his garden. Then if V is the total probable benefit to the community of gardeners we have:

$$V = p_1(a - f(1)) + p_2(2a - f(2)) + \ldots p_m(ma - f(m))$$

Assuming that numerical values can be given to a and to values of the function $f(n)$ we calculate the value of p for which $\dfrac{dV}{dp} = 0$. This gives the value of p which maximizes the total probable benefit. In practical cases of course numerical values of $f(n)$ and a cannot be determined, but a good approximation can usually be got by taking p as equal to zero. However the mathematical analysis is of theoretical interest for the discussion of utilitarianism. Too many writers mistakenly suppose that the only two relevant alternatives are that no one does something and that everyone does it.

I now pass on to a type of case which may be thought to be the trump card of restricted utilitarianism. Consider the rule of the road. It may be said that since all that matters is that everyone should do the same it is indifferent which rule we have, "go on the left hand side" or "go on the right hand side." Hence the only *reason* for going on the left hand side in British countries is that this is the rule. Here the rule does seem to be a reason, in itself, for acting in a certain way. I wish to argue against this. The rule in itself is not a reason for our actions. We would be perfectly justified in going on the right hand side if (*a*) we knew that the rule was to go on the left hand side, and (*b*) we were in a country peopled by super-anarchists who always on principle did the opposite of what they were told. This shows that the rule does not give us a reason for acting so much as an indication of the probable actions of others, which helps us to find out what would be our own most rational course of action. If we are in a country not peopled by anarchists, but by non-anarchist extreme utilitarians, we expect, other things being equal, that they will keep rules laid down for them. Knowledge of the rule enables us to predict their behavior and to harmonize our own actions with theirs. The rule "keep to the left hand side," then, is not a logical *reason* for action but an anthropological *datum* for planning actions.

I conclude that in every case if there is a rule R the keeping of which is in general optimific, but such that in a special sort of circumstances the optimific behavior is to break R, then in these circumstances we should break R. Of course we must consider all the less obvious effects of breaking R, such as reducing people's faith in the moral order, before coming to the conclusion that to break R is right: in fact we shall rarely come to such a conclusion. Moral rules, on the extreme utilitarian view, are rules of thumb only, but they are not bad rules of thumb. But if we *do* come to the conclusion that we should break the rule and if we have weighed in the balance our own fallibility and liability to personal bias, what good reason remains for keeping the rule? I can understand "it is optimific" as a reason for action, but why should "it is a member of a class of actions which are usually optimific" or "it is a member of a class of actions which as a class are more optimific than any alternative general class" be a good reason? You might as well say that a person ought to be picked to play for Australia just because all his brothers have been, or that the Australian team should be composed entirely of the Harvey family because this would be better than composing it entirely of any other family. The extreme utilitarian does not appeal to artificial feelings, but only to our feelings of benevolence, and what better feelings can there be to appeal to? Admittedly we can have a pro-attitude to anything, even to rules, but such artificially begotten pro-attitudes smack of superstition. Let us get down to realities, human happiness and misery, and make these the objects of our pro-attitudes and anti-attitudes.

The restricted utilitarian might say he is talking only of *morality*, not of such things as rules of the road. I am not sure how far this objection, if valid, would affect my argument, but in any case I would reply that as a philosopher I conceive of ethics as the study of how it would be *most rational* to act. If my opponent wishes to restrict the word "morality" to a narrower use he can have the word. The fundamental question is the question of rationality of action *in general.* Similarly if the restricted utilitarian were to appeal to ordinary usage and say "it might be most rational to leave Hitler to drown but it would surely not be *wrong* to rescue him," I should again let him have the words "right" and "wrong" and should stick to "rational" and "irrational." We already saw that it would be rational to praise Hitler's rescuer, even though it would have been most rational not to have rescued Hitler. In ordinary language, no doubt, "right" and "wrong" have not only the meaning "most rational to do" and "not most rational to do" but also have the meaning "praiseworthy" and "not praise-worthy." Usually to the utility of an action corresponds utility of praise of it, but as we saw, this is not always so. Moral language could thus do with tidying up, for example by reserving "right" for "most rational" and "good" as an epithet of praise for the motive from which the action sprang. It would be more becoming in a philosopher to try to iron out illogicalities in moral language and to make suggestions for its reform than to use it as a court of appeal whereby to perpetuate confusions.

One last defense of restricted utilitarianism might be as follows. "Act optimifically" might be regarded as itself one of the rules of our system (though it would be odd to say that this rule was justified by its optimificality). According to Toulmin (*The Place of Reason in Ethics,* pp. 146-48) if "keep promises," say, conflicts with another rule we are allowed to argue the case on its merits, as if we were extreme utilitarians. If "act optimifically" is itself one of our rules then there will always be a conflict of rules whenever to keep a rule is not itself optimific. If this is so, restricted utilitarianism collapses into extreme utilitarianism. And no one could read Toulmin's book or Urmson's article on Mill without thinking that Toulmin and Urmson are of the opinion that they have thought of a doctrine which does *not* collapse into extreme utilitarianism, but which is, on the contrary, an improvement on it.

JUSTICE
AS
FAIRNESS*
John Rawls

1. It might seem at first sight that the concepts of justice and fairness are the same, and that there is no reason to distinguish them, or to say that one is more fundamental than the other. I think that this impression is mistaken. In this paper I wish to show that the fundamental idea in the concept of justice is fairness; and I wish to offer an analysis of the concept of justice from this point of view. To bring out the force of this claim, and the analysis based upon it, I shall then argue that it is this aspect of justice for which utilitarianism, in its classical form, is unable to account, but which is expressed, even if misleadingly, by the idea of the social contract.

To start with I shall develop a particular conception of justice by stating and commenting upon two principles which specify it, and by considering the circumstances and conditions under which they may be thought to arise. The principles defining this conception, and the conception itself, are, of course, familiar. It may be possible, however, by using the notion of fairness as a framework, to assemble and to look at them in a new way. Before stating this conception, however, the following preliminary matters should be kept in mind.

Throughout I consider justice only as a virtue of social institutions, or what I shall call practices.[2] The principles of justice are regarded as formulating restrictions as to how practices may define positions and offices, and assign thereto powers and liabilities, rights and duties. Justice as a virtue of particular actions or of persons I do not take up at all. It is important to distinguish these various subjects of justice, since the meaning of the concept varies according to whether it is applied to practices, particular actions, or persons. These meanings are, indeed, connected, but they are not identical. I shall confine my discussion

*Reprinted by permission from John Rawls, "Justice as Fairness," *Philosophical Review,* April 1958.

to the sense of justice as applied to practices, since this sense is the basic one. Once it is understood, the other senses should go quite easily.

Justice is to be understood in its customary sense as representing but *one* of the many virtues of social institutions, for these may be antiquated, inefficient, degrading, or any number of other things, without being unjust. Justice is not to be confused with an all-inclusive vision of a good society; it is only part of any such conception. It is important, for example, to distinguish that sense of equality which belongs to a more comprehensive social ideal. There may well be inequalities which one concedes are just, or at least not unjust, but which, nevertheless, one wishes, on other grounds to do away with. I shall focus attention, then, on the usual sense of justice in which it is essentially the elimination of arbitrary distinctions and the establishment, within the structure of a practice, of a proper balance between competing claims.

Finally, there is no need to consider the principles discussed below as *the* principles of justice. For the moment it is sufficient that they are typical of a family of principles normally associated with the concept of justice. The way in which the principles of this family resemble one another, as shown by the background against which they may be thought to arise, will be made clear by the whole of the subsequent argument.

2. The conception of justice which I want to develop may be stated in the form of two principles as follows: first, each person participating in a practice, or affected by it, has an equal right to the most extensive liberty compatible with a like liberty for all; and second, inequalities are arbitrary unless it is reasonable to expect that they will work out for everyone's advantage, and provided the positions and offices to which they attach, or from which they may be gained, are open to all. These principles express justice as a complex of three ideas: liberty, equality, and reward for services contributing to the common good.[3]

The term "person" is to be construed variously depending on the circumstances. On some occasions it will mean human individuals, but on others it may refer to nations, provinces, business firms, churches, teams, and so on. The principles of justice apply in all these instances, although there is a certain logical priority to the case of human individuals. As I shall use the term "person," it will be ambiguous in the manner indicated.

The first principle holds, of course, only if other things are equal: that is, while there must always be a justification for departing from the initial position of equal liberty (which is defined by the pattern of rights and duties, powers and liabilities, established by a practice), and the burden of proof is placed on him who would depart from it, nevertheless, there can be, and often there is, a justification for doing so. Now, that similar particular cases, as defined by a practice, should be treated similarly as they arise, is part of the very concept of a practice; it is involved in the notion of an activity in accordance with rules.[4] The first principle expresses an analogous conception, but as applied to the structure of practices themselves. It holds, for example, that there is a presumption against the distinctions and classifications made by legal systems and other practices to the extent that they infringe on the original and equal liberty of the persons participating in them. The second principle defines how this presumption may be rebutted.

It might be argued at this point that justice requires only an equal liberty If, however, a greater liberty were possible for all without loss or conflict, then it would be irrational to settle on a lesser liberty. There is no reason for circumscribing rights unless their exercise would be incompatible, or would render the practice defining them less effective. Therefore no serious distortion of the concept of justice is likely to follow from including within it the concept of the greatest equal liberty.

The second principle defines what sorts of inequalities are permissible; it specifies how the presumption laid down by the first principle may be put aside. Now by inequalities it is best to understand not *any* differences between offices and positions, but differences in the benefits and burdens attached to them either directly or indirectly, such as prestige and wealth, or liability to taxation and compulsory services. Players in a game do not protest against there being different positions, such as batter, pitcher, catcher, and the like, nor to there being various privileges and powers as specified by the rules; nor do the citizens of a country object to there being the different offices of government such as president, senator, governor, judge, and so on, each with their special rights and duties. It is not differences of this kind that are normally thought of as inequalities, but differences in the resulting distribution established by a practice, or made possible by it, of the things men strive to attain or avoid. Thus they may complain about the pattern of honors and rewards set up by a practice (e.g., the privileges and salaries of government officials) or they may object to the distribution of power and wealth which results from the various ways in which men avail themselves of the opportunities allowed by it (e.g., the concentration of wealth which may develop in a free price system allowing large entrepreneurial or speculative gains).

It should be noted that the second principle holds that an inequality is allowed only if there is reason to believe that the practice with the inequality, or resulting in it, will work for the advantage of *every* party engaging in it. Here it is important to stress that *every* party must gain from the inequality. Since the principle applies to practices, it implies that the representative man in every office or position defined by a practice, when he views it as a going concern, must find it reasonable to prefer his condition and prospects with the inequality to what they would be under the practice without it. The principle excludes, therefore, the justification of inequalities on the grounds that the disadvantages of those in one position are outweighed by the greater advantages of

425

those in another position. This rather simple restriction is the main modification I wish to make in the utilitarian principle as usually understood. When coupled with the notion of a practice, it is a restriction of consequence,[5] and one which some utilitarians, e.g., Hume and Mill, have used in their discussions of justice without realizing apparently its significance, or at least without calling attention to it.[6] Why it is a significant modification of principle, changing one's conception of justice entirely, the whole of my argument will show.

Further, it is also necessary that the various offices to which special benefits or burdens attach are open to all. It may be, for example, to the common advantage, as just defined, to attach special benefits to certain offices. Perhaps by doing so the requisite talent can be attracted to them and encouraged to give its best efforts. But any offices having special benefits must be won in a fair competition in which contestants are judged on their merits. If some offices were not open, those excluded would normally be justified in feeling unjustly treated, even if they benefited from the greater efforts of those who were allowed to compete for them. Now if one can assume that offices are open, it is necessary only to consider the design of practices themselves and how they jointly, as a system, work together. It will be a mistake to focus attention on the varying relative positions of particular persons, who may be known to us by their proper names, and to require that each such change, as a once for all transaction viewed in isolation, must be in itself just. It is the system of practices which is to be judged, and judged from a general point of view: unless one is prepared to criticize it from the standpoint of a representative man holding some particular office, one has no complaint against it.

3. Given these principles one might try to derive them from a priori principles of reason, or claim that they were known by intuition. These are familiar enough steps and, at least in the case of the first principle, might be made with some success. Usually, however, such arguments, made at this point, are unconvincing. They are not likely to lead to an understanding of the basis of the principles of justice, not at least as principles of justice. I wish, therefore, to look at the principles in a different way.

Imagine a society of persons amongst whom a certain system of practices is *already* well established. Now suppose that by and large they are mutually self-interested; their allegiance to their established practices is normally founded on the prospect of self-advantage. One need not assume that, in all senses of the term "person," the persons in this society are mutually self-interested. If the characterization as mutually self-interested applies when the line of division is the family, it may still be true that members of families are bound by ties of sentiment and affection and willingly acknowledge duties in contradiction to self-interest. Mutual self-interestedness in the relations between families, nations, churches, and the like, is commonly associated with intense loyalty and devotion on the part of individual members. Therefore, one can form a more realistic conception of this society if one thinks of it as consisting of mutually self-interested families, or some other association. Further, it is not necessary to suppose that these persons are mutually self-interested under all circumstances, but only in the usual situations in which they participate in their common practices.

Now suppose also that these persons are rational: they know their own interests more or less accurately; they are capable of tracing out the likely consequences of adopting one practice rather than another; they are capable of adhering to a course of action once they have decided upon it; they can resist present temptations and the enticements of immediate gain; and the bare knowledge or perception of the difference between their condition and that of others is not, within certain limits and in itself, a source of great dissatisfaction. Only the last point adds anything to the usual definition of rationality. This definition should allow, I think, for the idea that a rational man would not be greatly downcast from knowing, or seeing, that others are in a better position than himself, unless he thought their being so was the result of injustice, or the consequence of letting chance work itself out for no useful common purpose, and so on. So if these persons strike us as unpleasantly egoistic, they are at least free in some degree from the fault of envy.[7]

Finally, assume that these persons have roughly similar needs and interests, or needs and interests in various ways complementary, so that fruitful cooperation amongst them is possible; and suppose that they are sufficiently equal in power and ability to guarantee that in normal circumstances none is able to dominate the others. This condition (as well as the others) may seem excessively vague; but in view of the conception of justice to which the argument leads, there seems no reason for making it more exact here.

Since these persons are conceived as engaging in their common practices, which are already established, there is no question of our supposing them to come together to deliberate as to how they will set these practices up for the first time. Yet we can imagine that from time to time they discuss with one another whether any of them has a legitimate complaint against their established institutions. Such discussions are perfectly natural in any normal society. Now suppose that they have settled on doing this in the following way. They first try to arrive at the principles by which complaints, and so practices themselves, are to be judged. Their procedure for this is to let each person propose the principles upon which he wishes his complaints to be tried with the understanding that, if acknowledged, the complaints of others will be similarly tried, and that no complaints will be heard at all until everyone is roughly of one mind as to how complaints are to be judged. They each understand further that the principles proposed and acknowledged on this occasion are binding on future occasions. Thus each will be wary of proposing a principle which would give him a peculiar advantage, in his present circumstances, supposing it to be

427

accepted. Each person knows that he will be bound by it in future circumstances the peculiarities of which cannot be known, and which might well be such that the principle is then to his disadvantage. The idea is that everyone should be required to make *in advance* a firm commitment, which others also may reasonably be expected to make, and that no one be given the opportunity to tailor the canons of a legitimate complaint to fit his own special condition, and then to discard them when they no longer suit his purpose. Hence each person will propose principles of a general kind which will, to a large degree, gain their sense from the various applications to be made of them, the particular circumstances of which being as yet unknown. These principles will express the conditions in accordance with which each is the least unwilling to have his interests limited in the design of practices, given the competing interests of the others, on the supposition that the interests of others will be limited likewise. The restrictions which would so arise might be thought of as those a person would keep in mind if he were designing a practice in which his enemy were to assign him his place.

The two main parts of this conjectural account have a definite significance. The character and respective situations of the parties reflect the typical circumstances in which questions of justice arise. The procedure whereby principles are proposed and acknowledged represents constraints, analogous to those of having a morality, whereby rational and mutually self-interested persons are brought to act reasonably. Thus the first part reflects the fact that questions of justice arise when conflicting claims are made upon the design of a practice and where it is taken for granted that each person will insist, as far as possible, on what he considers his rights. It is typical of cases of justice to involve persons who are pressing on one another their claims, between which a fair balance or equilibrium must be found. On the other hand, as expressed by the second part, having a morality must at least imply the acknowledgment of principles as impartially applying to one's own conduct as well as to another's, and moreover principles which may constitute a constraint, or limitation, upon the pursuit of one's own interests. There are, of course, other aspects of having a morality: the acknowledgment of moral principles must show itself in accepting a reference to them as reasons for limiting one's claims, in acknowledging the burden of providing a special explanation, or excuse, when one acts contrary to them, or else in showing shame and remorse and a desire to make amends, and so on. It is sufficient to remark here that having a morality is analogous to having made a firm commitment in advance; for one must acknowledge the principles of morality even when to one's disadvantage.[8] A man whose moral judgments always coincided with his interests could be suspected of having no morality at all.

Thus the two parts of the foregoing account are intended to mirror the kinds of circumstances in which questions of justice arise and the constraints which having a morality would impose upon persons so situated. In this way one can see how the acceptance of the principles of justice might come about, for given all these conditions as described, it would be natural if the two principles of justice were to be acknowledged. Since there is no way for anyone to win special advantages for himself, each might consider it reasonable to acknowledge equality as an initial principle. There is, however, no reason why they should regard this position as final; for if there are inequalities which satisfy the second principle, the immediate gain which equality would allow can be considered as intelligently invested in view of its future return. If, as is quite likely, these inequalities work as incentives to draw out better efforts, the members of this society may look upon them as concessions to human nature: they, like us, may think that people ideally should want to serve one another. But as they are mutually self-interested, their acceptance of these inequalities is merely the acceptance of the relations in which they actually stand, and a recognition of the motives which lead them to engage in their common practices. *They* have no title to complain to one another. And so provided that the conditions of the principle are met, there is no reason why they should not allow such inequalities. Indeed, it would be short-sighted of them to do so, and could result, in most cases, only from their being dejected by the bare knowledge, or perception, that others are better situated. Each person will, however, insist on an advantage to himself, and so on a common advantage, for none is willing to sacrifice anything for the others.

These remarks are not offered as a proof that persons so conceived and circumstanced would settle on the two principles, but only to show that these principles could have such a background, and so can be viewed as those principles which mutually self-interested and rational persons, when similarly situated and required to make in advance a firm commitment, could acknowledge as restrictions governing the assignment of rights and duties in their common practices, and thereby accept as limiting their rights against one another. The principles of justice may, then, be regarded as those principles which arise when the constraints of having a morality are imposed upon parties in the typical circumstances of justice.

4. These ideas are, of course, connected with a familiar way of thinking about justice which goes back at least to the Greek Sophists, and which regards the acceptance of the principles of justice as a compromise between persons of roughly equal power who would enforce their will on each other if they could, but who, in view of the equality of forces amongst them and for the sake of their own peace and security, acknowledge certain forms of conduct insofar as prudence seems to require. Justice is thought of as a pact between rational egoists the stability of which is dependent on a balance of power and a similarity of circumstances.[9] While the previous account is connected with this tradition, and with its most recent variant, the theory of games,[10] it differs from it in

429

several important respects which, to forestall misinterpretations, I will set out here.

First, I wish to use the previous conjectural account of the background of justice as a way of analyzing the concept. I do not want, therefore, to be interpreted as assuming a general theory of human motivation: when I suppose that the parties are mutually self-interested, and are not willing to have their (substantial) interests sacrificed to others, I am referring to their conduct and motives as they are taken for granted in cases where questions of justice ordinarily arise. Justice is the virtue of practices where there are assumed to be competing interests and conflicting claims, and where it is supposed that persons will press their rights on each other. That persons are mutually self-interested in certain situations and for certain purposes is what gives rise to the question of justice in practices covering those circumstances. Amongst an association of saints, if such a community could really exist, the disputes about justice could hardly occur; for they would all work selflessly together for one end, the glory of God as defined by their common religion, and reference to this end would settle every question of right. The justice of practices does not come up until there are several different parties (whether we think of these as individuals, associations, or nations and so on, is irrelevant) who do press their claims on one another, and who do regard themselves as representatives of interests which deserve to be considered. Thus the previous account involves no general theory of human motivation. Its intent is simply to incorporate into the conception of justice the relations of men to one another which set the stage for questions of justice. It makes no difference how wide or general these relations are, as this matter does not bear on the analysis of the concept.

Again, in contrast to the various conceptions of the social contract, the several parties do not establish any particular society or practice; they do not covenant to obey a particular sovereign body or to accept a given constitution.[11] Nor do they, as in the theory of games (in certain respects a marvelously sophisticated development of this tradition), decide on individual strategies adjusted to their respective circumstances in the game. What the parties do is to *jointly* acknowledge certain *principles* of appraisal relating to their common *practices* either as already established or merely proposed. They accede to standards of judgment, not to a given practice; they do not make any specific agreement, or bargain, or adopt a particular strategy. The subject of their acknowledgment is, therefore, very general indeed; it is simply the acknowledgment of certain principles of judgment, fulfilling certain general conditions, to be used in criticizing the arrangement of their common affairs. The relations of mutual self-interest between the parties who are similarly circumstanced mirror the conditions under which questions of justice arise, and the procedure by which the principles of judgment are proposed and acknowledged reflects the constraints of having a morality. Each aspect, then, of the preceding hypothetical account serves the

430

purpose of bringing out a feature of the notion of justice. One could, if one liked, view the principles of justice as the "solution" of this highest order "game" of adopting, subject to the procedure described, principles of argument for all coming particular "games" whose peculiarities one can in no way foresee. But this comparison, while no doubt helpful, must not obscure the fact that this highest order "game" is of a special sort.[12] Its significance is that its various pieces represent aspects of the concept of justice.

Finally, I do not, of course, conceive the several parties as necessarily coming together to establish their common practices for the first time. Some institutions may, indeed, be set up *de novo*; but I have framed the preceding account so that it will apply when the full complement of social institutions already exists and represents the result of a long period of development. Nor is the account in any way fictitious. In any society where people reflect on their institutions they will have an idea of what principles of justice would be acknowledged under the conditions described, and there will be occasions when questions of justice are actually discussed in this way. Therefore if their practices do not accord with these principles, this will affect the quality of their social relations. For in this case there will be some recognized situations wherein the parties are mutually aware that one of them is being forced to accept what the other would concede is unjust. The foregoing analysis may then be thought of as representing the actual quality of relations between persons as defined by practices accepted as just. In such practices the parties will acknowledge the principles on which it is constructed, and the general recognition of this fact shows itself in the absence of resentment and in the sense of being justly treated. Thus, one common objection to the theory of the social contract, its apparently historical and fictitious character, is avoided.

5. That the principles of justice may be regarded as arising in the manner described illustrates an important fact about them. Not only does it bring out the idea that justice is a primitive moral notion in that it arises once the concept of morality is imposed on mutually self-interested agents similarly circumstanced, but it emphasizes that, fundamental to justice, is the concept of fairness which relates to right dealing between persons who are cooperating with or competing against one another, as when one speaks of fair games, fair competition, and fair bargains. The question of fairness arises when free persons, who have no authority over one another, are engaging in a joint activity and amongst themselves settling or acknowledging the rules which define it and which determine the respective shares in its benefits and burdens. A practice will strike the parties as fair if none feels that, by participating in it, they or any of the others are taken advantage of, or forced to give in to claims which they do not regard as legitimate. This implies that each has a conception of legitimate claims which he thinks it reasonable for others as well as himself to acknowledge. If one thinks of the principles of justice as arising in the manner described,

then they do not define this sort of conception. A practice is just or fair, then, when it satisfies the principles which those who participate in it could propose to one another for mutual acceptance under the aforementioned circumstances. Persons engaged in a just, or fair, practice can face one another openly and support their respective positions, should they appear questionable, by reference to principles which it is reasonable to expect each to accept.

It is this notion of the possibility of mutual acknowledgment of principles by free persons who have no authority over one another which makes the concept of fairness fundamental to justice. Only if such acknowledgment is possible can there be true community between persons in their common practices; otherwise their relations will appear to them as founded to some extent on force. If, in ordinary speech, fairness applies more particularly to practices in which there is a choice whether to engage or not (e.g., in games, business competition), and justice to practices in which there is no choice (e.g., in slavery), the element of necessity does not render the conception of mutual acknowledgment inapplicable, although it may make it much more urgent to change unjust than unfair institutions. For one activity in which one can always engage is that of proposing and acknowledging principles to one another supposing each to be similarly circumstanced; and to judge practices by the principles so arrived at is to apply the standard of fairness to them.

Now if the participants in a practice accept its rules as fair, and so have no complaint to lodge against it, there arises a prima facie duty (and a corresponding prima facie right) of the parties to each other to act in accordance with the practice when it falls upon them to comply. When any number of persons engage in a practice, or conduct a joint undertaking according to rules, and thus restrict their liberty, those who have submitted to these restrictions when required have the right to a similar acquiescence on the part of those who have benefited by their submission. These conditions will obtain if a practice is correctly acknowledged to be fair, for in this case all who participate in it will benefit from it. The rights and duties so arising are special rights and duties in that they depend on previous actions voluntarily undertaken, in this case on the parties having engaged in a common practice and knowingly accepted its benefits.[13] It is not, however, an obligation which presupposes a deliberate performative act in the sense of a promise, or contract, and the like.[14] An unfortunate mistake of proponents of the idea of the social contract was to suppose that political obligation does requires some such act, or at least to use language which suggests it. It is sufficient that one has knowingly participated in and accepted the benefits of a practice acknowledged to be fair. This prima facie obligation may, of course, be overridden: it may happen, when it comes one's turn to follow a rule, that other considerations will justify not doing so. But one cannot, in general, be released from this obligation by denying the justice of the practice only when it falls on one to obey. If a persons rejects a practice, he should, so far as possible, declare his intention in advance, and avoid participating in it or enjoying its benefits.

This duty I have called that of fair play, but it should be admitted that to refer to it in this way is, perhaps, to extend the ordinary notion of fairness. Usually acting unfairly is not so much the breaking of any particular rule, even if the infraction is difficult to detect (cheating), but taking advantage of loopholes or ambiguities in rules, availing oneself of unexpected or special circumstances which make it impossible to enforce them, insisting that rules be enforced to one's advantage when they should be suspended, and more generally, acting contrary to the intention of a practice. It is for this reason that one speaks of the sense of fair play: acting fairly requires more than simply being able to follow rules; what is fair must often be felt, or perceived, one wants to say. It is not, however, an unnatural extension of the duty of fair play to have it include the obligation which participants who have knowingly accepted the benefits of their common practice owe to each other to act in accordance with it when their performance falls due; for it is usually considered unfair if someone accepts the benefits of a practice but refuses to do his part in maintaining it. Thus one might say of the tax-dodger that he violates the duty of fair play: he accepts the benefits of government but will not do his part in releasing resources to it; and members of labor unions often say that fellow workers who refuse to join are being unfair: they refer to them as "free riders," as persons who enjoy what are the supposed benefits of unionism, higher wages, shorter hours, job security, and the like, but who refuse to share in its burdens in the form of paying dues, and so on.

The duty of fair play stands beside other prima facie duties such as fidelity and gratitude as a basic moral notion; yet it is not to be confused with them.[15] These duties are all clearly distinct, as would be obvious from their definitions. As with any moral duty, that of fair play implies a constraint on self-interest in particular cases; on occasion it enjoins conduct which a rational egoist strictly defined would not decide upon. So while justice does not require of anyone that he sacrifice his interests in that *general position* and procedure whereby the principles of justice are proposed and acknowledged, it may happen that in particular situations, arising in the context of engaging in a practice, the duty of fair play will often cross his interests in the sense that he will be required to forego particular advantages which the peculiarities of his circumstances might permit him to take. There is, of course, nothing surprising in this. It is simply the consequence of the firm commitment which the parties may be supposed to have made, or which they would make, in the general position, together with the fact that they have participated in and accepted the benefits of a practice which they regard as fair.

Now the acknowledgment of this constraint in particular cases, which is manifested in acting fairly or wishing to make amends, feeling ashamed, and the like, when one has evaded it, is one of the forms of conduct by which participants in a common practice exhibit their recognition of each other as persons with similar interests and capacities. In the same way that, failing a special explanation, the criterion for the recognition of suffering is, helping one who suffers, acknowledging the duty of fair play is a necessary part of the criterion for recognizing another as a person with similar interests and feelings of oneself.[16] A person who never under any circumstances showed a wish to help others in pain would show, at the same time, that he did not recognize that they were in pain; nor could he have any feelings of affection or friendship for anyone; for having these feelings implies, failing special circumstances, that he comes to their aid when they are suffering. Recognition that another is a person in pain shows itself in sympathetic action; this primitive natural response of compassion is one of those responses upon which the various forms of moral conduct are built.

Similarly, the acceptance of the duty of fair play by participants in a common practice is a reflection in each person of the recognition of the aspirations and interests of others to be realized by their joint activity. Failing a special explanation, their acceptance of it is a necessary part of the criterion for their recognizing one another as persons with similar interests and capacities, as the conception of their relations in the general position supposes them to be. Otherwise they would show no recognition of one another as persons with similar capacities and interests, and indeed, in some cases perhaps hypothetical, they would not recognize one another as persons at all, but as complicated objects involved in a complicated activity. To recognize another as a person one must respond to him and act towards him in certain ways; and these ways are intimately connected with the various prima facie duties. Acknowledging these duties in *some* degree, and so having the elements of morality, is not a matter of choice, or of intuiting moral qualities, or a matter of the expression of feelings or attitudes (the three interpretations between which philosophical opinion frequently oscillates); it is simply the possession of one of the forms of conduct in which the recognition of others as persons is manifested.

These remarks are unhappily obscure. Their main purpose here, however, is to forestall, together with the remarks in Section 4, the misinterpretation that, on the view presented, the acceptance of justice and the acknowledgement of the duty of fair play depends in everyday life solely on there being a *de facto* balance of forces between the parties. It would indeed be foolish to underestimate the importance of such a balance in securing justice; but it is not the only basis thereof. The recognition of one another as persons with similar interests and capacities engaged in a common practice must, failing a special explanation, show itself in the acceptance of the principles of justice and the acknowledgment of the duty of fair play.

The conception at which we have arrived, then, is that the principles of justice may be thought of as arising once the constraints of having a morality are imposed upon rational and mutually self-interested parties who are related and situated in a special way. A practice is just if it is in accordance with the principles which all who participate in it might reasonably be expected to propose or to acknowledge before one another when they are similarly circumstanced and required to make a firm commitment in advance without knowledge of what will be their peculiar condition, and thus when it meets standards which the parties could accept as fair should occasion arise for them to debate its merits. Regarding the participants themselves, once persons knowingly engage in a practice which they acknowledge to be fair and accept the benefits of doing so, they are bound by the duty of fair play to follow the rules when it comes their turn to do so, and this implies a limitation on their pursuit of self-interest in particular cases.

Now one consequence of this conception is that, where it applies, there is no moral value in the satisfaction of a claim incompatible with it. Such a claim violates the conditions of reciprocity and community amongst persons, and he who presses it, not being willing to acknowledge it when pressed by another, has no grounds for complaint when it is denied; whereas he against whom it is pressed can complain. As it cannot be mutually acknowledged it is a resort to coercion; granting the claim is possible only if one party can compel acceptance of what the other will not admit. But it makes no sense to concede claims the denial of which cannot be complained of in preference to claims the denial of which can be objected to. Thus in deciding on the justice of a practice it is not enough to ascertain that it answers to wants and interests in the fullest and most effective manner. For if any of these conflict with justice, they should not be counted, as their satisfaction is no reason at all for having a practice. It would be irrelevant to say, even if true, that it resulted in the greatest satisfaction of desire. In tallying up the merits of a practice one must toss out the satisfaction of interests the claims of which are incompatible with the principles of justice.

6. The discussion so far has been excessively abstract. While this is perhaps unavoidable, I should now like to bring out some of the features of the conception of justice as fairness by comparing it with the conception of justice in classical utilitarianism as represented by Bentham and Sidgwick, and its counterpart in welfare economics. This conception assimilates justice to benevolence and the latter in turn to the most efficient design of institutions to promote the general welfare. Justice is a kind of efficiency.[17]

Now it is said occasionally that this form of utilitarianism puts no restrictions on what might be a just assignment of rights and duties in that there might be circumstances which, on utilitarian grounds, would justify institutions highly offensive to our ordinary sense of justice. But the classical utilitarian conception is not totally unprepared for this objection. Beginning with the notion that the general happiness can be represented by a social utility function

435

consisting of a sum of individual utility functions with identical weights (this being the meaning of the maxim that each counts for one and no more than one),[18] it is commonly assumed that the utility functions of individuals are similar in all essential respects. Differences between individuals are ascribed to accidents of education and upbringing, and they should not be taken into account. This assumption, coupled with that of diminishing marginal utility, results in a prima facie case for equality, e.g., of equality in the distribution of income during any given period of time, laying aside indirect effects on the future. But even if utilitarianism is interpreted as having such restrictions built into the utility function, and even if it is supposed that these restrictions have in practice much the same result as the application of the principles of justice (and appear, perhaps, to be ways of expressing these principles in the language of mathematics and psychology), the fundamental idea is very different from the conception of justice as fairness. For one thing, that the principles of justice should be accepted is interpreted as the contingent result of a higher order administrative decision. The form of this decision is regarded as being similar to that of an entrepreneur deciding how much to produce of this or that commodity in view of its marginal revenue, or to that of someone distributing goods to needy persons according to the relative urgency of their wants. The choice between practices is thought of as being made on the basis of the allocation of benefits and burdens to individuals (these being measured by the present capitalized value of their utility over the full period of the practice's existence), which results from the distribution of rights and duties established by a practice.

Moreover, the individuals receiving these benefits are not conceived as being related in any way: they represent so many different directions in which limited resources may be allocated. The value of assigning resources to one direction rather than another depends solely on the preferences and interests of individuals as individuals. The satisfaction of desire has its value irrespective of the moral relations between persons, say as members of a joint undertaking, and of the claims which, in the name of these interests, they are prepared to make on one another;[19] and it is this value which is to be taken into account by the (ideal) legislator who is conceived as adjusting the rules of the system from the center so as to maximize the value of the social utility function.

It is thought that the principles of justice will not be violated by a legal system so conceived provided these executive decisions are correctly made. In this fact the principles of justice are said to have their derivation and explanation; they simply express the most important general features of social institutions in which the administrative problem is solved in the best way. These principles have, indeed, a special urgency because, given the facts of human nature, so much depends on them; and this explains the peculiar quality of the moral feelings associated with justice.[20] This assimilation of justice to a higher

436

order executive decision, certainly a striking conception, is central to classical utilitarianism; and it also brings out its profound individualism in one sense of this ambiguous word. It regards persons as so many *separate* directions in which benefits and burdens may be assigned; and the value of the satisfaction or dissatisfaction of desire is not thought to depend in any way on the moral relations in which individuals stand, or on the kinds of claims which they are willing, in the pursuit of their interests, to press on each other.

7. Many social decisions are, of course, of an administrative nature. Certainly this is so when it is a matter of social utility in what one may call its ordinary sense: that is, when it is a question of the efficient design of social institutions for the use of common means to achieve common ends. In this case either the benefits and burdens may be assumed to be impartially distributed, or the question of distribution is misplaced, as in the instance of maintaining public order and security or national defense. But as an interpretation of the basis of the principles of justice, classical utilitarianism is mistaken. It *permits* one to argue, for example, that slavery is unjust on the grounds that the advantages to the slaveholder as slaveholder do not counterbalance the disadvantages to the slave and to society at large burdened by a comparatively inefficient system of labor. Now the conception of justice as fairness, when applied to the practice of slavery with its offices of slaveholder and slave, would not allow one to consider the advantages of the slaveholder in the first place. As that office is not in accordance with the principles which could be mutually acknowledged, the gains accruing to the slaveholder, assuming them to exist, cannot be counted as in *any* way mitigating the injustice of the practice. The question whether these gains outweigh the disadvantages to the slave and to society cannot arise, since in considering the justice of slavery these gains have no weight at all which requires that they be overridden. Where the conception of justice as fairness applies, slavery is *always* unjust.

I am not, of course, suggesting the absurdity that the classical utilitarians approved of slavery. I am only rejecting a type of argument which their view allows them to use in support of their disapproval of it. The conception of justice as derivative from efficiency implies that judging the justice of a practice is always, in principle at least, a matter of weighing up advantages and disadvantages, each having an intrinsic value or disvalue as the satisfaction of interests, irrespective of whether or not these interests necessarily involve acquiescence in principles which could not be mutually acknowledged. Utilitarianism cannot account for the fact that slavery is always unjust, nor for the fact that it would be recognized as irrelevant in defeating the accusation of injustice for one person to say to another, engaged with him in a common practice and debating its merits, that nevertheless it allowed of the greatest satisfaction of desire. The charge of injustice cannot be rebutted in this way. If justice were derivative from a higher order executive efficiency, this would not be so.

437

But now, even if it is taken as established that, so far as the ordinary conception of justice goes, slavery is always unjust (that is, slavery by definition violates commonly recognized principles of justice), the classical utilitarian would surely reply that these principles, as other moral principles subordinate to that of utility, are only generally correct. It is simply for the most part true that slavery is less efficient than other institutions; and while common sense may define the concept of justice so that slavery is unjust, nevertheless, where slavery would lead to the greatest satisfaction of desire, it is not wrong. Indeed, it is then right, and for the very same reason that justice, as ordinarily understood, is usually right. If, as ordinarily understood, slavery is always unjust, to this extent the utilitarian conception of justice might be admitted to differ from that of common moral opinion. Still the utilitarian would want to hold that, as a matter of moral principle, his view is correct in giving no special weight to considerations of justice beyond that allowed for by the general presumption of effectiveness. And this, he claims, is as it should be. The everyday opinion is morally in error, although, indeed, it is a useful error, since it protects rules of generally high utility.

The question, then, relates not simply to the analysis of the concept of justice as common sense defines it, but the analysis of it in the wider sense as to how much weight considerations of justice, as defined, are to have when laid against other kinds of moral considerations. Here again I wish to argue that reasons of justice have a *special* weight for which only the conception of justice as fairness can account. Moreover, it belongs to the concept of justice that they do have this special weight. While Mill recognized that this was so, he thought that it could be accounted for by the special urgency of the moral feelings which naturally support principles of such high utility. But it is a mistake to resort to the urgency of feeling; as with the appeal to intuition, it manifests a failure to pursue the question far enough. The special weight of considerations of justice can be explained from the conception of justice as fairness. It is only necessary to elaborate a bit what has already been said as follows.

If one examines the circumstances in which a certain tolerance of slavery is justified, or perhaps better, excused, it turns out that these are of a rather special sort. Perhaps slavery exists as an inheritance from the past and it proves necessary to dismantle it piece by piece; at times slavery may conceivably be an advance on previous institutions. Now while there may be some excuse for slavery in special conditions, it is never an excuse for it that it is sufficiently advantageous to the slaveholder to outweigh the disadvantages to the slave and to society. A person who argues in this way is not perhaps making a wildly irrelevant remark; but he is guilty of a moral fallacy. There is disorder in his conception of the ranking of moral principles. For the slaveholder, by his own admission, has no moral title to the advantages which he receives as a slaveholder. He is no more prepared than the slave to acknowledge the principle upon which is founded the respective positions in which they both stand. Since slavery does not accord with principles which they could mutually acknowledge, they each may be supposed to agree that it is unjust: it grants claims which it ought not to grant and in doing so denies claims which it ought not to deny. Amongst persons in a general position who are debating the form of their common practices, it cannot, therefore, be offered as a reason for a practice that, in conceding these very claims that ought to be denied, it nevertheless meets existing interests more effectively. By their very nature the satisfaction of these claims is without weight and cannot enter into any tabulation of advantages and disadvantages.

Furthermore, it follows from the concept of morality that, to the extent that the slaveholder recognizes his position vis-à-vis the slave to be unjust, he would not choose to press his claims. His not wanting to receive his special advantages is one of the ways in which he shows that he thinks slavery is unjust. It would be fallacious for the legislator to suppose, then, that it is a ground for having a practice that it brings advantages greater than disadvantages, if those for whom the practice is designed, and to whom the advantages flow, acknowledge that they have no moral title to them and do not wish to receive them.

For these reasons the principles of justice have a special weight; and with respect to the principle of the greatest satisfaction of desire, as cited in the general position amongst those discussing the merits of their common practices, the principles of justice have an absolute weight. In this sense they are not contingent; and this is why their force is greater than can be accounted for by the general presumption (assuming that there is one) of the effectiveness, in the utilitarian sense, of practices which in fact satisfy them.

If one wants to continue using the concepts of classical utilitarianism, one will have to say, to meet this criticism, that at least the individual or social utility functions must be so defined that no value is given to the satisfaction of interests the representative claims of which violate the principles of justice. In this way it is no doubt possible to include these principles within the form of the utilitarian conception; but to do so is, of course, to change its inspiration altogether as a moral conception. For it is to incorporate within it principles which cannot be understood on the basis of a higher order executive decision aiming at the greatest satisfaction of desire.

It is worth remarking, perhaps, that this criticism of utilitarianism does not depend on whether or not the two assumptions, that of individuals having similar utility functions and that of diminishing marginal utility, are interpreted as psychological propositions to be supported or refuted by experience, or as moral and political principles expressed in a somewhat technical language. There are, certainly, several advantages in taking them in the latter fashion.[21] For one thing, one might say that this is what Bentham and others really meant by them, at least as shown by how they were used in arguments for social reform.

More importantly, one could hold the best way to defend the classical utilitarian view is to interpret these assumptions as moral and political principles. It is doubtful whether, taken as psychological propositions, they are true of men in general as we know them under normal conditions. On the other hand, utilitarians would not have wanted to propose them merely as practical working principles of legislation, or as expedient maxims to guide reform, given the egalitarian sentiments of modern society.[22] When pressed they might well have invoked the idea of a more or less equal capacity of men in relevant respects if given an equal chance in a just society. But if the argument above regarding slavery is correct, then granting these assumptions as moral and political principles makes no difference. To view individuals as equally fruitful lines for the allocation of benefits, even as a matter of moral principle, still leaves the mistaken notion that the satisfaction of desire has value in itself irrespective of the relations between persons as members of a common practice, and irrespective of the claims upon one another which the satisfaction of interests represents. To see the error of this idea one must give up the conception of justice as an executive decision altogether and refer to the notion of justice as fairness: that participants in a common practice be regarded as having an original and equal liberty and that their common practices be considered unjust unless they accord with principles which persons so circumstanced and related could freely acknowledge before one another, and so could accept as fair. Once the emphasis is put upon the concept of the mutual recognition of principles by participants in a common practice the rules of which are to define their several relations and give form to their claims on one another, then it is clear that the granting of a claim the principle of which could not be acknowledged by each in the general position (that is, in the position in which the parties propose and acknowledge principles before one another) is not a reason for adopting a practice. Viewed in this way, the background of the claim is seen to exclude it from consideration; that it can represent a value in itself arises from the conception of individuals as separate lines for the assignment of benefits, as isolated persons who stand as claimants on an administrative or benevolent largesse. Occasionally persons do so stand to one another; but this is not the general case, nor, more importantly, is it the case when it is a matter of the justice of practices themselves in which participants stand in various relations to be appraised in accordance with standards which they may be expected to acknowledge before one another. Thus however mistaken the notion of the social contract may be as history, and however far it may overreach itself as a general theory of social and political obligation, it does express, suitably interpreted, an essential part of the concept of justice.[23]

8. By way of conclusion I should like to make two remarks: first, the original modification of the utilitarian principle (that it require of practices that the offices and positions defined by them be equal unless it is reasonable

to suppose that the representative man in *every* office would find the inequality to his advantage), slight as it may appear at first sight, actually has a different conception of justice standing behind it. I have tried to show how this is so by developing the concept of justice as fairness and by indicating how this notion involves the mutual acceptance, from a general position, of the principles on which a practice is founded, and how this in turn requires the exclusion from consideration of claims violating the principles of justice. Thus the slight alteration of principle reveals another family of notions, another way of looking at the concept of justice.

Second, I should like to remark also that I have been dealing with the *concept* of justice. I have tried to set out the kinds of principles upon which judgments concerning the justice of practices may be said to stand. The analysis will be successful to the degree that it expresses the principles involved in these judgments when made by competent persons upon deliberation and reflection.[24] Now every people may be supposed to have the concept of justice, since in the life of every society there must be at least some relations in which the parties consider themselves to be circumstanced and related as the concept of justice as fairness requires. Societies will differ from one another not in having or in failing to have this notion but in the range of cases to which they apply it and in the emphasis which they give to it as compared with other moral concepts.

A firm grasp of the concept of justice itself is necessary if these variations, and the reasons for them, are to be understood. No study of the development of moral ideas and of the differences between them is more sound than the analysis of the fundamental moral concepts upon which it must depend. I have tried, therefore, to give an analysis of the concept of justice which should apply generally, however large a part the concept may have in a given morality, and which can be used in explaining the course of men's thoughts about justice and its relations to other moral concepts. How it is to be used for this purpose is a large topic which I cannot, of course, take up here. I mention it only to emphasize that I have been dealing with the concept of justice itself and to indicate what use I consider such an analysis to have.

NOTES

1. An abbreviated version of this paper (less than one-half the length) was presented in a symposium with the same title at the American Philosophical Association, Eastern Division, December 28, 1957, and appeared in the *Journal of Philosophy,* LIV, 653-662.

2. I use the word "practice" throughout as a sort of technical term meaning any form of activity specified by a system of rules which defines offices, roles, moves, penalties, defenses, and so on, and which gives the activity its structure. As examples one may think of games and rituals, trials and parliaments, markets and systems of property. I have attempted a partial analysis of the notion of a practice in a paper "Two Concepts of Rules," *Philosophical Review,* LXIV (1955), 3-32.

3. These principles are, of course, well-known in one form or another and appear in many analyses of justice even where the writers differ widely on other matters. Thus if the principle of equal liberty is commonly associated with Kant (see *The Philosophy of Law,* tr. by W. Hastie, Edinburgh, 1887, pp. 56 f.), it may be claimed that it can also be found in J. S. Mill's *On Liberty* and elsewhere, and in many other liberal writers. Recently H. L. A. Hart has argued for something like it in his paper "Are There Any Natural Rights?," *Philosophical Review,* LXIV (1955), 175-191. The injustice of inequalities which are not won in return for a contribution to the common advantage is, of course, widespread in political writings of all sorts. The conception of justice here discussed is distinctive, if at all, only in selecting these two principles in this form; but for another similar analysis, see the discussion by W. D. Lamont, *The Principles of Moral Judgment* (Oxford, 1946), ch. v.

4. This point was made by Sidgwick, *Methods of Ethics,* 6th ed. (London, 1901), Bk. III, ch. v, sec. I. It has recently been emphasized by Sir Isaiah Berlin in a symposium, "Equality," *Proceedings of the Aristotelian Society,* n.s. LVI (1955-56), 305 f.

5. In the paper referred to above, footnote 2, I have tried to show the importance of taking practices as the proper subject of the utilitarian principle. The criticisms of so-called "restricted utilitarianism" by J. J. C. Smart, "Extreme and Restricted Utilitarianism," *Philosophical Quarterly,* VI (1956), 344-354, and by H. J. McCloskey, "An Examination of Restricted Utilitarianism," *Philosophical Review,* LXVI (1957), 466-485, do not affect my argument. These papers are concerned with the very general proposition, which is attributed (with what justice I shall not consider) to S. E. Toulmin and P. H. Nowell-Smith (and in the case of the latter paper, also, apparently, to me); namely, the proposition that particular moral actions are justified by appealing to moral rules, and moral rules in turn by reference to utility. But clearly I meant to defend no such view. My discussion of the concept of rules as maxims is an explicit rejection of it. What I did argue was that, in the *logically special* case of practices (although actually quite a common case) where the rules have special features and are not moral rules at all but legal rules or rules of games and the like (except, perhaps, in the case of promises), there is a peculiar force to the distinction between justifying particular actions and justifying the system of rules themselves. Even then I claimed only that restricting the utilitarian principle to practices as defined strengthened it. I did not argue for the position that this amendment alone is sufficient for a complete defense of utilitarianism as a general theory of morals. In this paper I take up the question as to how the utilitarian principle itself must be modified, but here, too, the subject of inquiry is not all of morality at once, but a limited topic, the concept of justice.

6. It might seem as if J. S. Mill, in paragraph 36 of Chapter V of *Utilitarianism,* expressed the utilitarian principle in this modified form, but in the remaining two paragraphs of the chapter, and elsewhere, he would appear not to grasp the significance of the change. Hume often emphasizes that *every* man must benefit. For example, in discussing the utility of general rules, he holds that they are requisite to the "well-being of every individual"; from a stable system of property "every individual person must find himself a gainer in balancing the account...." "Every member of society is sensible of this interest; everyone expresses this sense to his fellows along with the resolution he has taken of squaring his actions by it, on the conditions that others will do the same." *A Treatise of Human Nature,* Bk. III, Pt. II, Sec. II, par. 22.

7. It is not possible to discuss here this addition to the usual conception of rationality. If it seems peculiar, it may be worth remarking that it is analogous to the modification of the utilitarian principle which the argument as a whole is designed to explain and justify. In the same way that the satisfaction of interests, the representative claims of which violate the principles of justice, is not a reason for having a practice (see sec. 7), unfounded envy, within limits, need not to be taken into account.

8. The idea that accepting a principle as a moral principle implies that one generally acts on it, failing a special explanation, has been stressed by R. M. Hare, *The Language of Morals* (Oxford, 1952). His formulation of it needs to be modified, however, along the lines suggested by P. L. Gardiner, "On Assenting to a Moral Principle," *Proceedings of the*

Aristotelian Society, n.s. LV (1955), 23-44. See also C. K. Grant, "Akrasia and the Criteria of Assent to Practical Principles," *Mind*, LXV (1956), 400-407, where the complexity of the criteria for assent is discussed.

9. Perhaps the best known statement of this conception is that given by Glaucon at the beginning of Book II of Plato's *Republic*. Presumably it was, in various forms, a common view among the Sophists; but that Plato gives a fair representation of it is doubtful. See K. R. Popper, *The Open Society and Its Enemies*, rev. ed. (Princeton, 1950), pp. 112-118. Certainly Plato usually attributes to it a quality of manic egoism which one feels must be an exaggeration; on the other hand, see the Melian Debate in Thucydides, *The Peloponnesian War*, Book V, ch. VII, although it is impossible to say to what extent the views expressed there reveal any current philosophical opinion. Also in this tradition are the remarks of Epicurus on justice in *Principal Doctrines*, XXXI-XXXVIII. In modern times elements of the conception appear in a more sophisticated form in Hobbes, *The Leviathan*, and in Hume, *A Treatise of Human Nature*, Book III, Pt. II, as well as in the writings of the school of natural law such as Pufendorf's *De jure naturae et gentium*. Hobbes and Hume are especially instructive. For Hobbes' argument see Howard Warrender's *The Political Philosophy of Hobbes* (Oxford, 1957). W. J. Baumol's *Welfare Economics and the Theory of the State* (London, 1952), is valuable in showing the wide applicability of Hobbes' fundamental idea (interpreting his natural law as principles of prudence), although in this book it is traced back only to Hume's *Treatise*.

10. See J. von Neumann and O. Morgenstern, *The Theory of Games and Economic Behavior*, 2nd ed. (Princeton, 1947). For a comprehensive and not too technical discussion of the developments since, see R. Duncan Luce and Howard Raiffa, *Games and Decisions: Introduction and Critical Survey* (New York, 1957). Chs. VI and XIV discuss the developments most obviously related to the analysis of justice.

11. For a general survey see J. W. Gough, *The Social Contract*, 2nd ed. (Oxford, 1957), and Otto von Gierke, *The Development of Political Theory*, tr. by B. Freyd (London, 1939), Pt. II, ch. II.

12. The difficulty one gets into by a mechanical application of the theory of games to moral philosophy can be brought out by considering among several possible examples, R. B. Braithwaite's study, *Theory of Games as a Tool for the Moral Philosopher* (Cambridge, 1955). On the analysis there given, it turns out that the fair division of playing time between Matthew and Luke depends on their preferences, and these in turn are connected with the instruments they wish to play. Since Matthew has a threat advantage over Luke, arising purely from the fact that Matthew, the trumpeter, prefers both of them playing at once to neither of them playing, whereas Luke, the pianist, prefers silence to cacophony, Matthew is alloted 26 evenings of play to Luke's 17. If the situation were reversed, the threat advantage would be with Luke. See pp. 36 f. But now we have only to suppose that Matthew is a jazz enthusiast who plays the drums, and Luke a violinist who plays sonatas, in which case it will be fair, on this analysis, for Matthew to play whenever and as often as he likes, assuming, of course, as it is plausible to assume, that he does not care whether Luke plays or not. Certainly something has gone wrong. To each according to his threat advantage is hardly the principle of fairness. What is lacking is the concept of morality, and it must be brought into the conjectural account in some way or other. In the text this is done by the form of the procedure whereby principles are proposed and acknowledged (Section 3). If one starts directly with the particular case as known, and if one accepts as given and definitive the preferences and relative positions of the parties, whatever they are, it is impossible to give an analysis of the moral concept of fairness. Braithwaite's use of the theory of games, insofar as it is intended to analyze the concept of fairness, is, I think, mistaken. This is not, of course, to criticize in any way the theory of games as a mathematical theory, to which Braithwaite's book certainly contributes, nor as an analysis of how rational (and amoral) egoists might behave (and so as an analysis of how people sometimes actually do behave). But it is to say that if the theory of games is to be used to analyze moral concepts, its formal structure must be interpreted in a special and general

443

manner as indicated in the text. Once we do this, though, we are in touch again with a much older tradition.

13. For the definition of this prima facie duty, and the idea that it is a special duty, I am indebted to H. L. A. Hart. See his paper "Are There Any Natural Rights?," *Philosophical Review*, LXIV (1955), 185 f.

14. The sense of "performative" here is to be derived from J. L. Austin's paper in the symposium, "Other Minds," *Proceedings of the Aristotelian Society,* Supplementary Volume (1946), pp. 170-174.

15. This, however, commonly happens. Hobbes, for example, when invoking the notion of a "tacit covenant," appeals not to the natural law that promises should be kept but to his fourth law of nature, that of gratitude. On Hobbes' shift from fidelity to gratitude, see Warrender, *op. cit.,* pp. 51-52, 233-237. While it is not a serious criticism of Hobbes, it would have improved his argument had he appealed to the duty of fair play. On his premises he is perfectly entitled to do so. Similarly Sidgwick thought that a principle of justice, such as every man ought to receive adequate requital for his labor, is like gratitude universalized. See *Methods of Ethics,* Bk. III, ch. V, Sect. 5. There is a gap in the stock of moral concepts used by philosophers into which the concept of the duty of fair play fits quite naturally.

16. I am using the concept of criterion here in what I take to be Wittgenstein's sense. See *Philosophical Investigation,* (Oxford, 1953); and Norman Malcolm's review, "Wittgenstein's *Philosophical Investigations," Philosophical Review,* LXIII (1954), 543-547. That the response of compassion, under appropriate circumstances, is part of the criterion for whether or not a person understands what "pain" means, is, I think, in the *Philosophical Investigations.* The view in the text is simply an extension of this idea. I cannot, however, attempt to justify it here. Similar thoughts are to be found, I think, in Max Scheler, *The Nature of Sympathy,* tr. by Peter Heath (New Haven, 1954). His way of writing is often so obscure that I cannot be certain.

17. While this assimilation is implicit in Bentham's and Sidgwick's moral theory, explicit statements of it as applied to justice are relatively rare. One clear instance in *The Principles of Morals and Legislation* occurs in ch. X, footnote 2 to section XL: ". . . justice, in the only sense in which it has a meaning, is an imaginary personage, feigned for the convenience of discourse, whose dictates are the dictates of utility, applied to certain particular cases. Justice, then, is nothing more than an imaginary instrument, employed to forward on certain occasions, and by certain means, the purposes of benevolence. The dictates of justice are nothing more than a part of the dictates of benevolence, which, on certain occasions, are applied to certain subjects. . . ." Likewise in *The Limits of Jurisprudence Defined,* ed. by C. W. Everett (New York, 1945), pp. 117 f., Bentham criticizes Grotius for denying that justice derives from utility; and in *The Theory of Legislation,* ed. by C. K. Ogden (London, 1931), p. 3, he says that he uses the words "just" and "unjust" along with other words "simply as collective terms including the ideas of certain pains or pleasures." That Sidgwick's conception of justice is similar to Bentham's is admittedly not evident from his discussion of justice in Book III, ch. V of *Methods of Ethics.* But it follows, I think, from the moral theory he accepts. Hence C. D. Broad's criticisms of Sidgwick in the matter of distributive justice in *Five Types of Ethical Theory* (London, 1930), pp. 249-253, do not rest on a misinterpretation.

18. This maxim is attributed to Bentham by J. S. Mill in *Utilitarianism,* ch. V, paragraph 36. I have not found it in Bentham's writings, nor seen such a reference. Similarly James Bonar, *Philosophy and Political Economy* (London, 1893), p. 234 n. But it accords perfectly with Bentham's ideas. See the hitherto unpublished manuscript in David Baumgardt, *Bentham and the Ethics of Today* (Princeton, 1952), Appendix IV. For example, "the total value of the stock of pleasure belonging to the whole community is to be obtained by multiplying the number expressing the value of it as respecting any one person, by the number expressing the multitude of such individuals" (p. 556).

19. An idea essential to the classical utilitarian conception of justice. Bentham is firm in his statement of it: "It is only upon that principle [the principle of asceticism], and not from the principle of utility, that the most abominable pleasure which the vilest of malefactors ever reaped from his crime would be reprobated, if it stood alone. The case is, that it never does stand alone; but is necessarily followed by such a quantity of pain (or, what comes to the same thing, such a chance for a certain quantity of pain) that the pleasure in comparison of it, is as nothing: and this is the true and sole, but perfectly sufficient, reason for making it a ground for punishment" (*The Principles of Morals and Legislation,* ch. II, sec. iv. See also ch. X, sec. x, footnote I). The same point is made in *The Limits of Jurisprudence Defined,* pp. 115 f. Although much recent welfare economics, as found in such important works as I. M. D. Little, *A Critique of Welfare Economics,* 2nd ed. (Oxford 1957) and K. J. Arrow, *Social Choice and Individual Values* (New York, 1951), dispenses with the idea of cardinal utility, and uses instead the theory of ordinal utility as stated by J. R. Hicks, *Value and Capital,* 2nd ed. (Oxford, 1946), Pt. I, it assumes with utilitarianism that individual preferences have value as such, and so accepts the idea being criticized here. I hasten to add, however, that this is no object to it as a means of analyzing economic policy, and for that purpose it may, indeed, be a necessary simplifying assumption. Nevertheless it is an assumption which cannot be made in so far as one is trying to analyze moral concepts, especially the concept of justice, as economists would, I think, agree. Justice is usually regarded as a separate and distinct part of any comprehensive criterion of economic policy. See, for example, Tibor Scitovsky, *Welfare and Competition* (London, 1952), pp. 59-69, and Little, *op. cit.,* ch. VII.

20. See J. S. Mill's argument in *Utilitarianism,* ch. V, pars. 16-25.

21. See D. G. Ritchie, *Natural Rights* (London, 1894), pp. 95 ff., 249 ff. Lionel Robbins has insisted on this point on several occasions. See *An Essay on the Nature and Significance of Economic Science,* 2nd ed. (London, 1935), pp. 134-43, "Interpersonal Comparisons of Utility: A Comment," *Economic Journal,* XLVIII (1938), 635-41, and more recently, "Robertson on Utility and Scope," *Economica,* n.s. XX (1953), 108 f.

22. As Sir Henry Maine suggested Bentham may have regarded them. See *The Early History of Institutions* (London, 1875), pp. 398 ff.

23. Thus Kant was not far wrong when he interpreted the original contract merely as an "Idea of Reason"; yet he still thought of it as a *general* criterion of right and as providing a general theory of political obligation. See the second part of the essay, "On the Saying 'That may be right in theory but has no value in practice' " (1793), in *Kant's Principles of Politics,* tr. by W. Hastie (Edinburgh, 1891). I have drawn on the contractarian tradition not for a general theory of political obligation but to clarify the concept of justice.

24. For a further discussion of the idea expressed here, see my paper, "Outline of a Decision Procedure for Ethics," in the *Philosophical Review,* LX (1951), 177-197. For an analysis, similar in many respects but using the notion of the ideal observer instead of that of the considered judgment of a competent person, see Roderick Firth, "Ethical Absolutism and the Ideal Observer," *Philosophy and Phenomenological Research,* XII (1952), 317-345. While the similarities between these two discussions are more important than the differences, an analysis based on the notion of a considered judgment of a competent person, as it is based on a kind of judgment, may prove more helpful in understanding the features of moral judgment than an analysis based on the notion of an ideal observer, although this remains to be shown. A man who rejects the conditions imposed on a considered judgment of a competent person could no longer profess to *judge* at all. This seems more fundamental than his rejecting the conditions of observation, for these do not seem to apply, in an ordinary sense, to making a moral judgment.

EQUALITY
AS
AN IDEAL*
Isaiah Berlin

I

"Every man to count for one and no one to count for more than one."
This formula, much used by utilitarian philosophers, seems to me to form the
heart of the doctrine of equality or of equal rights, and has colored much liberal
and democratic thought. Like many familiar phrases of political philosophy it is
vague, ambiguous, and has changed in connotation from one thinker and society
to another. Nevertheless, it appears, more than any other formula, to constitute
the irreducible minimum of the ideal of equality. Moreover it is not self-evident
in the sense in which many simple empirical propositions seem so; it has not
been universally believed; and it is not uniquely connected with any one philosophical system. The notion of each man counting for one and only one, does
not depend on belief in rights, either natural or positive, either divinely
bestowed or adopted by convention. The statement that each man is to count
for one may, of course, be conceived as flowing from the recognition of natural
rights possessed by all men as such—rights "inherent" in being a man at all—
whether innate, or conferred at birth by a divine act—and so an "inalienable"
element in the "ultimate structure" of reality. But equally it can be held without
any metaphysical views of this kind. Again, it may be regarded as a rule, whether
universal or confined to certain defined classes of persons, deriving its validity
from a system of rights based on specific legal enactments, or custom, or some
other identifiable source of human authority. But again, it need not depend on
this. One can perfectly well conceive of a society organized on Benthamite or
Hobbesian lines, in which rights did not exist, or played a small part, and in
which the principle of "every man to count for one" was rigorously applied for

*Reprinted by permission of The Aristotelian Society, vol. 56 (1955-56).

utilitarian reasons, or because such was the will of the despot, or of the majority, or of the legislator or whoever held sovereignty in a given society. It is doubtless true that the most ardent champions of equality were, in fact, believers in human rights in some sense. Some were theists who believed that all men had immortal souls every one of which possessed infinite value and had claims which consequently must not be set aside in favor of objectives of lower value; some of these in addition believed in absolute standards of justice, divinely sanctioned, from which the doctrine of equality was directly deducible. Others were liberals and democrats, some of them deists or atheists or others ignorant of, or opposed to, the Judaeo-Christian tradition, who believed in the principle of equality a priori, as being revealed by natural light or whatever other source or method of knowledge was regarded as being the most certain. This was the foundation of the faith of the framers of the declarations of human rights in the American and the French revolutions; and has indeed been perhaps the strongest single element in egalitarian doctrines from the days of the Gracchi to the socialists and anarchists of modern times. But the connection between "counting for one" and the doctrines of Christian theology or the French *philosophes,* or this or that view of reason or of nature is rather more historical and psychological than logical. At any rate it is not one of mutual entailment. For this reason it may be of some use to enquire what this principle will look like if it is detached from its normal historical and psychological setting—whether it possesses any inherent plausibility of its own and whence it derives its universal and perennial appeal.

I should like to suggest that there is a principle of which the egalitarian formula is a specific application: namely, that similar cases call for, that is, should be accorded, similar treatment. Then, given that there is a class of human beings, it will follow that all members of this class, namely, men, should in every respect be treated in a uniform and identical manner, unless there is sufficient reason not to do so.[1] But since more than a finite degree of social and personal uniformity is in practice difficult or impossible to achieve, the principle ordains that the rule should be applied in, at any rate, important respects—those respects in which the type of treatment accorded to each other by human beings makes a great deal of difference to them, affects them deeply, forwards or frustrates their desires or interests in a significant degree. The assumption here seems to be that unless there is some sufficient reason not to do so, it is "natural" or "rational" to treat every member of a given class (in this case, men) as you treat any one member of it. To state the principle in this way leaves open crucial issues: thus it may be justly objected that unless some specific sense is given to "sufficient reason," the principle can be reduced to a trivial tautology (it is reasonable to act in manner X save in circumstances Y, in which it is not rational, and *any* circumstances may be Y); furthermore that since all entities are members of more than one class—indeed of a theoretically

447

limitless number of classes—*any* kind of behavior can be safely subsumed under the general rule enjoining equal treatment—since unequal treatment of various members of class A can always be represented as equal treatment of them viewed as members of some other class B, which in extreme circumstances can be so constructed as to contain no more than one actual member; which can reduce this rule to vacuity. There obviously can exist no formal method of avoiding such reductions to absurdity; they can be rebutted only by making clear what reasons are sufficient and why; and which attributes are alone relevant and why; and this will depend on the outlooks and scales of values of different persons, and the purposes of a given association or enterprise, in terms of which alone general principles can retain any degree of significance—whether in theory or practice. In concrete cases we distinguish good reasons from bad, central characteristics from irrelevant ones. Some inequalities (say, those based on birth) are condemned as arbitrary and irrational, others (say, those based on efficiency) are not, which seems to indicate that values other than equality for its own sake affect the ideals even of passionate egalitarians. A part of what we mean by rationality is the art of applying, and combining, reconciling, choosing among general principles in a manner for which complete theoretical explanation (or justification) can never, in principle, be given.

To return to the principle in the form in which it is normally applied: if I have a voice in settling the destinies of my society I think it unfair that all other members of it should not also have a similar voice; if I own property, it is unfair that others (situated in relevant respects as I am) should not do so too, and if I am allowed to leave it to my children in my will it is unfair that others should not have a similar opportunity; if I am permitted to read or write or express my opinion freely it is wrong, unjust, unfair, etc., that others should not be permitted to do so too. If someone is not to be allowed to do these things, or have these advantages, then sufficient reasons must be given; but no reason need be given for not withholding them, that is, for an equal distribution of benefits— for that is "natural"—self-evidently right and just, and needs no justification, since it is in some sense conceived as being self-justified. A society in which every member holds an equal quantity of property needs no special justification; only a society in which property is unequal needs it. So too with the distribution of other things—power or knowledge, or whatever else can be possessed in different quantities or degrees. I can justify the fact that the commander of an army is to be given more power than his men by the common purposes of the army, or of the society which it is defending—victory or self-protection—which can best be achieved by this means; I can justify the allocation of more than an equal share of goods to the sick or the old (to secure equality or satisfactions), or to the specially meritorious (to secure a deliberately intended inequality); but for all this I must provide reasons. If I believe in a hierarchical society, I may try to justify the special powers or wealth or position of persons of a certain origin, or of castes or classes or ranks, but for all this I am expected to give reasons—divine authority, a natural order, or the like. The assumption is that equality needs no reasons, only inequality does so; that uniformity, regularity, similarity, symmetry, the function correlation of certain characteristics with corresponding rights of which Mr. Wollheim speaks, need not be specially accounted for, whereas differences, unsystematic behavior, change in conduct, need explanation and, as a rule, justification. If I have a cake and there are ten persons among whom I wish to divide it, then if I give exactly one tenth to each, this will not, at any rate automatically, call for justification; whereas if I depart from this principle of equal division I am expected to produce a special reason. It is some sense of this, however latent, that makes equality an ideal which has never seemed intrinsically eccentric, even though extreme forms of it may not have been wholly acceptable to either political thinkers or ordinary men throughout recorded human history. There seem to me to be at least two conceptions which are involved in this love of order, each of which Mr. Wollheim has touched upon (although not by name or directly). These are the notions (a) of rules, and (b) of equality proper. I should like to say something about each of these.

(A) Rules

All rules, by definition, entail a measure of equality. In so far as rules are general instructions to act or refrain from acting in certain ways, in specified circumstances, enjoined upon persons of a specified kind, they enjoin uniform behavior in identical cases. To fall under a rule is *pro tanto* to be assimilated to a single pattern. To enforce a rule is to promote equality of behavior or treatment. This applies whether the rules take the form of moral principles and laws, or codes of positive law, or the rules of games or of conduct adopted by professional associations, religious organizations, political parties, wherever patterns of behavior can be codified in a more or less sytematic manner. The rule which declares that tall persons are permitted to cast five times as many votes as short ones creates an obvious inequality. Nevertheless, in the framework of this inequality it ensures equality of privilege within each of the two discriminated classes—no tall man may have more votes than any other tall man, and similarly with short men. This is Mr. Wollheim's first sense of "equality," in which, although the commodities or liberties, be they power or property or status, may not be owned in equal quantities or to an equal degree by everyone, yet every member of each class has an equal right to that which has been accorded to the class as a whole. This type of equality derives simply from the conception of rules as such—namely, that they allow of no exceptions. Indeed what is meant by saying that a given rule exists is that it should be fully, that is, equally fully,

449

obeyed by those who fall under it, and that any inequality in obedience would constitute an exception, that is, an offense against the rules. In so far as some minimum degree of prevalence of rules is a necessary condition for the existence of human societies (and this seems to be an almost universal, but still empirical, law), and in so far as morality, both personal and political, is largely conceived of in terms of rules, the kind of equality with which obedience to rules is virtually identical is among the deepest needs and convictions of mankind. In this sense equality is coextensive with social morality as such—that is to the degree to which social morality is conceived as a system of coherent, that is, not internally contradictory (and, according to some moralists, mutually entailing) sets of rules. A plea for equality in this sense is therefore a plea for life in accordance with rules as opposed to other standards, for example, the ad hoc orders of an inspired leader, or arbitrary desires. In this sense, then, to say that inequality is wrong is, in effect, to say that it is wrong to obey no rules in a given situation, or to accept a rule and break it; and a situation in which some men, for no stated reason, and in accordance with no rule, consistently obtain more than other men with the same, or sufficiently similar, relevant characteristics (however this is determined) is then described as being unfair. To provide no reasons for breaking a rule is described as irrational; to give reasons for obeying rules—save in terms of other rules—is regarded as unnecessary—rules are their own justification. In a moral system which entirely consists of rules, and is definable in terms of them, adequate reasons for breaking rule X must take the form of rule Y, which in certain circumstances may come into collision with Rule X, and, in accordance with Rule Z, will then cancel or modify it or, at any rate, be allowed to do so. A society which accepts a morality, whether personal or social and political, analysable into sets of rules of varying orders of stringency, some independent of each other, some connected by relations of entailment or mutual exclusion, may then be open to at least three kinds of criticism.

1. I may accept the rules and complain that too many exceptions are being made without specific rules to back the exceptions. If I merely object to the exceptions as such, I am merely complaining of the infringement of moral or social laws, as such. If the exceptions fulfill the desires of some people to the detriment of the fulfilment of the desires of others—for example where the desires are for some commodity in scarce supply, be it property, or power or status, or the fruits of civilization, then, if there is no rule governing such distribution (or if there is a rule but exceptions to it are made arbitrarily, that is, without being deducible from, or justifiable in terms of, other accepted rules) I complain, in addition, of unfairness, that is, that similar cases are being treated dissimilarly, when the whole essence of the rules is that this should be avoided.

2. I may complain that the rules themselves are bad or iniquitous. This may take several forms: I may complain that a given rule offends against some

other rule or principle which seems to me more important or morally superior. A rule consistently favoring the tall as against the short, would offend against the rule which I regard as superior, according to which physical characteristics must not be considered in, let us say, the distribution of honors, or against a rule which lays it down that all men, or all Englishmen, or all members of the Aristotelian society, must be treated as being equal in this regard. Then again, someone may say that equal treatment only for members of the Aristotelian society offends against equal treatment for all Englishmen, or that equal treatment for all Englishmen offends against the principle of equal treatment for all Europeans, or all men. In short, a rule may be condemned as offending against some wider rule to which it is then regarded as forming an irrational exception. Or it may be attacked on the ground that it conflicts with some rule not necessarily wider but merely incompatible with it: in cases of such conflict egalitarianism seems to entail that any rule which includes under it a larger number of persons or a larger number of types of persons[2] shall always be preferred to rules which ensure identical treatment only for smaller numbers or a smaller number of types; and a society will not be egalitarian to the degree to which in the formulation of its rules, or in its system of deciding which rules win in cases of conflict, it is influenced by principles other than those of the intrinsic desirability of identical treatment of the largest possible numbers of persons or classes of persons; for example if it is bent on the maximization of happiness, which may well entail gross inequalities.[3] And of course there are many other goals or values which may deflect the course of strict egalitarianism, as, for instance, the desire to encourage the arts and sciences, or a predominant desire to increase the military or economic power of the state, or a passion for the preservation of ancient traditions, or a strong taste for change and variety and new forms of life. All these may or may not breed rules that conflict with the principle that every man is to count for one and only one. This principle will indeed be preserved by the mere existence of rules within each area dominated by the rules themselves; but rules cannot guarantee its extension each beyond its own field. For the rules themselves may create inequalities, and the conflict between the rules still greater ones. To say, as we often do of a rule, that it is itself unfair, is, in effect, to say that it contradicts some other rule with a wider area of equal treatment—a rule which, if obeyed, will ensure that a larger number of persons (or classes of persons) shall receive similar treatment in specified circumstances. But to say of the rule that it is bad or iniquitous need not mean this; it need mean only that it is in conflict with some other rule or principle not necessarily itself tending toward greater equality. In case this seems too abstract, let me illustrate: although Bentham's doctrine about each man to count for one was in fact embodied by him in his utilitarian teachings, it seems plain that equality is not itself entailed by utilitarian principles, and might, indeed, on occasion conflict with them. Thus it can be argued that societies organized

451

hierarchically, certain types of medieval society, for example, or theocratic societies or even societies founded on slavery, may conceivably offer their members a greater degree of happiness (however this is calculated) than societies in which there is a greater degree of social or economic equality. When Montesquieu or Rousseau, for example, declare that the objection to slavery is not that it makes men unhappy—for it may not—the slaves may prefer to remain slaves—but that it is slavery, that men have no right to enslave other men, that it is unworthy of human beings to create such forms of life, they are pleading for equality for equality's sake. They are, in effect, saying that any society which has rules or laws enjoining or permitting slavery, even though its members may be happier than if they had been free, and even though Aristotle may be right and men exist whose faculties are realized best in slavery, is yet a society to be condemned, not for breaking the rules under which it lives, but for obeying the wrong kind of rules, pursuing the wrong kind of values. This implies that equality—that is, the rule that each man is to count for one and for no more than one, whether in the distribution of property or in the number of votes he has in the sovereign assembly or in the opportunities for education or pleasure, or in whatever respect—is an end in itself, in possible conflict with other ends, but higher than they, and, in cases of conflict, to be preferred.

3. Finally, someone may attack a society not indeed for breaking the rules that it affects to respect; nor yet for living by rules that are bad, or in conflict with some other ends or ideals which the critic regards as of greater moral authority; but that it lives by rules at all, that it is rule ridden. And if it is pointed out to him that a certain minimum of rules is an empirical necessity for the preservation of any degree of human organization, then he may retreat to the position that the rules in use go far beyond this minimum, and that a morality not compounded out of rules, but consisting of the pursuit of some ideal in a spontaneous and imaginative way, analogous to the creative activity of a painter or a composer, or to even less disciplined forms of self-expression, where both the use and recognition of rules is at a minimum, is to be preferred. It is salutary to be reminded that moral and political outlooks are not coextensive with systems of moral or political rules. The Romantic attack on the moral systems both of rationalists and empiricists at times took precisely this form of denunciation of the propositions and imperatives of the classical ethical systems, not because they were mistaken or deleterious, but because they were general. The Romantic philosophers, particularly in Germany,[4] assailed their predecessors for imposing rules, amalgamating cases, whether individual characters or moral situations or moral actions, that were necessarily unique and incommensurable, under the umbrella of some universal formula. They attacked all those who seemed to them bent on forcing the teeming multiplicity and variety of human activity into a Procrustean bed of symmetrical sets of moral rules, which, precisely because they were rules, tended to represent differences

as being relatively unimportant, and similarities as being alone relevant; and especially those who, so it was maintained, by following a false analogy with the natural sciences, ignored, or misrepresented vital individual differences, in virtue of which alone things and persons possessed their unique value, and did this in order to achieve an egalitarian society, dominated by rules—a society directed against the existence of all those elements which the Romantics regarded as alone worth preserving.

All three types of attack upon a given social or political order are, to say the least, relevant to the belief in equality. Let me recapitulate them: they take the form of saying:

(*a*) that rules are broken for no sufficient reason; or

(*b*) that the rules are themselves bad or iniquitous or otherwise inadequate; or

(*c*) that the rules are deplorable simply because they are rules.

Of these (*a*) represents the most direct demand for equality, for any protest against exceptions, because they are exceptions, is a genuine plea for equality; (*b*) springs from a demand for equality only if the rules are attacked on the ground that they are in conflict with other rules aimed at producing a greater degree of general equality; (*c*) is a direct attack upon the ideal of social equality as such. It is clear that this ideal is not solely the equality which all rules entail as such (even though it may derive much force from an intimate connection with moral systems to which universality, order, rules, laws, etc., are central), since otherwise rules could not themselves be criticized as leading to inequality, as we have seen that they can be. What, then, is this ideal?

II

(B) Equality Proper

In its simplest form the ideal of complete social equality embodies the wish that everything and everybody should be as similar as possible to everything and everybody else. It may serve to make this concept clearer if we try to conceive of some of the characteristics of a world in which no type of egalitarian would have anything to complain of. I doubt whether anyone has ever seriously desired to bring such a society into being, or even supposed such a society to be capable of being created. Nevertheless, it seems to me that the demands for human equality which have been expressed both by philosophers and by men of action who have advocated or attempted to reform society can best be represented as modifications of this absolute and perhaps absurd ideal. In the ideal egalitarian

453

society, inequality—and this must ultimately mean dissimilarity—would be reduced to a minimum. The greatest single cause of complaint has been disparity in the possession, or enjoyment, of characteristics or commodities which have been strongly desired by men at most times—such as property, political or social power, status, opportunities for the development of faculties or the obtaining of experiences, social and personal liberties and privileges of all kinds. And the attack has taken the form of maintaining that a society in which some men are much richer or stronger or freer than others; in which some men possess the power of acquiring what they want and of preventing others from acquiring these same things or other things which they in turn want; or in which some men are paid homage and deferred to and permitted to live as they wish in ways and degrees which set them off from other men; all these are societies which offend either against the principle of natural rights, which according to those who hold this principle, belong to all men as such; or against some rational principles whereby these differences may indeed be justified, but only by the provision of sufficient reasons for instituting or maintaining them. Disputes occur about what these rights are; or what reasons are sufficient or good; and whether such characteristics as differences of birth or of color or of religion or of wealth are true sources of unequal rights, or furnish good reasons for instituting political or social or other similar inequalities. There is, of course, a significant difference between these two ways of approach. Those who believe in natural rights differ mainly in establishing what these rights are, how their existence can be verified, whether all of them belong to all men, or only some to all, or only some to some; and whether equality is desirable in fields other than those covered by the claims created by the existence of natural rights. The other school—those who appeal to reason (though historically their views have over-lapped with and become inextricably mingled with those of the believers in natural rights) if they are to be consistent, must believe that equality should stretch over the entire field of human relations, and be modified only when there is sufficient reason to do so. Then disagreement may arise as to what constitutes a sufficient reason, and how great a modification a given reason justifies, and so forth. The first school, if it is consistent, will not object to inequalities, providing these do not infringe natural rights. But the second must protest against any inequality, unless a sufficient reason for it is produced. It is the latter, therefore, who go further, and are nearer to the extreme ideal which I should now like briefly to mention. Apart from the crucial question of what are and what are not sufficient reasons in such cases, it seems plain that inequalities of wealth or power are merely some among the possible inequalities which can excite opposition; they tend to be so prominent because they matter—affect human lives—more deeply, as things are, than other forms of inequality. But this is not always necessarily so. Even the most convinced social egalitarian does not normally object to the authority wielded by, let us

454

say, the conductor of an orchestra. Yet there is no obvious reason why he should not. And there have been occasions—few and far between—when this has actually happened. Those who maintain that equality is the paramount good, may not wish to be fobbed off with the explanation that the purpose of orchestral playing will not be served if every player is allowed equal authority with the conductor in deciding what is to be done. Inequality in the organization of an orchestra there patently is; the reason for it is the purpose of orchestral playing— the production of certain sounds in certain ways which cannot, in fact, be achieved without a measure of discipline which itself entails some degree of inequality in the distribution of authority. But a fanatical egalitarian could maintain that the inequality of the players in relation to the conductor is a greater evil than a poor performance of a symphonic work, and that it is better that no symphonic music be played at all if a conductorless orchestra is not feasible, than that such an institution should be allowed to offend against the principle of equality. To be more serious, the unequal distribution of natural gifts is a well-known obstacle to economic equality: in societies where there is a high degree of equality of economic opportunity, the strong and able and ambitious and cunning are likely to acquire more wealth or more power than those who lack these qualities. The fanatical egalitarian will look on this with horror; and because differences of natural talent will always tend towards the creation of inequalities, if only of prestige or influence, he will consequently wish—if equality is the paramount goal—to root out the evil at the source. He will tend to wish so to condition human beings that the highest degree of equality of natural properties is achieved, the greatest degree of mental and physical, that is to say, total uniformity—which alone will effectively preserve society, as far as possible, from the growth of inequalities of whatever kind. Only in a society where the greatest degree of similarity between the members occurs—where physical characteristics, mental endowment, emotional disposition, and conduct, are as uniform as possible—where people differ as little as possible from each other in any respect whatever, will true equality be attainable. Only in such a society will it be possible to reduce to a minimum those differences of treatment, or of power, or of position, or of natural or acquired characteristics, that are liable to lead people to complain that they have not what others have, and to ask for reasons why this should be so. It may be that the creation of so uniform a society, whether or not it is intrinsically desirable, may not, in fact, be feasible. It may also be that even the attempt to approach it as closely as is humanly possible, requires a degree of radical reorganization which cannot be carried out without a highly centralized and despotic authority—itself the cause of the maximum of inequality. Some convinced egalitarians have, as everyone knows, in practice accepted this as unavoidable, and have defended the institution of violent inequalities and the total suppression of many normal human claims as a necessary prerequisite for the creation of an ultimate equality. The moral and practical value of this is not relevant to the issue before us. What seems worth emphasizing is that so long as there are differences between men, some degree of inequality may occur; and that there is no kind of inequality against which, in principle, a pure egalitarian may not be moved to protest, simply on the ground that he sees no reason for tolerating it, no argument which seems to him more powerful than the argument for equality itself—equality which he regards not merely as end in itself, but as *the* end, the principle goal of human life. I do not suppose that extreme equality of this type—the maximum similarity of a body of all but indiscernible human beings—has ever been consciously put forward as an ideal by any serious thinker. But if we ask what kinds of equality have in fact, been demanded, we shall see, I think, that they are specific modifications of this absolute ideal, and that it therefore possesses the central importance of an ideal limit or idealized model at the heart of all egalitarian thought.

To examine some of these modifications, there are those who believe that natural human characteristics either cannot or should not be altered and that all that is necessary is equality of political and juridical rights. Provided that there exists equality before the law, such normal democratic principles as that of one man one vote, some form of government arrived at by consent (actual or understood) between the members of the society, or at any rate the majority of them, and, finally, a certain minimum of liberties—commonly called civil liberties—deemed necessary in order to enable men freely to exercise the legal and political rights entailed by this degree of equality, then, according to this view, no interference in other regions of activity (say, the economic) should be permitted. This is a common liberal doctrine of the last century. If it is complained that in a society where a large degree of political and legal equality is insured, the strong and the clever and the ambitious may succeed in enriching themselves, or acquiring political power, "at the expense of"—that is to say, in such a way as to keep these goods from—other members of the society, and that this leads to patent inequalities, liberals of this school reply that this is the price for ensuring political and legal equality, and that the only method of preventing economic or social inequalities is by reducing the degree of political liberty or legal equality between men. This amounts to an admission that we must choose one of several ways of treating men as counting for only one; that they can be "counted for one" only in some respects, but not in others. For we are told, with considerable empirical evidence, that to count men for one and only one in every respect whatever, is impracticable, that the full degree of, let us say, legal and political equality often results in economic and other forms of inequality, given the different endowments of men, and that only in an absolutely uniform, robot-like society, which no one wants, can this be effectively prevented. Those who believe this commonly maintain that the only inequality which should be avoided is an inequality based on characteristics which the individual cannot alter—unequal treatment based, for instance, on birth, or color, which human beings cannot alter at will. Given that all human beings start off with equal rights to acquire and hold property, to associate with each other in whatever ways they wish, to say whatever they will, and all the other traditional objectives of liberalism, and with no special rights or privileges attached to birth, color and other physically unalterable characteristics, then even though some human beings, by skill or luck or natural endowment, do manage to acquire property or power or ascendancy which enables them to control the lives of others, or to acquire objects which the others are not in a position to acquire, then, since there is nothing in the constitution of the society that actually forbids such acquisitiveness, the principle of equality has not been infringed. This is a pure form of laissez faire society which its proponents freely admit may lead to inequalities, but defend upon the ground that it gives an equal opportunity to all, a career genuinely open to all the talents—whereas any attempt to secure a greater degree of ultimate equality can only be obtained by interfering with this initial equalization of opportunity for all. In effect, this is, of course, tantamount to a plea for liberty at the expense of total equality; for it is only pure anarchists who believe that the maximum degree of liberty is wholly compatible with the maximum degree of equality in all important respects, and are called mistaken or utopian to the degree to which this proposition has in fact been falsified by experience. The distinction between general rights and special rights of which Professor H.L.A. Hart has spoken[5] and to which Mr. Wollheim refers, seems to be relevant to this kind of belief. One could easily conceive of a society in which all special rights (rights based on contract or on paternity, for example) will be instances of general rights—particular cases of them—because in such a society, at least in theory, any member can enter into a contract, any member can be a father, any member can enrich himself. There are no rights which belong to individuals in virtue of some characteristics—birth, blood, or color—which other members cannot in principle possess. In this schema certain types of traditional inequality have certainly been ruled out. But to maintain that this is the kind of society that true egalitarians desire would be disingenuous; for if one asks why some types of equality are protected in this case, initial equality whereby all men start off theoretically equal, while other types of equality are not protected, e.g., economic or social equality—equality in respect of whatever men can acquire by their own efforts, the answer is that the criterion of equality has plainly been influenced by something other than the mere desire for equality as such, namely, desire for liberty or the full development of human resources, or the belief that men deserve to be as rich or as powerful or as famous as they can make themselves—beliefs which are not connected with the desire for equality at all.

It is at this point that it becomes clear that in considering what kind of society is desirable, or what are "sufficient reasons" for either demanding equality or, on the contrary, modifying it or infringing it in specific cases, ideals other than equality conspicuously play a vital role.

This is clearly noticeable even in the writings of the most impassioned champions of the widest possible equality. Almost every argument favorable to equality, and in particular the assumption that everything that is scarce should be distributed as equally as possible unless there is strong reason against it, is to be found in the writings of Condorcet. The doctrine of equality in the Declaration of the Rights of Man and Citizen which heralded the French Revolution owes at least as much to him as it does to Rousseau or other thinkers. Yet even Condorcet contemplates the necessity for the government of human beings by men of enlightenment, above all by experts, men versed in the new, not yet created sciences of the behavior of men—sociology, anthropology and psychology—who alone can create an organization in which the greatest number of the desires of rational men will not be frustrated, as they have been hitherto, by prejudice, superstition, stupidity, and vice. Yet this elite is plainly to have greater powers than those whom they are to govern disinterestedly. And the reason for this is not merely that without this true equality cannot be achieved for the majority of men, but also that certain other ends must be striven for, such as happiness, virtue, justice, progress in the arts and sciences, the satisfaction of various moral and spiritual wants, of which equality, of whatever kind, is only one. Condorcet does not himself seem to be troubled by the problem of whether the quest for equality will clash with the need to seek these other ends, for, in common with many thinkers of his day, he took it for granted all too easily that all good things were certainly compatible, and indeed interlocked, with each other. We need not go into the reasons for this peculiar belief which has dominated much western thought at all times. While the principal assumption which underlies it is the view that since political and moral questions are factual in character, they are each answered by one true proposition and one only (otherwise they are not genuine questions); and since no true propositions can be inconsistent with one another, all the propositions which describe what should be done (no logical distinction is drawn between normative and descriptive statements by these thinkers) must be compatible with one another, and in the perfect harmony which Nature is thought to be, not merely compatible, but mutually entailing and entailed—for that defines a system, and Nature is known a priori to be such a—indeed *the*—harmonious system.

Whether or not this is the correct explanation of this central assumption, Condorcet did not allow the possibility of a collision between various human ends. It was left to others to emphasize the fact that in life as normally lived, the ideals of one society and culture clash with those of another, and at times come into conflict within the same society and, often enough, within the moral experience of a single individual; that such conflicts cannot always, even in principle be wholly resolved; that this can be traced to empirical causes, and does not entail either such theological doctrines as those of original sin, or the relevant beliefs of Buddhist doctrines, nor yet such pessimistic views of human character as those of Hobbes or Schopenhauer, or the ideologies of modern irrationalism. It follows that when the pursuit of equality comes into conflict with other human aims, be they what they may—such as the desire for happiness or pleasure, or for justice or virtue, or color and variety in a society for their own sake, or for liberty of choice as an end in itself, or for the fuller development of all human faculties, it is only the most fanatical egalitarian that will demand that such conflicts invariably be decided in favor of equality alone, with relative disregard of the other "values" concerned.

III

Equality is one value among many. The degree to which it is compatible with other ends depends on the concrete situation, and cannot be deduced from general laws of any kind; it is neither more nor less rational than any other ultimate principle, indeed it is difficult to see what is meant by considering it either rational or nonrational.

Yet the principle that every man shall count for one and no more than one demands a little more consideration before we finally abandon it as one of the ends pursued by men, needing neither explanation nor justification, being itself that which explains other rules or ethical principles. It seems, as we have seen above, intimately bound up with the belief in general rules of conduct. This belief may rest upon religious or metaphysical or utilitarian grounds, or derive from the love of order or system as such. However that may be, it often takes the form of a demand for fairness. The notions of equality and fairness are closely bound up: if as a result of breaking a rule a man derives benefits which he can obtain only so long as other men do not break but keep the rule, then no matter what other needs are being served by such a breach, the result is an offense against a principle best described as that of fairness, which is a form of desire for equality for its own sake. If I enter a train and do not pay for my ticket, and conceal this fact from the conductor and the other passengers, giving the sum withheld to a pauper whose situation is thereby improved materially, it may be argued that at any rate from a utilitarian point of view I have done what is right. The railway company will not know of its loss; nor would so small a loss noticeably decrease "its" happiness; I possess a strong will and shall not fall into bad habits; the collector has not noticed that he was not paid, and will not even so much as suffer from a sense of failure to carry out his duties; the passengers in their ignorance will not be led into temptation and demoralization, nor will there ensue any weakening of confidence between the persons concerned in the transaction leading, in the end, to the discontinuance of the train service. The general sum of happiness—in this case via that of the subsidized pauper—will surely have gone up to a greater degree than if I had paid my fare to the train conductor. Nevertheless, quite apart from the morally relevant fact that, having entered into a quasi-contractual obligation to pay, I have broken my promise, my act would be condemned as unfair, for it would rightly be maintained that I can only gain advantage (or the pauper can only gain advantage) so long as the other passengers continue to behave as they did before—since if my act were generally followed no one would pay, and the trains would stop running. So long as my advantage directly depends on the fact that others continue to obey the rule which applies to me as much as to them, so that I alone profit by the exception which I have made in my own favor, such a relaxation of the rule for my benefit would be rightly stigmatized as unfair (as well as dishonest); and although critical situations can be easily imagined in which it would be morally better that I should act in this way and break my contract, or cheat, yet it is clear that a person of normal moral sensitiveness would cheat in this manner only with considerable qualms—qualms derived not merely from the fact that he has broken a contract, but from the sense of the unfairness of what he was doing. Indeed liability to such qualms is among the very criteria of what we call moral sensitiveness. If, despite them, a man resolved to commit such an act, his moral justification would necessarily take the form of invoking, and attempting to balance the claims of, ends or values other than those of equality. He would be drawn in one direction by such considerations as the sanctity of promises; the social need to keep one's word and preserve the rule of law and the social order; the intrinsic desirability of avoiding unfairness; and so on. These factors he would have to weigh against such others as the desirability of increasing happiness (in this case of the pauper) or of avoiding the creation of misery; the claims, say, of scientific curiosity; the desire to follow some romantic impulse or vision of life, and so on. And the same kind of considerations will apply when exceptions are made to rules for "good" or "sufficient" reasons. The goodness of the reasons will depend upon the degree of value or importance attached to the purposes or motives adduced in justifying the exception, and these will vary as the moral convictions—the general outlooks—of different individuals or societies vary. I may consider it right to reward ability and achievement, and not, for example, honesty and kindness when they are accompanied by stupidity or ineptitude or failure. But others may well think this wrong, and the opposite morally right. I may think it right to reward the bearers of celebrated names or the descendants of famous families as such or to deny certain rights to Negroes which I grant freely to Englishmen, and I may try to defend this policy by maintaining that a society in which this is the normal practice seems to me intrinsically better, or more stable, or accords more closely with some pattern sanctioned by my religion, or my metaphysical beliefs about the structure of the universe, or the laws of history, whereas you

460

will reject a society dedicated to such practices as iniquitous because, let us assume, you reject my religion, or my metaphysics; or because you believe me to be interpreting them falsely, or think that a society constructed on such principles is intrinsically bad, or politically precarious; or simply because you believe so passionately in equality for its own sake, that you are not deterred by the realization that the consequences which I (and perhaps you too) wish to avert may well be brought about by opposing my policies. There are many ways in which such basic disagreements can manifest themselves: one man or sect or political party may desire equality in one sphere of life, say in social or in legal relationships or legal status, and ignore the economic consequences; another may regard economic relationships as being supremely important, and be prepared to tolerate lack of social or legal equality for the sake of a given economic structure. Some may regard exceptions made in favor of specific gifts or genius as justifiable by social results. Others may regard this as unfair, but, in their turn, believe in some natural social hierarchy, like Burke, and demand full equality of treatment upon each rung of the ladder—the only "true" equality— but bitterly oppose as being contrary to the natural order any attempt to deny the existence or relevance of such rungs or hierarchies, with its accompaniment of demands for equal treatment for all.[6] Consequently when, as often happens, a man admits that a law is administered fairly—that is to say with due regard to the principle of equality—but complains that the law itself is bad or iniquitous, we cannot always be clear about what is meant. The critic may wish to say that the more fairly the law in question is administered, the more this frustrates a principle of wider equality in which he himself believes, as when a law based upon the principle of discrimination between colored and white men is admini- stered fairly, with scrupulous regard to equal treatment within each category, but is thereby itself the cause of inequality between colored and white men. But the critic may have other reasons for complaint. He may attack this law because it offends against some value other than equality—because it promotes misery, because it frustrates talent, because it makes for social instability, because it insists upon equality in what the attacker thinks unimportant matters, but ignores equality in what he regards as more important aspects of human life (the scale of importance being decided in terms of values other than equality itself); because it ignores the claims of a religion; because it fulfills the claims of religion; because it is obscure or vague or too difficult to obey; and for an infinity of other possible reasons. Very commonly, because as in the instance given above, it permits one kind of equality at the expense of another, which can be a matter of fine nuance. In Mr. Wollheim's very ingenious example, where all the members of a community have equal rights and one vote per head, and each votes for some end different from those of the others, but two members by constantly voting in the same way are enabled theoretically to overrule all the others, what we object to is not the inequality of such a system, for in legal and even in political, terms, complete equality is clearly ensured. The unfairness of which Mr. Wollheim speaks is caused by our recognition that in this situation too great a majority of the voters find themselves permanently frustrated; we desire to see some degree of equality, not only of choices but of satisfactions, and regard it as "fairer" if some system of chance, for example, lot, were adopted, which by equalizing the chances of success, would prevent, at any rate, this type of systematic dissatisfaction. We should regard a system in which each person were permitted to have "his day" as fairer still. This is a typical clash between two systems incompatible in practice, each of which can claim to promote equality; one in the matter of the machinery of self-government, the other in the matter of the distribution of rewards. Similarly there is a conflict between those for whom equality means nondiscrimination in fields of human activity deemed important (however these are identified) on the basis of unalterable characteristics, for example, origins or physical characteristics, and the like, and those who reject this as an inadequate criterion and desire equality of treatment to remain unaffected even by such "alterable" attributes as religious or political views, personal habits and the like. We seem to choose as we choose because one solution seems to us to embody a blend of satisfaction of claims and desires (or to contain or omit other factors) which we prefer as a total pattern to the blend provided by the other solution. Indeed, the intervention of considerations of equity in the rigorous workings of some deductive legal system are due to our desire for justice that we are not always able to analyze too closely, into which the principle of "every man to count for one" does indeed enter, but without any clear understanding whether he is to count for one in the sphere of legislative rights, or of responsibility for action, or the receipt of benefits, or other respects, between any of which conflict all too easily occurs. And, of course, even in matters of equity the "counting for one" principle is, as often as not, modified by other ends and beliefs, in whatever combination they occur in a given culture or ethical system or within the outlook of an individual thinker.

Finally, those must not be forgotten who, as we said above, object to all rules as such and desire a society, whether this is practicable or not, governed in an unsystematic manner by the will of an inspired leader, or by the unpredictable movement of the Volksgeist, or the "spirit" of a race, a party, a church. This amounts to rejection of rules, and of equality as an end valuable in itself, and it is as well to recognize that this attitude is not as rare or as ineffective as liberal and socialist thinkers have sometimes assumed. In its conflicts with the traditional western principles of equality or justice or natural rights, or that minimum of civil liberties which is required to protect human beings from degradation and exploitation, romantic irrationalism has at times won easily enough. I cite this only as a warning against the thesis that the commandment to treat all men alike in like situations needs no independent argument to

462

support it, and that the proper criteria for what constitutes likeness cannot be doubted or conflict with each other, but are something taken for granted by reasonable men, a form of the working of natural reason which needs no justification, but is as self-evident as the principle of identity or that red is different from green. This is far from being so; and the vicissitudes of liberal principles in the last, and especially this, century, seem partly due to the unwarranted assumption on the part of their defenders that those who reject these principles only do so through ignorance or intellectual indolence or mental perversity or blindness.[7] Belief in equality—fairness—the view that unless there is a reason for it, recognized as sufficient by some identifiable criterion, one man should not be preferred to another, is a deep-rooted principle in human thought. It has been assimilated into many systems, those of the utilitarians and the theories of natural right, as well as various religious doctrines, but can be isolated from them, and has entered them less by way of logical connection, than by psychological affinity or because those who believed in these utilitarian or religious or metaphysical doctrines also in fact—perhaps from a craving for symmetry and unity that is at the root of all these views—believed in equality for its own sake, and therefore considered any society which did not make sufficient room for this principle to be to that degree worth less than one that did. In its extreme form egalitarianism requires the minimization of all differences between men, the obliteration of the maximum number of distinctions, the greatest possible degree of assimilation and uniformity to a single pattern. For all differences are capable of leading to irregularities of treatment. If this ideal is on the whole rejected in actual political doctrines, this seems mainly due to the fact that it conflicts with other ideals with which it cannot be wholly reconciled; indeed most ethical and political views are forms of less or more uneasy compromise between principles which in their extreme form cannot coexist.

Equality is one of the oldest and deepest elements in liberal thought, and is neither more nor less "natural" or "rational" than any other constituent in them. Like all human ends it cannot itself be defended or justified, for it is itself that which justifies other acts—means taken toward its realization. Many policies and views of life, themselves not particularly wedded to the ideal of equality, have been surreptitiously smuggled in under its cover, sometimes, as Mr. Wollheim suggests, with a certain measure of disingenuousness or hypocrisy. To isolate the pure ore of egalitarianism proper from those alloys which the admixture of other attitudes and ideals has at various times generated, is a task for the historian of ideas.

NOTES

1. In this formulation the principle will cover both of the forms of equal rights to property distinguished by Mr. Wollheim, i.e., both absolute equality of property, and

equality conditional upon specific qualifications, say, sufficient means to enable a man to buy it, or legal rights of inheritance, and the like. The notion of "sufficient reason" can be made to cover almost any type of situation, and is suspect for that very reason.

2. A policy of equal treatment for the largest number of persons may easily conflict with a policy of equal treatment of the largest number of classes of persons. Thus a reformer bent on abolishing discriminatory legislation may find himself faced with a choice between incommensurables, e.g., of emancipating either one large class of "inferiors," say, the poor, or several such classes, say, religious or racial minorities, which between them contain fewer members than the single large class. The first policy will give equality to more human beings; the second will abolish a greater number of class distinctions. Since either course can correctly be said to increase equality, and both cannot (for some practical reason) be adopted, the choice of a conscientious egalitarian will depend on the type of equality preferred. As it stands the question before him cannot be answered.

3. With the exception, I suppose, of those societies in which the desire for equality is itself so much stronger than all other desires, that inequality automatically breeds greater misery than any other possible arrangement.

4. This, or something like it, was also advocated by M. Bergson in one of his last works—that on the *Two Sources of Morality and Religion.*

5. *Philosophical Review,* 1955.

6. Or, like Plato and Aristotle, insist only on the natural hierarchy and appropriate differences of treatment at each level, without apparently caring whether there is social or economic equality between inhabitants of the same level, implying clearly that within each class unbridled competition can take place. Classical thought seems to be deeply and "naturally" inegalitarian.

7. As, for instance, by Locke, when in the *Second Treatise of Government,* he says "nothing more evident than that creatures of the same species and rank promiscuously born to all the same advantages of nature and the use of the same faculties, should also be equal one amongst another." This is the equality that the judicious Hooker is then praised for regarding as "evident in itself, and beyond all question." This, of course, is the pure doctrine of Natural Law, which Locke himself questioned (in the same year) in the *Essay* where he tells us that "there cannot any one moral rule be proposed whereof a man may not justly demand a reason" and contrasts "that most unshaken rule of morality and foundation of all social virtue, 'That one should do as he would be done unto' " which can "without any absurdity" be questioned and "a reason why?" demanded—with such genuinely senseless questions as why "it is impossible for the same thing to be and not to be." Locke's hesitations and confusions mark the beginning of the breakdown of the notion that at least some moral or political principles are as self-evident as those of logic or that "red is different from blue." An excellent discussion of this and related topics is to be found in Professor Morton White's article on "Original Sin, Natural Law and Politics," in *The Partisan Review,* Spring, 1956.

A
DEFENSE
OF
ABORTION*[1]
Judith Jarvis Thompson

Most opposition to abortion relies on the premise that the fetus is a human being, a person, from the moment of conception. The premise is argued for, but, as I think, not well. Take, for example, the most common argument. We are asked to notice that the development of a human being from conception through birth into childhood is continuous; then it is said that to draw a line, to choose a point in this development and say "before this point the thing is not a person, after this point it is a person" is to make an arbitrary choice for which in the nature of things, no good reason can be given. It is concluded that the fetus is—or anyway, that we had better say it is—a person from the moment of conception. But this conclusion does not follow. Similar things might be said about the development of an acorn into an oak tree, and it does not follow that acorns are oak trees or that we had better say they are. Arguments of this form are sometimes called "slippery slope arguments"—the phrase is perhaps self-explanatory—and it is dismaying that opponents of abortion rely on them so heavily and uncritically.

I am inclined to agree, however, that the prospects for "drawing a line" in the development of the fetus look dim. I am inclined to think also that we shall probably have to agree that the fetus has already become a human person well before birth. Indeed, it comes as a surprise when one first learns how early in its life it begins to acquire human characteristics. By the tenth week, for example, it already has a face, arms and legs, fingers and toes; it has internal organs, and brain activity is detectable.[2] On the other hand, I think that the premise is false, that the fetus is a person from the moment of conception. A newly fertilized

*Reprinted by permission from "A Defense of Abortion," by Judith Jarvis Thomson, *Philosophy and Public Affairs*, vol. 1, no. 1, pp. 47-66; copyright © 1971 by Princeton University Press.

ovum, a newly implanted clump of cells, is no more a person than an acorn is an oak tree. But I shall not discuss any of this, for it seems to me to be of great interest to ask what happens if, for the sake of argument, we allow the premise. How precisely are we supposed to get from there to the conclusion that abortion is morally impermissible? Opponents of abortion commonly spend most of their time establishing that the fetus is a person and hardly any time explaining the step from there to the impermissibility of abortion. Perhaps they think the step too simple and obvious to require much comment. Or perhaps, instead, they are simply being economical in argument. Many of those who defend abortion rely on the premise that the fetus is not a person, but only a bit of tissue that will become a person at birth, and why pay out more arguments than you have to? Whatever the explanation, I suggest that the step they take is neither easy nor obvious, that it calls for closer examination than it is commonly given, and that when we do give it this closer examination we shall feel inclined to reject it.

I propose, then, that we grant that the fetus is a person from the moment of conception. How does the argument go from here? Something like this, I take it. Every person has a right to life, so the fetus has a right to life. No doubt the mother has a right to decide what shall happen in and to her body; everyone would grant that. But surely a person's right to life is stronger and more stringent than the mother's right to decide what happens in and to her body, and so outweighs it. So the fetus may not be killed; an abortion may not be performed.

It sounds plausible. But now let me ask you to imagine this. You wake up in the morning and find yourself back to back in bed with an unconscious violinist. A famous unconscious violinist. He has been found to have a fatal kidney ailment, and the Society of Music Lovers has canvassed all the available medical records and found that you alone have the right blood type to help. They have therefore kidnapped you, and last night the violinist's circulatory system was plugged into yours, so that your kidneys can be used to extract poisons from his blood as well as your own. The director of the hospital now tells you, "Look, we're sorry the Society of Music Lovers did this to you—we would never have permitted it if we had known. But still, they did it, and the violinist is now plugged into you. To unplug you would be to kill him. But never mind, it's only for nine months. By then he will have recovered from his ailment and can safely be unplugged from you."

Is it morally incumbent on you to accede to this situation? No doubt it would be very nice of you if you did, a great kindness. But do you *have* to accede to it? What if it were not nine months, but nine years? Or longer still? What if the director of the hospital says, "Tough luck, I agree, but you've now got to stay in bed, with the violinist plugged into you, for the rest of your life. Because remember this: All persons have a right to life, and violinists are persons. Granted you have a right to decide what happens in and to your body, but a person's right to life outweighs your right to decide what happens in and to your body. So you cannot ever be unplugged from him." I imagine you would regard this as outrageous, which suggests that something really is wrong with that plausible-sounding argument I mentioned a moment ago.

In this case, of course, you were kidnapped; you didn't volunteer for the operation that plugged the violinist into your kidneys. Can those who oppose abortion on the grounds I mentioned make an exception for a pregnancy due to rape? Certainly. They can say that persons have a right to life only if they didn't come into existence because of rape, or they can say that all persons have a right to life but that some have less of a right to life than others, in particular, that those who came into existence because of rape have less. But these statements have a rather unpleasant sound. Surely the question of whether you have a right to life at all, or how much of it you have, shouldn't turn on the question of whether or not you are the product of a rape. In fact, the people who oppose abortion on the grounds I mentioned do not make this distinction, and hence do not make an exception in case of rape.

Nor do they make an exception for a case in which the mother has to spend the nine months of her pregnancy in bed. They would agree that would be a great pity, and hard on the mother; but all the same, all persons have a right to life, the fetus is a person, and so on. I suspect, in fact, that they would not make an exception for a case in which, miraculously enough, the pregnancy went on for nine years, or even the rest of the mother's life.

Some won't even make an exception for a case in which continuation of the pregnancy is likely to shorten the mother's life; they regard abortion as impermissible even to save the mother's life. Such cases are nowadays very rare, and many opponents of abortion do not accept this extreme view. All the same, it is a good place to begin: a number of points of interest come out in respect to it.

1. Let us call the view that abortion is impermissible even to save the mother's life "the extreme view." I want to suggest first that it does not issue from the argument I mentioned earlier without the addition of some fairly powerful premises. Suppose a woman has become pregnant, and now learns that she has a cardiac condition such that she will die if she carries the baby to term. What may be done for her? The fetus, being a person, has a right to life, but as the mother is a person too, so has she a right to life. Presumably they have an equal right to life. How is it supposed to come out that an abortion may not be performed? If mother and child have an equal right to life, shouldn't we perhaps flip a coin? Or should we add to the mother's right to life her right to decide what happens in and to her body, which everybody seems to be ready to grant—the sum of her rights now outweighing the fetus' right to life?

The most familiar argument here is the following. We are told that performing the abortion would be directly killing[3] the child, whereas doing nothing would not be killing the mother, but only letting her die. Moreover, in killing the child, one would be killing an innocent person, for the child has committed no crime, and is not aiming at his mother's death. And then there are a variety of ways in which this might be continued. (1) But as directly killing an innocent person is always and absolutely impermissible, an abortion may not be performed, or (2) as directly killing an innocent person is murder, and murder is always and absolutely impermissible, an abortion may not be performed,[4] or (3) as one's duty to refrain from directly killing an innocent person is more stringent than one's duty to keep a person from dying, an abortion may not be performed, or (4) if one's only options are directly killing an innocent person or letting a person die, one must prefer letting the person die, thus an abortion may not be performed.[5]

Some people seem to have thought that these are not further premises which must be added if the conclusion is to be reached, but that they follow from the very fact that an innocent person has a right to life.[6] But this seems to me to be a mistake; perhaps the simplest way to show this is to bring out that while we must certainly grant that innocent persons have a right to life, the theses in (1) through (4) are all false. Take (2), for example. If directly killing an innocent person is murder and thus is impermissible, then the mother's directly killing the innocent person insider her is murder and thus is impermissible. But it cannot seriously be thought to be murder if the mother performs an abortion on herself to save her life. It cannot seriously be said that she *must* refrain, that she *must* sit passively by and wait for her death. Let us look again at the case of you and the violinist. There you are in bed with the violinist, and the director of the hospital says to you: "It's all most distressing, and I deeply sympathize, but, you see, this is putting an additional strain on your kidneys, and you'll be dead within the month. But you *have* to stay where you are all the same, because unplugging you would be directly killing an innocent violinist, and that's murder, and that's impermissible." If anything in the world is true, it is that you do not commit murder, you do not do what is impermissible, if you reach around to your back and unplug yourself from that violinist to save your life.

The main focus of attention in writings on abortion has been on what a third party may or may not do in answer to a request from a woman for an abortion. This is in a way understandable. Things being as they are, there isn't much a woman can safely do to abort herself. So the question asked is what a third party may do, and what the mother may do, if it is mentioned at all, is deduced, almost as an afterthought, from what it is concluded that third parties may do. But is seems to me that to treat the matter in this way is to refuse to grant to the mother that very status of person which is so firmly insisted on for the fetus. We cannot simply read off what a person may do from what a third party may do. Suppose you find yourself trapped in a tiny house with a growing child. I mean a very tiny house, and a rapidly growing child—you are already up against the wall of the house and in a few minutes you'll be crushed to death. The child, on the other hand, won't be crushed to death; if nothing is done to stop him from growing he'll be hurt, but in the end he'll simply burst open the house and walk out a free man. Now I could well understand it if a bystander were to say, "There's nothing we can do for you. We cannot choose between your life and his, we cannot be the ones to decide who is to live, we cannot intervene." But it cannot be concluded that you too can do nothing, that you cannot attack it to save your life. However innocent the child may be, you do not have to wait passively while it crushes you to death. Perhaps a pregnant woman is vaguely felt to have the status of house, to which we don't allow the right of self-defense. But if the woman houses the child, it should be remembered that she is a person who houses it.

I should perhaps stop to say explicitly that I am not claiming that people have a right to do anything whatever to save their lives. I think, rather, that there are drastic limits to the right of self-defense. If someone threatens you with death unless you torture someone else to death, I think you have not the right, even to save your life, to do so. But the case under consideration here is very different. In our case there are only two people involved, one whose life is threatened, and one who threatens it. Both are innocent: the one who is threatened is not threatened because of any fault, the one who threatens does not threaten because of any fault. For this reason we may feel that we bystanders cannot intervene. But the person threatened can.

In sum, a woman surely can defend her life against the threat to it posed by the unborn child, even if doing so involves its death. This shows not merely that the theses in (1) through (4) are false, it shows also that the extreme view of abortion is false. So we need not canvass any other possible ways of arriving at it from the argument I mentioned at the outset.

2. The extreme view could, of course, be weakened to say that while abortion is permissible to save the mother's life, it may not be performed by a third party, but only by the mother herself. But this cannot be right either, for what we have to keep in mind is that the mother and the unborn child are not like two tenants in a small house which has, by an unfortunate mistake, been rented to both: the mother *owns* the house. The fact that she does adds to the offensiveness of deducing that the mother can do nothing from the supposition that third parties can do nothing. But it does more than this: it casts a bright light on the supposition that third parties can do nothing. Certainly it lets us see that a third party who says "I cannot choose between you" is fooling himself if he thinks this is impartiality. If Jones has found and fastened on a certain coat which he needs to keep him from freezing but which Smith also needs to keep himself from freezing, then it is not impartiality that says "I cannot choose between you" when Smith owns the coat. Women have said again and again "This body is *my* body!" and they have reason to feel angry, reason to feel that

it has been like shouting into the wind. Smith, after all, is hardly likely to bless us if we say to him, "Of course it's your coat, anybody would grant that it is. But no one may choose between you and Jones who is to have it."

We should really ask what it is that says "no one may choose" in the face of the fact that the body that houses the child is the mother's body. It may be simply a failure to appreciate this fact. But it may be something more interesting, namely the sense that one has a right to refuse to lay hands on people, even where it would be just and fair to do so, even where justice seems to require that somebody do so. Thus justice might call for somebody to get Smith's coat back from Jones, and yet you have a right to refuse to be the one to lay hands on Jones, a right to refuse to do physical violence to him. This, I think, must be granted. But then what should be said is not "no one may choose," but only "*I* cannot choose," and indeed not even this, but "*I* will not *act*," leaving it open that somebody else can or should, and in particular that anyone in a position of authority, with the job of securing people's rights, both can and should. So this is no difficulty. I have not been arguing that any given third party must accede to the mother's request that he perform an abortion to save her life, but only that he may.

I suppose that in some views of human life the mother's body is only on loan to her, the loan not being one which gives her any prior claim to it. One who held this view might well think it impartiality to say "I cannot choose." But I shall simply ignore this possibility. My own view is that if a human being has any just, prior claim to anything at all, he has a just, prior claim to his own body. Perhaps this needn't be argued for here anyway, since, as I mentioned, the arguments against abortion we are looking at do grant that the woman has a right to decide what happens in and to her body.

But although they do grant it, I have tried to show that they do not take seriously what is done in granting it. I suggest the same thing will reappear even more clearly when we turn away from cases in which the mother's life is at stake, and attend, as I propose we now do, to the vastly more common cases in which a woman wants an abortion for some less weighty reason than preserving her own life.

3. Where the mother's life is not at stake, the argument I mentioned at the outset seems to have a much stronger pull. "Everyone has a right to life, so the unborn person has a right to life." Isn't the child's right to life weightier than anything other than the mother's own right to life, which she might put forward as grounds for an abortion?

This argument treats the right to life as if it were unproblematic. It is not, and this seems to me to be precisely the source of the mistake.

We should now, at long last, ask what it comes to, to have a right to life. In some views having a right to life includes having a right to be given at least the bare minimum one needs for continued life. But suppose that what in fact *is* the

470

bare minimum a man needs for continued life is something he has no right at all to be given? If I am sick unto death, and the only thing that will save my life is the touch of Henry Fonda's cool hand on my fevered brow, then all the same, I have no right to be given the touch of Henry Fonda's cool hand on my fevered brow. It would be frightfully nice of him to fly in from the West Coast to provide it. It would be less nice, though no doubt well meant, if my friends flew out to the West Coast and carried Henry Fonda back with them. But I have no right at all against anybody that he should do this for me. Or again, to return to the earlier example, the fact that for continued life that violinist needs the continued use of your kidneys does not establish that he has a right to be given the continued use of your kidneys. He certainly has no right against you that *you* should give him continued use of your kidneys, for nobody has any right to use your kidneys unless you give him such a right. Nobody has the right against you that you shall give him this right—if you do allow him to go on using your kidneys, this is a kindness on your part, and not something he can claim from you as his due. Nor has he any right against anybody else that *they* should give him continued use of your kidneys. Certainly he had no right against the Society of Music Lovers that they should plug him into you in the first place. If you now start to unplug yourself, having learned that you will otherwise have to spend nine years in bed with him, there is nobody in the world who must try to prevent you, in order to see to it that he is given something he has a right to be given.

Some people are stricter about the right to life. In their view, it does not include the right to be given anything, but amounts to, and only to, the right not to be killed by anybody. But here a related difficulty arises. If everybody is to refrain from killing that violinist, then everybody must refrain from doing a great many different sorts of things. Everybody must refrain from slitting his throat, everybody must refrain from shooting him—and everybody must refrain from unplugging you from him. But does he have a right against everybody that they shall refrain from unplugging you from him? To refrain from doing this is to allow him to continue to use your kidneys. It could be argued that he has a right against us that *we* should allow him to continue to use your kidneys. That is, while he had no right against us that we should give him the use of your kidneys, it might be argued that he anyway has a right against us that we shall not now intervene and deprive him of the use of your kidneys. (I will come back to third-party interventions later.) But certainly the violinist has no right against you that *you* shall allow him to continue to use your kidneys. As I said, if you do allow him to use them, it is a kindness on your part and not something you owe him.

The difficulty I point to here is not peculiar to the right to life. It reappears in connection with all the other natural rights, and it is something which an adequate account of rights must deal with. For present purposes it is enough just

471

to draw attention to it. But I would stress that I am not arguing that people do not have a right to life—quite to the contrary, it seems to me that the primary control we must place on the acceptability of an account of rights is that it should turn out in that account to be a truth that all persons have a right to life. I am arguing only that having a right to life does not guarantee having either a right to be given the use of or a right to be allowed continued use of another person's body—even if one needs it for life itself. So the right to life will not serve the opponents of abortion in the very simple and clear way in which they seem to have thought it would.

4. There is another way to bring out the difficulty. In the most ordinary case, to deprive someone of what he has a right to is to treat him unjustly. Suppose a boy and his small brother are jointly given a box of chocolates for Christmas. If the older boy takes the box and refuses to give his brother any of the chocolates, he is unjust to him, for the brother has been given a right to half of them. But suppose that, having learned that otherwise it means nine years in bed with that violinist, you unplug yourself from him. You surely are not being unjust to him, for you gave him no right to use your kidneys, and no one else can have given him any such right. But we have to notice that in unplugging yourself, you are killing him; and violinists, like everybody else, have a right to life, and thus, in the view we were considering just now, the right not to be killed. So here you do what he supposedly has a right you shall not do, but you do not act unjustly to him in doing it.

The emendation which may be made at this point is this: the right to life consists not in the right not to be killed, but rather in the right not to be killed unjustly. This runs a risk of circularity, but never mind: it would enable us to square the fact that the violinist has a right to life with the fact that you do not act unjustly toward him in unplugging yourself, thereby killing him. For if you do not kill him unjustly, you do not violate his right to life, so it is no wonder you do him no injustice.

But if this emendation is accepted, the gap in the argument against abortion stares us plainly in the face: it is by no means enough to show that the fetus is a person and to remind us that all persons have a right to life. We need to be shown also that killing the fetus violates its right to life, that is, that abortion is unjust killing. And is it?

I suppose we may take it as a datum that in a case of pregnancy due to rape the mother has not given the unborn person a right to the use of her body for food and shelter. Indeed, in what pregnancy could it be supposed that the mother has given the unborn person such a right? It is not as if there were unborn persons drifting about the world, to whom a woman who wants a child says "I invite you in."

It might be argued that there are other ways one can have acquired a right to the use of another person's body than by having been invited to use it by that person. Suppose a woman voluntarily indulges in intercourse, knowing of the chance it will issue in pregnancy, and then she does become pregnant. Is she not in part responsible for the presence, in fact the very existence, of the unborn person inside her? No doubt she did not invite it in. But doesn't her partial responsibility for its being there give it a right to the use of her body?[7] If so, then her aborting it would be more like the boy's taking away the chocolates, and less like your unplugging yourself from the violinist—doing so would be depriving it of what it does have a right to, and thus would be doing it an injustice.

Then, too, it might be asked whether or not she can kill it even to save her own life: If she voluntarily called it into existence, how can she now kill it, even in self-defense?

The first thing to be said about this is that it is something new. Opponents of abortion have been so concerned to make out the independence of the fetus, in order to establish that it has a right to life, just as its mother does, that they have tended to overlook the possible support they might gain from making out that the fetus is *dependent* on the mother, in order to establish that she has a special kind of responsibility for it, a responsibility that gives it rights against her which are not possessed by any independent person—such as an ailing violinist who is a stranger to her.

On the other hand, this argument would give the unborn person a right to its mother's body only if her pregnancy resulted from a voluntary act, undertaken in full knowledge of the chance a pregnancy might result from it. It would leave out entirely the unborn person whose existence is due to rape. Pending the availability of some further argument, then, we would be left with the conclusion that unborn persons whose existence is due to rape have no right to the use of their mothers' bodies, and thus that aborting them is not depriving them of anything they have a right to and hence is not unjust killing.

We should also notice that it is not at all plain that this argument really does go even as far as it purports to. For there are cases and cases, and the details make a difference. If the room is stuffy, and I therefore open a window to air it, and a burglar climbs in, it would be absurd to say, "Ah, now he can stay, she's given him a right to the use of her house—for she is partially responsible for his presence there, having voluntarily done what enabled him to get in, in full knowledge that there are such things as burglars and that burglars burgle." It would be still more absurd to say this if I had had bars installed outside my windows, precisely to prevent burglars from getting in, and a burglar got in only because of a defect in the bars. It remains equally absurd if we imagine it is not a burglar who climbs in, but an innocent person who blunders or falls in. Again, suppose it were like this: people-seeds drift about in the air like pollen, and if you open your windows, one may drift in and take root in your carpets or upholstery. You don't want children, so you fix up your windows with fine mesh screens, the very best you can buy. As can happen, however, and on very, very rare occasions does happen, one of the screens is defective; and a seed drifts in and takes root. Does the person-plant who now develops have a right to the use of your house? Surely not, despite the fact that you voluntarily opened your windows, you knowingly kept carpets and upholstered furniture, and you knew that screens were sometimes defective. Someone may argue that you are responsible for its rooting, that it does have a right to your house, because after all you *could* have lived out your life with bare floors and furniture, or with sealed windows and doors. But this won't do—for by the same token anyone can avoid a pregnancy due to rape by having a hysterectomy, or anyway by never leaving home without a (reliable!) army.

It seems to me that the argument we are looking at can establish at most that there are *some* cases in which the unborn person has a right to the use of its mother's body, and therefore *some* cases in which abortion is unjust killing. There is room for much discussion and argument as to precisely which, if any. But I think we should sidestep this issue and leave it open, for at any rate the argument certainly does not establish that all abortion is unjust killing.

5. There is room for yet another argument here, however. We surely must all grant that there may be cases in which it would be morally indecent to detach a person from your body at the cost of his life. Suppose you learn that what the violinist needs is not nine years of your life, but only one hour: all you need do to save his life is to spend one hour in that bed with him. Suppose also that letting him use your kidneys for that one hour would not affect your health in the slightest. Admittedly you were kidnapped. Admittedly you did not give anyone permission to plug him into you. Nevertheless it seems to me plain you *ought* to allow him to use your kidneys for that hour; it would be indecent to refuse.

Again, suppose pregnancy lasted only an hour, and constituted no threat to life or health. Suppose that a woman becomes pregnant as a result of rape. Admittedly she did not voluntarily do anything to bring about the existence of a child. Admittedly she did nothing at all which would give the unborn person a right to the use of her body. All the same it might well be said, as in the newly emended violinist story, that she *ought* to allow it to remain for that hour—that it would be indecent in her to refuse.

Some people are inclined to use the term "right" in such a way that it follows from the fact that you ought to allow a person to use your body for the hour he needs, that he has a right to use your body for the hour he needs, even though he has not been given that right by any person or act. They may say that it follows also that if you refuse, you act unjustly toward him. This use of the term is perhaps so common that it cannot be called wrong; nevertheless it seems to me to be an unfortunate loosening of what we would do better to keep a tight rein on. Suppose that box of chocolates I mentioned earlier had not been given to both boys jointly, but was given only to the older boy. There he sits, stolidly eating his way through the box, his small brother watching enviously. Here we are likely to say "You ought not to be so mean. You ought to give your brother some of those chocolates." My own view is that it just does not follow from the truth of this that the brother has any right to any of the chocolates. If the boy refuses to give his brother any, he is greedy, stingy, callous—but not unjust. I suppose that the people I have in mind will say it does follow that the brother has a right to some of the chocolates, and thus that the boy does act unjustly if he refuses to give his brother any. But the effect of saying this is to obscure what we should keep distinct, namely the difference between the boy's refusal in this case and the boy's refusal in the earlier case, in which the box was given to both boys jointly, and in which the small brother thus had what was from any point of view clear title to half.

A further objection to so using the term "right" that from the fact that A ought to do a thing for B, it follows that B has a right against A that A do it for him, is that it is going to make the question of whether or not a man has a right to a thing turn on how easy it is to provide him with it; this seems not merely unfortunate, but morally unacceptable. Take the case of Henry Fonda again. I said earlier that I had no right to the touch of his cool hand on my fevered brow even though I needed it to save my life. I said it would be frightfully nice of him to fly in from the West Coast to provide me with it, but that I had no right against him that he should do so. But suppose he isn't on the West Coast. Suppose he has only to walk across the room, place a hand briefly on my brow, and lo, my life is saved. Then surely he ought to do it, it would be indecent to refuse. Is it to be said "Ah, well it follows that in this case she has a right to the touch of his hand on her brow, and so it would be an injustice in him to refuse?" So that I have a right to it when it is easy for him to provide it, though no right when it's hard? It's rather a shocking idea that anyone's rights should fade away and disappear as it gets harder and harder to accord them to him.

So my own view is that even though you ought to let the violinist use your kidneys for the one hour he needs, we should not conclude that he has a right to do so—we should say that if you refuse, you are, like the boy who owns all the chocolates and will give none away, self-centered and callous, indecent in fact, but not unjust. And similarly, that even supposing a case in which a woman pregnant due to rape ought to allow the unborn person to use her body for the hour he needs, we should not conclude that he has a right to do so; we should conclude that she is self-centered, callous, indecent, but not unjust, if she refuses. The complaints are no less grave; they are just different. However, there is no need to insist on this point. If anyone does wish to deduce "he has a right" from "you ought," then all the same he must surely grant that there are cases in which it is not morally required of you that you allow that violinist to use your kidneys, and in which he does not have right to use them, and in which you do not do him an injustice if you refuse. And so also for mother and unborn child. Except in such cases as the unborn person has a right to demand it—and we are leaving open the possibility that there may be such cases—nobody is morally *required* to make large sacrifices, of health, of all other interests and concerns, of all other duties and commitments, for nine years, or even for nine months, in order to keep another person alive.

6. We have, in fact, to distinguish between two kinds of Samaritan: the Good Samaritan and what we might call the Minimally Decent Samaritan. The story of the Good Samaritan, you will remember, goes like this:

> A certain man went down from Jerusalem to Jericho, and fell among thieves, which stripped him of his raiment, and wounded him, and departed, leaving him half dead.
>
> And by chance there came down a certain priest that way; and when he saw him, he passed by on the other side.
>
> And likewise a Levite, when he was at the place, came and looked on him, and passed by on the other side.
>
> But a certain Samaritan, as he journeyed, came where he was; and when he saw him he had compassion on him.
>
> And went to him, and bound up his wounds, pouring in oil and wine, and set him on his own beast, and brought him to an inn, and took care of him.
>
> And on the morrow, when he departed, he took out two pence, and gave them to the host, and said unto him, "Take care of him; and whatsoever thou spendest more, when I come again, I will repay thee."
>
> (Luke 10:30-35)

The Good Samaritan went out of his way, at some cost to himself, to help one in need of it. We are not told what the options were, that is, whether or not the priest and the Levite could have helped by doing less than the Good Samaritan did, but assuming they could have, then the fact they did nothing at all shows they were not even Minimally Decent Samaritans, not because they were not Samaritans, but because they were not even minimally decent.

These things are a matter of degree, of course, but there is a difference, and it comes out perhaps most clearly in the story of Kitty Genovese, who, as you will remember, was murdered while 38 people watched or listened, and did nothing at all to help her. A Good Samaritan would have rushed out to give direct assistance against the murderer. Or perhaps we had better allow that it would have been a Splendid Samaritan who did this, on the ground that it would have involved a risk of death for himself. But the 38 not only did not do this, they did not even trouble to pick up a phone to call the police. Minimally Decent Samaritanism would call for doing at least that, and their not having done it was monstrous.

After telling the story of the Good Samaritan, Jesus said "Go, and do thou likewise." Perhaps he meant that we are morally required to act as the Good

Samaritan did. Perhaps he was urging people to do more than is morally required of them. In any event, it seems plain that it was not morally required of any of the 38 that he rush out to give direct assistance at the risk of his own life, and that it is not morally required of anyone that he give long stretches of his life—nine years or nine months—to sustaining the life of a person who has no special right (we were leaving open the possibility of this) to demand it.

Indeed, with one rather striking class of exceptions, no one in any country in the world is *legally* required to do anywhere near as much as this for anyone else. The class of exceptions is obvious. My main concern here is not the state of the law with respect to abortion, but it is worth drawing attention to the fact that in no state in this country is any man compelled by law to be even a Minimally Decent Samaritan to any person. There is no law under which charges could be brought against the 38 who stood by while Kitty Genovese died. By contrast, in most states in this country women are compelled by law to be not merely Minimally Decent Samaritans, but Good Samaritans to unborn persons inside them. This doesn't, by itself, settle anything one way or the other, because it may well be argued that there should be laws in this country—as there are in many European countries—compelling at least Minimally Decent Samaritanism.[8] But it does show that there is a gross injustice in the existing state of the law. It shows also that the groups currently working against liberalization of abortion laws, in fact working toward having it declared unconstitutional for a state to permit abortion, had better start working for the adoption of Good Samaritan laws generally or earn the charge that they are acting in bad faith.

I should think, myself, that Minimally Decent Samaritan laws would be one thing, Good Samaritan laws quite another, and in fact highly improper. But we are not here concerned with the law. What we should ask is not whether anybody should be compelled by law to be a Good Samaritan, but whether we must accede to a situation in which somebody is being compelled—by nature, perhaps—to be a Good Samaritan. We have, in other words, to look now at third-party interventions. I have been arguing that no person is morally required to make large sacrifices to sustain the life of another who has no right to demand them, and this even where the sacrifices do not include life itself. We are not morally required to be Good Samaritans or anyway Very Good Samaritans to one another, but what if a man cannot extricate himself from such a situation? What if he appeals to us to extricate him? It seems plain that there are cases in which we can, cases in which a Good Samaritan would extricate him. There you are, you were kidnapped, and nine years in bed with that violinist lie ahead of you. You have your own life to lead. You are sorry, but you simply cannot see giving up so much of your life to the sustaining of his. You cannot extricate yourself and ask us to do so. I should have thought that—in light of his having no right to the use of your body—it was obvious that we do not have to accede to your being forced to give up so much. We can do what you ask. There is no injustice to the violinist in our doing so.

7. Following the lead of the opponents of abortion, I have throughout been speaking of the fetus merely as a person, and what I have been asking is whether or not the argument we began with, which proceeds only from the fetus' being a person, really does establish its conclusion. I have argued that it does not.

But of course there are arguments and arguments, and it may be said that I have simply fastened on the wrong one. It may be said that what is important is not merely the fact that the fetus is a person, but that it is a person for whom the woman has a special kind of responsibility issuing from the fact that she is its mother. And it might be argued that all my analogies are therefore irrelevant—for you do not have that special kind of responsibility for that violinist, Henry Fonda does not have that special kind of responsibility for me. And our attention might be drawn to the fact that men and women both *are* compelled by law to provide support for their children.

I have, in effect, dealt (briefly) with this argument in section 4 above, but a (still briefer) recapitulation now may be in order. Surely we do not have any such "special responsibility" for a person unless we have assumed it explicitly or implicitly. If a set of parents do not try to prevent pregnancy, do not obtain an abortion, and then at the time of birth of the child do not put it up for adoption but rather take it home with them, then they have assumed responsibility for it, they have given it rights, and they cannot *now* withdraw support from it at the cost of its life because they now find it difficult to go on providing for it. But if they have taken all reasonable precautions against having a child, they do not simply by virtue of their biological relationship to the child who comes into existence have a special responsibility for it. They may wish to assume responsibility for it, or they may not wish to. I am suggesting that if assuming responsibility for it would require large sacrifices, then they may refuse. A Good Samaritan would not refuse—or anyway, a Splendid Samaritan, if the sacrifices that had to be made were enormous. But then so would a Good Samaritan assume responsibility for that violinist; so would Henry Fonda, if he is a Good Samaritan, fly in from the West Coast and assume responsibility for me.

8. My argument will be found unsatisfactory on two counts by many of those who want to regard abortion as morally permissible. First, while I do argue that abortion is not impermissible, I do not argue that it is always permissible. There may well be cases in which carrying the child to term requires only Minimally Decent Samaritanism of the mother and this is a standard we must not fall below. I am inclined to think it a merit of my account precisely that it does *not* give a general yes or a general no. It allows for and supports our sense that, for example, a sick and desperately frightened 14-year-old schoolgirl, pregnant due to rape, may *of course* choose abortion, and that any

law which rules this out is an insane law. It also allows for and supports our sense that in other cases, resort to abortion is even positively indecent. It would be indecent in the woman to request an abortion, and indecent in a doctor to perform it, if she is in her seventh month and wants the abortion just to avoid the nuisance of postponing a trip abroad. The very fact that the arguments I have been drawing attention to treat all cases of abortion, or even all cases of abortion in which the mother's life is not at stake, as morally on a par ought to have made them suspect at the outset.

Second, while I am arguing for the permissibility of abortion in some cases, I am not arguing for the right to secure the death of the unborn child. It is easy to confuse these two things in that up to a certain point in the life of the fetus it is not able to survive outside the mother's body; hence removing it from her body guarantees its death. But they are importantly different. I have argued that you are not morally required to spend nine months in bed, sustaining the life of that violinist. But to say this is by no means to say that if, when you unplug yourself, there is a miracle and he survives, you then have a right to turn round and slit his throat. You may detach yourself even if this costs him his life; you have no right to be guaranteed his death, by some other means, if unplugging yourself does not kill him. There are some people who will feel dissatisfied by the thought of a child, a bit of herself, put up for adoption and never seen or heard of again. She may therefore want not merely that the child be detached from her, but more, that it die. Some opponents of abortion are inclined to regard this as beneath contempt—thereby showing insensitivity to what is surely a powerful source of despair. All the same, I agree that the desire for the child's death is not one which anybody may gratify, should it turn out to be possible to detach the child alive.

At this place, however, it should be remembered that we have only been pretending throughout that the fetus is a human being from the moment of conception. A very early abortion is surely not the killing of a person, and so is not dealt with by anything I have said here.

NOTES

1. I am very much indebted to James Thomson for discussion, criticism, and many helpful suggestions.

2. Daniel Callahan, *Abortion: Law, Choice and Morality* (New York, 1970), p. 373. This book gives a fascinating survey of the available information on abortion. The Jewish tradition is surveyed in David M. Feldman, *Birth Control in Jewish Law* (New York, 1968), Part 5, the Catholic tradition in John T. Noonan, Jr., "An Almost Absolute Value in History," in *The Morality of Abortion,* ed. John T. Noonan, Jr. (Cambridge, Mass., 1970).

3. The term "direct" in the arguments I refer to is a technical one. Roughly, what is meant by "direct killing" is either killing as an end in itself, or killing as a means to some end, for example, the end of saving someone else's life. See note 6, below, for an example of its use.

4. Cf. *Encyclical Letter of Pope Pius XI on Christian Marriage,* St. Paul Editions (Boston, n.d.), p. 32: "however much we may pity the mother whose health and even life is gravely imperiled in the performance of the duty allotted to her by nature, nevertheless what could ever be a sufficient reason for excusing in any way the direct murder of the innocent? This is precisely what we are dealing with here." Noonan (*The Morality of Abortion,* p. 43) reads this as follows: "What cause can ever avail to excuse in any way the direct killing of the innocent? For it is a question of that."

5. The thesis in (4) is in an interesting way weaker than those in (1), (2), and (3): they rule out abortion even in cases in which both mother *and* child will die if the abortion is not performed. By contrast, one who held the view expressed in (4) could consistently say that one needn't prefer letting two persons die to killing one.

6. Cf. the following passage from Pius XII, *Address to the Italian Catholic Society of Midwives*: "The baby in the maternal breast has the right to life immediately from God. Hence there is no man, no human authority, no science, no medical, eugenic, social, economic or moral 'indication' which can establish or grant a valid juridical ground for a direct deliberate disposition of an innocent human life, that is a disposition which looks to its destruction either as an end or as a means to another end perhaps in itself not illicit.— The baby, still not born, is a man in the same degree and for the same reason as the mother" (quoted in Noonan, *The Morality of Abortion,* p. 45).

7. The need for a discussion of this argument was brought home to me by members of the Society for Ethical and Legal Philosophy, to whom this paper was orginally presented.

8. For a discussion of the difficulties involved, and a survey of the European experience with such laws, see *The Good Samaritan and the Law,* ed. James M. Ratcliffe (New York, 1966).

THE RIGHTS
AND WRONGS
OF ABORTION:
A REPLY TO
JUDITH THOMSON*
John Finnis

Fortunately, none of the arguments for and against abortion *need* be expressed in terms of "rights." As we shall see, Judith Thomson virtually admits as much in her "A Defense of Abortion."[1] But since she has chosen to conduct her case by playing off a "right to life" against a "right to decide what happens in and to one's body," I shall begin by showing how this way of arguing about the rights and wrongs of abortion needlessly complicates and confuses the issue. It is convenient and appropriate to speak of "rights" for purposes and in contexts which I shall try to identify; it is most inconvenient and inappropriate when one is debating the moral permissibility of types of action—types such as "abortions performed without the desire to kill," which is the type of action Thomson wishes to defend as morally permissible under most circumstances. So in section I of this essay I shall show how her specification and moral characterization of this type of action are logically independent of her discussion of "rights." Then in section II I shall outline some principles of moral characterization and of moral permissibility, principles capable of explaining some of the moral condemnations which Thomson expresses but which remain all too vulnerable and obscure in her paper. In section III I shall show how the elaboration of those principles warrants those condemnations of abortion which Thomson thinks mistaken as well as many of those attributions of human rights which she so much takes for granted. In section IV I briefly state the reason (misstated by Thomson and also by Wertheimer[2]) why the fetus from conception has human rights, that is, it should be given the same consideration as other human beings.

*Reprinted by permission from "The Rights and Wrongs of Abortion," by John Finnis, *Philosophy and Public Affairs*, vol. 2, no. 2, pp. 117-45; copyright © 1973 by Princeton University Press.

I

Thomson's reflections on rights develop in three stages. (A) She indicates a knot of problems about what rights are rights to; she dwells particularly on the problem "what it comes to, to have a right to life" (p. 55). (B) She indicates, rather less clearly, a knot of problems about the source of rights; in particular she suggests that, over a wide range (left unspecified by her) of types of right, a person has a right only to what he has "title" to by reason of some gift, concession, grant or undertaking to him by another person. (C) She cuts both these knots by admitting (but all too quietly) that her whole argument about abortion concerns simply what is "morally required" or "morally permissible"; that what is in question is really the scope and source of the mother's responsibility (and only derivatively, by entailment, the scope and source of the unborn child's rights). I shall now examine these three stages a little more closely, and then (D) indicate why I think it useful to have done so.

(A) How do we specify the content of a right? What is a right a right to? Thomson mentions at least nine different rights which a person might rightly or wrongly be said to have.[3] Of these nine, seven have the same logical structure,[4] namely, in each instance, the alleged right is a right with respect to P's action (performance, omission) as an action which may affect Q. In some of these seven instances,[5] the right with respect to P's action is P's right (which Hohfeld[6] called a privilege and Hohfeldians call a liberty). In the other instances,[7] the right with respect to P's action is Q's right (which Hohfeldians call a "claim-right"). But in all these seven instances there is what I shall call a "Hohfeldian right": to assert a Hohfeldian right is to assert a three-term relation between two persons and the action of one of those persons insofar as that action concerns the other person.

The other two rights mentioned by Thomson have a different logical structure.[8] In both these instances, the alleged right is a right with respect to a thing (one's "own body," or the state of affairs referred to as one's "life"). Here the relation is two-term: between one person and some thing or state of affairs. Rights in this sense cannot be completely analyzed in terms of some unique combination of Hohfeldian rights.[9] P's right to a thing (land, body, life) can and normally should be secured by granting or attributing Hohfeldian rights to him or to others; but just which combination of such Hohfeldian rights will properly or best secure his single right to the thing in question will vary according to time, place, person and circumstance. And since moral judgments centrally concern *actions*, it is this specification of Hohfeldian rights that we need for moral purposes, rather than invocations of rights to things.

Since Thompson concentrates on the problematic character of the "right to life," I shall illustrate what I have just said by reference to the "right to one's own body," which she should (but seems, in practice, not to) regard as equally problematic. Now her two explicit versions of this right are: one's "just, prior claim to his own body," and one's "right to decide what happens in and to one's body." But both versions need much specification[10] before they can warrant moral judgments about particular sorts of action. For example, the "right to decide" may be *either* (1) a right (Hohfeldian liberty) to do things to or with one's own body (for example, to remove those kidney plugs, or that baby from it—but what else? anything? do I have the moral liberty to decide not to raise my hand to the telephone to save Kitty Genovese from her murderers?); *or* (2) a right (Hohfeldian claim-right) that other people shall not (at least without one's permission) do things to or with one's own body (for example, draw sustenance from, or inhabit, it—but what else? anything?); *or* (3) some combination of these forms of right with each other or with other forms of right such as (a) the right (Hohfeldian power) to change another person's right (liberty) to use one's body by making a grant of or permitting such use (*any such use?*), or (b) the right (Hohfeldian immunity) not to have one's right (claim-right) to be free from others' use of one's body diminished or affected by purported grants or permissions by third parties. As soon as we thus identify these possible sorts of right, available to give concrete moral content to the "right to one's body," it becomes obvious that the actions which the right entitles, disentitles or requires one to perform (or entitles, disentitles or requires others to perform) *vary* according to the identity and circumstances of the two parties to each available and relevant Hohfeldian right. And this, though she didn't recognize it, is the reason why Thomson found the "right to life" problematic, too.

(B) I suspect it was her concentration on non-Hohfeldian rights ("title" to things like chocolates or bodies) that led Thomson to make the curious suggestion which appears and reappears, though with a very uncertain role, in her paper. I mean, her suggestion that we should speak of "rights" only in respect of what a man has "title" to (usually, if not necessarily, by reason of gift, concession or grant to him).

This suggestion,[11] quite apart from the dubious centrality it accords to ownership and property in the spectrum of rights, causes needless confusion in the presentation of Thomson's defense of abortion. For if the term "right" were to be kept on the "tight rein" which she suggests, then (a) the popes and others whose appeal to "the right to life" she is questioning would deprive her paper of its starting point and indeed its pivot by simply rephrasing their appeal so as to eliminate all reference to rights (for, as I show in the next section, they are not alleging that the impropriety of abortion follows from any grant, gift or concession of "rights" to the unborn child); and (b) Thomson would likewise have to rephrase claims she herself makes, such as that innocent persons certainly have a right to life, that mothers have the right to abort themselves to save their lives, that P has a right not to be tortured to death by Q even if R is threatening to kill Q unless Q does so, and so on. But if such rephrasing is possible (as indeed it is), then it is obvious that suggestions about the proper or best way to use the term "a right" are irrelevant to the substantive moral defense or critique of abortion.

But this terminological suggestion is linked closely with Thomson's substantive thesis that we do not have any "special [scil. Good Samaritan or Splendid Samaritan] responsibility" for the life or well-being of others "unless we have assumed it, explictly or implicitly." It is this (or some such) thesis about *responsibility* on which Thomson's whole argument, in the end, rests.

(C) Thomson's explicit recognition that her defense of abortion *need* not have turned on the assertion or denial of rights comes rather late in her paper, when she says that there is "no need to insist on" her suggested reined-in use of the term "right":

> If anyone does wish to deduce "he has a right" from "you ought," then all the same he must surely grant that there are cases in which it is not morally required of you that you allow that violinist to use your kidneys. . . .[12] And so also for mother and unborn child. Except in such cases as the unborn person has a right to demand it . . . nobody is morally *required* to make large sacrifices . . . in order to keep another person alive (pp. 61-62).

In short, the dispute is about what is "morally required" (that is, about what one "must" and, for that matter, "may" or "can" [not] do: see p. 52); that is, about the rights and wrongs of abortion. True on page 61 there is still that "right to demand large sacrifices" cluttering up the margins of the picture. But when we come to the last pages of her paper (pp. 64-65) even that has been set aside, and the real question is identified as not whether the child has a "right to demand large sacrifices" of its mother, but whether the mother as a "special responsibility" to or for the child (since, if she has, then she may be morally required to make large sacrifices for it and *therefore* we will be able to assert, by a convenient locution, the child's "right to [demand] those sacrifices").

(D) So in the end most of the argument about rights was a red herring. I have bothered to track down this false trail, not merely to identify some very common sorts and sources of equivocation (more will come to light in the next two sections), but also to show how Thomson's decision to conduct her defense in terms of "rights" makes it peculiarly easy to miss a most important weak point in her defense. This weak point is the connection or relation between one's "special responsibilities" and one's ordinary (not special) responsibilities. One is enabled to miss it easily if one thinks (a) that the whole problem is essentially one of rights, (b) that rights typically or even essentially depend on grant, concession, assumption, etc., (c) that special responsibilities likewise depend on grants, concessions, assumptions, etc., and (d) that therefore the whole moral problem here concerns one's *special* responsibilities. Such a train of thought is indeed an enthymeme, if not a downright fallacy; but that is not surprising, since I am commenting here not on an argument offered by Thomson but on a likely effect of her "rhetoric."

What Thomson, then, fails to attend to adequately is the claim (one of the claims implicit, I think, in the papal and conservative rhetoric of rights) that the mother's duty not to abort herself is *not* an incident of any special responsibility which she assumed or undertook for the child, but is a straightforward incident of an ordinary duty everyone owes to his neighbor. Thomson, indeed, acknowledges that such ordinary nonassumed duties exist and are as morally weighty as duties of justice in her reined-in sense of "justice"; but I cannot discern the principles on which she bases, and (confidently) delimits the range of these duties.[13]

She speaks, for instance, about "the drastic limits to the right of self-defense": "If someone threatens you with death unless you torture someone else to death, I think you have not the right, even to save your life, to do so" (p. 53). Yet she also says: "If anything in the world is true, it is that you do not . . . do what is impermissible, if you reach around to your back and unplug yourself from that violinist to save your life" (p. 52). So why, in the first case, has one the strict responsibility not to bring about the death demanded? Surely she is not suggesting that the pain ("torture") makes the difference, or that it *is* morally permissible to kill *painlessly* another person on the orders of a third party who threatens you with death for noncompliance? And, since she thinks that "nobody is morally *required* to make large sacrifices, of health, of all other interests and concerns, of all other duties and commitments, for nine years, or even for nine months, in order to keep another person alive" (p. 62), will she go on to say that it is permissible, when a third party threatens you with such "large sacrifices" (though well short of your life), to *kill* (painlessly) another person, or two or ten other persons?

If Thomson balks at such suggestions, I think it must be because she does in the end rely on some version of the distinction, forced underground in her paper, between "direct killing" and "not keeping another person alive."

The more one reflects on Thomson's argument, the more it seems to turn and trade on some version of this distinction. Of course she starts by rejecting the view that it is always wrong to directly kill, because that view would (she thinks) condemn one to a lifetime plugged into the violinist. But she proceeds, as we have noted, to reject at least one form of killing to save one's life, on grounds that seem to have nothing to do with consequences and everything to do with the formal context and thus structure of one's action (the sort of formal considerations that usually are wrapped up, as we shall see, in the word "direct"). Indeed, the whole movement of her argument in defense of abortion is to assimilate abortion to the range of Samaritan problems on the basis that having an abortion is, or can be, justified as *merely* a way of *not rendering special assistance*. Again, the argument turns, not on a calculus of consequences, but on the formal characteristics of one's choice itself.

Well, why should this apparently *formal* aspect of one's choice determine one's precise responsibilities in a certain situation whatever the other circumstances and expected consequences or upshots? When we know *why*, on both sides of the debate about abortion, we draw and rely on these distinctions, then we will be better placed to consider (1) whether or not unplugging from the violinist is, after all, direct killing in the sense alleged to be relevant by popes and others, and (2) whether or not abortion is, after all, just like unplugging the captive philosopher from the moribund musician.

II

Like Thomson's moral language (setting off the "permissible" against the "impermissible"), the traditional rule about killing doubtless gets its peremptory sharpness primarily (historically speaking) from the injunction, respected as divine and revealed: "Do not kill the innocent and just."[14] But the handful of peremptory negative moral principles correspond to the handful of really basic aspects of human flourishing, which in turn correspond to the handful of really basic and controlling human needs and human inclinations. To be fully reasonable, one must remain *open* to every basic aspect of human flourishing, to every basic form of human good. For is not each irreducibly basic, and none merely means to end? Are not the basic goods incommensurable? Of course it is reasonable to concentrate on realizing those forms of good, in or for those particular communities and persons (first of all oneself), which one's situation, talents and opportunities most fit one for. But concentration, specialization, particularization, is one thing; it is quite another thing, rationally and thus morally speaking, to make a choice which cannot but be characterized as a choice *against* life (to kill), *against* communicable knowledge of truth (to lie, where truth is at stake in communication), *against* procreation, *against* friendship and the injustice that is bound up with friendship. Hence the strict negative precepts.[15]

The general sense of "responsibility," "duty," "obligation," "permissibility," is not my concern here, but rather the *content* of our responsibilities, duties, obligations, of the demands which human good makes on each of us. The general demand is that we remain adequately open to, attentive to, respectful of, and willing to pursue human good insofar as it can be realized and respected in our choices and dispositions. Most moral failings are not by way of violation of strict negative precepts, that is, they are not straightforward choices against basic values. Rather, they are forms of negligence, of *insufficent* regard for these basic goods or for the derivative structures reasonably created to support the basic goods. When someone is accused of violating directly a basic good, he will usually plead that he was acting out of a proper care and concern for the realization of that or another basic value in the *consequences* of his chosen act though not in the act itself. For example, an experimenter accused of killing children in order to conduct medical tests will point out that these deaths are necessary to these tests, and these tests to medical discoveries, and the discoveries to the saving of many more lives—so that, in view of the foreseeable consequences of his deed, he displays (he will argue) a fully adequate (indeed, the only adequate) and reasonable regard for the value of human life.

But to appeal to consequences in this fashion is to set aside one criterion of practical reasonableness and hence of morality—namely, that one remain open to each basic value and attentive to some basic value in each of one's chosen acts—in favor of quite another criterion—that one choose so to act as to bring about consequences involving a greater balance of good over bad than could be expected to be brought about by doing any alternative action open to one. Hare has observed that *"for practical purposes* there is no important difference" between most of the currently advocated theories in ethics; they all are "utilitarian," a term he uses to embrace Brandt's ideal observer theory, Richards' (Rawls'?) rational contractor theory, specific rule-utilitarianism, universalistic act-utilitarianism and his own universal prescriptivism.[16] All justify and require, he argues, the adoption of "the principles whose general inculcation will have, all in all, the best consequences."[17] I offer no critique of this utilitarianism here; Thomson's paper is not, on its face, consequentialist. Suffice it to inquire how Hare and his fellow consequentialists know the future that to most of us is hidden. How do they know what unit of computation to select from among the incommensurable and irreducible basic aspects of human flourishing; what principle of distribution of goods to commend to an individual considering his own interests, those of his friends, his family, his enemies, his *patria* and those of all men present and future? How do they know how to define the "situation" whose universal specification will appear in the principle whose adoption (singly? in conjunction with other principles?) "will" have best consequences;[18] whether and how to weigh future and uncertain consequences against present and certain consequences? And how do they know that net good consequences would in fact be maximized (even if *per impossibile* they were calculable) by general adoption of consequentialist principles of action along with consequentialist "principles" to justify nonobservance of consequentialist "principles" in "hard cases"?[19] One cannot understand the Western moral tradition with its peremptory negative (forbearance-requiring) principles (the positive principles being relevant in all, but peremptory in few, particular situations), unless one sees why that tradition rejected consequentialism as mere self-delusion—for Hare and his fellow consequentialists can provide no satisfactory answer to any of the foregoing lines of inquiry, and have no coherent rational account to give of any level of moral thought above that of the man who thinks how good it would be to act "for the best."[20] Expected total consequences of one's action do not provide a sufficient ground for making a choice that cannot but be regarded as *itself* a choice directly against a basic value (even that basic value which it is hoped will be realized in the *consequences*)—for expected total consequences cannot be given an evaluation sufficiently reasonable and definitive to be the decisive measure of our response to the call of human values, while a choice directly against a basic good provides, one might say, its own definitive evaluation of itself.

I do not expect these isolated and fragmentary remarks to be in themselves persuasive. I do not deny that the traditional Western willingness (in theory) to discount expected consequences wherever the action itself could not but be characterized as against a basic value, is or was supported by the belief that Providence would inevitably provide that "all manner of things shall be well" (that is, that the whole course of history would turn out to have been a fine thing, indisputably evil deeds and their consequences turning out to have been "all to the good" like indisputably saintly deeds and their consequences). Indeed the consequentialist moralist, who nourishes his moral imagination on scenarios in which by killing an innocent or two he saves scores, thousands, millions or even the race itself, rather obviously is a post-Christian phenomenon—such an assumption of the role of Providence would have seemed absurd to the pre-Christian philosophers[21] known to Cicero and Augustine. I am content to suggest the theoretical and moral context in which the casuistry of "direct" and "indirect" develops, within the wider context of *types* of action to be considered "impermissible" (I leave the term incompletely accounted for) because *inescapably* (that is, whatever the hoped-for consequences) choices *against* a basic value of human living and doing. In short, one's responsibility for the realization of human good, one's fostering of or respect for human flourishing in future states of affairs at some greater or lesser remove from one's present action, does not override one's responsibility to respect each basic form of human good which comes directly in question in one's present action itself.

But how does one choose "directly against" a basic form of good? When is it the case, for example, that one's choice, one's intentional act, "cannot but be" characterized as "inescapably" anti-life? Is abortion always (or ever) such a case? A way to tackle these questions can be illustrated by reference to three hard cases whose traditional "solutions" contributed decisively to the traditional judgment about abortion. The relevance of these "hard cases" and "solutions" to the discussion with Thomson should be apparent in each case, but will become even more apparent in the next section.

488

(1) Suicide

Considered as a fully deliberate choice (which it doubtless only rather rarely is), suicide is a paradigm case of an action that is always wrong because it cannot but be characterized as a choice directly against a fundamental value, life. The characterization is significant, for what makes the killing of oneself attractive is usually, no doubt, the prospect of peace, relief, even a kind of freedom or personal integration, and sometimes is an admirable concern for others; but no amount of concentration on the allure of these positive values can disguise from a clear-headed practical reasoner that it is *by* and *in* killing himself that he intends or hopes to realize those goods. And the characterization is given sharpness and definition by the contrast with heroic self-sacrifices in battle or with willing martyrdom.[22] Where Durkheim treated martyrdom as a case of suicide,[23] anybody concerned with the intentional structure of actions (rather than with a simplistic analysis of movements with foreseen upshots) will grant that the martyr is not directly choosing death, either as end or as means, for however certainly death may be expected to ensue from the martyr's choice not to accede to the tyrant's threats, still it will ensue through, and as the point of, *someone else's* deliberate act (the tyrant's or the executioner's), and thus the martyr's chosen act of defiance need not be interpreted as itself a choice against the good of life.

The case of suicide has a further significance. The judgments, the characterizations, and the distinctions made in respect of someone's choices involving his *own* death will be used in respect of choices involving the death of *others*. In other words, *rights* (such as the "right to life") are not the fundamental rationale for the judgment that the killing of other (innocent) persons is impermissible. What is impermissible is an intention set against the value of human life where that value is directly at stake in any action by virtue of the intentional and causal structure of that action; and such an impermissible intention may concern my life or yours—and no one speaks of his "right to life" as against himself, as something that would explain why *his* act of self-killing would be wrongful.

Indeed, I think the real justification for speaking of "rights" is to make the point that, when it comes to characterizing intentional actions in terms of their openness to basic human values, those human values are, and are to be, realized in the lives and well-being of others as well as in the life and well-being of the actor. That is, the point of speaking of "rights" is to stake out the relevant claims to equality and nondiscrimination (claims that are not to absolute equality, since *my* life and my well-being have some reasonable priority in the direction of *my* practical effort, if only because I am better placed to secure them). But the claims are to equality of *treatment*; so, rather than speak emptily of (say) a "right to life," it would be better to speak of (say, inter alia) a "right not to be killed intentionally"—where the meaning and significance of "intentional killing" can be illuminated by consideration of the right and wrong of killing oneself (that is, of a situation where no "rights" are in question and one is alone with the bare problem of the right relation between one's acts and the basic values that can be realized or spurned in human actions).

Finally, the case of suicide and its traditional solution remind us forcefully that traditional Western ethics simply does not accept that a person has "a right to decide what shall happen in and to his body," a right which Thomson thinks, astonishingly (since she is talking of Pius XI and Pius XII), that "everybody seems to be ready to grant" (p. 50). Indeed, one might go so far as to say that traditional Western ethics holds that, because and to the extent that one does *not* have the "right" to decide what shall happen in and to one's body, one *therefore* and to that extent does not have the right to decide what shall, by way of one's own acts, happen in and to anyone else's body. As I have already hinted and shall elaborate later, this would be something of an oversimplification, since one's responsibility for one's own life, health, etc., is reasonably regarded as prior to one's concern for the life, health, etc., of others. But the oversimplification is worth risking in order to make the point that the traditional condemnation of abortion (as something one makes happen in and to a baby's body) *starts* by rejecting what Thomson thinks everyone will admit.

(2) D's Killing an Innocent V in Order to Escape Death at the Hands of P, Who Has Ordered D to Kill V

This case has been traditionally treated on the same footing as cases such as D's killing V in order to save Q (or $Q_1, Q_2 \ldots Q_n$) from death (perhaps at the hands of P) or from disease (where D is a medical researcher); for all such cases cannot but be characterized as choices to act directly against human life. Of course, in each case, the reason for making the choice is to save life; but such saving of life will be effected, if at all, through the choices of other actors (e.g. P's choice not to kill D where D has killed V; or P's choice not to kill Q) or through quite distinct sequences of events (for example, Q's being given life-saving drugs discovered by D).

Hence the traditional ethics affirms that "there are drastic limits to the right of self-defense" in much the same terms as Thomson. "If someone threatens you with death when you torture someone else to death . . . you have not the right, even to save your own life, to do so" (p. 53). And it was this very problem that occasioned the first ecclesiastical pronouncement on abortion in the modern era, denying that "it is licit to procure abortion before animation of the fetus in order to prevent a girl, caught pregnant, being killed or dishonored."[24] The choice to abort here cannot but be characterized as a choice against life, since its intended good life- or reputation-saving effects are merely expected consequences, occurring if at all through the further acts of other persons, and thus are not what is being *done* in and by the act of abortion itself. But I do not know how one could arrive at any view of this second sort of hard case by juggling, as Thomson seems to be willing to, with a "right to life," a "right to determine what happens in and to your own body," a "right of self-defense" and a "right to refuse to lay hands on other people"—all rights shared equally by D, V, P, and Q, Q_1, Q_2 . . . !

(3) Killing the Mother to Save the Child

This was the only aspect of abortion that Thomas Aquinas touched on, but he discussed it three times.[25] For if it is accepted that eternal death is worse than mere bodily death, shouldn't one choose the lesser evil? So if the unborn child is likely to die unbaptized, shouldn't one open up the mother, rip out the child and save-it-from-eternal-death-by-baptizing-it? (If you find Aquinas' problem unreal, amend it—consider instead the cases where the child's life seems so much more valuable, whether to itself or to others, than the life of its sick or old or low-born mother.) No, says Aquinas. He evidently considers (for reasons I consider in section III) that the project involves a direct choice against life and is straightforwardly wrong, notwithstanding the good consequences.

So the traditional condemnation of therapeutic abortion flows not from a prejudice against women or in favor of children but from a straightforward application of the solution in the one case to the other case, on the basis that mother and child are *equally* persons in whom the value of human life is to be realized (or the "right to life" respected) and not directly attacked.[26]

III

But now at last let us look at this "traditional condemnation of abortion" a little more closely than Thomson does. It is not a condemnation of the administration of medications to a pregnant mother whose life is threatened by, say, a high fever (whether brought on by pregnancy or not), in an effort to reduce the fever, even if it is known that such medications have the side effect of inducing miscarriage. It is not a condemnation of the removal of the malignantly cancerous womb of a pregnant woman, even if it is known that the fetus within is not of viable age and so will die. It is quite doubtful whether it is a condemnation of an operation to put back in its place the displaced womb of a pregnant woman whose life is threatened by the displacement, even though the operation necessitates the draining off of the amniotic fluids necessary to the survival of the fetus.[27]

But why are these operations not condemned? As Foot has remarked, the distinction drawn between these and other death-dealing operations "has evoked particularly bitter reactions on the part of non-Catholics. If you are permitted to bring about the death of the child what does it matter how it is done?"[28] Still, she goes some way to answering her own question; she is not content to let the matter rest where Hart has left it, when he said:

> Perhaps the most perplexing feature of these cases is that the overriding aim in all of them is the same good result, namely ... to save the mother's life. The differences between the cases are differences of causal structure leading to the applicability of different verbal distinctions. There seems to be no relevant moral difference between them on any theory of morality ... [to attribute moral relevance to distinctions drawn in this way] in cases where the ultimate purpose is the same can only be explained as the result of a legalistic conception of morality as if it were conceived in the form of a law in rigid form prohibiting all intentional killing as distinct from knowingly causing death.[29]

Foot recognizes that attention to "overriding aim" and "ultimate purpose" is not enough if we are to keep clear of moral horrors such as saving life by killing innocent hostages, etc. As a general though not exclusive and not (it seems) at-all-costs principle, she proposes that one has a duty to refrain from doing injury to innocent people and that this duty is stricter than one's duty to aid others; this enables her to see that "we might find" the traditional conclusion correct, that we must not crush the unborn child's skull in order to save the mother (in a case where the child could be saved if one let the mother die): "for in general we do not think that we can kill one innocent person to rescue another."[30] But what is it to "do injury to" innocent people? She does not think it an injury to blow a man to pieces, or kill and eat him, in order to save others trapped with him in a cave, *if he is certain to die soon anyway.*[31] So I suppose that, after all, she *would* be willing (however reluctantly) to justify the killing by D of hostages, V, V_1, V_2, whenever the blackmailer P threatened to kill *them too*, along with Q, Q_1, Q_2, unless D killed them himself. One wonders whether this is not an unwarranted though plausible concession to consequentialism.

In any event, Foot was aware, not only that the "doctrine of the double effect" "should be taken seriously in spite of the fact that it sounds rather odd ...,"[32] but also of what Thomson has not recorded in her brief footnote (p. 479 n. 3) on the technical meaning given to the term "direct" by moralists using the "doctrine" to analyze the relation between choices and basic values,

492

namely that the "doctrine" requires more than that a certain bad effect or aspect (say, someone's being killed) of one's deed be not intended either as end or as means. If one is to establish that one's death-dealing deed need not be characterized as directly or intentionally against the good of human life, the "doctrine" requires further that the good effect or aspect, which *is* intended, should be proportionate (say, saving someone's life), that is, sufficiently good and important relative to the bad effect or aspect: otherwise (we may add, in our own words) one's choice, although not directly and intentionally to kill, will reasonably be counted as a choice inadequately open to the value of life.[33] And this consideration alone might well suffice to rule out abortions performed in order simply to remove the unwanted fetus from the body of women who conceived as a result of forcible rape, even if one were to explicate the phrase "intended directly as end or as means" in such a way that the abortion did not amount to a directly intended killing (for example, because the mother desired only the removal, not the death of the fetus, and would have been willing to have the fetus reared in an artificial womb had one been available).[34]

Well, how *should* one explicate these central requirements of the "doctrine" of double effect? When *should* one say that the expected bad effect or aspect of an action is not intended either as end or as means and hence does not determine the moral character of the act as a choice not to respect one of the basic human values? Since it is in any case impossible to undertake a full discussion of this question here, let me narrow the issue down to the more difficult and controverted problem of "means." Clearly enough, D intends the death of V *as a means* when he kills him in order to conform to the orders of the blackmailer P (with the object of thereby saving the lives of Q et al.), since the good effect of D's act will follow only by virtue of *another* human act (here P's). But Grisez (no consequentialist!) argues that the bad effects or aspects of some *natural* process or chain of causation need not be regarded as intended as means to the good effects or aspects of that process even if the good effects or aspects *depend* on them in the causal sense (and provided that those good effects could not have been attained in some other way by that agent in those circumstances).[35] So he would, I think, say that Thomson could rightly unplug herself from the violinist (at least where the hook-up endangered her life) even if "unplugging" could only be effected by chopping the violinist in pieces. He treats the life-saving abortion operation in the same way, holding that there is no direct choice against life involved in chopping up the fetus if what is intended as end is to save the life of the mother and what is intended as means is no more than the removal of the fetus and the consequential relief to the mother's body.[36] As a suasive, he points again to the fact that *if* an artificial womb or restorative operation were available for the aborted fetus, a right-thinking mother and doctor in such a case would wish to make these available to the fetus; this shows, he says, that a right-thinking mother and doctor, even where such facilities are *not* in fact available, need not be regarded as intending the death of the fetus they kill.[37] For my part, I think Grisez' reliance on such counter-factual hypotheses to specify the morally relevant meaning or intention of human acts is excessive, for it removes morally relevant "intention" too far from common-sense intention, tends to unravel the traditional and common-sense moral judgments on suicide (someone would say: "It's not death I'm choosing, only a long space of peace and quiet, after which I'd willingly be revived, if that were possible"!), and likewise disturbs our judgments on murder and in particular on the difference between administering (death-hastening) drugs to relieve pain and administering drugs to relieve-pain-by-killing.

In any event, the version of traditional nonconsequentialist ethics which has gained explicit ecclesiastical approval in the Roman church these last ninety years treats the matter differently; it treats a bad or unwanted aspect or effect of act A_1 as an *intended* aspect of A_1, not only when the good effect (unlike the bad) follows only by virtue of another human act A_2, but also *sometimes* when both the good effect and the bad effect are parts of one natural causal process requiring no further human act to achieve its effect. *Sometimes*, but not always; so when?

A variety of factors are appealed to explicitly or relied on implicitly in making a judgment that the bad effect is to count as intended-as-a-means. Bennett would call the set of factors a "jumble,"[38] but they are even more various than he has noted. It will be convenient to set them out while at the same time observing their bearing on the two cases centrally in dispute, the craniotomy to save a mother's life and that notable scenario in which "you reach around to your back and unplug yourself from that violinist to save your life."

(1) Would the chosen action have been chosen if the victim had not been present? If it would, this is ground for saying that the bad aspects of the action, namely, its death-dealing effects on the victim (child or violinist), are not being intended or chosen either as end or means, but are genuinely incidental side effects that do not necessarily determine the character of one's action as (not) respectful of human life. This was the principal reason the ecclesiastical moralists had for regarding as permissible the operation to remove the cancerous womb of the pregnant woman.[39] And the "bitter" reaction which Foot cites and endorses—"If you are permitted to bring about the death of the child, what does it matter how it is done?"—seems, here, to miss the point. For what is in question, here, is not a mere matter of technique, of different ways of doing something. Rather it is a matter of the very reason one has for acting in the way one does, and such reasons can be constitutive of the act as an intentional performance. One has no reason even to want to be rid of the fetus within the womb, let alone to want to kill it; and so one's act, though certain, causally, to kill, is not, intentionally, a choice against life.

494

But of course, *this* factor does not serve to distinguish a craniotomy from unplugging that violinist; in both situations, the oppressive presence of the victim is what makes one minded to do the act in question.

(2) Is the person making the choice the one whose life is threatened by the presence of the victim? Thomson rightly sees that this is a relevant question, and Thomas Aquinas makes it the pivot of his discussion of self-defensive killing (the discussion from which the "doctrine" of double effect, as a theoretically elaborated way of analyzing intention, can be said to have arisen). He says:

> Although it is not permissible to intend to kill someone else in order to defend oneself (since it is not right to do the act "killing a human being," except [in some cases of unjust aggression] by public authority and for the general welfare), still it is not morally necessary to omit to do what is strictly appropriate to securing one's own life simply in order to avoid killing another, for to make provision for one's own life is more strictly one's moral concern than to make provision for the life of another person.[40]

As Thomson has suggested, a bystander, confronted with a situation in which one innocent person's presence is endangering the life of another innocent person, is in a different position; to choose to intervene, in order to kill one person to save the other, involves a choice to make himself a master of life and death, a judge of who lives and who dies; and (we may say) this context of his choice prevents him from saying, reasonably, what the man defending himself can say: "I am not choosing to kill; I am just doing what—as a single act and not simply by virtue of remote consequences or of someone else's subsequent act—is strictly needful to protect my own life, by forcefully removing what is threatening it." Now the traditional condemnation of abortion[41] concerns the bystander's situation: a bystander cannot but be choosing to kill if (a) he rips open the mother, in a way foreseeably fatal to her, in order to save the child from the threatening enveloping presence of the mother (say, because the placenta has come adrift and the viable child is trapped and doomed unless it can be rescued, or because the mother's blood is poisoning the child, in a situation in which the bystander would prefer to save the child, either because he wants to save it from eternal damnation, or because the child is of royal blood and the mother low born, or because the mother is in any case sick, or old, or useless, or "has had her turn," while the child has a whole rich life before it); or if (b) he cuts up or drowns the child in order to save the mother from the child's threatening presence. "Things being as they are, there isn't much a woman can safely do to abort herself," as Thomson says (p. 52)—at least, not without the help of bystanders, who by helping (directly) would be making the same choice as if they did it themselves. But the unplugging of the violinist is done by the very person defending herself. Thomson admits (p. 52) that this gives quite a different flavor to the situation, but she thinks that the difference is not decisive, since bystanders have a decisive reason to intervene in favor of the *mother* threatened by her child's presence. And she finds this reason in the fact that the mother *owns* her body, just as the person plugged in to the violinist owns his own kidneys and is entitled to their unencumbered use (p. 53). Well, this too has always been accounted a factor in these problems, as we can see by turning to the following question.

(3) Does the chosen action involve not merely a denial of aid and succor to someone but an actual intervention that amounts to an assault on the body of that person? Bennett wanted to deny all relevance to any such question,[42] but Foot[43] and Thomson have rightly seen that in the ticklish matter of respecting human life in the persons of others, and of characterizing choices with a view to assessing their respect for life, it *can* matter that one is directly injuring and not merely failing to maintain a life-preserving level of assistance to another. Sometimes, as here, it is the causal structure of one's activity that involves one willy-nilly in a choice for or against a basic value. The connection between one's activity and the destruction of life may be so close and direct that intentions and considerations which would give a different dominant character to mere nonpreservation of life are incapable of affecting the dominant character of a straightforward taking of life. This surely is the reason why Thomson goes about and about to represent a choice to have an abortion as a choice *not* to provide assistance or facilities, *not* to be a Good or at any rate a Splendid Samaritan; and why, too, she carefully describes the violinist affair so as to minimize the degree of intervention against the violinist's body, and to maximize the analogy with simply refusing an invitation to volunteer one's kidneys for his welfare (like Henry Fonda's declining to cross America to save Judith Thomson's life). "If anything in the world is true, it is that you do not commit murder, you do not do what is impermissible, if you reach around to your back and unplug yourself from that violinist to save your life" (p. 52). Quite so. It might nevertheless be useful to test one's moral reactions a little further: suppose, not simply that "unplugging" required a *bystander's* intervention, but also that (for medical reasons, poison in the bloodstream, shock, etc.) unplugging could not safely be performed unless and until the violinist had first been dead for six hours and had moreover been killed outright, say by drowning or decapitation (though not necessarily while conscious). Could one then be *so* confident, as a bystander, that it was right to kill the violinist in order to save the philosopher? But I put forward this revised version, principally to illustrate *another* reason for thinking that, within the traditional casuistry, the violinist-unplugging in Thomson's version is *not* the "direct killing" which she claims it is, and which she *must* claim it is if she is to make out her case for rejecting the traditional principle about direct killing.

Let us now look back to the traditional rule about abortion. If the mother needs medical treatment to save her life, she gets it, subject to one proviso, even if the treatment is certain to kill the unborn child—for after all, her body is *her* body, as "women have said again and again" (and they have been heard by the traditional casuists!). And the proviso? That the medical treatment not be via a straightforward assault on or intervention against the child's body. After all, the *child's body is the child's body, not the woman's.* The traditional casuists have admitted the claims made on behalf of one "body" up to the very limit where those claims become *mere (understandable) bias, mere (understandable) self-interested* refusal to listen to the *very same* claim ("This body is *my* body") when it is made by or on behalf of another person.[44] Of course, a traditional casuist would display an utter want of feeling if he didn't most profoundly sympathize with women in the desperate circumstances under discussion. But it is vexing to find a philosophical Judith Thomson, in a cool hour, unable to see when an argument cuts both ways, and unaware that the casuists have seen the point before her and have, unlike her, allowed the argument to cut both ways impartially. The child, like his mother, has a "just prior claim to his own body," and abortion involves laying hands on, manipulating, that body. And here we have perhaps the decisive reason why abortion cannot be assimilated to the range of Samaritan problems and why Thomson's location of it within that range is a mere (ingenious) novelty.

(4) But is the action action against someone who had a duty not to be doing what he is doing, or not to be present where he is present? There seems no doubt that the "innocence" of the victim whose life is taken makes a difference to the characterizing of an action as open to and respectful of the good of human life, and as an intentional killing. Just how and why it makes a difference is difficult to unravel; I shall not attempt an unraveling here. We all, for whatever reason, recognize the difference and Thomson has expressly allowed it relevance (p. 52).

But her way of speaking of "rights" has a final unfortunate effect at this point. We can grant, and have granted, that the unborn child has no Hohfeldian *claim-right* to be allowed to stay within the mother's body under all circumstances; the mother is not under a strict duty to allow it to stay under all circumstances. In *that* sense, the child "has no right to be there." But Thomson discusses also the case of the burglar in the house. He, too, has "no right to be there," even when she opens the window! But beware of the equivocation! The burglar not merely has no claim-right to be allowed to enter or stay; he also has a strict duty *not* to enter or stay; that is, he has no Hohfeldian *liberty*—and it is *this* that is uppermost in our minds when we think that he "has no right to be there." It is actually unjust for him to be there. Similarly with Jones who takes Smith's coat, leaving Smith freezing (p. 53), and similarly with the violinist. He and his agents had a strict duty not to make the hook-up to Judith Thomson or her gentle reader. Of course, the violinist himself may have been unconscious and so not himself at fault; but the whole affair is a gross injustice to the person

497

whose kidneys are made free with, and the injustice to that person is not measured simply by the degree of moral fault of one of the parties to the injustice. Our whole view of the violinist's situation is colored by this burglarious and persisting wrongfulness of his presence plugged into his victim.

But can any of this reasonably be said or thought of the unborn child? True, the child has no *claim-right* to be allowed to come into being within the mother. But it was not in breach of any *duty* in coming into being nor in remaining present within the mother; Thomson gives no arguments at all in favor of the view that the child is in breach of duty in being present (though her counter examples show that she is often tacitly assuming this). (Indeed, if we are going to use the wretched analogy of owning houses, I fail to see why the unborn child should not with justice say of the body around it: "That is my house. No one *granted* me property rights in it, but equally no one *granted* my mother any property rights in it." The fact is that both persons *share* in the use of this body, both by the same sort of title, namely, that this is the way they happened to come into being. But it would be better to drop this ill-fitting talk of "ownership" and "property rights" altogether.) So though the unborn child "had no right to be there" (in the sense that it never had a claim-right to be allowed to *begin* to be there), in another straightforward and more important sense it *did* "have a right to be there" (in the sense that it was not in breach of duty in being or continuing to be there). All this is, I think, clear and clearly different from the violinist's case. Perhaps forcible rape is a special case; but even then it seems fanciful to say that the child is or could be in any way at fault, as the violinist is at fault or would be but for the adventitious circumstance that he was unconscious at the time.

Still, I don't want to be dogmatic about the justice or injustice, innocence or fault, involved in a rape conception. (I have already remarked that the impermissibility of abortion in any such case, where the mother's life is not in danger, does not depend necessarily on showing that the act is a choice directly to kill.) It is enough that I have shown how in three admittedly important respects the violinist case differs from the therapeutic abortion performed to save the life of the mother. As presented by Thomson, the violinst's case involves (1) no bystander, (2) no intervention against or assault upon the body of the violinist, and (3) an indisputable injustice to the agent in question. Each of these three factors is absent from the abortion cases in dispute. Each has been treated as relevant by the traditional casuists whose condemnations Thomson was seeking to contest when she plugged us into the violinist.

When all is said and done, however, I haven't rigorously answered my own question. When should one say that the expected bad effect or aspect of an act is not intended even as a means and hence does not determine the moral character of the act as a choice not to respect one of the basic human values? I have done no more than list some factors. I have not discussed how one decides which combinations of these factors suffice to answer the question one way rather than the other. I have not discussed the man on the plank, or the man off the plank; or the woman who leaves her baby behind as she flees from the lion, or the other woman who feeds *her* baby to the lion in order to make good her own escape; or the "innocent" child who threatens to shoot a man dead, or the man who shoots that child to save himself;[45] or the starving explorer who kills himself to provide food for his fellows, or the other explorer who wanders away from the party so as not to hold them up or diminish their rations. The cases are many, various, instructive. Too generalized or rule-governed an application of the notion of "double effect" would offend against the Aristotelean, common law, Wittgensteinian wisdom that here "we do not know how to draw the boundaries of this concept"—of intention, of respect for the good of life, and of action as distinct from consequences—"except for a special purpose."[46] But I think that those whom Aristotle bluntly calls wise can come to clear judgments on most of the abortion problems, judgments that all will not coincide with Thomson's.

IV

I have been assuming that the unborn child is, from conception, a person and hence is not to be discriminated against on account of age, appearance or other such factors insofar as such factors are reasonably considered irrelevant where respect for basic human values is in question. Thomson argues against this assumption, but not, as I think, well. She thinks (like Wertheimer,[47] mutatis mutandis) that the argument in favor of treating a newly conceived child as a person is merely a "slippery slope" argument (p. 47), rather like (I suppose) saying that one should call all men bearded because there is no line one can confidently draw between beard and clean shavenness. More precisely, she thinks that a newly conceived child is like an acorn, which after all is not an oak! It is discouraging to see her relying so heavily and uncritically on this hoary muddle. An acorn can remain for years in a stable state, simply but completely an acorn. Plant it and from it will sprout an oak sapling, a new, dynamic biological system that has nothing much in common with an acorn save that it came from an acorn and is capable of generating new acorns. Suppose an acorn is formed in September 1971, picked up on 1 February 1972, and stored under good conditions for three years, then planted in January 1975; it sprouts on 1 March 1975 and 50 years later is a fully mature oak tree. Now suppose I ask: When did that oak begin to grow? Will anyone say September 1971 or February 1972? Will anyone look for the date on which it was first noticed in the garden? Surely not. If we know it sprouted from the acorn on 1 March 1975, that is enough (though a biologist could be a trifle more exact about "sprouting");

499

that is when *the oak* began. *A fortiori* with the conception of a child, which is no *mere* germination of a seed. Two sex cells, each with only 23 chromosomes, unite and more or less immediately fuse to become a new cell with 46 chromosomes providing a unique genetic constitution (not the father's, not the mother's, and not a mere juxtaposition of the parents') which thenceforth throughout its life, however long, will substantially determine the new individual's makeup.[48] This new cell is the first stage in a dynamic integrated system that has nothing much in common with the individual male and female sex cells, save that it sprang from a pair of them and will in time produce new sets of them. To say that *this* is when a person's life began is not to work backward from maturity, sophistically asking at each point "How can one draw the line *here*?" Rather it is to point to a perfectly clear-cut beginning to which each one of us can look back and in looking back see how in a vividly intelligible sense, "in my beginning is my end." Judith Thomson thinks she began to "acquire human characteristics" "by the tenth week" (when fingers, toes, etc. became visible). I cannot think why she overlooks the most radically and distinctively human characteristic of all—the fact that she was conceived of human parents. Then there is Hendry Fonda. From the time of his conception, though not before, one could say, looking at his unique personal genetic constitution, not only that "by the tenth week" Henry Fonda would have fingers, but also that in his 40th year he would have a cool hand. That is why there seems no rhyme or reason in waiting "ten weeks" until his fingers and so on actually become visible before declaring that he *now* has the human rights which Judith Thomson rightly but incompletely recognizes.

NOTES

1. *Philosophy & Public Affairs* I, no. 1 (Fall 1971): 47-66. Otherwise unidentified page references in the text are to this article.

2. Roger Wertheimer, "Understanding the Abortion Argument," *Philosophy & Public Affairs* I, no. 1 (Fall 1971): 67-95.

3. Rights which Thomson is willing to allow that a person has:
   R1. a right to life (p. 51);
   R2. a right to decide what happens in and to one's body (p. 50) (to be equated, apparently, with a just prior claim to one's own body, p. 54);
   R3. a right to defend oneself (i.e. to self-defense, p. 53);
   R4. a right to refuse to lay hands on other people (even when it would be just and fair to do so, p. 54)—more precisely, a right not to lay hands on other people. . . .
Rights which she thinks it would be coherent but mistaken to claim that a person has or in any event always has:
   R5. a right to demand that someone else give one assistance (p. 63)—more precisely, a right to be given assistance by . . . ;
   R6. a right to be given whatever one needs for continued life (p. 55);
   R7. a right to the use of (or to be given, or to be allowed to continue, the use of) someone else's body (or house) (p. 56);

R8. a right not to be killed by anybody (p. 56);

R9. a right to slit another's throat (an instance, apparently, of a "right to be guaranteed his death") (p. 66).

4. Namely, R3 through R9 in the list of note 3 above.

5. Namely, R3, R4 and, in one of their sesnes, R7 and R9.

6. W. N. Hohfeld, *Fundamental Legal Conceptions* (New Haven, 1923).

7. Namely, R5, R6, R8 and, in another of their senses, R7 and R9.

8. Namely, R1 and R2.

9. This proposition is elaborated in a juridical context by A. M. Honoré "Rights of Exclusion and Immunities against Divesting," *University of Tulane Law Review* 34 (1960): 453.

10. Insufficient specification causes needless problems, besides those mentioned in the text. For example, against "so using the term 'right' that from the fact that A ought to do a thing for B, it follows that B has a right against A that A do it for him," Thomson objects that any such use of the term "right" is "going to make the question of whether or not a man has a right to a thing turn on how easy it is to provide him with it" (pp. 60-61); and she adds that it's "rather a shocking idea that anybody's rights should fade away and disappear as it gets harder and harder to accord them to him" (p. 61). So she says she has no "right" to the touch of Henry Fonda's cool hand, *because,* although he ought to cross the room to touch her brow (and thus save her life), he is not morally obliged to cross America to do so. But this objection rests merely on inadequate specification of the rights as against Henry Fonda. For if we say that she has a right that Henry Fonda should cross-the-room-to-touch-her-fevered-brow, and that she has no right that he should cross-America-to-touch-her-fevered brow, then we can (if we like!) continue to deduce rights from duties.

11. It is perhaps worth pointing out that, even if we restrict our attention to the rights involved in gifts, concessions, grants, contracts, trusts and the like, Thomson's proposed reining-in of the term "right" will be rather inconvenient. Does only the donee have the "rights"? Suppose that uncle U gives a box of chocolates to nephew N1, with instructions to share it with nephew N2, and asks father F to see that this sharing is done. Then we want to be able to say that U has a right that N1 and N2 shall each get their share, that N1 shall give N2 that share, that F shall see to it that this is done, and so on; and that N1 has the right to his share, the right not to be interfered with by F or N2 or anyone else in eating his share, and so on; and that N2 has a similar set of rights; and that F has the right to take steps to enforce a fair distribution, the right not to be interfered with in taking those steps, and so on. Since disputes may arise about any one of these relations between the various persons and their actions and the chocolates thereby affected, it is convenient to have the term "right" on a loose rein, to let it ride round the circle of relations, picking up the action in dispute and fitting the competing claims about "the right thing to do" into intelligible and typical three-term relationships. Yet some of the rights involved in the gift of the chocolates, for example U's rights, are not acquired by any grant to the right-holder.

12. The sentence continues: "and in which he does not have a right to use them, and in which you do not do him an injustice if you refuse." But these are merely remnants of the "rhetoric" in which she has cast her argument. Notice, incidentally, that her suggestion that "justice" and "injustice" should be restricted to respect for and violation of rights in her reined-in sense is of no importance since she grants that actions not in her sense unjust may be self-centered, callous and indecent, and that these vices are "no less grave" (p. 61).

13. Perhaps this is the point at which to note how dubious is Thomson's assertion that "in no state in this country is any man compelled by law to be even a Minimally Decent Samaritan to any person," and her insinuation that this is a manifestation of discrimination against women. This sounds so odd coming from a country in which a young man, not a young woman, is compelled by law to "give up long stretches of his life" to defending his country at considerable "risk of death for himself." True, he is not doing this for "a person who has no special right to demand it"; indeed, what makes active military service tough

is that one is not risking one's life to save *anybody* in particular from any *particular* risk. And are we to say that young men have *assumed* a "special responsibility" for defending other people? Wouldn't that be a gross fiction which only a lame moral theory could tempt us to indulge in? But it is just this sort of social contractarianism that Thomson is tempting us with.

14. Exodus 23:7, cf. Exodus 20:13, Deuteronomy 5:17, Genesis 9:6, Jeremiah 7:6 and 22:3.

15. These remarks are filled out somewhat in my "Natural Law and Unnatural Acts," *Heythrop Journal* 11 (1970): 365. See also Germain Grisez, *Abortion: the Myths, the Realities and the Arguments* (New York, 1970), chap. 6. My argument owes much to this and other works by Grisez.

16. R. M. Hare, "Rules of War and Moral Reasoning," *Philosophy & Public Affairs* 1, no. 2 (Winter 1972); 167, 168.

17. *Ibid.,* p. 174.

18. Cf. H.-N. Castañeda, "On the Problem of Formulating a Coherent Act-Utilitarianism," *Analysis* 32 (1972): 118; Harold M. Zellner, "Utilitarianism and Derived Obligation," *Analysis* 32 (1972): 124.

19. See D. H. Hodgson, *Consequences of Utilitarianism* (Oxford, 1967).

20. Cf. Hare, "Rules of War and Moral Reasoning," p. 174: "The defect in most deontological theories . . . is that they have no coherent rational account to give of any level of moral thought above that of the man who knows some good simple moral principles and sticks to them. . . . [The] simple principles of the deontologist . . . are what we should be trying to inculcate into ourselves and our children if we want to stand the best chance . . . of doing what is for the best."

21. Not to mention the Jewish moralists: see D. Daube, *Collaboration with Tyranny in Rabbinic Law* (Oxford, 1965).

22. Note that I am not asserting (or denying) that self-sacrificial heroism and martyrdom are moral duties; I am explaining why they need not be regarded as moral faults.

23. *Le Suicide* (Paris, 1897), p. 5. Cf. also Daube's remarks on Donne in "The Linguistics of Suicide," *Philosophy & Public Affairs* 1, no. 4 (Summer 1972): pp. 418ff.

24. Decree of the Holy Office, 2 March 1679, error no. 34; see Denzinger and Schönmetzer, *Enchiridion symbolorum definitionum et declarationum de rebus fidei et morum* (Barcelona, 1967), par. 2134; Grisez, *Abortion: the Myths, the Realities and the Arguments,* p. 174; John T. Noonan, Jr., "An Almost Absolute Value in History," in *The Morality of Abortion,* ed. John T. Noonan, Jr. (Cambridge, Mass., 1970), p. 34.

25. See *Summa Theologiae* III, q. 68, art. 11; *in 4 Senteniarum* d.6, q.1, a.1, q.1, ad 4; d.23, q.2, a.2, q.1, ad 1 & 2; Grisez, *op. cit.,* p. 154; Noonan, *op. cit.,* p. 24.

26. Pius XII's remark, quoted by Thomson, that "the baby in the maternal breast has the right to life immediately from God" has its principal point, not (*pace* Thomson, p. 51) in the assertion of a premise from which one could deduce the wrongfulness of direct killing, but in the assertion that *if* anybody—e.g. the mother—has the right not to be directly killed, *then* the baby has the same right, since as Pius XII goes on immediately "the baby, still not born, is a man in the same degree and for the same reason as the mother."

27. The three cases mentioned in this paragraph are discussed in a standard and conservative Roman Catholic textbook: Marcellino Zalba, *Theorogiae Moralis Compendium* (Madrid, 1958), 1, p. 885.

28. Philippa Foot, "The Problem of Abortion and the Doctrine of Double Effect," *The Oxford Review* 5 (1967): 6.

29. H.L.A. Hart, "Intention and Punishment," *The Oxford Review* 4 (1967): 13; reprinted in Hart, *Punishment and Responsibility* (Oxford, 1968), pp. 124-125.

30. Foot, "The Problem of Abortion and the Doctrine of Double Effect," p. 15.

502

31. *Ibid.*, p. 14.

32. *Ibid.*, p. 8.

33. *Ibid.*, p. 7. This is the fourth of the four usual conditions for the application of the "Doctrine of Double Effect"; see e.g. Grisez, *Abortion: the Myths, the Realities and the Arguments*, p. 329. G.E.M. Anscome, "War and Murder," in *Nuclear Weapons and Christian Conscience*, ed. W. Stein, (London, 1961), p. 57, formulates the "principle of double effect," in relation to the situation where "someone innocent will die unless I do a wicked thing," thus: "you are no murderer if a man's death was neither your aim nor your chosen means, *and if you had to act in the way that led to it or else do something absolutely forbidden*" (emphasis added).

34. Grisez argues thus, *op. cit.*, p. 343; also in "Toward a Consistent Natural-Law Ethics of Killing," *American Journal of Jurisprudence* 15 (1970): 95.

35. *Ibid.*, p. 333 and pp. 89-90 respectively.

36 *Ibid.*, p. 341 and p. 94 respectively.

37. *Ibid.*, p. 341 and p. 95 respectively. I agree with Grisez that the fact that, if an artificial womb were available, many women would *not* transfer their aborted offspring to it shows that those women are directly and wrongfully intending the *death* of their offspring. I suspect Judith Thomson would agree; cf. p. 66.

38. Jonathan Bennett, " 'Whatever the Consequences,' " *Analysis* 26 (1966): p. 92 n. 1.

39. See the debate between A. Gemelli and P. Vermeersch, summarized in *Ephemerides Theologicae Lovaniensis* 11 (1934): 525-561; see also Noonan, *The Morality of Abortion*, p. 49; Zalba, *Theologiae Moralis Compendium* 1, p. 885.

40. *Summa Theologiae* II-II, q. 64, art. 7: "Nec est necessarium ad salutem ut homo actum moderatae tutelae praetermittat ad evitandum occisionem alterius: quia plus tenetur homo vitae suae providere quam vitae alienae. Sed quia occidere hominem non licet nisi publica auctoritate propter bonum commune, ut ex supra dictis patet [art. 3], illicitum est quod homo intendat occidere hominem ut seipsum defendat."

41. *Ibid.*, arts. 2 and 3.

42. Bennett, " 'Whatever the Consequences.' "

43. Foot, "The Problem of Abortion and the Doctrine of Double Effect," pp. 11-13.

44. Not, of course, that they have used Thomson's curious talk of "owning" one's own body with its distracting and legalistic connotations and its dualistic reduction of subjects of justice to objects.

45. This case is (too casually) used in Brody, "Thomson on Abortion," *Philosophy & Public Affairs* 1, no. 3 (Spring 1972): 335.

46. Cf. Wittgenstein, *Philosophical Investigations* (Oxford, 1953), sec. 69.

47. "Understanding the Abortion Argument."

48. See Grisez, *Abortion: the Myths, the Realities and the Arguments*, chap. 1 and pp. 273-287, with literature there cited.

7

FREEDOM AND CONTROL OF MAN

A Wild Horse, meeting a Domestic One, taunted him with his condition of servitude. The tamed animal swore that he was as free as the wind.

"If that is so," said the other, "pray what is the office of that bit in your mouth?"

"That," was the answer, "is iron, one of the best tonics known."

"But what is the meaning of the rein attached to it?"

"That keeps it from falling from my mouth when I am too indolent to hold it."

"How about the saddle?"

"It spares me fatigue: When I am tired I mount and ride."

— Ambrose Bierce

"Freedom is a system based on courage."

— Charles Péguy

INTRODUCTION

The oblate is the geometrical form best suited to the representation of certain philosophical debates. It is spheroid, so it calls to mind an inevitable return to fixed positions, and flattened at both poles.

Perplexities that arise when the concept of human freedom is brought under discussion are characteristically philosophical in that the human mind finds itself naturally and to some extent irresistably drawn to positions which when conjoined turn out to be inconsistent. On the one hand, there is the thesis of determinism, a principle which sees in the regular patterns of cause and effect postulates for human psychology as well as for the motions of particles in a field of force. And on the other hand, there is the deeply felt and almost universal experience of personal freedom, at least with respect to certain chosen activities under certain appropriate conditions. But how can human beings be free if their every action is determined? This, of course, is still a rhetorical question, given the unclarity with which an intended opposition between freedom and determinism has been phrased. And I raise it only to suggest the fierce and hopelessly paradoxical character of the discussions that can ensue when these issues are systematically treated.

Incompatible positions in philosophy often evoke brutal and radical responses, engineered usually with the emotional aim of liberating the scholar from endless debate. With respect to human freedom, the psycholgist B. F. Skinner, whose professional work has involved the pigeon, has come to play a popular role as an over-simplifier. Given a paradox forged between freedom and determinism, he holds quite baldly that the first does not exist. That freedom is an illusion follows, Skinner believes, from the research of behavioral psychologists; and while these conclusions may evoke some of the inevitable sadness that attends the destruction of illusion, at the same time it affords the behaviorist an opportunity for arranging the circumstances of human behavior in ways that might provoke socially desirable ends.

Philosophers and even linguists have not failed to respond to such declarations even when made with all of Skinner's inevitable authority. On their own, they are professionally concerned with arguments that arise when concepts such as freedom and determinism are brought close enough to each other to cause friction. Thus Professors C. A. Campbell and R. E. Hobart, both 20th century British philosophers, argue jointly that free will rules out determinism and that there is perfect harmony between free will and determinism. Obviously they cannot both be right and since their positions seem flatly contradictory they cannot both be wrong either. The trick, of course, is knowing which is which—an enterprise made no easier by the fact that both philosophers bring to bear a series of skillful and persuasive arguments in defense of their central claims. It is just this effortless production of paradox that gives philosophy a bad name, especially among students whose tolerance of ambiguity is low. A more charitable interpretation, and one that I favor, has it simply that these issues are of such underlying complexity, that even the wrong analysis can be strongly supported, at least for a time.

A distinction is sometimes drawn between fatalism and determinism. The fatalist is described as holding to the thesis that the Universe in its main elements hews to some fixed and unalterable scheme of things. This seems to me an obvious consequence of determinism and I see fatalism as determinism raised to the second emphatic power. Richard Taylor's paper is a defense of fatalism in a special sense. Usually we are inclined to argue that as between the past and the future there is an important difference, we can affect the second but not the first. To deny this Taylor assumes, is to affirm fatalism; and his paper constructs the case in favor of the

508

thesis that human beings are as powerless to affect the future as they are to affect the past.

I have set Michael Dummett's paper in opposition to Taylor's only because Dummet does not reject out of hand the possibilities involved in changing the past. More accurately Dummet and Taylor stand to each other in a relationship best described by topologists as orthogonal—this is something very much like a conceptual right angle. Dummet is a contemporary British philosopher, a student of Frege's work, and an exceptionally delicate and subtle thinker.

The section, and this book, ends with an essay drawn from Erwin Schrodinger's little book *What is Life?*. Schrodinger was no philosopher, still less a biologist. His great work was all in quantum theory and the development of modern physics. *What is Life?* is, however, the most interesting and beautiful book ever written on the philosophy of biology, and the remarks that bring it to a close in their seriousness and moodiness strike just the right tone with which to bring to a close the inevitably inconclusive debates on the nature of human freedom.

B. F. Skinner has expressed his views on human freedom at greater length in a book entitled *Beyond Freedom and Dignity* (Random House). Skinner has been criticized often, with varying degrees of success. The most important of his critics has been the indefatigable linguist Noam Chomsky and his views may be found in Berlinski and Bever's collection *Against Behaviorism* (Aldine). Debates between the two have become a virtual commodity and as such subject to the laws of diminishing marginal utility. The purely philosophical discussions of freedom and determinism proceed with no sign of flagging. Some useful collections, with good biographical references, are: Bernard Berofsky's *Free Will and Determinism* (Harper & Row); Sidney Hook's *Determinism and Freedom in the Age of Modern Science* (Collier Books) and Herbert Morris's *Freedom and Responsibility* (Stanford University Press).

FREEDOM
AND
THE CONTROL
OF MEN*

B. F. Skinner

The second half of the twentieth century may be remembered for its solution of a curious problem. Although Western democracy created the conditions responsible for the rise of modern science, it is now evident that it may never fully profit from that achievement. The so-called "democratic philosophy" of human behavior to which it also gave rise is increasingly in conflict with the application of the methods of science to human affairs. Unless this conflict is somehow resolved, the ultimate goals of democracy may be long deferred.

I

Just as biographers and critics look for external influences to account for the traits and achievements of the men they study, so science ultimately explains behavior in terms of "causes" or conditions which lie beyond the individual himself. As more and more causal relations are demonstrated, a practical corollary becomes difficult to resist: it should be possible to *produce* behavior according to plan simply by arranging the proper conditions. Now, among the specifications which might reasonably be submitted to a behavioral technology are these: Let men be happy, informed, skillful, well behaved and productive.

This immediate practical implication of a science of behavior has a familiar ring, for it recalls the doctrine of human perfectibility of 18th and 19th-century humanism. A science of man shares the optimism of that philosophy and supplies striking support for the working faith that men can build a better world and, through it, better men. The support comes just in time, for there has been

*Reprinted from *American Scholar,* vol. 25, no. 1 (Winter 1955-56), by permission of the author and the *American Scholar.*

little optimism of late among those who speak from the traditional point of view. Democracy has become "realistic," and it is only with some embarrassment that one admits today to perfectionistic or utopian thinking.

The earlier temper is worth considering, however. History records many foolish and unworkable schemes for human betterment, but almost all the great changes in our culture which we now regard as worthwhile can be traced to perfectionistic philosophies. Governmental, religious, educational, economic and social reforms follow a common pattern. Someone believes that a change in a cultural practice—for example, in the rules of evidence in a court of law, in the characterization of man's relation to God, in the way children are taught to read and write, in permitted rates of interest, or in minimal housing standards—will improve the condition of men: by promoting justice, permitting men to seek salvation more effectively, increasing the literacy of a people, checking an inflationary trend, or improving public health and family relations, respectively. The underlying hypothesis is always the same: that a different physical or cultural environment will make a different and better man.

The scientific study of behavior not only justifies the general pattern of such proposals; it promises new and better hypotheses. The earliest cultural practices must have originated in sheer accidents. Those which strengthened the group survived with the group in a sort of natural selection. As soon as men began to propose and carry out changes in practice for the sake of possible consequences, the evolutionary process must have accelerated. The simple practice of making changes must have had survival value. A further acceleration is now to be expected. As laws of behavior are more precisely stated, the changes in the environment required to bring about a given effect may be more clearly specified. Conditions which have been neglected because their effects were slight or unlooked for may be shown to be relevant. New conditions may actually be created, as in the discovery and synthesis of drugs which affect behavior.

This is no time, then, to abandon notions of progress, improvement or, indeed, human perfectibility. The simple fact is that man is able, and now as never before, to lift himself by his own bootstraps. In achieving control of the world of which he is a part, he may learn at last to control himself.

II

Timeworn objections to the planned improvement of cultural practices are already losing much of their force. Marcus Aurelius was probably right in advising his readers to be content with a haphazard amelioration of mankind. "Never hope to realize Plato's republic," he sighed, ". . . for who can change the opinions of men? And without a change of sentiments what can you make but reluctant slaves and hypocrites?" He was thinking, no doubt, of contemporary patterns of control based upon punishment or the threat of punishment which, as he correctly observed, breed only reluctant slaves of those who submit and hypocrites of those who discover modes of evasion. But we need not share his pessimism, for the opinions of men can be changed. The techniques of indoctrination which were being devised by the early Christian Church at the very time Marcus Aurelius was writing are relevant, as are some of the techiques of psychotherapy and of advertising and public relations. Other methods suggested by recent scientific analyses leave little doubt of the matter.

The study of human behavior also answers the cynical complaint that there is a plain "cussedness" in man which will always thwart efforts to improve him. We are often told that men do not want to be changed, even for the better. Try to help them, and they will outwit you and remain happily wretched. Dostoevsky claimed to see some plan it it. "Out of sheer ingratitude," he complained, or possibly boasted, "man will play you a dirty trick, just to prove that men are still men and not the keys of a piano. . . . And even if you could prove that a man is only a piano key, he would still do something out of sheer perversity— he would create destruction and chaos—just to gain his point. . . . And if all this could in turn be analyzed and prevented by predicting that it would occur, then man would deliberately go mad to prove his point." This is a conceivable neurotic reaction to inept control. A few men may have shown it, and many have enjoyed Dostoevsky's statement because they tend to show it. But that such perversity is a fundamental reaction of the human organism to controlling conditions is sheer nonsense.

So is the objection that we have no way of knowing what changes to make even though we have the necessary techniques. That is one of the great hoaxes of the century—a sort of booby trap left behind in the retreat before the advancing front of science. Scientists themselves have unsuspectingly agreed that there are two kinds of useful propostions about nature—facts and value judgments—and that science must confine itself to "what is," leaving "what ought to be" to others. But with what special sort of wisdom is the nonscientist endowed? Science is only effective knowing, no matter who engages in it. Verbal behavior proves upon analysis to be composed of many different types of utterances, from poetry and exhortation to logic and factual description, but these are not all equally useful in talking about cultural practices. We may classify useful propositions according to the degrees of confidence with which they may be asserted. Sentences about nature range from highly probable "facts" to sheer guesses. In general future events are less likely to be correctly described than past. When a scientist talks about a projected experiment, for example, he must often resort to statements having only a moderate likelihood of being correct; he calls them hypotheses.

Designing a new cultural pattern is in many ways like designing an experiment. In drawing up a new constitution, outlining a new educational program, modifying a religious doctrine, or setting up a new fiscal policy, many state-ments must be quite tentative. We cannot be sure that the practices we specify will have the consequences we predict, or that the consequences will reward our efforts. This is in the nature of such proposals. They are not value judgments—they are guesses. To confuse and delay the improvement of cultural practices by quibbling about the word *improve* is itself not a useful practice. Let us agree, to start with, that health is better than illness, wisdom better than ignorance, love better than hate, and productive energy better than neurotic sloth.

Another familiar objection is the "political problem." Though we know what changes to make and how to make them, we still need to control certain relevant conditions, but these have long since fallen into the hands of selfish men who are not going to relinquish them for such purposes. Possibly we shall be permitted to develop areas which at the moment seem unimportant, but at the first signs of success the strong men will move in. This, it is said, has happened to Christianity, democracy and communism. There will always be men who are fundamentally selfish and evil, and in the long run innocent goodness cannot have its way. The only evidence here is historical, and it may be misleading. Because of the way in which physical science developed, history could until very recently have "proved" that the unleashing of the energy of the atom was quite unlikely, if not impossible. Similarly, because of the order in which processes in human behavior have become available for purposes of control, history may seem to prove that power will probably be appropriated for selfish purposes. The first techniques to be discovered fell almost always to strong, selfish men. History led Lord Acton to believe that power corrupts, but he had probably never encountered absolute power, certainly not in all its forms, and had no way of predicting its effect.

An optimistic historian could defend a different conclusion. The principle that if there are not enough men of good will in the world the first step is to create more seems to be gaining recognition. The Marshall Plan (as originally conceived), Point Four, the offer of atomic materials to power-starved countries—these may or may not be wholly new in the history of international relations, but they suggest an increasing awareness of power of governmental good will. They are proposals to make certain changes in the environments of men for the sake of consequences which should be rewarding for all concerned. They do not exemplify a disinterested generosity, but an interest which is the interest of everyone. We have not yet seen Plato's philosopher-king, and may not want to, but the gap between real and utopian government is closing.

III

But we are not yet in the clear, for a new and unexpected obstacle has arisen. With a world of their own making almost within reach, men of good will have been seized with distaste for their achievement. They have uneasily rejected opportunities to apply the techniques and findings of science in the service of men, and as the import of effective cultural design has come to be understood, many of them have voiced an outright refusal to have any part in it. Science has been challenged before when it has encroached upon institutions already engaged in the control of human behavior; but what are we to make of benevolent men, with no special interests of their own to defend, who nevertheless turn against the very means of reaching long-dreamed-of goals?

What is being rejected, of course, is the scientific conception of man and his place in nature. So long as the findings and methods of science are applied to human affairs only in a sort of remedial patchwork, we may continue to hold any view of human nature we like. But as the use of science increases, we are forced to accept the theoretical structure with which science represents its facts. The difficulty is that this structure is clearly at odds with the traditional democratic conception of man. Every discovery of an event which has a part in shaping a man's behavior seems to leave so much the less to be credited to the man himself; and as such explanations become more and more comprephesive, the contribution which may be claimed by the individual himself appears to approach zero. Man's vaunted creative powers, his original accomplishments in art, science and morals, his capacity to choose and our right to hold him responsible for the consequences of his choice—none of these is conspicuous in this new self-portrait. Man, we once believed, was free to express himself in art, music and literature, to inquire into nature, to seek salvation in his own way. He could initiate action and make spontaneous and capricious changes of course. Under the most extreme duress some sort of choice remained to him. He could resist any effort to control him, though it might cost him his life. But science insists that action is initiated by forces impinging upon the individual, and that caprice is only another name for behavior for which we have not yet found a cause.

In attempting to reconcile these views it is important to note that the traditional democratic conception was not designed as a description in the scientific sense but as a philosophy to be used in setting up and maintaining a governmental process. It arose under historical circumstances and served political purposes apart from which it cannot be properly understood. In rallying men against tyranny it was necessary that the individual be strengthened, that he be taught that he had rights and could govern himself. To give the common man a new conception of his worth, his dignity, and his power to save himself, both here and hereafter, was often the only resource of the revolutionist. When democratic principles were put into practice, the same doctrines were used as a working formula. This is exemplified by the notion of personal responsibility in Anglo-American law. All governments make certain forms of punishment contingent upon certain kinds of acts. In democratic countries these contingencies

515

are expressed by the notion of responsible choice. But the notion may have no meaning under governmental practices formulated in other ways and would certainly have no place in systems which did not use punishment.

The democratic philosophy of human nature is determined by certain political exigencies and techniques, not by the goals of democracy. But exigencies and techniques change; and a conception which is not supported for its accuracy as a likeness—is not, indeed, rooted in fact at all—may be expected to change too. No matter how effective we judge current democratic practices to be, how highly we value them or how long we expect them to survive, they are almost certainly not the *final* form of government. The philosophy of human nature which has been useful in implementing them is also almost certainly not the last word. The ultimate achievement of democracy may be long deferred unless we emphasize the real aims rather than the verbal devices of democratic thinking. A philosophy which has been appropriate to one set of political exigencies will defeat its purpose if, under other circumstances, it prevents us from applying to human affairs the science of man which probably nothing but democracy itself could have produced.

IV

Perhaps the most crucial part of our democratic philosophy to be reconsidered is our attitude toward freedom—or its reciprocal, the control of human behavior. We do not oppose all forms of control because it is "human nature" to do so. The reaction is not characteristic of all men under all conditions of life. It is an attitude which has been carefully engineered, in large part by what we call the "literature" of democracy. With respect to some methods of control (for example, the threat of force), very little engineering is needed, for the techniques or their immediate consequences are objectionable. Society has suppressed these methods by branding them "wrong," "illegal" or "sinful." But to encourage these attitudes toward objectionable forms of control, it has been necessary to disguise the real nature of certain indispensable techniques, the commonest examples of which are education, moral discourse, and persuasion. The actual procedures appear harmless enough. They consist of supplying information, presenting opportunities for action, pointing out logical relationships, appeal to reason or "enlightened understanding," and so on. Through a masterful piece of misrepresentation, the illusion is fostered that these procedures do not involve the control of behavior; at most, they are simply ways of "getting someone to change his mind." But analysis not only reveals the presence of well-defined behavioral processes, it demonstrates a kind of control no less inexorable, though in some ways more acceptable, than the bully's threat of force.

516

Let us suppose that someone in whom we are interested is acting unwisely—he is careless in the way he deals with his friends, he drives too fast, or he holds his golf club the wrong way. We could probably help by issuing a series of commands: don't nag, don't drive over sixty, don't hold your club that way. Much less objectionable would be "an appeal to reason." We could show him how people are affected by his treatment of them, how accident rates rise sharply at higher speeds, how a particular grip on the club alters the way the ball is struck and corrects a slice. In doing so we resort to verbal mediating devices which emphasize and support certain "contingencies of reinforcement"—that is, certain relations between behavior and its consequences—which strengthen the behavior we wish to set up. The same consequences would possibly set up the behavior without our help, and they eventually take control no matter which form of help we give. The appeal to reason has certain advantages over the authoritative command. A threat of punishment, no matter how subtle, generates emotional reactions and tendencies to escape or revolt. Perhaps the controllee merely "feels resentment" at being made to act in a given way, but even that is to be avoided. When we "appeal to reason," he "feels freer to do as he pleases." The fact is that we have exerted *less* control than in using a threat; since other conditions may contribute to the result, the effect may be delayed or, possibly in a given instance, lacking. But if we have worked a change in his behavior at all, it is because we have altered relevant environmental conditions, and the processes we have set in motion are just as real and just as inexorable, if not as comprehensive, as in the most authoritative coercion.

"Arranging an opportunity for action" is another example of disguised control. The power of the negative form has already been exposed in the analysis of censorship. Restriction of opportunity is recognized as far from harmless. As Ralph Barton Perry said in an article which appeared in the Spring 1953 *Pacific Spectator,* "Whoever determines what alternatives shall be made known to man controls what that man shall choose *from.* He is deprived of freedom in proportion as he is denied access to *any* ideas, or is confined to any range of ideas short of the totality of relevant possibilities." But there is a positive side as well. When we present a relevant state of affairs, we increase the likelihood that a given form of behavior will be emitted. To the extent that the probability of action has changed, we have made a definite contribution. The teacher of history controls a student's behavior (or, if the reader prefers, "deprives him of freedom") just as much in *presenting* historical facts as in suppressing them. Other conditions will no doubt affect the student, but the contribution made to his behavior by the presentation of material is fixed and, within its range, irresistible.

The methods of education, moral discourse, and persuasion are acceptable not because they recognize the freedom of the individual or his right to dissent, but because they make only *partial* contributions to the control of his behavior.

The freedom they recognize is freedom from a more coercive form of control. The dissent which they tolerate is the possible effect of other determiners of action. Since these sanctioned methods are frequently ineffective, we have been able to convince ourselves that they do not represent control at all. When they show too much strength to permit disguise, we give them other names and suppress them as energetically as we suppress the use of force. Education grown too powerful is rejected as propaganda or "brain-washing," while really effective persuasion is decried as "undue influence," "demogoguery," "seduction" and so on.

If we are not to rely solely upon accident for the innovations which give rise to cultural evolution, we must accept the fact that some kind of control of human behavior is inevitable. We cannot use good sense in human affairs unless someone engages in the design and construction of environmental conditions which affect the behavior of men. Environmental changes have always been the condition for the improvement of cultural patterns, and we can hardly use the more effective methods of science without making changes on a grander scale. We are all controlled by the world in which we live, and part of that world has been and will be constructed by men. The question is this: Are we to be controlled by accident, by tyrants, or by ourselves in effective cultural design?

The danger of the misuse of power is possibly greater than ever. It is not allayed by disguising the facts. We cannot make wise decisions if we continue to pretend that human behavior is not controlled, or if we refuse to engage in control when valuable results might be forthcoming. Such measures weaken only ourselves, leaving the strength of science to others. The first step in a defense against tyranny is the fullest possible exposure of controlling techniques. A second step has already been taken successfully in restricting the use of physical force. Slowly, and as yet imperfectly, we have worked out an ethical and governmental design in which the strong man is not allowed to use the power deriving from his strength to control his fellow men. He is restrained by a superior force created for that purpose—the ethical pressure of the group, or more explicit religious and governmental measures. We tend to distrust superior forces, as we currently hesitate to relinquish sovereignty in order to set up an international police force. But it is only through such counter-control that we have achieved what we call peace—a condition in which men are not permitted to control each other through force. In other words, control itself must be controlled.

Science has turned up dangerous processes and materials before. To use the facts and techniques of a science of man to the fullest extent without making some monstrous mistake will be difficult and obviously perilous. It is no time for self-deception, emotional indulgence, or the assumption of attitudes which are no longer useful. Man is facing a difficult test. He must keep his head now, or he must start again—a long way back.

518

V

Those who reject the scientific conception of man must, to be logical, oppose the methods of science as well. The position is often supported by predicting a series of dire consequences which are to follow if science is not checked. A book by Joseph Wood Krutch, *The Measure of Man,* is in this vein. Mr. Krutch sees in the growing science of man the threat of an unexampled tyranny over men's minds. If science is permitted to have its way, he insists, "we may never be able really to think again." A controlled culture will, for example, lack some virtue inherent in disorder. We have emerged from chaos through a series of happy accidents, but in an engineered culture it will be "impossible for the unplanned to erupt again." But there is no virtue in the accidental character of an accident, and the diversity which arises from disorder can not only be duplicated by design but vastly extended. The experimental method is superior to simple observation just because it multiplies "accidents" in a systematic coverage of the possibilities. Technology offers many familiar examples. We no longer wait for immunity to disease to develop from a series of accidental exposures, nor do we wait for natural mutations in sheep and cotton to produce better fibers; but we continue to make use of such accidents when they occur, and we certainly do not prevent them. Many of the things we value have emerged from the clash of ignorant armies on darkling plains, but it is not therefore wise to encourage ignorance and darkness.

It is not always disorder itself which we are told we shall miss but certain admirable qualities in men which flourish only in the presence of disorder. A man rises above an unpropitious childhood to a position of eminence, and since we cannot give a plausible account of the action of so complex an environment, we attribute the achievement to some admirable faculty in the man himself. But such "faculties" are suspiciously like the explanatory fictions against which the history of science warns us. We admire Lincoln for rising above a deficient school system, but it was not necessarily something *in him* which permitted him to become an educated man in spite of it. His educational environment was certainly unplanned, but it could nevertheless have made a full contribution to his mature behavior. He was a rare man, but the circumstances of his childhood were rare too. We do not give Franklin Delano Roosevelt the same credit for becoming an educated man with the help of Groton and Harvard, although the same behavioral processes may have been involved. The founding of Groton and Harvard somewhat reduced the possibility that fortuitous combinations of circumstances would erupt to produce other Lincolns. Yet the founders can hardly be condemned for attacking an admirable human quality.

Another predicted consequence of a science of man is an excessive uniformity. We are told that effective control—whether governmental, religious, educational, economic or social—will produce a race of men who differ from each other only through relatively refractory genetic differences. That would probably be bad design, but we must admit that we are not now pursuing another course from choice. In a modern school, for example, there is usually a syllabus which specifies what every student is to learn by the end of each year. This would be flagrant regimentation if anyone expected every student to comply. But some will be poor in particular subjects, others will not study, others will not remember what they have been taught, and diversity is assured. Suppose, however, that we someday possess such effective educational techniques that every student will in fact be put in possession of all the behavior specified in a syllabus. At the end of the year, all students will correctly answer all questions on the final examination and "must all have prizes." Should we reject such a system on the grounds that in making all students excellent it has made them all alike? Advocates of the theory of a special faculty might contend that an important advantage of the present system is that the good student learns *in spite of* a system which is so defective that it is currently producing bad students as well. But if really effective techniques are available, we cannot avoid the problem of design simply by preferring the status quo. At what point should education be deliberately inefficient?

Such predictions of the havoc to be wreaked by the application of science to human affairs are usually made with surprising confidence. They not only show a faith in the orderliness of human behavior; they presuppose an established body of knowledge with the help of which it can be positively asserted that the changes which scientists propose to make will have quite specific results—albeit not the results they foresee. But the predictions made by the critics of science must be held to be equally fallible and subject also to empirical test. We may be sure that many steps in the scientific design of cultural patterns will produce unforeseen consequences. But there is only one way to find out. And the test must be made, for if we cannot advance in the design of cultural patterns with absolute certainty, neither can we rest completely confident of the superiority of the status quo.

VI

Apart from their possibly objectionable consequences, scientific methods seem to make no provision for certain admirable qualities and faculties which seem to have flourished in less explicitly planned cultures; hence they are called "degrading" or "lacking in dignity." (Mr. Krutch has called the author's *Walden Two* an "ignoble Utopia.") The conditioned reflex is the current whipping boy. Because conditioned reflexes may be demonstrated in animals, they are spoken of as though they were exclusively subhuman. It is implied, as we have seen, that no behavioral processes are involved in education and moral discourse or, at least, that the processes are exclusively human. But men do show conditioned reflexes (for example, when they are frightened by all instances of the control of human behavior because some instances engender fear), and animals do show processes similar to the human behavior involved in instruction and moral discourse. When Mr. Krutch asserts that " 'Conditioning' is achieved by methods which by-pass or, as it were, short-circuit those very reasoning faculties which education proposes to cultivate and exercise," he is making a technical statement which needs a definition of terms and a great deal of supporting evidence.

If such methods are called "ignoble" simply because they have no room for certain admirable attributes, then perhaps the practice of admiration needs to be examined. We might say that the child whose education has been skillfully planned has been deprived of the right to intellectual heroism. Nothing has been left to be admired in the way he acquires an education. Similarly, we can conceive of moral training which is so adequate to the demands of the culture that men will be good practically automatically, but to that extent they will be deprived of the right to moral heroism, since we seldom admire automatic goodness. Yet if we consider the end of morals rather than certain virtuous means, is not "automatic goodness" a desirable state of affairs? Is it not, for example, the avowed goal of religious education? T. H. Huxley answered the question unambiguously: "If some great power would agree to make me always think what is true and do what is right, on condition of being a sort of clock and wound up every morning before I got out of bed, I should close instantly with the offer." Yet Mr. Krutch quotes this as the scarcely credible point of view of a "proto-modern" and seems himself to share T. S. Eliot's contempt for ". . . systems so perfect / That no one will need to be good."

"Having to be good" is an excellent example of an expendable honorific. It is inseparable from a particular form of ethical and moral control. We distinguish between the things we *have* to do to avoid punishment and those we *want* to do for rewarding consequences. In a culture which did not resort to punishment we should never "have" to do anything except with respect to the punishing contingencies which arise directly in the physical environment. And we are moving toward such a culture, because the neurotic, not to say psychotic, by-products of control through punishment have long since led compassionate men to seek alternative techniques. Recent research has explained some of the objectionable results of punishment and has revealed resources of at least equal power in "positive reinforcement." It is reasonable to look forward to a time when man will seldom "have" to do anything, although he may show interest, energy, imagination and productivity far beyond the level seen under the present system (except for rare eruptions of the unplanned).

What we have to do we do with *effort*. We call it "work." There is no other way to distinguish between exhausting labor and the possibly equally energetic

521

but rewarding activity of play. It is presumably good cultural design to replace the former with the latter. But an adjustment in attitudes is needed. We are much more practiced in admiring the heroic labor of a Hercules than the activity of one who works without having to. In a truly effective educational system the student might not "have to work" at all, but that possibility is likely to be received by the contemporary teacher with an emotion little short of rage.

We cannot reconcile traditional and scientific views by agreeing upon *what* is to be admired or condemned. The question is whether anything is to be so treated. Praise and blame are cultural practices which have been adjuncts of the prevailing system of control in Western democracy. All peoples do not engage in them for the same purposes or to the same extent, nor, of course, are the same behaviors always classified in the same way as subject to praise or blame. In admiring intellectual and moral heroism and unrewarding labor, and in rejecting a world in which these would be uncommon, we are simply demonstrating our own cultural conditioning. By promoting certain tendencies to admire and censure, the group of which we are a part has arranged for the social reinforcement and punishment needed to assure a high level of intellectual and moral industry. Under other and possibly better controlling systems, the behavior which we now admire would occur, but not under those conditions which make it admirable, and we should have no reason to admire it because the culture would have arranged for its maintenance in other ways.

To those who are stimulated by the glamorous heroism of the battlefield, a peaceful world may not be a better world. Others may reject a world without sorrow, longing or a sense of guilt because the relevance of deeply moving works of art would be lost. To many who have devoted their lives to the struggle to be wise and good, a world without confusion and evil might be an empty thing. A nostalgic concern for the decline of moral heroism has been a dominating theme in the work of Aldous Huxley. In *Brave New World* he could see in the application of science to human affairs only a travesty on the notion of the Good (just as George Orwell, in *1984*, could foresee nothing but horror). In an issue of *Esquire,* Huxley has expressed the point this way: "We have had religious revolutions, we have had political, industrial, economic and nationalistic revolutions. All of them, as our descendants will discover, were but ripples in an ocean of conservatism—trivial by comparison with the psychological revolution toward which we are so rapidly moving. *That* will really be a revolution. When it is over, the human race will give no further trouble." (Footnote for the reader of the future: This was not meant as a happy ending. Up to 1956 men had been admired, if at all, either for causing trouble or alleviating it. Therefore—)

It will be a long time before the world can dispense with heroes and hence with the cultural practice of admiring heroism, but we move in that direction whenever we act to prevent war, famine, pestilence and disaster. It will be a long time before man will never need to submit to punishing environments or engage in exhausting labor, but we move in that direction whenever we make food, shelter, clothing and labor-saving devices more readily available. We may mourn the passing of heroes but not the conditions which make for heroism. We can spare the self-made saint or sage as we spare the laundress on the river's bank struggling against fearful odds to achieve cleanliness.

VII

The two great dangers in modern democratic thinking are illustrated in a paper by former Secretary of State Dean Acheson. "For a long time now," writes Mr. Acheson, "we have gone along with some well-tested principles of conduct: That it was better to tell the truth than falsehoods; . . . that duties were older than and as fundamental as rights; that, as Justice Holmes put it, the mode by which the inevitable came to pass was effort; that to perpetrate a harm was wrong no matter how many joined in it . . . and so on. . . . Our institutions are founded on the assumption that most people follow these principles most of the time because they want to, and the institutions work pretty well when this assumption is true. More recently, however, bright people have been fooling with the machinery in the human head and they have discovered quite a lot. . . . Hitler introduced new refinements [as the result of which] a whole people have been utterly confused and corrupted. Unhappily neither the possession of this knowledge nor the desire to use it was confined to Hitler. . . . Others dip from this same devil's cauldron."

The first dangerous notion in this passage is that most people follow democratic principles of conduct "because they want to." This does not account for democracy or any other form of government if we have not explained why people *want* to behave in given ways. Although it is tempting to assume that it is human nature to believe in democratic principles, we must not overlook the "cultural engineering" which produced and continues to maintain democratic practices. If we neglect the conditions which produce democratic *behavior,* it is useless to try to maintain a democratic *form* of government. And we cannot expect to export a democratic form of government successfully if we do not also provide for the cultural practices which will sustain it. Our forebears did not discover the essential nature of man; they evolved a pattern of behavior which worked remarkably well under the circumstances. The "set of principles" expressed in that pattern is not the only true set or necessarily the best. Mr. Acheson has presumably listed the most unassailable items; some of them are probably beyond question, but others—concerning duty and effort—may need revision as the world changes.

The second—and greater—threat to the democracy which Mr. Acheson is

523

defending is his assumption that knowledge is necessarily on the side of evil. All the admirable things he mentions are attributed to the innate goodness of man, all the detestable to "fooling with the machinery in the human head." This is reminiscent of the position, taken by other institutions engaged in the control of men, that certain forms of knowledge are in themselves evil. But how out of place in a democratic philosophy! Have we come this far only to conclude that well-intentioned people cannot study the behavior of men without becoming tyrants or that informed men cannot show good will? Let us for once have strength and good will on the same side.

VIII

Far from being a threat to the tradition of Western democracy, the growth of a science of man is a consistent and probably inevitable part of it. In turning to the external conditions which shape and maintain the behavior of men, while questioning the reality of inner qualities and faculties to which human achievements were once attributed, we turn from the ill-defined and remote to the observable and manipulable. Though it is a painful step, it has far-reaching consequences, for it not only sets higher standards of human welfare but shows us how to meet them. A change in a theory of human nature cannot change the facts. The achievements of man in science, art, literature, music and morals will survive any interpretation we place upon them. The uniqueness of the individual is unchallenged in the scientific view. Man, in short, will remain man. (There will be much to admire for those who are so inclined. Possibly the noblest achievement to which man can aspire, even according to present standards, is to accept himself for what he is, as that is revealed to him by the methods which he devised and tested on a part of the world in which he had only a small personal stake.)

If Western democracy does not lose sight of the aims of humanitarian action, it will welcome the almost fabulous support of its own science of man and will strengthen itself and play an important role in building a better world for everyone. But if it cannot put its "democratic philosophy" into proper historical perspective—if, under the control of attitudes and emotions which it generated for other purposes, it now rejects the help of science—then it must be prepared for defeat. For if we continue to insist that science has nothing to offer but a new and more horrible form of tyranny, we may produce just such a result by allowing the strength of science to fall into the hands of despots. And if, with luck, it were to fall instead to men of good will in other political communities, it would be perhaps a more ignominious defeat; for we should then, through a miscarriage of democratic principles, be forced to leave to others the next step in man's long struggle to control nature and himself.

FREE WILL
RULES
OUT
DETERMINISM*
C. A. Campbell

1. During the greater part of the last lecture, which was concerned with the defense of the notion of self-activity and with the classification of its main species, we were operating on the very threshold of the problem of Free Will; and in its later stages, particularly in connection with the analysis of moral-decision activity, we may perhaps be judged to have passed beyond the threshold. The present lecture, in which we address ourselves formally to the Free Will problem, is in fact so closely continuous with its predecessor that I should wish the two lectures to be regarded as constituting, in a real sense, a single unit.

In the later, more constructive part of my programme today this intimate dependence upon what has gone before will become very apparent. My initial task, however, must be one of elucidation and definition. The general question I have to try to answer, a question which is very far indeed from admitting of a ready answer, is, What precisely *is* the Free Will problem?

It is something of a truism that in philosophic enquiry the exact formulation of a problem often takes one a long way on the road to its solution. In the case of the Free Will problem I think there is a rather special need of careful formulation. For there are many sorts of human freedom; and it can easily happen that one wastes a great deal of labor in proving or disproving a freedom which has almost nothing to do with the freedom which is at issue in the traditional problem of Free Will. The abortiveness of so much of the argument for and against Free Will in contemporary philosophical literature seems to me due in the main to insufficient pains being taken over the prelininary definition of the problem. There is indeed, one outstanding exception, Professor Broad's

*From Lecture IX, "Has the Self 'Free Will'?" of *On Selfhood and Godhood,* London: George Allen & Unwin Ltd, 1957; reprinted by permission of the publisher.

brilliant inaugural lecture entitled, "Determinism, Indeterminism, and Libertarianism,"[1] in which 43 pages are devoted to setting out the problem, as against seven of its solution! I confess that the solution does not seem to myself to follow upon the formulation quite as easily as all that[2] but Professor Broad's eminent example fortifies me in my decision to give here what may seem at first sight a disproportionate amount of time to the business of determining the essential characteristics of the kind of freedom with which the traditional problem is concerned.

Fortunately we can at least make a beginning with a certain amount of confidence. It is not seriously disputable that the kind of freedom in question is the freedom which is commonly recognized to be in some sense a precondition of moral responsibility. Clearly, it is on account of this integral connection with moral responsibility that such exceptional importance has always been felt to attach to the Free Will problem. But in what precise sense is free will a precondition of moral responsibility, and thus a postulate of the moral life in general? This is an exceedingly troublesome question; but until we have satisfied ourselves about the answer to it, we are not in a position to state, let alone decide, the question whether "Free Will" in its traditional, ethical significance is a reality.

Our first business, then, is to ask, exactly what kind of freedom is it which is required for moral responsibility? And as to method of procedure in this inquiry, there seems to me to be no real choice. I know of only one method that carries with it any hope of success, namely the critical comparison of those acts for which, on due reflection, we deem it proper to attribute moral praise or blame to the agents, with those acts for which, on due reflection, we deem such judgments to be improper. The ultimate touchstone, as I see it, can only be our moral consciousness as it manifests itself in our more critical and considered moral judgments. The "linguistic" approach, by way of the analysis of moral *sentences,* seems to me, despite its present popularity, to be an almost infallible method for reaching wrong results in the moral field; but I must reserve what I have to say about this for the next lecture.

2. The first point to note is that the freedom at issue (as indeed the very name "Free *Will* Problem" indicates) pertains primarily not to overt acts but to inner acts. The nature of things has decreed that, save in the case of one's self, it is only overt acts which one can directly observe. But a very little reflection serves to show that in our moral judgments upon others their overt acts are regarded as significant only in so far as they are the expression of inner acts. We do not consider the acts of a robot to be morally responsible acts; nor do we consider the acts of a man to be so save in so far as they are distinguishable from those of a robot by reflecting an inner life of choice. Similarly, from the other side, if we are satisfied (as we may on occasion be, at least in the case of ourselves) that a person has definitely elected to follow a course which he believes to be wrong, but has been prevented by external circumstances from

translating his inner choice into an overt act, we still regard him as morally blameworthy. Moral freedom, then, pertains to *inner* acts.

The next point seems at first sight equally obvious and uncontroversial; but as we shall see, it has awkward implications if we are in real earnest with it (as almost nobody is). It is the simple point that the act must be one of which the person judged can be regarded as the *sole* author. It seems plain enough that if there are any *other* determinants of the act, external to the self, to that extent the act is not an act which the *self* determines, and to that extent not an act for which the self can be held morally responsible. The self is only part-author of the act, and his moral responsibility can logically extend only to those elements within the act (assuming for the moment that these can be isolated) of which he is the *sole* author.

The awkward implications of this apparent truism will be readily appreciated. For, if we are mindful of the influences exerted by heredity and environment, we may well feel some doubt whether there is any act of will at all of which one can truly say that the self is sole author, sole determinant. No man has a voice in determining the raw material of impulses and capacities that constitute his hereditary endowment, and no man has more than a very partial control of the material and social environment in which he is destined to live his life. Yet it would be manifestly absurd to deny that these two factors do constantly and profoundly affect the nature of a man's choices. That this is so we all of us recognize in our moral judgments when we "make allowances," as we say, for a bad heredity or a vicious environment, and acknowledge in the victim of them a diminished moral responsibility for evil courses. Evidently we do *try*, in our moral judgments, however crudely, to praise or blame a man only in respect of that of which we can regard him as *wholly* the author. And evidently we do recognize that, for a man to be the author of an act in the full sense required for moral responsibility, it is not enough merely that he "wills" or "chooses" the act, since even the most unfortunate victim of heredity or environment does, as a rule, "will" what he does. It is significant, however, that the ordinary man, though well enough aware of the influence upon choices of heredity and environment, does not feel obliged thereby to give up his assumption that moral predicates *are* somehow applicable. Plainly he still believes that there is *something* for which a man is morally responsible, something of which we can fairly say that he is the sole author. *What is this something?* To that question common sense is not ready with an explicit answer—though an answer is, I think, implicit in the line which its moral judgements take. I shall do what I can to give an explicit answer later in this lecture. Meantime it must suffice to observe that, if we are to be true to the deliverances of our moral consciousness, it is very difficult to deny that *sole* authorship is a necessary condition of the morally responsible act.

Third, we come to a point over which much recent controversy has raged.

527

We may approach it by raising the following question. Granted an act of which the agent is sole author, does this "sole authorship" suffice to make the act a morally free act? We may be inclined to think that it does, until we contemplate the possibility that an act of which the agent is sole author might conceivably occur as a necessary expression of the agent's nature; the way in which, for example, some philosophers have supposed the Divine act of creation to occur. This consideration excites a legitimate doubt; for it is far from easy to see how a person can be regarded as a proper subject for moral praise or blame in respect of an act which he *cannot help* performing—even if it be his own nature which necessitates it. Must we not recognize it as a condition of the morally free act that the agent "could have acted otherwise" than he in fact did? It is true, indeed, that we sometimes praise or blame a man for an act about which we are prepared to say, in the light of our knowledge of his established character, that he "could no other." But I think that a little reflection shows that in such cases we are not praising or blaming the man strictly for what he does *now* (or at any rate we ought not to be), but rather for those past acts of his which have generated the firm habit of mind from which his *present* act follows necessarily. In other words, our praise and blame, so far as justified, are really retrospective, being directed not to the agent *qua* performing *this* act, but to the agent *qua* performing those past acts which have built up his present character, and in respect to which we presume that he *could* have acted otherwise, that there really *were* open possibilities before him. These cases, therefore, seem to me to constitute no valid exception to what I must take to be the rule, namely, that a man can be morally praised or blamed for an act only if he could have acted otherwise.

Now philosophers today are fairly well agreed that it is a postulate of the morally responsible act that the agent "could have acted otherwise" in *some* sense of that phrase. But sharp differences of opinion have arisen over the way in which the phrase ought to be interpreted. There is a strong disposition to water down its apparent meaning by insisting that it is not (as a postulate of moral responsibility) to be understood as a straightforward categorical proposition, but rather as a disguised hypothetical proposition. All that we really require to be assured of, in order to justify our holding X morally responsible for an act, is, we are told, that X could have acted otherwise *if* he had *chosen* otherwise (Moore, Stevenson); or perhaps that X could have acted otherwise *if* he had had a different character, or *if* he had been placed in different circumstances.

I think it is easy to understand, and even, in a measure, to sympathize with, the motives which induce philosophers to offer these counter-interpretations. It is not just the fact that "X could have acted otherwise," as a bald categorical statement, is incompatible with the universal sway of causal law—though this is, to some philosophers, a serious stone of stumbling. The more widespread objection is that it at least looks as though it were incompatible with that causal continuity of an agent's character with his conduct which is implied when we believe (surely with justice) that we can often tell the sort of thing a man will do from our knowledge of the sort of man he is.

We shall have to make our accounts with that particular difficulty later. At this stage I wish merely to show that neither of the hypothetical propositions suggested—and I think the same could be shown for *any* hypothetical alternative—is an acceptable substitute for the categorical proposition "X could have acted otherwise" as the presupposition of moral responsibility.

Let us look first at the earlier suggestion—"X could have acted otherwise *if* he had chosen otherwise." Now clearly there are a great many acts with regard to which we are entirely satisfied that the agent is thus situated. We are often perfectly sure that—for this is all it amounts to—if X had chosen otherwise, the circumstances presented no external obstacle to the translation of that choice into action. For example, we often have no doubt at all that X, who in point of fact told a lie, could have told the truth *if* he had so chosen. But does our confidence on this score allay all legitimate doubts about whether X is really blameworthy? Does it entail that X is free in the sense required for moral responsibility? Surely not. The obvious question immediately arises: "But *could* X have *chosen* otherwise than he did?" It is doubt about the true answer to *that* question which leads most people to doubt the reality of moral responsibility. Yet on this crucial question the hypothetical proposition which is offered as a sufficient statement of the condition justifying the ascription of moral responsibility gives us no information whatsoever.

Indeed this hypothetical substitute for the categorial "X could have acted otherwise" seems to me to lack all plausibility unless one contrives to forget why it is, after all, that we ever come to feel fundamental doubts about man's moral responsibility. Such doubts are born, surely, when one becomes aware of certain reputable world-views in religion or philosophy, or of certain reputable scientific beliefs, which in their several ways imply that man's actions are necessitated, and thus could not be otherwise than they in fact are. But clearly a doubt so based is not even touched by the recognition that a man could very often act otherwise *if* he so chose. That proposition is entirely compatible with the necessitarian theories which generate our doubt: indeed it is this very compatibility that has recommended it to some philosophers, who are reluctant to give up either moral responsibility or Determinism. The proposition which we *must* be able to affirm if moral praise or blame of X is to be justified is the categorical proposition that X could have acted otherwise because—not if—he could have chosen otherwise; or, since it is essentially the inner side of the act that matters, the proposition simply that X could have chosen otherwise.

For the second of the alternative formulae suggested we cannot spare more than a few moments. But its inability to meet the demands it is required to meet is almost transparent. "X could have acted otherwise," as a statement of a precondition of X's moral responsibility, really means (we are told) "X could have acted otherwise *if* he were differently constituted, or *if* he had been placed in different circumstances." It seems a sufficient reply to this to point out that the person whose moral responsibility is at issue is X; a specific individual, in a specific set of circumstances. It is totally irrelevant to X's moral responsibility that we should be able to say that some person differently constituted from X, or X in a different set of circumstances, could have done something different from what X did.

3. Let me, then, briefly sum up the answer at which we have arrived to our question about the kind of freedom required to justify moral responsibility. It is that a man can be said to exercise free will in a morally significant sense only in so far as his chosen act is one of which he is the sole cause or author, and only if—in the straightforward, categorical sense of the phrase—he "could have chosen otherwise."

I confess that this answer is in some ways a disconcerting one, disconcerting, because most of us, however objective we are in the actual conduct of our thinking, would *like* to be able to believe that moral responsibility is real: whereas the freedom required for moral responsibility, on the analysis we have given, is certainly far more difficult to establish than the freedom required on the analyses we found ourselves obliged to reject. If, for example, moral freedom entails only that I could have acted otherwise *if* I had chosen otherwise, there is no real "problem" abut it at all. I am "free" in the normal case where there is no external obstacle to prevent my translating the alternative choice into action, and not free in other cases. Still less is there a problem if all that moral freedom entails is that I could have acted otherwise *if* I had been a differently constituted person, or been in different circumstances. Clearly I am *always* free in *this* sense of freedom. But, as I have argued, these so-called "freedoms" fail to give us the preconditions of moral responsibility, and hence leave the freedom of the traditional free-will problem, the freedom that people are really concerned about, precisely where it was. . . .

5. That brings me to the second, and more constructive, part of this lecture. From now on I shall be considering whether it is reasonable to believe that man does in fact possess a free will of the kind specified in the first part of the lecture. If so, just how and where within the complex fabric of the volitional life are we to locate it?—for although free will must presumably belong (if anywhere) to the volitional side of human experience, it is pretty clear from the way in which we have been forced to define it that it does not pertain simply to volition as such; not even to all volitions that are commonly dignified with the name of "choices." It has been, I think, one of the more serious impediments to profitable discussion of the Free Will problem that Libertarians and Determinists alike have so often failed to appreciate the comparatively narrow area within which the free will that is necessary to "save" morality is required

to operate. It goes without saying that this failure has been gravely prejudicial to the case for Libertarianism. I attach a good deal of importance, therefore, to the problem of locating free will correctly within the volitional orbit. Its solution forestalls and annuls, I believe, some of the more tiresome clichés of Determinist criticism.

We saw earlier that Common Sense's practice of "making allowances" in its moral judgments for the influence of heredity and environment indicates Common Sense's conviction, both that a just moral judgment must discount determinants of choice over which the agent has no control, and also (since it still accepts moral judgments as legitimate) that *something* of moral relevance survives which can be regarded as genuinely self-originated. We are now to try to discover what this "something" is. And I think we may still usefully take Common Sense as our guide. Suppose one asks the ordinary intelligent citizen *why* he deems it proper to make allowances for X, whose heredity and/or environment are unfortunate. He will tend to reply, I think, in some such terms as these: that X has more and stronger temptations to deviate from what is right than Y or Z, who are normally circumstanced, so that he must put forth *a stronger moral effort* if he is to achieve the same level of external conduct. The intended implication seems to be that X is just as morally praiseworthy as Y or Z *if* he exerts an equivalent moral effort, even though he may not thereby achieve an equal success in conforming his will to the "concrete" demands of duty. And this implies, again, Common Sense's belief that *in moral effort* we have something for which a man is responsible *without qualification,* something that is *not* affected by heredity and environment but depends *solely* on the self itself.

Now in my opinion Common Sense has here, in principle, hit upon the one and only defensible answer. Here, and here alone, so far as I can see, in the act of deciding whether to put forth or withhold the moral effort required to resist temptation and rise to duty, is to be found an act which is free in the sense required for moral responsibility; an act of which the self is sole author, and of which it is true to say that "it could be" (or, after the event, "could have been") "otherwise." Such is the thesis which we shall now try to establish.

6. The species of argument appropriate to the establishment of a thesis of this sort should fall, I think, into two phases. First, there should be a consideration of the evidence of the moral agent's own inner experience. What *is* the act of moral decision, and what does it imply, from the standpoint of the actual participant? Since there is no way of knowing the act of moral decision—or for that matter any other form of activity—except by actual participation in it, the evidence of the subject, or agent, is on an issue of this kind of palmary importance. It can hardly, however, be taken as in itself conclusive. For even if that evidence should be overwhelmingly to the effect that moral decision does have the characteristics required by moral freedom, the question is bound to

be raised—and in view of considerations from other quarters pointing in a contrary direction is *rightly* raised—Can we *trust* the evidence of inner experience? That brings us to what will be the second phase of the argument. We shall have to go on to show, if we are to make good our case, that the extraneous considerations so often supposed to be fatal to the belief in moral freedom are in fact innocuous to it.

In the light of what was said in the last lecture about the self's experience of moral decision as a *creative* activity, we may perhaps be absolved from developing the first phase of the argument at any great length. The appeal is throughout to one's own experience in the actual taking of the moral decision in the situation of moral temptation. "Is it possible," we must ask, "for anyone so circumstanced to *dis*believe that we could be deciding otherwise?" The answer is surely not in doubt. When we decide to exert moral effort to resist a temptation, we feel quite certain that we *could* withhold the effort; just as if we decide to withhold the effort and yield to our desires, we feel quite certain that we *could* exert it—otherwise we should not blame ourselves afterwards for having succumbed. It may be, indeed, that this conviction is mere self-delusion. But that is not at the moment our concern. It is enough at present to establish that the act of deciding to exert or to withhold moral effort, as we know it from the inside in actual moral living, belongs to the category of acts which "could have been otherwise."

Mutatis mutandis, the same reply is forthcoming if we ask, "Is it possible for the moral agent in the taking of his decision to *dis*believe that he is the *sole* author of that decision?" Clearly he cannot disbelieve that it is *he* who takes the decision. That, however, is not in itself sufficient to enable him, on reflection, to regard himself as *solely* responsible for the act. For his "character" as so far formed might conceivably be a factor in determining it, and no one can suppose that the constitution of his "character" is uninfluenced by circumstances of heredity and environment with which *he* has nothing to do. But as we pointed out in the last lecture, the very essence of the moral decision as it is experienced is that it is a decision whether or not to *combat* our strongest desire, and our strongest desire *is* the expression in the situation of our character as so far formed. Now clearly our character cannot be a factor in determining the decision whether or not to *oppose* our character. I think we are entitled to say, therefore, that the act of moral decision is one in which the self is for itself not merely "author" but "sole author."

7. We may pass on, then, to the second phase of our constructive argument; and this will demand more elaborate treatment. Even if a moral agent *qua* making a moral decision in the situation of "temptation" cannot help believing that he has free will in the sense at issue—a moral freedom between real alternatives, between genuinely open possibilities—are there, nevertheless, objections to a freedom of this kind so cogent that we are bound to distrust the evidence of "inner experience"?

532

I begin by drawing attention to a simple point whose significance tends, I think, to be underestimated. If the phenomenological analysis we have offered is substantially correct, no one while functioning as a moral agent can help believing that he enjoys free will. Theoretically he may be completely convinced by Determinist arguments, but when actually confronted with a personal situation of conflict between duty and desire he is quite certain that it lies with him here and now whether or not he will rise to duty. It follows that if Determinists could produce convincing theoretical arguments against a free will of this kind, the awkward predicament would ensue that man has to deny as a theoretical being what he has to assert as a practical being. Now I think the Determinist ought to be a good deal more worried about this than he usually is. He seems to imagine that a strong case on general theoretical grounds is enough to prove that the "practical" belief in free will, even if inescapable for us as practical beings, is mere illusion. But in fact it proves nothing of the sort. There is no reason whatever why a belief that we find ourselves obliged to hold *qua* practical beings should be required to give way before a belief which we find ourselves obliged to hold *qua* theoretical beings; or, for that matter, vice versa. All that the theoretical arguments of Determinism can prove, unless they are reinforced by a refutation of the phenomenological analysis that supports Libertarianism, is that there is a radical conflict between the theoretical and the practical sides of man's nature, an antimony at the very heart of the self. And this is a state of affairs with which no one can easily rest satisfied. I think therefore that the Determinist ought to concern himself a great deal more than he does with phenomenological analysis, in order to show, if he can, that the assurance of free will is not really an inexpugnable element in man's practical consciousness. There is just as much obligation upon him, convinced though he may be of the soundness of his theoretical arguments, to expose the errors of the Libertarian's phenomenological analysis, as there is upon us, convinced though we may be of the soundness of the Libertarian's phenomenological analysis, to expose the errors of the Determinist's theoretical arguments.

8. However, we must at once begin the discharge of our own obligation. The rest of this lecture will be devoted to trying to show that the arguments which seem to carry most weight with Determinists are, to say the least of it, very far from compulsive.

Fortunately a good many of the arguments which at an earlier time in the history of philosophy would have been strongly urged against us make almost no appeal to the bulk of philosophers today, and we may here pass them by. That applies to any criticism of "open possibilities" based on a metaphysical theory about the nature of the universe as a whole. Nobody today *has* a metaphysical theory about the nature of the universe as a whole! It applies also, with almost equal force, to criticisms based on the universality of causal law as a supposed postulate of science. There have always been, in my opinion, sound philosophic reasons for doubting the validity, as distinct from the convenience, of the causal postulate in its universal form, but at the present time, when scientists themselves are deeply divided about the need for postulating causality even within their own special field, we shall do better to concentrate our attention on criticisms which are more confidently advanced. I propose to ignore also, on different grounds, the type of criticism of free will that is sometime advanced from the side of religion, based on religious postulates of divine omnipotence and omniscience. So far as I can see, a postulate of human freedom is every bit as necessary to meet certain religious demands (for example, to make sense of the "conviction of sin"), as postulates of divine omniscience and omnipotence are to meet certain other religious demands. If so, then it can hardly be argued that religious experience as such tells more strongly against than for the position we are defending: and we may be satisfied, in the present context, to leave the matter there. It will be more profitable to discuss certain arguments which contemporary philosophers do think important, and which recur with a somewhat monotonous regularity in the literature of anti-Libertarianism.

These arguments can, I think, be reduced in principle to no more than two: first, the argument from "predictability"; second, the argument from the alleged meaninglessness of an act supposed to be the self's act and yet not an expression of the self's character. Contemporary criticism of free will seems to me to consist almost exclusively of variations of these two themes. I shall deal with each in turn.

9. On the first we touched in passing at an earlier stage. Surely it is beyond question (the critical urges) that when we know a person intimately we can foretell with a high degree of accuracy how he will respond to at least a large number of practical situations. One feels safe in predicting that one's dog-loving friend will not use his boot to repel the little mongrel that comes yapping at his heels; or again that one's wife will not pass with incurious eyes (or indeed pass at all) the new hat-shop in the city. So to behave would not be (as we say) "in character." But, so the criticism runs, you with your doctrine of "genuinely open possibilities," of a free will by which the self can diverge from its own character, remove all rational basis from such prediction. You require us to make the absurd supposition that the success of countless predictions of the sort in the past has been mere matter of chance. If you *really* believed in your theory, you would not be surprised if tomorrow your friend with the notorious horror of strong drink should suddenly exhibit a passion for whisky and soda, or if your friend whose taste for reading has hitherto been satisfied with the sporting columns of the newspapers should be discovered on a fine Saturday afternoon poring over the works of Hegel. But of course you *would* be surprised. Social life would be sheer chaos if there were not well-grounded social expectations; and social life is not sheer chaos. Your theory is hopelessly wrecked upon obvious facts.

534

Now whether or not this criticims holds good against some versions of Libertarian theory I need not here discuss. It is sufficient if I can make it clear that against the version advanced in this lecture, according to which free will is localized in a relatively narrow field of operation, the criticism has no relevance whatsoever.

Let us remind ourselves briefly of the setting within which, on our view, free will functions. There is X, the course which we believe we ought to follow, and Y, the course towards which we feel our desire is strongest. The freedom which we ascribe to the agent is the freedom to put forth or refrain from putting forth the moral effort required to resist the pressure of desire and do what he thinks he ought to do.

But then there is surely an immense range of practical situations—covering by far the greater part of life—in which there is no question of a conflict within the self between what he most desires to do and what he thinks he ought to do? Indeed such conflict is a comparatively rare phenomenon for the majority of men. Yet over that whole vast range there is nothing whatever in our version of Libertarianism to prevent our agreeing that character determines conduct. In the absence, real or supposed, of any "moral" issue, what a man chooses will be simply that course which, after such reflection as seems called for, he deems most likely to bring him what he most strongly desires; and that is the same as to say the course to which his present character inclines him.

Over by far the greater area of human choices, then, our theory offers no more barrier to successful prediction on the basis of character than any other theory. For where there is no clash of strongest desire with duty, the free will we are defending has no business. There is just nothing for it to do.

But what about the situations—rare enough though they may be—in which there *is* this clash and in which free will does therefore operate? Does our theory entail that there at any rate, as the critic seems to suppose, "anything may happen"?

Not by any manner of means. In the first place, and by the very nature of the case, the range of the agent's possible choices is bounded by what he thinks he ought to do on the one hand, and what he most strongly desires on the other. The freedom claimed for him is a freedom of decision to make or withhold the effort required to do what he thinks he ought to do. There is no question of a freedom to act in some "wild" fashion, out of all relation to his characteristic beliefs and desires. This "freedom of caprice," so often charged against the Libertarian, is, to put it bluntly, a sheer figment of the critic's imagination, with no *habitat* in serious Libertarian theory. Even in situations where free will does come into play it is perfectly possible, on a view like ours, given the appropriate knowledge of a man's character, to predict within certain limits how he will respond.

But "probable" prediction in such situations can, I think, go further than this. It is obvious that where desire and duty are at odds, the felt "gap" (as it were) between the two may vary enormously in breadth in different cases. The moderate drinker and the chronic tippler may each want another glass, and each deems it his duty to abstain, but the felt gap between desire and duty in the case of the former is trivial beside the great gulf which is felt to separate them in the case of the latter. Hence it will take a far harder moral effort for the tippler than for the moderate drinker to achieve the same external result of abstention. So much is matter of common agreement. And we are entitled, I think, to take it into account in prediction, on the simple principle that the harder the moral effort required to resist desire the less likely it is to occur. Thus in the example taken, most people would predict that the tippler will very probably succumb to his desires, whereas there is a reasonable likelihood that the moderate drinker will make the comparatively slight effort needed to resist them. So long as the prediction does not pretend to more than a measure of probability, there is nothing in our theory which would disallow it.

I claim, therefore, that the view of free will I have been putting forward is consistent with predictability of conduct on the basis of character over a very wide field indeed. And I make the further claim that that field will cover all the situations in life concerning which there is any empirical evidence that successful prediction is possible.

10. Let us pass on to consider the second main line of criticism. This is, I think, much the more illuminating of the two, if only because it compels the Libertarian to make explicit certain concepts which are indispensable to him, but which, being desperately hard to state clearly, are apt not to be stated at all. The critic's fundamental point might be stated somewhat as follows:

"Free will as you describe it is completely unintelligible. On your own showing no *reason* can be given, because there just *is* no reason why a man decides to exert rather than withhold moral effort, or vice versa. But such an act—or more properly, such an 'occurrence'—it is nonsense to speak of as an act of a *self*. If there is nothing in the self's character to which it is, even in principle, in any way traceable, the self has nothing to do with it. Your 'freedom,' therefore, so far from supporting the self's moral responsibility, destroys it as surely as the crudest Determinism could do."

If we are to discuss this criticism usefully, it is important, I think, to begin by getting clear about two different senses of the word "intelligible."

If, in the first place, we mean by an "intelligible" act one whose occurrence is in principle capable of being inferred, since it follows necessarily from something (though we may not know in fact from what), then it is certainly true that the Libertarian's free will is unintelligible. But that is only saying, is it not, that the Libertarian's "free" act is not an act which follows necessarily from something! This can hardly rank as a *criticism* of Libertarianism. It is just a description of it. That there can be nothing unintelligible in *this* sense is precisely what the Determinist has got to *prove*.

Yet it is surprising how often the critic of Libertarianism involves himself in this circular mode of argument. Repeatedly it is urged against the Libertarian, with a great air of triumph, that on his view he can't say *why* I now decide to rise to duty, or now decide to follow my strongest desire in defiance of duty. Of course he can't. If he could he wouldn't *be* a Libertarian. To "account for" a "free" act is a contradiction in terms. A free will is *ex hypothesi* the sort of thing of which the request for an *explanation* is absurd. The assumption that an explanation must be in principle possible for the act of moral decision deserves to rank as a classic example of the ancient fallacy of "begging the question."

But the critic usually has in mind another sense of the word "unintelligible." He is apt to take it for granted that an act which is unintelligible in the *above* sense (as the morally free act of the Libertarian undoubtedly is) is unintelligible in the *further* sense that we can attach no meaning to it. And this is an altogether more serious matter. If it could really be shown that the Libertarian's "free will" were unintelligible in this sense of being meaningless, that, for myself at any rate, would be the end of the affair. Libertarianism would have been conclusively refuted.

But it seems to me manifest that this can *not* be shown. The critic has allowed himself, I submit, to become the victim of a widely accepted but fundamentally vicious assumption. He has assumed that whatever is meaningful must exhibit its meaningfulness to those who view it from the standpoint of external observation. Now if one chooses thus to limit one's self to the role of external observer, it is, I think, perfectly true that one can attach no meaning to an act which is the act of something we call a "self" and yet follows from nothing in that self's character. But then *why should we* so limit ourselves, when what is under consideration is a subjective activity? For the apprehension of subjective acts there is *another* standpoint available, that of *inner experience,* of the practical consciousness in its actual functioning. If our free will should turn out to be something to which we can attach a meaning from *this* standpoint, no more is required. And no more ought to be expected. For I must repeat that only from the inner standpoint of living experience *could* anything of the nature of "activity" be directly grasped. Observation from without is in the nature of the case impotent to apprehend the active *qua* active. We can from without observe sequences of states. If into these we read activity (as we sometimes do), this can only be on the basis of what we discern in ourselves from the inner standpoint. It follows that if anyone insists upon taking his criterion of the meaningful simply from the standpoint of external observation, he is really deciding in advance of the evidence that the notion of activity, and a fortiori the notion of a free will, is "meaningless." He looks for the free act through a medium which

537

is in the nature of the case incapable of revealing it, and then, because inevitably he doesn't find it, he declares that it doesn't exist!

But if, as we surely ought in this context, we adopt the inner standpoint, then (I am suggesting) things appear in a totally different light. From the inner standpoint, it seems to me plain, there is no difficulty whatever in attaching meaning to an act which is the self's act and which nevertheless does not follow from the self's character. So much I claim has been established by the phenomenological analysis, in this and the previous lecture, of the act of moral decision in face of moral temptation. It is thrown into particularly clear relief where the moral decision is to make the moral effort required to rise to duty. For the very function of moral effort, as it appears to the agent engaged in the act, is to enable the self to act against the line of least resistance, against the line to which his character as so far formed most strongly inclines him. But if the self is thus conscious here of *combating* his formed character, he surely cannot possibly suppose that the act, although his own act, *issues from* his formed character? I submit, therefore, that the self knows very well indeed— from the inner standpoint—what is meant by an act which is the *self's* act and which nevertheless does not follow from the self's *character*.

What this implies—and it seems to me to be an implication of cardinal importance for any theory of the self that aims at being more than superficial— is that the nature of the self is for itself something more than just its character as so far formed. The "nature" of the self and what we commonly call the "character" of the self are by no means the same thing, and it is utterly vital that they should not be confused. The "nature" of the self comprehends, but is not without remainder reducible to, its "character"; it must, if we are to be true to the testimony of our experience of it, be taken as including *also* the authentic creative power of fashioning and refashioning "character."

The misguided, and as a rule quite uncritical, belittlement, of the evidence offered by inner experience has, I am convinced, been responsible for more bad argument by the opponents of Free Will than has any other single factor. How often, for example, do we find the Determinist critic saying, in effect, *"Either* the act follows necessarily upon precedent states, *or* it is a mere matter of chance and accordingly of no moral significance." The disjunction is invalid, for it does not exhaust the possible alternatives. It seems to the critic to do so only because he *will* limit himself to the standpoint which is proper, and indeed alone possible, in dealing with the physical world, the standpoint of the external observer. If only he would allow himself to assume the standpoint which is not merely proper for, but necessary to, the apprehension of subjective activity, the inner standpoint of the practical consciousness in its actual functioning, he would find himself obliged to recognize the falsity of his disjunction. Reflection on the act of moral decision as apprehended from the inner standpoint would force him to recognize a *third* possibility, as remote from chance as from necessity, that, namely, of *creative activity,* in which (as I have ventured to express it) nothing determines the act save the agent's doing of it.

11. There we must leave the matter. But as this lecture has been, I know, somewhat densely packed, it may be helpful if I conclude by reminding you, in bald summary, of the main things I have been trying to say. Let me set them out in so many successive theses.

1. The freedom which is at issue in the traditional Free Will problem is the freedom which is presupposed in moral responsibility.

2. Critical reflection upon carefully considered attributions of moral responsibility reveals that the only freedom that will do is a freedom which pertains to inner acts of choice, and that these acts must be acts (*a*) of which the self is *sole* author, and (*b*) which the self could have performed otherwise.

3. From phenomenological analysis of the situation of moral temptation we find that the self as engaged in this situation in inescapably convinced that it possesses a freedom of precisely the specified kind, located in the decision to exert or withhold the moral effort needed to rise to duty where the pressure of its desiring nature is felt to urge it in a contrary direction.

Passing to the question of the *reality* of this moral freedom which the moral agent believes himself to possess, we argued:

4. Of the two types of Determinist criticism which seem to have most influence today, that based on the predictability of much human behavior fails to touch a Libertarianism which confines the area of free will as above indicated. Libertarianism so understood is compatible with all the predictability that the empirical facts warrant. And:

5. The second main type of criticism, which alleges the "meaninglessness" of an act which is the self's act and which is yet not determined by the self's character, is based on a failure to appreciate that the standpoint of inner experience is not only legitimate but indispensable where what is at issue is the reality and nature of a subjective activity. The creative act of moral decision is inevitably meaningless to the mere external observer; but from the inner standpoint it is as real, and as significant, as anything in human experience.

THE HARMONY OF FREE WILL AND DETERMINISM*

R. E. Hobart

The thesis of this article is that there has never been any ground for the controversy between the doctrine of free will and determinism, that it is based upon a misapprehension, that the two assertions are entirely consistent, that one of them strictly implies the other, that they have been opposed only because of our natural want of the analytical imagination. In so saying I do not tamper with the meaning of either phrase. That would be unpardonable. I mean free will in the natural and usual sense, in the fullest, the most absolute sense in which for the purposes of the personal and moral life the term is ever employed. I mean it as implying responsibility, merit and demerit, guilt and desert. I mean it as implying, after an act has been performed, that one "could have done otherwise" than one did. I mean it as conveying these things also, not in any subtly modified sense but in exactly the sense in which we conceive them in life and in law and in ethics. These two doctrines have been opposed because we have not realized that free will can be analyzed without being destroyed, and that determinism is merely a feature of the analysis of it. And if we are tempted to take refuge in the thought of an "ultimate" and "innermost" liberty that eludes the analysis, then we have implied a deterministic basis and constitution for this liberty as well. For such a basis and constitution lie in the idea of liberty.

I am not maintaining that determinism is true; only that it is true insofar as we have free will. That we are free in willing is, broadly speaking, a fact of experience. That broad fact is more assured than any philosophical analysis. It is therefore surer than the deterministic analysis of it, entirely adequate as that in the end appears to be. But it is not here affirmed that there are no small

*From *Mind*, vol. 43, no. 169 (January 1934), pp. 1-27; reprinted by permission of the publisher, Basil Blackwell, Oxford.

540

exceptions, no slight undetermined swervings, no ingredient of absolute chance. All that is here said is that such absence of determination, if and so far as it exists, is no gain to freedom, but sheer loss of it; no advantage to the moral life, but blank subtraction from it. When I speak below of "the indeterminist" I mean the libertarian indeterminist, that is, he who believes in free will and holds that it involves indetermination.

By the analytical imagination is meant, of course, the power we have, not by nature but by training, of realizing that the component parts of a thing or process, taken together, each in its place, with their relations, are identical with the thing or process itself. If it is "more than its parts," then this "more" will appear in the analysis. It is not true, of course, that all facts are susceptible of analysis, but so far as they are, there is occasion for the analytical imagination. We have been accustomed to think of a thing or a person as a whole, not as a combination of parts. We have been accustomed to think of its activities as the way in which, as a whole, it naturally and obviously behaves. It is a new, an unfamiliar and an awkward act on the mind's part to consider it, not as one thing acting in its natural manner, but as a system of parts that work together in a complicated process. Analysis often seems at first to have taken away the individuality of the thing, its unity, the impression of the familiar identity. For a simple mind this is strikingly true of the analysis of a complicated machine. The reader may recall Paulsen's ever significant story about the introduction of the railway into Germany. When it reached the village of a certain enlightened pastor, he took his people to where a locomotive engine was standing, and in the clearest words explained of what parts it consisted and how it worked. He was much pleased by their eager nods of intelligence as he proceeded. But on his finishing they said: "Yes, yes, Herr Pastor, but there's a horse inside, isn't there?" They could not *realize* the analysis. They were wanting in the analytical imagination. Why not? They had never been trained to it. It is in the first instance a great effort to think of all the parts working together to produce the simple result that the engine glides down the track. It is easy to think of a horse inside doing all the work. A horse is a familiar totality that does familiar things. They could no better have grasped the physiological analysis of a horse's movements had it been set forth to them.

Now the position of the indeterminist is that a free act of will is the act of the self. The self becomes through it the author of the physical act that ensues. This volition of the self causes the physical act but it is not in its turn caused, it is "spontaneous." To regard it as caused would be determinism. The causing self to which the indeterminist here refers is to be conceived as distinct from character; distinct from temperament, wishes, habits, impulses. He emphasizes two things equally: the physical act springs from the self through its volition, and it does not spring merely from character, it is not simply the result of character and circumstances. If we ask, "Was there anything that induced the self thus to act?" we are answered in effect, "Not definitively. The self feels motives but its act is not determined by them. It can choose between them."

The next thing to notice is that this position of the indeterminist is taken in defense of moral conceptions. There would be not fitness, he says, in our reproaching ourselves, in our feeling remorse, in our holding ourselves or anyone guilty, if the act in question were not the act of the self instead of a product of the machinery of motives.

We have here one of the most remarkable and instructive examples of something in which the history of philosophy abounds—of a persistent, an age-long deadlock due solely to the indisposition of the human mind to look closely into the meaning of its terms.

How do we reproach ourselves? We say to ourselves, "How negligent of me!" "How thoughtless!" "How selfish!" "How hasty and unrestrained!" "That I should have been capable even for a moment of taking such a petty, irritated view!" etc. In other words, we are attributing to ourselves at the time of the act, in some respect and measure, a bad character, and regretting it. And that is the entire point of our self-reproach. We are turning upon ourselves with disapproval and it may be with disgust; we wish we could undo what we did in the past, and, helpless to do that, feel a peculiar thwarted poignant anger and shame at ourselves that we *had it in us* to perpetrate the thing we now condemn. It is self we are reproaching, that is, self that we are viewing as bad in that it produced bad actions. Except insofar as what-it-is produced these bad actions, there is no ground for reproaching it (calling it bad) and no meaning in doing so. All self-reproach is self-judging, and all judging is imputing a character. We are blaming ourselves. If spoken, what we are thinking would be dispraise. And what are praise and dispraise? Always, everywhere, they are *descriptions* of a person (more or less explicit) with favorable or unfavorable feeling of what is described—descriptions in terms of value comporting fact, or of fact comporting value, or of both fact and value. In moral instances they are descriptions of his character. We are morally characterizing him in our minds (as above) with appropriate feelings. We are attributing to him the character that we approve and like and wish to see more of, or the contrary. All the most intimate terms of the moral life imply that the act has proceeded from *me*, the distinctive me, from the manner of man I am or was. And this is the very thing on which the libertarian lays stress. What the indeterminist prizes with all his heart, what he stoutly affirms and insists upon, is precisely what he denies, namely, that I, the concrete and specific moral being, am the author, the source of my acts. For, of course, that is determinism. To say that they come from the self is to say that they are determined by the self—the moral self, the self with a moral quality. He gives our preferrings the bad name of the machinery of motives, but they are just what we feel in ourselves when we decide. When he maintains that the self at the moment of decision may act to some extent independently of motives, *and is good or bad according as it acts in this direction or that,* he is simply setting up one character within another, he is separating the self from what he understands by the person's character as at first mentioned, only thereupon to attribute to it a character of its own, *in that he judges it good or bad.*

The whole controversy is maintained by the indeterminist in order to defend the validity of the terms in which we morally judge—for example, ourselves. But the very essence of all judgment, just so far as it extends, asserts determination.

If in conceiving the self you detach it from all motives or tendencies, what you have is not a morally admirable or condemnable, not a morally characterizable self at all. Hence it is not subject to reproach. You cannot call a self good because of its courageous free action, and then deny that its action was determined by its character. In calling it good because of that action you have implied that the action came from its goodness (which means its good character) and was a sign thereof. By their fruits ye shall know them. The indeterminist appears to imagine that he can distinguish the moral "I" from all its propensities, regard its act as arising in the moment undetermined by them, and yet can then (for the first time, in his opinion, with propriety!) ascribe to this "I" an admirable quality. At the very root of his doctrine he contradicts himself. How odd that he never catches sight of that contradiction! He fights for his doctrine in order that he may call a man morally good, on account of his acts, with some real meaning; and his doctrine is that a man's acts (precisely so far as "free" or undetermined) do not come from his goodness. So they do not entitle us to call him good. He has taken his position in defense of moral conceptions, and it is fatal to all moral conceptions.

We are told, however, that it is under determinism that we should have no right any more to praise or to blame. At least we could not do so in the old sense of the terms. We might throw words of praise to a man, or throw words of blame at him, because we know from observation that they will affect his action; but the old light of meaning in the terms has gone out. Well, all we have to do is to keep asking what this old meaning was. We praise a man by saying that he is a good friend, or a hard worker, or a competent man of business, or a trusty assistant, or a judicious minister, or a gifted poet, or one of the noblest of men—one of the noblest of characters! In other words, he is a being with such and such qualities. If it is moral praise, he is a being with such and such tendencies to bring forth good acts. If we describe a single act, saying, for instance: "Well done!" we mean to praise the person for the act as being the author of it. It is he who has done well and proved himself capable of doing so. If the happy act is accidental we say that no praise is deserved for it. If a person is gratified by praise it is because of the estimate of him, in some respect or in general, that is conveyed. Praise (once again) means description, with expressed or implied admiration. If any instance of it can be found which does not consist in these elements our analysis fails. "Praise the Lord, O my soul, *and forget not all His benefits*"—and the Psalm goes on to tell His loving and guarding acts toward humankind. To praise the Lord is to tell His perfections, especially the perfections of His character. This is the old light that has always been in words of praise and there appears no reason for its going out.

Indeterminism maintains that we need not be impelled to action by our wishes, that our active will need not be determined by them. Motives "incline without necessitating." We choose amongst the ideas of action before us, but need not choose solely according to the attraction of desire, in however wide a sense that word is used. Our inmost self may rise up in its autonomy and moral dignity, independently of motives, and register its sovereign decree.

Now, *insofar* as this "interposition of the self" is undetermined, the act is not *its* act, it does not issue from any concrete continuing self; it is born at the moment, of nothing, hence it expresses no quality; it bursts into being from no source. The self does not register *its* decree, for the decree is not the product of just that *it*. The self does not rise up *its* moral dignity, for dignity is the quality of an enduring being, influencing its actions, and therefore expressed by them, and that would be determination. *In proportion* as an act of volition starts of itself without cause it is exactly, so far as the freedom of the individual is concerned, as if it had been thrown into his mind from without—"suggested" to him—by a freakish demon. It is exactly like it in this respect, that in neither case does the volition arise from what the man is, care for or feels allegiance to; it does not come out of him. *In proportion* as it is undetermined, it is just as if his legs should suddenly spring up and carry him off where he did not prefer to go. Far from constituting freedom, that would mean, in the exact measure in which it took place, the loss of freedom. It would be an interference, and an utterly uncontrollable interference, with his power of acting as he prefers. In fine, then, *just so far* as the volition is undetermined, the self can neither be praised nor blamed for it, since it is not the act of the self.

The principle of free will says: "*I* produce my volitions." Determinism says: "My volitions are produced by *me*." Determinism is free will expressed in the passive voice.

After all, it is plain what the indeterminists have done. It has not occurred to them that our free will may be resolved into its component elements. (Thus far a portion only of this resolution has been considered.) When it is thus resolved they do not recognize it. The analytical imagination is considerably taxed to perceive the identity of the free power that we feel with the component parts that analysis shows us. We are gratified by their nods of intelligence and their bright, eager faces as the analysis proceeds, but at the close are a little disheartened to find them falling back on the innocent supposition of a horse inside that does all the essential work. They forget that they may be called upon to analyze the horse. They solve the problem by forgetting analysis. The solution they offer is merely: "There is a self inside which does the deciding." Or, let us say, it is as if the *Pfarrer* were explaining the physiology of a horse's motion. They take the whole thing to be analyzed, imagine a duplicate of it reduced in size, so to speak, and place this duplicate-self inside as an explanation—making it the elusive source of the "free decisions." They do not see that they are merely pushing the question a little further back, since the process of deciding, with its constituent factors, must have taken place within that inner self. Either it decided in a particular way because, on the whole, it preferred to decide in that way, or the decision was an underived event, a rootless and sourceless event. It is the same story over again. In neither case is there any gain in imagining a second self inside, however wonderful and elusive. Of course, it is the first alternative that the indeterminist is really imagining. If you tacitly and obscurely conceive the self as deciding *its own way,* that is, according to its preference, but never admit or recognize this, then you can happily remain a libertarian indeterminist; but upon no other terms. In your theory there is a heart of darkness.

Freedom

In accordance with the genius of language, free will means freedom of persons in willing, just as "free trade" means freedom of persons (in a certain respect) in trading. The freedom of anyone surely always implies his possession of a power, and means the absence of any interference (whether taking the form of restraint or constraint) with his exercise of that power. Let us consider this in relation to freedom in willing.

Can

We say, "I can will this or I can will that, whichever I choose." Two courses of action present themselves to my mind. I think of their consequences, I look on this picture and on that, one of them commends itself more than the other, and I will an act that brings it about. I knew that I could choose either. That means that I had the power to choose either.

What is the meaning of "power"? A person has a power if it is a fact that when he sets himself in the appropriate manner to produce a certain event that event will actually follow. I have the power to lift the lamp; that is, if I grasp it and exert an upward pressure with my arm, *it will rise.* I have the power to will so and so; that is, if I want, that act of will will take place. That and none other is the meaning of power, is it not? A man's being in the proper active posture of body or of mind is the cause, and the sequel in question will be the effect. (Of course, it may be held that the sequel not only does but must follow, in a sense opposed to Hume's doctrine of cause. Very well; the question does not here concern us.)

Thus power depends upon, or rather consists in, a law. The law in question takes the familiar form that if something happens a certain something else will ensue. If A happens then B will happen. The law in this case is that if the man definitively so desires then volition will come to pass. There is a series, wish—will—act. The act follows according to the will (that is a law—I do not mean an underived law) and the will follows according to the wish (that is another law). A man has the power (sometimes) to act as he wishes. He has the power (whenever he is not physically bound or held) to act as he wills. He has the power always (except in certain morbid states) to will as he wishes. All this depends upon the laws of his being. Whenever there is a power there is a law. In it the power wholly consists. A man's power to will as he wishes is simply the law that his will follows his wish.

What, again, does freedom mean? It means the absence of any interference with all this. Nothing steps in to prevent my exercising my power.[1]

All turns on the meaning of "can." "I can will either this or that" means, I am so constituted that if I definitively incline to this, the appropriate act of will will take place, and if I definitively incline to that, the appropriate act of will will take place. The law connecting preference and will exists, and there is nothing to interfere with it. My free power, then, is not an exemption from law but in its inmost essence, an embodiment of law.

Thus it is true, after the act of will, that I could have willed otherwise. It is most natural to add, "if I had wanted to": but the addition is not required. The point is the meaning of "could." I could have willed whichever way I pleased. I had the power to will otherwise, there was nothing to prevent my doing so, and I should have done so if I had wanted. If someone says that the wish I actually had prevented my willing otherwise, so that I could not have done it, he is merely making a slip in the use of the word "could." He means, that wish could not have produced anything but this volition. But "could" is asserted not of the wish (a transient fact to which power in this sense is not and should not be ascribed) but of the person. And the person *could* have produced something else than that volition. He could have produced any volition he wanted; he had the power to do so.

But the objector will say, "The person as he was at the moment—the person as animated by that wish—could not have produced any other volition." Oh, yes, he could. "Could" has meaning not as applied to a momentary actual phase of a person's life, but to the person himself of whose life that is but a phase; and it means that (even at that moment) he had the power to will just as he preferred. *The idea of power, because it is the idea of a law, is hypothetical, carries in itself hypothesis as part of its very intent and meaning—"if he should prefer this, if he should prefer that"—and therefore can be truly applied to a person irrespective of what at the moment he does prefer. It remains hypothetical even when applied.*[2] This very peculiarity of its meaning is the whole point of the idea of power. It is just because determinism is true, because a law obtains, that one "could have done otherwise."

Sidgwick set over against "the formidable array of cumulative evidence" offered for determinism the "affirmation of consciousness" "that I can now choose to do" what is right and reasonable, "however strong may be my inclination to act unreasonably."[3] But it is not against determinism. It is a true affirmation (surely not of immediate consciousness but of experience), the affirmation of my power to will what I deem right, however intense and insistent my desire for the wrong. I can will anything, and can will effectively anything that my body will enact. I can will it despite an inclination to the contrary of any strength you please—strength as felt by me before decision. We all know cases where we have resisted impulses of great strength in this sense and we can imagine them still stronger. I have the power to do it, and shall do it, shall exercise that power, if I prefer. Obviously in that case (be it psychologically remarked) my solicitude to do what is right will have proved itself even stronger (as measured by ultimate tendency to prevail, though not of necessity by sensible vividness or intensity) than the inclination to the contrary, for that is what is meant by my preferring to do it. I am conscious that the field for willing is open; I can will anything that I elect to will. Sidgwick did not analyze the meaning of "can," that is all. He did not precisely catch the outlook of consciousness when it says, "I can." He did not distinguish the function of the word, which is to express the availability of the alternatives I see when, before I have willed, and perhaps before my preference is decided, I look out on the field of conceivable volition. He did not recognize that I must have a word to express my power to will as I please, quite irrespective of what I shall please, and that "can" is that word. It is no proof that I cannot do something to point out that I shall not do it if I do not prefer. A man, let us say, can turn on the electric light; but he will not turn it on if he walks away from it; though it is still true that he can turn it on. When we attribute power to a man we do not mean that something will acomplish itself without his wanting it to. That would never suggest the idea of power. We mean that if he makes the requisite move the thing will be accomplished. It is part of the idea that the initiative shall rest with him. The initiative for an act of will is a precedent phase of consciousness that we call the definitive inclination, or, in case of conflict, the definitive preference for it. If someone in the throes of struggle with temptation says to himself, "I can put this behind me," he is saying truth and precisely the pertinent truth. He is bringing before his mind the act of will, unprevented, quite open to him, that would deliver him from what he deems noxious. It may still happen that the noxiousness of the temptation does not affect him so powerfully as its allurement, and that he succumbs. It is no whit less true, according to determinism, that he could have willed otherwise. To analyze the fact expressed by "could" is not to destroy it.

But it may be asked, "Can I will in opposition to my strongest desire at the moment when it is strongest?" If the words "at the moment when it is strongest" qualify "can," the answer has already been given. If they qualify "will," the suggestion is a contradiction in terms. Can I turn-on-the-electric-light-at-a-moment-when-I-am-not-trying-to-do-so? This means, if I try to turn on the light at a moment when I am not trying to, will it be turned on? A possible willing as I do not prefer to will is not a power on my part, hence not to be expressed by "I can."

Everybody knows that we often will what we do not want to will, what we do not prefer. But when we say this we are using words in another sense than that in which I have just used them. In *one* sense of the words, whenever we act we are doing what we prefer, on the whole, in view of all the circumstances. We are acting for the greatest good or the least evil or a mixture of these. In the *other* and more usual sense of the words, we are very often doing what we do not wish to do, that is, doing some particular thing we do not wish because we are afraid of the consequences or disapprove of the moral complexion of the particular thing we do wish. We do the thing that we do not like because the other thing has aspects that we dislike yet more. We are still doing what we like best on the whole. It is again a question of the meaning of words.

Compulsion

The indeterminist conceives that according to determinism the self is carried along by wishes to acts which it is thus necessitated to perform. This mode of speaking distinguishes the self from the wishes and represents it as under their dominion. This is the initial error. This is what leads the indeterminist wrong on all the topics of his problem. And the error persists in the most recent writings. In fact, the moral self is the wishing self. The wishes are its own. It cannot be described as under their dominion, for it has no separate predilections to be overborne by them: they themselves are its predilections. To fancy that because the person acts according to them he is compelled, a slave, the victim of a power from whose clutches he cannot extricate himself, is a confusion of ideas, a mere slip of the mind. The answer that has ordinarily been given is surely correct; all compulsion is causation, but not all causation is compulsion. Seize a man and violently force him to do something, and he is compelled—also caused—to do it. But induce him to do it by giving him reasons and his doing it is caused but not compelled.

Passivity

We have to be on our guard even against conceiving the inducement as a cause acting like the impact of a billiard ball, by which the self is precipitated into action like a second billiard ball, as an effect. The case is not so simple. Your reasons have shown him that his own preferences require the action. He does it of his own choice; he acts from his own motives in the light of your reasons. The sequence of cause and effect goes on within the self, with contributory information from without.

It is not clarifying to ask, "Is a volition free or determined?" It is the person who is free, and his particular volition that is determined. Freedom is something that we can attribute only to a continuing being, and he can have it only so far as the particular transient volitions within him are determined. (According to the strict proprieties of language, it is surely events that are caused, not things or persons; a person or thing can be caused or determined only in the sense that its beginning to be, or changes in it, are caused or determined.)

It is fancied that, owing to the "necessity" with which an effect follows upon its cause, if my acts of will are caused I am not free in thus acting. Consider an analogous matter. When I move I use ligaments. "Ligament" means that which binds, and a ligament does bind bones together. But *I* am not bound. *I* (so far as my organism is concerned) am rendered possible by the fact that my bones are bound one to another; that is part of the secret of my being able to act, to move about and work my will. If my bones ceased to be bound one to another I should be undone indeed. The human organism is detached, but it is distinctly important that its component parts shall not be detached. Just so my free power of willing is built up of tight cause-and-effect connections. The point is that when I employ the power thus constituted nothing determines the particular employment of it but *me.* Each particular act of mine is determined from outside itself, that is, by a cause, a prior event. But not from outside me. I, the possessor of the power, am not in my acts passively played upon by causes outside me, but am enacting my own wishes in virtue of a chain of causation within me. What is needed is to distinguish broadly between a particular effect, on the one hand, and, on the other, the detached, continuous life of a mental individual and his organism; a life reactive, but reacting according to its own nature.

What makes the other party uncontrollably reject all this—let us never forget—is the words. They smell of sordid detail, of unwinsome psychological machinery. They are not bathed in moral value, not elevated and glowing. In this the opponents' instinct is wholly right; only when they look for the value they fail to focus their eyes aright. It is in the whole act and the whole trait and the whole being that excellence and preciousness inhere; analysis must needs show us elements which, taken severally, are without moral expressiveness;

as would be even the celestial anatomy of an angel appearing on earth. The analytic imagination, however, enables us to see the identity of the living fact in its composition with the living fact in its unity and integrity. Hence we can resume the thought of it as a unit and the appropriate feelings without fancying that analysis threatens them or is at enmity with them.

Prediction

If we knew a man's character thoroughly and the circumstances that he would encounter, determinism (which we are not here completely asserting) says that we could foretell his conduct. This is a thought that repels many libertarians. Yet to predict a person's conduct need not be repellent. If you are to be alone in a room with $1000 belonging to another on the table and can pocket it without anyone knowing the fact, and if I predict that you will surely *not* pocket it, that is not an insult. I say, I know you, I know your character; you will not do it. But if I say that you are "a free being" and that I really do not know whether you will pocket it or not, that is rather an insult. On the other hand, there are cases where prediction is really disparaging. If I say when you make a remark, "I knew you were going to say that," the impression is not agreeable. My exclamation seems to say that your mind is so small and simple that one can predict its ideas. That is the real reason why people resent in such cases our predicting their conduct; that if present human knowledge, which is known to be so limited, can foresee their conduct, it must be more naive and stereotyped than they like to think it. It is no reflection upon the human mind or its freedom to say that one who knew it through and through (a human impossibility) could foreknow its preferences and its spontaneous choice. It is of the very best of men that even we human beings say, "I am sure of him." It has perhaps in this controversy hardly been observed how much at this point is involved, how far the question of prediction reaches. The word "reliable" or "trustworthy" is a prediction of behavior. Indeed, all judgment of persons whatever in the measure of its definitude, is such a prediction.

Material Fate

The philosopher in the old story, gazing at the stars, falls into a pit. We have to notice the pitfall in our subject to which, similarly occupied, Eddington has succumbed.

"What significance is there in my mental struggle tonight whether I shall or shall not give up smoking, if the laws which govern the matter of the physical universe already pre-ordain for the morrow a configuration of matter consisting of pipe, tobacco, and smoke connected with my lips?"[4]

No laws, according to determinism, pre-ordain such a configuration, unless I give up the struggle. Let us put matter aside for the moment, to return to it. Fatalism says that my morrow is determined no matter how I struggle. This is of course a superstition. Determinism says that my morrow is determined through my struggle. There is significance in my mental effort, that it is deciding the event. The stream of causation runs through my deliberations and decision, and, if it did not run as it does run, the event would be different. The past cannot determine the event except through the present. And no past moment determined it any more truly than does the present moment. In other words, each of the links in the causal chain must be in its place. Determinism (which, the reader will remember, we have not here taken for necessarily true in all detail) says that the coming result is "pre-ordained" (literally, caused) at each stage, and therefore the whole following series for tomorrow may be described as already determined; so that did we know all about the struggler, how strong of purpose he was and how he was influenced (which is humanly impossible) we could tell what he would do. But for the struggler this fact (supposing it to be such) is not pertinent. If, believing it, he ceases to struggle, he is merely revealing that the forces within him have brought about that cessation. If on the other hand he struggles manfully he will reveal the fact that they have brought about his success. Since the causation of the outcome works through his struggle in either case equally, it cannot become for him a moving consideration in the struggle. In it the question is, "Shall I do this or that?" It must be answered in the light of what there is to recommend to me this or that. To this question the scientific truth (according to determinism) that the deliberation itself is a play of causation is completely irrelevant; it merely draws the mind delusively away from the only considerations that concern it.

Self as Product and Producer

We can at this stage clearly see the position when a certain very familiar objection is raised. "How can anyone be praised or blamed if he was framed by nature as he is, if heredity and circumstance have given him his qualities? A man can surely be blamed only for what he does himself, and he did not make his original character; he simply found it on his hands." A man is to be blamed only for what he does himself, for that alone tells what he is. He did not make his character; no, but he made his acts. Nobody blames him for making such a character, but only for making such acts. And to blame him for that is simply to say that he is a bad act-maker. If he thinks the blame misapplied he has to prove that he is not that sort of an act-maker. Are we to be told that we may not recognize what he is, with appropriate feelings of its quality, because he did not create himself—a mere contortion and intussusception of ideas? The moral

551

self cannot be *causa sui.* To cause his original self a man must have existed before his original self. Is there something humiliating to him in the fact that he is not a contradiction in terms? If there were a being who made his "original character," and made a fine one, and we proceeded to praise him for it, our language would turn out to be a warm ascription to him of a still earlier character, so that the other would not have been original at all. To be praised or blamed you have to be; and be a particular person; and the praise or blame is telling what kind of person you are. There is no other meaning to be extracted from it. Of course, a man does exist before his later self, and in that other sense he can be a moral *causa sui.* If by unflagging moral effort he achieves for himself better subsequent qualities, what can merit praise but the ingredient in him of aspiration and resolution that was behind the effort? If he should even remake almost his whole character, still there would be a valiant remnant that had done it. These are commonplaces, precisely of the moral outlook upon life. When we come to the moral fountainhead we come to what the man is, at a particular time, as measured by what he does or is disposed to do with his power of volition.

The indeterminist, we noticed, requires a man to be "an absolute moral source" if we are to commend him. Well, if he were so, what could we say about him but what kind of a source he was? And he is so in fact. Suppose now that this source has in turn a source—or that it has not! Does that (either way) change what it is?

"But moral severity! How can we justly be severe toward a mere fact in nature—in human nature?" Because it is evil, because it must be checked. If somebody takes pleasure in torturing an innocent person, we spring to stop the act, to hold back the perpetrator, if need be with violence; to deter him from doing it again, if need be with violence; to warn any other possible perpetrators. "This shall not be done; we are the enemies of this conduct; this is evil conduct." At what could we be indignant but as a fact in somebody's human nature? Our severity and enmity are an active enmity to the evil: they are all part of that first spring to stop the act. "Society is opposed in every possible manner to such cruelty. You shall be made to feel that society is so, supposing that you cannot be made to feel yourself the vileness of the act." It does not remove our sense of its vileness to reflect that he was acting according to his nature. That is very precisely why we are indignant at him. We intend to make him feel that his nature is in that respect evil and its expression insufferable. We intend to interfere with the expression of his nature. That what he did proceeded from it is not a disturbing and pause-giving consideration in the midst of our conduct, but the entire basis of it. The very epithet "vile" assumes that his behavior arose from an intention and a moral quality in the man. How can we justly be severe? Because he *ought* to be checked and deterred, made to feel the moral estimate of what he has been doing. This we consider more fully under the topic of Desert.

552

Compare a case where the wrongdoing, whatever it be, is one's own. Catch a man in a moment of fierce self-reproach, and bring the objection above before him. Would it relieve him of his feeling? It would be an irrelevant frivolity to him. He is shocked at a wrong that was done and at himself for doing it; he repents of the acts of will that brought it about; he would gladly so change himself as never to do the like again; he is ready to "beat himself with rods." With all that the metaphysical entanglement has simply nothing to do.

"Still, does not determinism force us to face a fact in some sort new to us, that the offending person came to act so from natural causes; and does not that of necessity alter somewhat our attitude or state of mind about moral judgment?" Why, the fact is not new at all. In daily life we are all determinists, just as we are all libertarians. We are constantly attributing behavior to the character, the temperament, the peculiarities of the person and expecting him to behave in certain fashions. The very words of our daily converse, as we have so amply observed, are full of determinism. And we see nothing inconsistent in being aware at the same time that he is free in choosing his course, as we know ourselves to be. We merely form expectations as to what he *will* freely choose. Nor do we see anything inconsistent in blaming him. At the very moment when we do so we often shake our heads over the environment or mode of life or ill-omened pursuits that have brought him to such ways and to being a blame worthy person.

To be sure, determinism as a philosophic doctrine, determinism so named, may come as a new and repellent idea to us. We have been thinking in the right terms of thought all the while, but we did not identify them with terms of causation; when the philosophical names are put upon them we recoil, not because we have a false conception of the facts, but a false conception of the import of the philosophical terms. When we feel that somebody could have done otherwise but chose to do a wrong act knowingly, then we one and all feel that he is culpable and a proper object of disapproval, as we ought to feel. We merely have not been schooled enough in the applications of general terms to call the course of mental events within him causation. So again, goodness consists in qualities, but the qualities express themselves in choosing, which is unfettered and so often trembles in the balance; when we are suddenly confronted with the abstract question, "Can we be blamed for a quality we did not choose?" the colors run and the outlines swim a little; some disentanglement of abstract propositions is required, though we think aright in practice on the concrete cases. So all that philosophic determinism "forces us to face" is the meaning of our terms.

No, it is the opposite doctrine that must revolutionize our attitude toward moral judgments. If it is true, we must come to see that no moral severity towards the helpless subject of an act of will that he suddenly finds discharging itself within him, though not emanating from what he is or prefers, can be deserved or relevant. To comprehend all is to pardon all—so far as it is undetermined. Or, rather, not to pardon but to acquit of all.

However, in face of the actual facts, there is something that does bring us to a larger than the usual frame of mind about indignation and punishment and the mood of severity. And that is thought, sympathetic thought, any thought that enters with humane interest into the inner lives of others and pursues in imagination the course of them. In an outbreak of moral indignation we are prone to take little cognizance of that inner life. We are simply outraged by a noxious act and a noxious trait (conceived rather objectively and as it concerns the persons affected) and feel that such act should not be and that such a trait should be put down. The supervening of a sympathetic mental insight upon moral indignation is not a displacement, but the turning of attention upon facts that call out other feelings too. To comprehend all is neither to pardon all nor to acquit of all; overlooking the disvalue of acts and intentions would not be comprehension; but it is to appreciate the human plight; the capacity for suffering, the poor contracted outlook, the plausibilities that entice the will. This elicits a sympathy or concern co-existing with disapproval. That which is moral in moral indignation and behind it, if we faithfully turn to it and listen, will not let us entirely wash our hands even of the torturer, his feelings and his fate; certainly will not permit us to take satisfaction in seeing him in turn tortured, merely for the torture's sake. His act was execrable because of its effect on sentient beings, but he also is a sentient being. The humanity that made us reprobate his crime has not ceased to have jurisdiction. The morality that hates the sin has in that very fact the secret of its undiscourageable interest in the sinner. We come, not to discredit indignation and penalty, nor to tamper with their meaning, but to see their office and place in life and the implications wrapped up in their very fitness. Of this more presently.

Responsibility

Again, it is said that determinism takes from man all responsibility. As regards the origin of the term, a man is responsible when he is the person to respond to the question why the act was performed, hw it is to be explained or justified. That is what he must answer; he is answerable for the act. It is the subject of which he must give an account; he is accountable for the act. The act proceeded from him. He is to say whether it proceeded consciously. He is to give evidence that he did or did not know the moral nature of the act and that he did or did not intend the result. He is to say how he justifies it or if he can justify it. If the act proceeded from him by pure accident, if he can show that he did the damage (if damage it was) by brushing against something by inadvertence, for example, then he has not to respond to the question what he did it for—he is not consciously responsible—nor how it is justified—he is not morally responsible, though of course he may have been responsible in these respects for a habit of carelessness.

But why does the peculiar moral stain of guilt or ennoblement of merit belong to responsibility? If an act proceeds from a man and not merely from his accidental motion but from his mind and moral nature, we judge at once that like acts may be expected from him in the future. The color of the act for good or bad is reflected on the man. We see him now as a living source of possible acts of the same kind. If we must be on our guard against such acts we must be on our guard against such men. If we must take steps to defend ourselves against such acts we must take steps to defend ourselves against such men. If we detest such acts, we must detest that tendency in such men which produced them. He is guilty in that he knowingly did evil, in that the intentional authorship of evil is in him. Because the act proceeded in every sense from him, for that reason he is (so far) to be accounted bad or good according as the act is bad or good, and he is the one to be punished if punishment is required. And that is moral responsibility.

But how, it is asked, can I be responsible for what I will if a long train of past causes has made me will it—the old query asked anew in relation to another category, responsibility, which must be considered separately. Is it not these causes that are "responsible" for my act—to use the word in the only sense, says the objector, that seems to remain for it?

The parent past produced the man, none the less the man is responsible for his acts. We can truly say that the earth bears apples, but quite as truly not resent the claim of the trees to bear the apples, or try to take the business out of the trees' hands. Nor need the trees feel their claim nullified by the earth's part in the matter. There is no rivalry between them. A man is a being with free will and responsibility; where this being came from, I repeat, is another story. The past finished its functions in the business when it generated him as he is. So far from interfering with him and coercing him the past does not even exist. If we could imagine it as lingering on into the present, standing over against him and stretching out a ghostly hand to stay his arm, then indeed the past would be interfering with his liberty and responsibility. But so long as it and he are never on the scene together they cannot wrestle; the past cannot overpower him. The whole alarm is an evil dream, a nightmare due to the indigestion of words. The past has created, and left extant, a free-willed being.

Desert

But we have not come to any final clearness until we see how a man can be said to *deserve* anything when his acts flow from his wishes, and his wishes flow from other facts further up the stream of life. There is a peculiar element in the idea of deserving. This is the element of "ought." A man deserves punishment or reward if society ought to give it to him; he deserves the punishment or reward that he ought to receive. We cannot say universally that he deserves what he ought to receive, but only when it is a question of reward or punishment.

What treatment of a man should receive from society as a result of wrong-doing is a question of ethics. It is widely held that an evildoer deserves punishment, not only for the defense of society but because there is an ultimate fitness in inflicting natural evil for moral evil. This, as we know, has been maintained by determinists. Since the idea of desert collapses altogether on the indeterminist's conception of conduct, this theory of the ground of desert cannot be said to be logically bound up with indeterminism. For my own part, however, owing to reasons for which I have no space here, I cannot hold the theory. I believe that the ideal ends of the administration of justice are (1) to see that all possible restitution is made, (2) to see as far as possible that the malefactor does not repeat the act, and (3) so far as possible to render the act less likely on the part of others. And these ends should be sought by means that will accomplish them. Morality is humane. It is animated by good-will toward humanity. Our instinctive impulse to retaliation must be interpreted with a view to its function in society, and so employed and regulated to the best purpose. Being a part of the defensive and fighting instinct, its functional aim is evidently to destroy or check the threatening source of evil—to destroy the culprit or change his temper. Our common and natural notion of desert is in harmony with either of these views; only on the second it receives a supplement, a purposive interpretation.

We discover punishment not only in combat but in nature at large. If a child puts its hand into flames it is burnt. After that it puts its hand into flames no more. Nature teaches us to respect her by punishments that deter. Society, to preserve itself, must find deterrents to administer to men. It must say, "I'll teach you not to do that." Already nature has taught it such deterrents. Society must shape men's actions or at least rough-hew them, to the extent of striking off certain jagged and dangerous edges, and the most obvious way to do so is by penalties. A secondary way is by rewards, and these nature has taught also.

When a man needlessly injures others, society by punishment injures him. It administers to him a specimen of what he has given to others. "This," it says, "is the nature of your act; to give men suffering like this. They rebel at it as you rebel at this. You have to be made more acutely conscious of the other side; the side of the feelings and the forces that you have outraged. You have to be made to feel them recoil upon you, that you may know that they are there. You have to be made to respect them in advance. And others like-minded to respect them in some degree better by seeing how they recoil upon you."

But this is only a method of working upon him and them; it is justified by effectiveness alone. It supposes two things; that society has been just in the first instance to these men themselves, that is, that they were not drawn by unjust conditions of life into the acts for which they are made to suffer; and that the suffering will in fact improve their conduct or that of others. The truth is that society often punishes when it is itself the greater malefactor, and that the penalty, instead of reforming, often confirms the criminality. It is due to nothing but the crude state of civilization that we have added so little of a more sagacious and effectual mode of influencing criminals and preventing crime than the original and natural method of hitting back.

Out of this situation arises a subsidiary sense of deserving. A man may be said to deserve a punishment in the sense that, in view of the offense, it is not too severe to give him if it would work as above conceived; though if we believe it will not so work it ought not to be given him.

If the general view here taken, which seems forced upon us in the prosaic process of examining words, is correct, then as we look back over the long course of this controversy and the false antithesis that has kept it alive, how can we help exclaiming, "What waste!" Waste is surely the tragic fact above all in life; we contrast it with the narrow areas where reason and its economy of means to ends in some measure reign. But here is huge waste in the region of reasoning itself, the enemy in the citadel. What ingenuity, what resource in fresh shifts of defense, what unshaken loyalty to inward repugnances, what devotion to ideal values, have here been expended in blind opposition instead of analysis. The cause of determinism, seeming to deny freedom, has appeared as the cause of reason, of intelligence itself, and the cause of free will, seeming to exclude determination, has appeared that of morals. The worst waste is the clash of best things. In our subject it is time this waste should end. Just as we find that morality requires intelligence to give effect and remains rudimentary and largely abortive till it places the conscience of the mind in the foreground, so we find that determinism and the faith in freedom meet and are united in the facts, and that the long enmity has been a bad dream.

NOTES

1. A word as to the relation of power and freedom. Strictly power cannot exist without freedom, since the result does not follow without it. Freedom on the other hand is a negative term, meaning the absence of something, and implies a power only because that whose absence it signifies is interference, which implies something to be interfered with. Apart from this peculiarity of the term itself, there might be freedom without any power. Absence of interference (of what would be interference if there were a power) might exist in the absence of a power; a man might be free to do something because there was nothing to interfere with his doing it, but might have no power to do it. Similarly and conveniently we may speak of a power as existing though interfered with; that is, the law may exist that would constitute a power if the interference were away.

2. I am encouraged by finding in effect the same remark in Prof. G. E. Moore's *Ethics*, ch. vi., at least as regards what he terms one sense of the word "could." I should hazard saying, the only sense in this context.

3. *Methods of Ethics*, 7th ed., 65.

4. *Philosophy,* Jan., 1933, p. 41.

FATE*
Richard Taylor

We all, at certain dramatic moments of pain, threat, or bereavement, entertain the idea of fatalism, the thought that what is then happening just had to be, that we are powerless to prevent it. Sometimes we find ourselves in circumstances not of our own making, circumstances in which our destinies and our very being are thoroughly anchored, and then the thought of fatalism can be quite overwhelming and sometimes consoling. Whatever then happens, one feels, and however good or ill, will be what those circumstances yield, and we are helpless. There is nothing for you or me to do about it, hence nothing for us to think or deliberate about; we can only wait and see. Soldiers, it is said, are sometimes possessed by such thoughts. Perhaps all men would feel more inclined to such thoughts if they paused to think more often of how little they ever had to do with bringing themselves to wherever they have arrived in life, of how much their fortunes and destinies were decided for them by sheer circumstance, and how the entire course of their lives is often set, once for all, by the most trivial incidents, which they did not produce and could not even have foreseen. If we are free to work out our destinies at all, which is doubtful, it is a freedom that is at best exercised within exceedingly narrow paths. The important things—when we are born, of what parents, into what culture, of what sex and temperament, of what intelligence or stupidity, indeed everything that makes for the bulk of our happiness and misery—is decided for us by the most casual and indifferent circumstances, by sheer coincidences, chance encounters, and seemingly insignificant fortuities. One can see this in retrospect if he searches, but few search to find it. The fate that has given us our very being and human natures has thereby made us so that, being human, we congratulate

*From Richard Taylor, *Metaphysics,* 2nd edition © 1974. Reprinted by permission of Prentice-Hall, Inc., Englewood Cliffs, New Jersey.

ourselves on our blessings, which we can deem our achievements, blame the world for our deficiencies, which we call our ill luck, and scarcely think of the fate which arbitrarily dispenses both.

FATALISM AND DETERMINISM

A theory of fatalism is often distinguished academically from the theory of determinism by noting that, whereas determinism is a theory about all things and events, fatalism is a theory about some events only; the theory, namely, that these events could never have been otherwise, regardless of whatever else happened; or that certain events are such that they cannot fail to occur, no matter what else occurs. But this distinction is only academic. A determinist is simply, if he is consistent, a fatalist about everything; or at least, he should be. For the essential idea that a man would be expressing by saying that his attitude was one of fatalism with respect to this or that event—his own death, for instance—is that it is not up to him whether, or when or where, this event will occur, that it is not within his control. But the theory of determinism, as we have seen, once it is clearly spelled out and not hedged about with unresolved "ifs," entails that this is true of everything that ever happens, that it is never really up to any man what he does or what he becomes, and that nothing ever can happen, except what does in fact happen. One can indeed find verbal formulas for distinguishing the two theories, but if we think of a fatalist as one who has a certain attitude toward certain events, we find that it is the attitude that a thoroughgoing believer in determinism should, in consistency, assume toward all events.

FATALISM WITH RESPECT TO THE FUTURE AND THE PAST

A fatalist is best thought of, quite simply, as someone who thinks he cannot do anything about the future. He thinks it is not up to him what will happen next year, tomorrow, or the very next moment. He thinks that even his own behavior is not in the least within his power, any more than the motions of distant heavenly bodies, the events of remote history, or the political developments in faraway countries. He supposes, accordingly, that it is pointless for him to deliberate about anything, for a man deliberates only about those future things he believes to be within his power to do and forego. He does not pretend always to know what will happen. Hence, he might try sometimes to read signs and portents, or contemplate the effects upon him of the various things that might, for all he knows, be fated to occur. But he does not suppose that, whatever will happen, it will ever have been really avoidable.

560

A fatalist, then, thinks of the future in the manner in which we all think of the past, for all men are fatalists as they look *back* upon things. He thinks of both past and future "under the aspect of eternity," the way God is supposed to view them. We all think of the past in this way, as something once for all settled and fixed, to be taken for just what it is. We are never in the least tempted to modify it, or even to suppose that we ever can. We all believe that it is not in the least now up to us what happened last year, yesterday, or even a moment ago; that these things are no longer within our power, any more than the motions of the heavens or the political developments in China. And of course we are not ever tempted to deliberate about what we have done or left undone. At best we can speculate on these things, try to figure out what they were in case we do not know, or we can rejoice over them or repent. If we are not fatalists about the future, we can extract lessons from the past to apply in the future. But as for what has in fact happened, we do, and feel we certainly must, simply take it as given. The possibilities for action, if there are any at all, do not lie there. We might, indeed, believe that some past things *were* once within our power to do or avoid, while they were still future—but this expresses our attitude toward the future, not the past.

Such is surely our conception of the whole past, whether near or remote. But the true fatalist thinks of the future in just the same way. We all think things past are no longer within our power; the fatalist thinks they never were. It is a consoling doctrine, as many contemplative minds have discovered; but it somehow seems to violate the common sense of the greater part of mankind.

There are various ways in which one might get thinking fatalistically about the future, but they are most apt to arise from certain theological ideas, or from the metaphysical theory of determinism. Thus, if God is really all-knowing and all-powerful, then it is not hard to suppose that he has already arranged for everything to happen just as it is going to happen, and there is nothing left for you and me to do about it, except to watch things unfold and see what is to become of us, in the here or hereafter. Religious systems have used this thought as a cornerstone, and it is a firm one indeed for those who have this kind of faith. But without bringing God into the picture, it is not hard to suppose, as we have seen, that everything that happens is wholly determined by what went before it, and hence that whatever happens at any future time is the only thing that can then happen, given that certain other things will happen just before then, and that these, in turn, are the only things that can happen then, given the state of the world just before that, and so on, through the infinite past. So again, there is no more left for us to do about what is to be than about what already has been. What we do in the meantime will, to be sure, determine how some things eventually turn out; but these things that we are going to do will, on this conception, be only the causal consequences of what will be happening just before we do them, and so on back to a not distant point at which it seems obvious that we have nothing to do with what happens then.

No man needs convincing that fatalism is the only proper attitude to hold toward things past, but we want to see whether we should think in the same way of the future. The consequences of doing so are obviously momentous. To say nothing of the consolation of fatalism—a consolation which enables one to view all things as they arise, with the same undisturbed mind with which he contemplates even the horrors of remote history—the attitude of fatalism relieves one's mind of all tendency toward both blame and approbation of others and of both guilt and conceit in himself. It promises one that a perfect understanding of everything is at least possible, even if never actually possessed. This thought alone, once firmly grasped, yields a sublime complacency toward everything that life offers, whether to oneself or to his fellows; and while it thereby reduces one's pride, it simultaneouly enhances the feelings, opens the heart, and enormously broadens one's understanding.

PRESUPPOSITIONS

Like any metaphysical theory, the theory of fatalism cannot be evaluated apart from one's presuppositions or data. Theological conceptions obviously cannot be invoked here, for they are far more doubtful than any metaphysical theory that one might try to erect on them. At best, they could only serve to convey the theory of fatalism more easily to an unphilosophical imagination. Similarly, the theory of determinism will be of no use to us, for it is not a datum but a theory, and a controversial one too.

For our data we shall use only six claims, each of which recommends itself to the ordinary understanding as soon as it is understood, and hardly any of which have very often been doubted even by the most critical philosophical minds, many of whom, however, have failed to see their implications. These six suppositions, with some explanation of each, are simply these.

First, we suppose that any proposition or statement whatever is either true or, if not true, then false. If anyone affirms anything whatever, as distinguished from merely uttering nonsense, then what he affirms is, if not false, true; and if not true, false. There is no middle ground. This is simply the standard interpretation (*tertium non datur*) of what is called in logic "the law of excluded middle." It has generally been thought to be a necessary truth, and an indisputable law of logical thought. It seems, in any case, quite unexceptionable.

Second, we suppose that if any change or state of affairs is *sufficent* for the occurrence of some other change or state of affairs at the same or any other time, then the former cannot occur without the latter occurring also, even though the two are logically unconnected. This is simply the standard way in which the concept of *sufficiency* is explained in philosophy. A perhaps clearer way of saying the same thing is that if one state of affairs *ensures* another, then the former cannot exist without the other occurring too. The ingestion of cyanide, for instance, ensures death under certain familiar circumstances, which only means that one cannot normally swallow cyanide without dying, even though it is not logically impossible to do so.

Third, we suppose that if any change or state of affairs is *necessary* for some other change or state of affairs at the same or any other time, then the latter cannot occur without the former occurring too, even though they are logically unconnected. This is simply the standard way in which the concept of a *necessary condition* is explained in philosophy. A perhaps clearer way of saying the same thing is that if one state of affairs is *essential* for another, then the latter cannot occur without it. Oxygen, for instance, is essential for life, which means that we cannot normally live without it, even though it is not logically impossible that we should.

Fourth, we suppose that if some change or state of affairs is sufficient for (ensures) another, then that other is necessary (essential) for it; and conversely, if some change or state of affairs is necessary (essential) for another, then that other is sufficient for (ensures) it. This is simply a logical consequence of our second and third data; it follows from the definitions themselves.

Fifth, we suppose that no agent can perform any given action if there is lacking, at the same or any other time, some condition or state of affairs necessary for the occurrence of that act. This follows simply from the idea of anything being necessary or essential for the accomplishment of something else. For example, I cannot live without oxygen, or swim five miles without ever having been in water, or win a certain election without having been nominated, or fly to the moon without some sort of rocket, and so on, for these are all conditions that are necessary, or essential, for doing the things in question. Something is always necessary for the accomplishment of anything at all, and without the thing that is needed, nothing can be done. This is no law of logic, and in fact cannot be expressed even in the contemporary modal logics, but it is nonetheless manifestly true.

And *sixth,* we suppose that time is not "efficacious," that is, that the mere passage of time does not augment or diminish the powers or capacities of anything and, in particular, that it does not enhance or decrease an agent's powers or abilities. This means that if any substance or agent gains or loses powers or abilities over the course of time, then such a gain or loss is always due to something other than the mere passage of time. For instance, if a substance loses or gains in its power to corrode things, or if a man loses or gains the power to do push-ups, or lift weights, or what not, then such gains and losses are always due to certain things that happen over the course of time.

563

They are not due *merely* to the passage of time alone, which has no causal effect upon anything. This cannot be proved, but it is never doubted in physical science, and can hardly be doubted by anyone who thinks on it.

With these data before us, we are now going to compare two simple situations in turn. The relations involved in both situations will be identical except for certain relations of time, and we want to see whether an examination of each situation warrants similar inferences in both cases.

THE FIRST SITUATION

Let us assume that I am going to open my morning newspaper and glance over the headlines. There have for weeks been rumors of an impending naval battle, and I am intensely interested to learn from the paper whether any such battle has occurred. I have a son who is a sailor, we may suppose, and I am anxious for his safety. Assume further, then, that conditions are such that only if there was such a battle yesterday does my newspaper carry a certain kind of headline—i.e., that such a battle is, in the sense defined, necessary or essential for that kind of headline—whereas if it carries a certain different sort of headline, this will ensure that there was no such battle. Of course newspapers are not always that reliable, but we shall suppose that this one is, at least this time.

Now then, I am about to perform one or the other of two acts; namely, seeing a headline of the first kind or seeing one of the second kind. We shall call these alternative possible acts S and S' respectively And let us call the two propositions, "A naval battle occurred yesterday" and "No naval battle occurred yesterday," P and P' respectively. We can now assert that if I perform act S, then my doing so will ensure that there was a naval battle yesterday (i.e., that P is true), whereas if I perform S' then my doing that will ensure that no such battle occurred (or, that P' is true). This logically follows from the description of the situation.

With reference to this example, then, let us now ask whether it is up to me which sort of headline I read as I open the newspaper. More precisely, let us consider whether the following statement is true:

(A) It is now within my power to do S, and it is also now within my power to do S'.

It seems quite obvious that this is not true. For if both these acts were equally within my power, that is, if it were up to me which one to do, then it would also be up to me whether or not a naval battle has taken place yesterday, giving me a power over the past which I plainly do not possess. It will be well, however, to express this point in the form of a proof, as follows:

Argument I:

1. If *P* is true, then it is not within my power to do *S'* (for in case *P* is true, then there is, or was, lacking a condition essential for my doing *S'*, the condition, namely, of there being no naval battle yesterday).
2. But if *P'* is true, then it is not within my power to do *S* (for a similar reason).
3. But either *P* is true or *P'* is true.
4. Either it is not within my power to do *S*, or it is not within my power to do *S'*;

and A is accordingly false. A common-sense way of expressing this is to say that what sort of headline I see depends, among other things, on whether a naval battle took place yesterday, and that in turn is not now up to me.

Now this conclusion is perfectly in accordance with common sense, for we all are, as noted, fatalists with respect to the past. We sometimes try to find out what has happened by reading newspapers and so on, but no one ever supposes that he can determine or in any way influence what has happened, or that the past is in any way within his power to control. We simply have to take past things as they have happened and make the best of them.

It is significant to note incidentally that in the hypothetical sense in which statements of human power or ability are often formulated by philosophers, one *does* have power over the past. For we can surely assert that *if* I do *S*, this will ensure that a naval battle occurred yesterday; whereas *if*, alternatively, I do *S'*, this will equally ensure the nonoccurrence of such a battle, for these acts are, in the conditions assumed in our example, quite sufficient for the truth of *P* and *P'* respectively. Or we can say that I can ensure the occurrence of such a battle yesterday simply by doing *S*, and that I can ensure its non-occurrence simply by doing *S'*. Indeed, if I should ask *how* I can go about ensuring that no naval battle occurred yesterday, perfectly straightforward instructions can be given; namely, the instruction to do *S'* and by all means to avoid doing *S*. But of course the hitch is that I cannot do *S'* unless *P'* is true, the occurrence of the battle in question rendering me quite powerless to do it.

THE SECOND SITUATION

Now let us imagine that I am a naval commander about to issue my order of the day to the fleet. We assume, further, that within the totality of other conditions prevailing, my issuing of a certain kind of order will ensure that a naval battle will occur tomorrow, whereas if I issue another kind of order this will ensure that no such battle occurs.

Now then, I am about to perform one or the other of these two acts; namely, one of issuing an order of the first sort or one of the second sort.

We shall call these alternative possible acts O and O' respectively And let us call the two propositions "A naval battle will occur tomorrow" and "No naval battle will occur tomorrow," Q and Q' respectively. We can now assert that if I do act O, then my doing such will ensure that there will be a naval battle (i.e., that Q is true), whereas if I do O' my doing that will ensure that no naval battle will ocur (or, that Q' is true).

With reference to this example, then, let us now ask whether it is up to me which sort of order I issue. More precisely, let us consider whether the following statement is true:

> (B) It is now within my power to do O, and is also now within my power to do O'.

Anyone except a fatalist would surely want to say that, in the situation we have envisaged, this statement might well be true; that is, that each of these acts is quite within my power. In the circumstances we assume to prevail, it is, one would think, up to me as the commander whether the naval battle occurs tomorrow or not. It depends only on what kind of order I issue, given all the other conditions as they are; and what kind of order is issued is something for me to decide, something wholly within my power. It is precisely the denial that such statements are ever true that renders one a fatalist.

But we have, alas, exactly the same argument to show that B is false that we had for proving the falsity of A; namely:

> Argument II:
> 1. If Q is true, then it is not within my power to do O' (for in case Q is true, then there is, or will be, lacking a condition essential for my doing O', the condition, namely, of there being no naval battle tomorrow).
> 2. But if Q' is true, then it is not within my power to do O (for a similar reason).
> 3. But either Q is true or Q' is true.
> 4. Either it is not within my power to do O, or it is not within my power to do O';

and B is accordingly false. Another way of expressing this is to say that what kind of order I issue depends, among other things, on whether a naval battle takes place tomorrow—for in this situation a naval battle tomorrow is a necessary condition of my doing O, whereas no naval battle tomorrow is equally essential for my doing O'.

In view of the fact that probably everything anyone does, and certainly everything of any significance that anyone ever does, has consequences for the future, so that, his act being sufficient for those consequences, they are in turn necessary conditions of his act, we can generalize upon this conclusion by saying that, for any such act *A,* either it is not within one's power to do *A,* or it is not within his power to refrain from doing it, depending of course on which consequences are in fact going to ensue.

At this point most persons are apt to feel most intensely that something has gone wrong, that a piece of sophistry has been concocted merely to puzzle and bewilder; but this is only because most persons are not fatalists about the future. No one feels the slightest suspicion about the first argument. Indeed, the logic of it seems so obvious that one might well wonder what can be the point of spelling it all out so exactly. But that is because everyone is already a fatalist about the past—no one supposes it is up to him what has happened, or that past things are still within his power.

The thing to note, however, is that these two arguments are formally identical, except only for tenses. If the occurrence of a naval battle yesterday is a necessary condition of my reading a certain kind of headline today, then it logically follows that my reading that headline today is a sufficient condition for the prior occurrence of that battle. This is obvious and indisputable. But, similarly, if my issuing a certain kind of order today is a sufficient condition for the occurrence of a naval battle tomorrow, then the occurrence of that naval battle tomorrow is a necessary condition of my issuing that order. This too is indisputable but somehow not so obvious. If, then, either argument is a good one—and surely the first one is—then the other is just as good no matter how anyone might feel about its conclusion.

People do nevertheless seem to have an almost deathless conviction that fatalism about the future has got to be false, though no one, it seems, has ever given a very good reason for thinking so. Men do, as we noted when considering the theory of determinism, have a conviction that future things are within their control, that what is going to happen is somehow up to them, at least sometimes. What they have failed to note, and what it in fact takes considerable sophistication to see, is that the very reasons that can be given for being a fatalist about the past can be given for being a fatalist about the future. Similarly, whatever arguments can be given for rejecting fatalism with respect to the future turn out to be just as conclusive for rejecting it with respect to the past. This is a consequence of the fact that the relations of necessity and sufficiency are perfectly timeless, and hold in exactly the same way, whether from past to future or from future to past, together with the fact that time, by itself, makes no difference to things.

Fatalism is nevertheless an odious philosophy to most persons. It is repellent only to the will, however, and not to the intellect, for men's wills do not normally crave the serenity to which a fatalist is rightly entitled upon his doctrine. Still, the question can only be settled by intelligence, and we shall therefore consider the arguments against this view that some persons are always eager to press.

BRINGING
ABOUT
THE PAST*

Michael Dummet

I observe first that there is a genuine sense in which the causal relation has a temporal direction: it is associated with the direction earlier-to-later rather than with the reverse. I shall not pause here to achieve a precise formulation of the sense in which this association holds; I think such a formulation can be given without too much difficulty, but it is not to my present purpose to do this. What I do want to assert is the following: so far as I can see, this association of causality with a particular temporal direction is not merely a matter of the way we speak of causes, but has a genuine basis in the way things happen. There is indeed an asymmetry in respect of past and future in the way in which we describe events when we are considering them as standing in causal relations to one another; but I am maintaining that this reflects an objective asymmetry in nature. I think that this asymmetry would reveal itself to us even if we were not *agents* but mere *observers*. It is indeed true, I believe, that our concept of cause is bound up with our concept of intentional action: if an event is properly said to cause the occurrence of a subsequent or simultaneous event, I think it necessarily follows that, if we can find any way of bringing about the former event (in particular, if it is itself a voluntary human action), then it must make sense to speak of bringing it about *in order* that the subsequent event should occur. Moreover, I believe that this connection between something's being a cause and the possibility of using it in order to bring about its effect plays an essential role in the fundamental account of how we ever come to accept causal laws: that is, that we could arrive at any causal beliefs only by beginning with those in which the cause is a voluntary action of ours. Nevertheless, I am inclined to think that we could have some kind of concept of cause, although

---

*From *The Philosophical Review* (1964). Reprinted by permission of *The Philosophical Review*.

one differing from that we now have, even if we were mere observers and not agents at all—a kind of intelligent tree. And I also think that even in this case the asymmetry of cause with respect to temporal direction would reveal itself to us.

To see this, imagine ourselves observing events in a world just like the actual one, except that the order of events is reversed. There are indeed enormous difficulties in describing such a world if we attempt to include human beings in it, or any other kind of creature to whom can be ascribed intention and purpose (there would also be a problem about memory). But, so far as I can see, there is no difficulty whatever if we include in this world only plants and inanimate objects. If we imagine ourselves as intelligent trees observing such a world and communicating with one another, but unable to intervene in the course of events, it is clear that we should have great difficulty in arriving at causal explanations that accounted for events in terms of the processes which had *led up to* them. The sapling grows gradually smaller, finally reducing itself to an apple pip; then an apple is gradually constituted around the pip from ingredients found in the soil; at a certain moment the apple rolls along the ground, gradually gaining momentum, bounces a few times, and then suddenly takes off vertically and attaches itself with a snap to the bough of an apple tree. Viewed from the standpoint of gross observation, this process contains many totally unpredictable elements: we cannot, for example, explain, by reference to the conditions obtaining at the moment when the apple started rolling, why it started rolling at that moment or in that direction. Rather, we should have to substitute a system of explanations of events in terms of the processes that led back to them from some subsequent moment. If through some extraordinary chance we, in this world, could consider events from the standpoint of the microscopic, the unpredictability would disappear theoretically ("in principle") although not in practice; but we should be left—so long as we continued to try to give causal explanations on the basis of what leads up to an event—with inexplicable coincidences. "In principle" we could, by observing the movements of the molecules of the soil, predict that at a certain moment they were going to move in such a way as to combine to give a slight impetus to the apple, and that this impetus would be progressively reinforced by other molecules along a certain path, so as to cause the apple to accelerate in such a way that it would end up attached to the apple tree. But not only could we not make such predictions in practice: the fact that the "random" movements of the molecules should happen to work out in such a way that all along the path the molecules always happened to be moving in the same direction at just the moment that the apple reached that point, and, above all, that these movements always worked in such a way as to leave the apple attached to an *apple* tree and not to any other tree or any other object—these facts would cry out for explanation, and we should be unable to provide it.

I should say, then, that, so far as the concept of cause possessed by mere

569

observers rather than agents is concerned, the following two theses hold: (1) the world is such as to make appropriate a notion of causality associated with the earlier-to-later temporal direction rather than its reverse; (2) we can conceive of a world in which a notion of causality associated with the opposite direction would have been more appropriate and, so long as we consider ourselves as mere observers of such a world, there is no particular conceptual difficulty about the conception of such a backwards causation. There are, of course, regions of which we are mere observers, in which we cannot intervene: the heavens, for example. Since Newton, we have learned to apply the same causal laws to events in this realm; but in earlier times it was usually assumed that a quite different system of laws must operate there. It *could* have turned out that this was right; and then it could also have turned out that the system of laws we needed to explain events involving the celestial bodies required a notion of causality associated with the temporal direction from later to earlier.

When, however, we consider ourselves as agents, and consider causal laws governing events in which we can intervene, the notion of backwards causality seems to generate absurdities. If an event C is considered as the cause of a preceding event D, then it would be open to us to bring about C in order that the event D should have occurred. But the conception of doing something in order that something else should have happened appears to be intrinsically absurd; it apparently follows that backwards causation must also be absurd in any realm in which we can operate as agents.

We can affect the future by our actions: so why can we not by our actions affect the past? The answer that springs to mind is this: you cannot *change* the past; if a thing has happened, it has happened, and you cannot make it not to have happened. This is, I am told, the attitude of orthodox Jewish theologians to retrospective prayer. It is blasphemous to pray that something should *have* happened, for, although there are no limits to God's power, He cannot do what is logically impossible; it is logically impossible to alter the past, so to utter a retrospective prayer is to mock God by asking Him to perform a logical impossibillity. Now I think it is helpful to think about this example, because it is the only instance of behavior, on the part of ordinary people whose mental processes we can understand, designed to affect the past and coming quite naturally to us. If one does not think of this case, the idea of doing something in order that something else should previously have happened may seem sheer raving insanity. But suppose I hear on the radio that a ship has gone down in the Atlantic two hours previously, and that there were a few survivors; my son was on that ship, and I at once utter a prayer that he should have been among the survivors, that he should not have drowned; this is the most natural thing in the world. Still, there are things which it is very natural to say which make no sense; there are actions which can naturally be performed with intentions which *could* not be fulfilled. Are the Jewish theologians right in stigmatizing my prayer as blasphemous?

570

They characterize my prayer as a request that, if my son has drowned, God should make him not have drowned. But why should they view it as asking anything more self-contradictory than a prayer for the future? If, before the ship set sail, I had prayed that my son should make a safe crossing, I should not have been praying that, if my son was going to drown, God should have made him not be going to drown. Here we stumble on a well-known awkwardness of language. There is a use of the future tense to express present tendencies: English news-papers sometimes print announcements of the form "The marriage that was arranged between X and Y will not now take place." If someone did not understand the use of the future tense to express present tendencies, he might be amazed by this "now"; he might say, "Of course it *will* not take place *now*; either it *is* taking place *now*, or it *will* take place *later*." The presence of the "now" indicates a use of the future tense according to which, if anyone had said earlier, "They are going to get married," he would have been right, even though their marriage never subsequently occurred. If, on the other hand, someone had offered a bet which he expressed by saying, "I bet they will not be married on that date," this "will" would normally be understood as expressing the *genuine* future tense, the future tense so used that what happens on the future date is the decisive test for truth or falsity, irrespective of how things looked at the time of making the bet, or at any intervening time. The future tense that I was using, and that will be used throughout this paper, is intended to be understood as this genuine future tense.

With this explanation, I will repeat: when, before the ship sails, I pray that my son will make the crossing safely, I am not praying that God should perform the logically impossible feat of making what will happen not happen (that is, not be-going-to happen); I am simply praying that it will not happen. To put it another way: I am not asking God that He should now make what is going to happen not be going to happen; I am asking that He *will* at a future time make something not to happen at that time. And similarly with my restrospective prayer. Assuming that I am not asking for a miracle—asking that if my son has died, he should now be brought to life again—I do not have to be asking for a logical impossibility. I am not asking God that, even if my son has drowned, He should *now* make him not to have drowned; I am asking that, at the time of the disaster, He should then have made my son not to drown at that time. The former interpretation would indeed be required if the list of survivors had been read out over the radio, my son's name had not been on it, and I had not envisaged the possibility of a mistake on the part of the news service: but in my ignorance of whether he was drowned or not, my prayer will bear another interpretation.

But this still involves my trying to affect the past. On this second interpreta-tion, I am trying by my prayer *now* to bring it about that God made something not to happen: and is not this absurd? In this particular case, I can provide a

571

rationale for my action—that is why I picked this example—but the question can be raised whether it is not a bad example, on the ground that it is the only kind for which a rationale *could* be given. The rationale is this. When I pray for the future, my prayer makes sense because I know that, at the time about which I am praying, God will remember my prayer, and may then grant it. But God knows everything, both what has happened and what is going to happen. So my retrospective prayer makes sense, too, because at the time about which I am praying, God knew that I was going to make this prayer, and may then have granted it. So it seems relevant to ask whether foreknowledge of this kind can meaningfully be attributed only to God, in which case the example will be of a quite special kind, from which it would be illegitimate to generalize, or whether it could be attributed to human beings, in which case our example will not be of purely theological interest.

I have heard three opinions expressed on this point. The first, held by Russell and Ayer, is that foreknowledge is simply the mirror image of memory, to be explained in just the same words as memory save that "future" replaces "past," and so forth, and as such is conceptually unproblematic: we do not have the faculty but we perfectly well might. The second is a view held by a school of Dominican theologians. It is that God's knowledge of the future should be compared rather to a man's knowledge of what is going to happen, when this lies in his intention to make it happen. For example, God knows that I am going to pray that my son may not have drowned because He is going to make me pray so. This leads to the theologically and philosophically disagreeable conclusion that everything that happens is directly effected by God, and that human freedom is therefore confined to wholly interior movements of the will. This is the view adopted by Wittgenstein in the *Tractatus,* and there expressed by the statement, "The world is independent of my will." On this view, God's foreknowledge is knowledge of a type that human beings do have; it would, however, be difficult to construct a nontheological example of an action intelligibly designed to affect the past by exploiting this alleged parallelism. The third view is one of which it is difficult to make a clear sense. It is that foreknowledge is something that can be meaningfully ascribed only to God (or perhaps also to those He directly inspires, the prophets; but again perhaps these would be regarded not as themselves possessing this knowledge, but only as the instruments of its expression). The ground for saying this is that the future is not something of which we could, but merely do not happen to, have knowledge; it is not, as it were, *there* to be known. Statements about the future are, indeed, either-true-or-false; but they do not yet have a particular one of these two truth values. They have present truth-or-falsity, but they do not have present truth or present falsity, and so they *cannot* be known: there is not really anything to be known. The nontheological part of this view seems to me to rest on a philosophical confusion; the theological part I cannot interpret, since it appears to involve ascribing to God the performance of a logical impossibility.

We saw that retrospective prayer does not involve asking God to perform the logically impossible feat of changing the past, any more than prayer for the future involves asking Him to change the future in the sense in which that is logically impossible. We saw also that we could provide a rationale for retrospective prayer, a rationale which depended on a belief in God's foreknowledge. This led us to ask if foreknowledge was something which a man could have. If so, then a similar rationale could be provided for actions designed to affect the past, when they consisted in my doing something in order that someone should have known that I was going to do it, and should have been influenced by this knowledge. This inquiry, however, I shall not pursue any further. I turn instead to more general considerations: to consider other arguments designed to show an intrinsic absurdity in the procedure of attempting to affect the past—of doing something in order that something else should have happend. In the present connection I remark only that if there is an intrinsic absurdity in *every* procedure of this kind, then it follows indirectly that there is also an absurdity in the conception of foreknowledge, human or divine.

Suppose someone were to say to me, "Either your son has drowned or he has not. If he has drowned, then certainly your prayer will not (cannot) be answered. If he has not drowned, your prayer is superfluous. So in either case your prayer is pointless: it cannot make any *difference* to whether he has drowned or not." This argument may well appear quite persuasive, until we observe that it is the exact analogue of the standard argument for fatalism. I here characterize fatalism as the view that there is an intrinsic absurdity in doing something in order that something else should subsequently happen; that any such action—that is, any action done with a further purpose—is necessarily pointless. The standard form of the fatalist argument was very popular in London during the bombing. The siren sounds, and I set off for the air-raid shelter in order to avoid being killed by a bomb. The fatalist argues, "Either you are going to be killed by a bomb or you are not going to be. If you are, then any precautions you take will be ineffective. If you are not, all precautions you take are superfluous. Therefore it is pointless to take precautions." This belief was extended even to particular bombs. If a bomb was going to kill me, then it "had my number on it," and there was no point in my attempting to take precautions against being killed by *that* bomb; if it did not have my number on it, then of course precautions were pointless too. I shall take it for granted that no one wants to accept this argument as cogent. But the argument is formally quite parallel to the argument supposed to show that it is pointless to attempt to affect the past; only the tenses are different. Someone may say, "But it just the difference in tense that makes the difference between the two arguments. Your son has either *already* been drowned or else *already* been saved; whereas you haven't *yet* been killed in the raid, and you haven't *yet* come through it." But this is just to reiterate that the one argument is about the future: we want to know what, if anything, there is *in* this fact which makes the one valid, the other invalid. The best way of asking this question is to ask, "What refutation is there of the fatalist argument, to which a quite parallel refutation of the argument to show that we cannot affect the past could not be constructed?"

Let us consider the fatalist argument in detail. It opens with a tautology, "Either you are going to be killed in this raid or you are not." As is well known, some philosophers have attempted to escape the fatalist conclusion by faulting the argument at this first step, by denying that two-valued logic applies to statements about future contingents. Although this matter is worth investigating in detail, I have not time to go into it here, so I will put the main point very briefly. Those who deny that statements about future contingents need be either true or false are under the necessity to explain the meaning of those statements in some way; they usually attempt to do so by saying something like this: that such a statement is not true or false now, but *becomes* true or false at the time to which it refers. But if this is said, then the fatalist argument can be reconstructed by replacing the opening tautology by the assertion, "Either the statement 'You will be killed in this raid' is going to become true, or it is going to become false." The only way in which it can be consistently maintained not only that the law of excluded middle does not hold for statements about the future, but that there is no other logically necessary statement which will serve the same purpose of getting the fatalist argument off the ground, is to deny that there is, or could be, what I called a "genuine" future tense at all: to maintain that the only intelligible use of the future tense is to express present tendencies. I think that most people would be prepared to reject this as unacceptable, and here, for lack of space, I shall simply assume that it is. (In fact, it is not quite easy to refute someone who consistently adopts this position; of course, it is always much easier to make out that something is not meaningful than to make out that it is.) Thus, without more ado, I shall set aside the suggestion that the flaw in the fatalist argument lies in the very first step.

The next two steps stand or fall together. They are: "If you are going to be killed in this raid, you will be killed whatever precautions you take" and "If you are not going to be killed in this raid, you will not be killed whatever precautions you neglect." These are both of the form, "If *p*, then if *q* then *p*"; for example, "If you *are* going to be killed, then you will be killed even if you take precautions." They are clearly correct on many interpretations of "if"; and I do not propose to waste time by inquiring whether they are correct on "the" interpretation of "if" proper to well-instructed users of the English language. The next two lines are as follows: "Hence, if you are going to be killed in the raid, any precautions you take will be ineffective" and "Hence, if you are not going to be killed in the raid, any precautions you take will have been superfluous." The first of these is indisputable. The second gives an appearance of sophistry. The fatalist argues from "If you are not going to be killed, then you won't be killed even if you have taken no precautions" to "If you are not going to be killed, then any precautions you take will have been superfluous"; that is, granted the truth of the statement "You will not be killed even if you take no precautions," you will have no motive to take precautions; or, to put it another way, if you would not be killed even if you took no precautions, then any precautions you take cannot be considered as being effective in bringing about your survival—that is, as effecting it. This employs a well-known principle. St. Thomas, for instance, says it is a condition for ignorance to be an excuse for having done wrong that, if the person had not suffered from the ignorance, he would not have committed the wrongful act in question. But we want to object that it may be just the precautions that I am going to take which save me from being killed; so it cannot follow from the mere fact that I am not going to be killed that I should not have been going to be killed even if I had not been going to take precautions. Here it really does seem to be a matter of the way in which "if" is understood; but, as I have said, I do not wish to call into question the legitimacy of a use of "if" according to which "(Even) if you do not take precautions, you will not be killed" follows from "You will not be killed." It is, however, clear that, on any use of "if" on which this inference is valid, it is possible that both of the statements "If you do not take precautions, you will be killed" and "If you do not take precautions, you will not be killed" should be true. It indeed follows from the truth of these two statements together that their common antecedent is false; that is, that I am in fact going to take precautions. (It may be held that on a, or even the, use of "if" in English, these two statements cannot both be true; or again, it may be held that they can both be true only when a stronger consequence follows, namely, that not only am I as a matter of fact going to take precautions, but that I could not fail to take them, that it was not in my power to refrain from taking them. But, as I have said, it is not my purpose here to inquire whether there are such uses of "if" or whether, if so, they are important or typical uses.) Now let us say that it is correct to say of certain precautions that they are capable of being effective in preventing my death in the raid if the two conditional statements are true that, if I take them, I shall not be killed in the raid, and that, if I do not take them, I shall be killed in the raid. Then, since, as we have seen, the truth of these two statements is quite compatible with the truth of the statement that, if I do not take precautions, I shall not be killed, the truth of this latter statement cannot be a ground for saying that my taking precautions will not be effective in preventing my death.

Thus, briefly, my method of rebutting the fatalist is to allow him to infer from "You will not be killed" to "If you do not take precautions, you will not be killed"; but to point out that, on any sense of "if" on which this inference is valid, it is impermissible to pass from "If you do not take precautions, you will not be killed" to "Your taking precautions will not be effective in preventing your death." For this to be permissible, the truth of "If you do not take precautions, you will not be killed" would have to be incompatible with that of "If you do not take precautions, you will be killed"; but, on the sense of "if" on which the first step was justified, these would not be incompatible. I prefer to put the matter this way than to make out that there is a sense of "if" on which these two are indeed incompatible, but on which the first step is unjustified, because it is notoriously difficult to elucidate such a sense of "if."

Having arrived at a formulation of the fallacy of the fatalist argument, let us now consider whether the parallel argument to demonstrate the absurdity of attempting to bring about the past is fallacious in the same way. I will abandon the theological example in favor of a magical one. Suppose we come across a tribe who have the following custom. Every second year the young men of the tribe are sent, as part of their initiation ritual, on a lion hunt: they have to prove their manhood. They travel for two days, hunt lions for two days, and spend two days on the return journey; observers go with them, and report to the chief upon their return whether the young men acquitted themselves with bravery or not. The people of the tribe believe that various ceremonies, carried out by the chief, influence the weather, the crops, and so forth. I do not want these ceremonies to be thought of as religious rites, intended to dispose the gods favorably towards them, but simply as performed on the basis of a wholly mistaken system of causal beliefs. While the young men are away from the village the chief performs ceremonies—dances, let us say—intended to cause the young men to act bravely. We notice that he continues to perform these dances for the whole six days that the party is away, that is to say, for two days during which the events that the dancing is supposed to influence have already taken place. Now there is generally thought to be a *special* absurdity in the idea of affecting the past, much greater than the absurdity of believing that the perform-ance of a dance can influence the behavior of a man two days' journey away; so we ought to be able to persuade the chief of the absurdity of his continuing to dance after the first four days without questioning his general system of causal beliefs. How are we going to do it?

Since the absurdity in question is alleged to be a *logical* absurdity, it must be capable of being seen to be absurd however things turn out; so I am entitled to suppose that things go as badly for us, who are trying to persuade the chief of this absurdity, as they can do; we ought still to be able to persuade him. We first point out to him that he would not think of continuing to perform the dances after the hunting party has returned; he agrees to that, but replies that that is because at that time he *knows* whether the young men have been brave or not, so there is no longer any point in trying to bring it about that they have

576

been. It is irrelevant, he says, that during the last two days of the dancing they have already either been brave or cowardly: there is still a point in his trying to make them have been brave, because he does not yet know which they have been. We then say that it can be only the first four days of the dancing which could possibly affect the young men's performance; but he replies that experience is against that. There was for several years a chief who thought as we did, and danced for the first four days only; the results were disastrous. On two other occasions, he himself fell ill after four days of dancing and was unable to continue, and again, when the hunting party returned, it proved that the young men had behaved ignobly.

The brief digression into fatalism was occasioned by our noticing that the standard argument against attempting to affect the past was a precise analogue of the standard fatalist argument against attempting to affect the future. Having diagnosed the fallacy in the fatalist argument, my announced intention was to discover whether there was not a similar fallacy in the standard argument against affecting the past. And it indeed appears to me that there is. We say to the chief, "Why go on dancing now? Either the young men have already been brave, or they have already been cowardly. If they have been brave, then they have been brave whether you dance or not. If they have been cowardly, then they have been cowardly whether you dance or not. If they have been brave, then your dancing now will not be effective in making them have been brave, since they have been brave even if you do not dance. And if they have not been brave, then your dancing will certainly not be effective. Thus your continuing to dance will in once case be superfluous, and in the other fruitless: in neither case is there any point in your continuing to dance." The chief can reply in exactly the way in which we replied to the fatalist. He can say, "If they have been brave, then indeed there is a sense in which it will be true to say that, even if I do not dance, they will have been brave; but this is not incompatible with its also being true to say that, if I do not dance, they will not have been brave. Now what saying that my continuing to dance is effective in causing them to have been brave amounts to is that it is true both that, if I go on dancing, they have been brave, and that, if I do not dance, they have not been brave. I have excellent empirical grounds for believing both these two statements to be true; and neither is incompatible with the truth of the statement that if I do not dance, they have been brave, although, indeed, I have no reason for believing *that* statement. Hence, you have not shown that, from the mere hypothesis that they have been brave, it follows that the dancing I am going to do will not be effective in making them have been brave; on the contrary, it may well be that, although they have been brave, they have been brave just *because* I am going to go on dancing; that, if I were not going to go on dancing, they would not have been brave." This reply sounds sophistical; but it cannot be sophistical if our answer to the fatalist was correct, because it is the exact analogue of that answer.

We now try the following argument: "Your *knowledge* of whether the young men have been brave or not may affect whether you *think* there is any point in performing the dances; but it cannot really make any difference to the *effect* the dances have on what has happened. If the dances are capable of bringing it about that the young men have acted bravely, then they ought to be able to do that even after you have learned that the young men have *not* acted bravely. But that is absurd, for that would mean that the dances can change the past. But if the dances cannot have any effect after you have learned whether the young men have been brave or not, they cannot have any effect before, either; for the mere state of your knowledge cannot make any difference to their efficacy." Now since the causal beliefs of this tribe are so different from our own, I could imagine that the chief might simply deny this: he might say that what had an effect on the young men's behavior was not merely the performance of the dances by the chief as such, but rather their performance by the chief when in a state of ignorance as to the outcome of the hunt. And if he says this, I think there is really no way of dissuading him, short of attacking his whole system of causal beliefs. But I will not allow him to say this, because it would make his causal beliefs so different in kind from ours that there would be no moral to draw for our own case. Before going on to consider his reaction to the argument, however, let us first pause to review the situation.

Suppose, then, that he agrees to our suggestion: agrees, that is, that it is his dancing as such that he wants to consider as bringing about the young men's bravery, and not his dancing in ignorance of whether they were brave. If this is his belief, then we may reasonably challenge him to try dancing on some occasion when the hunting party has returned and the observers have reported that the young men have *not* been brave. Here at last we appear to have hit on something which has no parallel in the case of affecting the future. If someone believes that a certain kind of action is effective in bringing about a subsequent event, I may challenge him to try it out in all possible circumstances: but I cannot demand that he try it out on some occasion when the event is *not* going to take place, since he cannot identify any such occasion independently of his intention to perform the action. Our knowledge of the future is of two kinds: prediction based on causal laws and knowledge in intention. If I think I can predict the nonoccurrence of an event, then I cannot consistently also believe that I can do anything to bring it about; that is, I cannot have good grounds for believing, of any action, both that it is in my power to do it, and that it is a condition of the event's occurring. On the other hand, I cannot be asked to perform the action on some occasion when I believe that the event will not take place, when this knowledge lies in my intention to prevent it taking place; for as soon as I accede to the request, I thereby abandon my intention. It would, indeed, be different if we had foreknowledge; someone who thought, like

Russell and Ayer, that it is a merely contingent fact that we have memory but not foreknowledge would conclude that the difference I have pointed to does not reveal a genuine asymmetry between past and future, but merely reflects this contingent fact.

If the chief accepts the challenge, and dances when he knows that the young men have not been brave, it seems that he must concede that his dancing does not *insure* their bravery. There is one other possibility favorable to us. Suppose that he accepts the challenge, but when he comes to try to dance, he unaccountably cannot do so: his limbs simply will not respond. Then we may say, "It is not your dancing (after the event) which causes them to have been brave, but rather their bravery which makes possible your dancing; your dancing is not, as you thought, an action which it is in your power to do or not to do as you choose. So you ought not to say that you dance in the last two days in order to make them have been brave, but that you try to see whether you can dance, in order to find out whether they have been brave."

It may seem that this is conclusive; for are not these the only two possibilities? Either he does dance, in which case the dancing is proved not to be a sufficient condition of the previous bravery; or he does not, in which case the bravery must be thought a causal condition of the dancing rather than vice versa. But in fact the situation is not quite so simple.

For one thing, it is not justifiable to demand that the chief should either consider his dancing to be a sufficient condition of the young men's bravery, or regard it as wholly unconnected. It is enough, in order to provide him with a motive for performing the dances, that he should have grounds to believe that there is a significant positive correlation between his dancing and previous brave actions on the part of the young men; so the occurrence of a certain proportion of occasions on which the dancing is performed, although the young men were not brave, is not a sufficient basis to condemn him as irrational if he continues to dance during the last two days. Secondly, while his being afflicted with an otherwise totally inexplicable inability to dance may strongly suggest that the cowardice of the young men renders him unable to dance, and that therefore dancing is not an action which it is in his power to perform as he chooses, any failure to dance that is explicable without reference to the outcome of the hunt has much less tendency to suggest this. Let us suppose that we issue our challenge, and he accepts it. On the first occasion when the observers return and report cowardly behavior on the part of the young men, he performs his dance. This weakens his belief in the efficacy of the dancing, but does not disturb him unduly; there have been occasions before when the dancing has not worked, and he simply classes this as one of them. On the second occasion when the experiment can be tried, he agrees to attempt it, but, a few hours before the experiment is due to be carried out, he learns that a neighboring tribe is marching to attack his, so the experiment has to be abandoned; on the

579

third occasion, he is bitten by a snake, and so is incapacitated for dancing. Someone might wish to say, "The cowardice of the young men caused those events to happen and so prevent the chief from dancing," but such a description is far from mandatory: the chief may simply say that these events were accidental, and in no way *brought about* by the cowardice of the young men. It is true that if the chief is willing to attempt the experiment a large number of times, and events of this kind repeatedly occur, it will no longer appear reasonable to dismiss them as a series of coincidences. If accidents which prevent his dancing occur on occasions when the young men are known to have been cowardly with much greater-frequency than, say, in a control group of dancing attempts, when the young men are known to have been brave, or when it is not known how they behaved, then this frequency becomes something that must itself be explained, even though each particular such event already has its explanation.

Suppose now, however, that the following occurs. We ask the chief to perform the dances on some occasion when the hunting party has returned and the observers have reported that the young men have not acquitted themselves with bravery. He does so, and we claim another weakening of his belief that the dancing is correlated with preceding bravery. But later it turns out that, for some reason or other, the observers were lying (say they had been bribed by someone): so after all this is not a counterexample to the law. So we have a third possible outcome. The situation now is this. We challenge the chief to perform the dances whenever he knows that the young men have not been brave, and he accepts the challenge. There are three kinds of outcome: (1) he simply performs the dances; (2) he is prevented from performing the dances by some occurrence which has a quite natural explanation totally independent of the behavior of the young men and (3) he performs the dances, but subsequently discovers that this was not really an occasion on which the young men had not been brave. We may imagine that he carries out the experiment repeatedly, and that the outcome always falls into one of these three classes; and that outomes of class (1) are sufficiently infrequent not to destroy his belief that there is a significant correlation between the dancing and the young men's bravery, and outcomes of class (2) sufficiently infrequent not to make him say that the young men's cowardice renders him incapable of performing the dances. Thus our experiment has failed.

On the other hand, it has not left everything as before. I have exploited the fact that it is frequently possible to discover that one had been mistaken in some belief about the past. I will not here raise the question whether it is *always* possible to discover this, or whether there are beliefs about the past about which we can be *certain* in the sense that nothing could happen to show the belief to have been mistaken. Now before we challenged the chief to perform this series of experiments, his situation was as follows. He was prepared to perform the dancing in order to bring it about that the young men had been brave, but only when he had no information about whether they had been brave or not. The rationale of his doing so was simply this: experience shows that there is a positive correlation between the dancing and the young men's bravery; hence the fact that the dances are being performed makes it more probable that the young men have been brave. But the dancing is something that is in my power to do if I choose: experience does not lead me to recognize it as a possibility that I should try to perform the dances and fail. Hence it is in my power to do something, the doing of which will make it more probable that the young men have been brave: I have therefore every motive to do it. Once he had information, provided by the observers, about the behavior of the young men, then, under the old dispensation, his attitude changed: he no longer had a motive to perform the dances. We do not have to assume that he was unaware of the possibility that the observers were lying or had made a mistake. It may just have been that he reckoned the probability that they were telling the truth as so high that the performance of the dances after they had made their report would make no significant difference to the probability that the young men had been brave. If they reported the young men as having been brave, there was so little chance of their being wrong that it was not worth while to attempt to diminish this chance by performing the dances; if they reported that the young men had been cowardly, then even the performance of the dances would still leave it overwhelmingly probable that they *had* been cowardly. That is to say, until the series of experiments was performed, the chief was prepared to discount completely the probability conferred by his dancing on the proposition that the young men had been brave in the face of a source of information as to the truth of this proposition of the kind we ordinarily rely upon in deciding the truth or falsity of statements about the past. And the reason for this attitude is very clear: for the proposition that there was a positive correlation between the dancing and the previous bravery of the young men could have been established in the first place only by relying on our ordinary sources of information as to whether the young men had been brave or not.

But if we are to suppose that the series of experiments works out in such a way as not to force the chief either to abandon his belief that there is such a positive correlation or that the dancing is something which it is in his power to do when he chooses, we must suppose that it fairly frequently happens that the observers are subsequently proved to have been making false statements. And I think it is clear that in the process the attitude of the chief to the relative degree of probability conferred on the statement that the young men have been brave by (1) the reports of the observers and (2) his performance of the dances will alter. Since it so frequently happens that, when he performs the dances *after* having received an adverse report from the observers, the observers prove to have been misreporting, he will cease to think it pointless to perform the dances after having received such an adverse report: he will thus cease to think that he can decide whether to trust the reports of the observers independently of whether he is going to perform the dances or not. In fact, it seems likely that he will come to think of the performance of the dances as itself a ground for distrusting, or even for denying outright, the adverse reports of the observers, even in the absence of any *other* reason (such as the discovery of their having been bribed, or the reports of some other witness) for believing them not to be telling the truth.

The chief began with two beliefs: (1) that there was a positive correlation between his dancing and the previous brave behavior of the young men; and (2) that the dancing was something in his power to do as he chose. We are tempted to think of these two beliefs as incompatible, and I described people attempting to devise a series of experiments to convince the chief of this. I tried to show, however, that these experiments could turn out in such a way as to allow the chief to maintain both beliefs. But in the process a third belief, which we naturally take for granted, has had to be abandoned in order to hang onto the first two: the belief, namely, that it is possible for me to find out what has happened (whether the young men have been brave or not) independently of my intentions. The chief no longer thinks that there is any evidence as to whether he intends subsequently to perform the dances. And now it appears that there really is a form of incompatibility among these *three* beliefs, in the sense that it is always possible to carry out a series of actions which will necessarily lead to the abandonment of at least one of them. Here there is an exact parallel with the case of affecting the future. We *never* combine the beliefs (1) that an action A is positively correlated with the subsequent occurrence of an event B; (2) that the action A is in my power to perform or not as I choose; and (3) that I can know whether B is going to take place or not independently of my intention to perform or not to perform the action A. The difference between past and future lies in this: that we think that, of any past event, it is in principle possible for me to know whether or not it took place independently of my present intentions; whereas, for many types of future event, we should admit that we are never going to be in a position to have such knowledge independently of our intentions. (If we had foreknowledge, this might be different.) If we insist on hanging onto this belief, for all types of past event, then we cannot combine the two beliefs that are required to make sense of doing something in order that some event should have previously taken place; but I do not know any reason why, if things were to turn out differently from the way they do now, we *could* not reasonably abandon the first of these beliefs rather than either of the other two.

My conclusion therefore is this. If anyone were to claim, of some type of action A, (1) that experience gave grounds for holding the performance of A as increasing the probability of the previous occurrence of a type of event E; and

(2) that experience gave no grounds for regarding A as an action which it was ever not in his power to perform—that is, for entertaining the possibility of his trying to perform it and failing—then we could either force him to abandon one or other of these beliefs, or else to abandon the belief (3) that it was ever possible for him to have knowledge, independent of his intention to perform A or not, of whether an event E had occurred. Now doubtless most normal human beings would rather abandon either (1) or (2) than (3), because we have the prejudice that (3) must hold good for every type of event: but if someone were, in a particular case, more ready to give up (3) than (1) or (2), I cannot see any argument we could use to dissuade him. And so long as he was not dissuaded, he could sensibly speak of performing A in order that E should have occurred. Of course, he could adopt an intermediate position. It is not really necessary, for him to be able to speak of doing A in order that E should have occurred, that he deny all possibility of his trying and failing to perform A. All that is necessary is that he should not regard his being informed by ordinary means, of the nonoccurrence of E as making it more probable that if he tries to perform A, he will fail: for, once he does so regard it, we can claim that he should regard the occurrence of E as making possible the performance of A, in which case his trying to perform A is not a case of trying to bring it about that E has happened, but of finding out whether E has happened. (Much will here depend on whether there is an ordinary causal explanation for the occurence of E or not.) Now he need not really deny that learning, in the ordinary way, that E has not occurred makes it at all more probable that, if he tries to perform A, he will fail. He may concede that it makes it to some extent more probable, while at the same time maintaining that, even when he has grounds for thinking that E has not occurred, his intention to perform A still makes it more probable than it would otherwise be that E has in fact occurred. The attitude of such a man seems paradoxical and unnatural to us, but I cannot see any rational considerations which would force him out of this position. At least, if there are any, it would be interesting to know what they are: I think that none of the considerations I have mentioned in this paper could serve this purpose.

My theological example thus proves to have been a bad—that is, untypical—example in a way we did not suspect at the time, for it will never lead to a discounting of our ordinary methods of finding out about the past. I may pray that the announcer has made a mistake in not including my son's name on the list of survivors; but once I am convinced that no mistake has been made, I will not go on praying for him to have survived. I should regard this kind of prayer as something to which it was possible to have recourse only when an ordinary doubt about what had happened could be entertained. But just because this example is untypical in this way, it involves no tampering with our ordinary conceptual apparatus at all: this is why it is such a natural thing to do. On my view, then, orthodox Jewish theology is mistaken on this point.

583

I do not know whether it could be held that part of what people have meant when they have said "You cannot change the past" is that, for every type of event, it is in principle possible to know whether or not it has happened, independently of one's own intentions. If so, this is not the mere tautology it appears to be, but it does indeed single out what it is that makes us think it impossible to bring about the past.

ON
DETERMINISM
AND
FREE WILL*
Erwin Schrödinger

As a reward for the serious trouble I have taken to expound the purely scientific aspect of our problem *sine ira et studio,* I beg leave to add my own, necessarily subjective, view of the philosophical implications.

According to the evidence put forward in the preceding pages the space time events in the body of a living being correspond to the activity of its mind, to its self-conscious or any other actions, are (considering also their complex structure and the accepted statistical explanation of physico-chemistry) if not strictly deterministic at any rate statistico-deterministic. To the physicist I wish to emphasize that in my opinion, and contrary to the opinion upheld in some quarters, *quantum indeterminacy* plays no biologically relevant role in them, except perhaps by enhancing their purely accidental character in such events as meiosis, natural and X-ray-induced mutation and so on—and this is in any case obvious and well recognized.

For the sake of argument, let me regard this as a fact, as I believe every unbiased biologist would, if there were not the well-known, unpleasant feeling about "declaring oneself to be a pure mechanism." For it is deemed to contradict Free Will as warranted by direct introspection.

But immediate experiences in themselves, however various and disparate they be, are logically incapable of contradicting each other. So let us see whether we cannot draw the correct, non-contradictory conclusion from the following two premises:

(1) My body functions as a pure mechanism according to the Laws of Nature.

(2) Yet I know, by incontrovertible direct experience, that I am directing

*From Erwin Schrödinger, *What is Life and Mind and Matter,* Cambridge, England: Cambridge University Press, 1967; reprinted by permission of the publisher.

its motions, of which I foresee the effects, that may be fateful and all-important, in which case I feel and take full responsibility for them.

The only possible inference from these two facts is, I think, that I—I in the widest meaning of the word, that is to say, every conscious mind that has ever said or felt "I"—am the person, if any, who controls the "motion of the atoms" according to the Laws of Nature.

Within a cultural milieu (*Kulturkreis*) where certain conceptions (which once had or still have a wider meaning amongst other peoples) have been limited and specialized, it is daring to give to this conclusion the simple wording that it requires. In Christian terminology to say: "Hence I am God Almighty" sounds both blasphemous and lunatic. But please disregard these connotations for the moment and consider whether the above inference is not the closest a biologist can get to proving God and immortality at one stroke.

In itself, the insight is not new. The earliest records to my knowledge date back some 2,500 years or more. From the early great Upanishads the recognition ATHMAN—BRAHMAN (the personal self equals the omnipresent, all-comprehending eternal self) was in Indian thought considered, far from being blasphemous, to represent the quintessence of deepest insight into the happenings of the world. The striving of all the scholars of Vedanta was, after having learned to pronounce with their lips, really to assimilate in their minds this grandest of all thoughts.

Again, the mystics of many centuries, independently, yet in perfect harmony with each other (somewhat like the particles in an ideal gas) have described, each of them, the unique experience of his or her life in terms that can be condensed in the phrase: DEUS FACTUS SUM (I have become God).

To Western ideology the thought has remained a stranger, in spite of Schopenhauer and others who stood for it and in spite of those true lovers who, as they look into each other's eyes, become aware that their thought and their joy are *numerically* one—not merely similar or identical; but they, as a rule, are emotionally too busy to indulge in clear thinking, in which respect they very much resemble the mystic.

Allow me a few further comments. Consciousness is never experienced in the plural, only in the singular. Even in the pathological cases of split consciousness or double personality the two persons alternate, they are never manifest simultaneously. In a dream we do perform several characters at the same time, but not indiscriminately: we *are* one of them; in him we act and speak directly, while we often eagerly await the answer or response of another person, unaware of the fact that it is we who control his movements and his speech just as much as our own.

How does the idea of plurality (so emphatically opposed by the Upanishad writers) arise at all? Consciousness finds itself intimately connected with, and dependent on, the physical state of a limited region of matter, the body.

(Consider the changes of mind during the development of the body, as puberty, ageing, dotage, etc., or consider the effects of fever, intoxication, narcosis, lesion of the brain and so on.) Now, there is a great plurality of similar bodies. Hence the pluralization of consciousnesses or minds seems a very suggestive hypothesis. Probably all simple, ingenuous people, as well as the great majority of Western philosphers, have accepted it.

It leads almost immediately to the invention of souls, as many as there are bodies, and to the question whether they are mortal as the body is or whether they are immortal and capable of existing by themselves. The former alternative is distasteful, while the latter frankly forgets, ignores or disowns the facts upon which the plurality hypothesis rests. Much sillier questions have been asked: Do animals also have souls? It has even been questioned whether women, or only men, have souls.

Such consequences, even if only tentative, must make us suspicious of the plurality hypothesis, which is common to all official Western creeds. Are we not inclining to much greater nonsense, if in discarding their gross superstitions we retain their naive idea of plurality of souls, but "remedy" it by declaring the souls to be perishable, to be annihilated with the respective bodies?

The only possible alternative is simply to keep the immediate experience that consciousness is a singular of which the plural is unknown; that there *is* only one thing and that what seems to be a plurality is merely a series of different aspects of this one thing, produced by a deception (the Indian MAJA); the same illusion is produced in a gallery of mirrors, and in the same way Gaurisankar and Mt. Everest turned out to be the same peak seen from different valleys.

There are, of course, elaborate ghost-stories fixed in our minds to hamper our acceptance of such simple recognition. E.G. it has been said that there is a tree there outside my window but I do not really see the tree. By some cunning device of which only the initial, relatively simple steps are explored, the real tree throws an image of itself into my consciousness, and that is what I perceive. If you stand by my side and look at the same tree, the latter manages to throw an image into your soul as well. I see my tree and you see yours (remarkably like mine), and what the tree in itself is we do not know. For this extravagance Kant is responsible. In the order of ideas which regards consciousness as a *singulare tantum* it is conveniently replaced by the statement that there is obviously only *one* tree and all the image business is a ghost story.

Yet each of us has the indisputable impression that the sum total of his own experience and memory forms a unit, quite distinct from that of any other person. He refers to it as "I." *What is this "I"*?

If you analyze it closely you will, I think, find that it is just a little bit more than a collection of single data (experiences and memories), namely the canvas *on which* they are collected. You will, on close introspection, find that

587

what you really mean by "I" is that ground-stuff on which they are collected You may come to a distant country, lose sight of all your friends, may all but forget them; you acquire new friends, you share life with them as intensely as you ever did with your old ones. Less and less important will become the fact that, while living your new life, you still recollect the old one. "The youth that was I," you may come to speak of him in the third person, indeed the protagonist of the novel you are reading is probably nearer to your heart, certainly more intensely alive and better known to you. Yet there has been no intermediate break, no death. And even if a skilled hypnotist succeeded in blotting out entirely all your earlier reminiscences, you would not find that he had killed *you*. In no case is there a loss of personal existence to deplore.

Nor will there ever be.

GLOSSARY

GLOSSARY

ABSOLUTE A generally senseless emphatic term, as in the statement, "There are no absolute truths," which is always uttered as an absolute truth.

AD HOC Hypotheses that have been cooked up to cover special cases; a term that generally functions to describe the premises in arguments advanced by those philosophers with whom you disagree.

AD HOMINEM In Latin: against the man; an argument that achieves its effect by insult; the form of argument chosen by those with whom you disagree to describe your own arguments.

ANALYTIC A sentence true in virtue of the meaning of its terms; for example, "A vixen is a female fox." According to Quine, one of the two chief kinds of sentences that cannot be distinguished from each other; the second are the *synthetic*.

AGNOSTICISM The doctrine that God keeps Himself sufficiently well hidden so as to prevent authoritative opinions concerning His existence.

ANSELM 11th century English philosopher and theologian, originator of the ontological argument.

ANALYSANS/ANALYSANDUM A pair of Latin terms used in elementary logic. In the theory of definitions, the analysandum is what is to be defined, the analysans, what does the defining.

ARTIFICIAL INTELLIGENCE Intelligence as it might appear if a computer had it.

ATHEISM The doctrine that God does not exist.

A PRIORI Sentences that may be judged true before (prior to) any particular experience, as in the case of "Everything colored is extended." Analytic truths, if they exist, are a priori truths, if they exist.

ARGUMENT FROM ILLUSION Sceptical argument against the thesis that objects are directly perceived.

ARGUMENT FROM ANALOGY The argument that I am entitled to conclude from your behavior that you have sensations similar to mine since I have those sensations when I display behavior similar to yours. In overall form, the argument from analogy recalls the inference that since grapefruits and basketballs both have pebbled skins and are round, it follows that they are both nourishing and good to eat.

591

BEHAVIORISM In psychology, the doctrine that a scientific study of human behavior must restrict itself solely to what happens to an organism physically, and what an organism does when what happens, happens.

BI-CONDITIONAL A statement of the form *P if and only if Q:* "Snow is white" is true if and only if snow is white.

CONDITIONAL A statement of the form *If P then Q:* "If whales are mammals then some mammals live in saltwater."

CONTRADICTORY Pairs of sentences that cannot be jointly true or false.

CONTRARY Pairs of sentences that cannot be jointly true but which may be jointly false.

DETERMINISM The view that for every event there exists a cause such that if the cause occurs the event must follow.

DILEMMA The predicament of a philosophical opponent after an imaginary confrontation with oneself. A dilemma is fashioned from a pair of conditions each of which lead to unacceptable conclusions and which jointly exhaust all of the possibilities. For example, if you fail to eat foods that are low in fat and scrupulously nourishing, you will probably die early of coronary artery disease. If on the other hand you confine your diet to boiled groats, tuna packed in water and organically grown peanut butter, you will not lead a life worth living.

DUALISM The doctrine that minds as well as bodies exist.

EMPIRICISM The doctrine in epistemology that knowledge arises only through the senses.

EMOTIVISM The doctrine in ethics that moral discourse functions to express emotion.

ETHICS Moral Philosophy; the analysis of such concepts as goodness, rightness obligation and justice.

EPISTEMOLOGY The theory of knowledge; the analysis of such concepts as knowledge, belief, probability, certainty and evidence.

FATALISM The thesis that everything that happens occurs in accordance with a fixed, general and unalterable plan; determinism made emphatic.

FALLACY An error in reasoning.

FEEDBACK Any process in which adjustments are continually made as the result of a sampling performed on the outputs of the process; an ordinary thermostat is a feedback regulator.

FREE WILL Our will as we like to see it—genuinely capable of choosing between alternatives; what we do not have according to some philosophers if determinism is true; and what we do not have according to still other philosophers if determinism is false.

IDEALISM The doctrine, as found in Berkeley, that reality is made up of ideas or perceptions.

INDUCTION Reasoning from evidence to conclusions that logically go beyond the evidence: from the fact the most samples chosen at random have a certain property, the inductivist argues that the chances are good that they all do; statistical inference generally.

INTUITIONISM In moral philosophy, the doctrine that moral truths are cognitively accessible to the morally tuned intellect.

INNATE IDEAS Those ideas, according to rationalist philosophers, that we come glued to at birth and points before.

KNOWLEDGE Traditionally, justified true belief, what one would have if the traditional definition were acceptable, which it isn't.

LOGIC The science of correct reasoning and inference.

LOGICAL POSITIVISM A middle and anti-metaphysical stage in the development of 20th century philosophy; a movement devoted to the doctrine that only the propositions of science and mathematics are meaningful. Enthusiasts included for a time A. J. Ayer, Otto Neurath, Rudolf Carnap and M. Schlick. The movement flourished in the two decades just prior to the Second World War and found itself hopelessly shattered both by the war and the rise of linguistic philosophy.

MATERIALISM The doctrine that the Universe is made up of matter and nothing else.

METAPHYSICS That branch of philosophy dealing with the ultimate nature of reality.

NATURAL RIGHTS Those rights that come to a man quite apart from those that he derives from the state; according to many contemporary philosophers precisely those rights of a sort that do not exist.

NATURALISTIC FALLACY The term used by G. E. Moore to describe the impression that goodness was the name of some property such as being pleasant; the general sort of mistake involved in confusing moral and factual terms.

NAIVE REALISM The doctrine that the acts of perception put a man directly in touch with the external world.

ONTOLOGICAL ARGUMENT The argument, first formulated by Anselm, that God must exist since He numbers all perfections and existence is a perfection.

PHENOMENALISM Idealism is the theory of perception; the doctrine that all knowledge is built up from such stuff as sense data.

593

PROBLEM OF OTHER MINDS The problem of justifying our instinctive conviction that human beings acting in ways that we might act are pretty likely to be feeling the way we might feel; generally, the problem of justifying belief in the existence of minds other than one's own.

PRINCIPLE OF VERIFIABILITY The positivist principle that aimed to separate the meaningful from the meaningless sentences of a given language: only those sentences whose truth could be empirically verified turned up as meaningful; a principle which when self-applied self-destructs.

RATIONALISM The doctrine in epistemology that knowledge arises as the result of the operation of a series of innate ideas or schemata which give to the knowing agent access to a set of a priori truths.

REALISM With respect to abstract objects, the denial of nominalism; with respect to perception, the denial of idealism.

REDUCTIONISM The view in the philosophy of science that in the end all of the sciences, including sociology and biology, will turn out to be special instances merely of those sciences which deal with the fundamental properties of matter, such as particle physics.

RELATIVISM The doctrine in moral philosophy that the man who defends his conviction that Mantovani is a finer composer than Mozart by arguing that while he knows nothing about music he certainly knows what he likes is entitled to use much the same argument in coming to the defense of his moral principles; any thesis in moral philosophy which entails the denial that moral principles are true or false.

SCEPTICISM The doctrine in epistemology that it is not possible to obtain knowledge.

SOLIPSISM The doctrine in epistemology that reality has so contracted as to leave real only an agent's thoughts and immediate perceptions.

SENSE DATA What the epistemologist believes he directly perceives just after he has given up as hopeless the doctrine of naive realism; the immediate data of consciousness in perception.

SOUNDNESS One of the two chief dimensions according to which an argument is evaluated: the other is validity. A sound argument is one that is valid and whose premises are true.

UTILITARIANISM The doctrine in moral philosophy that acts and institutions alike are to be judged with an eye toward the balance of pain over pleasure in the consequences that they yield.

VALIDITY What an argument displays in virtue of correctness of form.